Within the Palazzo Ducale Di Urbino, a five hundred-year-old treasure, the music room of Isabella D'Este reveals a coved gold-leaf ceiling, a carved marble doorway, a silk damask wall, and wooden marquetry paneling that combine to create a pleasing environment for moments spent with Renaissance music played on the lute and recorder. Exquisite detail reflected the refined arts and crafts expressed through commission work for the pleasure and patronage of the Italian Renaissance aristocracy. Photo by Ted Spiegel.

To Asa and to Kristine and to all our kids, at home and at school

The design of an interior has often utilized the talents of the era's greatest artists and craftsmen, involving thousands of hours of painstaking labor; its success then meriting hundreds of years of preservation. Transported from late eighteenth-century Worcestershire, England, and preserved along with other masterpieces of art at New York's Metropolitan Museum, the Tapestry Room from Croome Court is an opulent expression of wealth and culture. Tapestries here, made of wool and silk, were designed during 1758 to 1767 by François Boucher (1703–1770) and woven from 1764 to 1771 in the workshop of Jacques Neilson (1714–1788) at the French Gobelins Tapestry Works for George William, sixth Earl of Coventry. Neoclassic styling is evident in the floor rug, gold-leaf armchairs and settee, and candelabra pedestals. Photo courtesy of Metropolitan Museum of Art, New York City.

INTERIORS

A N I N T R O D U C T I O N

Karla J. Nielson
Brigham Young University

David A. Taylor
Brigham Young University

Wm. C. Brown Publishers

Book Team

Editor   *Meredith Morgan*
Developmental Editor   *Raphael Kadushin*
Designer   *Mark E. Christianson*
Production Editor   *Ann Fuerste*
Art Editor   *Janice Roerig*
Photo Editor   *Carol M. Smith*
Permissions Editor   *Vicki Krug*
Visuals Processor   *Jodi Wagner*

WCB   Wm. C. Brown Publishers

President   *G. Franklin Lewis*
Vice President, Editor-in-Chief   *George Wm. Bergquist*
Vice President, Director of Production   *Beverly Kolz*
Director of Marketing   *Thomas E. Doran*
Advertising Manager   *Ann M. Knepper*
Marketing Manager   *Kathleen Nietzke*
Production Editorial Manager   *Colleen A. Yonda*
Production Editorial Manager   *Julie A. Kennedy*
Publishing Services Manager   *Karen J. Slaght*
Manager of Visuals and Design   *Faye M. Schilling*

Cover images and photo essays: © 1990 Ted Spiegel

Printed in the United States of America by
Wm. C. Brown Publishers
2460 Kerper Boulevard, Dubuque, IA 52001

10   9   8   7   6   5   4   3

The dining room from the Lansdowne House, 1765–1768, Berkeley Square, London; moved to the Metropolitan Museum of Art in 1932. One of the greatest British architects and interior designers of the eighteenth century, Robert Adam (1728–1792), designed every component of his interiors, from floor motifs to mantle pieces to furniture to area rugs and to cast-plaster anaglypta set into wall and ceiling panels. Based on soft colors with white raised figures as seen in the wall and ceiling decoration, the virtuosity of Adam extended even to Josiah Wedgewood's Jasperware, which today are highly prized as accessory pieces. Although Adam

CONTENTS

Preface xiii
A Look Forward xiv

PART 1
THE DESIGN
FOUNDATION 1

CHAPTER 1
THE PROCESS OF
DESIGN 3

Why Study Interior Design 10
When Do We Need Interior
    Design 10
Interiors and Well-Being 10
Homes of Character 11
Developing Sensitivity and
    the Ability to
    Discriminate 11
Interior Design Is Where You
    Find It 12
The Design Process 12
    The Design Statement 12
    Research and Programming 12
    Writing a Program 20
    *Design Development: Solving
        the Problem 20*
Nonresidential
    Considerations 22
    Notes 23
    Bibliography 23

CHAPTER 2
DESIGN PRINCIPLES AND
ELEMENTS 25

The Principles of Design 30
    Scale 30
    Proportion 31
    Balance 32
    Rhythm 35
    Emphasis 36
    *Harmony: Variety and
        Unity 36*
The Elements of Design 37
    Space 38
    Shape or Form 39

    Mass 40
    Line 41
    Texture 44
    Pattern 45
    Light 46
    Color 46
Evaluating Design 47
    Function 48
    Cultural Context 48
    Appropriateness 49
    *Structural and Decorative
        Design 49*
Discernment and Design
    Excellence 52
    The Power of Discernment 52
    Good Taste and Style 53
Nonresidential
    Considerations 54
    Notes 55
    Bibliography 56

CHAPTER 3
COLOR 57

The Role of Color in History 61
    Color in the Ancient World 61
    The Middle Ages 61
    Renaissance Color 61
    Historic Color in America 61
    The Modern Era 62
The Color Trend Market 63
Color Theory 64
    *The Standard Color Wheel
        Theory 64*
    The Munsell Theory 66
    Other Color Theories 67
Color Harmony 68
Neutralized Colors 69
Neutrals 69
Color-Influencing Factors 70
Color Psychology 72
Color in Residential
    Interiors 75
Nonresidential
    Considerations 75
    Notes 76
    Bibliography 76
    Color Organizations 77

was unique in his interpretation of
classical elements, he did not invent
them but spent years studying,
drawing, and interpreting the ruins
and preserved masterpieces of
Imperial Rome and Classical Greece.
Nor was his exposure to the source
unique. Much of what is considered
refined English taste is a result of the
aristocracy and gentry taking the
grand tour of the Continent,
primarily France, Italy, and Austria,
to visit important museums and
architecture, thereby becoming
cultured. Photo courtesy of
Metropolitan Museum of Art, New
York City.

The Van Cortland Manor in the Hudson River Valley bears witness to America's Dutch Colonial architectural heritage. In the parlor, the Queen Anne tea table and Sheraton/Hepplewhite urn-back chair are placed in front of a Chippendale camel-back sofa and classic Dutch Renaissance cupboard filled with fine Continental porcelain. The wooden plank floor has been skillfully painted to become faux (imitation) marble. The mixed influences in this American interior befit New York as a trade capital with contacts in the West Indies as well as Europe.

Mr and Mrs. Pierre Van Cortland, lord and lady petrunes (landlords), owned tens of thousands of acres, yet the opulence attached with European aristocracy was not emulated by their American counterparts. A marked disparity between the haves and have-nots would not have been well received in a society that revered egalitarian qualities. The lords could not flaunt it, even before independence, and the interior design reflects that fundamental aspect of the society. Forbearance is a quality we respected in early Colonial days; the hallmark of success was having money and not showing it off. Furnishings are original Van Cortland possessions. Photo by Ted Spiegel. Courtesy of Historic Hudson Valley, Tarrytown, NY.

PART 2
THE INTERIOR 79

CHAPTER 4
LIGHTING 81

The Way We See Color 87
Natural Light 87
  Combustion Lighting 87
Artificial Lighting 88
  Incandescent Lighting 89
  Fluorescent Lighting 89
  Power Terminology and Units
    of Measurement 90
Categories of Lighting
    Effects 91
  Ambient and General
    Lighting 91
  Task Lighting 91
  Accent and Mood Lighting 92
  Lighting as Art 92
Lighting Economy 92
Lighting Effects in the
    Interior 93
Light and the Mind and
    Body 94
  Glare 94
Wiring Plans 95
  Switches and Outlets 95
Lighting Luminaires 96
  Architectural Lighting 96
  Luminous Panels 96
Lighting for the Future 98
Nonresidential
    Considerations 99
  Natural Daylighting 99
  HID Lighting 99
  Cold Cathode Lighting 99
  Motivational Lighting 99
  Safety Lighting 100
  Wiring 100
  Lighting Economy 100
  Lighting for the Future 101
  Notes 102
  Bibliography 102
  Lighting Associations 102

CHAPTER 5
SPACE PLANNING 103

Space Planning and the Design
    Process 109
Function and Zoning 109
  Interrelating Functions 109
Diagramming and Floor
    Plans 110
  Measurement of Space: Cubic
    and Square Footage 110
  Shaping the Space 111
  Site, Orientation, and
    Climate 112
Economy 112
  Other Factors That Affect
    Economy in Planning
    Home Space 112
Living with Less Space 113
Stretching Space 114
Traffic Patterns 115
Storage 115
Space Planning Rooms with
    Permanent Fixtures 116
  Kitchens 116
  Bathrooms 120
  Laundry Rooms 121
Planning for Independent
    Living 123
Emotion and Psychology 123
Space Planning and the
    Principles and Elements
    of Design 123
Types of Floor Plan
    Drawings 124

Custom Floor Plans 124
  Stock Plans 124
Floor Plans and Housing 124
  Floor Plan Types 124
Types of Housing 124
  The Single Detached
    Dwelling 124
  The Mobile Home 125
  High-rise Dwellings 125
  Town Houses 125
  Twin Homes and Multiplex
    Dwellings 125
Types of Ownership 126
  Private Ownership 126
  Condominium 126
  Rental 127
  Multi-Level Living 128
Nonresidential
    Considerations 129
  Function and Zoning 129
  Cubic and Square Footage 130
  Traffic Patterns 130
  Space Planning for the
    Handicapped 131
  Psychology of Nonresidential
    Spaces 131
  Floor Plan Symbols 131
  Notes 132
  Bibliography 132

CHAPTER 6
FURNITURE
ARRANGEMENT 133

Function 139
  Combining Functions 140
  Mechanical Functions 140
  Circulation 140
Human Factors 141
  Anthropometry and Barrier-
    Free Planning 141
    Standard Clearances 141
    Proxemics 142
    Crowding 143
    Territoriality 143
The Elements and Principles of
    Design 144
  Balance and Scale 144
  Rhythm 146
  Emphasis 146
  Line and Harmony 148
  Form and Space 148
  Proportion 150
Basic Groupings 150
Nonresidential
    Considerations 153
  Function 153
  Nonresidential Furniture
    Types 153
  Planning Unseen Areas 155
  Planning for Systems
    Furniture 155
  Circulation 155
  Barrier-Free Public Spaces 155
  Notes 156
  Bibliography 156

CHAPTER 7
FURNITURE
SELECTION 157

Furniture as a Symbol 164
Determining Quality 164
Wooden Furniture 165
  Hardwood and Softwood 165
  Other Forms of Wood 166
  Case Goods 167
  Wood Grains 168
  Joining Methods 168
  Wood Finishes 168
Metal Furniture 169
  Types of Metal 169

Other Furniture Materials 170
  Plastic 170
  Wicker, Rattan, Cane, and
    Rush 171
Upholstered Furniture 171
  Frames 172
  Springs 172
  Cushioning 172
  Coverings 172
Human Factors 173
  Function 173
  Anthropometrics, Ergonomics,
    and Biotechnology 173
The Classics 174
  Pieces from History 174
Modern Classics 180
Nonresidential
    Considerations 183
  Custom Designs 183
  Systems Furniture 183
  Ergonomic Superchairs 185
  Notes 185
  Bibliography 185

CHAPTER 8
ARCHITECTURAL
DETAIL 187

Walls 192
  Wood Paneling 192
  Moldings 193
Doors 194
Windows 196
Stairs 201
Fireplaces and
    Chimneypieces 203
Ceilings 206
Cabinetwork 208
Nonresidential
    Considerations 209
A Historical Overview 210
  Notes 213
  Bibliography 213

CHAPTER 9
WALL, CEILING,
AND WINDOW
TREATMENTS 215

Wall and Ceiling Materials 220
  Making the Right Choice 220
Hard or Rigid Wall
    Materials 220
Paint 227
  Painting Guidelines and
    Cautions 228
  Paint Types 230
  Preparation, Finishes, and
    Textures 230
  Paint Texturizing
    Techniques 230
Wall Coverings 232
  Wall Covering Guidelines and
    Cautions 232
  Types of Wall Coverings 233
  Fabric Wall Coverings 235
Ceiling Treatments 235
Window Treatments 236
  Window Treatment
    Considerations 237
  Soft Window Coverings 240
  Hard Window Treatments 245
Nonresidential
    Considerations 248
  Durability 248
  Nonresidential Ceiling
    Treatments 250
  Nonresidential Window
    Treatments 250
  Safety Codes 251
  Notes 251
  Bibliography 251

CHAPTER 10
FLOOR MATERIALS AND
COVERINGS 253

Flooring Requirements and
    Specifications 260
Guidelines for Selecting Hard
    and Resilient Floor
    Materials 260
Hard Floor Materials 261
Resilient Floor Materials 265
Soft Floor Coverings 265
  Carpeting 265
  Oriental and Area Rugs 271
  Accent Rugs 276
Nonresidential
    Considerations 276
  Hard and Resilient
    Floorings 276
  Rugs and Carpeting 277
  Notes 278
  Bibliography 278

CHAPTER 11
FABRIC 279

The Fabric Industry 285
Fabric—The Champion of
    Versatility 285
  The Human Touch 286
  Fabric Aesthetics 287
Fabric Weight and
    Application 292
  Performance and
    Durability 292
Fibers 293
Fabric Maintenance 296
Fabric Construction 296
  Nonwoven textiles 300
  Needle Constructions 300
  Layered or Compounded
    Fabrics 300
Finishes 300
  Coloring 300
  Prefinishes 300
  Standard Finishes 301
  Decorative Finishes 301
Nonresidential
    Considerations 302
  Contract Specifications
    Tests 303
  Notes 303
  Decorative Fabrics
    Glossary 303
  Bibliography 307

CHAPTER 12
ART AND
ACCESSORIES 309

Fine Art 314
  Sculpture 314
  Painting 314
  Mosaic 315
  Drawing 315
  Printmaking 315
  Obtaining Fine Art 316
  Preparing Art for Display 317
Decorative Art 317
  Mirrors 318
  Tableware and Cookware 318
  Baskets 321
  Clocks 321
  Screens 321
  Decorative Lighting
    Fixtures 322
  Books 323
  Textiles 324
Objects from Nature 325
  Plants 325
  Flowers and Greenery 325
  Other Natural Objects 326
Other Accessories 326

The Use of Accessories 327
   Collections 327
   Emotionally Supportive
     Design 328
Nonresidential
   Considerations 328
   Notes 330
   Bibliography 330

PART 3
THE BUILDING 331

CHAPTER 13
BUILDING SYSTEMS 333

Plumbing Systems 334
Heating, Ventilation, and Air
   Conditioning 334
Other Built-In Systems 336
   Fire Alert Systems 336
   Security Systems 336
   Communication Systems 336
   The Smart House System 336
Passive and Active Solar
   Systems 337
Insulation 340
Identifying the Professional
   Roles 340
Constructing the Building 343
   Structural Building Compo-
     nents and Systems 344
   The Critical Path and the Punch
     List 347
Nonresidential
   Considerations 350
   The Professionals 350
   Structural Systems 350
   Heating, Ventilation, and Air
     Conditioning 351
   Communication and Safety
     Systems 351
   Notes 352
   Bibliography 352

CHAPTER 14
EXTERIOR STYLE 353

Early Influences 360
   Greece (Fifth Century
     B.C.) 360
   Rome (750 B.C.–
     A.D. 476) 361
   The Middle Ages
     (325–1453) 362
   The Renaissance
     (1420–1650) 365
The English Influence in
   America 365
   The Seventeenth-Century
     English Medieval Style
     (1608–1695) 365
   The Early Georgian Style
     (1695–1750) 367
   The Late Georgian Style
     (1750–1790) 368
   The Federal Style
     (1790–1830) 370
   Jeffersonian Federal 370
   The Vernacular Tradition
     (Seventeenth Century-
     Present) 371

The Cape Cod Cottage
   (Seventeenth-Twentieth
   Centuries) 371
   The Greek Revival Style
     (1820–1845) 372
   The Victorian Age in America
     (1837–1901) 373
Other Influences in
   America 376
   The Swedish Influence 376
   The German Influence 377
   The Dutch Influence 377
   The French Influence 377
   The Spanish Influence 378
   The Beaux Arts Influence
     (1881–1945) 380
The Modern Styles (1885-
   Present) 381
   The Skyscraper
     (1857-Present) 381
   Organic Architecture (1908-
     Present) 382
   The International Style (1932-
     Present) 383
   Art Deco (1925–1940) 384
Preservation 384
   Notes 385
   Bibliography 385

PART 4
THE DESIGNER 387

CHAPTER 15
THE PROFESSION 389

The Evolution of the Design
   Profession 395
The Design Profession
   Today 395
   Attributes and Skills
     of Contemporary
     Designers 396
   Tasks Required of the Skilled
     Designer 396
   Professional Development and
     Continuing Education 397
Interior Design Resources 399
Interior Design Tools 400
   Computers in the Design
     Profession 400
Careers in Interior Design 402
   Interior Design 402
   Residential Interior
     Design 402
   Retailing 403
   Interior Design Education 403
   Specialized Design 403
   Careers in Related Fields 403
Working with a Professional
   Designer 407
The Future of Interior
   Design 408
Nonresidential
   Considerations 408
   Responsibilities of
     the Nonresidential
     Designer 408
   Nonresidential Design
     Fees 409
   Notes 410
   Bibliography 410

An exquisite Philadelphia highboy, c. 1780, from the Ford museum in Dearborn, Michigan. The flowering of American furniture craftsmanship came into full bloom during the Late Georgian period (c. 1750–1790), as Philadelphia and Newport craftsmen turned out fine furniture rivaled only in Europe. In this piece, the carver felt free to render a restrained Rococo touch to the decoration. The eternal flame in a Grecian torch is set as a beacon finial within the broken scroll pediment at the top, whose arms end in a carved rose motif. The highboy became an important piece of furniture during eighteenth-century America, certainly a success in the combination of good design, fine proportions, and superb craftsmanship. Photo by Ted Spiegel.

Appendix 411
Glossary 412
Index 440

The treasure of simple, eloquent design, admired since its nineteenth-century introduction to the American lifestyle, is witnessed in this Shaker ladder-back chair and stacked wooden boxes. Woven fabric tapes form a sturdy webbed seat that becomes an integral part of the structural design statement. Clean lines and superb quality craftsmanship have established Shaker furnishings as classic standards of design excellence. Photo by Ted Spiegel, taken at the Shaker Museum in Chatham, New York.

A gracious Saratoga Springs, New York, parlor indulges in the spontaneity of Belter Rococo-style Victorian furniture. Here the contemporary interior designer has taken a traditional matched suite and specified upholstery in a lighthearted chinoiserie toile fabric that serves as a perfect foil for the daily prescribed dose of fresh flowers. Part of interior design is creating a setting for fresh flowers and living plants, placed there for the continual enjoyment of those sensitive to the beauty and vitality of growing and blooming flora. This room is used for after-dinner conversation and refreshments with family and guests, providing delight to the eye and spirit with charming curved forms and stimulating colors and patterns. Photo by Ted Spiegel.

A private home designed by Frank Lloyd Wright in his native Wisconsin is seen here. Wright's work as the foremost American organic architect shows in his interior design a clear concern for the impact of the environment on the occupants. His home designs inevitably included furniture and textiles he custom designed and had created for each space. This fundamental concern for consistent aesthetics sprang from the sensitive relationship of landscape to the house, a philosophy that set Wright's work apart as an ensign to the architectural world. His unique architectural commissions are documented in book form and found in most design libraries. The work of Frank Lloyd Wright is a source influencing the framework of many contemporary interior designers and architects. Photo Norman McGrath © 1989.

PREFACE

Interiors: An Introduction is a beginning point for a lifetime of design education, appreciation, and enjoyment. The fact that you now hold this book in your hand indicates that to some degree, interior design is a value to you. That value is like a seed that needs to be nourished and cultivated with knowledge, training, and experience. As design awareness grows and matures, we see our world with fresh new eyes. Life can be richer and better for this effort, and that is the real value of studying interior design. From this book, a deeper appreciation and understanding of interior design may be obtained. It is a complex and intriguing subject, yet one in which personal satisfaction and enrichment are available to all who seek and study.

Interiors is a book for the beginning college or university student of interior design and for all who wish to acquaint themselves with the foundation of the major aspects of interior design. As such, the goals of this book are threefold:

1. to introduce a philosophy of and encourage an appreciation of fine design wherever and whenever is it found
2. to present the timeless design principles and elements and their application to interiors, and
3. to make the student aware of the numerous choices of materials, furnishings, and components that are used in interior design.

Because the main emphasis of introductory courses in interior design is the home, this book presents all topics as they relate to residential interiors. Home is the most important interior in our personal lives. Individual expression and the greatest satisfaction

in design can be found there. At the end of each chapter is a section entitled "Nonresidential Considerations," which relates the information to interiors we visit, where we do business, or where we obtain services beyond the home. This organized, twofold approach will be a starting point for those who will become interior designers. For those who do not go further in design than an introductory class, this book will form a basis for judging and understanding good design in both the home and all nonresidential public spaces. Indeed, most of us will spend a great deal of our waking hours in places where we work or do business. The person who can appreciate good design wherever it is found and who can evaluate why poor design is not pleasing will find life more rewarding and interesting. With the understanding gleaned from Interiors we can seek to personalize our homes and work spaces with greater skill and sensitivity to beauty.

Interiors is planned for flexibility. Because beginning interior design courses are so different in approach, every section of the text may not be applicable to every course. Some sections may be eliminated for a given course if desired. Much technical data has been incorporated into charts that may be utilized according to the teacher's preference and may find continued use as a reference for years to come. A glossary is provided at the conclusion of the book for convenience, understanding, and clarity.

The illustration program is also planned for understanding fine design and the processes that bring design to reality. The chapters begin with photo essays by editorial photographer Ted Spiegel, showing the process of

design in operation and illustrating that designs are created in a logical and sequential manner. The essays bear witness to the everyday challenges facing interior designers and design trade professionals as they transform flat plans into 3-dimensional environments. The bringing of people into the scene in an interior design book is a unique departure from the traditional approach. This is as it should be, for people are the very reason interior design exists at all. Our spaces should not be just museums but must function viably for those who occupy them. And last, the quality line drawings help the student understand the numerous terms that are so important to the vocabulary and comprehension of interior design.

Acknowledgments

This book is the result of the efforts of many talented and supportive people. We would like to express our thanks to our spouses, Asa S. Nielson and Kristine B. Taylor, and to our families and peers for their moral and thoughtful support.

Jim Park, who did the line artwork, has been a tremendous help in the preparation of the book. As a Bachelor of Fine Arts in Interior Design graduate from Brigham Young University, his knowledge of interior design, combined with his training as a skilled renderer and illustrator, brought insightful dimension to his inkline illustrations. He was also wonderful to work with as a professional and as a friend.

Ted Spiegel photographed the visual essays which introduce each chapter. His broad exposure to fine architecture and interiors, combined with a deep appreciation of historic preservation and understanding of contemporary

life-styles, gave unique dimension to each chapter's concepts. Ted was the mastermind behind the visual pedagogy of the book and served as wise mentor and helpful critic, as well as a great example of professionalism and friendship. Thanks, Ted. Our thanks also to Signy Spiegel, Donna Wisecup, Pauline Delli-Carpini, and K.C. Wetherall for assistance in obtaining photography or doing layout work utilized in the body of the text.

Our appreciation goes to the many fine people at Wm. C. Brown Publishers, who have worked on the text. Particularly we would like to thank early on editors Karen Speerstra and Carol Mills and the editors who wrapped up the project, Raphael Kadushin and Meredith Morgan, Art Director Marilyn Phelps, Designer Mark Christianson, and Production Editor Ann Fuerste for their assistance in bringing this book to reality.

Finally, we would like to thank the reviewers, who provided such an objective eye and such cogent feedback. They include: L. Annah Abbott, Ball State University; James Riley Avery, University Tennessee-Chattanooga; Susan M. Coleman, Orange Coast College; Edward Dorsa, Iowa State University; Ben D. Gunter, Virginia Commonwealth University; Doris Katz, Bellevue Community College; Jean M. Klopfer, Washington State University; Lavinia H. Kubiak, Eastern Kentucky University; LuAnn Nissen, University of Nevada; and Jill D. Smith, Seminole Community College.

Karla J. Nielson
Orem, Utah

David A. Taylor
Provo, Utah

A LOOK FOREWORD

"Seeing with a child's eye," fresh to new horizons, is the most important asset you bring to the field of interior design. Visual curiosity leads as you probe color, pattern, form and mass, space, structure, texture, and symmetry. What you explore within this book should further inform your eye and enhance your professional exploration of the world about you.

The design of interior space for family living, for work and for marketing, for public and ecclesiastical enjoyment, draws upon the fullness of perception. The photo essays that I have contributed to this text were conceived as visual bridges to the design community. Reservoirs of design creativity can be found in magazines, books, and museums. Visits to home shows, show houses, and interior design centers can broaden your visual experience and inspire your designs to draw upon the good taste and function of yesterday as well as the technology and aesthetics of today.

As varied as the resources are for each individual designer, there can be only one criteria for the finished interior: "it works." This means that knowledgeable, intelligent, and skilled planning and implementation yields space that pleases the client's taste, fulfills the client's needs, and maintains the submitted budget. The voyage to a project's completion requires patience, human engineering, and the mastery of financial and time budgets.

Though some designers become known for specific styles and are asked to reproduce that style continuously, this is not how most interior designers work. Versatility is the hallmark of the professional: commissions are done for a variety of clients in a variety of spaces for a variety of needs. One client's desire for chintz may be succeeded by another's enchantment with linen. What is inappropriate for one is ideal for the next, and the pursuit of the fresh and exciting keeps one's mind—and eye— alive.

Interior design decisions often involve the employment of thousands of dollars of the client's money and a myriad of trade talents and resources. The management of all these elements is a true life's challenge. Enriched by the experience that Karla Nielson and David Taylor have brought together on these pages, you can "look forward" to the excitement of designing interiors.

Ted Spiegel
South Salem, New York

THE DESIGN FOUNDATION

The process and principles and elements form the foundation of interior design. Design skills that develop from an understanding of these are used to plan interiors and make aesthetic and functional selections of materials and components. The carpet and fabric samples shown here are being considered by interior designer Lynn Lemone for use in the project on the drafting board.

Even after the selections are made, much effort goes into specification, scheduling, and follow-through—making the project a reality. Photo by Alejandro Ruvalcaba.

THE PROCESS
OF DESIGN

At the studio of Daroff Design, Inc., in Philadelphia, a designer's desk drawer offers insights into the basic materials of any interior design commission—technical proficiency, aesthetic judgment, and patience under fire. Photo by Ted Spiegel.

LACK OF PLANNING ON YOUR PART DOES NOT NECESSARILY MEAN AN EMERGENCY ON MY PART.

Page 4: Daroff Design's commission to redesign the interior of the venerable Sagamore Hotel in Bolton's Landing, New York, offered numerous challenges. Public spaces had to be in keeping with the classic sense of the Adirondack Mountain resort, built at the turn of the century. Bedrooms needed to have a homey feeling to put vacationers at ease. Contract work often combines both public and private spaces to be done by the same designer. Photo by Ted Spiegel. *Page 5, bottom left:* In the design studio of Susan Thorn, ASID, in Cross River, New York, the drawing board is at the heart of preparation for the execution of an interior design commission. Since many projects involve restructuring interior spaces or fitting built-in furniture specified by the designer, accurate working drawings are essential for the client's approval

and on-site execution. Photo by Ted Spiegel. *Page 5, top right:* The client conference initiates the design process. Apart from the functions of the spaces to be designed, materials to be used must be selected with the clients' taste and budget in mind. Susan Thorn (left) and her clients are conferring about color schemes and fabrics for a city apartment. Photo by Ted Spiegel. *Page 5, middle right:* Susan Thorn's studio wall offers the materials being considered for her clients' daughter's bedroom. Photo by Ted Spiegel. *Page 5, bottom right:* Interior designers must see the aesthetics and the functional success of the new interior into reality. The reality of interior design includes meticulous attention to detail, successful and timely management of subcontractors, and continual follow-through by phone. Photo by Ted Spiegel.

The Process of Design   5

Page 6, top left: The interior designer manages the timely execution of the design by a host of subcontractors. The painter can be called upon not only for flat and textured surface painting but also for an infinite variety of painting techniques and even stenciling for walls, ceilings, floors, and furnishings. Photo by Ted Spiegel.
Page 6, top right: Fabrics appropriate to a design scheme can be chosen at design centers such as the D & D Building in New York City. Taken out "on memo" they are presented to the client for consideration. Susan Thorn maintains a large file of textiles in her studio but makes weekly trips to New York to keep abreast of new possibilities. Each of the hundreds of fabric companies offers dozens of new lines both spring and fall, making the possibilities nearly limitless. Many of the major companies have regional showrooms in major cities, with sales representatives supplying samples to interior designers around the country. Photo by Ted Spiegel. Page 6, bottom left: When interior designers specify window treatments with special fabrics and designs, they must have fine workrooms where orders can be executed in a skilled and timely manner. A host of suppliers and professional tradespeople back up each interior designer. The clients benefit greatly through the designer's management of all the working relationships with subcontractors. Photo by Ted Spiegel. Page 6, bottom right: Carpet installation is both an art and a craft. By using a broadloom carpet with contrasting border, the floor covering adds special elegance to a living room. Patterned carpets and borders, such as these, are often used in nonresidential settings,

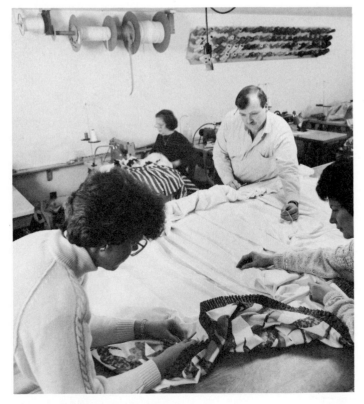

such as hotels, banks, and fine restaurants, where the pattern conceals both soil and traffic-wear. Photo by Ted Spiegel.
Page 7, top left: The right electric fixture is imperative for correct illumination for personal grooming in this bathroom, which is being remodeled. The electrician's arrival must be coordinated with the orderly flow of other work being done on the project. The written schedule is called the critical path.

When one subcontractor begins or finishes a job late, it may prevent others on the critical path from beginning the next phase of structural work or installation on time. Further, it is often not an easy matter to reschedule contractors without several days' or even weeks' notice and follow-through. Photo by Ted Spiegel. *Page 7, top right:* Drawing upon the skills of a specialist in painting furniture, walls, and floors, Susan Thorn is

able to enhance her projects with small flourishes that fit into the big picture. Photo by Ted Spiegel. *Page 7, bottom left:* In a world given to foam furniture, the professional designer's relationship with skilled upholsterers offers her clients furniture that bears the right fabric on its surface and the right feel and longevity beneath the surface. Here the coil springs are hand tied eight ways, giving the best support to

spring-constructed furniture. Photo by Ted Spiegel. *Page 7, bottom right:* Cabinetry for kitchen, bath, library, office, or other special installations is designed to meet the client's needs and to coordinate with the overall design of the project. Cabinetry is often a major capital investment; quality and installation are part of the overall supervisory job undertaken by the interior designer.

Page 8, top: Susan Thorn's responsiveness to her clients' needs is indicative of the flexibility and resourcefulness all designers must bring to their field. Her own living room is done in a classic French manner. Trompe l'oeil walls set the tone echoed in the carpet, draperies, and exquisite furnishings. Photo by Ted Spiegel. *Page 8, bottom:* Taking her theme from the broad-ranging tastes of her clients, as evidenced in the collection of primitive masks, the ethnic quality is repeated in the artwork and in the coffee table's form. Susan Thorn selected more refined pieces of modern furniture to create an eclectic interior that bridges the gap from distant to modern times. Photo by Ted Spiegel.

Page 9, top: *Casual and country themes are mixed here to bring warmth to a great room fashioned out of three tight, remodeled spaces. Extensive alterations were supervised after the initial design* phase. *To enhance her clients' satisfaction with the project, Thorn added barn beams to establish a rustic and homey architectural background to this informal living space. Custom cushions and top-* grade wicker were used. Photo by Ted Spiegel. **Page 9, bottom:** *A modern art collection and spectacular woodland setting are reflected in the overall modern interior of this Westchester, New* York, living room. Modern architecture is often enhanced by deep textures contrasted with smooth ones and unique elemental furnishings, such as the cabinet at the left. Photo by Ted Spiegel.

Why Study Interior Design

Like getting dressed, interior design is inevitable. Each morning we reach into the closet and select items of clothing that were chosen basically to cover our bodies. However, some dress with great style and verve, whereas others merely get dressed. So too, every interior can be planned with great concern and sensitivity or with capriciousness and lack of care. Because the investment required to furnish an interior is not trivial and since it will be done either for good or ill anyway, it makes sense to do it well. If well planned, the design not only will be appealing to the senses but will also meet the needs of those who use it and will create a safe and satisfying environment.

Many people are finding rewarding careers in interior design. For these, studying and learning are necessary prerequisites to professional practice. Their study of interior design must be thorough and detailed because they are responsible to all of us for the development of interiors that are safe and functional as well as beautiful. Interior design is an exciting discipline that makes life better through effective solutions to problems. The satisfaction and pride that come with a well-designed interior are worth the effort it takes to learn, study, and assimilate the rather vast body of knowledge that comprises interior design.

When Do We Need Interior Design

The reasons for getting involved in an interior design project are varied.

- New homes require complete designs. A new home must be completely planned from the arrangement and allocation of space to the selection of new materials and furnishings. The extent of the selection and the purchase of new furnishings will often depend on whether one is moving from an existing home or starting a new home from scratch. Those starting fresh will have to select every item, whereas those who move from a more settled situation may be able to use existing furnishings if they are in character with the new home.
- Interiors need refurbishing. With time, materials and furnishings become worn and are no longer suitable. The average life span for better-than-average soft goods (upholstery, draperies, and floor coverings), paint, and wall coverings is six to twelve years; when they wear out, they will need to be replaced.
- The program changes. As the composition of a household changes, a home may need remodeling or refurnishing. For example, as children are born into a family, more bedroom space may be required. As the children grow and move on to college and out of the home, their rooms may be given to younger brothers

and sisters, or they may become long-desired personal spaces for Mom or Dad, requiring further design alterations. Environments that are created in response to change are satisfying because they function better and are suited to real needs.

- Fashions change. No matter how carefully our interiors are designed, we may find ourselves longing for a change. As exciting new materials and furnishings become available, we can see expanded possibilities for change that will bring freshness to our homes. This is an area that requires careful balance. The interior furnishings industry thrives on changes in fashion, and new directions in design are frequently exciting. Yet if durable furnishings are carefully chosen with an eye to classic styling, they will not date and will not need replacing. If furnishings are well chosen, then a new color or fabric or a new piece of furniture or an accessory may satisfy the craving for new fashion.

Interiors and Well-Being

It has often been said that we shape our environments and then our environments mold us. This principle is nowhere more true than in the home. The home is where we come for shelter from the elements and the pressures of everyday life. It is the place where children can be nurtured. Here they can be taught the value of work and cleanliness and the satisfaction that comes from a job well done. They can learn honesty, integrity, dependability, and service to their fellow men and women by taking appropriate responsibility for the home, its maintenance, and the quality of life it provides. The home is where we come for entertainment and relaxation. It is a place where we seek physical rest and sleep—no bed feels as good as the one at home. Here we can cook in order to feed and fortify ourselves for the onslaught of daily living. Home should be a place of refreshment and support, and it should be important to us as a place where the finest values can be espoused and reinforced.

Interior design is the means to making homes pleasant and functional. In our fast-paced society, life is often filled with stress and sometimes even unhappiness. Poorly planned interiors can add to this emotional burden and can be an unnecessary source of frustration. Well-planned and lovely homes are no guarantee of happiness, but a well-designed interior certainly helps smooth the rough edges of life. It is also significant to note that there is no relationship between the size and luxury of a home and its ability to function. A tiny but well-planned apartment may make a better home than an enormous mansion. Likewise, a modest cottage, if it meets the needs of those who call it home, can be a pleasant and lovely place to live. It is up to us to create the kind of interior that best meets our needs and our expectations of what will take place there.

Figure 1.1 (A) Over the mantel is a portrait of Franklin Delano Roosevelt, son of Sara Delano Roosevelt. (B) Interior designer Carole H. Price planned the rejuvenation of this family room in the Sara Delano Roosevelt House, a designated historic landmark now open to the

Homes of Character

Our homes represent what we are or what we want people to think we are. Louis XIV of France built the Palace of Versailles not because he needed a home but as a symbol of his power and a monument to a unified France. To a lesser degree, our interiors also say who we are. It is this principle, when followed honestly, that results in the most charming and appealing interiors. When interiors are designed purely as an expression of wealth and status, they will often be pretentious and unsatisfying.

(A)
Figure 1.1

Homes filled with objects and materials of personal value will be unlike any other home anywhere. It is pleasant to sit in the home of a musician or theater professional, for example, and sense their interests and experiences merely by looking around. When homes have the good fortune of growing and evolving with their occupants over a number of years, the charm will likely be even greater. This is the reason model homes often lack the emotional warmth of real home environments. Even though they may be designed and furnished with great sensitivity and filled with exciting objects and ideas, they may still lack the sense of ownership and distinction that comes to a home that is lived in with love and care over a period of years.

Developing Sensitivity and the Ability to Discriminate

Merely surrounding oneself with things of personal value will not guarantee an aesthetically pleasing environment. Such environments may be quite personal, but they may also be rather unattractive. Beauty is most certainly in the eye of the beholder. However, knowledgeable people with a trained and an experienced eye can appreciate a good design even if it is not what they would personally choose. Developing this ability to discriminate and sensitively evaluate is one of the most important reasons for studying interior design. True enough, some people seem to be gifted with an innate sense of style, but like an appreciation for fine art or music, it is cultivated and carefully developed through education, exposure, and real effort over a period of time. Developing the ability to discriminate is a lifetime pursuit.

The art and music/design analogy is apt. To decide to study and learn about art or music, the discipline must be of value to us. When well-designed interiors become important to us, we will take the time to study and observe. The more we are exposed to design and its principles, the better we can sense the rightness or wrongness of a design. This exposure comes through the deliberate study of design, by taking classes, reading books, and visiting design showrooms, to observe style options and quality levels.

It is also important to the development of discrimination to study historical exteriors and interiors to gain an appreciation for those designs that have passed the test of time to become classics that are loved and appreciated still today. Museums and historic homes and buildings can provide such a laboratory. As we travel we should be aware of opportunities to learn and observe what such experiences provide. Study and exposure will sharpen the senses and increase the ability to make educated judgments about architecture and its furnishings.

Education is the key to developing the ability to discriminate. Interior design is a very complex discipline that goes far beyond the selection of beautiful fabrics and well-designed pieces of furniture. These decorative aspects are certainly an important part of the process of interior design, but interior design is also founded in the knowledge of a wide range of technical information and a creative capacity to solve design problems.

(B)

(C)

public in New York City, as a reflection of the home's venerable and original colors. Cherished family heirlooms and rich colors and textile applications make this interior speak of its noble heritage. (C) Katherine Stephens pays tribute to "a man of our time" with the Franklin Roosevelt barrier-free den/bedroom. Designed for the handicapped, this room in the Sara Delano Roosevelt House gives ample maneuvering space and state-of-the-art computer equipment within easy reach for the wheelchair-bound occupant. The rejuvenation of the Sara Delano Roosevelt House gave opportunity to designers to create spaces that would reflect a particular life-style and particular needs. In this case, this interior would have met the needs of the late President Franklin Delano Roosevelt and, as such, reflects the needs of a sizable population today—the handicapped. Photos courtesy of DuPont "Teflon" soil and stain repellent.

The principles and elements of design—principles of lighting, space planning, building systems, architectural detail, materials and their application as well as art and accessories—are building blocks that are used to create understanding and a discriminating individual. In order to be fully sensitive to every aspect of design, we must have exposure to its principles, concepts, and components. This exposure comes best through education.

Interior Design Is Where You Find It

Although the focus of our interest in interior design is often personal, it certainly need not be limited just to our personal home environment. The development of nonresidential interiors is often the emphasis of professional interior designers. Life-styles today often dictate that we spend many of our waking hours in working situations, obtaining medical services, as well as shopping and dealing with various types of business services. We also spend time eating out, traveling, and staying in hotels. These nonresidential environments should be planned with as much sensitivity to human needs as the home environment, though often the nonresidential interior, by its very nature, will be less personal. As we study interior design, we develop the ability to sensitively evaluate a finished interior design or design solution. We then should be able to apply our powers of discrimination to the appreciation and evaluation of designs wherever we find them—in medical facilities, restaurants, hotels or resorts, offices, banks, shopping centers, schools, and every place we go. The lifelong study of interior design, even for those who do not become professional interior designers, can be a joyful experience.

The Design Process

Design is the process of solving problems. Design training and skills are necessary to develop designs that function properly and also meet the emotional needs of those who will use the interior. A successful design must carefully be researched to provide adequate understanding of all the factors that will make the design function well. The research data becomes the basis for the solution to the problem, and the more information we obtain, the better the design is likely to be.

The information becomes a compass or guide for the creation of a concept or idea for the solution to the problem. If the creative concept for the design is acceptable to those who commissioned it, then the design development can be continued by making working drawings and compiling lists of specific products and materials with which a contractor can execute the design. In order to be functional and aesthetically satisfying, the design must carefully be researched, creatively developed, and well executed. All of these factors are in the control of the designer.

The Design Statement

As the design process begins, the three basic questions *who, what,* and *where* are answered in a short and simple declaration called a *design statement.* The design statement identifies the design project before the actual research, problem solving, and creative design aspects of the process begin.

The design statement answers the question "Who" by identifying the individual or group who commissioned the design. It does not provide any detailed information about these people, it merely identifies them. These could be, but do not necessarily have to be, those who will use the interior. The design statement must also address the question of purpose. For example, Will the design be a primary, year-round residence, a weekend retreat, or a winter ski condominium? Is it new construction or remodeling? What is the reason for the design? The last question answered is, Where will the design be? The design statement specifies the country, state, province, city, specific area, development, building, and even the address when possible. The design statement succinctly identifies the problem to be researched and developed.

Research and Programming

The *program* is the sum total of what goes on in an interior, including the activities, needs, and requirements of those who will use the design as well as any external factors that could affect its planning. Programming is the research phase of the design process when the program is explored in great depth, clarifying everything necessary for an effective solution to the problem identified in the design statement.

Users

The research process begins with identification of each of the *users.* The users, as the name implies, are those who will use the design directly or indirectly, from principal occupants to service people to guests and friends.

In a residential design, a *profile* is developed for each of the principal residents who will live in the home. The profile should include such things as age, sex, background, culture, values, temperament, personality, personal habits, need for privacy, style preferences, responses to color as well as an inventory of possessions and furnishings that need to be accommodated.

The profile helps the designer understand the *life-style* of the principal users. Life-style is a term frequently used in residential design to describe part of the program for a home. It represents the constantly changing way a person or group of people live and how they use their time. It includes the consideration of traditional two-parent families as well as nontraditional families, such as combined households, single-parent families, the elderly, and those with handicaps. It includes such considerations as whether they like to read, write, or use a computer or whether they

Figure 1.2 The media room in the home of Robert Bradford, a film producer, has padded and sound-proofed walls. Mr. Bradford uses the room to screen films and videotapes. A custom-designed media wall includes a tape deck, a stereo and computerized receiver, an access

Figure 1.2

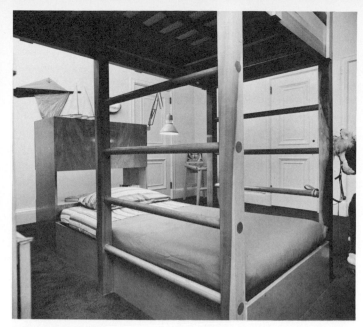

Figure 1.3

have special hobbies such as sewing, crafts, or woodworking or to what extent they enjoy and participate in sports. The way people choose to entertain; how they prepare, serve, and eat meals; whether or not a grandparent lives with them; the way they use their leisure time; the type of instruments they play; the routine they use for dressing and their personal toilette; the amount and type of interaction they want with their children—all are examples of life-style considerations. As the composition of families or groups changes and as people grow older, interests, needs, and life-styles also change. Consequently, flexibility in planning for potential modification is very important in order to meet changes without major upheaval.

Since life-styles are in a constant state of flux as household *demographics* change, it is important to be aware of the effect such changes will have. For example, many families with small children may find a playroom well suited to their needs. Tiny children can use the space for toys and for play. As children begin to bring friends into the home, the room will provide space for playing games with peers. As children become teenagers and young adults, the playroom can become a game room with music and entertainment and even space for parties and dancing. When the young adults leave home to begin families of their own, the room may start the cycle all over again with space for grandchildren.

Another example of accommodating a changing life-style might be the evolution of a bedroom from nursery into a child's room and from a child's room into an environment for a teenager or young adult. When the young adult leaves home, the room could be used for hobbies, study, television, a home office, a guest room, or a combination of uses.

The foresight to project changes in life-style and the ingenuity to plan for flexibility are invaluable assets in the research and design process.[1]

Function

In order for a design to be effective, it is essential to determine in a methodical and thorough manner what tasks or activities will take place in a given space and what is needed to accomplish each task. Examples of questions that might apply to the planning of function for a kitchen might be

- How many of the users will be cooking at once?
- What kinds of equipment will be needed?
- Will there be minimal or gourmet cooking?
- What kind of supplies must be accommodated?
- How should supplies be stored?
- What kind of dining, if any, should be planned?

In a bedroom we might ask

- Do the users like to read in bed?
- Does the bedroom need to accommodate study facilities?
- Is an area for seating desirable?
- Will there be television or other forms of entertainment?
- What are the storage needs?

In living areas we might want to know

- Is the space used by company, family, or both?
- Will there be a piano or other musical instruments?
- Will television and entertainment be included here?
- Should books and reading be part of the planning?
- Will conversation be an important function?
- Will the space be used to display art?

tuner for TV, and recorders and cassette recorders. All system controls are in the lacquered coffee table and can be concealed with the sliding tambour door. A beam-projecting unit is overhead in what looks like a duct system. Behind the sofa, the table acts as an office desk for correspondence and film-critiquing work. This interior has been carefully tailored to meet the needs of Mr. Bradford's profession, as well as to provide a luxurious standard of home media planning. Photo courtesy of the International Linen Promotion Commission.

Figure 1.3 Demographics—the age, gender, and number of people that will occupy the interior—make up a substantial portion of the design program. This room accommodates two young children, with bunk beds in an L arrangement in the center of the room, leaving plenty of space to move around the perimeter. As the children grow, the beds can be arranged side by side; one can be removed later on if privacy is sought. Accommodating flexibility and change in the design program is intelligent planning. Photo by Norman McGrath © 1989.

The Process of Design   13

Determinations should be made regarding every space and its use. For example, a bedroom could accommodate study or sewing space as well as sleeping. The family room could be used for dining, television, and stereo as well as conversation and games. The laundry and sewing could be accommodated in the same space. The dining room or guest room could double as a library or hobby room. This kind of flexibility is crucial because the cost of space is high and infrequently used rooms need to be made more useful by planning for several functions. Every life-style will dictate different kinds of functions for each area; thorough inquiry will determine precisely what the functions are. With this exact data, planning can be effective and accurate, and life-style differences can be well accommodated.

Relationships

When the functions for each space have been assessed, the relationships of each function must be determined. Important lines of communication and the need for proximity must be identified. For example, it might be convenient to plan sewing and ironing near the laundry. The laundry needs to be close to the kitchen for daytime convenience, or it could be near the bedrooms and bathrooms where soiled clothes are removed. Bedrooms should have a well-planned relationship with bathrooms. Easy access from the nursery to the master bedroom may be ideal for some, but other parents might want children's rooms and activities isolated from their own. Kitchens and dining areas where food will be served should have logical and convenient relationships. A home office might most appropriately be located near the front door and close to a seating area such as a living room, for the convenience of those who visit the office.

The consideration of relationships should even extend to the location of areas outside the building. For example, the convenient relationship of garbage containers to the kitchen or of kitchen to patio or garden is important. When bringing in groceries, the relationship of the garage or car park to the kitchen or pantry is significant. Identifying these types of relationships helps the use of space become more efficient and makes the design more effective because of its convenience. Well-planned relationships also smooth lines of communication, cut building costs, and make traffic patterns more efficient.

Space Requirements

When function and relationships are clearly identified, the next step is to determine how much space will be allotted to each function or related functions. Space is costly and must be used wisely, but care must also be taken to ensure sufficient space for priority items and functions or the design will be inadequate.

Often the consideration of space is a matter of counting and measuring. We should know minimum and maximum numbers of people who will use a given space in a variety of hypothetical situations and how many possessions must be accommodated. A typical checklist might include such things as

- How is entertaining handled, and how much space does that require?
- How many people might need to be seated for formal dining?
- What is the maximum number of guests that might stay at one time?
- What pieces of equipment need to be accommodated in the kitchen?
- How many cans, jars, bags, or boxes of food will be stored in the pantry?
- What kind of vacuums, mops, brooms, and other cleaning supplies are there?

Figure 1.4

Figure 1.4 Completely retractable glass walls make this room an extension of the outdoor living area with its covered patio, swimming pool, and the sea beyond. This type of planning is well adapted to the life-style of tropical areas, where ocean breezes cool and refresh the interior and where the weather continually invites us out of doors. Interior design by John Saladino. Photo by Norman McGrath © 1989.

- Are there collections of slides, videos, or movies that require space?
- Do card tables and folding chairs need to be stored?
- How many books, records, tapes does the user have?
- How many skis, golf clubs, balls, bats need storage?
- How many shirts, sweaters, pairs of stockings, underwear does the user own?
- How many pairs of shoes need to be accommodated?
- Are there seasonal decorations that will require storage?

Everything that can be inventoried and quantified should be listed and counted as space is planned. When *inventories* are complete, then actual physical measurements should be taken where possible. The dimensions of furniture pieces, fixtures, equipment, clothing, and even storage boxes should all be noted so they can be given adequate space in the plan.

Planning sufficient space for circulation or movement through an interior is important to make the environment functional. Insufficient area for actual physical movement will make the design unusable and frustrating. The mind must also be able to move through an interior. Inadequate visual space where the eye and mind cannot expand may result in an environment that is unpleasant for many and even claustrophobic for some.

In order to create comfortable and functional designs, space considerations must carefully be reviewed so that space can be allocated according to the priorities of the users. These types of priorities can only be determined if the research of space needs is complete and accurate. Chapter 5, Space Planning, deals with these and other considerations, as it follows the planning process through to the floor plan and housing stages of the design process.

Environmental Factors

As the factors that will influence the design are researched, environmental considerations, such as climate and weather and physical location, must be explored. Some designs that seem to be aesthetically pleasing are failures because they ignore important environmental questions. Environmental concerns cannot be given second place to aesthetics and achieve a successful design. There must be a sympathetic compromise between the two.

Climate and Weather   Problems of climate and weather are generally straightforward. Climates with extremes of heat and/or cold will require ample forms of insulation as well as adequate heating and/or cooling systems. These require careful planning in order to function properly and to integrate aesthetically with the design of the interior. Climate and weather also influence the placement of a building to take advantage of favorable climate conditions or to avoid unpleasant conditions. Weather and climate should also be

(A)
Figure 1.5

(B)

Figure 1.6

Figure 1.5 Grand-scale spaces suggest a formal life-style befitting elegant entertaining at Oheka Castle, Cold Springs Hills, New York. *(A)* The dining room, laid out to graciously serve eighteen, is set in an exquisite Neoclassic-paneled area. *(B)*

The ballroom with round, skirted tables is designed for the continuing entertainment of guests, including the serving of light refreshments and, of course, ample space for dancing. Photo by Norman McGrath © 1989.

Figure 1.6 This home office is carved out of a nooklike attic space, made light and airy with triple skylights. Built-in shelves make the best use of wall space for slide carousels, whereas limited desk area allows

utilization of the Macintosh computer and its compatible printer. A compact, yet efficient, space meets the needs of the program. Photo by Norman McGrath © 1989.

keys to determining the type of structure to be built. Building materials should be suitable to the climate so they will not be subject to excessive deterioration.

Physical Location Physical location involves factors such as site, view, prevailing winds, solar exposure, noise, and environmental hazards.

Figure 1.7

- The site of a building should influence its design. The building should be compatible with its neighbors, though the style need not be the same, merely harmonious. Where conservation and preservation of the environment are important, the design should be well suited to, and harmonious with, the natural surroundings. Plans should be developed to do the least possible damage to nature and to integrate the building with existing natural features.

    In other cases, the design may be created to stand out in contrast with its environment; the environment may even be altered and reworked by the designer. Good and responsible judgment is paramount in such situations. Building and development are the natural results of growth and change and should be planned so that in years to come they will have improved with age.
- Delightful daytime or nighttime views are a valuable asset to an interior and should be featured in the design of the building. They should not be hidden by excessively ornate window treatments. Where views are unpleasant or nonexistent, attention should be focused inward away from windows, and treatments should be planned to hide unpleasant views.
- Prevailing winds can be a positive or negative feature of a location. They can provide cooling breezes or cold disturbing winter winds. When pleasant breezes prevail, buildings should be oriented to use them for natural cooling. When winds are icy cold, the building and its landscaping should provide shelter and protection. *Berms* (small hills) of earth or trees planted in a *windbreak* can help minimize the effect of cold winter winds.
- Like the wind, the sun can be both a positive and negative factor with its winter warmth and summer heat. In the winter, the sun streaming through south windows may be warm and comforting, but without adequate protection from the summer sun, an interior may become too hot and difficult to cool. Chapter 13, Building Systems, contains a thorough discussion of solar factors.

Figure 1.8

- Some types of noise are pleasant. The tumbling of a small creek or brook, the sound of waves breaking at the seashore, the crackle of a warm fire in the fireplace, or a breeze rustling leaves can be comforting and pleasant sounds. However, most people enjoy an environment free from loud annoying noise. It is amazing how the human organism can adapt to noise. Those who sleep in rooms facing busy city streets may soon become accustomed to the city sounds and find it difficult to sleep in a completely quiet environment.

    Noise from the outside and noise through interior walls can be controlled with extra insulation, adequate construction, and insulated glass. Noise within an environment can be controlled by the use

Figure 1.7 The informal adobe building style of New Mexico is nicely adapted to the local terrain, where sagebrush, rabbitbrush, western cedars, and cottonwood trees abound. Rough stucco, projecting vigas, and flat roofs are in harmony with the natural environment. Photo by Markus Fant.

Figure 1.8 Vertical louvered shutters bring a wonderful view into this interior design scheme. Simple lines and panels that can stack off the glass are two elements that make these shutters a good choice. View is an important program consideration and should be preserved because of the visual satisfaction it can bring to the occupants. Photo courtesy of Pinecrest, Inc.

Figure 1.9

Figure 1.11

Figure 1.10

of materials that *refract* (bend) or absorb sound waves. Textile applications (upholstery and floor, wall, and window coverings) refract and absorb sound waves and can largely eliminate echo noise, or *reverberation*.

- When planning, it is important to be aware of hazardous conditions, some serious enough to warrant selection of a new site. Fault lines, slide areas, eroding waterfronts, areas subject to flooding, high-power lines, railroad lines, heavy industries, areas of extreme pollution, and even former pollution sites—all are examples of potential hazards. Streets with heavy traffic may be hazards that should be considered so that planning will keep children free from danger and injury.

Mechanical Considerations

Mechanical considerations include heating, ventilation, air-conditioning (HVAC), plumbing, lighting, and telephone. A basic knowledge of the way these systems function will be helpful in understanding how they must integrate with the completed interior. Such understanding will also make working with the skilled technicians who install these systems smoother and more productive. Mechanical systems are also discussed in chapter 4, Lighting, and chapter 13, Building Systems.

Psychological and Sociological Considerations

Psychological and sociological needs also must carefully be considered because the design of an interior has tremendous power to make people feel good about their environments and can even affect the way they feel about each other. Most people recognize the effect that an interior environment can have (for both good and ill) on our well-being and even on some aspects of our character. As stated earlier, we create our interior environments and they determine our feelings and attitudes. That means that the use of space, color, texture, pattern, scale, balance, furnishings, and all the other design elements and principles that constitute our interiors make us feel and act in certain ways. Knowledgeable use of these elements can lead to the creation of environments that make us feel emotional responses such as cool, warm, happy, romantic, nostalgic, awed, compassionate, hungry, full, restless, soothed, stimulated, or relaxed. That is why an interior design must be considerate of subtle manipulations that do affect us so strongly.

Other sociological and psychological considerations include the need for privacy and interaction, cultural relationships, security and safety, and familiarity and stability.

Figure 1.9 The sun pouring through the skylight makes this swimming area pleasant and appealing, even though the temperature outside may be well below freezing. Photo by John Wang.
Figure 1.10 Frank Lloyd Wright's Guggenheim Museum in New York City, pictured here with its ascending circular display area, is beautiful because of its exciting form and is uplifting because of the way its design leads the eye upward. It is a good example of the way interiors can produce positive emotional responses and make being in an interior a pleasure. Photo by Ted Spiegel.

Figure 1.11 Intimate, personalized space that provides privacy and emotional response is created here by the Laura Ashley Company, with a master bedroom that is decorative and comforting, suggesting old-fashioned coziness. The selection of furnishings fills the needs for the program for this room—sleeping, seclusion, and domestic activities such as reading, conversation, and handwork. The emotional response is clearly romantic—the occupant feels transported into the Victorian era. Textiles by and photo courtesy of Laura Ashley.

Privacy and Interaction   Some people are rather private by nature, whereas others are more gregarious. Regardless of our basic social nature, we all have times when we need to be alone, and other times we need to interact with others. Spaces such as living rooms, family rooms, game rooms, dining rooms, and even kitchens should be planned for interaction. In many homes the kitchen is the heart. Even when homes are provided with areas for individual study, many times the family will end up studying around the kitchen table. When guests arrive for parties, they frequently gravitate to the kitchen. It is this tendency that has led to the popularity of *great rooms* which are large kitchen/dining/family room spaces where most of the day-to-day living is centered.

It is equally important to plan spaces where members of the household can be alone. Libraries, studies, workrooms, or bedrooms are logical places for privacy. When children share a room, some means of division or separation should be planned so that a degree of privacy can be achieved when needed. A desire for solitude and introspection is a basic human need that must be planned for and respected.

Cultural Relationships   Distinctive aspects of local culture or family history can enhance the quality of an interior. For example, the Pueblo Indian design of New Mexico with its adobe construction has been adapted into a local style that is charming and well suited to its environment. It is also strongly tied into the history and culture of the area and provides a strong emotional link with the prevailing culture. Some families may have strong ties to foreign cultures that should be considered in the design of the home. Displaying art or collections of crafts from those cultures makes the home an extension of personal history and experience.

Figure 1.12

(A)
Figure 1.13

(B)

Figure 1.12 This interior shows the New Mexico influence as it has been interpreted across the country. The curved stucco of the seating area and the video display unit are adapted from the softly curved forms of the New Mexico style. The tile floors and the whitewashed stucco walls, together with the Indian-style pottery and textiles, all help to create a casual Southwest mood. Photo by Bill Rothschild.

Figure 1.13 (A) The culture of New Mexico, with its distinctive mix of Pueblo Indian, Spanish, and American influence, is exemplified by the adobe architecture of Santa Fe, New Mexico. (B) Santa Fe residents have incorporated elements of the local style into their contemporary interiors. The round adobe corner fireplace shown here is adapted from earlier historical types and enhances the relationship with local history and culture. Photos by Markus Fant.

Security and Safety   The physical safety of the occupants and possessions can affect the psychological well-being of a home. There are few things that compare with the feeling of terror and despair associated with a fire or other disaster. To help prevent accidents and fire danger, government agencies have established guidelines and rules (codes) for safety and fire prevention. Smoke detectors and fire extinguishers offer even greater security, both physical and emotional.

The need for protection is one of the most basic reasons for seeking the shelter of a home. Home security has become a multimillion dollar industry providing alarm systems and other means of securing homes. These security systems may utilize complex equipment and sophisticated electronic surveillance, while others are as basic as well-engineered locking mechanisms. For many, these kinds of measures provide a sense of calm and well-being that makes a home the center of security that it should be.

Familiarity and Stability   The design of an interior can include items that create stability and reassurance through their familiarity. For example, space might be designated for family photographs and other personal mementos. Art, accessories, and furnishings collected while traveling also have the same effect of tying us to our personal histories and experiences. Such personal belongings are often reminders of events or people and are part of an emotional support system. The use or display of cherished collections, objects, or furnishings should be included as part of the planning process. Because of their familiarity and warm associations, our environments can support better mental and emotional health (see also chapter 12, Art and Accessories).

Economic Factors

The last consideration is one of the most important because it has such an impact on the extent of the design. Without proper funding a design can remain forever on paper. It is essential to know how much money can be used to research, develop, and execute the design because economic considerations will govern the quality of materials and furnishings, the lavishness of space utilization, and in reality, the total parameters of the project.

There are some considerations that will make designs more economical. For example, building materials that are plentiful or indigenous to an area will usually be economical. This means that brick is less costly near the factory because shipping costs are generally less. Where brick has to be transported many hundreds of miles, the cost will escalate. Wood is a natural choice in wooded areas and adds the economical quality of good insulation as well. Building and finish materials that require the least upkeep and give the greatest length of service or durability for the climate and location are also economical choices, a justification for selecting brick or siding instead of wood.

Specification of exterior and interior building components that are standard sizes, including doors, windows, and ceiling heights, and standard "in stock" items such as appliances and plumbing fixtures that are available are more economical than those special ordered or custom manufactured.

The cost of replacement when materials wear out is also an important factor in planning for economy. It is sad when a home that has been mortgaged for fifteen, twenty, or even thirty years is outfitted with materials that need replacing in as soon as five years. For example, a lower grade vinyl flooring or carpet will likely wear out and cost

Figure 1.14

Figure 1.15

Figure 1.14 These pieces of ceramic, glass, and linen, collected and loved over a lifetime, are the kinds of pieces that create familiarity and stability in an interior. Because they are often associated with people or events, they are the basis for warm memories. They also have fine decorative qualities and certainly may be functional as well. There is something satisfying about serving soup to family or guests from a tureen that was inherited from family or friends, or even acquired while traveling. Photo courtesy of Motif Design.

Figure 1.15 The British and Scottish military collection of Angus MacAulay gives his Inc. Magazine office both distinction and personality. Not only is the office unlike any other, it is also a source of familiarity and stability for its user. Photo by Ted Spiegel.

more to replace than a better quality, durable flooring would have cost in the beginning. Hardwood, tile, or even stone floors, which are initially expensive, will seldom wear out or need replacing. In the long run, cheap may cost more than expensive because poor quality will have to be replaced. If the lower quality goods wear out before replacement is economically feasible, then those who use the design must live with shabby goods. The credo "buy once and buy good quality" will serve well all choices for design materials and furnishings.

The cost of maintenance or upkeep of materials is another factor in planning for economy. If a finish or material requires constant dusting, cleaning, polishing, waxing, or some other strenuous form of maintenance, it may not be the best choice. The cost is counted in two ways—the money for repair or hired cleaning help and the time and effort spent in maintaining it yourself.

Economy may also include planning ahead for future changes or additions. Plumbing and wiring can be installed for central vacuum systems, intercom units, or for entertainment and sound systems that will be added later. Planning ahead saves costly remodeling, with its accompanying inconvenience and frustration. The list of projected changes and additions should include any item that is built-in and must be planned for in advance.

Writing a Program

This list of considerations may seem lengthy, yet raising and answering as many questions as possible establish a clear understanding or mastery of the problem. Such mastery becomes the basis for a good design solution. The only limiting factor in asking questions is the time limitation. At some point the design must move forward. When each of these aspects has been completely explored and the data has been confirmed by the users, then the data can be analyzed and compiled into a written document known as the *program*. (Note that the term *program* describes both what goes on in an interior and the written compilation of that data.)

Since the program is a constantly changing set of circumstances, the analysis of the research data previously discussed will only reveal the program at a given point in time. The program is the set of factors that indicates the direction the design solution must take. The written program is the road map that helps the design stay on course. The length of the written program will vary according to the size of the project. The critical aspect is not its length but its completeness and accuracy. The finished design will only be as good as the quality of research and articulation of the data. A fine design is the result of spending adequate time to analyze and organize before beginning to create.

Design Development: Solving the Problem

The creative mind will be generating ideas for design solutions all the way through the research phase of the design process. However, only after the research data has been analyzed and clearly articulated in the written program can the development of the ideas, or *concepts*, be formulated with accuracy.

Initial Concept Development

Concept development usually begins with *brainstorming*, which is the process of generating ideas without restriction and without making judgment as to the goodness or badness of the idea. The ideas can be verbal, sketched, or written. Some very good design solutions have been scrawled on table napkins and scraps of building lumber. The important part of brainstorming is the flow of ideas as one idea often triggers another and the two may suggest a third or a combination idea. When the best ideas emerge, they are put on paper as the basis for the design solution.

The ideas take the form of quick drawings called *schematics*, which are used to help visualize space plans, traffic patterns, details, or even possible color schemes. These can be modified as the process continues until the parts begin to form the whole. As the design starts to come together, the brainstorming process continues as one scheme generates variations. These ideas must be examined, and at some point decisions must be made. Some ideas must be rejected and those that survive can be accepted, altered, or expanded. This process continues until the pile of drawings reaches the ceiling or until time runs out. The ideation stage could go on indefinitely since solutions are limited only by imagination.

At some point, the best ideas are brought to a degree of completion and the design concept begins to emerge. A commitment is then made to the ideas, and they are refined to a level where they can be presented for analysis. The presentation of the proposed interior design is generally made with a series of boards (mat board, foam-core, or illustration board) displaying

- *Conceptual drawings,* which quickly demonstrate the ideas for the plan of the design without the time-consuming precision of finished drawings. These include scaled drawings showing furniture placement.
- *Materials and finishes boards,* which are mounted with actual materials suggesting color schemes and other selections.
- *Renderings,* colored perspective drawings of the space, which help to visualize how the finished design will appear.

Based on the presentation, the client approves the concept, or if it is not agreeable, the design must go back to the drawing board and the process begins again with additional client input. When the concept is approved, the design work may proceed.

Working Drawings and Specifications

With the approval of the concept, final design development begins with working drawings and written specifications. When approved and signed, these may become part of the agreement or legal document between the client and the designer. The working drawings are the finished mechanical drawings or plans prepared for use by the contractors in making bids and completing the construction of the design.

The working drawings are often prepared in blueprint form showing the details as they are to be executed. The furnishings and materials to be used in the design must be itemized in written, documented lists called *specifications*. The specifications include

- identification of the item
- its manufacturer
- pricing per unit and extended total; labor costs
- quantities and types of materials
- standards of durability or fire resistance
- types of finishes
- special instructions for construction or installation
- dimensions (sizes) and shipping weights
- any other necessary data

If these are not carefully and completely spelled out, the item or construction will not turn out as intended because it was subject to interpretation. Bids may also be inaccurate and inconsistent. When the working drawings and specifications are complete and approved and the contract arrangements have been made, the design process moves into its final phase.

Execution

The *execution* is the implementation of the design. During the execution, the actual construction begins, and the materials and furnishings orders are finalized. Ordering can be time-consuming, yet like each step in the design process, it must be done with great care and accuracy. When work-ing to meet a deadline, nothing is more frustrating than receiving fewer materials or different furnishings than what was intended.

During this phase of the design process, the work of the contractors should be inspected to ensure that the plans are being carried out properly. This might entail work with builders who do the actual construction and with electricians and plumbers to make sure the electrical, lighting, and plumbing systems are installed as planned and specified. It usually includes meeting with the carpenters and cabinetmakers who construct and install custom woodwork to verify style, dimensions, and quality. It is necessary to check with window treatment fabricators and installers as well as wallcovering and flooring installers to assure that the goods are correctly fabricated and installed. All of this supervision is a sort of a juggling act, but it is a crucial part of the process that will help guarantee success. This process is discussed further in chapter 13, Building Systems, where scheduling, critical path, and punch lists are explained and illustrated.

During the installation procedures, furnishings must be inspected for damage, in which case any necessary insurance claims with shipping firms and manufacturers must be processed without delay. Unfortunately, damage or flaws are somewhat common, and when they occur, attention is required to arrange for repairs or replacement.

Although there are inevitable frustrations during the execution phase, it can also be the most exciting part of the design process. There is great satisfaction when the research and design development finally come together into a completed design. It is exciting to witness what was once a few scrawls on a scrap of paper emerging into something very real, innovative, beautiful, and functional.

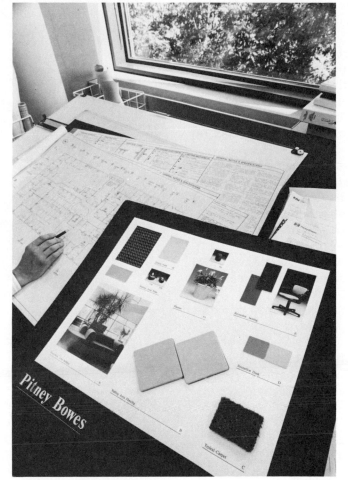

Figure 1.16

Figure 1.16 A commitment to design ideas is reflected in the presentation of materials and finishes boards. These boards, laid over the blueprints and specification booklets, were prepared for the branch offices of the Pitney Bowes corporation. Photo by Ted Spiegel.

Nonresidential Considerations

The design process for nonresidential interiors is largely the same as for a residence with the exception of the following considerations.

- Nonresidential design has a greater emphasis on the preparation of contracts and agreements between the client and designer. This is the reason nonresidential design is often referred to as contract design. However, contracts for residential projects are not uncommon today.
- Preparation of bids is a more common procedure in nonresidential design. The designer develops a concept and prepares an estimate of how much the implementation of the concept will cost. This information is presented to the client who can compare the concept and its cost with similar presentations by other designers.
- The specialties in nonresidential design are diverse, including health care, hospitality (hotels and restaurants), commercial (stores and businesses), and office planning. Specialization in different types of design allows the designer to stay current on issues within his or her area of focus. However, any designer willing to invest the time in research might be able to develop a suitable design solution for any area of specialty.
- The profile for a nonresidential design may be more generic. Because customers, employees, and guests are transient, the design of a nonresidential space may not be for a specific person but rather for any person who performs a certain task or uses a certain space. Consequently, it is more important to identify most nonresidential users in terms of numbers and functions, which are generic considerations. However, for others such as a president, a chairman of the board, or the senior partner of a law firm personal preferences will have to be assessed as they would for a residential user. Their offices might be more personal and costly, fitted with exclusive furnishings of personal preference.
- Nonresidential designs are often larger in scope, size, and budget as well as being less personal than residential designs. Consequently, their planning may be more complex. For example, on large projects, such as hotels or hospitals that require several years for completion, it is usually necessary to substitute items that may have been discontinued by the manufacturer in the interim and are no longer available. The designer will select substitutes that maintain the integrity of the original design.

Figure 1.17

- *Codes* and restrictions are laws established by federal, state, and local governments and their agencies for the health, safety and welfare of the consumer. They are exacting and often complex and tie the designer to a considerable amount of liability. Codes provide requirements for mechanical systems that will function both safely and properly and for fire and occupational safety with certain types of materials, equipment, and structures. Codes and restrictions also force the designer to be aware of the needs of the handicapped. Today, all areas of a public building must be easily accessible to those with physical limitations (see also chapter 6, Furniture Arrangement). Codes are contained in documents available from state building boards, from health, safety, and welfare departments, and from agencies such as the American National Standards Institute who have prepared specifications for making buildings accessible to the physically handicapped. The International Conference of Building Officials has prepared a document called the *Uniform Building Code (UBC).* This is a set of guidelines for construction that is accepted nationwide.[2]

Figure 1.17 This well-planned reception area on the floor of the Lenox Hill Hospital shows clean, sleek lines and smooth functioning of duties that make the medical center run well. Well-placed task lighting and ergonomic seating help personnel work efficiently. Photo by Norman McGrath, © 1988.

Figure 1.18

- After a period of time when users have lived with and tested the effectiveness of the design, the *post-occupancy evaluation (POE)* reveals how well the design functions. The evaluation can be accomplished by on-location interviews and open-ended questionnaires. It might seem that the information from such evaluations would be too late to be of any value. The value lies in future improvements and in the benefit of vital information that can be implemented in other projects. The evaluation is a tool that helps the designer perform better because of the added insight such information provides.[3]

Notes

1. For a more complete set of life-style considerations, see June Curran's *Profile Your Lifestyle* (Los Altos: Brooks, 1979).
2. The UBC is available from International Conference of Building Officials, 5360 So. Workman Rd., Whittier, CA 90601.
3. ASID Report. Vol. XII, No. 4, pp. 13–16.

Bibliography

Brill, Michael. *"Better Interior Design through Post-Occupancy Evaluation."* ASID Report, Vol. XII, No. 4, pp. 13–16.
Curran, June. *Profile Your Life-Style.* Los Altos: Brooks, 1979.
Faulkner, Sarah. *Planning a Home.* New York: Holt, Rinehart and Winston, 1979.
Preiser, Wolfgang. *Post-Occupancy Evaluation.* New York: Van Nostrand Reinhold, 1988.
Reznikoff, S.C. *Specifications for Commercial Interiors.* New York: Whitney Library of Design, 1979.

Chart 1.1   The Design Process

Letter of Agreement (contract)

Design Statement

Identifies
- Who
- What
- Where

Research and Programming

Identifies and asks questions about
- Users
- Function
- Relationships
- Space requirements
- Environmental factors
- Mechanical considerations
- Psychological and sociological considerations
- Economic factors
- Codes and restrictions

Writing a Program

Includes
- Analysis of research data
- Organizing the data into a written program

Design Development

The program is implemented through
- Initial concept development
- Working drawings and specifications
- Execution of the design

Post-Occupancy Evaluation

Figure 1.18 The design of this hotel atrium lobby and reception space is generic; it is planned to be appealing to many types of users. The large scale space is made to feel even more expansive through the use of a skylighted ceiling that allows the eye to move upward. The choice of materials and finishes is calculated to create a feeling of contemporary elegance and class common to much of today's hospitality design. Photo by John Wang.

DESIGN PRINCIPLES
AND ELEMENTS

CHAPTER 2

The AT&T building, a Post-Modernist design by the champion of Post-war Modernism, Philip Johnson. This building has been nicknamed his "Chippendale" building because it resembles many Late Georgian furniture pieces with its stately broken pediment. The integration of timeless principles and elements is the basis of all fine design, beginning with the building itself, and equally important, in the building's interior design. Photo by Ted Spiegel.

Page 26, top: In the lobby of International Business Machines (IBM) in Arkmonk, New York, the I.M. Pei Interior design firm created a three-story atriumlike interior with dramatic lines and vertical space. The frankly structural ceiling with diagonal lines in the skylights makes the design live with the rhythms of the sun. The light and pattern cast on the walls and floor change as the sun moves, making the design kinetic—living, changing, migratory. Line is the most forceful element of design. It is dramatic and dynamic. Large-scale furniture has been wisely chosen for the spacious area defined under the one-story area ceiling. The focal point is clearly the tree and skylight glazing. Photo courtesy of I.M. Pei, Architects and Planners. Photo by Steve Rosenthal. Page 26, bottom: This lobby, also by I.M. Pei, is in the Arco Oil Tower in Dallas, Texas. Here there are fixed elements—gridlike patterns on the floor, walls, and ceilings—that relieve the smooth skin of the exterior. Rich blue granite gives textural depth and interest in the space; shapes and forms are expansive and carry the eye along the vista. A form of kinetic energy is also seen in this lobby, this time through color and smooth, reflective textures and repeating shapes and moving transitionary lines. Photo courtesy of I.M. Pei. Photo by Richard Payne. Page 27, top: Although some interiors are created from the architectural blueprint stage as previously seen in the I.M. Pei lobby, most interior design work is accomplished in a given, established space. The sensitivity to the existing character of the space will help to bring about the best possible design solution. Here, designer Beverly Jacomini sought to express the warm, cheerful, and poetic native beauty of Texas by furnishing a nineteenth-century cookhouse at Austin's Windedale Historical Center as a country hideaway. Rusticated boards and beams provide a history-rich setting for the new furnishings that illustrate turn-of-the-century expression filled with comforting memories of a recognizable past. Subdued hues and elegant patterns turn a humble setting into an interior of great sophistication. Photo courtesy of Brunschwig & Fils. Page 27, bottom: Studied symmetrical balance on each side of the Georgian dog-ear window molding is in perfect harmony with the exquisite architectural detail integral to this home. The Champion House, an architectural gem in East Haddam, Connecticut, was updated by interior designer Robert K. Lewis for its restoration. Smooth textures, a contemporary Federal stripe in the balloon shade, and historical elements such as the prints of architectural engravings placed below acanthus leaf sconces and white porcelain vases contribute to the sympathetic beauty of compatible elements. The furniture was designed by John Saladino for the Facade collection by Baker Furniture and upholstered in fabric by Jack Lenor Larsen and Yves Gonnet. The Greek fretwork border is by Clarence House. Reprinted by permission from HOUSE BEAUTIFUL, © July 1985. The Hearst Corporation. All Rights Reserved. Lizzie Himmel, photographer.

Page 28, top: Inside the glass house designed and owned by architect Philip Johnson, minimal but elemental furnishings make a strong, structurally designed statement. Here the Barcelona chair, chaise, stool, and table by Mies van der Rohe are classic selections of the highest design caliber in a setting where fine design is paramount because of the clarity of the setting. The furniture, however, must not demand attention because the landscape plays the dominant role, uniting the breathtaking beauty of the New England landscape with the simplicity of the architecture. Photo by Norman McGrath. **Page 28, bottom:** *The bedroom of the glass house consists only of a stark, white-covered bed; the storage unit behind the bed forms the wall partition, eliminating chests, dressers, and nightstands. An essential group of seating completes the furnishings so that line, space, and textural background elements can take center stage. Photo by Norman McGrath.* **Page 29, top:** *A landmark in modern design, this exterior view of Philip Johnson's glass house reveals that space is the essential element, restricted as little as possible by the framework of transparent curtain wall construction. The compact size and stark lines are based on Bauhaus ideals of structural simplicity, utilizing modern materials in the finest of clean design compositions. The beauty of the planned and natural landscape is a part of this house, not an arbitrary addition. The exterior literally becomes at one with the masterfully planned spacial divisions and transparency. Privacy is assured in the bath and kitchen area in the central core of the home. Photo by Norman McGrath.* **Page 29, bottom:** *Before an interior design can become reality, much planning goes into the design process, resulting in a visual image of the space often presented by the designer to the client. This plan for Westwind Imports, a fictitious importing firm, won honors in the International Furnishings and Design Association (IFDA) 1988 National Design Fellowship Competition. The designer was Kevin Wooley, Bachelor of Fine Arts candidate in Interior Design at Brigham Young University, who executed the plan as seen here and wrote the program that accompanied the design. Specification and arrangement of elements are based on a thorough understanding of the principles and elements of design. The integration of time-honored and proven principles and elements forms the basis for decisions made by all professional interior designers in producing spaces that are not only aesthetically pleasing but function soundly for the parameters of the program, thereby meeting the needs of its occupants. Photo courtesy of International Linen Promotion Commission.*

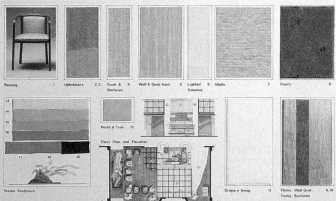

The Principles of Design

The principles of design—*scale and proportion, balance, rhythm, emphasis,* and *harmony (variety and unity)*—are somewhat abstract concepts that have been in existence and important to great architecture, art, furnishings, textiles, and hard materials for many centuries. The principles form the theory of *design*. Ideally, the theory of design implies that truly fine interior design incorporates appropriate scale and good proportion, carefully achieved balance, continuity through rhythm, areas of importance through emphasis, and harmony of all the elements, which is achieved through sensitive balance of variety and unity. These design principles are the bylaws that are universally accepted as the philosophy or rules that should govern the use of the elements of design. Furthermore, each element can be judged right or wrong in its use and placement through an evaluation of the principles of design.

For example, the use of color, an important and emotive element of design, can be judged or evaluated in this way according to each principle of design.

- Scale: Is the size or amount of the color appropriate for the decorative scheme, or is it used in too large or too small a quantity or an area?
- Proportion: Do colors complement each other, or is one ill-proportioned by too much or too little intensity or quantity?
- Balance: Is the color balanced with other colors in terms of size and intensity, and is the color distributed throughout the interior to create a balanced effect?
- Rhythm: Does the color carry the eye along with rhythmic smoothness, or is it too punctuated and abrupt in its use?
- Emphasis: Does the color create or support a focal point, or does it detract from the area of emphasis?
- Harmony: Does the use of color yield harmony through the adherence to a unified theme (unity) with enough subtle or dramatic difference to maintain interest in the scheme (variety), or does the interior lack harmony because the colors are too weak or competitive?

Chart 2.1 Principles and Elements of Design

NOTE: In-depth discussion of the principles and elements follows in the body of the chapter.

Design Principles

The principles constitute the design theory, bylaws, or governing concepts that work together to make a design composition successful.

Scale: The size of a space or an object, such as the overall dimensions or the largeness or smallness of a room, an object, or a pattern.

Proportion: The size relationship or ratio of parts to the whole, such as the size and placement of the arm compared to the chair.

Balance: The state of equilibrium achieved by arranging architectural components, furnishings, or patterns either symmetrically (exactly the same on each side of a center point), asymmetrically (different on each side), or radially (spokes or concentric circles).

Rhythm: The smooth flow of elements that carries the eye around the room. Types include repetition and alternation, progression or gradation, transition, opposition or contrast, and radiation.

Emphasis: An enhanced point of interest, or a focal point. A room may contain more than one and in varying degrees of dominance.

Harmony (variety and unity): The selection of compatible elements and furnishings that create a pleasing whole.

Design Elements

The elements are the components that can be manipulated to give form to the principles of design. The elements are seen in the arrangement of architectural structure and details and compositions of materials, furnishings, and accessory items.

Space: The defining of open and closed areas and positive (filled) space versus negative (empty) space to create a building, interior, or furnishings composition.

Shape or form: Shape is the two-dimensional outline often seen as a geometric figure, such as a rectangle, triangle, or circle. Form is three-dimensional as seen in cubes, cones, and spheres.

Mass: The actual or visual weight, density, or relative solidity of a form.

Line: The connection of two points that gives direction: vertical, horizontal, angular, or curved. Each has a psychological impact.

Texture: The relative smoothness or roughness of a surface; texture is read physically (by touch) or visually. Very small pattern is often read as texture.

Pattern: The arrangement of motifs to create a unified design, such as a pattern seen in an area rug or upholstery textile.

Light: Natural sunlight and artificial (man-made) lamps (bulbs) that affect the appearance of all other elements of design.

Color: Hues such as red, yellow, and blue that can vary from light to dark, from intense to dull, can be mixed with other colors, and can be combined in color schemes or hue combinations to create a psychological impression within interior design.

Scale

Scale deals with actual and relative size and visual weight. Scale is generally categorized as small or light, medium, large or heavy, or grand (extra large). One of the goals of pleasing interior design is to select furnishings that are in scale with one another. This implies a similarity of objects in overall dimensions or in mass (density), in pattern, or in other forms of visual weight. When objects are out of scale with each other, they will not be appropriate or harmonious selections. To evaluate the compatibility of objects in relation to scale is of paramount importance in interior design.

Although the actual dimensions of two objects may be similar, one may be a visually heavier scale than the other because of its weight or mass and the selection of material. For example, a glass table on legs will appear smaller scaled than a solid wooden chest table. While the overall dimensions might be exactly the same, the glass-and-leg table allows us to see through the piece, which visually scales it down and makes it appear smaller than the wooden piece.

Pattern and ornament also visually determine scale. A pattern with large motifs may appear visually heavy or massive, while a pattern of the same overall dimensions filled with small motifs and empty areas will appear smaller scaled overall. Likewise, color will affect our impression of scale. Bright, bold colors will appear larger than light, pastel ones (see also chapter 3, Color).

Figure 2.1

Figure 2.2

The scale, or size, of the architecture will often determine the scale of furnishings; small-scale furnishings are used in small interiors and large-scale furnishings are used in large or lofty interiors. This rule can be broken to provide drama or excitement, such as a large-scale pattern in a small area (which will also make the space seem much smaller). Conversely, small scale in a large interior might look tailored and may visually expand the space even further. When floor plans are drawn, they are reduced to scale, or drawn to scale, with 1/4, 1/8, or 1/16 inch usually equaling one foot.

In choosing or judging scale, perhaps the most important consideration is human scale. Very large scale and very small scale often feel awkward to people. Although grand scale is impressive and dramatic in public architecture, and small scale is wonderful for children, for the majority of adults, scale is most appropriate when it complements and easily accommodates the average human form. Because we are most comfortable with these dimensions, the standard ceiling height in homes is eight feet, and chairs and sofas generally have a standard seating height and depth.

Often we need to determine if the scale is right for the setting. This is done by comparing the scale of the object to other objects and to the architecture where it is found. This comparison tells us if the scale is well chosen. When parts of the object are compared to other parts of itself, the comparison forms the basis for proportion, and is the reason the two principles—scale and proportion—are frequently termed together; they are interdependent.

Proportion

Proportion is closely related to scale and is usually expressed in terms of the size relationship of parts to each other and to the whole. Proportion also deals with shapes and forms and their dimensions. It is, for example, the relationship of a chair seat or back to its base or arms or the size and scale of the tabletop to its legs. When the relationship or ratio is pleasing, the furniture is well proportioned. The evaluation of proportion is based on ratios, or the comparison of sizes. For example, a table that is well proportioned has side dimensions (width and length) that relate well to each other, creating a nicely shaped rectangle—neither too wide nor too narrow for the function of the piece.

Figure 2.1 Lightly scaled furnishings in the dining room at Boscobel reveal succinct compatibility in the two Sheraton/Hepplewhite sideboards and the dining table and the delicately scaled faux bamboo (wood made to imitate bamboo) Regency-inspired chairs. The Neoclassic architectural detail seen in the delicate mirror and transom light tracery and woodwork establishes the need for restraint in the scale of furniture and accessories; harmony results from a pleasing relationship of size and scale. Photo courtesy of Boscobel.
Figure 2.2 Frankly structural architecture in the window and wood floor grid dictates large-scale furnishings in this skyline penthouse suite. The fabric-covered screens are divided into an orderly sequence of big squares. Against this background, the overstuffed furnishings make a commanding, but appropriately scaled, presence. Geometric patterns in the sofa and chair are subtle in comparison to the ottoman upholstered in boldly patterned, large-scale "tree-of-life" crewel design. Accessories seen in massive pottery and broad-leaved foliage complete this substantial vignette. Fabric and furniture by and photo courtesy of Brunschwig & Fils.

Another example might be a sofa table (placed behind the back of the sofa and the same height as the back), which must be relatively narrow or it will be cumbersome and ill proportioned. Likewise, a family dining table that is wider than three and one-half feet may be too wide for food to be comfortably passed across it. Tables for other uses should have sizes evaluated according to their use or function.

Throughout the centuries that humans have worked toward pleasing proportions, many theories of what is good and acceptable have been espoused. One of the best known is that of the ancient Egyptians and later the classical Greeks who stated that pleasing proportions were termed golden. The *golden mean* is a line of division that visually divides an object, a wall, a tieback drapery treatment, or other furnishings into two unequal but harmonious parts; that line falls somewhere between one-half and one-third (vertically or horizontally). For example, the placement of a chair rail or dado molding (see chapter 8) creates pleasing proportions above and below the molding when it is placed not in the middle of the wall nor at the one-third mark but somewhere between one-third and one-half way up from the floor. Tieback draperies or curtains are also divided into pleasing proportions somewhere between one-third to one-half way up from the bottom or down from the top of the treatment.

The *golden section* refers to proportions of parts to each other and to the whole. The progressions, 3 to 5 to 8 to 13 to 21, and so on, are considered pleasing ratios or proportions as they relate to each other and roughly equate the theory of the golden mean. Further, these increments can be translated into sides of rectangles, called *golden rectangles,* which form the basis for a study of good proportions. For example, a table or art piece three feet by five feet is a pleasing proportion, as are multiples (or divisions) of those dimensions: twelve by twenty (four times three and four times five) or fifteen by twenty-five (five times three and five times five). A room with golden rectangle dimensions will theoretically be the easiest in which to arrange furnishings, and a golden rectangle window should pose few aesthetic window treatment problems. The golden mean, golden section, and golden rectangle are examples of how harmonious proportions can be calculated.

Many other philosophies of good proportion exist, but the bottom line is the "sense of rightness" that we feel or recognize when good proportion is evident. Recognizing good proportion is an intuitive ability for some people, and for others, it may take time and deliberate study to learn to recognize and to sense pleasing proportion. Much of what we learn about good proportion comes from studying classic architectural exteriors and interior detail, classic furniture, great works of art, and the beautiful application of finish materials and other furnishings, where the design has been recognized for years or even centuries as good or of pleasing proportions.

Figure 2.3

Balance

Balance is *equilibrium* or the arrangement of objects physically or visually to reach a state of stability and poise. Balance is an important concept because of the human need for balance in our lives. Balance is not only necessary for physical confidence in our actions and movements but balance is a guidepost in achieving satisfaction and fulfillment in life itself, and so we naturally seek it in our interiors. This state of equilibrium is achieved in one of three ways: through *symmetrical or formal balance*, through *asymmetrical or informal balance*, or by *radial balance*.

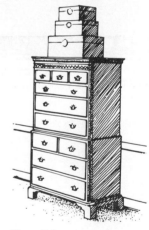

Figure 2.4

Symmetrical Balance

Symmetrical balance is also known as *bisymmetrical, formal, or passive balance.* Symmetrical balance creates a mirror image by the placement of items that are exactly the same on both sides of a central point. This might be a matching pair of mantel vases on each side of a painting or mirror. Or formal balance can be seen as matching nightstands or end

Figure 2.3 Country French architectural backgrounds and furnishings continue to be a favorite for dining spaces. This breakfront china cabinet is methodically divided into pleasing sections that approach golden proportions—the base is just over one-third of the height of the entire piece. Curved lines are also sensitively placed to be

pleasing to the eye. The armchair and dining table in front are in sympathetic relationship to each other; overall size, scale, and mass are refined and fluid. Photo courtesy of Hickory/Kaylynn.
Figure 2.4 This historic chest-on-chest is divided according to the golden section, just below the halfway mark. The lower portion is slightly larger, creating a heavier scale

and pleasing proportions. Rhythm by gradation is seen in the progressively larger boxes stacked on top of the chest.
Figure 2.5 The remodeling of the Levitas house in Martha's Vineyard, Massachusetts, by architect Armstrong Cumming, utilized mirror-image windows. A central wicker sofa framed in the foreground with wicker rocking chairs creates unusually interesting

Figure 2.5

Figure 2.6

Figure 2.7

tables with matching lamps placed on them. It could be a formal dining table where the chairs are placed exactly across from each other. Symmetrical balance suggests restraint, refinement, orderliness, and formality. Bisymmetrical balance is passive because it requires no judgment; we know exactly what to expect. Because formal balance is predictable, it adds a type of steadiness and durability to interior design. Much classical design from the Greeks and Romans to the Renaissance, Baroque, and subsequent periods was symmetrical. The symmetry created a sense of power and grandeur.

However, because of its unchanging nature, symmetrical balance can become stale and boring. In fact, it has been said that a really good symmetrical composition always contains elements of asymmetry. The symmetrical nature of historic designs was broken by asymmetric placement of figures in a frieze or by inclusion of dissimilar sculptural pieces in symmetrical niches. Rigid symmetry is less suitable to today's less formal and more relaxed life-style.

Figure 2.8

symmetrical balance. In addition to the space planning of other areas in the house such as stairs to one side and a dining area on the other, the mammoth butterflies between the walls and pillows on the sofa add elements of asymmetry to lessen the predictability of the formal balance. Symmetrical balance establishes stability and security in interior design. Photo by Norman McGrath 1988.

Figure 2.6 Studied symmetry seen in the matching bookcases, chairs, and accessories emphasizes the importance of the fireplace and mirror as a dramatic focal point. The asymmetrical placement of the plants, art, and door provides variety and relief from the exactness of the arrangement.
Figure 2.7 The stately quality of symmetrical or bisymmetrical balance welcomes all visitors to eighteenth-century

Colonial Williamsburg, Virginia. This restored village, based on classic placement, proportions, clean lines, and straightforward yet unpretentious architecture, holds charm and eternal appeal. Dividing the building vertically in half, the windows, dormers, and each half of the front door and transom exactly match each other in form and placement. Photo by Ted Spiegel.

Figure 2.8 Over one hundred years later, the Victorian era saw creative uses for design principles. Here, symmetrical balance is seen in a pyramid of round-headed windows framed with capped bull's-eye corner blocks supported with decorative brackets. The effect is intriguing. Photo courtesy of Anderson Windows.

Design Principles and Elements 33

Asymmetrical Balance

Asymmetrical balance is also known as *informal, active, optical,* or *occult balance.* Asymmetrical balance can be accomplished in two different ways:

1. Dissimilar objects can be placed so that their center points are at varying distances from the center point, or

2. Objects of similar visual weight or form may be balanced at equal distance from an imaginary central dividing line.

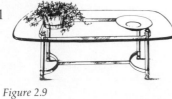

Figure 2.9

Asymmetrical balance is often difficult to accomplish. It requires finding objects that are compatible yet varied enough to be interesting, then arranging the objects, judging the arrangement, and often rearranging them over and over until the sense of equilibrium is judged to "feel right." This effort justifies the nickname active, because it requires active participation to accomplish. The term *optical balance* is derived from the necessity of judging the composition with the eye, or the optic sense. Achieving asymmetrical balance demands patience and sensitivity and certainly comes easier to some people than to others. Yet the results are definitely worth the efforts because asymmetrical balance can be deeply pleasing and does not readily become tiresome.

Although informal balance is the most common of the alternative names of asymmetrical balance, it is also known as occult balance because it has no set rules of what is right and is, therefore, a type of mystery in interior design. The Western world has learned much of asymmetrical balance from the strong Japanese influence in architecture and design. Oriental philosophies are based on the intrinsic, harmonious, and asymmetrical arrangement seen in nature, then translated through careful study and application to interior design compositions.

Radial Balance

Radial balance is a state of equilibrium that is based on the circle. It is seen as chairs surrounding a round table; as concentric circles in a chandelier or lighting fixture or, on a small scale, on the round dial of a clock; or on a larger scale, as circular furniture arrangements of comfortable chairs for group gathering. Radial balance can also be seen as spokes extending from a wheel or pedestal table or chair base. A form of radial balance can be seen in the grain of a dining table where the veneer (top layer) is laid in quarter sections that meet in the center. Historic wooden pieces frequently

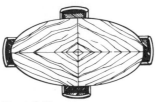

Figure 2.10

Figure 2.11

Figure 2.12

Figure 2.9 The plant visually balances the plate in this simple asymmetrical grouping. The glass tabletop and slender brass legs classify the table as a lightly scaled, or small-scaled, piece.

Figure 2.10 Radial balance is apparent in the placement of chairs around this oval dining table. The bird's-eye view reveals

wood grain laid to create rhythm by radiation in concentric flowing diagonal lines.

Figure 2.11 The living area of this Long Island, N.Y. home demonstrates the principle of asymmetrical balance in the placement of furnishings and architectural elements. Though they are very different, the windows at the far end of the room

balance with the stairway in the foreground, and the sofa balances with the two upholstered chairs. The furniture grouping also has an asymmetrical relationship with the architectural detail of the fireplace wall. Further, the arrangements on the mantel and coffee table also show asymmetrical relationships. Interior design by Jane Victor. Photo by Norman McGrath, © 1988.

Figure 2.12 Radial balance ascends from the main floor to the second story in this spiraling staircase in Summit, New Jersey, designed by the architectural firm Chapman & Biber. Based on the circle, this flowing linear form has spokelike stair treads extending out from the center shaft. Rhythm

incorporated radial balance with inlaid pieces of wood. Spiraling forms can also create a type of radial balance.

Rhythm

Rhythm is a concept familiar in music as the beat that continually carries along the melody. In interior design, rhythm carries the eye along a path at a pace determined by the elements that illustrate it. For example, rhythm might be found in the repetitive use of a color, pattern, texture, line, or furniture piece or style. Architectural detail such as stairs, window panes, and moldings illustrate rhythm. Rhythm is also a matter of expectation and anticipation and is a major part in the concept of emphasis or surprise. There are five types of rhythm:

1. repetition and alternation,
2. progression or gradation,
3. transition,
4. opposition or contrast, and
5. radiation.

Repetition establishes rhythm through the repetitive use of an element of design, as previously suggested. Repetition not only establishes a continuity and flow of rhythm but it also provides unity, or sameness, a part of the principle of harmony. For example, a color repeated throughout an interior can establish rhythm if the eye can smoothly connect rather than jumping or leaping from colored object to colored object. Repetition is seen in rows of seats in a church or theater, in a set of books bound to match, or in the same style of lighting fixture used many times in a public space. In architectural detail, repetition may be seen in the same window in classic architecture such as the elegant Georgian home (see chapter 14) or in moldings such as dentil trim or in the classic egg-and-dart sequence (see chapter 14). The egg-and-dart motif repeats two shapes symbolizing birth and death, and they are used in alternation, where every other design is the same. Alternation is the

Figure 2.13

Figure 2.14

sequence of two or more components where the eye can follow a rhythmic pattern. It is also seen in historic buildings with coffered ceilings, where a wafflelike pattern has both high and low areas.

Progression, or gradation, is seen in shapes progressing from large to small or small to large, such as the front steps leading to the *piano nobile* in classic architecture, or a set of nesting tables, where each smaller table fits beneath its next larger counterpart. A collection of different-sized boxes or a candelabrum (descending branched candlestick) are accessory items that can create rhythm by progression, or gradation.

Progressive rhythm (rhythm by gradation) can also be seen in the value of color, where a color scheme contains shades that vary from very light values (perhaps on the ceiling) to medium values (on the wall) to dark values (on the floor) and where the values are further expanded in the furnishings. This light-to-medium-to-dark progressive sequence is also discussed in chapter 3, Color, as the concept of value distribution.

Transition is a rhythm that leads the eye without interruption from one point to another. Rhythm by transition can be established by a continuous line, usually an architectural element such as a crown or dado molding or an arched doorway. A stenciled or wallpaper border or a painted graphic or a long carpet runner are methods of creating an uninterrupted visual, rhythmically flowing line.

Opposition or contrast is an abrupt change that forms interesting, repetitive rhythm and is seen in three ways. First, as repetitive 90-degree angles, such as window frames or grids, as built-in units, such as cabinetry and luminous ceilings, and in the corners of angular furniture or framed artwork. Second, opposition or contrast can be seen in patterns: open and closed, busy and plain, light and dark combinations of fabric, area

by radiation is also a result of lines and forms brought into a radial design. Lines in this interior are well balanced: horizontal and vertical in the glass grids; diagonal in the skylights; and graceful curves in the spiral staircase, inviting the eye upward. Photo by Norman McGrath, © 1988.

Figure 2.13 Romanesque Victorian influence is seen in the roundheaded (top and middle) and Tuscan (bottom) arches of the historic courthouse in Tell City, Indiana (c. 1969). This venerable public building clearly illustrates a rhythmic eye movement through repetition of shapes and materials and through gradation of sizes and forms. Photo courtesy of the Vinyl Window and Door Institute.

Figure 2.14 The grand staircase at Boscobel unveils myriad rhythmic patterns. Repetition is abundant in the faux building blocks and contrasting vertical progression of the balusters. The dark edging of the stair treads and risers seems to be an underlying beat, following the melodically smooth line of the banister that ascends to the landing

and onward to the second story. The banisters and treads that lead the eye upward yield rhythm by transition. The prismatic chandelier in the Neoclassic/ Empire style of the period illustrates rhythm by radiation—in this case, as concentric circles of light. Photo courtesy of Boscobel.

rugs, or other textiles or wall coverings. Third, forms can be placed to contrast in a pleasing rhythm. Angular shapes placed next to rounded shapes not only create rhythm by contrast or opposition, they also give relief and a type of asymmetrical balance.

Radiation, which is essentially the same as *radial balance,* is the final type of rhythm. The type of rhythm that is established by radiating concentric or spokelike lines or forms can be dramatic and impressive. It is sometimes employed as designs in large, custom floor coverings in places such as hotel lobbies and ballrooms or in grand ceilings where architectural carving or cast plaster creates a radial effect. As such, it can be very beautiful and give the room a circular, sweeping, rhythmic movement. On a smaller scale, radiation can be seen in place settings at a round or oval table or as furniture forms in a circular grouping. (See figure 2.10.)

Emphasis

Emphasis is the creation of a *focal point*—an area visually important enough to draw and hold attention. Examples of dramatic, demanding focal points include a beautiful fireplace, a view from a window (or even an art glass window), a wall of dramatic art, or an impressive piece or grouping of furniture. A rhythmic progression—a many-doored hallway, for example, ending in a vista such as a fine furniture piece or artwork—is the principle of emphasis.

Some interiors may have multiple focal points, each one with a different level of emphasis, progressing from the most to the least dominant in order to avoid conflict. Logically, smaller areas can handle fewer focal points than larger areas. An exception might be an art gallery, where each piece of art is given equal opportunity to be a point of interest and emphasis. (See figure 2.16.)

Where varying levels of emphasis are planned, the dominant focal point could migrate. For example, in the winter the fireplace is a logically comforting focal point that dominates interest. In warmer seasons, through rearrangement of the furnishings, the most dominant focal point might become a large window with a view. Where no focal point exists, one can be created in the guise of bookcases, china cabinets, artwork (displayed individually or in group arrangements), tapestries, rugs, quilts or other art fabrics, and mirrors.

Figure 2.15

The elements of design can be manipulated to give greater emphasis to a focal point. Arranging furniture shapes to face the focal point, directing lines toward the focal point, grouping or massing objects to give visual weight to the focal point, or using more dramatic color at the area of the focal point are ways to increase emphasis.

Harmony: Variety and Unity

Harmony is the combination of design elements, architecture, and furnishings into a pleasing or orderly whole—a state of agreement or a feeling of rightness. Harmony is the result of a delicate balance of two subprinciples: variety and unity.

Variety is the absence of monotony or sameness, yet it is much more. Variety is a healthy, positive influence that brings about vitality, interest, and diversity. It can be seen through a selection of differing colors, textures, furniture and accessory styles, through the contrast of hard materials with soft materials, and through the combination of seemingly divergent old (historic) and new (modern) architecture and furnishings. Yet variety without some order or a master plan can become confusing and dissonant.

Unity, the other component of harmony, complements and balances variety. Unity suggests a oneness and uniformity—an identity that establishes a master plan.

Figure 2.16

Figure 2.15 Rhythm by opposition is seen in the right angles of this window fenestration. Right angles are further echoed in the chest and screen.
Figure 2.16 Rhythm by opposition is seen in this innovative kitchen/dining area in three ways. First,

ninety-degree angles are replete in the ziggurat-type step forms and in the kitchen cabinetry. Second, strips of light- and dark-colored tiles edge the terraced walls and banquette (dining bench), creating rhythmic opposition through value contrast. Shapes are the third way to accomplish rhythm

by opposition, evidenced here in the circular forms of the table base, pendant lighting, plant forms, and basketry as opposed to the severe rectilinear lines. This New York City apartment was designed by architect Peter Wilson. Photo by Norman McGrath, © 1979.

Figure 2.17 (A) The arrangement of furnishings is important in the creation of a focal point. In this great room (kitchen, dining room, family room) designed by Nina Hughes, ASID, contemporary furnishings and lighting make a pleasant U-shaped conversion area. (B) The furniture

Unity is the goal that is being sought and, hopefully, achieved when all the various elements and furnishings are brought together.

Unity can be achieved by carrying out a cohesive color scheme or by keeping the character and style of the furniture consistent. Unity dictates selecting background materials, fabrics, and accessories that all have a similar feeling. This means that the use of pattern or ornament, color and value, surface textures (smooth or rough), and even the grain of the wood (coarse or fine) is consistent in character with the master plan.

Unity is established at the beginning of a design project as a part of the design statement, discussed in chapter 1. At the outset, every planned interior should have

goals of identity and oneness. This design statement, master plan, or set of goals should be organized and set forth on paper in written and graphic form, so that every furnishing item, whether purchased at once or over a period of years, will be selected to complement all other furnishings specified. It is wise and thoughtful planning that sets apart fine design from interiors that lack harmony. True harmony is within the reach of everyone who studies, plans, and directs their efforts toward design of the highest caliber.

The Elements of Design

The *elements of design—space, shape* or *form, mass, line, texture, pattern, light,* and *color—*are used by every designer in every discipline, from interior design to fashion design to landscape design to architecture to community planning. These elements were not invented but discovered and skillfully incorporated and balanced by artisans and designers over the course of history. Because of the basic and crucial nature of the elements of design, they are discussed in nearly every fine art textbook and wherever the education or evaluation of a designed work takes place.

Keep in mind that every element of design can be used effectively or ineffectively and that many compositions exist that are not perfect in their use of the elements. For example, an interior may have dramatic space, perfectly balanced light, well-proportioned form or mass, and appropriate line but may be filled with poorly selected pattern, texture, or color. Or perhaps the pattern, texture, and color are well chosen, yet some of the other elements are used ineffectively. As students of design, we seek to recognize and to perfect the skillful use of the elements of design in interiors.

(A)
Figure 2.17

(B)

Figure 2.18

grouping faces a complex focal point, or area of visual emphasis, in the television/stereo wall, eating bar, cabinetry, and handsome window with sophisticated balloon shade. The view out the window is pleasant during the day, and the wood cabinets and fabric lighted by track

luminaries make the room pleasing in the evening as well. This interior was part of the designers' show house, Castles on the Sound, at Sands Point, Long Island. Photos courtesy of Nina Hughes Associates, Inc., Interior Planning and Design.

Figure 2.18 Harmony is the design principle resulting from balancing variety and unity. In this interior furnished with Laura Ashley textiles and wall coverings, color and a repetitive use of a printed floral fabric unite the scheme, while vintage

antique furnishings and accessories from various historic periods give lively interest and character. The successful result suggests an interior occupied for many years by aesthetically sensitive people. Photo courtesy of Laura Ashley.

Figure 2.19

Figure 2.20

Figure 2.21

Space

Although the elements of design are equally important, space is perhaps the cornerstone of interior design elements, because space exists as a diffuse, endless entity until it is defined. The definition of space occurs with building construction, resulting in exterior and interior spacial allotments. Space-restricting devices within the building—walls, floors, ceilings, and furnishings—create a series of spaces with individual dimensions and qualities. These qualities can only be discovered as a person moves through spaces and perceives them one at a time: one space flowing into another or one abruptly ending and another beginning. When the space/time movement is complete, the perceptions are mentally assembled to give a true picture and judgment of the space.

The divisions and restrictions of space form the foundation of architectural planning. Interior designers often create unequal space allotments within buildings not only for aesthetic reasons but to answer human needs, as well. Treating spaces of different sizes addresses two basic human needs. First is the need to be protected, enclosed, and comforted. Small spaces give a sense of security from intruders and from the buffeting of the outside world. Small spaces establish territory; they give a sense of pride, of ownership, and offer opportunity to personalize our own space. Conversely, small spaces can be restricting or confining and can spawn restlessness and frustration. Small spaces that are inadequate for functions that are performed there may visually be expanded through the use of light colors, wall-to-wall neutral floor coverings, small-scaled furnishings, mirrors, and smoothly textured surfaces or textures with little pattern. Generous light from more than one source can also give the impression of more space than actually exists.

Large space fills a second basic human need as an outgrowth of the confinement of small space. This is the need to be free, to mentally soar into a space devoid of restrictions, to be stimulated by the immensity of space as compared to the insignificance of human scale. After a while, however, the lack of restriction can create feelings of insecurity and inadequacy and a desire to return to the safe, secure quarters of small spaces. Large interior spaces

Figure 2.19 In this Fire Island, New York, home, architect Peter Wilson divided space into interesting shapes and planes as seen in this dramatic view of a two-story descent. Open spaces in the guise of cutouts, balconies, and vaulted areas make a strong architectural statement. The visual expanse allowed here is both stimulating and exhilarating; the window at the lower landing allows a view into a wooded landscape. Photo by Norman McGrath, © 1979.
Figure 2.20 A small landing near a back door lends charm and intimacy through its restricted dimensions. Photo courtesy of Laura Ashley.
Figure 2.21 In this Nantucket, Massachusetts, house, architect Edward Knowles has planned a large space for informal living, containing not only generous square footage but ample cubic footage through vaulted beamed ceilings and the arched doorway and window. The dark wood trim establishes a linear definition of space indicating where the room ends, even though the floor through the archway has no such divisions. The expanse of glass seen in the background serves to bring the exterior into the interior, further

can be difficult to handle; often there is a need to make the space seem smaller than it is. Effective ways of creating more intimacy in large spaces include using medium- to large-scale patterns and dark or vivid colors that visually advance, furniture that is heavy or solid-looking, area rugs (particularly patterned or colored ones that visually break the floor space), large-scale artwork, and multiple furniture groupings (see also chapter 6, Furniture Arrangement).

Many well-planned interiors incorporate both small and large spaces. We see this in homes where a living area or solarium has a high ceiling, where a family room or great room has generous square footage, or where several rooms open onto a solarium, deck, or covered patio. In nonresidential interiors, such as business and professional centers, shopping malls, or hotels, the small, enclosed quarters are offices, boutiques, shops, or hotel rooms, and these are often grouped around a courtyard, atrium, ballroom, or multistoried open lobby area. To emerge from small spaces into large or tall spaces can be exhilarating and satisfying, yet the return to the small areas can bring about a needed sense of personal belonging, security, and safety.

Interior designers create interesting areas of *positive and negative space.* Positive space is space that is filled with color, texture, form, or mass. This could be architectural walls, furnishings, art, area rugs, or even graphics or scenes painted on walls. Negative space is the empty space surrounding the positive space—the windows between walls, the floor around the area rug, the wall around and between works of art, the space between furniture pieces or even the cubic footage. In a successful interior, the positive and negative spaces should be balanced both in terms of amount and in terms of placement. Some areas may be primarily positive space, others primarily negative and some areas may be equally distributed between filled and unfilled space. For example, the proportion of negative (empty wall) space between works of art hanging on walls may remain relatively even or it may be unevenly distributed.

Shape or Form

While we sometimes think of shape as only a two-dimensional outline, form (which is an extension of shape) is the three-dimensional configuration of the objects within the interior. For example, furniture seen in silhouette has shape that can be perceived, and as we move around the furniture, the silhouette changes and we begin to comprehend the three-dimensional quality of the form.

Figure 2.22

Figure 2.23

expanding the line of vision and, hence, the feeling of even greater visual freedom and spaciousness. Photo by Norman McGrath, © 1988.
Figure 2.22 The fish tank at the end of this waiting room is form; empty walls are negative space, whereas all areas that are occupied, including the plants and frankly structural

furniture, become part of the positive space. The bay window brings vintage character to this fine old house adaptively reused as a professional space—a family dentistry practice. Interior design by Carolyn Close and Signy Spiegel. Photo by Signy and Ted Spiegel.

Figure 2.23 Oheka Castle in New York is replete with shapes and forms that span the centuries to be appreciated and loved today. The series of Roman keystone arches in the facade are two-dimensional shapes whereas the arch becomes an imposing three-dimensional form in the carriage drive-through. Steep

hipped roofs are dramatic three-dimensional triangular forms. Vast strips of grass form flat planes that prelude the cobblestone courtyard, both important rectilinear shapes that give respect to the monumental architecture. Photo by Norman McGrath © 1989.

Often an interior is successful because the forms that fill it are beautifully shaped and well proportioned one to another. There are several kinds of shapes: two-dimensional outline shapes or planes such as rectangles, squares, triangles, circles, and other geometric shapes or meandering, curved, or angular shapes that do not fit neatly into geometry. When these geometric planes are given a third dimension, they become forms such as cubes, cones, or spheres and forms that are sinuous or curving.

For example, a rectangular table can be an appreciated form and shape that is simple and pleasing, yet if the entire room were filled with similar shapes and forms, the room would become boring and repetitious. Certainly there needs to be a balance of form—a curved chair, perhaps with upholstery covering, to soften the straight lines of the table form. The forms that are placed next to each other will have considerable effect on each other. Sometimes the juxtaposition of unlikely elements, such as the tandem placements of a vintage piece of furniture with a thoroughly modern piece, can create a delightful and charming surprise. On the other hand, certain forms destroy the integrity of each other and prove disastrous to both objects. This might be the placement of a delicate and lacy plant next to the abstract lines of a modern painting where the incongruity is jolting and disturbing. Perhaps a sculptural, abstract plant form, such as a cactus, would be better suited to the shapes in the painting.

The key to selecting forms is to balance them against the proportion and scale of the architecture for the desired psychological effect or feeling and to select each form to complement other nearby forms, as previously discussed.

The sensitive and careful selection and arrangement of forms is crucial in an interior because forms have great power to persuade us to feel certain ways, such as alert and attentive, or relaxed and secure. Shapes and forms appeal to the senses and can have amazing impact on the person who enters the room. For example, a person entering a room

(A)
Figure 2.24

(B)

(C)

filled with cubes will probably perceive the interior as a no-nonsense one where, perhaps, business takes place. Curved forms are gracious, may make people feel more relaxed, and are commonly used in residential living rooms and bedrooms.

Being sensitive to sculptural forms can increase our appreciation for classical beauty and modern abstract expression. Classic furniture pieces (see chapter 7) are sculptural forms that are so important that the character of an interior can become impressive with their added presence. Furniture pieces that have endured decades or centuries are revered and appreciated today as fine decorative art largely because of their timeless and appealing forms.

Mass

Mass is the solidity, matter, or density that is defined by shape or form. In furniture, mass is *actual density* when the material is filled in, such as a solid block of wood. Mass can also be *visual density* where the material may not be solid. Heavier or more solid mass will make furniture pieces look larger than furniture with the same overall dimensions but with empty areas instead of solid areas. Examples of furniture with solid or heavy mass include sofas, chairs, and ottoman stools with skirts to the floor and/or with oversized cushions; end tables and nightstands supported with bracket feet or no feet or with doors or solid fronts; dining room tables with heavy solid legs or pedestals; bookcases filled with books (as compared to bookcases with empty areas or areas of art or sculpture).

Heavy mass is desirable where the room is large and furnishings need to visually take up as much space as possible or where furniture needs to appear dignified or commanding. (See figure 2.39.)

Massing means grouping together components such as accessories or furniture or blocks of architecture to create a unified "group mass." Massing will give a weighted, more solid or imposing appearance. For example, several framed art pieces on a wall will create an important,

Figure 2.24 The shape and form of new modern design. *(A)* The Tric-Trac table lamp imported from Italy makes a bold Art Deco statement. The oversized, white-speckled black fabric shade is a perfect counterbalance to the swirl created by the paler,

asymmetrical funnel-shaped ceramic column and its rotated, triple-tiered, triple-toned gray base. Photo courtesy of Calger Lighting, Inc. *(B)* The Piccolo chair, with leather-upholstered seat, arm, and back. Its small scale is adaptable to both

residential and nonresidential seating. Eight colors are offered for both the enameled metal frame and leather, allowing for either tone-on-tone or contrasting combinations, making the form and shape take on even more flexible dimensions. Photo courtesy of Cy Mann Designs, Ltd. *(C)* The Flou-

Flou sofa is a plump sumptuous cover draping fluidly over a puffy upholstered base. Inside, sectioned fiberfill keeps the cover fluffed all over; outside, simple seaming polishes the soft, unconstricted look—a welcoming, appealing form. Photo courtesy of Ligne Roset/Gonin, Inc.

heavier looking arrangement than just one or two isolated small pieces. On the coffee table, a book, potted plant, and objects of art grouped into an interesting composition will draw more attention than would the book alone. And, certainly, two sofas placed in an L shape or parallel to each other will become more impressive than a single sofa.

Furniture, accessories, and artwork can be massed together to balance other larger pieces or architectural components such as windows or fireplaces or to fit into the scale of a room. For example, a low chest with a table lamp could be massed together with a framed art piece to become a visual unit. This unit could then balance a larger case piece such as a breakfront or secretary-type cabinet. Massing can be instrumental in giving richness and completeness to the other components that otherwise might look empty or unfinished when used alone. Certainly a framed artwork by itself on the wall may float awkwardly without something (a table, chair, or chest) to visually anchor it; this is the role of massing.

Architects use massing as a tool to create emphasis or to draw attention. For example, when an exterior is analyzed, it is often clear that the architect has manipulated window openings or wings or shapes of roof in such a way as to create areas of emphasis and balance.

Line

Line is the connection of two or more points. The eye also perceives line when two planes meet and when shape is seen in silhouette as an outline. Lines may be *straight* (horizontal or vertical), *angular* (diagonal or zigzag), and *curved* (circular, flowing, or tightly curved). Lines are used by interior designers to create effects such as increased height, width, or the impression of movement. The psychology of line is important to creating ambience or a particular mood in interior design. The types of line are listed in Chart 2:2, along with the psychological effect of each.

Figure 2.25

Figure 2.26

Figure 2.27

Figure 2.25 These ottomans illustrate heavy mass—density or solidity that fill the overall dimensions of an object. There are no see-through areas, as the upholstery covers the seats to the floor. The dense mass is accentuated by massing, or grouping, three ottomans. Massing brings together like objects to produce a weightier effect through volume or numbers. Further, the darkly colored, complex fabric suggests an even heavier mass because it draws attention to its bold, heavy-appearing designs. Fabric and furniture by and photo courtesy of Brunschwig & Fils.

Figure 2.26 This charming Victorian collection of accessories or whatnots is massed together to give greater importance and a larger grouped scale. The three frames on the wall are hung in symmetry, whereas the table grouping is clearly a cluttered asymmetrical mélange.

Figure 2.27 Massing can be seen even on a small scale in this handsome collection of accessories atop an Empire chest. Individual pieces yield their identity to merge into a single visual unit, asymmetrically balanced, where each piece is important to the entire arrangement. Laura Ashley linens; photo courtesy of J. P. Stevens & Co., Inc.

Chart 2.2   Psychological Effects of Line

Straight Lines

Horizontal Lines: Weighty, Secure, Restful, Repose.

Horizontal lines suggest a solid, harmonious relationship with the earth; earth's gravity has no further pull. Long horizontal lines can visually expand space, making rooms appear wider or longer. When found in a connecting architectural detail such as a molding, horizontal lines provide a smooth transition between rooms or areas. If they lead to a focal point, they help to emphasize it; when they stop at a window, the eye is guided to the exterior view. Too many horizontal lines in an interior may become boring and lack interest.

Figure 2.28

Figure 2.29

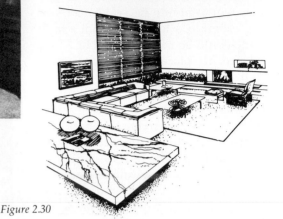

Vertical Lines: Imposing, Lofty, Solid, Formal, Restrained.

Vertical lines lift the eye upward. They have the ability to lift the mind and the spirit as well. As such, vertical lines are a purposeful tool for architects and designers of churches and public buildings because they inspire awe and tend to diminish the significance of human scale. The use of vertical lines can make an interior seem higher, apparently increasing vertical space. Vertical lines are stable because they represent a perpendicular resistance to earth's gravity. They convey a feeling of strength and dignity and are quite appropriate in formal dining rooms, entryways, and formal living areas. This formality can bring a stiffness or commanding feeling to the interior. Too many vertical lines can cause a feeling of uneasiness, of too much confinement and predictability.

Angular Lines

Diagonal Lines: Action, Movement, Interest, Angular Stability.

Diagonal lines are flexible because their exact direction may vary from shallow to steep angles. Diagonal lines generally suggest movement, action, or dynamism, perhaps because diagonal lines are associated with going places: up or down a diagonal staircase or an escalator, the taking off or landing of an airplane. Interest is usually sustained longer in diagonal lines than in horizontal or vertical lines, possibly because the angles appear to defy gravity and the eye and mind are stimulated. Yet diagonal lines can also be secure, such as the reinforcing diagonals of an angled roof truss system. Too many diagonal lines, particularly on the wall, can be overstimulating and perhaps tiresome.

Zigzag Lines: Exciting, Lively, Rhythmic Movement.

Zigzag lines are short diagonal lines that reverse upon themselves and form a regular or irregular pattern. A zigzag line can be one single line or several in a set. A set of regular zigzag lines is called a chevron or herringbone pattern, and irregular zigzag lines are called a flamestitch pattern. Angular zigzag lines can add energy and life to an interior. If too many zigzag lines are incorporated, however, the effect can be frenzied and agitating.

Curved Lines

Curved or Circular Lines: Soft, Humanizing, Repetitive Tempo, Gracefulness.

Curved or circular lines provide relief and softness to straight and angular lines and balance the harshness of too many straight lines. Curved lines give a human quality to interiors; they can be easy on the eyes and pleasant to view. A series of curved lines, such as in an arcade (a procession of arches) (see Fig. 2.39), gives a rhythmic cadence to the room, suggesting graceful movement. In architectural components, round or elliptic segments (sections of circles or ovals) such as archways provide graceful dignity to interiors. Generously curved lines are viewed as feminine. An excess of curved lines may become too decorative and, consequently, visually disturbing.

Figure 2.30

Figure 2.31

Flowing Lines: Gentle Movement, Growth, Linear Development.

Flowing lines are irregularly curved lines that move gently in a random or spiraling manner. Flowing lines may be seen in large, live interior trees, in spiral or curved staircases, or in the lines of fine, Oriental rugs, for example. Inspiration may be taken from the graceful curved lines of growing and changing plant forms. Because we are never certain where the line will end, flowing lines can provide a great deal of interest. (See Fig. 2.34.)

Figure 2.28 Horizontal lines clearly predominate in this Japanese-inspired home. The beams and clerestory windows with shoji screens attract the eye movement across the ceiling, while dark wood trim spans the windows and fireplace mantle and visually provides a transitionary

rhythm, connecting the room's perimeter. In the background is seen the tokonoma, or ceremonial niche, for displaying symbolic artwork. Even furniture pieces and ashlar masonry echo the horizontal theme, giving the room a sense of restraint and repose. Photo by Ted Spiegel, courtesy of Paul Kramer Construction.

Figure 2.29 This glass sculpture, entitled *Linear Moon* is made of horizontal strips of art glass on a solid base. Horizontal lines suggest tranquility, as evidenced in this artistic accessory. Photo courtesy of Run Stadler Studio and Opus II.
Figure 2.30 Horizontal lines dominate this ultrasleek modern room.

Figure 2.31 Vertical lines are effectively used in the traditional architecture and volumes of this library, creating a feeling of formality and attention. The verticality is balanced by the floor and ceiling lines and given some action and movement by the ascending staircase.

Figure 2.32

Figure 2.33

Tightly Curved or Busy Lines: Playful Activity, Zest, Lively Visual Stimulation.

Tightly curved or busy lines are most often seen in textiles and in wall and floor coverings as complicated patterns that are lively, busy or active. Tightly curved lines can add frivolity and fun to interiors and can make up a pattern that conceals soil and visually closes in space. Complicated tightly curved compositions, such as those in vivid floral fabric patterns or in area rugs, add life and may be visually stimulating and even aesthetically satisfying. As such, busy lines may save interiors from becoming dull or boring, yet control over the quality of the design is imperative. Colors and contrast that are bold or too much obvious pattern might prove displeasing and detract from the harmony of the interior.

Figure 2.34

Figure 2.35

Figure 2.32 Pairs of French windows determine vertical line dominance, giving dignity and seriousness to this bedroom. The effect of pilasters between the sets of windows is made possible by fluting the custom cabinetwork. The lines are balanced with the horizontally restful lines selected for the bed by interior designer Cindy Muffson. Carpeting is Anso V Worry Free Nylon by and photo courtesy of Cabin Craft Carpets.

Figure 2.33 Curved lines dominate the staircase and unusual window arrangement with its series of rhythmic circular shapes. Architect Jeff Riley of Centerbrook planned eye interest high in the wall as the asymmetrical placement of the curved and flowing lines mingles pleasantly with diagonal, horizontal, and vertical lines in this Essex, Connecticut, home. Photo by Norman McGrath, © 1988.

Figure 2.34 Curved, flowing lines are graciously employed in this sitting area. From gently curved to flowing to tightly curved lines, the effect is genteel and refined.

Figure 2.35 Flowers in a Basket, a traditional English floral handwoven rug, is a tightly curved, busy pattern that would add lively interest and a note of frivolity to an interior. Some lighthearted pattern underfoot can be visually satisfying, can make spaces appear smaller and more cozy, and can conceal soil. Photo courtesy of Saxony Carpet Company, Inc.

Design Principles and Elements   **43**

Combining Lines

Lines are used in combination in every interior, yet often one line will be planned to dominate in order to accomplish a desired effect, such as the vertical lines that produce awe and lift the eye heavenward in a church. Furthermore, vertical and horizontal lines generally form the structural foundation for a building in the form of perpendicular floors, walls, and ceilings. Angular and curved lines are utilized for reinforcement, strength, interest, movement, and relief, as seen in triangular roof truss systems and angled ceilings or walls and in dignified archways and domed ceilings.

Texture

Texture is the surface characteristics and appearance inherent in every element and component of interior design. As the relative smoothness or roughness of a surface, texture is determined in two ways: by touching the surface to feel the physical texture or by visually reading the surface, which may appear quite a different texture to the eye than it actually is to the touch. Some textures that read as rough are painted or printed tiny patterns that give the impression of a texture when it does not actually exist. An example is the painting of surfaces to appear as rock, brick, or tile.

Smooth textures generally are associated with more formal, high-style interiors, while rough textures are often thought to be more casual. Textures generally need to be handled in a unified manner, with a compatible feeling to every other texture selected for the interior. However, some contrast in texture is vital for relief and for emphasis. If every texture reads as smooth and glassy, for example, the interior would seem cold and unwelcoming. If every texture is rough, the interior may become harsh and irritating. A balance or a variety of textures is necessary within the unified theme or ambience in order to achieve harmony.

Texture is an element where different individuals may express different preferences. It is an element that can prove to be deeply pleasing to the occupant.

Figure 2.36

Figure 2.37

Figure 2.36 In the Robert house in Nantucket, Massachusetts, architect Edward Knowles has masterfully accomplished a pleasing combination of lines in this structural kitchen. Horizontal and vertical lines in the walls are counterpointed with the vaulted ceiling and well-placed skylight. Curved lines and forms are seen in perimeter spotlights, hanging pots, countertop appliances, and hand-thrown ceramic dinnerware. Flowing curved lines are the most important relief to the geometric shapes seen in the ceramic fish on the shelves and suspended from a block-and-tackle pulley system. These fish are symbolic and culturally important, as Nantucket has been a fishing village for over two hundred years. Photo by Norman McGrath, © 1988.

Figure 2.37 Visual texture is the byword in this attic retreat. Hand-printed and painted wall coverings and daybed cover resemble batik or tie-dyed techniques. The ribbed carpet is wrapped around the end-table cube and the apron of the daybed. The chair and footstool are upholstered in leather, completing the picture of commanding, upholstered textures. Photo by Norman McGrath.

Figure 2.38 (A) A variety of linen textures and subtle patterns in varying weaves and designs provide a close-up glimpse into the wide

Upkeep is also a consideration in selecting texture. Light-colored, rough textures will show very little dirt because the relief (high and low areas that produce highlight and shadow) will conceal soil. Smooth surfaces, such as flat walls, glass, or dark, polished wood, will reveal dust and fingerprints.

Pattern

Pattern is the arrangement of forms or designs to create an orderly whole. Pattern often consists of a number of motifs, or single design units, arranged into a larger design composition. Pattern is seen in printed and woven textiles such as upholstery and drapery fabric, floor rugs, and carpeting. Pattern is also seen in wall coverings and in carved or inlaid furniture designs. Very small pattern that is too small to distinguish may read as texture.

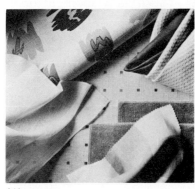 

(A) (B)

Figure 2.38

Figure 2.39

Combining Patterns

Patterns are frequently combined in interior design. While some combinations are very successful, we often sense incompatibility in other combined pattern schemes. To achieve a feeling of rightness, four things need to be evaluated: (1) the placement of emphasis, (2) the character of the pattern, (3) the color scheme, and (4) the scale of the patterns to be combined.

The placement of emphasis   Emphasis is giving importance to one pattern over another so that conflict is minimized. Emphasis is established by using a greater amount of one pattern or a larger scale of one pattern than another.

The character of the pattern   When two or more patterns are used in the same interior, the characters or styles must be compatible. For example, a dignified Georgian damask or brocade will not be compatible with a country Victorian printed cotton. They will have an entirely different look or character.

The color scheme   Generally, a closely related color scheme will greatly aid the achieving of harmony. If one pattern contains blues and yellows, for example, then other patterns should also contain exact, similar, or compatible hues, values, and intensities. If the colors are close but "off," then the patterns will not combine successfully.

Figure 2.40

world of fabric textures. Photo courtesy of the International Linen Promotion Commission. *(B)* Another close-up of a fabric texture and pattern. This one is handwoven for vertical blinds and Roman shades. The pattern results not only from the chevron pattern in the weave but also from the textured yarn and stained wooden sticks that interweave with the yarns. Photo courtesy of Window Modes/Modern Window, Inc.

Figure 2.39   The large scale of this interior, seen in the dramatic arcade and ceiling height, makes an appropriate setting for large-scale, definite-patterned upholstered pieces. The sofa and chair are coordinated in large- and small-scale patterns.

Figure 2.40   Coordinated patterns are combined in this vignette featuring Mary Gilliat's Edwardian Garden wall covering and fabric collection. The floral pattern used on the bedspread is coordinated with a striped floral bed curtain and echoed on the wall. The tieback curtains shirred onto a rod are ruffled in the floral pattern, evenly distributing the pattern. The plain or solid fabric curtain, bed valance, and dust ruffle balance the pattern, and an oriental rug on the floor with its own floral-based pattern complements the ensemble. Photo courtesy of Sandpiper Studios.

The scale of the pattern   Pattern scale or size can be similar if the style and the color are compatible. However, when the scale is the same, multiple patterns often seem to conflict. Varying the size or scale of the patterns by using, for example, a large pattern, a small pattern, a tiny pattern, a finely blended stripe or a compatible geometric shape, and appropriate textures can be a good means of achieving success in combining pattern.

Light

Light in interior design has two sources: natural light and artificial, or man-made, light. Although natural light admitted in a large quantity through expanses of glass windows may need some means of screening to prevent glare (too much bright light) or heat buildup, natural light is a desirable and an appreciated element of design. The quality, quantity, and color of light affects they way we see our surroundings and, as such, needs direction, control, and perhaps supplemental sources of light. When natural light cannot fully meet the needs of the interior design, artificial lighting is used to make up the difference. Artificial light is generally used in either incandescent form (the common light bulb with a tungsten element that glows to produce heat) or fluorescent (luminous lamps). Both natural and artificial light are discussed in further detail in chapter 4.

Figure 2.41

Light as an element of design affects all other elements. Light can make space appear large or small, friendly or cold. Areas well lit with clear, bright light will make spaces appear larger, whereas dim lights and shadows cast upon walls will seem to close in space.

Light can alter the apparent form or shape of furnishings. By lighting portions and leaving other areas in darkness, the form can appear much different than it actually is.

Low-wattage light sources or backlighting (throwing light behind an object) can affect mass by making objects appear heavier than they really are.

Light affects the way we interpret texture when it highlights textural relief (surface irregularities), and light affects pattern by clarifying or by submerging details. For example, a rough texture can appear even rougher when a light is cast on it at a parallel angle. Light directed onto a surface at a low, nearly parallel angle will emphasize the relief through highlight and shadow. A smooth texture will appear smoother with a directional band of light, such as a spotlight or a smooth wash of light. Likewise, clear light shining directly on a pattern will emphasize the pattern details, and low light casting shadows on a pattern will minimize the details.

Light can change the apparent identity of a color through the color and type of light that hits the surface. Further, different materials may reflect light and color in different ways, affecting the relationship of the colors to each other.

Color

Color, the last element of design, is the most emotional and personal of all the elements. Although everyone has individual preferences toward, and prejudices against, certain colors, humans generally respond similarly to color combinations within each culture. Here the psychology of color is based on the reaction of people in the United States and similar cultures to color hue, value, and intensity.

Color hues, or colors by their names, affect us in similar ways. Reds, oranges, and yellows are stimulating; blues, greens, and violets are calming. Color hues as seen on the standard color wheel can be divided into equal groups

Figure 2.41 This spacious kitchen, with its study in linear combination, uses two important forms of lighting. The natural light from the sink window and especially through the skylights makes working in this kitchen an enjoyable experience. The single-pendant luminaries will cast a mellow-light glow on the cooking and dining experience. Echoing design from the 1950s, this kitchen is up-to-the-minute in space planning, function, and aesthetics. Photo by Norman McGrath, © 1988.

where one-half of the wheel are warm colors that are the stimulating, friendly, cozy, and inviting hues and the other half consists of calming cool colors that suggest restraint, dignity, and formality.

Color values are the relative lightness or darkness of the hues; for example, a high value, light red is a pink; a low value, dark red is a burgundy. Lighter colors seem to recede, making space appear larger and giving a more airy look to the interior, whereas darker values do the opposite—close in and give a cavelike coziness. Distribution of value is sought after in most fine interior design, where some values of light, medium, and dark hues are carefully placed to achieve the desired effect. Light and dark values placed next to each other (*high contrast*) can be dramatic, whereas hues close in value (*low contrast*) create a subtly blended, calming environment.

Color intensity is the brightness versus the dullness of a hue. Pure colors can be lowered in intensity by adding a neighboring or a contrasting color or by adding white, black, gray, or any combination of these. Bright, bold, pure colors are exciting and happy. These need careful handling so as not to become overbearing through overuse or indiscriminate placement. Dull colors can be dark, medium, or light values but are generally easy to live with because they are undemanding. Often a good balance is found in rooms that utilize the law of chromatic distribution: The larger areas are dulled and neutralized, and the smallest areas are brightest, with the intensity becoming brighter as the areas become smaller.

Color is examined in greater depth in chapter 3, which covers historic applications, color theory, and psychology as well as residential and nonresidential uses of color.

Figure 2.42

Evaluating Design

The principles and elements of design are the foundation of every design discipline; they form the basis for judging design quality and integrity. All around us there is design that can be appreciated—from the intrinsically beautiful scenes of nature at any season and climate to great public and private architecture and their finely designed interiors, to the details of individual furnishings and accessories. Learning to evaluate design will help us be more objective about the way we feel in the interiors where we live, work, and obtain services.

The evaluation process begins with an understanding of the theory of design or, in other words, implementing the principles by asking questions such as, How do I feel in this room? and What principles of design cause me to feel this way? If the reaction is less than positive, then an evaluation of the application of the elements of design can enable us to see what changes could be made to improve the interior.

Further, there are four general considerations that serve to clarify and simplify design evaluation: function, cultural context, appropriateness, and criteria for good structural and decorative design. These form a basis for understanding whether or not architecture or furnishings are well designed and how well objects interrelate with other objects and with the interior and exterior design. Looking at the overall effect is important because no interior can fully be separated from the permanent features of its architecture.

Figure 2.42 As we evaluate design wherever it is found, we look at the historical and cultural context, the appropriateness of forms and materials used, and the placement of furnishings in relation to the existing architecture and to each other. In the apartment of the late artist Andy Warhol, unusual finds that symbolized segments of American design progression (both machine made and handmade) were zealously collected and combined to fill the senses. Photo by Norman McGrath, © 1987.

Function

Function is the way the elements perform in an interior—whether they are durable, operable, or serve the purpose for which they are intended. Each choice made in interior design, from the arrangement of the structural members (floors, walls, windows, ceilings) to the selection of furnishings, art and accessories, must fulfill the needs and purposes for which it is intended, or the design is inevitably frustrated.

The process of design (chapter 1) is one of problem solving. Therefore the evaluation of how well the finished design works as it was intended to work is of paramount importance. In nonresidential design, this is known as post-occupancy evaluation (POE) and is a thorough critique of how well the design fulfilled the needs of the program. In homes as well, good design can only be aesthetically pleasing if the goals of the design statement and program have been thoroughly satisfied.

Cultural Context

When an object is evaluated, it must first be viewed according to its original context. Context is defined as the whole situation, background, or environment relevant to a particular object. This means, for example, that to begin to truly appreciate Chippendale furniture, we need to see it in its original context in a Late Georgian setting. Then fine Chippendale furniture can be incorporated into more contemporary settings where it is appropriate and contributes beauty. Likewise, to initiate an appreciation for modern Scandinavian or Italian furnishings, we need to internalize the concept that "form follows function" (see pages 49–50).

Many accessory items that come from ethnic or primitive cultures can be genuinely appreciated for their beauty when we understand the society of their origin and its aesthetic views and cultural traditions surrounding decorative design. An example is the symbolic nature of the patterns and colors in Navajo rugs and other rugs from ethnic cultures.

When these authentic sources are misused or misrepresented or when the object is mass-produced in a material that is not suited for the purpose, the item is poorly

Figure 2.43

Figure 2.44

Figure 2.43 The function of this rescued space was originally a gardening greenhouse. In its reincarnated life, it serves the function of a dining area, set here for a formal dinner, but beguiling because of the furnishing elements that suggest a more common function of solarium greenhouse, complete with wicker furniture and a child's tricycle, that may have use beyond the appreciation of its classic form. Photo by Norman McGrath, © 1988.

Figure 2.44 The late champion of common Americana, artist Andy Warhol, brought to our attention the value of cherishing the reality of our past, however tacky it might seem to the modern discriminating eye. Here an array of ceramic dinnerware and cookie jars brings back warm memories to almost everyone who had a grandmother. The open cabinetry in the background proudly displays historic ceramic plates, cups, bowls, and saucers that bespeak a humble yet well-designed cultural context. Because our parents and grandparents used these items, we today collect them to tie ourselves to their time—an era that we think was somehow better, more romantic, or at least, less stressful. Photo by Norman McGrath © 1987.

Figure 2.45

swags and fringe that are placed over a wide expanse of a frankly modern picture window are simply not appropriate. It will cause both the window architecture and the window treatment to seem ill chosen and out of place. On the other hand, where an older, historic interior forms the background, it is often most appropriate to complement the existing interior architecture with colors, textiles, and furnishings that add to, not detract from, the richness of the period. This is not to say that furnishings should look antiquated, for fresh new design is always welcome when it is suitable and appropriate. It is only when the selections are inappropriate, poor choices that the design loses integrity and becomes either shocking or banal and distasteful at either extreme.

designed. For example, the classic Thonet bentwood rocker is attractive because of the beauty of the wood that is curved under heat and pressure to its well-known shape. When the curvature is duplicated in metal or plastic, it is out of its authentic context and loses much of its original design integrity (honesty and sincerity). Not only must the materials be suited for the design and the purpose to be good design but the colors, lines, patterns, and textures must also be appropriate and harmonious.

Appropriateness

Appropriateness means suitability, fitness, or rightness of components for a specific purpose. Every element in interior design can be used appropriately or inappropriately. It is often said, for example, that there is no such thing as an ugly color, only colors that are not used correctly. This means that we need to look at not only the hue itself but at intensity (brightness versus dullness), value (lightness versus darkness), placement (where is it located), and quantity (area to be covered) as well. Color is but one of the elements we scrutinize in terms of appropriateness. Each selection, from wall and floor materials to accessory items, needs to be a suitable choice for the particular interior if that design is to succeed.

Often the architecture determines which style of furnishing elements are appropriate or suitable. For example, sheers and tied-back layers of elegant fabric topped with

Selecting items that are appropriate often takes study and consideration, and a scanning of what is available on the market is an essential part of the process of selecting suitable components. We should observe interiors in magazines, public spaces, homes and models open to the public and continually ask, Is this appropriate? Do these furnishings and elements really feel right together and with the architecture? We often will sense the rightness of good design and feel fulfilled and satisfied when it is experienced. It is rewarding to experience appropriately selected, fine interior design.

Structural and Decorative Design

Structural and decorative or ornamentive design are two basic divisions of design that are not generally considered with the principles and elements, yet they are important concepts in evaluating the success of a design.

Structural Design

Structural design is seen in any element of interiors where the design is intrinsic to the structure and the form indicates the function of the piece. The concept of "form follows function" is a credo followed by architects and designers who have created modern classic works that are simple yet exactingly well-thought-out and executed. Form follows function means that the first priority in a design is its

Figure 2.45 The selection of furniture and window treatments is most appropriate in this interior. It reminisces the pre- and post-World War II days with rounded Art Deco forms and the then popular Hawaiian lanai look with old-fashioned venetian blinds. The natural feeling suggests a serene connection with nature in patterns, forms, textures, and materials. Photo by Norman McGrath, © 1988.

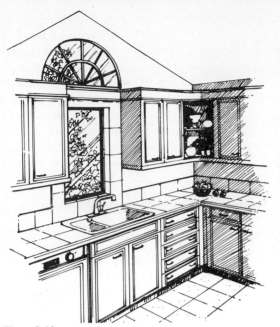

Figure 2.46

Figure 2.47

function, and the parameters of that purpose or function will dictate the shape or form of the design. For example, many modern chairs are designed primarily for the comfort and physical support of their users. The study of ergonomics or "ergofit" means that a chair (or even the entire range of furnishings and the building itself) is best suited for specific functions that will take place there. A chair designed to follow the dictum form follows function will be stripped of embellishment and fulfill only the needs of its function, with an eye to fine, albeit sleek and simplified, design.

Structural design has no added decoration, and the design cannot be removed from the structure without destroying both the design (form) and the purpose (function) of the piece. In order for structural design to be considered fine or high-quality design, certain criteria must be met.

* Structural design must be simple. The form and materials will never be complicated or arbitrary. Ironically, however, simplicity is often much more difficult to design and execute than ornate design. Every curve, angle, and part of the design are absolutely necessary to the form or design and to the function or purpose of the design.
* Structural design is unadorned. There will be no carving, decals, unnecessary color changes, or extras of any sort. The design is found in the form and the materials used—wood grain, for example, or stainless steel or plastic—all frankly exposed to reveal their real worth.
* The function of the piece must be apparent. For example, a well-designed structural clock will look exactly like a clock and not like anything else.

Figure 2.48

* A structural piece must be well proportioned to be good design. This is particularly true since there is no decoration to cover up the dimensions, the scale, and the relationship of parts.

Most of the classic modern chairs are structural design, and much of today's designs from Italy and Scandinavia are structural design.

Figure 2.46 Striking simplicity is evident in this structural room with European-styled cabinets, simple yet dramatic windows, angled ceiling, and tile floor and backsplash.
Figure 2.47 This structural building uses frankly exposed wooden beams and siding to present an angular-reinforced exterior. If the beams that

make the design were removed, then the building would not stand. The angles of the structural elements are integral to the structure itself. Photo courtesy of Anderson Windows.
Figure 2.48 A high-tech kitchen with frankly used man-made materials and sleek lines epitomizes structural design. Line plays an important role

in structural design, here through arrangement of forms. Horizontal lines are emphasized in the jalousie-type louvers of the upper cabinetry; curved lines on the ceiling define the lighting/exhaust unit; floor tiles are placed to yield a building-block design on the floor. Photo by Norman McGrath, © 1984.

Figure 2.49 Decorative conventional designs based on flowing plant forms enrich the architecture of this grand oval room. The balance of curved lines to straight lines is also effective. A French fauteuil armchair is an appropriate selection in harmony with the elegance evident here.

Figure 2.49

Figure 2.50

Figure 2.51

Decorative Design

Decorative design is also called applied or ornamentive design and refers to the ornamentation, or embellishment, of the object or structure. Some objects are in themselves decorative because of the way they are formed, whereas others may be structural pieces with decorative design added. The decoration can be accomplished by any other process of applying decoration such as painting, inlaying, firing, engraving, or carving. When decorative architec-

ture, interior architectural detail, or applied design on furnishings is well done, it will have the following characteristics:

- There must be a sympathetic relationship between the style and method of decoration and the object, such as precise etching or engraving of glass or carving or inlaying of wood.
- The decoration must be suitable for the function and/or style of the piece. If the object is a Rococo French form, for example, then the decoration should not be unrelated Victorian motifs. Also, truly fine decorative design will complement the function. The decoration of a clock face, for example, should not obscure the ability to read the time but should enhance the clock's design richness.
- The proportion of the decoration must be right for the size of the object. This means two things: (1) the scale of the decoration, which should be right for the scale of the object (not too large or too small in proportion), and (2) the amount of decoration compared to the size of the object. Certainly a piece too heavily ornamented will stand the chance of being considered poor design.
- The ornamentation should embrace the form and not interfere with its function.

Figure 2.50 Decorative design abounds in the loft of this Boston, Massachusetts, home. Naturalistic design is obvious in the realistic painting of the cow but less obvious in the pillow in the center of the love seat, where a man on a camel is led through the desert by a frond-carrying guide. Conventional design with stylized floral patterns appears in the rug and window shade and surrealistic painting on the brick wall. Geometric patterns appear in the chevron zigzag of the club chairs, in the plaid love seat pillows, and in the diamond-shaped design of the other pillows atop the striped seat cushion of the raised-panel settee. Abstract design makes a fascinating balcony balustrade and raised-panel back of the settee. Fabrics and furniture by and photo courtesy of Brunschwig & Fils.

Figure 2.51 Decorative design proliferates in this intimate sitting room. European and Chinese porcelain, filigree-inset wall panels and faux paintings are placed near a patterned sofa and chair fabrics atop a designer rug. All this pattern makes this a busy room that creates intimacy and personal comfort and satisfaction for its occupants. The mirrored wall that flanks the fireplace doubles the effect of all the decorative ornamentation. Photo by Norman McGrath, © 1986.

Discernment and Design Excellence

When we evaluate an object, we often label it a level of design. We may say the design of the object is excellent or fine; the design may be good, fair, mediocre, or poor; or the design may be pretentious and in bad taste, sometimes called kitsch. These labels are useful because they help us see that many aesthetic levels of design do indeed exist, and it clarifies our responsibility to select only design that will stand the test of time; that is, to select items of furnishing that will not only be appealing today but will seem just as beautiful many years later. Items that are beautifully, artistically, and sensitively designed will not become dated. Rather, they will endear themselves to us because the timelessness of their beauty, their classic lines, their excellence of forms, and their sensitive use of textures and colors appeal continually to our senses. This is just as true in well-designed structural objects as it is in well-designed objects that are decorative.

The Power of Discernment

The ability to recognize and appreciate fine design wherever it is found is known as the power of discernment. Discernment is the conscious effort required to make good choices and is of paramount importance in today's world of mass production, mass media, and instant information. We are barraged on every side with demanding decisions. We must choose from a vast array of furnishing products and art pieces to furnish our environments. Since much average and poor design exists, it becomes necessary that everything we choose should be selected only after evaluation with a discriminating eye. We can also evaluate selections that are beyond our control, as we see them in retail stores, in business offices, in medical facilities, in hotels, in public buildings and in churches. In short, we can become discerning by evaluating everything we see.

The key to developing discernment is to studiously look and expose ourselves to design at every opportunity, and then to critically evaluate the level of design we see. Visit museums and art galleries, great public and church architecture, quality furniture stores, and even fine gift shops. Most cities have groups that support museum homes, and sponsor home shows, and model homes exist in almost every community. It has been said that good design is there for the finding, which is to say that almost every place we look we will find good design in some form.

One of the easiest ways to develop the power of discernment or discrimination is to look through design periodicals—the magazines that appear monthly and tell us what is fashionable. However, not all that is fashionable will necessarily be good design, and the discriminating eye will be able to see through the fads and promotion to what is truly timeless and beautiful.

Another key to developing discernment is to observe, study, and value what nature has given to us. Not through pushing buttons was the majesty of nature scenes created but through time, wearing away, and evolution of the landscape. Nature possesses a patina, or mellow, warm, old glow, that speaks not only to our senses but to our souls.

Figure 2.52

Figure 2.52 Design that has withstood the test of time is still deeply appreciated today by those who favor classic forms from the past. Here a formal dining room utilizes Chippendale side chairs and armchairs and a Sheraton/Hepplewhite sideboard and a Baroque-inspired mirror. Details include botanical artwork, Chinese porcelain, and elegantly refined Georgian silver and crystal. Underfoot, the complex Persian oriental rug bespeaks thousands of hours of hand labor to produce a textile work of art. Renaissance designs in fine damask and sumptuous plain silk lined with a stripe are historically derived and clipped with café rings onto a European-designed drapery rod. The small curio cabinet is Regency in origin. The dark walls unite these various elements that have history as their common ground—all considered to be the best of the past, worth preserving for gracious interiors of the present and the future. Photo by Norman McGrath © 1989.
Figure 2.53 This handsome interior utilizes design elements from many historic periods and locales. Although the architecture is clearly structural, its owners did not want to divorce themselves from all historic and ethnic beauty. Rather, what was

Great interior design often parallels this. It is based on a commitment to time: time in research, programming, and deliberate effort; time in seeking until just the right furnishing elements are discovered; and time in putting the elements together so that it appears as though they have fallen into place because of the rightness of the design. Like a thrilling scene in nature, fine interior design can be uplifting and rewarding.

A final key to understanding discernment is to establish the relationship of cost to design. Whereas many items that are very costly are good design, it is just as true that expense often gets in the way of good design, because wealth urges us toward ostentation.[1] Often the more expensive of two alternatives is less acceptable to those who are visually aware.[2] It often reveals greater discrimination when a simple interior design holds evidence of good taste and true sophistication. Items that are simple and even roughly made can be just as beautiful as the most elegant and expensive furnishings. It is through the evaluation of the principles and elements and of good structural and decorative design and of the careful balance of beauty and craftsmanship that we discover real and individual worth. Also, the effect of the interior is not only based on the selection of individual items but in the composition or grouping that gives to each a meaning, or significance, and a rightness.

Good Taste and Style

The development of discernment will eventually lead to what we call good taste or style. When we say that certain people have good taste, we mean that they exhibit sound aesthetic judgment and thoroughly understand the needs of their individual life-style. It appears that people with good taste always make good choices and that perhaps it comes easy to them. However, anyone can develop good taste and can make good choices once they realize that it does require a conscious effort in every detail of our lives. From the clothes we wear to anything we buy to the books we read to the films we see to the food we eat—all are aspects of living that are governed by taste.[3]

Although many of us are uncertain about our tastes, we can be educated, we can elevate our tastes, and we can learn to judge good design. To begin with, we need to understand our life-style, the needs of our surroundings, and what choices are available in terms of style and material for every element that goes into the interior. This requires

Figure 2.53

Figure 2.54

created was an eclectic interior that reflects their travels and tastes. Hence we see influence from both the Georgian and early Modern eras in the fireplace and historically adapted furniture, including a Chinese coffee table. The owners' collection of accessories is largely English, including ceramic, crystal, and brass pieces. These diverse elements are brought together with the perceptively clean arrangement of lines and contemporary natural materials such as stucco, stone, wood, and nature-derived glass, as well as textured fabrics that are adapted from geometric Southwest patterns. Photo by Norman McGrath, © 1988.

Figure 2.54 A lavish use of this subtle-textured print fabric with pearlized finish creates an intimate area of fine design. The power of the understatement is often the most long-lived of the design elements. This design, intended for a master bedroom retreat away from the pressures of the world, does not overpower the viewer but rather allows the occupant to relax, free of stimulating design. An important part of design discrimination, then, is to evaluate the purpose of the design and to judge its effectiveness in meeting the needs of the program. Photo courtesy of John Wolf Decorative Fabrics.

careful attention to detail, and means that everything we choose serves to create harmony.

It is important to note that although people with great style do things that are totally unexpected and out of the ordinary, perhaps ahead of their time—seeming to abandon all trends and fads in favor of their own good choices—it is never done to shock, amaze, or impress anyone. True style is tuning into and following what is naturally right. It has little to do with what is in fashion, although an awareness of fashion is always evident in people with taste. Fashion passes, style remains. Style abhors the cliché, the cuteness, and, consciously, abhors conformity (doing it because everybody else is doing it) in favor of an uncompromising approach to first-class design quality and individuality. Truly great design is innovative yet demanding of the best.

People with style seem to know when to stop just short of excess. They often intuitively know that "less is more," that as Plato said, "beauty of style depends on simplicity." Perhaps the first step toward evolving a personal style is to pare back to the essentials before piling on any extraneous additions.

Style is most importantly an individual matter. You cannot copy another's style, even as we cannot copy another's personality. To create or copy an interior for the sake of correctness often falls short of style and appropriateness. In today's instant society, we are often impatient to have style developed immediately, but this is often not the way real beauty is made. Just as with nature who took time to create her masterpieces, it is worth waiting to find just the right accessory, fabric, or piece of furniture to fit your style. And in the process of looking, we develop a distinctive personal style. Certainly there are many nonresidential interiors that reflect good taste and great style, but it is in the home where these are most personally evident.

Of all the objectives we may choose to incorporate in life, the dedication to creating a warm, welcoming, attractive, and individual home is one of the most worthwhile and precious. It is upon the theory (principles) and application (elements) that selections in good taste are incorporated with style and cherished for years to come.

Figure 2.55

Nonresidential Considerations

The principles and elements of design are evident not only in the homes we view, visit, and live in but in public spaces as well. Those who have traveled abroad and visited castles and palaces have experienced the transcendence of exquisitely decorated large spaces along with the feelings of awe and grandeur that they give to their visitors. Although many of the castles and palaces that are open to the public were intended as private residences, they are today often used not only for tours but as places of gathering for civic events. In such places we can experience the large-scale handling of the design principles and elements, along with an evaluation of design in spaces that have carefully been preserved over decades or even hundreds of years. Similarly, museums are often grand places architecturally and contain glimpses of past eras that educate us in traditional and folk uses of the design principles and elements.

The often lofty spaces of church architecture with its predominance of vertical lines and often upward curving lines give a feeling of insignificance of the human status and lead thoughts to higher planes. This is particularly true in cathedrals, mosques, synagogues, and larger churches and temples.

Figure 2.55 Personal style is the reward of working through a design program. Here the interior reflects the tastes of its owners in this eclectic, one-of-a-kind master bedroom. Historic pieces all have vernacular adaptations such as the extended American Empire chaise lounge with caned sides and the shield-back

mirror from the Federal era. The clean architecture and natural broad-plank floor fits well with the natural environment outdoors, yet the expansive fanlight transom gives license to bring treasures from the past into present living spaces. The buzzword of the 1990s—appropriation—symbolizes the hunt and

successful obtaining of unique finds from our history, from both near and distant parts of the world, to create interiors that are eclectic *par excellence*. Photo by Norman McGrath, © 1988.
Figure 2.56 Wherever we go, into buildings that function as churches, government and public buildings, hotels, schools, and places of

business, we have an opportunity to evaluate design, to discern the rightness and success of the interior design and its background architecture. The refinement of our powers of discrimination will be immeasurably enhanced by simply observing and thinking through what we see based on our knowledge of the principles

Figure 2.56

(A)
Figure 2.57

(B)

There are many public spaces where we may have opportunity to evaluate the levels of good design. The principles and elements are used for better or for worse in retail spaces, in restaurants, in offices, in banks, and in medical facilities. We see design that bridges the gap between residential and nonresidential design when we stay in hotels and resorts where both small spaces and large spaces play important parts in the rest and recreation procedure. Time spent in theaters before and after the movie, play, or cultural event allows us to ponder the level and integrity of interior design there. The theatrical or stage "set" can be an experience of good design or form the basis for critique as well.

There is drama implicit in the lofty interiors of some federal, state, county, or local government headquarters and in large-scale office or corporate buildings. In large spaces meant to impress, we often see fascinating uses of natural hard materials such as stone that give texture, pattern, and color to the interior.

The working environment is perhaps the place where our best scrutiny can take place. At work stations, whether it is in the office, the medical facility, or the public service business, we can look around and see how the principles and elements make our working interiors more pleasant. We may also be able to see improvements that can be made to increase job efficiency, working or spacial relationships (proxemics), and job satisfaction.

The manipulation of the design principles and elements to create beautiful environments can even go beyond our homes and nonresidential interiors to the limitless variety of nature scenes where we escape when the pressures and confines of civilization become burdensome. In nature we view structural design at its finest, and through the careful orchestration of the elements, we see every principle of design illustrated in one form or another. Indeed, the beauty of nature has been accomplished over a long period of time, and through observation of this careful, deliberate effort, we glean beauty that is not simply voguish or stylish but see beauty that has been and can be appreciated for eons of time. From nature we can learn, as a final lesson in the use of design principles and elements, that beautiful interiors do take planning, thought, effort, and time and that when great interiors are accomplished they will stay pleasing for many years to come.

Notes

1. Whiton, Sherrill, *Interior Design and Decoration* (New York: Lippincott, 1973, pp. 749-756).
2. Hicks, David, *On Living—With Taste* (London: Leslie Frewin, 1968, pp. 10-11).
3. Ibid.

and elements of design. Here, at Paul Segal & Associates, a New York ad agency, space is divided into planes by lines and forms in pleasing proportional relationship. Each area has a specific purpose. Can you evaluate why each segment of this design exists as it does? Photo by Norman McGrath, © 1986.

Figure 2.57 The principles and elements of design are easily recognizable in nonresidential architecture; wherever we go we can appreciate the lines, shapes, and forms that create balance, rhythm, and fine proportion. By consciously looking at and analyzing what we see, our powers to not only recognize but

to discriminate will be increased. *(A)* A ground-floor exterior view of this high-rise office building reveals strong vertical lines, used to uplift the soul in ecclesiastical architecture since the Middle Ages. Today these vertical lines encourage the eye to soar with the dizzying height of today's skyrise cityscapes. Photo by John Wang. *(B)*

The long, low profile of the Art Center in Pasadena, California, is filled with reinforcing triangular trusslike shapes, at once visually stimulating with its strong sense of rhythm and aesthetically fulfilling with its statement of fine structural design. Photo by Alejandro Rubalcava.

Bibliography

Albers, Anni. *On Designing*. Middletown, CT: Wesleyan University Press, 1971.

Allen, Phyllis. *Beginnings of Interior Environment*. Minneapolis: Burgess Publishing Company, 1985.

Anderson, Donald M. *Elements of Design*. New York: Holt, Rinehart and Winston, 1961.

Ashley, Laura. *The Laura Ashley Book of Home Decorating*. London: Octopus Books, Ltd., 1985.

Bellinger, Louise, and Thomas Broman. *Design: Sources and Resources*. New York: Van Nostrand Reinhold, 1965.

Bevlin, Marjory. *Design Through Discovery*. New York: Holt, Rinehart and Winston, 1977.

Bloomer, Carolyn M. *Principles of Visual Perception*. New York: Van Nostrand Reinhold, 1976.

Bothwell, Dorr, and Marlys Frey. *Notan: The Dark-Light Principle of Design*. New York: Van Nostrand Reinhold, 1976.

Carpenter, James M. *Visual Art: A Critical Introduction*. New York: Harcourt Brace Jovanovich, 1982.

Cheatham, Frank, Jane Cheatham, and Sheryl Haler. *Design Concepts and Applications*. Englewood Cliffs, NJ: Prentice-Hall, 1983.

Collier, Graham. *Form, Space, and Vision*. Englewood Cliffs, NJ: Prentice-Hall, 1972.

De Lucio-Meyer, J. *Visual Aesthetics*. New York: Harper & Row, 1974.

De Sausmarez, Maurice. *Basic Design*. New York: Van Nostrand Reinhold, 1964.

Evans, Helen Marie, and Carla Davis Dumesnil. *An Invitation to Design*. New York: Macmillan, 1982.

Faulkner, Ray, and Edwin Zeigfeld. *Art Today*. New York: Holt, Rinehart and Winston, 1969.

Faulkner, Ray, LuAnn Nisson, and Sarah Faulkner. *Inside Today's Home*. New York: CBS College Publishing, 1986.

Gombrich, E.H. *Art and Illusion: A Study in the Psychology of Pictorial Representation*. Princeton, NJ: Princeton University Press, 1961.

Grillo, Paul. *Form, Function, and Design*. New York: Dover, 1975.

Hale, Nathan Cabot. *Abstraction in Art and Nature*. New York: Watson-Guptill Publications, 1972.

Hambridge, Jay. *Practical Applications of Dynamic Symmetry*. New York: Davin, 1965.

Harlan, Calvin. *Vision and Invention: A Course in Art Fundamentals*. Englewood Cliffs, NJ: Prentice-Hall, 1970.

Held, Richard, ed. *Image, Object, and Illusion, Readings from Scientific American*. San Francisco: Freeman.

Hicks, David. *On Living—with Taste*. London: Leslie Frewin, 1968.

Hicks, David. *Living with Design*. London: William Morrow and Company, 1979.

Itten, Johannes. *Design and Form*. New York: Litton Educational Publishing, Inc, 1975.

Kepes, Gyorgy. *Language of Vision*. Chicago: Paul Theobald, 1969.

Lauer David. *Design Basics*. New York: Holt, Rinehart and Winston, 1979.

Lowry, Bales. *The Visual Experience*. Englewood Cliffs, NJ: Prentice-Hall, 1975.

Maier, Manfred. *Basic Principles of Design*. New York: Van Nostrand Reinhold, 1977.

McHarg, Ian. *Design with Nature*. New York: Doubleday, 1971.

McKim, Robert H. *Thinking Visually*. Belmost, CA: Lifetime Learning Publications, 1980.

Ocvirk, Otto G., Robert O. Bone, Robert E. Stinson, and Philip R. Wigg. *Art Fundamentals, Theory and Practice*. Dubuque, Iowa: Wm. C. Brown Publishers, 1975.

Pile, John F. *Design Purpose, Form, and Meaning*. New York: W.W. Norton and Company, 1979.

Pile, John F. *Interior Design*. Englewood Cliffs, NJ: Prentice-Hall and New York: Harry N. Abrams. Inc, 1988.

Pye, David. *The Nature of Design*. New York: Van Nostrand Reinhold, 1964.

Renner, Paul. *Color, Order, and Harmony*. New York: Van Nostrand Reinhold, 1965.

Scott, Robert Gillam. *Design Fundamentals*. New York: McGraw-Hill, 1951.

Stix, et al. *The Shell: Five Hundred Million Years of Inspired Design*. New York: Ballantine, 1972.

Stoops, Jack, and Jerry Samuelson. *Design Dialogue*. Worcester, MA: Davis Publications, 1983.

Strache, Wolf. *Forms and Patterns in Nature*. New York: Pantheon, 1973.

Weismann, Donald I. *The Visual Arts as Human Experience*. Englewood Cliffs, NJ: Prentice-Hall, 1970.

Whiton, Sherrill. *Interior Design and Decoration*. New York: J.B. Lippincott Company, 1976.

Wong, Wucius. *Principles of Two-Dimensional Design*. New York: Van Nostrand Reinhold, 1972.

Young, Frank. *Visual Studies: A Foundation for Artists and Designers*. Englewood Cliffs, NJ: Prentice-Hall, 1985.

COLOR

Sometimes color plays a dominant role in the room, where the color, rather than pattern, texture, or furniture style, becomes the room's theme. Here red was chosen by interior designer Paula Perlini of Mark Hampton, Inc., for clients who selected her as a designer because of her penchant for making rooms come alive with color. The red paint is stippled (see chapter 9) over bubble gum pink, and elsewhere in the house, red accents remind one of the red living room. Of this interior, Ms. Perlini says, "Everyone's afraid strong color will make rooms small and dark, but it actually makes them rich and cozy, especially with lots of white woodwork." The owners, photographer Joe Standart and his wife, Clinton, chose this gutsy scheme because he says, "I'm used to looking through the camera and seeing what makes a room leap off a magazine page." Reprinted by permission from HOUSE BEAUTIFUL, copyright © August 1987. The Hearst Corporation. All Rights Reserved. Joe Standart, photographer.

Page 58, bottom: Jane Bescherer composed the interior design for this Westport, Connecticut, beach house. The magnificent antique quilt displayed on the mezzanine wall establishes a color scheme reflecting the colors of sea and sky and evoking a relaxing and refreshing ambience in the spacious room. Off-white walls emphasize the soaring and vistaed space, giving the impression of a simple, uncluttered life-style, a counterpoint to big-city living and business dealings. While furnishings are clean-lined contemporary, the tie to our cultural and historic heritage is brought home in classic Doric columns and, of course, the precious handmade quilt. *Page 58, top right:* Selecting colors from a paint "fan" or "deck" can be a bewilder-

ing experience since the painted surface can look lighter or darker than the paint chip. Often a solution is found in purchasing a quart of colored paint and applying it in situ to judge its behavior and appearance in the light of the proposed installation. Here, a clear aqua off-white was the choice for walls for the beach house's interior designed by Jane Bescherer, creating a calming background for the Brunschwig & Fils woven herringbone fabric and woven upholstery textile from Donghia. Soothing greens and browns are historic colors, set in a contemporary mode. Photo by Ted Spiegel. *Page 59, top:* Primary colors are stimulating to younger children, even intellectually, as has been found over many years of research.

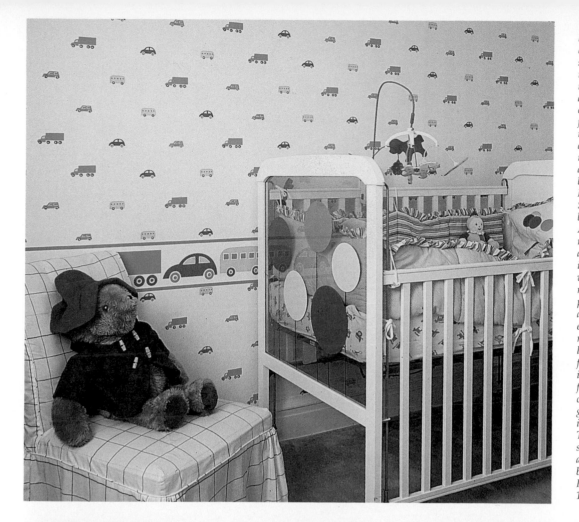

White as a medium for splashes of bright chroma gives crispness, clarity, and a not-to-be-taken-too-seriously statement. Although this room is clearly for the youngsters, it is equally as refreshing to the adults, who upon entering may change tones themselves. The feeling is whimsical, lighthearted, uplifting, and imaginative. Interior design by Motif Designs, Mamaroneck, New York. Wall coverings and textiles by Marimekko. Photo by Ted Spiegel. **Page 59, bottom:** In the library of Oheka Castle, Cold Springs Hills, New York, originally built for Wall Street magnate Adolph Kahn, color is brought to renewed life through wood graining and ocher hue. Real wood is found in the bookcases, where the natural wood tone becomes the key to the room's color impact. The rich brown paneling is an anomaly—it is faux, a painted imitation of wood, an effective, albeit costly, process. The rich red in a small, rather than a large, quantity (as in the chapter's first photo) is seen between the sofas in the Oriental rug and in the flowers. Red is a crucial and vibrant counterpoint to the dominant golden brown hue. In both cases, red is a powerful and emotional color. The result here is an interior wall suited to the status of its original and current owners. Interior design by Gail and Stephen Huberman. Photo by Norman McGrath, © 1987.

Page 60, top right: Color cannot exist without light; it is the phenomenon whereby surfaces absorb some light waves and reflect others, thereby allowing us to see color. Here, artisan John Byers of Philadelphia, Pennsylvania, works in his chosen medium—colored, beveled, and leaded art glass set into creative, original designs for interiors. When backlighted by natural or artificial light, the transmitted color sends messages of prismic mystique, holding us spellbound. As sunlight direction changes, coupled with seasonal environment factors that color natural light, art glass becomes living art, a delight to the mind and to the eye. Art glass can be utilized at the window, in cabinetry, and as screens or dividers. Photo by Ted Spiegel. *Page 60, bottom:* In the Lightolier Lighting Laboratory in New York City, a display graphically illustrates the varying impact of artificial light on colored surfaces. The source of each light box represents a light source commonly available on the market, ranging from sodium-vapor to tungsten incandescent and halogen to the spectrum to fluorescent tubing. The lighting showroom affords designers an opportunity to see light sources and fixtures and to become educated to the variation of the effects of light on color. Clearly, color is the creature of the light source that it is reflecting. When a material appears to be one color in one light and another color in another light, the phenomenon is termed metamerism and is a crucial reason for trying out paints, textiles, and hard materials in situ before the order for the goods is finalized. Colors may match in the design studio, but that does not assure they will do so in the home or contract setting. Photo by Ted Spiegel in cooperation with the Lightolier Company.

The Role of Color in History

Color has always played an important role throughout history. Colors have reflected climate, political and social atmosphere, trade with and exposure to other cultures. Today as we view the ruins of the world of antiquity, we have only a glimpse into the real colors enjoyed by peoples of every era in history. These colors are useful to interior designers today as historic interiors are re-created, restored, or adaptively reused.

Color In The Ancient World

The color palette of the great dynasties of *ancient Egypt* (4500–663 B.C.) included rust and henna red; bone ivory; dull gold; wood brown; pale, medium, and deep cobalt; pale and deep green; pale horizon blue; sun yellow; and soft purple. Colors of *ancient Greece*, whose *golden age* was in the fifth century B.C., included stellar, slate, and mist blues; scarlet; pale violet; pale and medium malachite and olive greens; sun yellow; ivory white; marble pink; clay beige; copper brown; and charcoal. Fragments of color on the Parthenon in Athens show us that blue was dominant, with figures in realistic tints of yellow, pink, and pale blue.

The mosaics of *Byzantium* (A.D. 330–1453), the ancient Roman eastern capital, still sparkle with rich golds, blues, greens, and flesh tones. *Classical Roman* interiors (200 B.C.–A.D. 100) were decorated with painted stucco and colorful mosaics, accented with rich fabrics. The brilliance and relative clarity of colors such as magenta (the Imperial purple), rich gold, Pompeii red, Roman greens, accented with black, surprised the Western world when excavations began in 1754 at *Pompeii* and *Herculaneum*, the Roman resort cities located at the Bay of Naples destroyed in A.D. 79.

The Middle Ages

Although color in castles and homes during the *Medieval era* or *Middle Ages* (A.D. 800–1500) was somewhat somber; the impact of color seen in the magnificent stained glass windows throughout Europe still impresses us today. Techniques used to create these colorful masterpieces were temporarily lost until research revived the production of colored stained glass during the Victorian era (A.D. 1842–1910). Colors of the Middle Ages and previous periods were governed by symbolism and were not freely and creatively used.

Renaissance Color

The Renaissance (Italy, A.D. 1400–1600) was a time of rebirth of artistic and architectural pursuits. No longer tied strictly to symbolic color, artists discovered the freedom to creatively use color. Color became a pleasing, decorative, and satisfying element for artists and patrons alike. Oil-painting colors such as garnet and persimmon reds, bright copper, deep cobalt blue, blue-green and medium blue, pale and deep greens, medium and deep malachite greens, rich and dull brown, marble and ivory cream and white, and metallic gold were rich, sensuous hues. Renaissance color elements migrated from Italy northward to Europe, notably France, Germany, the Lowlands, and England, then finally to America. In the colder climates and with more reserved attitudes, Renaissance colors tended to be more restrained.

Historic Color in America

Colonial American colors can be divided into *Early American* and *Early* and *Late Georgian* periods. Early American (c. 1650–1750) colors tended to be earth colors seen in pewter, wood, unbleached muslin, simple homespun checks in indigo blues, yellows, and madder reds. Colors, limited as they were, tended to be dull, natural, and faded.

Early Georgian (c. 1770–1750) colors were the Renaissance colors imported from England and France, with a preference for greens and dark dull blues, deep olive greens (examples of Colonial Williamsburg colors), and some golds, oranges, and browns reminiscent of English Medieval interiors.

Late Georgian (c.1750–1790) colors were peach, ivory, Wedgewood blue, opal pink, and green with clean and creamy white backgrounds of English garden-printed fabrics. More intense colors such as reds and golds and deep greens and blues were still often seen in rich imported textiles such as silks, fine cottons, and linens and in the increasingly popular Oriental rugs.

Colors during the *Neoclassic* or *Classic Revival* period (c.1760–1820) were light and pastel. Americans were influenced by the French Neoclassic colors such as palace cream; powder green and pink; French lilac and turquoise; Medici green (the Italian family who patronized the arts); Sevres blue (a French porcelain); Pompadour blue and DuBarry red (soft colors named after Louis XV's mistresses); and accentuated gold and silver tones. English and Americans added Robert Adam (A.D. 1728–1792, English Neoclassic architect and furniture designer) colors to the spectrum: a clear spring green called Adam green, dove gray, pale lavender, faded red, deep olive green, grayed green and blue, warm pink, and the Wedgwood jasperwear colors, which were tones of blue, warm coral pink, creamy sage or stark whites, and sometimes accentuated with gold leaf.

The *Empire style* (c. 1804–1860), which followed the French Revolution, was a reflection of Napoleon's campaigns and personal admiration for the classical interiors. Bright royal red and gold, emerald to olive green, majestic purple, brown, and accents of pale mauve, cream, white, or black predominated this era. In England the period was called *Règency*; in America, the interiors were called *Ameri-*

can Empire (c. 1820–1860), contained in *Greek Revival* and late Federal homes. The bold color statements were seen particularly in upholstery, draperies, and broadloom woven (Wilton and Axminster) carpeting.

Following the Civil War, other revivals brought color schemes from past eras. The *Victorian era* (c. 1842–1910) was an age of richly furnished eclecticism. This era is often referred to as the mauve decades, supporting colors such as deep old-looking red and faded rose red or mauve, wine and dark violet, taupe, and black. Also seen were sage, dark olive, clear green, dark and creamy gold, tobacco brown, rust, and accents of royal blue, bright red and magenta in traditionally designed textile patterns. From the turn of the century through the 1930s, many pure revivals were seen and colors were often documented to the era of the revival.[1]

Two styles that influenced color schemes in America after the Victorian era were *Art Nouveau* and *Art Deco*. Art Nouveau (c. 1890–1910) designs were based on growing plant forms with colors that may be described as the warm, late afternoon colors of plant growth in summer: many shades of green, yellow, and orange; the entire spectrum of floral colors from soft pink to deep violet; the colors seen in sunsets behind mountains or over lakes—blended, subtle, rich hues.

Art Deco (c. 1909–1939) was the ornate phase of the Modern era, with decoration that included sleek forms and geometric shapes. Favorite colors were rose, mauve, silver and black, and warm yellow-greens trimmed with gold and mustard yellow. Both Art Nouveau and Art Deco forms and colors are frequently revived in today's interiors.

The Modern Era

The outbreak of World War II effectively cut off America from European color influence. Many interior colors were neutral and comparatively drab during the 1940s. However, America turned its color attention to the optimistic bright and colorful south of the border—Latin American hues that were best represented in the interiors of Hollywood movies.

During the 1950s, research that was initiated before and during World War II was utilized for interior use. Dyestuffs chemically invented and applied to synthetic fibers gave rise to bright, clear, often gaudy colors: bright yellow, carnation and flamingo pink, Oriental blue, flower red, chartreuse, avocado and pine green, and gold. These colors were usually assigned to artwork or textiles, while backgrounds and even furniture remained monochromatic colors such as rose-beige, or pale turquoise, black or white, or neutrals. Colors and design from Scandinavia were introduced during the 1950s, and for the first time in America, blues and greens were used together. Scandinavian and Bauhaus designers brought the *Modern International style*, which began around the turn of the century, to America

from Europe. Frank use of metal and glass coupled with natural stone and brick gave interiors a stark, almost colorless effect.

Although some of the stark and neutral look of the *Early Modern era* persisted, the 1960s brought more textiles and color into interiors. Man-made fiber textiles accepted chemical dyes with great intensity and contributed to the bold, bright, even psychedelic colors that permeated the late 1960s and early 1970s. Bright colors in translucent draperies sometimes caused entire rooms to be bathed in orange, gold, or pink light, for example. Carpeting and upholstery fabrics were likewise intense, with reds, orange, shocking pink, vivid blue, and clear yellow at the forefront.

Figure 3.1

Figure 3.2

Figure 3.1 Color during the Federal and American Empire periods was often brilliant and intense, influenced greatly by the French revolution. This interior shows a Neoclassic treatment at the poster bed and window in a rich, vivid green, a color personally preferred by Napoleon. White sheers and white trim in the woodwork made the depth of the scheme come alive. Photo courtesy of Boscobel Restoration Incorporated.

Figure 3.2 A contemporary version of the cottage Victorian look where the textile brings light and cheery color in high contrast to deep values of dark-stained woodwork in a cluttered Victorian setting furnished with American Empire pieces. In recent years, the charm of Victoriana has caught the fancy of a great many people; it is rich and cozy, largely because of the depth of the colors used combined with patterns that range from serious to lighthearted. Textiles and J. P. Stevens & Co. bed linens by and photo courtesy of Laura Ashley.

Midway into the 1970s, two major color trends developed. The first was natural to neutrals, earth-toned beige. Textural interest replaced pattern and neutral replaced color. At the same time, America was celebrating the bicentennial anniversary, and although some interiors were done in vivid American flag colors, the major color thrust came from the renewed appreciation for and pride in colors of the American heritage. America turned to its historic roots and revived and adapted traditional colors to contemporary interiors.

There was also an Oriental color influence in the 1970s that came with the normalization of American relations with mainland China, opening of trade that contributed colors such as Ming and peacock blue, jade green, chrysanthemum yellow and orange, and peony pink.

During the late 1970s and early 1980s, the Post-Modern architectural movement brought vivid, contrasting colors to interior design. By the 1980s the path had been paved for multiple color trends in use at once, including the continuation of historic interior colors, sometimes freshened up with brighter intensity and varied value, and neutral schemes with bright or deep accents. Colors were influenced by grays and deep, rich, vibrant tone colors. Colors were influenced again by Europe, particularly Victorian Britain and Renaissance Italy. In the late 1980s, pastels of the earlier two decades also become more refined, clearer, and brighter. Earth tones, likewise, found depth and richness as warmed-up element colors.

The Color Trend Market

Today we see new color trends or palettes established by color forecasting as an eighteen-month or two-year consecutive and overlapping prediction. These changes are most evident in fashion apparel, yet they do permeate the interior design marketplace as well. Some explanations for the rapid change include the following:

1. The public responds to new colors introduced by the mass media—when fashion changes and a new look is introduced, people are generally quite receptive in order to stay in style or to stay on the forefront of fashion change.
2. The fast-paced society where we live makes us not only accept change but expect and even be impatient for it.
3. High technology—instant access to pools of computer or media-based information—has made us a change-oriented society.
4. Economic growth paves the way for expansion of the interior design profession. Consequently, further research into organizational and individual behavior based on color response is also possible.

There are associations that research color direction and forecast color trends with remarkable accuracy. These forecasts aid manufacturers who are anxious to keep products selling well in the marketplace, where appealing and popular color is of primary importance in item selection. Color trends for each year are established by professional groups. Three of the best known and most influential are the Color Marketing Group (CMG), the Color Association of the United States (C.A.U.S.), and the International Colour Authority (ICA).[2] As these groups trace the advance and recession of color

Figure 3.3

Figure 3.3 A hallmark of modern interiors is the absence of color. This interior, a study in minimalism, is also a study in the use of space neutrals and neutralized color. Off-white walls are clean and frank. Even the right angles at the ceiling are missing, so that the off-white can continue uninterrupted above the eye level. Natural materials—wood floors, wicker furniture, glass tabletop, faux stone pendant light—all utilize natural color or no color at all. At the windows are pleated shades in a pale, dull red violet, a soothing understatement. Window treatments by and photo courtesy of Del Mar.

popularity, they select or recognize new hues and freshen hues currently on the market. They also look at and decide which hues the public is most likely to accept. These decisions are based on

1. an awareness of color trend evolutions and past and present trends;
2. an awareness of the constant demand by consumers for change in color preference;
3. the input nationally and internationally by companies who are actually producing the colors and by association members who market these colors;
4. an understanding of human response or psychological reaction to specific hues and an intuition for color based on this understanding;
5. national or international events that affect color trends, as they have in the past;
6. creative designers and artists, whose works become well-known, influencing decisions; and
7. public personalities, such as political leaders, royalty, media personalities, and other high-profile people with charisma or controversial status who set a trend through their personal style.

These three groups are the organizations that establish color trends and forecasting. In addition, other organizations and corporations provide specific consulting services for groups or manufacturers. These companies may provide color swatches for marketing a specific product, they may perform color trend consulting, or they may help companies improve their public relations as they market the rapidly changing colors.

Color Theory

A good understanding of color theory provides a sound color expertise base in interior design. This basic information is as valuable to people in home or working environments as it is to professionals.

For centuries, artists, scientists, and observers of nature have theorized about color. They have studied how it is made; what it is made up of (pigment and light, for example); how nature uses color; how people use color; how colors affect one another; and how colors affect people emotionally, mentally, and physiologically. They observed what lightness and darkness and intensity do to color; how colors may be combined, blended, broken up, or otherwise manipulated to achieve specific end results; and what colors make pleasing harmonies, schemes, or set of combinations. Of the many who theorized about color, a few have made significant observations that even today guide our understanding and use of color in interiors. M.E. Chevruel (1786–1889), a French chemist and head of dyestuffs at the Gobelin Tapestry Works near Paris, published a book in

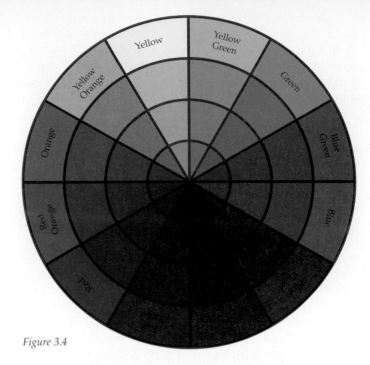

Figure 3.4

1825 that has been translated into English and is still in use today, *The Principles of Harmony and Contrast of Colors*. This book is considered one of the greatest works ever written on color; in it are found the roots of all our present theories.[3]

The Standard Color Wheel Theory

The *Standard Color Wheel theory* or system is also known as the *Palette theory*, the *Prang theory* and the *David Brewster Color theory*. This theory is based on a conventional color circle or wheel where three *primary hues*—red, yellow, and blue—are placed equidistant. *Secondary hues* are placed between these primaries and are a result of mixing any two of them: red plus yellow yields orange; yellow plus blue yields green; blue plus red yields violet. Hence, the secondary colors are orange, green, and violet and are placed on their proper places between the primaries. By mixing a primary and a secondary color on the color wheel, an *intermediate*, or *tertiary, color* emerges, for example, yellow plus orange yields yellow-orange. These colors are yellow-orange, yellow-green, blue-green, blue-violet, red-violet, and red-orange. Note that the primary color is written first.

When these primary, secondary, and intermediate colors are placed in a circle, there are twelve colors; this constitutes the conventional color wheel. However, with the addition of black and white and by mixing the colors on the wheel in various manners, an unlimited number of colors can be achieved; hence, the title the Palette theory. This method can be used to mix paint in literally any hue, value, and intensity, to match or blend with any wall covering or fabric, or to achieve any artistic result. We have only to observe the overwhelming number of choices of paint-chip colors on the market to see that this is so.

Figure 3.4 The color wheel.

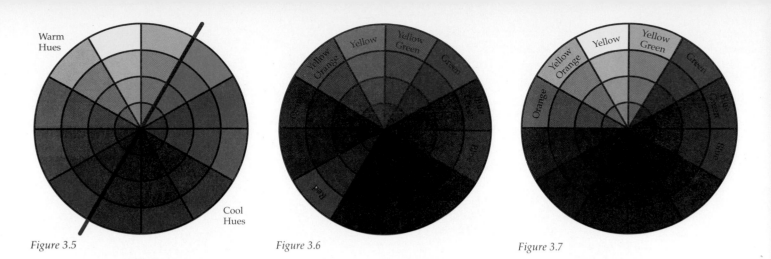

Figure 3.5

Figure 3.6

Figure 3.7

When a color wheel is divided down the center between red-violet and violet and across to green and yellow-green, some of the colors are considered *warm colors*—red-violet, red, red-orange, orange, yellow-orange, yellow and yellow-green. The other colors are considered *cool colors*—green, blue-green, blue, blue-violet, and violet. The warmth or coolness of a color is also relative to the amount of white or black added. For example, very light yellow may be rendered cool because it recedes away from the viewer and gives feelings of light and space. The visual temperature is also dependent on the strength or intensity of the color and by the placement of colors next to each other. The psychology of these warm and cool hues will be considered later in this chapter.

Chevreul discovered through his studies that color combinations could be divided into "analogous and contrasting harmonies." Today we have expanded this concept by the use of color schemes based on the standard color wheel.

Monochromatic color schemes are based on one color. Successful monochromatic schemes often utilize light, medium, and dark values, varieties of the color in intensity and dullness, and the addition of other hues such as the complement to neutralize or to vary the hue identity slightly. Ample amounts of white or off-white and small amounts of black or the complement hue added to a monochromatic interior can balance the color distribution or relieve a potentially overwhelming use of color.

Analogous harmonies or schemes are colors next, or adjacent, to each other on the color wheel. Generally, three to six colors are used, with one color being predominant, another being secondary in importance and usage, and a third and others up to six used as accents. Here, a key to success often lies in the variety of the lightness, darkness, intensity or clarity, dullness, and exactness of the hue and in the uneven use of the different colors. For example, in a

scheme of orange, yellow-orange, orange, and yellow-green, perhaps a softened or neutralized yellow would dominate, with yellow-orange used in smaller proportions and more neutralized tones and the orange and yellow-green as accent colors.

Complementary colors are those opposite on the color wheel.

- *Direct complement* colors are pairs exactly opposite—red and green; yellow and violet; blue and orange. Or they may be intermediate colors such as blue-green and red-orange, for example, that when lightened and/or dulled are a lovely combination.
- *Split complements* contain a base hue, or color, and the two colors on each side of its direct complement—yellow, red-violet, and blue-violet, for example.
- *Triadic complements* are three colors that are equidistant on the color wheel. Examples include the primary colors, (red, yellow, and blue) or the secondary colors (green, orange, and violet) or a set of intermediate hues (yellow-green, blue-violet, and red-orange).
- *Double complements* are two pairs of direct complements that are adjacent or next to each other, such as yellow and violet and yellow-orange and blue-violet.
- *Tetrad complements* are four colors that are equidistant on the color wheel, such as yellow-orange, green, blue-violet, and red.
- *Alternate complements* are triad schemes with a direct complement of one of the hues.

Chevreul noted that colors that are far apart on the wheel enhance the intensity of one another. In other words, the greater the difference, the more apparent or obvious the difference. He deemed complementary combinations more beautiful than analogous ones. Both analogous and com-

Figure 3.5 Warm colors and cool colors.

Figure 3.6 Monochromatic.

Figure 3.7 Analogous color scheme.

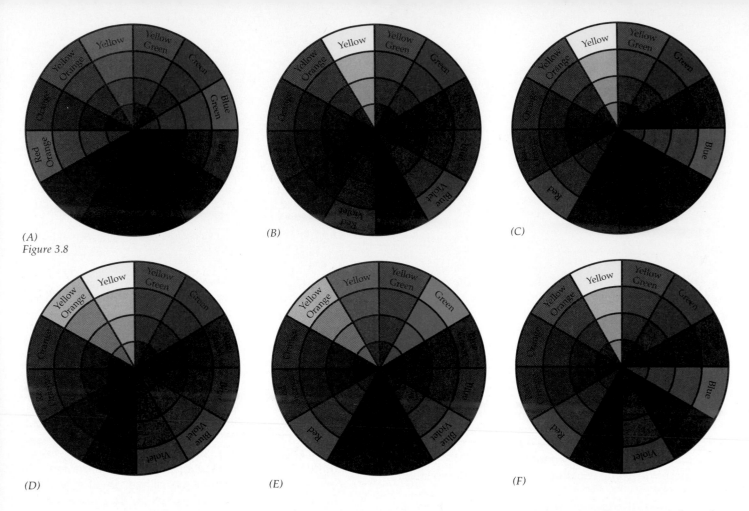

(A)
Figure 3.8

(B)

(C)

(D)

(E)

(F)

plementary harmonies are generally more aesthetically pleasing when the colors are used in unequal proportions with one color being clearly more dominant. When the colors in the scheme vary in intensity and value, then equal amounts of equal intensities and values cannot compete for attention.

Chevreul also did considerable research into afterimages, a concept that had a profound impact on modern art. Afterimages will be discussed later in the chapter under Color Psychology.

The Munsell Theory

The Munsell theory is a major color theory in general use for interior design today. *Munsell* (1858–1918), an American colorist, published his studies in several books. One study published in 1905 and still in use today is his *Color Notation.* His basic theory is widely used today in industry, manufacturing, interior design, and other fields such as science and medicine. Munsell "packets" are available today from Munsell Color for color study and implementation of exact color needs.[4]

The Munsell theory is a precise, formula-based system for notating specific colors. Munsell formulated a color wheel, then expanded it to a three-dimensional globe with leaves or pages of color variations. The system is based on three attributes that determine the exact color identity. These attributes are

1. *Hue*—the color name; for example, the hue red.
2. *Value*—the lightness or darkness of the hue, or color (the amount of white or black added to the hue). Hues with white added are called tints and hues with black added are called shades.
3. *Chroma* or *intensity*—the amount of pure chroma in a given hue; the relative brightness versus the dullness or neutralization of the hue.

The Munsell system is based on five hues; they are red, yellow, green, blue, and purple (not violet). The colors between these are red-yellow, yellow-green, blue-green, blue-purple, and red-purple. Hue families are given a letter and a numerical notation, 2.5, 5, 7.5, and 10, where 5 is the pure hue. Pure red (R), for example, without any of its neighbors to the left (purple hues) or to the right (yellow hues) is assigned a 5, hence 5R. If the red page or palette had some yellow in it, the hue page would be assigned 7.5R. This is essentially red-orange. If the red hue was slightly red-purple, the page is 2.5R. Therefore, the numerical designa-

Figure 3.8 (A) Direct complement colors. (B) Split complement colors. (C) Triadic complement scheme: three colors equidistant on the color wheel. (D) Double complement: side-by-side pair of direct complements. (E) Tetrad complements. (F) Alternate complement.

Figure 3.9 A horizontal cross section of the Munsell system of color notation "tree" showing hue symbols and their relation to one another. There are five primary hues and five intermediate hues, designated as a letter or letter combination—R for red, YR for yellow-red (there is no orange in Munsell). The hue without any undertones from its neighbor is a 5 hue, and colors to the right added to the hue increase the numerical designation (7.5R contains some yellow, for example), whereas colors with a lower designation have undertones from hues to the left (2.5R contains some purple). Photo courtesy of Munsell Color.

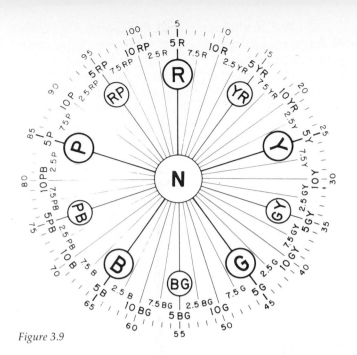

Figure 3.9

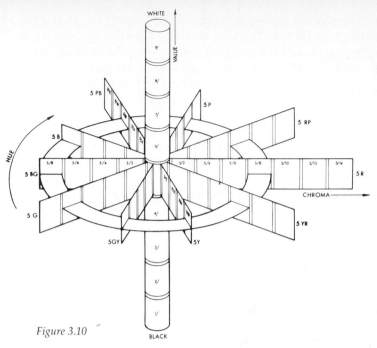

Figure 3.10

tion is based on the pureness of the hue. Yellow without any yellow-red or green added is 5Y, 5B is blue without any green or purple influence, and so on.

Value, the lightness or darkness, is geared to a central column of value. White, at the top, is given the number of 10; black, at the bottom, is designated as 0; in-between is a step series of grays going from dark gray or 1, next to black at the bottom, to light gray or 9, next to white at the top. Every color has what is termed a normal value. This means that every hue has a certain value level as it occurs naturally or in its most natural-appearing state. Yellow is naturally very light and has the lightest *natural saturation point.* Violet is the darkest.

Normal Values:

Yellow	-light value	8
Green	-medium light value	6
Blue	-medium value	5
Red	-medium dark value	4
Purple	-dark value	3

At the natural saturation point, more color chips will be found on the Munsell page. For example, more light yellows exist than dark yellows, and more darker purple than light purple.

Chroma or intensity, the brightness or purity of a hue, is also designated with a number,

following the value number and a slash. The numbers range from 1 to 16, with the lower numbers meaning neutralized or dulled colors. A color is dulled or lessened in intensity by adding its color-wheel complement. The higher numbers indicate less of that complementary color, so the color becomes clearer and purer, and sometimes brighter, as the numbers increase.

A sample of the Munsell notation for a pure, light, clear yellow would by 5Y 8/12; a clear, naturally occurring red would be 5R 4/14. A dull, medium-value purple would be 5P 5/2. A less pure red, one with some purple added and found in a light value and dull intensity, would be 2.5R 7/4. The advantage to this system is that it states clearly the attributes of a color. The precision of the system is also a boon to color use were exactness is paramount.

Other Color Theories

Many others have contributed to our knowledge of color. Some of the outstanding colorists who have strongly influenced interior design include *Wilhelm Ostwald, Johannes Itten,* and *Josef Albers.*

The *Ostwald theory* has some similarities to Munsell but is plotted as triangular

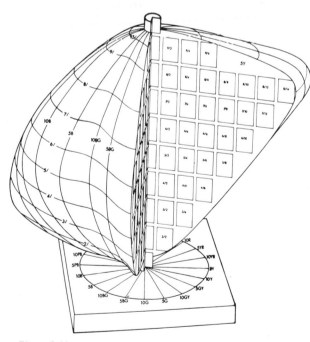

Figure 3.11

Figure 3.10 A center cutaway revealing the core of N, or neutrals, beginning with 1/ at the bottom (black) and ending at 9/ at the top (white). Here we see at the 5/ value level a comparison of how many hues extend to the greatest chroma, or brightness. Since 5 is normal for red, it contains the most color chips, up to fourteen steps out from the central core. As the chroma extends outward, it becomes more pure and intense. Thus the notation 5R 4/14 indicates the most natural, normal, and intense red in the Munsell system. Photo courtesy of Munsell Color.

Figure 3.11 A cutaway illustration of the Munsell color notation system in three-dimensional form, showing that colors with high-normal range, such as yellow, contain more chroma chips high in the tree. Colors with low-normal values, such as blue, contain more chips in the lower value spectrum. Each vertical curved line represents a different hue with its page of chips. The notation lists first hue then value then chroma. Munsell color is a system for exact color notation, matching, and comparison used throughout design, industry, and science. Photo courtesy of Munsell Color.

pages with hues varied not by chroma but by the amount of black and white. The formula bases pure hue or color (C) at one angle, white (W) at the second angle, and black (B) at the third. Harmonious colors are those that have the same content or amount of hue, white, and black—(C + W + B = 1). Further, harmonies can be established in parallels, where colors with the same whiteness work nicely with colors of the same content of black. Harmonies of verticals, of step values, called shadow series, are also harmonious. Complex ring-star and elliptic path harmonies were also plotted by Ostwald. Wilhelm Ostwald (1853–1932) was a physicist who won the Nobel Prize in 1909 for chemistry. He turned his research to color and produced a book *Die Farbenfibel*, which was translated into English as *The Color Primer*.[5]

Johannes Itten (1888–1967) was a teacher at the Bauhaus in Germany between the world wars who did comprehensive work in color theory. He became a great color teacher at Yale University and published two important works: *The Art of Color* and *The Elements of Color*.[6]

Josef Albers (1888–1976), who also taught at the Bauhaus and at Yale University, has become famous for his studies in simultaneous and successive contrast. He experimented with the optic of color. Together with his text *Interaction of Color* he is considered one of the most influential teachers of this century.[7]

Color Harmony

Color harmony is the arrangement of colors so that they are pleasing to the eye and to the senses. Color harmonizing is a skill that comes naturally to some people and only after a difficult struggle and through a constant effort for others. People generally see colors in the same way unless they are losing their eyesight and cannot see the less-intense colors as well or at all or are affected by color blindness. Color blindness to some degree affects roughly 1.5 percent of the population and is found more often in men than in women.

It has been said that there is no such thing as an ugly color; a color only becomes ugly to us if it is used incorrectly. Using colors correctly requires an understanding of how colors change identity and character as they are blended with other hues literally, and how colors are affected visually as they are placed next to other hues.

First, the hue identity itself must be examined closely to determine what its character really is. A blue, for example, is rarely just a blue. It may be a blue with black added (called navy); a blue with green added (called teal); a light and cool blue (called baby blue); a pure and deep blue (American blue); a blue leaning toward violet and darker in value (called royal blue); blues with varying amounts of green, red, yellow, white, black, orange, or violet added. Blue is often considered the most difficult of colors to work with since blue is so easily swayed by other hues or by the white or black that has been mixed into it.

All colors are influenced by other colors; other colors inherent in mixed hues are called *undertones*. Undertones can be evaluated according to whether the basic hue has become lighter or darker, warmer or cooler, more or less pure, or if the hue leans toward another identity or hue. Once the undertones have been discovered, then other colors with similar tendencies can be more successfully blended with or placed near to create color harmonies. Generally speaking, colors that are neutralized or grayed will harmonize as a family; colors that are browned will harmonize as a group, and colors that are pure and tints and/or shades of pure colors will harmonize well together. Undertones can also render a color warm or cool. Warm colors—yellow, orange, and red—become cooler when blues, greens, and violets are mixed into them, and vice versa.

An important fact in color harmony is that colors placed next to each other will be blended by the eye and will be influenced by the type and relative warmth or coolness of the light striking the combination. In small quantities, colors will actually blend into different colors from a distance. If the colored surface is a large area and if the colors surrounding it are not related via undertones, warmth, or clarity, then dissonance will likely result.

Small samples may make it difficult to select colors for a large area. A tiny paint chip is rarely the color of the entire wall when it is painted because of the large quantity of paint or color on the surface and because of the way the light affects the color. It may appear darker or lighter than the paint chip, often more intense, and the undertones will become more obvious. Likewise, floor coverings, textiles, and wall coverings sometimes produce a shock when the color installed looks different from the sample. Working with large samples is not always possible. However, a quart of paint applied to a portion of the wall *in situ* (on the site), where the effects of natural and artificial lighting can be evaluated, is a small price to pay compared to the dissatisfaction of an unproven choice. Fabric can be tested out as well; with only a yard or two placed next to a portion of painted wall, surprising results may emerge that could save anguish as well as money.

Color harmony can also apply to the completed interior as a whole, in addition to the ways individual components of color work together. The Japanese concept of Shibusa states that all elements and colors must interrelate to be subtly harmonious, so that nothing offends the eye. Contrary to this is the concept of color harmony, espoused by some designers, that colors should be bold, high contrast, or even shocking to be most effective. Either philosophy should be used only after evaluating the needs of the people who will occupy the space, the amount of time spent there, and what activities will be performed. For example, a peaceful shibui scheme would be a wise choice in a bedroom suite, whereas the bold, stimulating types of colors in a shopping plaza may be selected to encourage spending and to produce a feeling of euphoria.

Neutralized Colors

True color harmony cannot be achieved without understanding the roles that both neutralized colors and neutrals play in interior design. *Neutralized colors* are those that are made less pure, are dulled in intensity or grayed, and are influenced by other colors. Neutralized colors, or *tones,* are achieved in a number of ways.

1. By mixing any two hues on the color wheel, the resultant hue is less pure than either original color. By mixing colors that are far apart, such as complementary hues, these tones are rich and deep. A small amount of the complement will effectively neutralize in degrees, where the hue becomes less and less pure and finally becomes a deep tone that still maintains its identity. More of the complement renders it a murky, nondescript color, then the mixture progressively becomes tones of the complement.

2. By adding black to a hue, a shade is created, effectively neutralizing the hue. Adding white only to a hue yields tints, or pastels, which are also less pure than the hue but still rather intense.

3. By adding gray or brown, a color becomes neutralized. Grays, browns, or blacks with colored undertones will neutralize the color differently than will pure neutrals.

4. Adding one or more other hues will neutralize a color. Adding yellow and violet to blue, for example, will neutralize the blue and produce undertones. Some very interesting tones, shades, pastels, and tints can be achieved this way.

5. Adding white to neutralized tones yields beautiful soft or grayed pastels in medium to very light neutralized colors. These often make beautiful and livable wall colors.

The value of neutralization lies in the easy-to-live-with, nonassertive colors that can be effective in retail businesses, offices, medical facilities, hotels, restaurants, and, most especially, the home.

Figure 3.12

The *law of chromatic distribution* effectively utilizes neutralized colors. It states: The more neutralized colors of the scheme are found in the largest areas, and the smaller the area, the brighter or more intense the chroma becomes. This means that backgrounds such as floors, walls, ceilings, and draperies are less-intense colors or tones and pastels; large areas such as upholstery are somewhat brighter, intense colors and are used in smallest amounts.

Neutrals

Neutrals are the families of whites and off-whites, grays, and blacks and off-blacks. Browns and beiges are also often considered neutrals, even though they are actually neutralized colored hues.

Whites and off-whites give interiors increased visual space. Whitened floors, ceilings, and walls look light and spacious and seem farther away than they are. Interiors that are hues seem cleaner and crisper surrounded with whites. Off-whites are produced by adding other neutrals (gray, black, brown) to white or by mixing color and neutrals or color into white. These undertones produce off-whites that may be warm or cool, clean or dirty, more neutralized or more colored. Thousands of different off-whites are used in today's interiors. These are seen in paints, wall coverings, textiles, floor coverings, and accessories. It is usually wise to avoid using off-whites that are not similar in undertone. For example, a clear yellowish off-white and a dirty neutralized pinkish off-white will be disturbing; one will appear as the wrong color. However, off-whites with similar warmth, clarity, and color undertones will blend harmoniously.

Grays are achieved by mixing together various amounts of black and white, which makes true achromatic (no color) grays. As such, gray is often an ideal background color against which to show other colors. Grays are easily colored with other hues to produce a wide variety of pinkish grays, yellowish grays, greenish grays, brownish grays, and so on. Colored grays need to be carefully matched or

Figure 3.12 Browns, beiges, whites and off-whites, grays, and blacks and off-blacks make up the family of neutrals. These are livable and warm, yet they evoke none of the emotion that many colored interiors do. Neutrals let the occupant feel at ease and in harmony with nature. Here wood shutters, parquet floor, and adapted rush-seat Neoclassic chairs are all left in a natural wood value and hue. The table is a glass-topped black base. Walls and ceilings are off-white. Shutters by and photo courtesy of Pinecrest, Inc.

blended to be harmonious, and like off-white, gray may be rendered cool or warm, depending on the undertones. Warm grays can be welcoming and comforting; cool grays tend to be cold and uninviting.

Blacks and off-blacks give deep, dark value to the set of neutrals. Black sharpens and adds richness to other colors placed next to it. Black used generously may create a dramatic and theatrical setting, although it might produce feelings of depression in some people. Accents of black give richness to interiors. Off-blacks may be very dark grays or tinted blacks where the hue is barely discernible and can effectively tie into color schemes.

Browns and beiges are often favored because of the warm qualities that they bring to an interior. Browns are achieved by mixing several colors on the color wheel or by neutralizing orange. Often browns are introduced into an interior through stained woods, which do not need to match as long as they harmonize with one another. Used in large amounts, browns can produce a cavelike coziness or a feeling of oppression. Browns are often at their peak when good value distribution is employed, utilizing many steps of lightness from beige to very dark brown.

Rooms done entirely in neutrals is not a new idea nor will it readily be a dated one. Interiors of true neutrals, whites, grays, and blacks are termed *achromatic,* or without color. Many beautiful interiors are created using achromatic whites, grays, and blacks, and the brown/beige group. These environments make fine backgrounds for colorful artwork and accessories. One major advantage of selecting neutrals for interiors is the flexibility to change color schemes without being locked into a set color. Interiors where neutrals are used in every room allow furnishings to be moved from one room to another.

Color-Influencing Factors

Many factors influence the way we see color in interior design. Perhaps the most important are light, texture and material, color placement, and value distribution and contrast.

Light contains color. A light shown through a prism is simple proof of the rays of the color spectrum seen in light. The colors of the rainbow found in nature are arranged similarly to the color wheel, except that light rays are seen from the longest to the shortest: red, orange, yellow, green, blue, and violet. Since color exists in light, all light is colored. The degree of color, the warmth or coolness of the light, is a variable in each interior design installation and will affect the background and furnishing colors. Light influences color more, perhaps, than any single factor or element.

We perceive color in paint, materials, and furnishings because of the physics of light. When light strikes an item that has been colored with pigment or dye, then all the light rays are absorbed except those which are reflected by that pigment. We are therefore able to identify the material by color or hue.[8]

Natural light affects color in many ways: (1) according to the *orientation,* or direction, of light (east light is clear and bright; north light is cool; south light is constant and warm; west light is hazy and hot); (2) according to the season of the year; and (3) according to other environmental factors, such as humidity, and clarity versus fog, smog, or overcast conditions.

Interior *artificial lighting* also affects the way we see color. *Incandescent* light is usually warm and flattering; luminescent or *fluorescent* light can be warm or cool but is always clear and virtually shadowless.

Candlelight and firelight, used on occasion in homes and in contract settings such as restaurants and some hotel lobbies, is lighting by *combustion.* It is similar to incandescent lighting in that it is warm and flattering. It is, however, a darker light source, and because it flickers, colors will appear darker and less defined or precise.

The placement of the lighting and the direction from which it hits the color and even the time of the day can each give a different look or personality to color. *Metamerism* is the characteristic of color to appear as one color in one light and another color in another light (considering all the lighting factors). Testing color on the site and under every lighting condition is always the best avenue for success.

Texture and materials affect color because of the different ways light is caught and absorbed or because of the degree of reflection on the surface. Smooth surfaces will reflect more light, which makes colors appear lighter and more intense than normal. Materials that are grained, such as wood, or those textured in any way will absorb or refract (break up) the light, causing colors to appear somewhat darker than normal. Because of this factor, the exact match in colored samples will not appear as the same colors when installed. Paint, draperies, carpeting, upholstery, and laminates will never be exactly the same color, and the attempt to match may cause frustration and dissonance in the finished interior. It is wiser to blend color, purposefully selecting various values or harmonious undertones and allowing the inherent differences that come from the texturizing of materials to enhance the entire color scheme.

Wood is a colored material seen in so many interiors. Wood furniture sets, groups, or suites have been produced in single-colored stains for many years. This has sometimes caused the opinion that all wood furniture and backgrounds should match. Today we have come to realize that beautiful interiors often feature many different woods in varying stains and values. When the grain is similar and the undertones are compatible, then different woods can often be successfully used together in an interior.

Figure 3.13

Figure 3.13 Just as the quality, color, and direction of light from within and without can affect the appearance of color, so, too, can the effect of a great quantity of wood. Here the wealth of brown seen in the mill work (milled woodwork) and shutters set into the traceried round Victorian window influences the light, making it appear as a mellow, glowing room. Shutters by and photo courtesy of Pinecrest, Inc.

Figure 3.14

Figure 3.15

Color placement of hues in *juxtaposition,* or close together, will cause colors to affect one another. A color placed near green, for example, may take on a greenish cast or bring out a greenish undertone. When a color is selected alone then installed in combination with other hues, it may take on undertones that give a different character to that color. Sometimes the result is pleasing, and at other times, the color combination is disharmonious. Coordinating colored samples under similar lighting conditions or on the site before actual installation can avoid unpleasant surprises when the colors become permanent in the interior.

Similarly, the placement within the interior can yield surprising results. Traditionally, darkest colors were used on the floors, lighter colors on the walls, and lightest colors on the ceiling, imitative of the natural color placement in nature. However, dark value on the wall will visually close in the space and render the room more cozy. Dark values on the ceilings will visually lower the ceiling, which may be useful when the ceiling is very high and the volume of space is not welcoming. Conversely, lighter colors on the floor will visually expand space and may effectively unify the color schemes between rooms. Again, trying out an unusual placement of color where it is to be used will help to ensure success of the completed work.

Value distribution and contrast mean the degree of lightness of the hue (white added) versus the degree of darkness (or black). Light or *high values* are tints, and dark or *low values* are shades. When an interior is filled with a variety of values, from very light to very dark and the subsequent value steps are somewhat evenly distributed, then the room is said to have good *value distribution.* However, various types of *value contrast* can also be put to good use. Values that are similar, all light values (*high key*) or all middle values or all darker values (*low key*), for example, are termed *low-contrast values.* These interiors are generally soothing and calming. Light values produce an airy, somewhat carefree feeling. Middle-range values give a sense of normality and calm, and dark values give a stable or anchored mood to the interior. Very light and very dark values (no middle values) used in a single interior are termed *high-contrast values.* High-contrast schemes are dramatic, theatrical, or intense. They can look sophisticated and professional and they are stimulating but rarely are comforting or relaxing.

It is important to note that not only can colors be manipulated to achieve value distribution and contrast, but achromatics (black, white, and various shades of gray) and beiges and browns can also.

Color Psychology

Although nearly everyone sees or perceives color the same way, the way we interpret or feel about color can vary because of our experiences with color, our education of color, and our cultural associations with color through the years.

Figure 3.14 Interior designer Richard Napple used deep values to create low-key drama amidst reflective and textile surfaces and fabrics and sculpture from India. The effect of low-key interiors is cozy, reclusive, and theatrical. Photo by Norman McGrath, © 1980.

Figure 3.15 Predominantly light values at and above eye level in this filtered sunny room make a high-key value scheme. The effect is light-hearted and casual sophistication.

A fabulous Persian Oriental rug makes an exotic setting for the abundant use of wicker furniture. Photo courtesy of Bielecky Brothers, Inc.

Figure 3.16

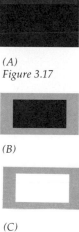

Figure 3.17

(B)

(C)

The psychology of color is a valuable tool to the interior designer in creating interiors tailored to the needs of the users. In the home as well as in any public situation, a knowledge of how colors are generally viewed and understood by humans can help create effective and efficient interiors.

Common color associations or *symbolisms* are based on the response people have to hues in general. These may be swayed by cultural and/or individual psychological associations. Based on intensities and values, some common associations in Western societies include the following listed in chart 3.1.

Color group moods can also be determined based on research. Philip Thiel, in his book *Visual Awareness and Design,* has discovered that groups of colors may produce emotional response:

1. Light value colors that are high in chroma (light and bright) produce feelings of spontaneity and happiness.
2. Colors light or high in value and dark or deep in chroma (light and dull or neutralized) produce feelings of calmness and relaxation.
3. Colors with deep values and dull chroma (dark and dull or neutralized) are serious and profound.
4. Colors dark in value and bright in chroma (jewel tones) suggest richness and strength.[9]

Warm and cool colors are a traditional method of determining color psychological effects. Warm colors are generally those on the color wheel that are adjacent from yellow-green, yellow, orange, red-orange, red, and red-violet. These colors will visually and psychologically warm the temperature of an interior to a remarkable degree. Warm colors are inviting, homey, optimistic, encouraging, stimulating to the appetite, and they blend objects, patterns, and textures. Warm colors also tend to close-in space and create more intimate interiors. Keep in mind that these are generalities. Depending on the value and the intensity of the chroma, colors can be very warm (high chroma), which will intensify these attributes, warm, or only slightly warm (middle to low chroma), which will deemphasize the qualities listed.

Cool colors are those adjacent on the other side of the color wheel: violet, blue-violet, blues, and greens. These colors generally calm and relax the mind and body, giving the impression of lack of pressure and plenty of time to wait or to accomplish tasks. Cool colors often suggest more formality and precision of detail, pattern, and color. These visually expand space, making them effective tools in small, cramped quarters. Cool colors subdue the appetite and

Figure 3.16 High contrast is seen in this achromatic kitchen with white cabinetry and black tile countertops. The only color is seen in the copper cooking pots and wood accessories and, of course, in the colors seen in food preparation. This type of scheme is sometimes referred to as an accented neutral. While this scheme is predominately high key, the dark elements bring crispness and vivid contrast to this vintage, remodeled kitchen. Countertop and floor tiles by and photo courtesy of Hastings Tile & Il Bagno Collection.

Figure 3.17 (A) Value scale indicating high key (light values), middle values, and low key (low values). (B) Low contrast—all light or all medium or all dark value. (C) High contrast—light versus dark values.

Chart 3:1 Common Color Associations

Red

Pure, intense: Danger, passion, love, excitement, stimulus, conspicuous.
Dark, neutralized: Wealth, power, sometimes evil.
Pure chroma pink: Cheerfulness, youth, festivity.
Light or pastel pink: Femininity, innocence, relaxation, delicacy.

Orange

Pure, intense: Friendliness, warmth, celebration, clarity.
Dark, neutralized: Wealth, success, fame, rich depth.
Light or pastel: Stimulation (to the appetites), security, relaxed euphoria (sense of well-being).

Yellow

Pure, bright: Optimism, sunshine, springtime, renewal, intensity, demanding, revealing, warmth (too much is hot), intellect, stimulation.
Dark, neutralized golden yellow: Wealth, affluence, status, distinction, high esteem. Too much is brash, garish, or ostentatious.
Middle to light value: Intelligence, wisdom, compassion, freshness, cheerfulness, optimism, goodness, clarity, cleanliness.

Green

Pure, bright: Nature, calmness, friendliness, integrity, practicality, frankness.
Dark, neutralized: Solidity, wealth, anchored tenacity, security.
Blue-green: Sea and sky, cleanliness, nostalgia, calmness.
Yellow-green: Youthfulness, freshness, happiness.

Blue

Pure, intense: Loyalty, honesty, integrity, royalty, stimulation, restlessness. These also apply to deep or neutralized blues.
Deep, neutralized: Sincerity, conservatism, safety, sense of peace, kindness, compassion. These also apply to pure or intense blues.
Light or pastel: Tentativeness, cleanliness, calm, expanded time and space, lack of security.

Purple or Violet

Pure, intense: Optimism, imagination, royalty, dignity, poise, renewal, commitment, dramatic, theatrical.
Dark, neutralized: Depth, richness, security, sternness, soberness, sobriety, dullness.
Light or pastel: Freshness, springtime, floral, imaginative, femininity, kindness, sensitivity.

emotions. Very cool colors are intense, cool colors are middle chroma, and slightly cool colors are low in chroma (neutralized).

Afterimages are physical phenomena that can affect anyone and potentially create a disturbing visual and, hence, emotional state of being. Humans are sensitive to complementary pairs of colors, directly across on the color wheel. (It is to pairs or colors that people may become color-blind—not just to red but to green as well, for example.) When the eye is focused on an intense color for as few as thirty seconds, if the eye is then focused on a neutral area, the complementary color appears in the same pattern as an afterimage. Pairs of intense, high-chroma complementary colors of equal value placed in juxtaposition will create a vibrating afterimage where they border, which can cause problems with eye focusing and be responsible for irritation or headaches after a period of time. Afterimages can be reduced by varying the intensity of colors placed together, by separating them in distance, or by carefully handling strong graphics and patterns. A stark white background is far more likely to create an afterimage than a neutralized color or a gray. A strong chroma of a hue will bring the complement into the visual area, which will be seen in the neutrals. Varying the value of colors will also reduce visual discomfort.

Figure 3.18

Figure 3.18 The way that value, or the relative lightness or darkness of hues, is distributed is important in an interior. A standard or acceptable value distribution is seen in this Laura Ashley interior furnished with Alba Roses fabric in which the ceiling is white, the walls a light value, and the floor is darker, producing a sense of stability. Darker colors will advance and lighter colors recede, making this interior seem spacious and airy above, tenacious below, and pleasant around the perimeter. Photo courtesy of Laura Ashley.

Color in Residential Interiors

Perhaps the most important application of color in interior design to most people is in the home, for it is there that we are free to select colors that are the most personally appealing to us. At home we have control over the selection of color in the major background elements and the application of color in the more flexible aspects of the design. When color schemes are neutral, children and extended-family members can express themselves with art and accessories without disturbing the general color scheme of the rest of the house. When neutrals or neutralized color schemes are used at home, its role as a place of rest and repose, and as a calming, peaceful sanctuary becomes even more important.

Color is a good way to change the look, mood, formality, or gender level without spending a lot of money. Although reupholstering furniture, replacing carpeting, and selecting custom window coverings often are costly, many other colored items are usually not. Paint, for example, is relatively inexpensive considering the square footage it covers. Bed, bath, and kitchen linens can change the look entirely when backgrounds are suitably neutralized. Likewise, art and accessories may be changed with the seasons or moods. Smaller, manipulatable colored areas that are bright and cheerful might be preferred by younger children who can benefit from them intellectually. Tailored for their needs, these same areas may provide a source of identity and individuality for teens and young adults, be soothing and relaxing for working adults, and be comforting and reminiscent for senior citizens.

Color in homes can be tailor-made to individual needs beyond age. Those who are housebound or prone to depression can be cheered with warm, encouraging colors. People with poor eyesight may benefit from light, clear color and value. Those who need reassuring environments in which to work at home can select colors that are calming or stable. Various task or hobby areas within the home can also be outfitted for individuality. However, living areas where people congregate or are entertained should be neutralized enough to be generally appealing to everyone.

Nonresidential Considerations

Color in public and in work spaces is a complex topic. Color in medical facilities will often be handled differently than in hospitality interiors, office interiors, retail businesses, or production or assembly-line facilities. The differences lie in the specialized needs that must be met for users of these various environments. Designers must be sensitive to these needs that govern emotional responses that affect behavior, attitude, productivity, or patronization. Often considerable research will be conducted to determine how to best serve the psychological responses of the users.

Medical facilities include hospitals, doctors' offices, outpatient facilities, and geriatric facilities. Here the philosophy of color has changed significantly in the past several years. Medical facilities used to be white or pale tints and cool looking, full of hard surfaces, an echo of the sterile environment, which was free from germs and the communication of disease. Today we have found that soft or neutralized colors in a variety of values from dark to light are relaxing yet encouraging of bodily repair. Also, colored background elements are no longer always hard. Often medical facilities will incorporate carpet on the floors, fireproof fabric or wall coverings on the partitions and walls, and warm wood textures. This atmosphere gives a more human, caring approach to sometimes frightening and bewildering circumstances.

Figure 3.19

Figure 3.19 Colors are often seen to be soothing in places such as medical facilities and hotel suites. At the Palio Restaurant in the New York City Equitable Building, however, the color is vivid and stimulating. Black and white tile on the floor and black chairs at the bar are a high-style, sophisticated use of color value, giving high visibility to those seated there. Against the walls, the black chairs blend more closely in low contrast to the rich browns of the wall paneling, giving a secluded and private feeling. Many vibrant colors are mixed and juxtaposed in the equestrian theme of the artwork on the upper walls, giving a sense of companionship to those alone in the restaurant and a suggestion of activity, strength, and movement. Downlights in the recessed coffered ceiling illuminate the general area, while base lighting washes the mural from brass casing below (above the paneling). The light/dark grid pattern in the ceiling echoes the floor, but since the value contrast is lower, it does not draw attention. Photo by Norman McGrath © 1989.

Hospitality interiors include hotels and motels, resorts and spas, and restaurants. These are areas where color and design are dictated by the culture and the climate. Often more lavish colors and patterns will dominate reception areas and rooms and suites. In restaurants, red- and orange-related hues are found to be the most stimulating to the appetite, although colors that complement the food color enhance the visual appeal and flavor of the food. Where climates are very warm, cooler colors are often used, and in colder climates, warmer colors are often more welcoming in hospitality interiors.

Office interiors in the past several years have become increasingly more sophisticated in terms of equipment and furniture systems and the use of computers to simplify procedures, storage, and retrieval systems. The whole complexion of office interiors has changed. Although color trends will always be reflected in contemporary office design, the major shift has been away from clear, obvious hues toward grayed tones and grays accented or coordinated with either pure chroma or neutralized hues. These types of colors reflect an attitude of increased professionalism in the business world.

Retail businesses have as the object of primary importance the enticement of customers to purchase goods and services. Two major color trends in recent years have developed to meet these goals. One trend is the use of stimulating warm, cheerful, and advancing colors, a technique often utilized in large stores and shopping malls where the bright colors help customers locate departments and services. To an extent, glitter or neon-bright color have been incorporated into retail businesses that appeal to youth.

The other retail business color trend reflects the hues in office interiors. It is the use of more subtle deep value tones and neutralized pastels, accented with jewel tones or pure chroma. The addition of polished wood or classic brass or chrome gives retail businesses an exclusive or rich appearance. This method does not necessarily limit the clientele to those with money. Rather, it is aimed toward making customers feel that they deserve quality merchandise and can somehow afford it.

Production plants have requirements of psychological comfort, productivity, and safety. Light pastel colors that reflect light are generally more pleasing than stark whites, intense colors, or dark values. Cheerful colors influence workers to be cheerful.

Productivity can be increased by eliminating eye fatigue caused by afterimages, intense chroma, stark whites or very dark values, or shiny or glossy surfaces at the workstation. Matte or dull surfaces that provide a pleasing contrast to the material or object being worked on will aid production and add some color and texture contrast also necessary for both comfort and productivity. Primary colors used to identify controls or parts of machinery will increase efficiency. Warm colors in cool environments and cool colors in warm environments will help workers feel more comfortable.

Safety can be enhanced by using bold or intense colors on dangerous parts of machinery or in areas of potential hazard. The use of color to reduce eye fatigue will help workers be more alert and help prevent accidents.

Notes

1. Faber Birren, *Color for Interiors: Historical and Modern* (New York: Whitney Library of Design, 1965), 23, 25, 27, 29, 31, 33, 37, 103.
2. Darlene Kinning, *"How Color Connects"* Draperies and Window Coverings Magazine (Vol. 2, No. 27, February 1985), 18–21.
3. M.E. Chevruel, *The Principles of Harmony and Contrast of Color and Their Applications* (New York: Van Nostrand Reinhold Company), 63–70.
4. Munsell Color. Macbeth. A division of Kollmorgen Corporation, 2441 North Calver Street, Baltimore, MD 21218, Telex 9–6480, Cable Macbeth NBUR.
5. Faber Birren, *Color and the Human Response* (New York: Van Nostrand Reinhold, 1978), 64–65.
6. Johannes Itten, *The Art of Color: The Subjective Experience and Objective Rationale of Color* (New York: Van Nostrand Reinhold Company, Inc., 1973), 11–17.
7. Josef Albers, *Interaction of Color* (New Haven, CT: Yale University Press, 1963), 1–74.
8. Arnold Friedman, John F. Pile, and Forrest Wilson, *Interior Design: An Introduction to Architectural Interiors* (New York: American Elsevier, Inc., 1970), 52.
9. Philip Theil, *Visual Awareness and Design* (Seattle: University of Washington Press, 1981), 189.

Bibliography

Albers, Josef. *Interaction of Color.* New Haven: Yale University Press, 1963.

Ball, Victoria Kloss. *The Art of Interior Design.* New York: John Wiley and Sons, 1982.

Birren, Faber. *Creative Color.* New York: Van Nostrand Reinhold Company, Inc., 1961.

    Color for Interiors: Historical and Modern. New York: Whitney Library of Design, 1965.

    Principles of Color. New York: Van Nostrand Reinhold Company, Inc., 1969.

    Color and the Human Response. New York: Van Nostrand Reinhold Company, Inc., 1978.

    Light, Color and Environment. New York: Van Nostrand Reinhold Company, Inc., 1982.

Evans, Ralph M. *An Introduction to Color.* New York: John Wiley and Sons, Inc., 1959.

Fabri, Ralph. *Color: A Complete Guide for Artists.* New York: Watson, Guptill, 1967.

Friedman, Arnold, John F. Pile, and Forrest Wilson. *Interior Design: An Introduction to Architectural Interiors.* New York: American Elsevier, Inc., 1970.

    Color Fundamentals. New York: McGraw Hill, 1952.

Gerstner, Karl. *The Spirit of Colors*. Cambridge, MA: The MIT Press, 1981.

Graves, Maitland. *The Art of Color and Design*. New York: McGraw-Hill Book Company, 1951.

Guptill, Arthur L. *Color Manual for Artists*. New York: Van Nostrand Reinhold Company, Inc., 1962.

Itten, Johannes. *The Art of Color*. New York: Van Nostrand Reinhold Company, Inc., 1961.

_____. *The Elements of Color*. New York: Van Nostrand Reinhold Company, Inc., 1970.

Klien, Dan. *All Color Book of Art Deco*. New York: Cresent Books, n.d.

Kueppers, Harald. *The Basic Law of Color Theory*. New York: Barron's, 1980.

Luscher, Dr. Max. *The Luscher Color Test*. New York: Simon and Schuster Pocket Books, 1969.

Munsell, A.H. *A Color Notation*. Baltimore: Munsell Color, 1981.

Ocvirk, Otto G., et al. *Art Fundamentals Theory and Practice*. Dubuque, IA: Wm. C. Brown Publishers, 1981.

Ostwald, Wilhelm. *The Color Primer*. New York: Van Nostrand Reinhold Company, Inc., 1969.

Sharpe, Deborah T. *The Psychology of Color and Design*. Chicago: Nelson-Hall, 1974.

Sidelinger, Stephen J. *Color Manual*. Englewood Cliffs, NJ: Prentice-Hall, 1985.

Thiel, Philip. *Visual Awareness and Design*. Seattle: University of Washington Press, 1981.

Venity, Enid. *Color Observed*. New York: Van Nostrand Reinhold Company, Inc., 1980.

Warren, Geoffrey. *All Color Book of Art Nouveau*. London: Octopus Books, 1972.

Color Organizations

Color Marketing Group, 1134 Fifteenth Street, NW, Washington, DC 20005, is a nonprofit organization with a membership of around eight hundred, all of whom are involved in the process of color selection. The association selected colors for the marketing services and products. Members pay an association fee and attend meetings—regional and semiannual national meetings. At the spring meeting, colors are chosen, and at the fall meeting, they are presented to the members. Members are sent resourceful newsletters and have access to workshops and educational seminars.

Color Association of the United States, 24 East 48th Street, New York, NY 10016, issues color charts for home and contract furnishings each September and apparel swatches each March and September, to be eighteen to twenty months ahead of the actual selling season. Members receive the charts and monthly color newsletters and may attend New York-based seminars. Colors each year are selected by a rotating panel of eight to ten members recognized for their color expertise and professionalism.

Members of the International Colour Authority, c/o Benjamin Dent & Company, 33 Bedford Place, London WC1B 5JX, England, meet in the spring and fall in London where forecasts emerge from international members' panels on both home furnishings and apparel. Members receive a continuous printout of ICA data that indicates colors to be promoted worldwide. Monthly reports telexed into London from subscribers are tabulated, divided into specific areas, and the information telexed back, followed up with a written report that evaluates and documents trend development and forecasted color use.

Munsell Color, 2441 N. Calvert Street, Baltimore, Maryland 21218, is a resource to designers and educators. Munsell Color can provide many tools and educational materials for use in defining, identifying, and recording or matching colors through the Munsell color notation system.

THE INTERIOR

Great interiors often are built upon venerable architectural detail. Interior designer John Saladino has captured the essence of fine design by selecting exquisite textiles, unusual furnishings, and handsome background treatments. These are destined to become hallmarks of a new era of interior design: reaching into the past, combining design for the present and future, composing interiors that will become unique classics.

The arrangement and integration of materials and components, as well as their selection, makes successful interior design. Fine interior design fills human needs of function, protection, and comfort, and also brings pleasure and delights the senses. Photo by Ted Spiegel.

This demonstration panel at Just Lights in New York City shows the broad range of effects that can be created by featuring any one of the many designer bulbs that can be used to enhance the look of the lighting itself. Each of these bulbs is available in various sizes and wattage outputs. Use of dimmers on these light bulbs changes their impact in the overall lighting scheme of the room, as well as in the perception of the bulb itself. Photo by Ted Spiegel.

Page 82, top left: For a Princeton University hall, Synergy, a New York City lighting consultant firm, was called in to work with acoustic engineers in the creation of a dual purpose floating panel, capable of focusing an orchestra's sound toward the audience and focusing light on the musicians. Photo by Ted Spiegel. *Page 82, top right:* Lighting's complexity—both in effect and installation—is immediately evident when you see the reference collection at Synergy. The computer in the foreground is displaying just one of hundreds of fixtures surveyed for Consolidated Edison. These fixtures, many from fifty years and more ago, are also inspiration for Synergy's own designs. Interior designers faced with lighting problems are often well advised to call on lighting consultants to aid in the design process or to suggest existing fixtures from within the lines that house consultants work for. Salespeople working with the trade are usually an excellent resource. Photo by Ted Spiegel. *Page 82, bottom:* Boyd Lighting's showroom in the D & D Building in New York often offers lighting workshops for visiting interior designers. Professional lighting sources that deal with the trade are an excellent source for advice on fixtures and their placement. Designers in the contract field will often work with manufacturers in modifying existing fixtures for a large building installation. Photo by Ted Spiegel. *Page 83, top:* At the Sign of the Dove restaurant in New York City, skylight filtered through a draped diffusing material projects a pleasant luncheon atmosphere. Photo by Ted Spiegel. *Page 83, bottom:* In the same room, dinnertime mood is enhanced by downlights, which illuminate the tables individually, and wall washes, which highlight the texture of the brick walls. Photo by Ted Spiegel.

Page 84, top: *At the Lightolier Corporation's New York City showroom, the Lighting Lab offers a flexible demonstration of the impact of specialized fixtures on a home dining room. A simple overhead light (often the illumination an interior designer is challenged to change) starts off our demonstration sequence. Photo by Ted Spiegel.*

Page 84, bottom left: *The first resource to be exploited in creating a design of lighting for the dining room is downlights that will bring controlled lighting to the place settings. Photo by Ted Spiegel.*
Page 84, bottom right: *Ceiling-mounted picture lights highlight the owner's art collection and are a second aspect of the total lighting design. Photo by Ted Spiegel.*

Page 85, top left: *Sconces that accent the wall itself are another option available for the lighting design. Photo by Ted Spiegel.* **Page 85, top right:** *Another option is a ceiling-mounted wall wash that throws the light down. (Sconces do this from the wall surface itself; wash lights do wall illumination from ceiling or floor mounts as well.) Photo by Ted Spiegel.* **Page 85, bottom:** *The final result is a room with mood and accent—not just illumination. The final touch is an uplight behind each of the plants in the corners, as well as a framing spot on the rear wall painting. Photo by Ted Spiegel.*

Page 86, top: The traveler is treated to a kinetic light show in the United Airlines connecting concourse at O'Hare Airport in Chicago, Illinois. As the exciting, changing colored lights go streaming past, the long, dull passage turns into a vital and artistic experience. Photo by Ted Spiegel. *Page 86, bottom:* Beneath dancing feet at Pogo's Disco in Kansas City, Missouri, the multihued light display actually pulses to the rhythm of the music. The lighting is an integral part of the interior design, making the room live with the music. Photo by Ted Spiegel.

The Way We See Color

The way color is perceived is part of the *physics of light* first discovered by *Sir Isaac Newton* in 1676. He experimented with a glass prism and found that sunlight is made of a *full spectrum* of colors that range from red to orange then yellow, green, blue, and violet. These colors are the portion of the electromagnetic spectrum we call the *visual spectrum* that allows us to see objects and their colors.

Three factors determine how we see color. These are (1) the color of the light source, (2) the color of the object, and (3) the combination of the eye and brain or the visual system as a decoder.

When light falls on an object, the object reflects certain wavelengths and absorbs others. The mixture of the wavelengths that are reflected make up the color that the eye sees. For example, an apple looks red because it reflects red light and absorbs all the other colors (or lengths) of light. If the red wavelengths were missing from a light source, the apple would appear without color or gray. Further, the eye sends the message to the brain, which decodes what the eye sees; each person can see a scene somewhat differently. Nearly 10 percent of the male population and 0.04 percent of the female population have a visual color deficiency or are color-blind to some degree.

Natural Light

Natural light, or light from the sun, has a full spectrum of colors. Natural light makes colors appear rich and vibrant and is a healthful, cheerful light necessary for living. A balance of natural light evenly distributed from two or more directions is desirable and helps reduce shadows in the interior and consequent visual and physical fatigue.

Yet even natural light can lean toward one color, depending on factors such as the time of day, season, weather conditions, orientation, climate, and location. The color of light at morning, noon, and evening will vary from each other and individually,

according to the season and weather conditions. The morning sun in the summer will be brighter and warmer than the morning winter sun and more brilliant and yellow on clear days than on overcast days. Orientation means the direction of the light. For example, southern-exposure light will be warmer and northern light will be cooler. Orientation also takes into account reflected surfaces. If that northern exposure faces a large orange building, then certainly that color will be reflected into the north-facing interior, rendering the light warmer than it would otherwise be. Light from a location where a sandy beach is near a deep blue sea or azure sky will reflect bluish light into the interior.

Natural light is not completely predictable. When there is no cloud cover or screening at the window, natural light can become too bright and intense, resulting in *glare,* excessive luminance in the visual field that can cause irritation and fatigue. Glare is a problem that requires interior shading or screening window treatments. Artificial glare will be discussed later on. There are also times when overcast conditions or the size and orientation of the window causes natural light to be inadequate. Too little natural light

Figure 4.1

for activities such as reading, writing, or other tasks where attention to detail is important can cause eye strain and fatigue. When natural light is too dim for the occupants to function well, it must be combined with an artificial light source to become fully effective. Most people turn on lights during the day when a heavy cloud cover, fog, or smog cuts the luminance of natural light.

Combustion Lighting

Firelight, candlelight, and lanterns are another natural source of lighting called combustion lighting. For centuries, combustion lighting was the only way to supplement daylight in the interior and at night the only source for reading light. Light from fires and candles flicker, as do lanterns when they are moved about. This inconsistency can be charming and create a low-lit mood that is amiable and cozy.

Figure 4.1 Wood blinds warmly filter daylight in this natural-theme restaurant. The dropped-pendant chandelier transmits task lighting through translucent glass trimmed with brass. Dining lights should be placed to give soft lighting to the table area but should not shine down unflattering light onto the heads and bodies of the diners. Wood blinds by and photo courtesy of Nanik.

The warmth from a combustion source is also an important reason for its existence. A fireplace draws people near it for warmth and comfort as much as for the light. Drawbacks to combustion lighting, however, include the mess of making fires or monitoring the melting candle wax. Many homes have "gas logs" installed that burn natural gas with a flickering flame imitative of a real fire but without the work and mess involved in fire building. *Luminaires* (lighting fixtures) may incorporate flame-shaped bulbs that flicker to copy the light of real candles.

Artificial Lighting

In *artificial* or *man-made lighting*, we select *lamps* (light bulbs) that contain color characteristics that will enhance or diminish the colors specified for an interior. It is necessary to match colors under both the natural light and artificial lamps in the actual setting. If this is impossible because, say, the actual installation is not finished or is in another city or location, then the hard and soft materials (floor, wall, window, ceiling, and furnishing materials) should be matched under at least two kinds of light. By doing this, we can prevent a *metameric shift*, or the appearance of an object or textile as one color in one light and another color in another light. The metameric shift is caused by the *spectral energy distribution*, or color characteristics of the material or object, that will absorb or reflect the light as previously explained. This is the reason colors may match perfectly in the store, but when they are installed at home, they do not match at all.

It is always important to bring samples of paint, carpeting, and so on, to the interior where they will be installed. Look at the colors during different times of the day and at night. Lighting can affect the way a paint chip appears compared to the actual painted surface. A quart of paint applied to a section of the wall is an inexpensive way to determine if the color is a good choice under all types of light in that interior. It can then be more realistically matched or harmoniously blended with samples under that lighting.

Artificial lighting can create moods, add sparkle and emphasis, and be directed and manipulated to meet the needs of the interior. Although artificial lighting is often considered a stable source of light, it is interesting to note that over the life of the lamp the lumen output or level of brightness does go down. There is also a color shift when dimming the lamp and a gradual color change over the life of the lamp.

Although many kinds of artificial lighting sources exist today, the most commonly used are *incandescent* (common filament light bulbs), *fluorescent* (tubes for general, luminous lighting), *HID* (high-intensity discharge) lighting, and *cold cathode lighting*. HID lighting and cold cathode lighting are discussed under Nonresidential Considerations at the end of this chapter.

Figure 4.2

Figure 4.3

Figure 4.2 Recessed downlighters wash the wall and highlight artwork in this eclectic interior. Behind the built-in sofa, uplighters cast interesting plant-form shadows and graze the surface of the vertical louvers. Candlelight contributes romantic combustion lighting, casting prismlike fingers of light through the Lucite table onto the velvety, cut pile carpet. Photo courtesy of Knoll Carpet of Anso IV Nylon.

Figure 4.3 Low-voltage lighting spotlights photography of unusual and intriguing Utah geological formations at the Salt Lake International Airport. The light-beam spread is directed at each individual photo, casting a pool of light that bathes the subject. The lighting is also motivational, leading both the eye and the traveler along the concourse toward the gates. Photo by Andrew Arnone and Darlene Langford.

Incandescent Lighting

Incandescent light is light produced by heating a high-resistance *tungsten filament* with an electric current until it glows intensely.[1] Incandescent light contains a continuous, warm, mellow color spectrum often utilized for mood lighting. Incandescent lighting is also effective for general, task, and accent or mood lighting, discussed later in the chapter.

Low-Voltage Lighting

Low-voltage lighting is a type of bulb or lamp that controls the beam spread. The lamp typically has a built-in reflector with a halogen bulb that produces superior accent lighting. *Low-voltage lamps* come in small and large sizes, depending on whether they are for indoor or outdoor use. Indoor low-voltage lighting is often a small size and used inside recessed or track fixtures. Low-voltage lighting incorporates transformers to reduce voltage to the source.

Tungsten Halogen Lighting

Another type of incandescent light is the *tungsten halogen lamp*. The filament of the small lamp is surrounded with halogen gas. As the tungsten burns off, the halogen reacts with the tungsten, creating a very bright light. Options of tungsten halogen light include the ability to direct light to a pinpointed area and to intensify the light by placing the lamp bulb inside a reflective (PAR) lamp. Tungsten halogen lights cost more than common incandescent lighting but will usually last longer.

Colored incandescent lighting can be achieved by using colored glass on the lamps or by placing a colored screen over the light. The most familiar are the colored Christmas lamp bulbs, those B torpedo-shaped bulbs that light our homes and spirits during the holidays.

Fluorescent Lighting

Fluorescent lamps produce light by establishing an arc between two electrodes inside a glass tube filled with very low-pressure mercury vapor. The arc or discharge produces ultraviolet (invisible) radiation in wavelengths that excite or activate the white powder (phosphorus crystals) lining the lamp. The phosphor *fluoresces* (glows), converting the ultraviolet energy into visible light energy.[2]

Fluorescent light is a relatively shadowless, even light making it ideal for general lighting (discussed later in this chapter) of environments where tasks are performed but where task light-

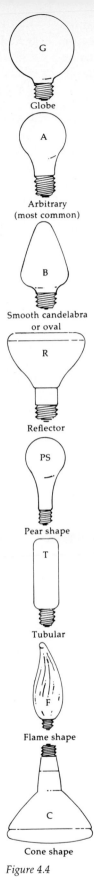

Figure 4.4

Chart 4.1 Types of Incandescent Lamps

Types of incandescent lamps (*bulbs*) vary according to shape and purpose. Commonly used lamps or bulbs are listed in this chart. These are available in a wide range of wattage. The numerical system that indicates the size of the lamp uses numbers such as *R-20, R-30, R-40* and indicates the diameter of the lamp in inches divided by one-eighth of an inch. For example, R-20 is a lamp two and one-half inches wide.

Lamp Shapes

A lamp: Arbitrary-shaped bulb; the most common lamp shape.

B lamp: Candelabra lamp—a smooth torpedo-shaped (oval or ovoid) bulb.

C lamp: Cone-shaped bulb.

F lamp: Flame-shaped bulb.

G lamp: Spherical or round globe-shaped bulb.

T lamp: Tubular lamp, also a designation for tungsten halogen lamps.

PS lamp: Pear-shaped lamp—a rounded, longer shape.

Reflective Lamps

R lamp: Common cone-shaped reflector is lighter and shaped to spread the beam wider.

ER lamp: Elliptic-shaped reflector lamps focus the light beam to two inches in front of the lamp, thereby saving energy with increased light in one spot.

PAR lamp: Parabolic aluminized reflector lamps have heavy, protective glass that makes them suitable for both interior and exterior (outdoor) use. Silvering is used to establish the beam spread and the reflective quality of the lamp and determines whether the beam will spread out into a *floodlight* or will be used for a spotlight. Silvering also creates *glare-free lamps*. The lamp face (the nonsilvered portion) also affects the beam spread.

HID lamps: Mercury vapor and high-pressure sodium are two of the most common high-intensity discharge lamps. Home use is commonly outdoors.

PL lamp: Compact twin fluorescent lamp bulb.

---

ing would be impractical or undesirable. In homes, fluorescent lighting is most commonly used in luminous ceiling panels, recessed into a dropped ceiling and covered with textured, translucent panels. Fluorescent lights are also commonly used in under-the-cabinet lighting over counters, in bathroom lighting, and over work surfaces in hobby rooms or offices. This type of even, clear light provides an environment where work can take place for a long period of time without lighting-caused fatigue.

Fluorescent lamps are available in straight, circular, U- or V-shaped tubes. Although they initially cost more than incandescent light bulbs, they require less energy to run and last longer than ordinary lamps. The exact difference in cost, energy saved, and longevity varies according to the type of fluorescent lamp and according to

Figure 4.4 Types of incandescent lamps or light bulbs.

which type of incandescent lamp it is compared against. Fluorescent tubes become less effective as they age because they lose lumens and may hum or flicker prior to burning out. *Rapid-start fluorescent lamps* have eliminated the problem of blinking when the lights are switched on.

Fluorescent lighting is available in both warm and cool color spectrums. The fluorescent lamps that are cold and unflattering are the cheaper lamps, and although they are cold, the lumens per watt are high and the light is cost efficient. *Cool white deluxe* and *warm white deluxe* lamps have a balanced spectrum and are more flattering to the skin. Cool or warm white deluxe fluorescent lighting is more pleasant because of the balanced light spectrum and will naturally cost more than standard fluorescent lamps. Fluorescent lamps are available in a wide range of styles and types; each dealer will have a chart with all the kinds of fluorescent lamps listed. When shopping for fluorescent lamps, it is wise to consult with the lighting personnel for help in selecting lamps that will be right for the needs of the installation.

Another colored fluorescent light is the cold cathode, or *neon* lamps that use different gases or vapors to produce colors. Neon lighting has traditionally been used to light exterior signs in business districts, but today, creative uses of neon lighting have brought this type of light indoors. Lighting as art (discussed later in this chapter) frequently incorporates neon lighting with surprising and intriguing effects.

Power Terminology and Units of Measurement

To understand how incandescent and fluorescent lighting is measured, it is necessary to understand basic power terminology and units of measurement.

Incandescent and fluorescent lighting is measured in *footcandles, footlamberts,* and *lumens* (see chart 4.2) These terms allow lighting engineers and designers to create and evaluate lamps for specific purposes. These terms are a part of the general body of interior design knowledge.

Incandescent lamps, or light bulbs, typically vary in wattage from 15, 25, 60, 75, 100, 120, 150, and 175. In a luminaire that contains two or more lamps, there is often a limitation on the wattage so that the fixture will not be overheated and risk catching fire. The wattage of fluorescent lamps ranges from 18, 20, 32, 40, 60, and 80 and delivers greater brightness per watt than incandescent lighting, making flourescent lamps more energy efficient.

Ordinary incandescent lamps (bulbs) last from 750 to 2,500 hours, and *long-life bulbs* (which cost more initially and deliver less light for the electricity used) last from 2,500 to 3,500 hours. *Low-voltage incandescent lamps* use less wattage or electric power and deliver greater control and a wider range of beam spread.

Note that it is not the size of the lamp or the level of wattage that makes an impact in lighting. Lighting becomes most interesting when the size of the beam is controlled to create pools of light or emphasize certain areas or focal

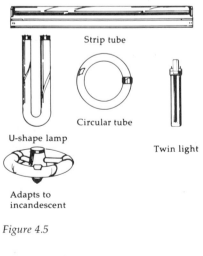

Figure 4.5

Figure 4.6

Figure 4.5 Shapes of discharge fluorescent lamps.

Figure 4.6 Natural daylight through a bank of windows washes this cheerful, modern kitchen by Kershaw, whereas luminous panels on the sloping ceiling give the effect of skylights. A pendant light provides task lighting for informal dining, and overhead ambient lighting provides clarity to the laundry closet. Photo courtesy of the Maytag Company.

points in the interior. This is the advantage of incandescent lighting types such as low-voltage lighting and some tungsten halogen and high-intensity discharge (HID) lighting over fluorescent.

Light Control

The control and economy of light is interrelated to light measurement and reflectance. The goal of lighting an interior is threefold:

1. to make lighting effective and practical for the activities or purposes of the interior,
2. to make the interior more aesthetically pleasing, and
3. to make the interior psychologically useful.

These goals are accomplished by the placement and control of lighting fixtures.

Categories of Lighting Effects

In order to accomplish the three goals of lighting, categories are useful in directing the design. In homes, these categories of lighting include: *ambient (general) lighting, task lighting, accent and mood lighting,* and *lighting as art.* These are discussed in the

---

Chart 4.2   Units of Mesurement

• Volts or voltage means the units for measuring electric potential, defining the force or pressure of electricity in the power line.

• Ampere or amp is the measurement of the current that is taken from the mainline and fed into a building as a circuit. A typical residence, for example, has a fifteen-amp circuit.

• Watt or wattage is the unit for measuring electric power that defines the energy consumed by a lamp or electric fixture.

• Footcandle is defined as the amount of direct light thrown by one candle on a square foot of flat surface and is a unit of measurement of light.

• Lumen is a unit of measurement for the flow of light. Lumens are listed on the package of a *fixture* or *luminaire.* Lumens per watt is the measure of *efficacy,* or efficiency, or how much energy is expended per watt.

• Foot lambert (fl) measures the light reflected off a surface. We actually see by foot lamberts. Reflectance is the amount of light that reflects, or bounces off, an object and can increase the apparent brightness of the light. A white wall will reflect 80 percent of the light, whereas a black wall will reflect only 2 percent of the light.[3]

(A)
Figure 4.7

(B)

(C)

(A)
Figure 4.8

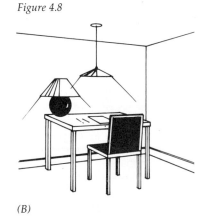
(B)

---

following paragraphs. Other categories are found at the end of the chapter under Nonresidential Considerations.

Ambient and General Lighting

Ambient and general lighting must be planned into the blueprints of the home (see Wiring Plans later in the chapter). General lighting provides a uniform or even, broad plane of light used for general occupation. It may be accomplished with *direct lighting* such as ceiling fixtures that shine outward and downward, illuminating the general area. *Direct general lighting* often takes the form of fluorescent or other utilitarian incandescent ceiling fixtures. These fixtures, particularly the fluorescent type, may provide good general lighting for kitchens, offices, workrooms, and classrooms, where tasks are performed throughout the space. However, one of the drawbacks of this type of lighting is that it may be bland or monotonous, making it unsuited for areas such as living rooms and bedrooms where aesthetics are an important part of the lighting plan.

Ambient lighting generally comes from an indirect source that throws light against a surface such as a wall or ceiling, reflecting the light back into the room. One popular *indirect general lighting* fixture is the *uplighter* that casts light onto the ceiling, where it is reflected back and creates a soft general illumination of the room or space. Another method of achieving indirect general or ambient lighting is the use of fixtures recessed into the ceiling around the perimeter of a room that "wash" the walls with light. This type of lighting creates a pleasant quality of illumination but may not provide enough light for specific tasks. For this reason ambient lighting is often combined with other types of task lighting.

Task Lighting

Task lighting is a pool of light where it is needed to perform tasks requiring hand-eye coordination. Some of these tasks are reading, typing or word processing, writing, drawing, assembling parts or working with tools, cooking, dining, sewing, and personal grooming. Task lighting should not constitute dramatic, high-contrast areas of light and dark. If the pool of

---

Figure 4.7 Ambient or general lighting. *(A)* The ceiling luminaire lights an area from above eye level. *(B)* Uplighters wash this wall with light, illuminating the ceiling and the area nearby. Light-colored walls will reflect and increase footlamberts. *(C)* Eyeball spotlights wash the wall from ceiling level.
Figure 4.8 Task lighting for specific purposes. *(A)* Personal grooming. *(B)* Reading, writing or studying.

light abruptly ends and darkness begins, unnecessary eye strain and fatigue will result. It is wise to combine task lighting with general or natural lighting whenever possible. In the kitchen, for example, the *luminous ceiling* (general lighting) is typically accompanied by task lighting, built into the ceiling or over the soffit or under the cupboard (which may be a portable light). Task lighting in the kitchen is desirable for the sink area, the range or hob, and the food preparation area.

Task lighting may also be seen as strip lights placed around a mirror or above a work area. *Track lighting* and *spotlights* are also favorite ways to focus light onto a task area.

Task lighting can also be accomplished with *portable luminaires*, such as table lamps, that can be moved from one area to another. These include floor and table lamps, plug-in wall sconces, and under-the-counter strips.

Accent and Mood Lighting

Accent lighting is sometimes referred to as *artistic lighting*. Accent lighting may focus on a piece of art or an accessory item, giving that object greater importance in the room. Accent lighting can create interest and drama through shadows created with small spots of light or by casting light in small areas against a dark background. This *high contrast* of dark and light areas gives interest and life to an interior through the patterns of light and dark. It is stimulating and may appear as a play of *brilliants*—a myriad of pinpoints of light.

Mood lighting creates a sense of inviting coziness. The contrast of soft, low, or even glittering light against a dark background (where the ambient or general lighting has been lowered) adds sparkle and excitement to interior design. In this sense, combustion lighting (discussed earlier) from a fireplace is an effective method of mood lighting. It emotionally draws people near for not only visual interest and comfort but for warmth as well. The heart of the home has long been its hearth, where meals were prepared and served for centuries. Today a seating area around a flickering fireplace is still inviting. It can become even more effective and beautiful with the addition of spotlights or directed low-voltage lighting.

General lighting, task lighting, and accent lighting are frequently combined, since each type of lighting fulfills different purposes. Lighting may overlap to fit the time of day or night and the particular activities that are taking place within the interior. For example, on a gloomy, overcast day, general lighting may be needed as

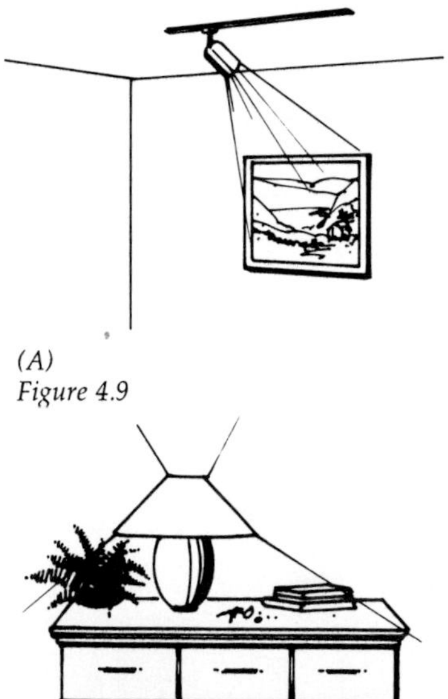

(A)
Figure 4.9

(B)

Figure 4.9 Accent or mood lighting. *(A)* Throwing track spotlight onto artwork. *(B)* Low lighting from a small luminaire (table lamp) to create softness or mellow, romantic mood lighting.

backup for natural lighting for daily activities. General lighting is mandatory in interiors where no windows exist and for general nighttime occupation and businesses or offices open after dark. Task lighting may supplement general lighting for specific work projects during the day or night; accent lighting is used primarily at night and in windowless interiors during the day. Because these types of lighting are often used concurrently, there needs to be some control of their usage for the sake of the life of the bulb and the energy each consumes.

Lighting as Art

There are new frontiers in planned lighting, and one of the most exciting is lighting as art where the light fixture and method of lighting become art itself. Besides traditional *decorative luminaire* lamps, there are several ways that lighting can become artistic.

- The fixture or luminaire itself may be the emphasized point of vision, as in a neon sign or artistic lighting fixture. Innovative artists are working with not only light but with other materials and textures and combining them for intriguing artistic effects.
- Colored light and patterns of light and dark from one or many sources can turn lighting into art.
- Lighted etched *acrylic sheets* allow light to shine through the etched areas, giving unlimited design possibilities to art, floors, walls, and other areas.
- *Light pipes* made of acrylic can conduct a variety of lights in artistic ways: by sunlight and by a selection of lamps that produce intense light up to 1,000 watts. Subtle and/or changing color can be inserted into the pipe. When the pipe is formed into shapes such as prisms, the effect can be multiplied, giving the interior designer phenomenal new freedom in creating color impressions.
- *Laser* lights, commonly used in light shows, can be made stationary or changeable and can project images of art, furniture, people, or even the illusion of more interior space.
- Already research and experimentation have shown that the *hologram* can produce phenomenal effects, even creating three-dimensional images in midair.[4]

Lighting Economy

The upward surge of electricity rates, predicted to continue on the rise, is the major factor in economizing with light. Lighting consumes less electricity than heat-producing appliances such as dryers, water heat-

Figure 4.10

Figure 4.11

ers, dishwashers, ovens, and ranges. However, lighting does consume more power than smaller appliances. Some ways that lighting can be more effectively and economically used are listed in chart 4.3.

Lighting Effects in the Interior

Lighting effects can be handled many ways in an interior; this aspect is perhaps the most enjoyable of all the aspects of interior lighting. Lighting can change the apparent shape, color, and texture of the interior by highlighting objects or areas and leaving other areas in shadow.

- An ambient *bank* or *plane of light* is a large, well-lit area. Although it may not encompass the entire interior, it can designate smaller areas within a large space.
- An even *wash* is a soft plane of light from spotlights or track lights aimed at a wall or ceiling that can illuminate artwork, for example.
- A light shining at a steep angle or very close to the object or to a surface *grazes* it with luminescence—an effective way of emphasizing texture.
- A *pool of light* is a round circle of light thrown by a downlighter or spotlight, for example, or it may be thrown onto the wall or the ceiling. Spotlighting from more than one direction can *balance light* and emphasize detail by eliminating harsh shadows.
- *Perimeter lighting,* around the outside of a room or an area, will visually expand the space.
- *Point or pinpoint* lighting spotlights a tiny area. Pinpoint lighting can emphasize or create shiny, glittery accents if it strikes a reflective surface.
- *Line or outline* lighting can emphasize a shape or light an area such as a dressing table and mirror. This may be done with a line of incandescent lamps or with fluorescent or neon tubes.

Chart 4.3 Suggestions for Lighting Economy

- Turn out lights when not in use.
- Put light only where it is needed, keeping in mind that a high contrast (a pool of light surrounded by dark) can cause fatigue and even distress, which can waste human energy.
- Use dimmer switches to control and lower the wattage.
- Use photoelectric cells or timers to turn outdoor lights on and off automatically.
- Open window treatments to allow natural light in, supplementing with artificial light only when needed.
- Use light-colored surfaces to reflect and thereby increase light and use textures that will not absorb much light.
- Use only some of the lights in an interior such as one, rather than two, table lamps.
- Switch on portable luminaires with fewer lamps or lower wattage to illuminate local tasks rather than using ambient or general overhead lighting.
- Use one higher wattage bulb rather than multiple lower wattage bulbs. For example, one 100-watt bulb will use less energy than two 60-watt bulbs.
- Install extra light switches so that at each doorway the light can be turned off without inconvenience.
- Use low-voltage or lower wattage lamps.
- Use new materials such as acrylic that will conduct and reflect light while using a fraction of the electricity required for traditional incandescent lighting.
- Use energy-saving fluorescent lighting in place of incandescent lighting where aesthetically practical. It is estimated that fluorescent lighting saves energy by using one-fifth to one-third as much electricity as incandescent lighting with comparable lumen ratings. Warm white deluxe fluorescent lamps are suggested as replacements for incandescent lighting in the home.
- Replace incandescent lamps with new compact fluorescent lamps that can be screwed in their place, using only about eighteen watts in place of a 75-watt incandescent lamp. These new fluorescent lamps are long life, lasting the life of ten average incandescent lamps when properly installed and ventilated. There is no humming of the ballast or interference with radio or television reception.

Figure 4.10 Perimeter spotlights shine downward on the food preparation area, producing an even wash at the countertop. Pendant lighting casts pools of light on the dining area. Photo courtesy of the American Home Lighting Institute.

Figure 4.11 Ambient lighting accented by perimeter strip or theatrical lighting illuminates the personal grooming area. A separate compartment for the water closet should have a ceiling or wall fixture using a 60 to 75 watt incandescent or 30 to 40 watt fluorescent. A wet location requires a recessed fixture with 60 watts incandescent. Local codes will govern safety placement in bathrooms. Photo courtesy of the American Home Lighting Institute.

- Lights shining directly downward will cause shadows beneath and around the object. Downward light on people casts unflattering shadows.
- Silhouette lighting is accomplished by shining a light directly on an object so that the shadow behind it echoes its shape.
- Lights that shine upward behind objects such as plants and art will "model" that shape, thereby creating patterns on the wall or ceiling.

Light and the Mind and Body

The psychological and physical effects of lighting, or the way light can affect the mind and body, is a fascinating and complex study because of the variety of ways that light can affect the human psyche. For example, nearly everyone has experienced a lighthearted, cheerful outlook on sunny spring days and a gloomy attitude on dark, dreary winter days in northern climates when clear, natural light is lacking.

Interior lighting can also affect our outlook and physical state. The size and source of the light, the direction of the light, the color of the light, and the color and texture of the objects being lit are the factors that determine the psychosocial and physical or physiological effects of lighting. For example, the plane or bank of light minimizes form and bulk, reduces the importance of objects and even people. It can fill a person with a sense of space and freedom and can be restful and reassuring. This type of general lighting is effective in open areas of public buildings, offices, hotels, and retail businesses. It is often used in homes in rooms such as kitchens, bathrooms, workrooms, or hobby rooms, where moderately bright light, whether from incandescent or fluorescent lighting, produces a general feeling of well-being.

Large areas of bright light are thought to stimulate a temporary psychological and physical surge of energy, which may cause undue fatigue after periods of prolonged exposure. Mentally, the mind will become bored or dulled after a barrage of continuous bright lights. If the light becomes too brilliant, it can cause malaise or a feeling of illness.

Moderate to low levels of indirect lighting are sometimes called mood lighting, meaning that the area is inviting, cozy, and intimate. This type of lighting is used in restaurants where the clientele come not only for good food but for a relaxed, private, and unhurried conversation. Mood lighting is also favored in the home in areas such as the formal living room and master bedroom. Mood lighting can also be accomplished with backlighting (placing lights behind furnishings) from *flickering light* from candles, fireplaces, or electric flame lamps. Flickering light is usually warm in color, casting a healthy glow on the skin.

Low lighting can give an impression of intrigue and intimacy. Low lighting is employed in lounges and nightclubs. In the home, low lighting can enhance the feeling of relaxation and privacy in a bedroom, for example. In media/presentation rooms (for television, slides, or films), low lighting diminishes eye strain. It helps establish the perimeter of the room and produces a sense of security.

Colored light also has profound effect on the mind and body. Warm white light and soft warm colored light generally are welcoming and uplifting. However, intensely colored light, such as bright red, orange, and yellow, produce considerable eye strain. This may lead to an eventual feeling of physical exhaustion as the mind struggles to avoid coping with the intensity.

Cool white light and colored lights that are cool color—blue, cool green, and violet—produce calm, restful environments but can become unfriendly, cold, or depressing after a period of time or when viewed in large amounts or intensities.

Glare

Glare means excessive light that causes irritation or fatigue. Heat buildup from excessive natural or incandescent lighting, as well as too much brightness, will cause discomfort and irritation. Natural daylighting often requires shading window treatments. Glare from artificial light can be con-

Figure 4.12

Figure 4.12 Recessed spotlights give soft ambient light to this quiet corner. Lighting is planned to accentuate art and give plenty of illumination to the reading area. Photo courtesy of the American Home Lighting Institute.

trolled by lowering the wattage or using a cool-beam lamp bulb or by adjusting the direction of the lighting source.

Another means of diverting or diffusing glare is through *baffles.* Baffles come in many forms.

1. A baffle or bracket could be a length of wood placed in front of lights to direct light upward or downward.
2. Louvers or grooves on or inside a luminaire or fixture can act as baffles.
3. A metal or wooden grid diffuses the light and can produce more even distribution.
4. The lens or glass covering can be textured or coated to diffuse glare.
5. Reflectors inside the lamp bulb itself can further control the light and glare.

The most common types of glare are listed in chart 4:4. These are *direct glare, reflecting glare,* and *veiling glare.*

Wiring Plans

The planning of lighting systems does require some training and experience. It also requires thinking through what lighting must accomplish in an interior. Interior designers are often actively involved in this process. A *wiring or lighting plan* is a part of the working drawings (see chapters 5 and 13) and is usually referred to as the reflected ceiling plan. The wiring plan indicates where outlets, switches, wall and ceiling light fixtures, or luminaires will be located.

Switches and Outlets

Light switches can be placed in one location or in two or even three locations. Switches should easily be accessible at the doorway on the open side so that lights can be turned on at the doorway. Careful thought should be given to the type and placement of switches, according to the needs of the users. If, for example, the user is an aged or infirm person, then a "rocker switch" may be easier to operate than a standard flip switch.

Dimmer switches are knob switches that are pushed to turn on the light and rotated to increase or decrease the level of illumination or brightness. Dimmers are effective for incandescent lighting. Only one kind of fluorescent light can be dimmed, that is the rapid-start lamp, which requires a specialized dimmer. Dimmers make it possible to create levels of interest and different moods in the interior. *Automatic sensor dimmers* are used to turn on interior lights automatically when needed to supplement natural daylight to a proportionate, preprogrammed level. Switched outlets are plugs that are activated by switches. This allows for table luminaires (commonly called lamps), lighting as art, or decorative lights, such as Christmas decorations, to be turned on at the flip of a switch by leaving the light plugged in and turned on at the source but controlled at the switch. Switched outlets contribute convenience and safety to the interior and its occupants. If, for example, a portable table luminaire is the only or desired source of light in the room, it can be turned on at the door. This will eliminate the necessity of first turning on general lighting to reach the portable light, then returning to turn off the general lighting. It also reduces the danger of walking across a dark room to reach the desired light. Also the inconvenience of fumbling over holiday packages, decorations, or tree to reach Christmas lights or walking outside to turn on exterior lights can be removed through switched outlets.

According to state and local building codes, outlets must be located from six to twelve feet along the wall for portable luminaires (floor, table, wall lamps). The frequent placement of outlets minimizes the need for extension cords and avoids the necessity of plugging too many lights or electric appliances or equipment into one outlet. Therefore, the building code helps ensure safety against tripping

---

Chart 4.4 Types of Glare

- Direct glare is bright light or insufficiently shielded light sources in the field of view. Placement of lighting sources is very important; light in the center of room a can produce direct glare, as can some accent lighting. Direct glare is a problem in offices where the desk faces the window. This may be corrected by turning the desk so that the light is coming from the side rather than the front. Note that light from behind a seated person will cause shadows on the work surface and will be equally unacceptable as direct glare.

- Reflecting glare is something shiny reflecting in the area of the task, such as a silver bowl or a mirror causing a distraction.

- Veiling glare prevents us from seeing a task clearly. It is caused by light reflecting off a surface, causing a blind spot. What we see is the reflected images of the light source rather than the task at hand, such as the writing, drawing, or typing. Veiling glare can make seeing extremely difficult and cause eye strain; it is due to incorrect placement of the lighting source or an inadequate baffle (screening device) of the light fixture.

- Areas of dark surrounding lighted areas cause eye strain, fatigue, and even depression as peripheral vision constantly has to deal with the dark-bright contrast.[5]

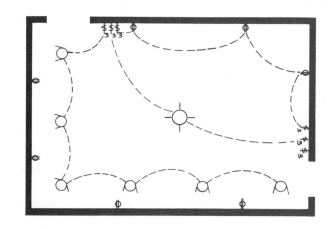

Figure 4.13

Figure 4.13 An electrical and wiring plan. Three-way light switches turn on or off lights from two switches. Wall plugs may also be controlled from wall switches for accent, mood, or task lighting, or for Christmas decorations. Wall plugs not connected with dashes are not switch controlled.

and falling and against fire from overloading a circuit and outlet. Stretching cords tight can also increase danger of damage, loose connections, and possibly tenuous circumstances where the luminaire is placed too close to the edge of a surface and could easily fall off, break, and perhaps even burst into flames.

Convenience is another major reason for including frequent outlets, making it easy to locate and place the luminaire, appliance, or piece of equipment where it is needed or can easily be used. An important part of planning outlets and switches is vertical placement. For example, a table-height outlet may be desirable for units such as entertainment components or computers. Appliances for kitchens and workrooms or hobby areas need outlets above counter height. Outlets should have a *grounding receiver* (three-prong plug outlet) as standard in all areas for high-electric use lights, appliances, and components. *Outlet strips,* casings with spaced outlets that are prewired or portable, are useful in home workbenches, home offices, and kitchens.

The exact placement of switches and outlets can be determined when the building has been framed. It is common for the client and/or interior designer to meet the electrician at the site and mark the exact location of fixtures, outlets, and switches. There is often a need to adjust placement because of the heat ducts. Before mechanical systems are installed, it is wise to go over any adjustments or compromises to be certain that the luminaires or fixtures, outlets, and switches can be placed where they are needed.

The planning of lighting systems in nonresidential complexes and high-rise buildings entails technical studies of lighting needs and electrical code requirements and restrictions.

Figure 4.14

Lighting Luminaires

Luminaires, sometimes called lighting fixtures, fall into two broad categories: *architectural* or *structural lighting* and *nonarchitectural lighting,* or *portable luminaires.* Architectural or structural luminaires are those permanently installed and planned for in the lighting or wiring plan. These include ceiling and wall fixtures that are installed to permanent wiring.

Many architectural luminaires are simple and inconspicuous. Their goal is to emphasize what they light and not call attention to themselves. Other luminaires are quite decorative and/or dramatic and can make up an important part of the design scheme.

Many styles, designs, colors, and finishes of luminaires are on the market today—metal, painted white or a color; bright or antique brass; pewter; or stainless steel, for example. The glass may be clear, white, colored, or bronzed. A large portion of the appeal of lighting interiors is the charm and/or character of the luminaires. Luminaires may be found in styles to match every kind of setting and in good, poor, and mediocre design and quality. Because of the many design quality levels, the power of discrimination discussed in chapter 2 becomes paramount when selecting luminaires.

Portable luminaires, also called nonarchitectural lighting, are those that plug in and either hang on the wall or from a ceiling hook, or they may be placed on a table or on the floor. *Decorative luminaires* are discussed in chapter 12, Art and Accessories.

Architectural Lighting

There are six main categories of architectural lighting. These include *luminous panels, built-in indirect lighting, recessed* and *adjustable fixtures,* and *surface-mounted* and *suspended fixtures.*

Luminous Panels

Luminous panels are strips or lines of lights, usually fluorescent, over which glass or plastic translucent panels are placed. The translucent panel seems to illuminate, or glow, producing a soft white or colored light, according to the texture and color of the glass or plastic. It can also cause glare in some situations. Luminous panels are quite common in kitchens, and are referred to as luminous ceilings.

Indirect Lighting

Indirect lighting is placing a light behind a built-in or portable feature. Types of indirect lighting placed behind deflectors illustrated in figure 4.15 include the following:

1. *cornice lighting*—a light behind a board mounted into the ceiling to wash light down onto the wall,
2. *valance lighting*—a light used over the top of windows and washes both the ceiling and the window treatment,

Figure 4.14 A warm-toned veneer boxes in a lighted soffit that illuminates favorite collectibles from sea and shore as Nantucket is brought home in this family retreat. Plywood wall paneling patterned with sea gulls and dune grass framed with horizontally applied real wood veneer creates a panoramic effect. A pharmacy lamp by the wing chair provides intimate task lighting, here for reading or handwork, whereas the window provides general illumination during daylight hours. Photo courtesy of Plywood Paneling Council.

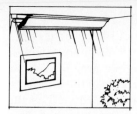 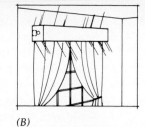 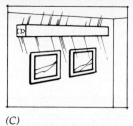  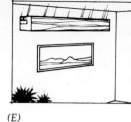

(A) (B) (C) (D) (E)

Figure 4.15

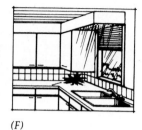

(F)

(G)

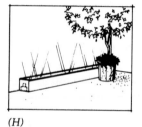

(H)

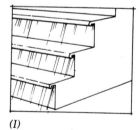

(I)

Figure 4.16

3. *bracket lighting*—valance lighting mounted lower on the wall to wash the upper (and perhaps lower) wall with light,

4. *cove lighting*—a light placed just below the ceiling with the board or deflector beneath it,

5. *soffit lighting*—a light built into the soffit, shining downward from the top of the cabinet overhead,

6. *base lighting*—a strip of light against the floor where a deflector directs the light upward or perhaps downward, giving the effect of theatrical usher lights, and

7. *Lighted toe mold*—lighting under the toe-kick area of cabinets or stairs.

Figure 4.15 Forms of architectural lighting. *(A)* Cornice lighting. *(B)* Valance lighting. *(C and D)* Bracket lighting. *(E)* Bracket lighting. *(F and G)* Soffit lighting. *(H)* Base or toe-mold lighting. *(I)* Toe-kick or riser lighting under stair treads.

Figure 4.16 Set between Roman-shaded windows, nonstructural columns house dramatic uplights that shine in front and behind the baffle to create artistic pools of light at the ceiling level. A recessed downlighter is seen over the curved sofa for more general illumination. Interior design by Vince Lattuca of Cenzo Custom Design for the Sara Delano Roosevelt House, New York City. Photo courtesy of DuPont "Teflon" soil and stain repellent.

Recessed and Adjustable Luminaires

This category includes various luminaires that are set into the ceiling called *recessed luminaires* and those that are adjustable. Adjustable luminaires can be recessed or surface mounted. Specifically, these types include the following:

1. *Recessed downlights*—canisters set into the ceiling that cast pools of light downward.
2. *High-hatters*—a recessed light that is very deep; the lamp is high inside the fixture.
3. *Surface-mounted fixtures*—canisters mounted on the ceiling and hang down. (These are used where there is insufficient ceiling clearance, or they are added later in a remodeling situation.)
4. *Recessed adjustable accent lighting*—lighting that projects only the lamp from the wall or ceiling and throws pools of light onto the wall or ceiling; the most common form is eyeball spotlights. A series of these can form *wall washers*.
5. *Track lighting*—flexible ceiling-mounted fixtures that can hold spotlights or floodlights mounted anywhere and at any position on a fixed track. (Track luminaires come in various sizes, shapes, colors, and finishes. They are ideal for accent lighting and wall-wash lighting.)

Surface-Mounted and Suspended Luminaires

These are luminaires that are clearly visible and perhaps even obvious to the eye. Translucent covers are called *diffusers* and serve to soften the light. Clear or tinted glass covers may require a decorative lamp.

Suspended fixtures such as *chandeliers* or *dropped-pendant luminaires* may be dropped only a few inches from the ceiling (over a dining or conference table) or be suspended several feet (in an open area such as a hotel atrium or an entrance). Sizes vary dramatically from about six inches to several feet in diameter. The size and placement are dependent upon the scale of the interior and the use. In the dining situation, the chandelier should be approximately thirty inches above the table. Suspended lamps are

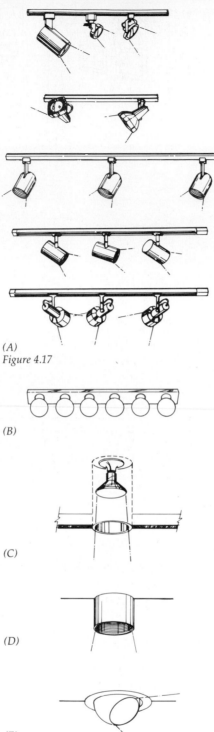

(A)
Figure 4.17

(B)

(C)

(D)

(E)

often used in reading corners; the lamp should drop to about forty inches from the floor or twenty inches above the seat level. These heights are, of course, dependent on the scale of the luminaire and the ceiling height as well as the scale and placement of the furniture.

Lighting for the Future

In many respects, the future is here today. Lighting experts have created such amazing effects with lighting that only a few years ago it would have been impossible to believe what we almost take for granted today. Lighting has perhaps advanced the most quickly in nonresidential settings—in theaters, museums, and other public places where special effects are desirable. Discussed in this chapter are laser lighting, light pipes and other materials that glow when lit, lighting as art, motivational and illusion lighting. In each of these areas we will see amazing developments in the very near future. No doubt there will also be new developments on the market that today are only being researched. Many experts feel that lighting is actually in its infancy and that the future holds ways of lighting that will become increasingly important to the success of interior design and to its occupants. Lighting experts are, quite naturally, excited to be a part of this rapidly changing, stimulating, and effective medium. Certainly lighting can make the difference in the effectiveness of the interior now; and in the future, it will do so in ever increasingly creative ways.

New developments in lighting control devices are already increasing energy efficiency. These include

* electronic sensors that can turn selected lights in an interior on and off,
* various control systems that include wall-mounted programmable control for total home or area control,
* hand-held controllers that operate on infrared frequencies to send instructions to wall receivers,
* switches that can turn lights off after preselected time periods, and

Figure 4.17 *(A)* Various types of adjustable tract lighting, used for throwing pools or spots of light. *(B)* Strip or theatrical lighting is often used for personal grooming areas. *(C)* Recessed high-hatter ceiling fixture.

(D) A surface-mounted downlighter, sometimes single or in rows. *(E)* An eyeball spotlight, used to highlight art or used in groups to wash a wall with ambient light.

- sensing devices that turn on lighting as a response to radiated heat caused by human presence and movement.[6]

In the future, lighting organizations such as the International Association of Lighting Designers, the Designers Lighting Forum, and the Illuminating Engineering Society of North America will continue in their role of providing state-of-the-art research and products to professionals in the design field. Communication through printed material and conferences and seminars as well as through marketing will make artistic and scientific advances readily accessible for tomorrow's interiors. For the layperson, the National Lighting Bureau publishes a variety of excellent guides on beneficial uses, cost effectiveness, and conservation. The addresses for these organizations are found at the end of the bibliography in this chapter.

Lighting is an area where science and the arts have come together to create illumination that is literally changing the shape of things to come.

Nonresidential Considerations

Many of the topics discussed in this chapter are also applicable to nonresidential situations. In addition, other considerations that apply specifically to nonresidential interiors are given in this section.

Natural Daylighting

In nonresidential settings such as offices, natural daylight is often desired by employees and sometimes considered a luxury. However, problems exist with natural daylighting, as we discussed under Glare. Temperature control is another major consideration linked to daylighting. Excessive heat and cold can be the result of poor insulation or large expanses of glass. Natural daylight almost always needs supplementing with artificial light; the lighting systems need careful control to maintain a healthy balance of light.

HID Lighting

HID, or high-intensity discharge, lighting is used for bright interior and exterior lighting. HID lamps establish an arc between two very close electrodes set in opposite ends of small, sealed, translucent or transparent glass tubes. The electric arc generates heat and pressure high enough to vaporize the atoms of various metallic elements inside the lamp, causing the atoms to emit large amounts of visible-range electromagnetic energy.[7]

HID lamps are used to "uplight" exteriors of large buildings and are being used more often in interiors of nonresidential buildings. HID lights are becoming smaller and more useful in many interior settings. They produce a greater quantity of light using less energy than an incandes-

Figure 4.18

cent lamp. The problems being overcome in HID lighting are the noise or hum of the arc or *ballast* and the length of time to restart the lamp after a power failure.

Cold Cathode Lighting

Cold cathode, or *neon*, lighting uses different gases or vapors to produce colors. Neon lighting is an important part of not only exterior lighting for advertising and storefronts but has been increasingly used in interiors such as restaurants and retail businesses to emphasize a color scheme and add drama and excitement to the interior. Lighting specialists are often consulted to design neon lighting for interior design.

Motivational Lighting

This is also a new area being examined by lighting specialists where the behavior of people can be altered or directed with *illusion lighting.* This can mean that people will be motivated to sit, walk, face, or otherwise motivate themselves in a particular direction because of the impressions given them by special lighting (particularly the manipulation of bright versus dark areas) and finishes. *Motivational*

Figure 4.18 Art Deco-inspired neon lighting in this Chicago nightclub takes the eye on a flight of fantasy with seemingly suspended concentric circles and squares in vivid, stimulating color. Neon lighting can be an exciting medium for creating artistic illumination. Interior design by Spiros Zakas. Photo courtesy of Zakaspace.

lighting can create environments where the quality, intensity, and angle of light create the appearance or disappearance of objects, walls, ceilings, and even entire rooms.[8] Lighting specialists are often called upon as consultants by interior designers to accomplish special effects in an interior. The manipulation of areas of intense brightness or darkness can affect both the mind and body, making us believe that something exists that really is not there (a wall, for example) or that something is not as close as it literally is. This can make spaces fit the needs of the people in the environment, as well as making us behave in a predicted manner.

Safety Lighting

Safety lighting is required in public spaces, such as restaurants and stores, where there are egress signs, such as Exit signs. Other safety lighting mandatory by lawful building codes includes aisle or egress lighting and lighting for stairs and landings. New developments in egress lighting will be discussed in Lighting for the Future.

Wiring

Nonresidential lighting plans constitute a *network of lighting* fixtures that are controlled from a central location or are automated. The interior designer will not visit the site to determine exact location in nonresidential lighting because placement is firmly established by the architectural plans.

However, special needs and considerations can be met through the collaboration of the designer with the electrical engineer. The designer determines the needs and specifies through calculations which lamps and levels of power are required. The engineer will work with the specifications, confirm or perform the necessary plans and calculations, then often oversee the actual installation of wiring components.

Wiring in newer nonresidential settings such as business offices is often carried not only in the wall but in the floor or in the ceiling. Office systems that are furniture modules that are prewired and contain outlets for business equipment and lighting can be hooked into the architectural wiring in the wall, ceiling, or floor. Where additional electric plugs are required, after the building is complete, *outlet strips* (a casing of spaced outlets) are commonly used.

Lighting Economy

In nonresidential interiors, lighting is a major monthly expense, and because of the tremendous amount of electricity used, nonresidential buildings are limited by law to the amount of electricity consumed per square foot. These limitations are roughly one-tenth of what they were before the energy crunch of the 1970s. The cost and the consumption limits of lighting do, therefore, constitute a legitimate reason for controlling lighting use augmenting effectiveness.

Figure 4.19

Figure 4.20

Figure 4.19 Portable spotlights draw the shopping professional's attention at the Italian Furniture Showcase at the Interior Design Center New York (IDCNY) in Long Island City. The rhythmic progression of spotlights form motivational lighting—it keeps the traffic moving from one innovative chair to the next. Photo by Ted Spiegel.

Figure 4.20 At the IBM showroom in New York City, pairs of spotlights illuminate the seemingly endless options in computer hardware and software. Faceted ceiling tiers form semicircular bracket lighting, giving dramatic emphasis to each concentric row of computers. Architectural lighting of this type requires permanent wiring, an important system in the design process of the building. Photo by Norman McGrath, © 1985.

In addition to the lighting economy suggestions in the main body of the chapter, there are other ways to control energy consumption and costs in nonresidential lighting. One is the addition of central programmable monitoring systems that will automatically turn off and on lights in various parts of a building when required. Another is the increased usage of sensing devices, listed previously under Lighting for the Future, that monitor light usage, turning it on and off according to time, daylight levels, or whether or not there are moving human bodies in the room.

Fluorescent luminaires in the ceiling can be retrofitted with reflective materials that make it possible to receive the same lumens for half the number of lamps. For example, a luminaire that ordinarily contained four 60W fluorescent lamps will give the same light output with only two 60W lamps after retrofitting. In this way, energy consumption can be cut in half, greatly reducing the cost of electricity.

Electric costs can be greatly reduced by retrofitting incandescent luminaires with compact, adaptable fluorescent lighting that delivers the same lumens or brightness for far fewer watts. These lamp bulbs connect to ballasts fitted into adapters that screw into incandescent fixtures, cutting costs immediately by up to 80 percent by producing greater light for less watts and for a longer life span. For example, PL-type fluorescent lamps that use 7 or 9 watts can replace 150-watt incandescent lighting. The PL-type lamp is a small, low-wattage fluorescent twin tube with a prong base that fits into the adapter containing a ballast. Lamps are now on the market that look like incandescent lamps and screw in like them but that contain fluorescent lamps inside the bulb.

Lighting for the Future

Motivational and illusion lighting may play key roles in nonresidential design in the future, as they are beginning to today. We will likely see more motivational lighting in public spaces such as banks, offices, medical facilities. We will see remarkable lighting effects in public places such as museums, theaters, and all types of staged events. The laser show has become a standard attraction in discotheques and planetariums and is now making its way into homes as well.

There are currently technological breakthroughs on the market in nonresidential interiors. One notable development is the introduction and marketing of LEDs—light-emitting diodes—that are solid state lamps without filaments whose life expectancy projections range from seven hundred thousand to over five million hours (eighty to 570 years). LEDs have application in areas such as emergency exits or where lights burn out or are shaken loose due to vibration (such as in airports, railway stations, industrial plants, and over doorways). Egress Exit signs can also be made of etched acrylic plates that eliminate the necessity of breakable glass.

Other developments will continue to become important to the future of lighting nonresidential spaces, specifically sensing devices and central computerized monitoring systems.

New developments are being marketed that reduce office glare by improving light dispersion at the work surface where the user can control the levels of illumination. Tilting fixtures are available to adjust the direction of light and control glare at workstations.

Lower maintenance through retrofitted longer life lamp bulbs and fluorescent lamps is another trend for the present and future.

Fluorescent luminaire fixtures are now available that screw into existing fixtures, as previously discussed.

Remote control devices are being developed and marketed that look like television remote controls or small radios that send instructions for reprogramming back to a central unit or that control lights from hallways, for example. Dimming controls can, likewise, be computer controlled.

New products such as oak wrap strips for fluorescent ceiling boxes and unbreakable diffuser lenses for luminous ceilings are two of the

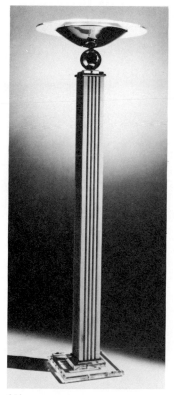

(A)
Figure 4.21

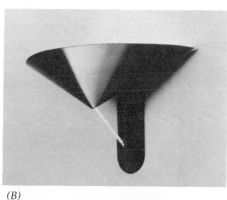

(B)

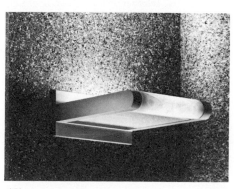

(C)

Figure 4.21 New directions in lighting, some based on lines of antiquity. *(A)* A Neoclassical torchere has a pickled oak column with acrylic base and brass shade balanced atop a solid brass ball. Photo courtesy of Calger Lighting, Inc. *(B)* The "Demetra" metal and glass halogen wall sconce is a high-tech look with a black metal screen shade that illuminates as well as projects a decorative pattern of light. The supporting glass triangle with its leading edge also catches the light, contrasting with the black metal. Photo by Robert Riggs, courtesy of Calger Lighting, Inc. *(C)* This sconce of translucent alabaster was designed to reflect the design trend employing natural materials and finishes in exquisite design quality and craftsmanship. Photo courtesy of Boyd Lighting Company.

ways that aesthetics continue to be improved in nonresidential design. In addition, exciting new designs are continually emerging in the lighting-as-art field and as decorative luminaire fixtures. Lighting design is a viable field for a design professional because of the continual demand for new products and designs in the marketplace.[9]

Notes

1. General Electric, Light and Color (Cleveland: General Electric Lighting Business Group, n.d.), 21.
2. Ibid.
3. *"Design Criteria for Interior Lighting Spaces"* (New York: Illuminating Engineering Society of North America, 1980), 6.
4. Fran Kellogg Smith, *"Light as Art, Today and Tomorrow"* (New York: ASID Report, Vol. XII, No. 3 Summer 1986), 8–9.
5. James L. Nuckolls, *"Glare-Free Workstation"* (New York: Interiors, August 1982), 74–75.
6. Fran Kellog Smith, and Fred J. Bertolone, *Bringing Interiors to Light* (New York: Watson-Guptill, 1986), 60–61.
7. General Electric, Light and Color (Cleveland: General Electric Lighting Business Group, n.d.), 21.
8. Fran Kellog Smith, *"Light as Art, Today and Tomorrow"* (New York: ASID Report, Vol. XII, No. 3 Summer 1986), 8–9.
9. *"Reflections/New Products/Applications"* (New York: Energy User News Magazine, November 1987), 8–22.

Bibliography

American Society of Interior Designers. *"Lighting Vertical Surfaces."* ASID Industry Foundation Bulletin, New York: American Society of Interior Designers, n.d.

DeBoer, J.B., and D. Fischer. *Interior Lighting.* Antwerp: Philips Technical Library, 1981.

Egan, David M. *Concepts in Architectural Lighting.* New York: McGraw-Hill, 1983.

Erhardt, Louis. *Radiation, Light and Illumination.* Camarillo: Camarillo Reproduction Center, 1977.

Evans, Benjamin H. *Daylight in Architecture.* New York: McGraw-Hill, 981.

Flynn, John E., and Samuel M. Mills. *Architectural Lighting Graphics.* New York: Reinhold, 1962.

Gebert, Kenneth L. *National Electrical Code Blueprint Reading.* Alsip: American Technical Publishers, 1977.

Gilliat, Mary, and Douglas Baker. *Lighting Your Home: A Practical Guide.* New York: Pantheon, 1979.

Helms, Ronald N. *Illumination Engineering for Energy Efficient Luminous Environments.* Englewood Cliffs, NJ: Prentice-Hall, 1980.

Hopkinson, R.G., and J.D. Kay. *The Lighting of Buildings.* London: Faber & Faber, 1972.

Horn, Richard. *"Task Lighting: Useful Hints for Lighting Up the Written Word."* Residential Interiors, August, 54–57, 90, 1980.

Illuminating Engineering Society of North America. *Design Criteria for Lighting Interior Living Spaces.* New York: Illuminating Engineering Society of North America, 1980.

Kaufmann, John E. *IES Lighting Handbook Reference Volume.* New York: Illuminating Engineering Society, 1981.

Kilpatrick, David. *Light and Lighting.* Kent: Focal, 1984.

Light and Color. Cleveland: General Electric Company Lighting Business Group, 1981.

"Lighting Your Life: A Home Lighting Guide" Chicago: American Home Lighting Institute, n.d.

Lightolier Incorporated. *Lessons in Lighting.* New Jersey: Lightolier Incorporated, 1982.

Marstellar, John. *"A Philosophy of Light."* Interior Design, March, 78–80, 1987.

Merrill, John J., W. Kenneth Hamblin, and James M. Thorne. *Physical Science Fundamentals.* Minneapolis: Burgess Publishing Company, 1972.

National Lighting Bureau. *Getting the Most From Your Lighting Dollar.* Washington, D.C.: National Lighting Bureau, 1982.

Nuckolls, James L. *Interior Lighting for Environmental Designers.* New York: John Wiley and Sons, 1983.

Office Lighting. Cleveland: General Electric Company Lighting Business Group, 1976.

Phillips, Derek. *Lighting in Architectural Design.* London: McGraw-Hill, 1964.

Rhiner, James L. *The Language of Lighting.* Elk Grove Village: McGraw-Edison, 1983.

Rooney, William R., ed. *Practical Guide to Home Lighting.* New York: Van Nostrand Reinhold, 1980.

Shemitz, Sylvan R. *"Designing with Light."* Interior Design, March, 284–97, 1983.

Smith, Fran Kellogg, and Fred J. Bertolone. *Bringing Interiors to Light.* New York: Whitney Library of Design, 1986.

Westinghouse Electric Corporation. *Westinghouse Lighting Handbook.* Bloomfield: Westinghouse, 1981.

Wilson, David Winfield. *The Control of Light, part 2.* Interior Design, Jan., 292–97; 1985. *The Control of Light, part 4.* Interior Design, May, 286–91, 1985.

Zimmerman, Maureen Williams. *Home Lighting.* Menlo Park: Lane Publishing Company, 1982.

Lighting Associations

American Home Lighting Institute (AHLI)
435 North Michigan Ave.
Chicago, IL 60611

Designer's Lighting Forum (DLF)
Contact: Illumineering Engineering Society of North America for information on local chapters (address follows)

Illumineering Engineering Society of North America (IESNA)
345 East 47th Street
New York, NY 10017

International Association of Lighting Designers (IALD)
c/o Wheel Gersztof Associates
30 West 22nd Street
New York, NY 10010

National Lighting Bureau (NLB)
2101 L Street NW
Washington, D.C. 20037

SPACE PLANNING

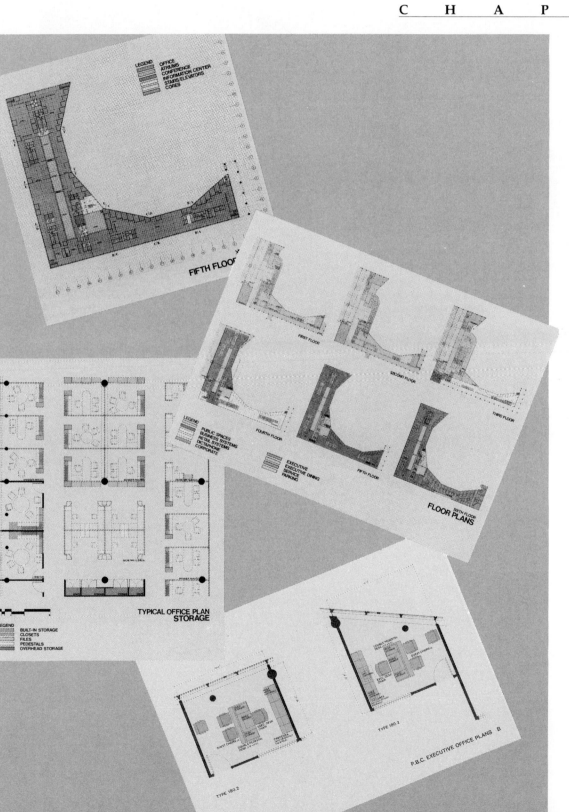

Four presentation boards depict space planning and furniture placement for the Pitney-Bowes home office seen on the following pages. These boards were accomplished by Abby Suckle of I. M. Pei and represent a crucial step in the process of design—the two-dimensional planning of space to meet the needs of its occupants and to enhance the orderly flow of daily activities. These four layouts show scale from overall view of the facility to detail of specific spaces. First, all six floors of the building (top), then one floor with all its spaces laid out in relationship to each other (middle left), then a typical office plan with storage (middle right), and details of two office plans (bottom). In non-residential design, additional requirements include building codes for workplace safety and space utilization as well as electrical and communication hookups. Photos courtesy of I.M. Pei, Architects and Planners.

Pages 104 and 105: *Pitney-Bowes home office in Stamford, Connecticut, was designed by I. M. Pei, Architects and Planners. Abbey Suckle of Pei's design group worked closely with the client to effectively deliver a comfortable working environment for thousands of employees. A headquarters building is at once a showplace for visiting clients and a workplace controlling countless diverse corporate activities. There is an open, friendly feel to this structure, from the outdoor dining area immediately adjacent to the low-lying cafeteria to the conversation areas lining the building's central atrium. Connecting walkways and glass walls lend a sense of intimacy to the space. Though the bays are common in size, effective space planning has tailored the offices to the needs of a score of operating management groups that are housed under the same roof in Stamford. Photos by Ted Spiegel.*

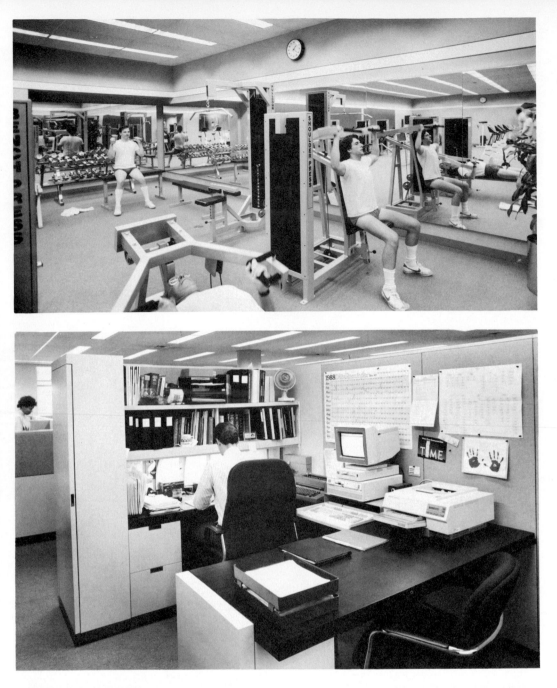

Page 106, top: *Recognizing that middays offer employees a chance for exercise as well as nourishment, many corporations will specify the need to create a fitness center in support of their employees' personal health. The interior design has taken into account the number of employees likely to use the facility to afford adequate locker, shower, and exercise positions. Mirrors in the basement space utilized enhance the spaciousness perceived.* **Page 106, middle and bottom:** *Common work space is broken into modules that are dependent upon the function and work space needs of the home office staff. In this communications staff office, a typewriter, computer, and laser printer as well as a telephone are in constant use. The back wall serves as worktable, bookshelf, and coat closet. Modular furniture can be relocated while still functioning as a corridor wall. The interior worktable doubles as a small conference table. Floor conduits afford delivery of electrical and communication cables. The core area accommodates secretarial staff, common–usage business equipment, and office files. On the right, the showplace function of a home office is highlighted in a Pitney-Bowes corporate poster. A leader in the corporate communications field, it benefits from having clients aware of their state-of-the-art offices. Photos by Ted Spiegel.*
Page 107, top and bottom: *The reception area for the chief executive officer also serves as a control point for the nearby board of directors meeting areas. Throughout the entire building, meeting rooms are in the corners. Effective space planning is detailed through the selected furnishings, which reflect each space's particular use. The boardroom is frequently used for presentations requiring multimedia support, all of which must be planned into the space. Photos by Ted Spiegel.*

Page 108: Office space for top management includes adequate space for small conferences; furniture selection frequently reflects the individual officer's management style. Photo by Ted Spiegel.

Space Planning and the Design Process

The *design process,* discussed in chapter 1, forms the basis for planning space and cannot be separated from it. The gathering of data, which results in a design direction or program, lays the foundation for planning the space. The program also identifies goals to be accomplished in the space—the creation of a sense of place (being surrounded with a feeling of belonging to the space). The architect or designer *allocates spaces* (assigns square footage and placement to rooms or areas) by following the design process. The process of design entails making many decisions through careful consideration of the factors that make *space planning* possible.

The factors that must be considered in intelligent space planning include

- function and zoning
- size and shape of the space
- site, orientation, and climate
- cubic and square footage
- economy
- stretching space
- traffic patterns
- storage
- permanent fixtures (kitchen and bath spaces)
- special needs for the elderly or handicapped
- emotion and psychology
- utilization of the principles and elements of design

These factors, together with the clients' needs, influence the decisions on how to plan and best utilize the space.

As these considerations are reviewed and satisfied, the floor plan evolves from a conceptual bubble diagram to a finished plan. Figure 5.1 illustrates this process with a floor plan that has evolved from the bubble diagram stage through three steps of refining to arrive at a finished floor plan. This floor plan is ready to be blueprinted with the addition of all necessary schedules and diagrams that general contractors and subcontractors must know in order to construct the

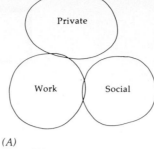

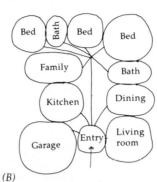

(A)
Figure 5.1

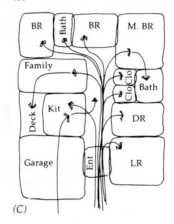

(B)

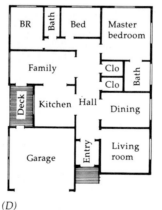

(C)

building and install its structural components correctly. Chapter 13 deals with the processes and systems of building.

Function and Zoning

Functional analysis is perhaps the most important of the space allotment criteria. *Function* means the intended use of the space; it can graphically be illustrated as *zones,* as seen in figure 5.1. In most homes there are typically four zones: *social zones* (*formal* or *informal areas*); *work zones* (kitchen, office, laundry, sewing, hobby, or other task-oriented rooms); *private zones* (bedrooms, retreat areas, bathrooms); and *storage zones* (cabinets and closets wherever they are needed). These zones may be large or small and may be repeated as necessary to meet the needs of the program.

Interrelating Functions

Zones within the home are located near or overlap other zones because of an *interrelationship of functions.* Typical is the placement of the formal living zone adjacent to the formal dining; the kitchen close to the service and dining areas; the bedrooms grouped around a shared bathroom. Part of the space-planning process includes a list of what areas or functions the user wishes to interrelate; there is great latitude for individual space planning in the design of custom homes. For example, a particular user may request a home office adjacent to the master bedroom, while another person may want a home office near the front door or near the kitchen. Some people prefer the family room open to the kitchen and informal dining, whereas others specify the informal social zone separate and away from the kitchen.

When functions interrelate, or smoothly flow from one zone or area to another, and, when the interior design is unique and sophisticated, we experience fine quality design. A skill worth developing is the ability to recognize what functions are being served by the design. It is then possible to evaluate how well the zoned areas interrelate and whether that relationship is smooth and effective.

Figure 5.1 Four phases of schematics or graphics in the evolution of the floor plan. *(A)* The general zones— private, work, and social. *(B)* Divisions within these zones for specific rooms and their relationship to one another. *(C)* The size and shape of the rooms and the traffic patterns. *(D)* The floor plan where doorways, windows, and walls are clearly defined.

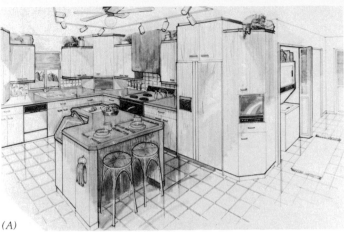

(A)
Figure 5.2

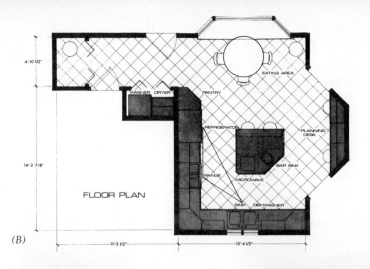

(B)

Diagramming and Floor Plans

Diagramming is the process of placing a two- or three-dimensional representation of the proposed space on paper. The *graphics* evolve by refining the *schematics* or drawings and allocation of space to finally become a finished *floor plan.* This process is represented in figure 5.1. The floor plan becomes the main element of the *blueprints* or *working drawings* discussed in chapter 13. The evolution of diagramming takes place as follows:

- *Bubble planning*—the placement of zones on paper according to function.
- *Size and shape determination*—the allocation of square footage and cubic footage and the shape of rooms and areas.
- *Refinement*—this step could take up to several *overlays,* the laying of tracing paper over the previous graphic to tighten and refine the sketch.
- *Perspective sketches and renderings*—three-dimensional pencil, pen-and-ink, or full-color representations of the proposed space or how a portion of the interior will appear upon completion. Drawing perspective sketches and renderings is a skill required of interior designers; perspective sketches are a tool for the designer in the planning process as much as for the client to visualize spaces and furnishings.
- *Floor plans*—the finished product that indicates specific and exact placement of walls and systems within the home (see chapter 13). Floor plans are drawn *to scale* (usually one-fourth inch equals one foot) and consist of symbols that make the plan understandable to the general contractor and subcontractors (see chapter 15). Floor plans are designed and produced by an architect, competent interior designer, or draftsman. While on paper, changes can be discussed and made with little effort and expense; once the construction has begun, every change requires sizable effort and cost.

Figure 5.3

Measurement of Space: Cubic and Square Footage

Three-dimensional space (the space we walk through) is measured in *cubic feet.* Cubic footage is determined by multiplying the room width by its length then by its height. Rooms with a typical eight-foot ceiling will contain fewer cubic feet than rooms with higher ceilings. Greater cubic footage suggests the possibility of vaulted (high, angled) ceilings and interesting vertical shapes with the accompanying illusion of greater square footage or floor space.

Two-dimensional space (floor area) is measured in *square footage,* which equals the length of the room or building multiplied by its width. Square footage may be the

Figure 5.2 Floor plan layout and rendering by Michael B. Laido, CKD (certified kitchen designer) of Laido Designs, Franklin Lakes, N.J., that won First Place in the 1987 CKD Excellence in Kitchen Design

Competition sponsored by Maytag, Wilsonart, and Home Magazine. The plan features a neat work triangle; an island for informal dining, food preparation, cooking, and cleanup; and a planning desk.

Figure 5.3 In this British artist's studio furnished in Queen Mary textiles by Laura Ashley, cubic footage is generous because of the loftiness of the ceiling. In vaulted or extended ceilings, some very exciting

architectural elements are possible, as evidenced here in the vaulted angled ceiling and unique arch-topped window. Photo courtesy of Laura Ashley.

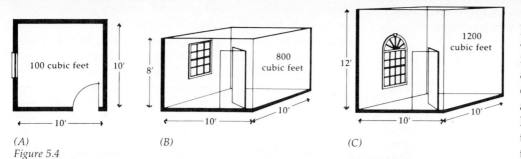

(A)

Figure 5.4

(B)

(C)

During the design process, part of the research phase is to ascertain the minimum square footage required for each task or area within the building. A breakdown is often based on a percentage for each general area. In homes, a general rule of thumb is that 80 percent of the space is allotted for living space, 10 percent for halls, and 10 percent for storage.

Another factor in determining square footage may be the number of people who will occupy the space. Psychological studies have repeatedly demonstrated that *overcrowding* can lead to serious emotional consequences as well as physical limitations and discomfort. It should be noted, however, that the number of square feet allotted per person will vary according to society. Whereas in Hong Kong sixty feet per person is considered adequate, in the United States four hundred to five hundred square feet per person is generally considered the minimum for comfortable living standards. In America, therefore, a family of six would ideally have three thousand square feet of living space.

Shaping the Space

The shape of the interior space can be discussed in two directions—horizontally and vertically. Although a rectangular room is certainly the easiest to build and the simplest to decorate, it can also be the most boring architecturally. Rooms with angled or curved walls, with vaulted or curved ceilings, with half walls or transparent walls, or even with cut out sections between rooms can add interest and visual expansion of the actual dimensions of the room. Altering room shapes has been a boon to new smaller homes and to the remodeling of older ones, as the alternatives give the impression of greater space and provide architectural interest where none may otherwise have existed.

The shape of interior spaces can also affect the exterior shape and dimensions of the home; this, too, must be taken into careful consideration when designing custom housing. From the interior living standpoint, it is ideal to first determine the spacial arrangements and shapes within the floor plan, then let the exterior shape be determined by the sizes and shapes of the interior spaces. However, the desired style or proportions of the exterior will often limit or restrict the interior shapes or sizes. Realistically, some compromise is often necessary. A room may need to be altered in dimension or size to make the exterior more pleasing, or the

Figure 5.5

determining factor of the building size based on an estimated *cost per square foot* (see Economy, later in this chapter). Square footage may also be limited by the size and building restrictions of the lot or location where it is to be constructed. In neighborhoods of newly constructed homes, there may also be a minimum acceptable square footage requirement. This may be part of the restrictive covenants, or standard rules for building sizes and materials, established by the developer or community residents to ensure a consistent level of quality and price range in the homes of that neighborhood.

Figure 5.4 (A) Square footage is derived by multiplying the width of a room by its length. Here ten feet by ten feet makes 100 square feet. (B) Cubic footage is the width multiplied by the length then by the height of the room. The 100 square feet multiplied by eight-foot walls makes 800 cubic feet. (C) The same room with a twelve-foot ceiling contains greater cubic footage and will cost more in both material and labor, even though the square footage remains the same as the typical eight-foot ceiling.

Figure 5.5 Appearing simple yet based on complex space planning is this nature-surrounded Guilford, Connecticut, home. Multilevel planning with various step-downs and angles seen in walls, half-walls, and fenestration (window arrangement) yields not only clean modern architectural interest blended with traditional in the upper background but exhilarating vaulted cubic space in the diagonal wall and window lines and soaring ceilings. Architect Jeff Riley of Centerbrook. Photo by Norman McGrath, © 1979.

placement of doors and windows in the rooms may be dictated by their fenestration, or arrangement, from the exterior.

Site, Orientation, and Climate

The shape of the space may also be dictated by the limitations or special considerations of the building site. The architect will look carefully at the direction of the prevailing breezes in both summer and winter; the slope of the lot; any natural vegetation, the location and types of nearby buildings; and property values of surrounding architecture. Also considered will be the orientation, or direction the site faces, so that solar aspects and fenestration can intelligently be incorporated to the advantage of the home. The orientation is also important in relation to the climate. A Sunbelt home will have different planning than a New England home, for example, because the former must provide control of heat from the sun and the latter must control excessive winter cold. The needs and criteria of the climate, then, are important aspects of planning a home.

Economy

Economy is an important consideration in planning space. In most cases, new construction will have a financial limit (a maximum amount that can be spent) imposed by the client or by the lending institution. Therefore, the architect, designer, and builder as well as the client or homeowner need to make careful and wise decisions concerning the amount of space. This is because the actual *square footage* is proportional to the cost of the building or home. Total price is estimated on a cost per square foot. The cost per square foot will vary according to the location, the building materials used, the amount of skilled labor involved, and the number of luxury items incorporated.

An illustration of the relationship of cost per square foot of space to the total building cost at $40.00 per square foot might be as follows (excluding the building lot or property costs):

1. an eight hundred square foot building would cost approximately $32,000;
2. a twelve hundred square foot building would be about $48,000; and
3. a two thousand square foot building would cost $80,000.

Therefore, smaller total square footage means lower building costs when building one-story or main level-only homes.

However, second-story and basement living space is less costly to construct than main floor living space. This is because the roof and foundation can serve all levels and because plumbing and electrical systems can be centralized and fireplaces stacked. Further, room inside an attic (termed a half story) can be quite economical since the attic space would often be there anyway. With the addition of dormer windows or skylights and perhaps a steeper pitch in the roof, the attic space can become not only livable but charming because of its angles and nooks. In the case of basements, there may necessarily be a crawl space or a deep frost line that would require sinking deep foundations that when extended can become living space. Basements are a modest addition to the initial building cost in most cases. The attic or basement space may be framed with the home but finished at a later date, giving added living space as the need arises. Thereby, the initial cost of the home would not reflect the potential of that addition of living space in a high initial cost per square foot. In this way, a home with half-story and basement space can be more affordable than a home of the same square footage on one level only.

Other Factors That Affect Economy in Planning Home Space

*   Interest rates also affect the cost of the payments and, hence, whether or not the home or building can be afforded. Examples are listed in chart 5.1 for monthly payments of fixed-interest loans of $60,000, $70,000, and $80,000 at 10 percent, 12 percent, and 14 percent for both a fifteen-year loan and a thirty-year loan. These amounts only represent the principle and interest and do not take into account escrow amounts required for taxes and insurance, which can easily add up to another $100 or $200 a month, depending on the location and value of the home and real estate. Taxes and insurance can be included in the monthly payment or, in some cases, can be paid directly to the government and insurance company by the homeowner.
*   The *cubic footage* affects the cost. Areas with very high ceilings will be more costly to construct because of the additional building materials required than those with the more typical eight-foot ceiling.
*   Simple building shapes also contribute to economy. A home or building with many jogs, angles, gables (roof points), and dormers (windows in the roof) will make the cost per square foot rise, making the interior space more expensive. The closer the home is to a simple box the more economical it will be to build. Some of the most beautiful houses in history have been simple rectangles or boxes. Some may find variations in the form of jogs or angles in the floor plans more appealing.
*   Long-range space planning can also be a boon to saving money in initial building or remodeling. When a space is to be finished or remodeled at a later date, structural planning or framing can accommodate those changes. For example, if a room will one day adjoin another via French doors, the framework for that doorway can be in place as the home is built thus avoiding major remodeling. Planning in advance for additions in this way is wise and economi-

cal space planning. The exterior style should always be taken into consideration when planning additions so that the home will look as though the addition belonged there all along, not as an awkward afterthought. Living with the construction of remodeling or adding on can be a strain, but if careful space planning has taken place, the frustrations can be minimal and the results most rewarding.

- Careful planning to avoid unusable wasted space or poor traffic patterns can increase economy.
- The proper scale and proportion of rooms appropriate to the particular interior space should be considered. This means judging the intended function of

the area and planning square and cubic footage to meet the demands for that space. Chart 5.5 lists several types of rooms or functions and the typical small- to moderate-sized rooms versus large-sized dimensions and/or square footage. This can be used as a guide in planning economy.

- Economy is evident when the size of rooms allows the function to take place without crowding or frustration. A space that is too small can necessitate costly expansion by remodeling.
- Economy can be accomplished by doubling up purposes in an area called a *multiuse area* and by making space appear larger than it is.

Chapter 13, Building Systems, contains further information on planning and building and on components that make up the structure of a home.

Living with Less Space

Smaller seems to be the direction of the future. This is not necessarily bad, since large spaces demand upkeep and extra furnishings and pose not only cleaning burdens but security problems as well.

Skillful and creative planning makes the best use out of what space is available. This can be done in advance in the blueprint stage. Multiuse space is generally open space as large as two or three rooms. The omission of walls is a cost-saving factor, and one large space rather than cubicles of smaller spaces can give the entire interior a more spacious and luxurious feeling. A large space allows for greater flexibility in meeting current needs and for different furniture pieces or arrangements as the function changes over time than do traditional small spaces.

In a home where the cost disallows space for every desired purpose, some rooms can double up, performing two or more functions. For example, a little-used but desired formal dining room can double as a library; the home office or den could act as a guest room. The most dramatic multiuse area, however, is the idea of the *great room,* a term taken from medieval England when the *great hall* was the place where dining, entertaining, conversation, and sleeping all took place. Today's great room frequently includes a kitchen; a snack bar or island for both food preparation and eating; a seating conversation area, often grouped around a fireplace, window, or other focal point; an entertainment system of television, videotape player, and stereo equipment; perhaps a sit-down eating area (in lieu of the formal dining room); and a desk for study, scheduling, and handling personal finances, which may contain space for a personal computer and filing system.

Reasons for the evolution of this area include not only rising building costs but today's life-style. People today are busy, often employed in or outside the home, and time is a precious commodity. Many rooms or a duplication of formal/informal spaces means time spent cleaning and main-

---

Chart 5.1 Comparison of Monthly Mortgage Payments

Principle and Interest Only—Fixed Rates

Loan Amount—15-Year Loan	10%	12%	14%
$60,000 ———————	$644.00	$720.00	$799.00
$70,000 ———————	$752.00	$840.00	$932.00
$80,000 ———————	$860.00	$960.00	$1065.00

Loan Amount—30-Year Loan	10%	12%	14%
$60,000 ———————	$526.00	$617.00	$710.00
$70,000 ———————	$614.00	$720.00	$829.00
$80,000 ———————	$702.00	$823.00	$947.00

Totals: When the loan is paid in full, the following amounts will have been paid:

Fifteen-Year Loan

The amount paid back will be a little more than twice the loan amount.

$60,000 at 10% ($644.00 X 180 payments) = $115,920.00
$60,000 at 12% ($720.00 X 180 payments) = $129,600.00
$60,000 at 14% ($799.00 X 180 payments) = $143,820.00

$70,000 at 10% ($752.00 X 180 payments) = $135,360.00
$70,000 at 12% ($840.00 X 180 payments) = $151,200.00
$70,000 at 14% ($932.00 X 180 payments) = $167,760.00

$80,000 at 10% ($860.00 X 180 payments) = $154,800.00
$80,000 at 12% ($960.00 X 180 payments) = $172,800.00
$80,000 at 14% ($1065.00 X 180 payments) = $191,700.00

Thirty-Year Loan

The amount paid back will be roughly three times the loan amount. NOTE: Most of the interest is paid at the beginning of the loan. By increasing the amount paid to the principle each month, the number of payments can be reduced. For example, an additional $50.00 a month paid to principle on any of these loans can reduce the years of payment to around fourteen to eighteen years rather than thirty years. Also, paying a half-monthly payment every two weeks rather than one payment each month can reduce the life of the loan significantly by increasing the amount paid to principle, as well. This works well for people who are paid every two weeks.

$60,000 at 10% ($526.00 X 360 payments) = $189,360.00
$60,000 at 12% ($617.00 X 360 payments) = $222,120.00
$60,000 at 14% ($710.00 X 360 payments) = $255,600.00

$70,000 at 10% ($614.00 X 360 payments) = $221,040.00
$70,000 at 12% ($720.00 X 360 payments) = $259,200.00
$70,000 at 14% ($829.00 X 360 payments) = $298,440.00

$80,000 at 10% ($702.00 X 360 payments) = $252,720.00
$80,000 at 12% ($823.00 X 360 payments) = $296,280.00
$80,000 at 14% ($947.00 X 360 payments) = $340,920.00

taining those spaces. Today's life-style is less formal than in past eras. Whereas a formal dinner party may have been the standard through the mid-twentieth century, today even the boss is entertained comfortably in the great room and may even enjoy pitching in and helping with the cooking. Further, hired help today is used in a different sense. The homeowner may have someone come in to clean but will rarely employ servants to prepare meals, serve, and clean up as was commonly the case in past eras among the well-to-do families. Convenience foods and equipment, such as microwave ovens and dishwashers, have simplified lifestyles and taken away much of the burden of food preparation and entertaining.

Figure 5.6

Stretching Space

Because of smaller spaces in today's homes, it is often desirable to make spaces seem larger than they actually are. A *space-saving device* is a method of making space appear larger. Some of these devices are

1. The use of open plans with few structural walls. Many a home has been remodeled to remove walls. However, a general contractor should be consulted first to determine if walls can safely be removed without posing a threat to the structural soundness of the building. In no case should load-bearing walls (discussed in chapter 13, Building Systems) be removed.
2. Vertical space, accomplished with vaulted (high, angled) ceilings, one- and one-half-story or two-story ceilings, or skylights.
3. Half walls that allow visual and audible communication to the upper area of an adjoining room.
4. Extensive use of glass windows, doors, and walls. In the past, glass building materials admitted too much heat and cold. Now, however, we are able to control solar gain and heat loss through new glass types, shading devices, and energy-conserving window treatments.

Once the building is complete, decorative space saving devices can also seem to expand space. These devices include the following:

1. Light colors seem to recede, as do dull colors.
2. Smooth textures expand space more than rough textures.
3. Mirrors properly used can expand space if, for example, the mirror reflects a view out a window and not a decoratively furnished or busy, patterned area.
4. Draperies from the ceiling to the floor make walls look taller, as do top treatments and strong vertical lines in the window treatments.
5. Long vertical or horizontal moldings carry the eye and expand visual space, giving the impression of greater height or width, respectively.
6. Floor coverings that are relatively plain and installed wall to wall will give the impression of greater floor area, particularly in contrast to patterned or layered floor coverings.
7. Furnishings that are small scale, are lighter in color, use small or no patterns, have legs rather than upholstered skirts or solid wood to the floor, and utilize glass or other see-through materials will also help

Figure 5.6 A great room has been created in this home by opening the kitchen, dining room, and informal family room to each other. Posts and railing visually divide the areas, while the openness, cathedral window wall, and vaulted ceiling apparently increase spaciousness. Photo courtesy of Frigidaire.

Figure 5.7

expand small spaces. A common design error is to place large, patterned upholstered pieces and large-scale wooden furniture in small spaces.

Traffic Patterns

Traffic patterns are also referred to as circulation or traffic flow. A traffic pattern is the repeatedly used walking path from room to room or area to area. Traffic patterns are necessary and unavoidable and require careful evaluation as an important part of space planning. Traffic patterns may be drawn in lines and arrows on the diagram or floor plan, indicating where people will be walking or where objects will be moved regularly through the space. These traffic patterns should be left free and kept as direct as possible. In a home, major traffic patterns typically go from

- front door to a central circulation system that leads to all areas of the house
- garage to kitchen for carrying groceries
- garage to mudroom or closet/locker area
- kitchen to formal, informal, and private living areas
- kitchen to service areas and entry areas
- laundry areas to bedrooms
- bedrooms to bathrooms
- garage to hall closet or service area
- back door to kitchen, mudroom, or service area

Some pitfalls to avoid:

- Rooms that act as hallways, where a room must be crossed to get to another room.
- Door locations that force circulation through conversation furniture groupings.
- Areas too small for furniture and circulation.
- Private areas, bathroom fixtures that are open to view from a traffic pattern.
- Work areas that tend to be untidy, such as the kitchen sink or laundry area, that are in plain view of traffic flow or can be viewed from the entry.

Traffic patterns must be planned for adequate width. Hallways and stairs in homes have typically been three to three and one-half feet wide. However, a four foot wide corridor and stairs will more comfortably allow two-way traffic.

Another traffic-planning feature is the location of doors and the direction the doors swing. Generally, doors should be placed toward the corner of a room to avoid cutting up the wall space, and the door should swing inward against the adjoining wall. Where *swinging doors* will be a problem, *pocket* doors or sliding doors may be a good choice that will not impede traffic.

Storage

Storage is a precious commodity; it fills up so quickly and is difficult to empty because possessions are hard to part with. A cardinal rule for storage is that storage should be located at the point of first or most frequent use. It has also been suggested that in order to determine real storage needs a list should be made of things owned and their corresponding sizes, then list where these items should be stored and what size that storage area should be. Storage zones are desirable in specific locations.

- The kitchen should include storage for dry goods (such as a wall or walk-in pantry) and ample storage for pots and pans, small appliances, serving bowls, informal and formal plates and dishes and glasses (stemware), silverware and utensils, linens, soaps and cleansers, and cleaning appliances—brooms, mops, or vacuums—all located within convenient reach.

Figure 5.7 The size of the California den designed by Noel Jeffrey, ASID, is visually doubled with ceiling-height mirrors, reflecting nineteenth-century Chinese screens used as wall panels. A collection of Chinese cinnabar (carved red porcelain) on the end table, and silk embroidered pillows, provide exotic pattern and hence interest to this otherwise sleek, modern setting. Photo courtesy of Noel Jeffrey, Inc.

- The laundry facility should have storage for extra soap, bleach, softener, and other cleaning preparations.
- The front hall closet is for family and/or guest coats. Depending on the weather and the life-style, there may be a place for wet outerwear such as raincoats, umbrellas, or boots. It may not always be possible, however, to accommodate all the guests' coats, scarves, and gloves when a sizable group is being entertained. In this case, the outerwear might be stacked up in a den or on a bed.
- Closets, lockers, a walk-in closet, or a wall of hooks near the back entrance or garage entrance or in the mudroom are for winter gear (coats, boots, school bags) and individual sports gear, again depending on life-style. In the summer, such an area could double for summer sports gear: tennis, baseball, and soccer equipment and even swimming towels and gear.
- A closet for the vacuum cleaner should be placed where it is needed. In two-story houses, a vacuum might be located in a closet on each floor.
- Linen closets are usually located in a hall near bedrooms to hold extra sheets, pillowcases, pillows, and blankets.
- Bathrooms need storage for a supply of paper goods, personal hygiene sundries, and extra towels.
- Bedrooms are often shortchanged in storage. Closets that are ample in size and compartmentalized will be appreciated.
- Any area where a hobby is performed requires individualized storage.
- Home offices need closets, shelves, and/or units that can hold reference books, files, paper, and other supplies. The personal computer demands certain storage items such as printer paper and disks.
- The family room or room where media entertainment is located will need storage for items such as cassette tapes, records or compact disks, and videotapes.
- The library, often combined with a home office or another room, will need plenty of shelves and perhaps some locking doors for valuable books or papers.
- The tool shed is a place for storage of lawn and garden tools and equipment, and tools for use in other maintenance projects.
- Where no tool shed or yard storage shed exists, the garage is often used for lawn and garden equipment and tools, bicycles, and a myriad of bulky items that found no place in the house. With careful planning, the garage that is also a storage area can be organized and avoid a cluttered appearance.

Space Planning Rooms with Permanent Fixtures

Rooms or areas in the home that require extra thought and planning are those where built-in cabinetry and fixtures are permanent. Permanent fixtures are a part of the floor plan and are treated as structural components that are specified by the architect or designer, built and installed by craftsmen, and ordered and installed through plumbing companies or contractors. Because the cabinets and fixtures do not move, it is important to give extra attention to their planning. The kitchen, bath, and laundry room each have specific and individual requirements. Other rooms that may have built-in cabinetry and require careful space planning and attention to detail might include dens or libraries, sewing rooms, and hobby areas.

Kitchens

The kitchen has rightfully been called the hub of the home, a place where most people build fond memories of watching or helping a parent or relative with the task of preparing food and where dining or visiting with friends and loved ones often takes place. The kitchen is where most people want to be not only because it contains food to feed the body but because kitchens set the stage for people to interact and bond loving friendships. Perhaps this is the underlying basis for today's great room.

Because the kitchen is the center for food preparation and storage, food service and/or dining, and cleaning up after meals, it is a room where much time is spent. Although the tasks that take place in the kitchen clearly are work, today's kitchen can masterfully be planned with labor-saving appliances and cabinetry that make storage and organization pleasant and cleanup much less of a strain. Kitchens are no longer a place of drudgery; they have become an important center of the home—a fashionable setting for the host and/or hostess to do the cooking. Today even the guests are often active participants in the food preparation process—it is a social experience in itself.

Certified kitchen designers take into account all aspects of life-style when helping clients with kitchen design. For example, when two or more people are preparing meals, rules such as the standard working triangle (discussed later in this chapter) are not as applicable. Family traffic patterns and clearance dimensions must then change to avoid congestion and confusion. If there is a hierarchy in the planning, such as an assistant to the chef, then the helper will need more space between sink and refrigerator to wash and prepare vegetables, for example. Specialty or gourmet cooking may further require extra space and perhaps a separate center. If two chefs are team cooking, each preparing individual dishes, then two separate working areas are called for—two sinks, two food preparation areas, two cooking areas, and a shared refrigerator.

Figure 5.8

Another trend in kitchen planning is to accommodate the growing number of latch-key children who arrive home before working parents and who help prepare food without assistance from an experienced adult. This new segment of the cooking population will have special needs such as lower placement of microwaves and dishes. Safe appliance and cabinet designs are also important. This could include locks on some cabinets and toe-kick areas that double as pull-out stepping stools.

The growing population of people aged sixty-five years and older is also demanding changes in traditional kitchen design. Safety here is an important factor to consider, as well as comfort and convenience. For those with bad backs, for example, shelving should be high enough to avoid bending. The aged and infirm also will have special needs as they maintain a longer period of independence. The kitchen must be planned for accessibility and size/height dimensions to meet individual needs. For the people who are aging and will age in good health, the demand for personalized work spaces as well as social spaces planned with or adjacent to kitchen areas will increase.

Another major trend is toward smaller spaces due to greater population density (more people and less land), limited funds, and higher energy costs. These factors require more efficient kitchens that combine work spaces and feature added storage over tall appliances, in the toe-kick space, as shelves on door interiors, or as shelves on the backsplash. Rollout or swing-out drawers, shelves, and pantries, pullout work and dining surfaces, and the elimination of unnecessary walkways are other ways to improve efficiency in smaller spaces.

Kitchens for the future will not necessarily become ultramodern and futuristic. Rather, with the emphasis on high-tech appliances, we will see more personalizing of the kitchen—the addition of art and accessories that give identity and reveal the style and values of those who work, eat, and socialize there. As the center of the home, kitchens will not necessarily become more fancy or more stark but will become a quiet backdrop where people are the real stars.[1]

With these current and predicted trends in mind, it is quite reasonable that the kitchen should become a center of attention, commanding more money in cabinetry, plumbing fixtures, and appliances than any other area of the home. Today people want beautiful kitchens with character and style —kitchens where cooking meals of any type or origin can be an enjoyable and a creative experience.

Kitchen planning includes working arrangements in zones or work areas. The three zones that are considered the basic working triangle include:

- the refrigerator zone
- the cooking zone (range and ovens)
- the sink/cleanup zone.

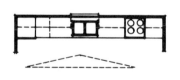
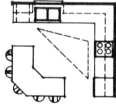

(A)
Figure 5.9

(B)

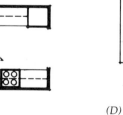
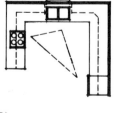

(C)

(D)

Figure 5.8 The ability to cook large meals with gas and bake with electricity is shown in this kitchen. The island provides work space and informal dining, or a snack bar. Closed, open, and glassed-in shelving give plenty of storage. Appliances by and photo courtesy of Dacor.

Figure 5.9 Four kitchen configurations and the work triangle. *(A)* The single-wall kitchen with refrigerator at the left, the stove/oven on the right of the sink. *(B)* The L-shaped kitchen with an eating bar and the stove and refrigerator on the opposing wall from the sink. *(C)* The galley kitchen works as a hallway—an economical use of space but potentially conflicting with traffic patterns. *(D)* The U-shaped kitchen eliminates the traffic problems and gives plenty of countertop space around each appliance.

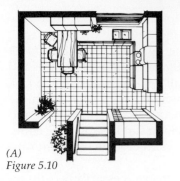

(A)
Figure 5.10

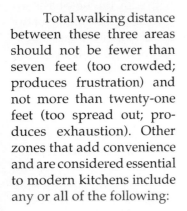

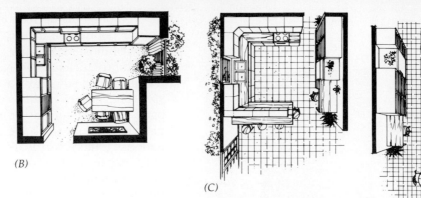

(B)

(C)

(D)

Total walking distance between these three areas should not be fewer than seven feet (too crowded; produces frustration) and not more than twenty-one feet (too spread out; produces exhaustion). Other zones that add convenience and are considered essential to modern kitchens include any or all of the following:

- additional food storage zones
- various specialized food preparation zones
- a second cooking zone and/or a quick-cooking zone
- a second cleanup/sink zone
- tableware storage zone(s)
- serving and service storage zone
- a cleaning supplies storage zone

These zones should be planned for the convenience and consideration of the family members who cook and should be laid out logically according to individual life-style needs. However, certain checkpoints are fairly consistent considerations in each area. These are presented in charts 5.2 and 5.3.

(E)

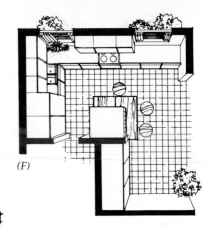

(F)

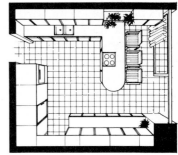

(G)

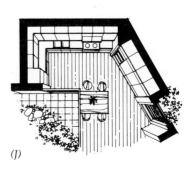

(H)

(I)

(J)

Figure 5.10 (A) An L-shaped kitchen with informal dining handy at the end of the cabinetry. Kitchen is closed to other living areas; stairs to upper floor are accessed in the kitchen. (B) An L-shaped kitchen with a long countertop for food preparation and serving. Dinette is away from the preparation area. Deep floor-to-ceiling storage forms a pantry. (C) A popular U-shaped kitchen with wide eating bar beneath overhead cabinetry. Pantry, refrigerator, and kitchen desk form the wall opposite the sink. (D) A U-shaped kitchen with island eating bar that doubles as food preparation area complete with small sink. Dining area is informal yet away from the cooking area and offers outside access through French doors. Cooktop range is separate from a built-in microwave/conventional oven pair. (E) This U-shaped kitchen has a food preparation island and ample counter space. Long desk-countertop provides convenient serving to the dining area. (F) This L-shaped galley kitchen is anchored around a peninsula eating bar. The kitchen opens up to the family room to create a "great room." (G) Easy access to the outside makes this U-shaped kitchen a pleasant environment. A long wall of cabinets

Food Storage Cabinetry

Food storage can be divided into three main categories.

1. Perishables: Those items that require refrigeration or freezing.

2. Regularly used dry food supplies: Foods used on a daily basis such as flour (flour bin drawers with metal liners are available), baking powders, spices and supplies, boxed cereal, various pastas, rice, and legumes. These should be located in the kitchen near the zone where they will be used in food preparation or cooking. Generally, the flour and heavy supplies go in the lower cabinets and smaller supplies above. A spice rack or specially designed cabinet is desirable to keep spices organized and handy. A cabinet or cupboard specifically for boxed cereal or for items such as sugar, cornmeal, popcorn, rice, beans, and other legumes is good planning. The shelf heights should be adjustable and the interiors of a material that can easily be cleaned.

3. Staples and canned goods: Occasionally used. These might be located in a pantry or larder—a wall of cabinets or a walk-in closet where occasionally used or extra containers of food or even utensils, serving pieces, and china are kept. By keeping extra supplies in the pantry, the cook can save kitchen space and save trips to the store. The pantry may also be located between the kitchen and dining room as a place from which to serve food to the formal dining room. An extension of the concept of the pantry is the food storage room that is located in a cool area (such as a basement), where staples, cases of food (such as canned goods), flour, cooking supplies, legumes, and other items with a long shelf life, which replenish the pantry supply, and bulky cooking pots and pans are stored. A root cellar is not often seen today, although some homes are planned to contain one. Historically, a root cellar was an underground room often away from the house, with stone or dirt floors, that was cool and

was used for keeping fruits, vegetables, and even cured meats. Today a root cellar can be added within the home if the floor is left dirt and if the room is properly ventilated (as it tends to smell).

Food Preparation Countertop/Cabinet-Top Areas

Determine the kind of food preparation that will take place and plan countertop areas accordingly. In kitchens where much food preparation takes place, a minimum of two long counters (over three feet) are required. An island or a peninsula often provides wide countertops. Where bread is frequently mixed, a large area near flour bins and cooking supplies is imperative. If vegetables are often chopped, cutting boards that are built into the countertop or that pull out near the sink will be appreciated. Some kitchens are planned with two or more cutting boards of various sizes— larger ones for mixing, smaller ones for cutting. The sink may be smaller for

Figure 5.11

food preparation and not cleanup (such as in an island or peninsula). As another example, if candymaking is a specialty, a separate area with supplies nearby and a counter of marble is ideal. The type of food preparation, then, should be the topic of careful consideration in planning the size and location of countertop or cabinet-top space.

Cooking containers such as pots and pans need to be close to the range or cooking top. Cupboards with sliding drawers eliminate awkward hunting situations. Vertical panels hold cooking sheets, dripper pans, muffin sheets, and other flat dishes upright and should be

located near (often above or below) the oven where they are used. Cooking utensils can be located in drawers near the stove or placed in a crock or hung on the wall. Items used everyday should be most convenient.

An appliance garage is cabinet doors on the countertop with space behind to hide portable appliances; sliding shelves in lower cabinets can also hold appliances, and electric plugs can be installed inside these special cupboards. Cabinets can be designed with solid or glass doors or without any doors at all and to hold any special item.

Cleanup Cabinetry

Cabinets need to be planned near the sink for cleaning supplies. Typically, the cabinet beneath the sink contains everyday cleaning supplies and often a trash can. A separate, taller cupboard keeps the smell away from the sink and allows for a larger trash can (trash compactors are discussed in chart 5.3). A broom closet should be planned to accommodate the equipment (brooms, mops, vacuum cleaner) and to be conveniently accessible.

Towels and washcloths should be handy to the sink. A rack for dish towels that slides into the lower cabinets is good to control clutter and to keep towels dry and more sanitary. A drawer or two should be allotted for clean kitchen linen. Drawers should be added for extra paper towels or cleaning cloths or rags, storage for paper or plastic garbage bags, and extra disposable items such as rubber gloves or scouring pads.

Tableware Storage Cabinetry

Cabinetry for tableware includes cupboards for plates and dishes and stemware (cups, glasses). Lower cabinets next to the dishwasher might hold dishes for everyday use (children can then easily set the table), and upper cabinets could contain special, breakable tableware. Drawers should be planned for silverware, placemats, cloth or paper napkins, and folded tablecloths and a closet for hanging tablecloths (pressed and ready for special occasions). A set of shelves for centerpieces and vases is valuable. Here the planning will proceed according to life-style and possessions.

Dining Cabinetry

Islands and peninsula eating bars are a common sight in today's kitchens. The bar may accommodate only two stools or chairs or many, depending on the number of people in the household. Today the meals served at the bar generally outnumber those at a conventional table, although both a bar and a kitchen table are still considered the ideal kitchen dining arrangement. The bar is planned and built as a part of the cabinets; it may contain drawers, cupboards, or appliances on one or two sides. It may double as a desk or contain a space for a computer. It may have no cabinets and function as a cabinet-top eating surface with bar stool space only beneath it. The bar, island, or peninsula may also be lowered where the eating surface is so that shorter bar stools or standard chairs can be used rather than tall bar stools.

Service/Storage Cabinetry

Planning cabinets for table service or serving dishes also takes some thought because some dishes, platters, and utensils are used on a regular basis and others may be used only occasionally, such as on holidays or at more formal meals. Therefore, the serving pieces most often used should be accessible, and the items seldom

Continued on next page.

---

ensures ample storage; the countertops give plenty of work and serving space. *(H)* A simple L-shaped kitchen and glass doors to the patio give emphasis to the dining area in this uncomplicated design. *(I)* A compact kitchen that separates dining from the working triangle. Little counter space is ideal for cooks who do little

cooking. Serving/storage cabinetry near the table gives a more formal and private feeling to the in-kitchen dining. *(J)* A dramatic storage wall angles around dining in this modified L-shaped kitchen. There is no traffic pattern crossing the working triangle.

Figure 5.11 Kitchen/pantry storage can be dramatically increased with well-planned cabinetry that offers features such as sliding shelves and drawers, lift-up doors, and storage in

the doors. Items stored can be more readily accessed, making them far more usable because they are conveniently located.

used can go in less accessible places, such as above the oven or the refrigerator. Keep in mind that lightweight items should go overhead, and heavier items should be placed in lower cabinets for reasons of physical ease and safety. Storage dishes, such as glass or plastic dishes with lids, used for storing perishable items in the refrigerator or freezing unit should be fairly close to the refrigerator and near a countertop or cabinet top. Consider drawers just for lids, perhaps one for plastic and one for glass, plus a drawer or two for plastic wrap and bags, aluminum foil, and waxed paper for storing food items.

It has often been said that there is never too much storage space, and although people

tend to fill up whatever kitchen storage is available, it is a far better approach to plan generous, rather than skimpy, storage space, which inevitably brings about frustration and discontent.

Figure 5.12

Part of the kitchen-planning process is deciding which types of appliances to purchase, making selections between the many makes, styles, and options of those appliances, and making sure the cabinetry dimensions will accommodate them with precision. Chart 5.3 lists the major types or categories of appliances that are on the market and surveys options and considerations in their selection and placement.

Bathrooms

The bath has come a long way since its sterile "sink/toilet/ tub-in-a-cubicle" days. The bath of today is a luxurious area both in terms of square footage and fixtures. Bathtubs include a vast selection of shapes, sizes, depths, and colors in plain water-holding devices or whirlpool bathtub styles. The shower is routinely located in a walk-in stall, sometimes oversized, perhaps with a seat or bench built in, and even with two nozzles if desired. The health spa can be brought home in the form of a combination sauna/steam room/bathing facility that is now available as a manufactured unit measuring around twelve feet long by five feet

Figure 5.13

Figure 5.12 Some possibilities in traditional and contemporary patterns of cabinetry drawer and door faces. Wood and plastic laminates are the most commonly used cabinet-face materials.

Figure 5.13 Despite the overall trend toward smaller homes, today's master baths are often planned with separated areas for bathing and grooming and even incorporate large dressing areas and closets, exercise equipment, and whirlpool, sauna, and spa facilities. Luxury and spacious-

ness are bywords of contemporary master baths. Here we see clean, modern design with fabric and flooring inspired by Southwestern motifs. Flooring by and photos courtesy of Armstrong World Industries, Inc.

wide by six feet high. Sinks vary from single to dual vanities to pedestal styles in sleek, sophisticated designs. The toilet, or *water closet,* takes on several stylish forms and can include a urinal. The bidet may be placed by a toilet, and is used for personal hygiene. The *compartmental bathroom* generally consists of two rooms: the vanity area and the tub and toilet area. In some residential settings, the toilet is further separated by an enclosure or closet. Minimum sizes for fixtures are found in chart 5.4.

With the surge of physical fitness as a vogue, the exercise area has become a part of many bathroom areas in not only spas but in homes as well. The exercise area may include one (or more) piece(s) of equipment such as the treadmill, a minitrampoline, an exercise bicycle, and a bench press (barbells), or other strengthening and endurance units. Even a mat and a television for doing aerobics may be included.

And finally, the bathroom may include a dressing area, often a large, walk-in closet with compartmentalized shelves, mirrors, and clothes bars for easy organization.

Laundry Rooms

The laundry room is also an area of permanent cabinetry and stationary appliances where flexibility in planning is possible. Sizes required for washers and dryers are listed in chart 5.4. Cabinets should contain shelves high enough for laundry detergents, whiteners, and softeners, and other fre-

---

Chart 5:3   Appliance Planning Considerations

Refrigerators and Freezers

There are many options in today's refrigerators, such as adjustable shelves, special compartments (for meat, vegetables, and dairy products), frost-free and energy-saving features, and textured doors in fashionable colors. Also available are automatic cold water and ice dispensers in the outside of the door to alleviate the need to continually open and close the door (saving energy). Keep in mind, however, that the more options, the greater the possibility of breakdown. Most refrigerators contain a freezer unit, which can be located at the top, bottom, or side (hence, side-by-side refrigerator). A second refrigerator may be desired for extra storage, and freezers are sometimes also located in the kitchen. Ordinarily a second refrigerator or large freezer will be placed in a garage, basement, or utility/storage area. Freezers come with side-hinged doors or as a chest where the lid lifts (keeps cold inside rather than rushing out but is more difficult to organize and access food). The area in front of the refrigerator or freezer needs a minimum of three feet to open and close the door and access the food without crowding. There should be a countertop nearby for loading and unloading food.

Ovens/Ranges/Cooking Tops

Conventional ovens may be a part of a range or stove unit where the oven is below, or the unit may also have a smaller conventional or microwave oven above as well. A cooking top contains cooking elements only and is placed in the countertop or cabinet top wherever it is desired—along the wall or in an island, for example.

Standard appliance sizes are listed in chart 5.4, although it should be noted that oven (and all appliance) sizes vary according to the manufacturer.

Few modern kitchens are planned without microwave ovens; three locations are the general rule: on the counter, suspended under the upper cabinets, or built into the wall. Microwaves are the least attractive placed on a counter; suspended types are smaller microwave units, and built-in units are often combined with a conventional oven (these should be able to slide out for repair). Ovens that are both microwave and conventional or convection are also available. Self-cleaning or continuous self-cleaning options are also worth considering in new ovens. (Toaster ovens are discussed under portable appliances.) Ovens and ranges or cooking tops can be located together or separately. The convection oven can be placed by itself in a wall away from the microwave, which may be in a quick-cooking center. Ample counter space on each side of a range is sound kitchen planning, and counter space on at least one side of an oven to place food before and after cooking while opening the door is also very important to avoid spills and burns.

Dishwashers

Most dishwashers are built-in units that slide under the countertop or cabinet top.

Portable dishwashers are rolled to the sink and attached to the faucet and drain there after meals. Dishwashers today have cycle length and energy-saving options as well as various color and finish options. A special frame can hold wood or laminate to match the kitchen cabinets. The dishwasher should be located just to the left or to the right of the sink and next to the storage area for tableware.

Garbage Disposal

The garbage disposal is a standard appliance in one side of the sink or in the center of a three-compartment sink.

Trash Compactor

Trash compactors are appliances that compress garbage and thereby eliminate frequent trips to an outside garbage can. Trash compactors are located next to the sink or virtually any place in the kitchen. For those who do not desire a trash compactor, the same space can contain a garbage container that slides or swings out.

Sinks

Many styles of sinks are available today in a variety of contemporary colors. Porcelain and stainless steel are the two most popular materials for sinks. Double sinks are common, and sinks with a third, central compartment for a garbage disposal is not uncommon. Sinks may have different-sized compartments and different depths. Smaller sinks for rinsing vegetables or alternate cleanup areas are a nice addition.

Portable Appliances

There are two major categories of portable appliances: **appliances for food preparation** and **food-cooking appliances.** The number of choices is increasing every year. When planning a kitchen, it is wise to make a list of the appliances to be used and to prioritize their location—the most frequently used will need to be most accessible, perhaps even on the countertop or cabinet top. To accommodate convenience and eliminate clutter, plan for appliance cubbyholes or compartments on the counter. An important fact to remember is that portable appliances will only be used if they are convenient and accessible. If it is necessary to move bulky items out of the way and reach to the back of low or high cabinets for an appliance, it will seldom be used.

Portable Appliances for Food Preparation: Blender, food processor, cabinet-top mixers, hand mixer, food mills, chopper/grinder, can opener, electric knife, knife sharpener, food slicer, pasta maker, dough roller, drink mixer, coffee grinder, juicer, plastic bag sealer, ice cream maker, weight scale, food dehydrator.

Portable Food-Cooking Appliances: Microwave oven, toaster, toaster oven, coffee maker, rice cooker, crock pot, electric skillet/grill, waffle iron, popcorn popper, electric wok, warming trays, hot plates/portable range, yogurt maker, deep fryer.

quently used items. Counter space for folding clothes and a closet for hanging permanent press clothing are important. The laundry room most often contains an ironing board, perhaps the built-in variety, which is excellent for saving space and keeping iron and board accessible and orderly. Drawers or cabinets for clothes to be ironed or mended and supplies for mending are good. Sewing rooms are favorite combinations with laundry facilities because the ironing board is necessary for laundry and sewing and because mending often takes place before or after laundering clothes. Sewing cabinetry can contain work surfaces that fold or slide behind doors, keeping the clutter out of sight when sewing is not being done. The laundry room may also double with a mudroom and may contain closets or "lockers" for coats, winter gear, or sports equipment according to the season. The laundry/utility room may hold a food freezer, and the cabinetry may be organized for tools such as hammers and nails or perhaps paint supplies. It could double as a storage room for bulky cooking appliances if the laundry room is located near the kitchen.

There are five options of laundry location in space planning a home. The first, and most typical, is to locate the laundry near the kitchen. Some smaller homes have the washer and dryer in the kitchen itself, although ideally, the laundry needs to be in a place where clothes sorting can take place and where the door can be closed on the mess if necessary. Placing it near the kitchen is convenient since much of the daily household work revolves around the kitchen and only a few steps are needed to tend to the laundry in progess.

A second location is in a basement. This location will keep the noise and clutter off the main floor but will necessitate climbing stairs with loads of dirty and clean laundry.

The third location is in the bedroom wing, next to the family bathroom. This location is popular in larger two-story homes and eliminates carrying laundry up and down stairs. In two-story homes where the laundry is on the main floor, careful planning can locate the laundry beneath at least one bathroom and over a clothes drop, which could empty into a cabinet above the washer and dryer. It is also possible to install two or three clothes drops so that sorting takes place as clothes are being dropped: one for whites, one for dark colors and jeans, and one for bright or light colors. This concept can be extended with the idea of drawers or baskets belonging to each family member. As clothes are folded,

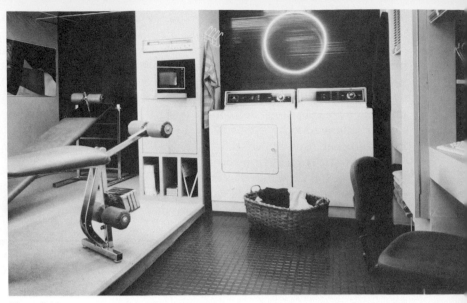

Figure 5.14

Chart 5.4   Standard Sizes of Fixtures and Cabinet Work

Item	Width/Length	Height	Depth	Special
Kitchen counter	as needed	36"	20-35"	28" high (handicap)
Refrigerator	28-36	5'-6'	2'6"	34"-36" high
Dishwasher	24"	34"	24"	
Range	30"-36"	36"	24"	
Oven	24"-30"	24"-30"	26"	two units make "double-oven" size
Washer	30"	36"	30"	
Dryer	30"	36"	30"	
Bathroom Counter	as needed	30"-34"	20"	28" high (wheelchair handicap)
Toilet	15" (seat)	28-30" (tank)	26"	
Regular Bathtub	5'0"	16"	2'8"	
Oversize Bathtub	6'-7'8"	to 24"	3'0"-4'0"	
Spa (sauna/steam room)	6'	8'	8'	8' wide X 16' long
Interior Door	2'6"-3'0"	6'8"	1 3/8"	
Exterior Door	3'0"	6'8"	1 3/8" (Wider as needed)	
Ceiling	-	-	8'0" (Higher as desired)	

they are put into the drawer and that individual is responsible to take the clothes and put them away.

A fourth location is in a hallway, which is not good planning since the clothes have to be sorted in the hall and a mess is created in the traffic pattern. The bathroom may also be a place for the laundry in smaller homes, which theoretically might be a good location since soiled clothing is often taken off there at bath time. Some conflict could easily arise between functions and users, however. Lack of space for laundry activities may also be a disadvantage.

Figure 5.14 One creative solution to laundry room design makes the laundry do double duty, as in this laundry/exercise/computer/sewing room. Note the built-in television and stereo component system with storage beneath. The fluorescent light behind the washer and dryer is art lighting. The flooring is quiet, resilient rubber. Appliances by and photo courtesy of the Maytag Company.

Figure 5.15

Planning for
Independent Living

Independent living refers to the physically handicapped and aged who could live at home rather than at rest homes if modifications were made at home. Those in wheelchairs, particularly, require modified spaces and dimensions. Halls should be a minimum of three feet to accommodate one wheelchair, sixty inches (five feet) for passage of two wheelchairs. A width of six feet is required for pivot-turning a wheelchair, a space required at the end of hallways and in bedrooms, bathrooms, work zones, and social zones. A change of floors, such as a step-down, is unthinkable when planning for the handicapped or aged, and a plane change is accomplished with ramps. The slope must not exceed a one-foot rise for every twelve feet of ramp, expressed in the ratio 1:12. (This, of course, will vary according to state building codes.) Slight change of flooring material (such as carpet to hard floor) should not exceed one-half inch, which would be an impediment for the wheelchair.

Countertops should be lowered to around thirty inches, and the under-the-counter area normally used for storage should be left free for the wheelchair to slide close and allow the person to work at the counter. Storage must also be lower, as the reach of a person in a wheelchair usually does not exceed forty-eight inches high. Light switches need to be lowered, and electric outlets need to be raised for independent living.

Figure 5.15 Louvered doors provide ventilation and conceal this compact arrangement of planning desk and stacking washer and dryer. The single touch-control microprocessor controls both the washer and dryer. The unit will fit in a space roughly half that needed for a conventional side-by-side washer and dryer pair. Many new space-saving laundry appliances feature full-capacity load sizes. Photo courtesy of the Maytag Company.

Emotion and Psychology

Spaces that are planned to be emotionally appealing, beautiful, or satisfying can accomplish specific goals of the interior. This appeal can be accomplished by the shape, size, and scale of the interior or with the use of materials, colors, and textures. It can also be accomplished to an extent with furnishings. Furniture arrangement as it relates to space manipulation is discussed in chapter 6.

This element of psychological or emotional appeal is so important that it cannot be ignored in planning space. It puts people into the picture, and it is the human touch that makes architecture and interior design meaningful.

The client profile, discussed in chapter 1, will form the basis for the architect and designer to make space-planning decisions that will be satisfactory to the user. The homeowner should never feel shy or insecure in expressing personal preferences concerning the size, shape, and layout of the rooms being commissioned to the architect or designer to create. In fact, the person who does not assert his or her needs for emotional satisfaction through the space planning may experience years of unnecessary frustration because those needs were not made known. The psychology of space was discussed in more detail in chapter 2, Design Principles and Elements.

Space Planning and
the Principles and
Elements of Design

Effective space planning incorporates careful consideration of the *principles* and *elements of design* (discussed in chapter 2) in order to create interiors that are pleasing and effective. And since people are the most important ingredient of the space, the *proportion* and *scale* in particular should always be judged according to that of the human body. With this in mind, the space can be planned to fit the purpose. A very large or grand scale, seen in places such as cathedrals, turn-of-the century banks, or open atrium areas of hotels, are awesome compared to the human scale. But in these places, that overwhelming feeling serves a purpose—to give a different perspective or alternative to viewing space. The perspective may create a feeling of reverence, awe, contemplation, or simply relief from closed, small-scale quarters. However, the overall size or scale of the space best relates to the human frame in most interiors. Chart 5.5 indicates typical sizes for living areas in homes that have proven their effectiveness in relating to the human scale.

Other design principles and elements are readily applied in the space-planning process. Scale, proportion, balance, rhythm, emphasis, and harmony (the principles of design) are sought in order to make space functional and pleasing for many years to come. These aspects of function and pleasantness in space planning are accomplished through the manipulation of the elements of design—the delineation of space with shape or form through mass, line, pattern, texture, light, and color.

Types of Floor Plan Drawings

There are two ways to obtain a set of blueprints for a floor plan: one is to have the plan custom drawn, and the other is to purchase a set of plans that has been mass-produced, called a stock plan. It is possible to make minor changes to a stock plan in order to customize it, and when the changes become structural or major, it usually becomes necessary to have it custom drawn, which will then cost several hundred dollars more or about the same as a custom floor plan. The specifics for each type of plan are discussed in the following paragraphs.

Custom Floor Plans

Custom floor plans are produced by an architect or designer, tailored to fit the needs of a particular site and client. Although a custom floor plan is costly and requires some time and effort, it is the best way to get exactly what you want in a home. The danger is that when a home has many features custom designed for a particular person or lifestyle, it may be difficult to resell the home if the need arises.

Stock Plans

Stock plans, as seen in floor plan magazines, have been mass-produced by architects or draftsmen and are usually obtained by mail order at a considerably lower cost than custom floor plans. An advantage is that if another home from the same plan has already been built in the vicinity it may be possible to walk through it for evaluation. Small alterations are possible to slightly customize the plan. Exterior building materials can also be varied in most cases. Disadvantages lie in the fact that a stock plan may be somewhat common and it may be difficult to find a plan that will exactly suit the program.

Floor Plans and Housing

Floor Plan Types

There are three types of floor plans: *open, closed, and combination.* A *closed floor plan* is one where most or all of the rooms are units that are opened to others only by a door, and when the door is shut, the room is completely enclosed. This gives privacy and control over sound, yet often it creates a chopped-up floor plan without flexibility.

An *open floor plan* has several areas that are open to each other without walls or with only partial walls or dividers. The cost to build may be less, and the space seems much larger than with a closed plan. There is flexibility in the use of the space. The disadvantages lie in the lack of privacy that may result and the transmitting of more sound than is desirable. These floor plans may open vertically (high ceilings), horizontally (few walls), or both.

Chart 5.5 Residential Space Planning for the Human Scale

Room/Function	Moderate	Large Size
Entry	35 sq. ft.	over 35 sq. ft.
Hall	3 feet wide	4 feet wide +
Living Room	13 X 15 (195 sq ft)	18 X 30 (540 sq ft)
Kitchen	8 X 12 (96 sq ft)	12 X 16 (192 sq ft)
Great Room	12 X 20 (240 sq ft)	20 X 30 (600 sq ft)
Family Room	13 X 18 (234 sq ft)	15 X 25 (375 sq ft)
Dining Room/Area	10 X 13 (130 sq ft)	13 X 16 (208 sq ft)
Bathroom	5 X 10 (50 sq ft)	10 X 15 (150 sq ft)
Bedroom	10 X 12 (120 sq ft)	15 X 20 (300 sq ft)
Two-Car Garage	22 X 22 (484 sq ft)	25 X 40 (1,000 sq ft)

Combination open and closed plans are types of plans that have both open and closed areas or areas that can be opened to permit a flexible use of the space. This can be accomplished with double doors such as a pair of pocket sliding doors, French doors, or accordion doors and with some areas with high ceilings that open to areas such as lofts or balconies or other living space.

Types of Housing

There are two major categories of residential housing. They are *detached* and *attached dwellings.* Within these two categories are several subcategories. Detached dwellings include the single detached family dwelling and the *mobile home.* The attached dwelling includes high-rise apartments and condominiums, *townhouses,* and *twin houses* or multiplexes. Each subcategory has its merits and is useful for a segment of the population and for particular periods of life development.

The Single Detached Dwelling

The single detached family dwelling—a home with a yard—has long been a part of the American dream. Although it is becoming less common because of rising building costs and less available land, it is still sought after by a large segment of the population. The single detached dwelling is particularly appealing because it has the greatest potential for self-expression in terms of location, style, and landscaping. It also is considered to be an investment in which funds can be retrieved by selling. In some urban areas of this country, and in countries such as Japan, where crowding and land prices are such a strong factor, a detached single family dwelling is an impossible dream.

These dwellings can be prefabricated on an assembly line, designed and built as part of a *planned development* built from stock plans, or custom built. A small home has between eight-hundred and twelve-hundred square feet of living space on one or more levels. A medium-sized home contains twelve-hundred to three-thousand square feet, and a large residence is anything over three-thousand square feet. Houses of any size or type with extra, luxurious features are considered *luxury homes*. These features might include saunas, spas, whirlpools, areas for workout and exercise equipment, greenhouse rooms, gourmet-equipped kitchens, formal dining rooms, built-in entertainment centers, central vacuum systems, stereo/intercom systems, or computerized controls for mechanical systems (lighting, heating, security.) These kinds of features are most often found in *custom design houses* (designed, built, and furnished for a specific user).

The Mobile Home

At one time the mobile home was commonly called a trailer. These were mobile dwellings, not unlike today's camping vehicles that could be pulled behind a car. Today the mobile home is a prefabricated residence assembled in a factory and moved to a *mobile home park,* where it usually becomes a permanent fixture. These parks vary from being cramped and ill-kept, to being spacious, well-groomed, and attractive. The park may even have a clubhouse, pool, or other recreation areas shared by all the occupants of the park. The mobile home is manufactured in twelve- to fifteen-foot widths; a *double-wide* mobile home is manufactured in two sections and assembled on its pad in the mobile home park. These are often as spacious as a small house. *Single-wide* mobile homes are not as large, with small rooms and narrow hallways. Like standard houses, mobile homes are available in a wide range of prices, depending on the number and quality of features. They do, however, tend to be much less expensive than standard houses. Originally intended as temporary and moveable, mobile homes are permanent housing for many people today.

High-rise Dwellings

High-rise buildings are multistoried structures designed to house large numbers of people in a relatively small area. They have been essentially an urban phenomenon, but they now exist in most areas of the country. High-rises have been used extensively for public housing in large cities, although such projects have been mostly unsuccessful because of deterioration, lack of satisfaction, and increases in crime. It may seem ironic that high-rise structures are also the setting for a great deal of luxury housing. Such luxury developments have all the *amenities* of the finest luxury homes, and sometimes as much space. Between these two extremes there are many moderate housing

situations also contained in high-rise structures. The principal disadvantages of high-rise housing are the lack of relationship to natural green space, the inconvenience of elevators and corridors, and problems associated with getting out in an emergency.

Town Houses

Town houses and *row houses* are attached houses generally built as a single development. This type of housing creates private homes in a small amount of space. Town houses do not have large yards but may have roof gardens or small private gardens behind. Row houses from the nineteenth-century were large and luxurious, but in more recent times some of these have been subdivided and broken up into separate apartments or *flats.* Many older town houses became slum dwellings and were destroyed. Fortunately, today, many of those that remain are being revitalized as single homes or multiple dwellings. Traditionally town houses were built in town right on the street, and they shared common walls with their neighbors. Today some town houses are being planned and built with jogs and setbacks so that they only share a portion of a wall with their neighbors. These are called *semidetached houses* and are often located in parklike settings or around golf courses.

Twin Homes and Multiplex Dwellings

Twin homes are double houses designed, like town houses, with common walls between units. They often are planned with the appearance of a single home. This double configuration is also called a *duplex.* Other examples of multiplex dwellings are the *four plex,* with four housing units, and the *eight plex,* with eight units.

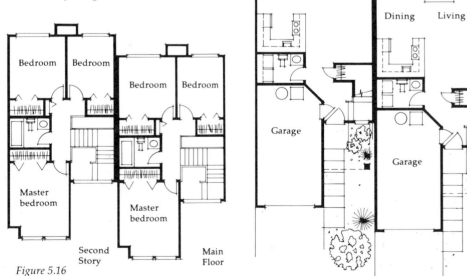

Bedroom Bedroom

Bedroom Bedroom

Master bedroom

Master bedroom

Second Story

Main Floor

Dining Living

Dining Living

Garage

Garage

Figure 5.16

Figure 5.16 A two-story town house, typically used for condominiums or apartments. The main floor houses an open floor plan with living room, dining area, and kitchen, plus a laundry/powder room combination and coat closet. Upstairs are three bedrooms around a common bath.

One (or more) bedroom(s) can be used for hobbies or office space. Note the thickness of the common wall between the town house units for extra insulation and privacy. There are approximately 600 square feet on the main floor and 800 square feet upstairs.

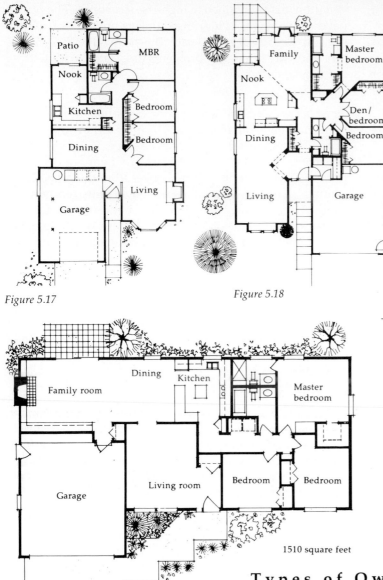

Figure 5.17

Figure 5.18

Figure 5.19

1510 square feet

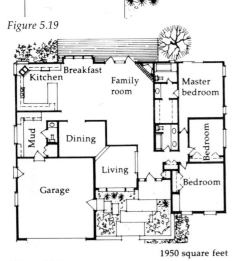

Figure 5.20

1950 square feet

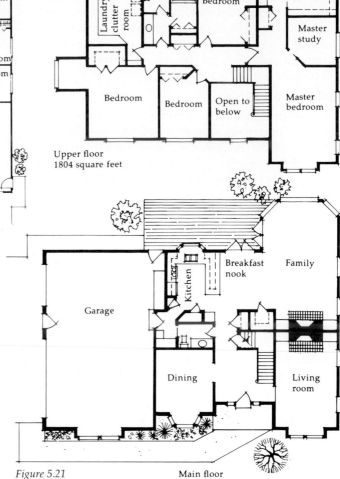

Upper floor
1804 square feet

Figure 5.21

Main floor
1499 square feet

Types of Ownership

Three principle forms of ownership are private, *condominium,* and rental. Each type has advantages and disadvantages for certain groups of people, and for those in different stages of life.

Private Ownership

Like the single detached house, private ownership—owning one's own home—is a part of the American dream that is becoming less and less obtainable. The cost of housing and financing is forcing this goal further out of reach (see chart 5.1). Private ownership brings with it a great deal of responsibility for upkeep, maintenance, security, and care of the house and grounds. For some, this responsi-

bility is an unwanted burden that is eliminated by other forms of ownership.

Condominium

The word condominium comes from Latin and literally means "ownership with." Condominiums are complexes of any type of dwelling, from high-rise to town house, that are owned privately but maintained and governed by groups of owners. These groups form homeowners' associations that provide for general maintenance, security, snow removal, and care of the landscape provided for by the payment of monthly fees. The homeowners' associations establish the rules and restrictions for the condomini-

---

Figure 5.17 A small patio home designed for a narrow building lot. This plan offers living room and dining room; breakfast nook; kitchen with a pass-through to the dining room; three bedrooms; and two baths. Approximately 1,100 square feet.
Figure 5.18 This patio home utilizes a large X-shaped angled approach. The kitchen opens to an informal family room area. The plan offers efficiency and good planning in

the use of limited space—approximately 1,500 square feet.
Figure 5.19 A rambler is a one-story home that is wide and shallow. This plan offers three bedrooms, formal and informal living, and two baths. The laundry is in the hallway near the bedrooms. The front door must be accessed through the living room. Approximately 1,500 square feet.
Figure 5.20 A moderate-sized rambler offers open planning in a spacious family room adjoining the breakfast area and an

open kitchen as a large great room. From the kitchen to the front door is a considerable distance, yet the mudroom/laundry and garage are very convenient to the kitchen. The bedroom wing is separated from the living areas with the back-to-back bathrooms. Approximately 1,950 square feet.
Figure 5.21 A large, two-story home with a grand two-story entrance flanked by formal living and dining rooms. A spacious family room opens to the breakfast nook and

kitchen. Back-to-back fireplaces share the main chimney with separate flues. Upstairs, three bedrooms surround a compartmented bath and large laundry room. The master suite offers a luxury bath, large walk-in closet, and private study. Approximate sizes: main floor—1,500 square feet; upstairs—1,800 square feet.
Figure 5.22 Sleek modern styling through curves and angles makes this large home unique. Glass block walls and pillars are contemporary luxury features. The formal

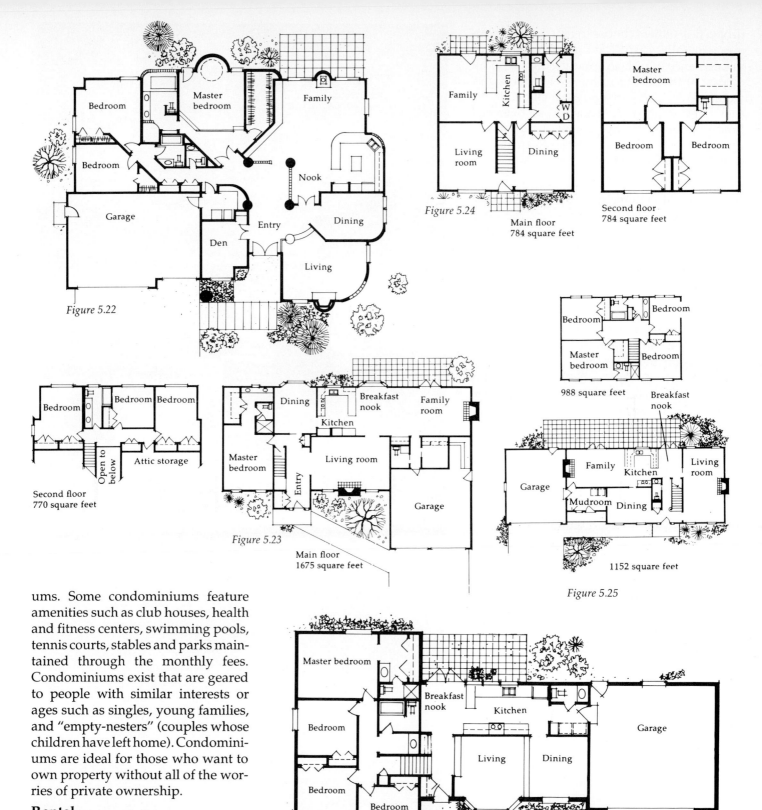

Figure 5.22

Figure 5.24

Main floor
784 square feet

Second floor
784 square feet

Second floor
770 square feet

Figure 5.23

Main floor
1675 square feet

988 square feet

1152 square feet

Figure 5.25

1629 square feet

Figure 5.26

ums. Some condominiums feature amenities such as club houses, health and fitness centers, swimming pools, tennis courts, stables and parks maintained through the monthly fees. Condominiums exist that are geared to people with similar interests or ages such as singles, young families, and "empty-nesters" (couples whose children have left home). Condominiums are ideal for those who want to own property without all of the worries of private ownership.

Rental

Those who are unable to afford condominiums or private ownership will usually rent housing from a landlord who owns and maintains the rental

living room and master bedroom have sunken floors. A spacious great room provides entertaining space. Approximately 2,500 square feet (excluding three-car garage).
Figure 5.23 This classic one-and-one-half-story home features a main-floor master bedroom, as well as formal and informal living and dining areas radiating around the kitchen. The laundry and lavatory are between the garage and family room. Upstairs three bedrooms share a bath in the

extended dormer-attic space at the rear of the home. Approximate sizes: main floor—1,675 square feet; upstairs—600 square feet.
Figure 5.24 A simple box forms this traditional two-story home, which could be detached or flanked by other row houses with similar plans. The main floor holds formal living and dining areas, kitchen/family great room, and laundry/mudroom. Upstairs are three bedrooms, including the master bedroom, which share one bath. A

compact, economical plan, since building vertically costs less than building laterally. Approximately 1,000 square feet on each floor.
Figure 5.25 A more spacious two-story home with four bedrooms and two baths upstairs. The laundry is a long walk from the bedrooms and bathrooms yet convenient to main-floor social and work zones. Approximately 1,200 square feet on the main floor and 990 square feet upstairs.

Figure 5.26 A split-level home with living, dining, and laundry on the main floor. Up one-half flight is the bedroom wing, down one-half flight is the family room area. Economical to build, this type of home provides logical zoning. Approximately 1,629 square feet on the main floor and upstairs.

properties. Others choose to rent because renting generally carries no responsibility for maintenance or upkeep, and in some cases all or part of the cost of utilities (electricity, gas, water, sewer, and garbage) are included in the rent. Any type of housing, from detached houses to high-rise apartments to duplexes, can be rented, although costs and quality of rental units vary greatly.

Multilevel Living

In traditional architecture, living space is assigned to predictable living areas: the main floor, the basement, the upstairs or second story, and perhaps a half story (rooms in the attic). The two-story home simplifies zoning; private living is usually upstairs. A small detached home with space on one floor (with or without a basement) is called a *rambler*. Today's architecture includes both these traditional styles, and frequently divides space into multi-level patterns, as well.

An early example still widely used today is the *split-level home,* which consists of up to four levels. This plan allows the feeling of a larger home by zoning on different levels, and the space can be economical to build, as well. Split-levels consist of a ground level that contains the living/dining/kitchen areas; up half a flight of stairs is the bedroom wing; down half a flight from the ground floor is the family room wing; and down yet another half flight (beneath the ground floor) is the basement/storage/extra bedroom area. Another typical multilevel floor plan is the *split-entry home,* which essentially is a home with a raised basement. The entrance directs traffic up half a flight to the living/dining/kitchen/bedroom/bath areas and down half a flight to the family room/bedroom/bath/storage areas.

As the cost of building has skyrocketed during the 1970s and 1980s, architects, interior designers, and builders have come up with ingenious solutions for cramped living by introducing new twists on multilevel living. The great room may be a step-down area; bedrooms or study may be in a loft; partial walls and vaulted ceilings give an impression of not only spaciousness but visual multilevel living space. It should be noted, however, that open areas do not screen out noise from one area to another; a lack of privacy may make this type of plan inappropriate for a household of varied ages of people.

(A)
Figure 5.27

(B)

Figure 5.27 *(A)* Space planning has reached a successful conclusion at the Toscana Ristoranté in New York City. Fluid curved lines carry the eye and foot traffic along to individual tables that radiate from the bar. Different levels are seen in the various soffits and the higher lighted ceiling, showing the architect's ability to utilize not only pleasing square footage arrangements but artistic manipulation of cubic footage space planning as well. Piero Sartogo, architect; photo by Norman McGrath © 1989. *(B)* Space planning in nonresidential interiors, such as this hotel lobby/restaurant area, requires creative solutions. There is often a need to physically divide areas without obstructing the visual expanse or cutting the area into small rooms. Here the answer was found in low, partial walls that allow the eye to enjoy the artistic surroundings and to be tempted by the fine dining experience. Photo by John Wang.

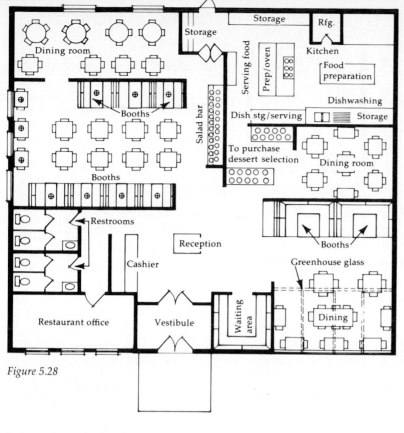

Figure 5.28

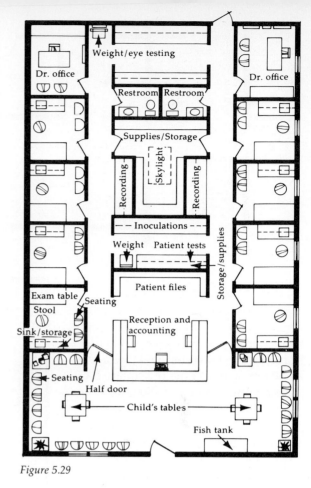

Figure 5.29

Nonresidential Considerations

The discipline of space planning nonresidential spaces is far more complex than planning residential spaces. Each area—medical facilities, hospitality, business and office space, retail space, and production plants—has highly complex and specialized considerations, often based on local or state building codes. As such, an evaluation of all nonresidential space is beyond the scope of this book. However, as most of us have opportunities to visit many or all of these spaces, it is possible to evaluate what we see as it pertains to space planning.

To this end, the following information is an extension of the space-planning principles discussed in this chapter; most of the information that applies to homes can, in some form or another, also apply to many nonresidential interiors. All of these are examples and not intended to be comprehensive considerations.

Function and Zoning

Although the exact arrangement and design of spaces may vary, there still exists a certain standard of space relationships in nonresidential design. This standard is seen in places such as restaurants, medical offices, and department stores.

In restaurants the specific spaces must be arranged in a logical interrelationship where the reception/waiting/payment zone or area is adjacent to the dining zones, and the serving zone overlaps the food preparation (kitchen) and storage zones.

In medical offices, the waiting rooms and reception areas must be situated so that they flow conveniently to one another and can easily be identified by the patient. Further, these areas must be conveniently located to the examination rooms, rest rooms, and payment area.

In department stores the planning of space creates the departments that carry a certain type of goods, from sports gear to clothing to children's toys, and placed by similar goods. Apparel (clothing) is customarily located near the jewelry and accessories; bath and bedding linens may be located near the sundries such as personal and health care items (shampoo and lotion). Space planning also includes designing the right size, color, and placement of *graphics* or signage that direct customers to each department. These departments must interrelate with stockrooms, dressing rooms, managerial offices, service counters, and cashier stations.

Figure 5.28 Restaurant space planning. Reception, waiting, and cashier areas are at the center; dining rooms extend outward. Kitchen is at the rear, with serving access to dining areas well planned.

Figure 5.29 Space planning for a pediatrics clinic. Examination rooms for two doctors are symmetrically placed with the central support core, reception, files, and secretarial help shared.

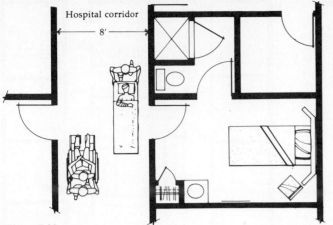

Figure 5.30

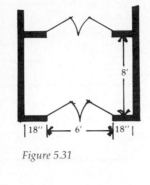

Figure 5.31

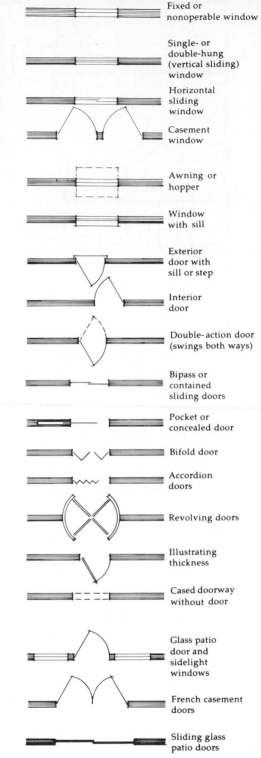

Fixed or nonoperable window

Single- or double-hung (vertical sliding) window

Horizontal sliding window

Casement window

Awning or hopper

Window with sill

Exterior door with sill or step

Interior door

Double-action door (swings both ways)

Bipass or contained sliding doors

Pocket or concealed door

Bifold door

Accordion doors

Revolving doors

Illustrating thickness

Cased doorway without door

Glass patio door and sidelight windows

French casement doors

Sliding glass patio doors

Figure 5.33

Cubic and Square Footage

In nonresidential spaces, the allotment of square feet may rely on the functions to be performed. In a business office the number of workstations may determine the square footage for one part of the office; the reception area, conference room, executive offices, library, lounge or kitchen, rest rooms, and storage are all areas that will demand specific allotments of square footage.

Traffic Patterns

The greater the volume of people or objects, the wider the traffic pattern or *corridors* will need to be. This is evident in public architecture such as hospitals and shopping centers where the traffic is heavy and corridors are wide. Local building codes must be met for corridor widths in nonresidential buildings.

Two separate sets of doors are often employed in nonresidential settings as air-lock entries, or vestibules, to keep out excess cold air, rain, and snow. The vestibule area should be sizable so that foot traffic will not pile up and there is room for shelter.

Traffic patterns in nonresidential settings such as department or specialty stores can be quite complex, and architects use visible markers or guideposts to aid the occupant.

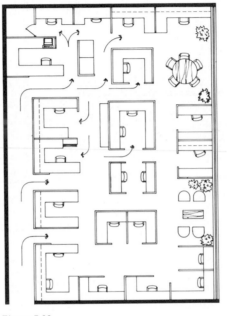

Figure 5.32

People entering nonresidential spaces need to know three things in order for traffic to flow smoothly:

1. how to get in,
2. how to find their way around, and
3. how to get out.

Some spaces do this quite effectively. For example, in a well-planned grocery store or supermarket, the buyer must be able to find grocery carts near the entrance, find items by looking up at the bright wall signs and

---

Figure 5.30 Extra wide corridors are needed in hospitals for dual passage of professionals, patients, and equipment. Private room has one bed, the life support panel anchored around the bed, and the sink and closet in the room. Bath contains a toilet (water closet) and shower and is back-to-back with the next room's bath.

Figure 5.31 Double doors forming a vestibule, or air-lock entry, help keep cold and heat out of nonresidential buildings and in homes where energy consciousness is paramount.

Figure 5.32 Open office planning divides the large area into efficient cubicle stations with excellent traffic flow. The partitions are approximately six feet high and give privacy and acoustic control without boxing in the employees to an uncomfortable extent. In this plan, how else could the stations have been arranged? What nonresidential spaces have you seen that have employed open office planning?

Figure 5.33 Architectural space-planning symbols.

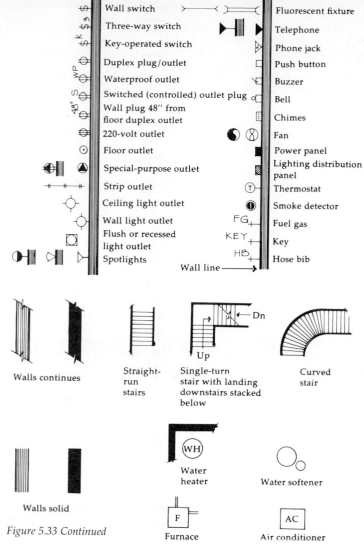

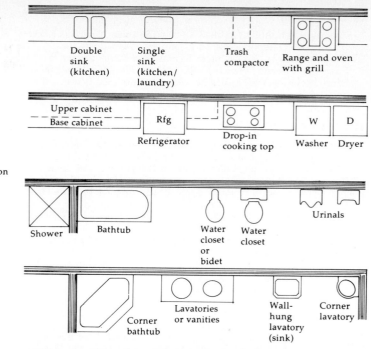

Figure 5.33 Continued

the smaller hanging signs over spacious aisles, then easily find the checkout counter with easy egress to the doors and onto the street or parking lot.

Open office planning is another example of multiuse space. Where several functions take place in one area, the furnishings or planning systems can be the delineators of space. A freestanding wall partition, desk, computer terminal desk, filing system, and shelves can be moved to accommodate changing needs, providing flexibility in the utilization of office space. Further, fewer structural walls allow for easier traffic flow, and the removal of visual obstructions makes spaces seem larger.

Space Planning for the Handicapped

State and local laws and building codes have made building *ingress* and *egress* (entrance and exit) accessible to occu-

pants of wheelchairs through ramps, automated door openers, extra wide doors, and elevators. In public rest rooms, there is generally a stall for those in wheelchairs.[2]

Psychology of Nonresidential Spaces

Space planning takes into account the effect of the space on the emotions of the people who occupy the space. Where small, closed, crowded spaces can cause people frustration and even claustrophobia, large spaces can give a feeling of insecurity (see Space in chapter 2). Further, when people enter a building and cannot find their way around or to the exit, a feeling of panic, confusion, or fear may result.

Floor Plan Symbols

Floor plan symbols are illustrated in figure 5.33.

- Exterior Walls
- Interior Walls
- Windows
- Swinging door (one way)
- Swinging door (two ways)
- Bifold doors
- Sliding closet doors
- Pocket door (sliding into wall)
- Stairs
- Stairs continue
- UP
- DN
- Sink
- Closet
- Cupboards and counter top (low)
- Cupboards above
- Washer and Dryer (W/D)

- Toilet/toilet stall
- Urinal
- Bathtub
- Vanity
- Free-standing sink
- Wall-mounted lavatory sink
- Water heater (WH)
- Water Softener (WS)
- Furnace (F)
- Air Conditioner/Cooling Unit (AC)
- Ceiling light
- Track lighting
- Light switch and connecting wiring to light (one-way)
- Various switches and outlets
- Schedule symbols for specifying doors and windows

Notes

1. Cheever, Ellen, ASID, Certified Kitchen Designer. *"Trends in Kitchen Design"* (ASID Report. New York, January, 1988.), pp. 8–10.
2. Johnson, Einar H., Jr., Architect. *Planning and Design Criteria to Prevent Architectural Barriers for the Aged and Physically Handicapped,* Fourth Revision. (Salt Lake City: Utah State Building Board, n.d.), pp. 31–37.

Bibliography

American National Standard, *Specifications for Making Buildings and Facilities Accessible to and Usable by Physically Handicapped People.* New York: American National Standards Institute, 1980. Available from ANSI, 1430 Broadway, New York, New York, 10018

Bennet, Corwin. *Spaces for People.* Englewood Cliffs, NJ: Prentice-Hall, Inc., 1977.

Curran, June. *Drawing Home Plans.* New York: McGraw-Hill, 1979.

Davern, Jeanne M. *Places for People: Hotels, Motels, Restaurants, Bars, Clubs, Community Recreation Facilities, Camps, Parks, Plazas, and Playgrounds.* New York: McGraw-Hill, 1976.

Deasy, C. M., FAIA. *Designing Places for People: A Handbook on Human Behavior for Architects, Designers, and Facility Managers.* New York: Whitney Library of Design, 1985.

Diffrient, Niels. *Human Scale 1/2/3.* Cambridge, MA: MIT Press, 1974.

Faulkner, Ray, LuAnn Nissen, and Sarah Faulkner. *Inside Today's Home.* New York: Holt, Rinehart, and Winston, 1986.

Friedman, Arnold, John F. Pile, and Forrest Wilson. *Interior Design: An Introduction to Architectural Interiors.* New York: American Elsevier Co., Inc., 1982.

Hall, Edward T. *Hidden Dimension.* Garden City: Doubleday & Co. Inc., 1966.

Hanks, Kurt, Larry Belliston, and Dave Edwards. *Design Yourself!* Los Altos: William Kaufmann, Inc., 1977.

Harkness, S., and J. Groom. *Building without Barriers for the Disabled.* New York: Whitney Library of Design, 1976.

Information Design, Inc. *Notes on Interior Design.* Los Altos: William Kauffman, Inc., 1981.

Johnson, Einar H., Jr., Architect. *Planning and Design Criteria to Prevent Architectural Barriers for the Aged and Physically Handicapped.* Fourth Revision. Salt Lake City: Utah State Building Board, n.d.

Klaber, Eugene Henry. *Housing Design.* New York: Reinhold Publishing Company, 1954.

Packard, Robert T., AIA. *Architectural Graphic Standards.* 7th ed. New York: John Wiley and Sons, 1981.

Panero, Julius. *Anatomy for Interior Designers.* 3rd ed. New York: Whitney Library of Design, 1962.

Panero, Juluis, and Martin Zelnik. *Human Dimensions and Interior Space.* New York: Whitney Library of Design, Watson-Guptill, 1979.

Pile, John F. *Open Office Planning: A Handbook for Interior Designers and Architects.* New York: John Wiley and Sons, Inc., 1978.

Pratt Institute. *An Investigation of the Small House.* New York: Pratt Institute of Architecture, n.d.

Ramsey, Charles George, and Harold Reeve Sleeper. *Architectural Graphic Standards.* 7th ed. New York: John Wiley and Sons, Inc., 1979.

Reznikoff, S.C. *Interior Graphic and Design Standards.* New York: Whitney Library of Design, 1986.

Wakita, Dr. Osamu A., and Richard M. Linde. *The Professional Practice of Architectural Working Drawings.* New York: John Wiley and Sons, 1984.

FURNITURE
ARRANGEMENT

When architect Myron Goldfinger and his interior designer-wife June moved into their dream house eighteen years ago, they created custom living spaces out of standard-shaped rooms through artful arranging of furniture and built-ins. Each of the living spaces measures fifteen feet by fifteen feet. Towering canted ceilings with dramatic windows add a sense of spaciousness, but it is artful furniture placement that customizes the space to fulfill a variety of domestic needs.

The dining room, on this page, faces onto an atrium/family room, but a mirrored interior wall affords a sense of internal spaciousness. Diagonal placement of a square table offers excellent access to all chairs while creating a natural circulation pattern. A custom-built half-circle breakfront offers easy storage, as well as a site for one of the Goldfingers' many groups of collectibles. Photo by Ted Spiegel.

Page 134, top left: First and foremost, a home is an environment for highly personalized living needs. Thira Goldfinger, the family's oldest daughter, enjoys a study space slightly separated from her bedroom area, with a large corkboard for memorabilia and a study desk (resting on a set of wide drawers) for her computer. The room divider is created with a bookcase, which has an instant cleanup door. Page 134, bottom: The bed itself is queen size, as much a living space as a sleeping space. Sliding drawers beneath hold bedclothes; the headboard is backed up by her dresser drawers, accessible from the room's perimeter. An exercise bike for active moments and an antique school desk for clear-space reading and sorting of school papers are placed by the room wall. Page 135: In the entrance hall sporting equipment used by Thira and her sister Djerba are immediately at hand, with professional cooking rack modules forming both storage and display space for their active sports life: Access for use is the key to these arrangements. Photos by Ted Spiegel.

Page 136, top: The architectural sense of space determines both furniture arrangement and selection. In the formal living room, on a lower level adjacent to the dining room, a conversational arrangement encourages the continuation of dinner companionship. *Page 136, bottom:* The informal atrium/family room, which joins the parent's wing to the two three-story towers containing common family space and the children's bedrooms, utilizes wicker furniture and overstuffed pillows—a perfect reflection of the scale of the room as well as its function as family-time space and a get-away-from-it-all media center. Photos by Ted Spiegel. *Page 137, top left:* June Goldfinger's office in the home harbors a collection of models of husband Myron's ultramodern commissions, many of which she decorates with her particular understanding of the flexibility of modern architectural space. The loft above her office affords her an escape from the day's demands and access to a treetop forest view. *Page 137, top right and bottom:* Utility dominates these three spaces. The kitchen module places the sink in the same unit as the breakfast counter. Wall units containing, respectively, refrigerator, food storage, cooking appliances, and dish storage surround the cook. Immediately adjacent is an all-purpose space, its walls festooned with gourmet cookware, its broad countertop as handy for buffet service as it is for Myron's electric train set. Formica laminate on the drawers beneath the counter makes for easy maintenance. Photos by Ted Spiegel.

Function

Function is the use an environment will have and the activities that will take place there. In chapter 1, The Process of Design, the term *life-style* was introduced. Life-style describes the way an individual or group lives and functions in an interior. Examining a life-style will help establish a list of functions for a space. Function will then dictate the selection and the arrangement of furniture. For example, a living room could be used to accommodate conversation, a library, musical instruments, a stereo, a television, video equipment, slides or movies, games, reading, resting, napping, formal or informal dining, writing letters, paying bills, growing plants, displaying art, or any combination of these or other functions. The arrangement of furniture should be planned to accommodate the appropriate activities in the amount of space available. If the primary use of the living room is conversation, then it is logical that the comfortable seating pieces should be placed in groupings that facilitate communication and maximize interaction between users. If the main function of the room is television viewing, the sofas and chairs should be arranged to face the screen. Reading will require the placement of lamps near seating pieces to avoid the eyestrain caused by inadequate lighting.

Figure 6.1

Page 138: *The exterior of Myron and June Goldfinger's New York home reveals vertical wood siding, integrating the home with its wooded site. The house is based on a fifteen foot by fifteen foot module—a series of fifteen foot square cubes (rooms) stacked and laid out side by side. The furniture arrangement for each room must be pleasing and fit well into this conformity. Photo by Ted Spiegel.*

Figure 6.1 The furniture in this library supports many functions such as research, writing, or studying at the desk and table; conversing or playing games; taking light refreshment with guests at the table; or enjoying the companionship of a good book near the warmth and reflective aura of the fireplace. Photo courtesy of Bielecky, Inc.

Combining Functions

Often, functions will have a strong relationship to each other. For example, the conversation area previously mentioned might also accommodate informal *buffet-style dining*, and the way those two activities interface should be considered. Tables should be arranged close enough to seating for easy placement of drinks or plates, and a serving table should be conveniently located near the seating area. Tables used with seating pieces should be approximately the same height as the arm of the seating piece so that food or drink can be reached without bending over the arm.

The combination of functions is an absolute necessity in small homes or apartments. Such spaces must often include both a dining table and comfortable seating in the same room. Some creative planning will not only solve the problem but will create a solution with a great deal of functional and aesthetic appeal. One such solution might include moving the sofa to the center of the room. A drop-leaf table could then be placed behind the sofa to provide dining space for one or two people. With the table pulled away from the sofa or with one leaf extended even more diners could be accommodated. When not being used for dining, the drop-leaf table could double as a sofa table.

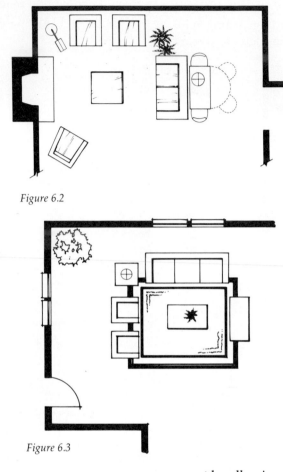

Figure 6.2

Figure 6.3

The consideration of function extends to every area of the home. A bedroom will naturally be used for sleeping, but it might also serve for dressing, conversation, a studio, a study, an office, a computer, a stereo, a library, an art gallery, a sewing room, and a number of other functions each requiring appropriate arrangement of the furniture. For example, if reading in bed is important, then a table must be placed close enough to the bedside to reach books, and the table should accommodate a lamp, or some other form of adequate lighting should be provided. Another very simple function that often takes place in a bedroom is putting on shoes and stockings. Something as obvious as a small chair or *ottoman* appropriately placed in or near the dressing area can make this simple task much more pleasant. Such considerations, though they may seem insignificant, can make life run much more smoothly.

Mechanical Functions

It is also important that furniture arrangement be planned so that furniture pieces do not interfere with the mechanical functions of an interior. Heating vents and *cold air returns* should not be covered by furniture. Blocking them causes the heating, ventilation, and air-conditioning systems to function much less efficiently. Doors should be able to swing and open freely without interference from furniture pieces, and furniture placement should not hinder the opening and closing of windows.

Furniture designed to hold lamps or telephones should be placed near electric outlets and phone hookups for convenience and safety and to prevent tripping over cords. Unless they are custom designed and carefully planned from the beginning, most residences do not offer the kind of flexibility that allows an electric outlet in the middle of the floor. Consequently, furniture groupings will have to be "anchored" to a wall where there are electric and phone connections. Careful planning before construction or during remodeling might include floor plugs for greater flexibility in arranging furniture.

Circulation

Furniture arrangement needs to accommodate free movement or *circulation* from one space to another. Furniture should be placed to enhance that movement by allowing *traffic* to flow or by restricting and redirecting the traffic when necessary. This kind of control provides the best utilization of space because it eliminates unnecessary traffic patterns. Free circulation requires specific amounts of space. These requirements are discussed later in this chapter under Human Factors.

Interiors have natural *traffic patterns*. These patterns can easily be seen by drawing lines on a floor plan with a pencil. The lines represent where we would walk to get from one space to another. It is as if the pencil represents us and traces our path as we walk through the plan. The beginning point of the line is where we enter the space. The path we might follow to leave the space or walk to a particular area within the space is the *natural traffic pattern*. The complexity and lack of organization in the completed pattern usually shows quite clearly the need to control traffic.

Figure 6.2 This drawing shows a plan with dining and seating combined.

Figure 6.3 This kind of a "floating" arrangement requires a floor plug so that electrical cords will not be a hazard.

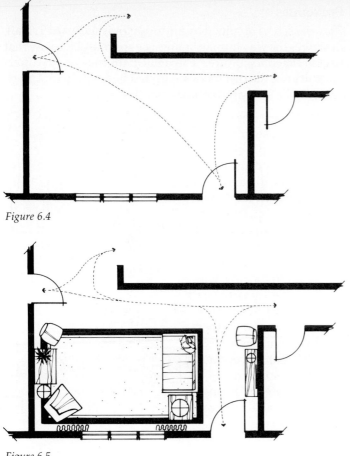

Figure 6.4

(A)
Figure 6.6

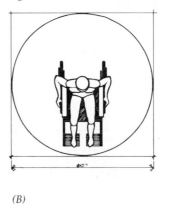

(B)

We can control the flow of traffic by placing furniture at key locations so that it forces traffic to flow away from areas that should be used for seating and conversation or other functions where traffic might be disruptive. These locations can be determined by preparing a corrected plan indicating where the traffic should flow. Laying the corrected plan over the natural traffic plan will show where furniture should be placed to control the flow; for example, many homes have no entries—the front door opens directly into the living area. In this kind of plan, a sofa or other large piece of furniture could be used to divide the seating area from the door area and establish a visual entry that redirects traffic behind the seating area instead of through it. Such placement avoids cutting the room in half with an unnecessary traffic pattern. A well-placed piece of furniture can be a simple deterrent to misdirected traffic.

Human Factors

Anthropometry and Barrier-Free Planning

Anthropometrics, the dimensions of the human form, are an important consideration in arranging furniture because human dimensions must be the standard of measure for interior design. Furniture arrangement must accommodate

the circulation of the human form, with its individual dimensions, into and through the design. One must also consider those whose conditions make their needs for circulation different from the norm. Those who are confined to wheelchairs and those who use canes, crutches, or walkers have special limitations that must be addressed if they are to be able to move freely in an interior. Today, awareness of people with these types of limitations is high, yet *barrier-free design* of residences is not common. We assume that we will always be free from such limiting conditions, but physical impairments often occur without warning. Some thought as to how a plan might be adapted for barrier-free access could make future adjustments more feasible.

Standard Clearances

Users without physical impairments also require variable amounts of space or *clearance* to circulate comfortably within an environment.[1]

- Major traffic paths should be three feet or wider.
- Minimal clearance for traffic is one foot six inches.
- Seating pieces used with coffee tables need slightly over one foot of clearance between the table and the front of the seat.

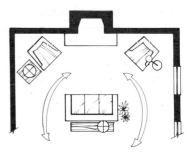

Figure 6.7

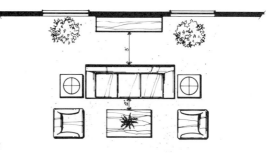

Figure 6.8

Figure 6.4 The natural traffic pattern of this room consumes nearly half of the available space.
Figure 6.5 The arrangement of furniture corrects the problem and makes the flow of traffic more efficient.

Figure 6.6 Dimensions for wheelchairs. *(A)* Hallway clearances must be a minimum of thirty-six inches to forty-two inches. *(B)* A radius of sixty inches is required to turn a wheelchair around.

Figure 6.7 Three feet clearance for circulation.
Figure 6.8 One foot clearance between coffee table and sofa. Three feet are necessary for traffic patterns between furniture pieces.

- For a user to be able to extend his or her legs in front of a seating piece, up to three feet five inches of space is required, depending on the length and the degree of extension of the legs.

- Desks and pianos require a minimum of three feet clearance for chairs, benches, and users.

Figure 6.9

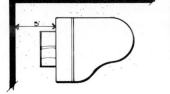

Figure 6.10

- Comfortable dining requires slightly more than two feet of space per user along the perimeter of the table.

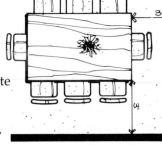

- In order to have room to accommodate a seated diner and space behind for passage and serving, three feet of space should be planned.

Figure 6.11

- Getting in and out of a dining chair requires about one foot six inches of space.

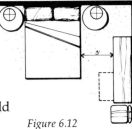

- Three feet is considered good clearance between a bed and dresser.
- Space between two beds should be from two feet six inches to three feet.

Figure 6.12

- Minimal clearance to facilitate bed making is one foot six inches between the bed and the wall.

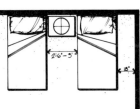

- In a bathroom, a two feet six inches to three feet six inches clearance provides adequate space for most functions.

Figure 6.13

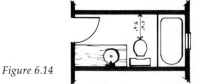

Figure 6.14

Figure 6.9 Three feet to extend legs.
Figure 6.10 Three feet clearance for desk or piano.
Figure 6.11 Two feet of space for each seated person is needed for dining. Three feet of space is needed for serving and clearance at the dining table.

Figure 6.12 Three feet clearance between bed and dresser.
Figure 6.13 Minimum clearance between beds and between bed and wall.
Figure 6.14 Minimum clearance for a bathroom.

Proxemics

Proxemics, a term coined by anthropologist Edward T. Hall, describes the way human beings use space and the way that use is related to culture.[2] Proxemic patterns vary in different cultures; the distances suggested here apply to Americans. Hall's study indentifies four distances.

1. The space from one foot six inches to actual physical contact is considered intimate distance and is reserved for displays of affection, comfort, protection, or physical aggression.

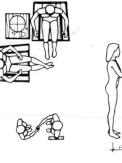

Figure 6.15

2. Personal distance is equal to the invisible "bubble" of space with which we separate ourselves from others. Everyone has a different perception of this space, and many are made uncomfortable by those with smaller bubbles who stand too close and violate *personal space*. In many cultures, particularly those of southern Europe, the Middle East, and South America, the personal space bubble is much smaller; people are customarily seen appropriately touching and even embracing without any feeling of threat or discomfort. Personal distance usually extends from one foot six inches to four feet.

Figure 6.16

The way people normally use furniture is also affected by their perception of personal space; for example, few people choose to sit in the center of a sofa. Most people sit at one end, and most often they prop one arm on the arm rest. In this way, a sofa that can comfortably hold three people is most often occupied by only two people, since no one wants to sit in the middle. Sitting on an eight-foot sofa between two people leaves only about one foot between each person. This comes very close to intimate distance, leaving people who are just friends or, worse yet, merely acquaintances or strangers in the uncomfortable position of being too close. Furthermore, there is no "anchor" in the form of an armrest to cling to for mental protection by retreating into one's personal space bubble.

When forced into close contact, we become uncomfortable because we perceive ourselves as starting with our personal space bubble. Those who use crowded public

Figure 6.15 Intimate distance—one foot six inches to contact.
Figure 6.16 Personal distance—one foot six inches to four feet.

transportation or elevators with strangers have methods of coping with the unnatural intimacy of such situations. Most will become immobile and avoid eye contact. Body contact is avoided, and when touching does occur, the tendency is to recoil quickly. Eyes are kept focused away from others; to help avoid eye contact, some people may keep their eyes fixed on a book or other reading material.

When strangers enter an empty seating space, they tend to take seats at opposite ends, gradually filling the space but leaving a seat between themselves and others. When the only spaces left are next to a stranger, some people will choose to stand or will hesitate before taking a seat. Many would consider a person aggressive who sits next to them when there are still areas of open seating available. Under difficult circumstances such as occasions when airports are filled with grounded travelers, many of these notions of personal space are repressed. In such conditions, strangers may be viewed as colleagues in discomfort and crowding perceived as more tolerable.

3. From four to twelve feet is considered social distance. At the far end of that scale, interaction tends to be more formal, and at the close end, interaction is characterized by greater involvement and less formality.

4. More than twelve feet is called public distance. In public distance there is little personal interaction.

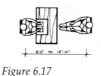
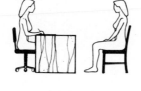

Figure 6.17

Figure 6.18

These distances can be helpful in planning interiors. For example, furniture groupings for conversation should be planned within the four- to twelve-foot bounds of social distance. Maximum distance for conversation is eight feet from the mouth of the speaker to the ear of the listener, to feel neither too close nor too distant.[3]

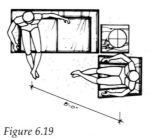

Figure 6.19

Figure 6.17 Social distance—four feet to twelve feet.
Figure 6.18 Public distance—more than twelve feet.
Figure 6.19 Eight feet conversation distance.

Crowding

The effects of *crowding* on animals are well known. In crowded conditions, animals begin to suffer stress, abnormal social behavior, illness, and in some cases, death. Studies of crowding in humans have shown confusing results. Hall cites a study by Frenchman Paul Chombart de Lauwe who discovered that when the subjects of his study had less than eight to ten square meters of space per person in their residences, their social and physical pathology doubled. He also discovered that when the space grew beyond fourteen square meters per person, the problems also increased, though not as dramatically. Hall hastens to note that there is nothing magical about ten to fourteen square meters.[4]

Crowding is not strictly a function of dimensions. It also seems to be closely related to culture, personality, and the desire for involvement with other people. Those of us who enjoy involvement and interaction with others tolerate and, in some cases, even enjoy crowding. We find a crowded, lively environment exciting. Shops, cafés, restaurants, clubs, shopping areas, and markets are areas where one might expect to see planned crowding. The crowded environment should also provide islands of tranquility for those who enjoy less involvement or for those who need to retreat periodically. This type of person may find the *effects of crowding* (sounds, smells, and touch) overstimulating.

In our home environments, some of us enjoy being surrounded by lots of furniture, books, and art objects. Others need more visual or actual space in which to mentally expand. We must be sensitive to these differences in personality and preferences when planning furniture arrangements because the amount of furniture and its placement will affect the way we feel about our homes.

Territoriality

Territoriality is an aspect of proxemics that deals with the need to have a space of our own. This need manifests itself in many ways. For example, you may have noticed that some people select a classroom seat at the beginning of a school term and sit in the same seat each time the class meets. When someone sits in our place, we are annoyed and feel displaced. The same kind of behavior occurs in families where adults and children have determined their places at the table or in the car. Any unauthorized variation from the normal seating pattern may lead to conflict. Those who share bedrooms may find that certain parts of the room or even a certain side of a bed belongs to one person. When it is time to clean or straighten the space, things not belonging to one person may end up in a pile somewhere in the area that is perceived as the other person's territory.

Animals have the same perception of territory as humans. When pets are part of an environment, they establish a place as their own. A cat or dog often owns a favored chair or spot normally reserved for a human. We do the

Figure 6.20

same thing. A study, a bedroom, a kitchen, a workroom, a shop, or even a comfortable chair may become personal territory to a particular person. When someone says, "Get out of my chair," or "Get out of my kitchen," they are stating that this area has become their personal territory. With time, even a tiny work space or cubicle becomes personal territory. Street vendors who use public sidewalks to conduct their business will claim a favorite spot as their personal territory. When someone intrudes, it is as if they have been deprived of their own property. These are the feelings that cause us to build fences and to consider trespassing a crime in most Western cultures.

It is important to understand this need, so that when placing furniture, space will be adequate for each person and shared areas will have space and amenities that give each user a sense of personal territory. It is interesting to note how quickly we personalize our spaces and establish territoriality. This is a natural process, and we should plan for this important human need.

A good look at why we use our furniture the way we do—physically, emotionally, and culturally—will help us arrange the furnishings so that they will most likely be used and appreciated. It should be noted that not only do we design interiors to look beautiful but, even more important, we design interiors so that people will feel good in using them.

The Elements and Principles of Design

Several of the elements and principles of design are directly applicable to the arrangement of furniture. Understanding how these important tools apply to furniture placement leads to attractive and pleasant furniture arrangements (also see chapter 2, Design Principles and Elements).

Balance and Scale

Furniture should be arranged to provide a feeling of balance within the interior. Both balance and scale deal with *visual weight* (how heavy the piece appears to be). Furniture is particularly effective in achieving equal distribution of

Figure 6.20 Territoriality, the establishing of areas or rooms that suggest domain or exclusive ownership, is a paramount psychological benefit in furniture arrangement. Here the master bedroom is clearly a private world, with important pieces of furniture that bespeak not only their purpose but reflect the need for an inner sanctuary for its occupants. Boscobel, a Neoclassic museum mansion in the Hudson River Valley, New York. Photo courtesy of Boscobel.

Figure 6.21

visual weight because
it is available in so
many different sizes,
shapes, materials,
and colors, which
are all factors
that influence
visual weight.
For example,
darker pieces
appear heavier
than lighter pieces;

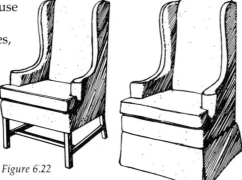

Figure 6.22

bold and large-scale patterns have more visual weight than
subdued or smaller scaled patterns; heavier textures are
visually weightier than smooth textures; and pieces the eye
can penetrate are visually lighter scaled than solid pieces.
For this reason a glass table appears to be lighter scaled than

a solid wood table, and a piece that sits up on legs has a
lighter appearance than a piece that is solid or upholstered
clear to the floor. Following are some guidelines for considering balance and scale in the arrangement of furniture:

- The visual weight or scale of the pieces are more
  important than actual dimensions in creating a well-
  balanced arrangement.
- Furniture can be balanced with other pieces of furniture. For example, two chairs of the same visual
  scale placed across from each other will be visually
  balanced.
- Furniture can also be used to balance *architectural
  elements* in an interior. For example, a sofa or love
  seat could be used opposite a fireplace to create
  balance.

Figure 6.21 This home office/
conversation area has interesting
shapes and angles that illustrate how
both light- and heavy-scaled furniture
can be utilized in different groupings
within the same interior. In the
background, the desk and accompanying chairs have lightly scaled,
Neoclassic-inspired lines. Stools

provide seating yet take small visual
space. In the foreground, the large-
scale and visually heavy sectional
sofa and stepped and carved stone
and Plexiglass accent tables establish
importance in this part of the room.
The commanding black fabric gives
the sectional sofa an even more
imposing look than its actual

dimensions. The selection and
arrangement of artwork and
accessories also balance the two
contrasting areas. In the background,
small, lightly scaled artwork is symmetrically hung, whereas the large
surrealist painting containing
asymmetrical balance within is

appropriate in completing the
visually heavy conversation area.
Photo by Norman McGrath © 1989.
Figure 6.22 These two chairs have
the same dimensions, yet the one with
the upholstery to the floor has heavier
visual weight because the eye does
not penetrate between the legs.

- *Massing* furniture together may create a heavier visual scale in order to achieve balance. For example, a large-scale wing chair does not balance with a small side chair. However, if the side chair is arranged with a table and lamp, the three pieces massed together may balance the heavier wing chair.

- Groupings may be arranged in symmetrical or asymmetrical balance. For example, a pair of matching sofas facing each other in front of a fireplace creates a symmetrical grouping. If one of the sofas were replaced with a pair of chairs, the grouping would be asymmetrical but balanced nonetheless. One form of balance is not better than the other—each type has its own appeal. In a symmetrical grouping when small details such as lamps, tables, or even small occasional seating pieces are varied, the feeling will still be one of symmetry, but the grouping will have the intriguing quality of asymmetry.

- Lighting should also be considered in planning the balance of a furniture arrangement. At night the balance of a room can drastically be altered by lighting. Artificial light will create areas of emphasis that should be balanced along with the furniture. If the lighting is well placed and the levels of light are appropriate, the balance will be maintained.

- The final judgment as to whether balance has been achieved will have to be personal, visual, and intuitive because no device exists for such measurement other than the eye.

Rhythm

The placement of furniture is an exercise in rhythm. One particularly important aspect of rhythm to consider when creating furniture arrangements is rhythm through alternation. Here are some considerations for the use of rhythm by alternation.

- An interior will be more interesting when upholstered and wooden pieces or hard and soft

textures are alternated. A long string of upholstered pieces without contrasting textures of wood or other hard materials to separate and break the flow may feel monotonous.

- The alternation of textures creates contrast, an element that makes any design more pleasing.

- Alternation of rectilinear and curvilinear forms will also make the interior more appealing. The addition of rounded forms in an otherwise rectilinear design softens the impact of the straight lines and lessens any harshness such lines may have implied.

- The same subtle appeal is created when high and low forms are alternated. Particularly when seen in *elevation* (a flat, straight-on view), an arrangement of furniture is more interesting when high and low pieces are mixed in such a way that wall space is broken into interesting shapes and proportions.

- Alternation of high and low pieces away from the walls, in the open space of an environment, helps relieve monotony and can provide interest. In large spaces this principle can be employed to create interest by creating raised and lowered areas that break up the horizontal and vertical space. For example, in a very large living room, a sunken area for conversation or a fireplace is used to create interest, and in a large bedroom, a raised dias (platform) for the bed area will divide the space.

Emphasis

Emphasis deals with the creation of a focal point. A focal point is the object or area where the eye is drawn first. Furniture arrangement is an important factor in creating an area of focus within an interior. The planning of *primary* and *secondary focal points* gives the environment a sense of purpose and subtly involves and stimulates the senses as the eye moves from one area of emphasis to another. Fireplaces, windows, and other architectural features are natural focal points that draw

Figure 6.23

(A)
Figure 6.24

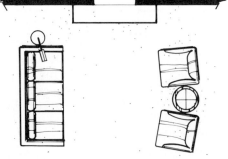

(B)

Figure 6.23 The pieces on the right are massed to create equal visual weight with the piece on the left.

Figure 6.24 Two arrangements showing symmetrical and asymmetrical arrangements. (A) Two sofas facing each other create symmetrical balance. (B) The sofa is asymmetrically balanced with two chairs.

Figure 6.25 Sometimes the success of a furniture arrangement is found in its empty spaces as much as its filled ones. Here the unused, or negative, space is crucial to set off the positive forms—an unusually angled but highly successful arrangement. The repetition of cylinders as artistic sculpture, together with the

the eye naturally. Following are some guidelines for creating emphasis:

- In rooms with natural focal points, furniture can be placed to emphasize and take advantage of them. A grouping around a window or fireplace will emphasize the fine natural features of the room.
- In rooms that lack natural focal points, furniture can be placed to create groupings that take their place. For example, a case piece such as a chest or secretary could be placed against a wall with a pair of sofas placed facing each other at right angles to the case piece. The seating area would then be focused on the case piece.
- Most rooms will have just one primary focal area and other secondary or minor focal areas. In a standard-sized living room, the area around the fireplace could be the primary focal area, and the secondary focal points could be a desk with a chair and a lamp, a console table with a painting or mirror and a lamp, or a comfortable chair with a table and lamp for reading tucked into a corner away from the primary grouping. A chest with an occasional chair could also be a secondary focal point. (An *occasional chair* is a small-scaled piece that sits away from the main seating area that can be drawn up on occasion when it is needed for additional seating.)
- Very large spaces may require more than one main focal area. Very large living rooms may need more than one main seating area to adequately fill the space.

Figure 6.25

Figure 6.26

alternation of materials such as wood, leather, steel, tin, and stone, creates studied rhythm. The stark simplicity of this grouping also allows the focal point—the leaded glass window—to become the most important feature. Largest seating areas face it, and low Barcelona chairs in front of the window do not compete but complement its craftsmanship and rhythmic linear composition. Photo by Norman McGrath © 1989.

Figure 6.26 A hand-carved Rococo bookcase is an obvious focal point. Louis XV side chairs with their fluid Rococo curves become a part of the linear frivolity, further emphasizing the bookcase. The awkward proportions of the room have been broken into two areas, each anchored by a designer rug. The conversation grouping in the foreground is in stark contrast with its no-nonsense angular lines and sleek forms. Yet the conversation grouping also seems to be the comfortable theater from which the focal point "on stage" can be enjoyed. Although the seating group seems distant from the bookcase, the complexity and commanding presence of the case goods bring it visually into the grouping without overwhelming it. Photo by Norman McGrath © 1989.

- In a dining room the table will be the primary focal point, and a serving piece with a painting or mirror and side chairs could be a secondary focal point.
- The bed will generally be the primary focal point in a bedroom, and a small area with comfortable seating, tables, and lighting could be the secondary focal point.

Line and Harmony

Whenever a piece of furniture is placed in an environment, a line is created where the piece meets the floor or where its silhouette is seen against the background. In *plan drawing* (a view drawn from above), the furniture arrangement is also a study in line. Line is a powerful tool and should be used judiciously to create harmonious furniture arrangements. Some points to consider about the harmony of line when planning furniture arrangements include the following:

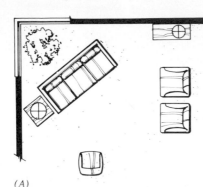

(A)
Figure 6.27

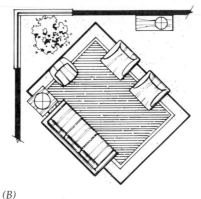

(B)

- When arranging furniture, it is important to remember that if a line is introduced into a space, it should relate harmoniously to the other existing lines. For example, a sofa or other large piece placed across the corner in a room feels awkward unless other elements repeat and enhance the diagonal line of the piece.
- Placing large pieces at an angle often disregards the basic lines of the architecture. However, if other elements are arranged in concert with the diagonal line, the result may be very harmonious and interesting. For example, if an area rug turned on an angle is used as the format for an arrangement in a room of sufficient scale, the grouping will feel right. If the other pieces or the architectural elements in a room follow the same diagonal format and repeat and accentuate the diagonal lines, the arrangement will be pleasing.

Figure 6.28

- Chairs in a grouping placed at a slight angle tend to make the arrangement feel less formal and rigid because they soften the solid feeling of a rectilinear composition.

Form and Space

The forms in a furniture arrangement are the individual pieces of furniture. The space is the empty area between the furniture pieces. The design of space is as important as the furniture forms themselves. Furniture arrangement is a two- and three-dimensional study in space and form and should be planned with sensitivity to *negative space.* Seen in plan, the arrangement should make interesting use of space, and seen in elevation, the furniture placement should also break the wall space into interesting forms. Art

Figure 6.27 Diagonal placement of furnishings works best when the diagonal line is repeated by other furnishings or architectural elements. *(A)* Incorrect diagonal placement. *(B)* Correct placement with rug, chairs, and table in harmony with the diagonal lines.

Figure 6.28 Line is a significant element of design in this unusual L-shaped corner grouping. The rough, heavy, horizontal lines of the wall and ceiling are balanced with a skirted sofa upholstered with a complex, curved patterned fabric daringly set at a diagonal across the corner. The

seeming disparity, however, creates a sophisticated country charm that is inviting and homey. This is due, in part, to the intimate scale and detail of the sofa and the anchoring of accessories behind the sofa. On the wall, unpretentious artwork in

handcrafted frames, anchored around a floral arrangement, and small table accessories create a charming, asymmetrical grouping. Furniture and fabric by, and photo courtesy of, Brunschwig and Fils.

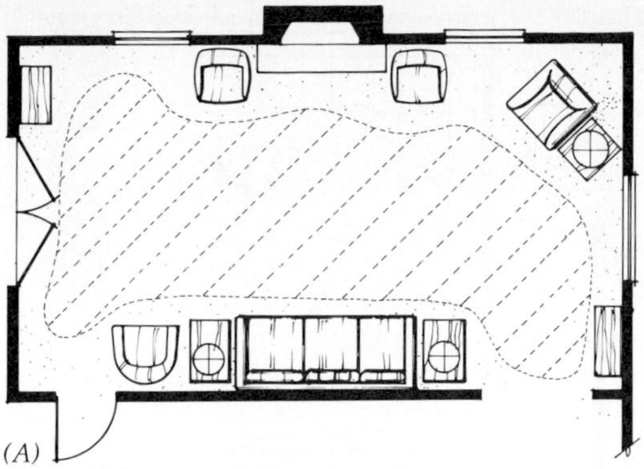

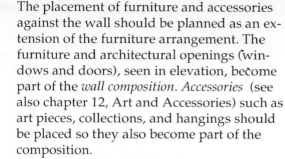

(A)
Figure 6.29

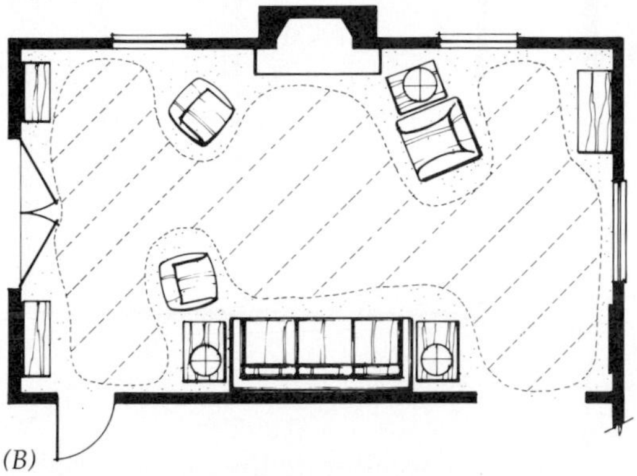

(B)

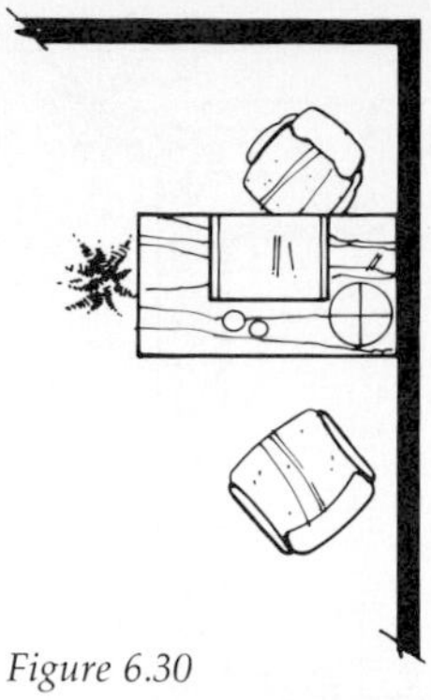

Figure 6.30

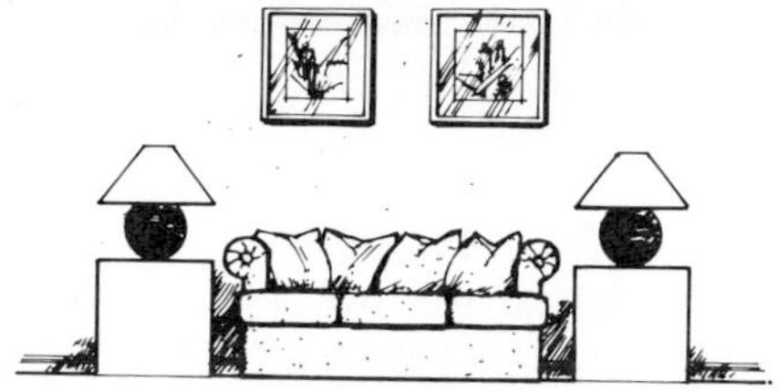

Figure 6.31 *(A)*

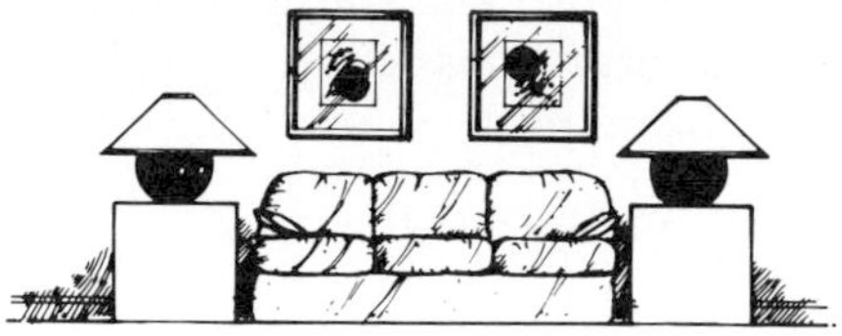

(B)

Figure 6.32

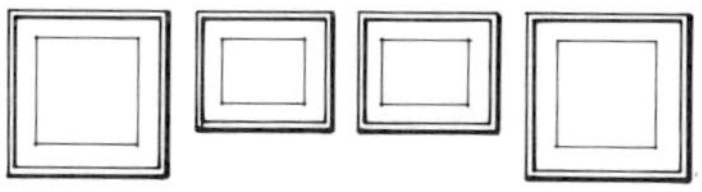

Figure 6.33

and accessories hung on the wall must be treated as part of the composition. Consider the following when arranging furniture and hanging accessories:

- Negative space needs to be interesting; avoid arrangements with the furniture "holding hands" dance hall fashion— around the perimeter of the room. This type of arrangement is often safe but without the interest it could have if some of the furniture were drawn into the room instead of being placed flat against the wall.

- Large pieces of furniture pushed tightly into corners are not as pleasing as pieces placed leaving some negative space. This is true in both plan and elevation—the piece needs breathing room to separate it from the corner or some negative space to separate it from a doorway or window.

- A desk that is placed perpendicular to a wall or actually moved out into the room may be more interesting than one that is pushed flat facing the wall. Turned perpendicularly, it extends into the negative space and changes the shape of the space, making it more interesting.

- The placement of furniture and accessories against the wall should be planned as an extension of the furniture arrangement. The furniture and architectural openings (windows and doors), seen in elevation, become part of the *wall composition. Accessories* (see also chapter 12, Art and Accessories) such as art pieces, collections, and hangings should be placed so they also become part of the composition.

- In many instances the accessories can be used to complete the composition and finish the balancing process. There are no rules governing the hanging of pictures and other accessories, only the consideration of form, negative space, and balance.

- When hanging more than one piece in a grouping, it is important to lay the pieces out on a table or on the floor just as we intend to hang them. By doing this, we can evaluate the composition and see how the pieces relate to each other and how the proportion of the negative spaces between the pieces relate to the pieces themselves.

- Accessories must be considered in relationship to the furniture with which they share a wall. Art pieces should not be hung so high above the furniture that the relationship between the pieces is lost.

- The scale of the accessory should relate well to the scale of the furniture with which it will be placed. If the scale of a piece is too small, several smaller pieces could be massed to create a grouping of appropriate scale for the furniture. For example, a mirror or painting can be massed together with a chest or table to balance a higher case piece on opposite sides of a fireplace.

- On walls without furniture or architectural openings, the accessory pieces could be massed in groupings or hung gallery fashion. Hanging pictures gallery fashion requires that the pieces be placed in a row at eye level with appropriate spacing between each piece. If the pieces are all close to the same size, an imaginary line could be traced along the wall to

Figure 6.29 A room will have more aesthetic and functional appeal when furnishings are placed to create interesting negative space. *(A)* Incorrect—negative space creates a large, awkward chasm. *(B)* Correct— better furniture arrangement yields interesting and better-distributed negative space.
Figure 6.30 A desk placed at a right angle to the wall makes a functional and an interesting composition.

Figure 6.31 Pieces placed on a wall work well when they relate to the furniture below. *(A)* Artwork is placed too high. *(B)* Art pieces have become a part of the grouping.

Figure 6.32 Art pieces placed on a wall can be massed together with careful consideration of composition and use of negative space.
Figure 6.33 Art can also be displayed gallery fashion in a straight line.

Furniture Arrangement   149

mark the top edge of the pictures. If this seems too rigid, then an imaginary line could be used instead to mark the center of each picture.

- The height of hangings should relate to other pieces in the room as well as to the composition of all the other walls. With training and practice the eye will sense when the arrangement is correct.

Proportion

Every space has its own shape and proportions. Some spaces are long and narrow, some are square, and others are well-proportioned rectangles. In a large-scale interior, the proportions will be less apparent and consequently of less concern when arranging furniture. However in most environments, the proportions of a room should be carefully considered when placing furniture. Furniture arrangements can be planned to make best use of awkward spaces, and in some cases, the proportions of a space can visually be altered by a good furniture arrangement. The following considerations may be helpful:

- Rectangular rooms, if not too narrow, are the most flexible and easy to arrange.
- A square room is more difficult but could be arranged with a rectangular grouping as a primary focal point on one side, with open space along the opposite side with room for secondary focal points to balance. An area rug could be used to help define the primary focal point.
- If the square room is large enough, an area rug could also be used to create a central focal point with a square or rectangular grouping placed in the center of the room. This would require careful planning of floor plugs or the use of recessed or other ceiling lighting.
- Long, narrow spaces can be challenging. The best way to handle this type of space is by dividing it into areas of function or use. For example, in long narrow family rooms or game rooms, part of the space could be devoted to conversation and music/video. The next section of the room could be planned for a game table, for a pool or Ping-Pong table, or for eating space. The back of a sofa could serve as a divider between the spaces and help alter the *visual proportion* of the room.
- A narrow living room could also be divided, according to use, into seating area, music area, dining area, or even into more than one area for conversation and seating.

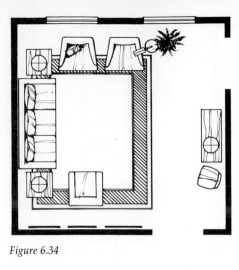

Figure 6.34

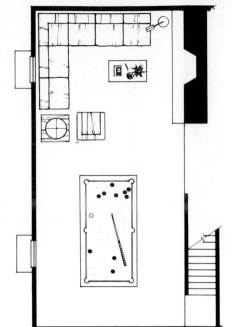

Figure 6.35

- Long narrow rooms do not need extra long sofas to match the proportion of the space. The long sofa only tends to exaggerate the uncomfortable proportions. It is wiser to divide the space into smaller modules with furniture groupings.

Basic Groupings

As we carefully observe interiors, we see that most seating arrangements fit into seven basic configurations. The seven groupings can be composed of any combination of benches, ottomans, chairs, sofas, lounges, or love seats, and each grouping will be appropriate for different functions.

1. Straight-line groupings are formed by arranging furniture in continuous lines. This configuration is the most efficient for seating the largest number of people in a space. This arrangement is used in theaters, airplanes, waiting rooms, classrooms, churches, arenas, and even in homes when they have been arranged for club meetings or other large gatherings. This type of grouping makes interaction difficult since it requires leaning forward, weaving back and forth, or craning one's neck to talk with anyone except the person next to you. Its principal advantage is its ability to handle crowds.

2. L-shaped groupings are more conducive to interaction and are formed with two seating pieces placed at right angles to each other. This could be an intimate arrangement of two chairs and a small table tucked into a corner or a pair of sofas capable of seating several people. The L could be formed by something as simple as a chair placed at a right angle to the end

Figure 6.34 A possible solution for furniture arrangement in a square room.

Figure 6.35 Long narrow spaces work best when they are divided into areas of function or use.

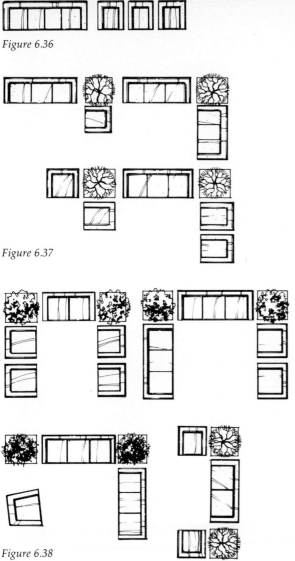

Figure 6.36

Figure 6.37

Figure 6.38

Figure 6.39

of a love seat or sofa. The L-shaped grouping allows people to converse easily because the angle of conversation is comfortable. They do not face each other directly but sit at a slight angle, elbow to elbow.

3. U-shaped groupings are an extension of the L shape. They can be formed by adding a chair, a sofa, a love seat, or any seating piece to the L. This configuration also enables interaction and further expands the space for seating.

4. Box-shaped groupings are formed by adding seating pieces to partially close the opening of the U-shaped grouping. This is the best configuration for interaction among the largest possible group of users. *Conversation pits,* which are built-in seating areas designed as an integral part of the environment, are often box shaped. If built around a fire pit, the

interaction is often diminished by the fire hood, which interferes with visual contact. But if the line of sight is carefully maintained, the interaction can be excellent. In more standard furniture groupings, the opening of the U will usually be closed with a chair or pair of chairs allowing sufficient room for users to enter and exit the grouping with ease.

5. Circular groupings are much like box-shaped groupings except that as the name implies they are arranged in circular shapes. Some modular furniture pieces and conversation pits are designed in a circular or curving fashion. These groupings, like the box-shaped groupings, are excellent for interaction because eye contact can be maintained with nearly everyone in the group. However, its unusual shape makes it unsuited to many situations.

Figure 6.36 Straight-line grouping, ideal for waiting areas or spectator theater seating.
Figure 6.37 L-shaped grouping.
Figure 6.38 U-shaped groupings.

Figure 6.39 A charming and intimate U-shaped furniture grouping is made more endearing through the selection of unmatched furnishings and rustic antiques. Textiles and wall coverings are from Victoria Morland's A Farmhouse in Provence. Photo courtesy of Raintree Designs, Inc.

Figure 6.40

6. Parallel groupings are an excellent arrangement for emphasizing a natural focal point or creating one where none exists. Two seating pieces are placed so they face each other at right angles to a window, fireplace, or other natural focal point. The seating pieces frame the focal point, and the users face each other for good interaction. Where no focal point exists, the grouping can focus on a case piece or some other object of interest to create a focal point.

7. Solo groupings may sound like a paradox—the ideas may not seem compatible. However, it is important to remember that single pieces placed away from main groupings of furniture generally need some form of accompaniment. For example, a reading chair at least needs a lamp and would be even better with a table to hold a book and a possible refreshment. The chair becomes more functional and feels more purposeful with the table and lamp. Consider also that when a single chair is placed in a particularly beautiful spot to complete a point of emphasis, it may never be occupied. Where the design may call for a chair as part of a vista—placed under a window or at the end of a hallway—people may feel "on stage" if they use it.

Seating pieces in some sleek, modern rooms may have no need for accompaniment. In such environments, the furniture is often treated as sculpture whose principal purpose is aesthetic. The lighting in these spaces will often be architectural and preclude the need for tables and lamps. The

Figure 6.40 When spaces are large, it is good to create more than one focal area. In this very large space in the Trump Parc Apartments, designer Noel Jeffrey has physically divided the space with large-scale columns. In the background a seating area incorporating an L-shaped sofa has been given definition with a room-sized area rug. The seating is expanded with a Louis XV chaise lounge, an Empire bergère, and an ottoman. In the foreground a smaller, box-shaped grouping is also defined by an area rug. The two areas are joined visually by the repeated use of soft blue. Photo courtesy of Noel Jeffrey.

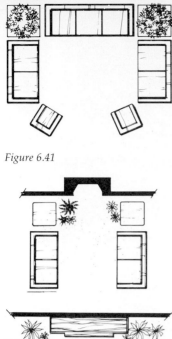

Figure 6.41

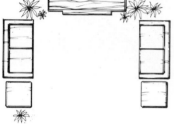

Figure 6.42

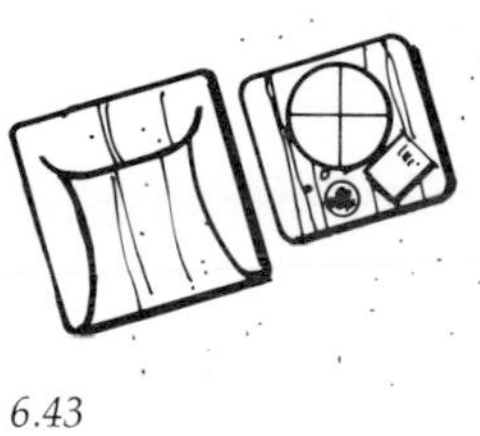

Figure 6.44

Figure 6.43

appeal of such designs is in their clarity and lack of embellishment; extra pieces of furniture would only detract. However, most rooms are designed with a wider range of purpose in mind and are made better by grouping pieces that extend the function of the furniture. Even a wall of books can be made more functional by placing an otto-man or occasional chair next to the bookcase for browsing.

Nonresidential Considerations

The process of arranging furniture in nonresidential design is based on the same principles as residential furniture arrangement, but some of the basic considerations will be different.

Function

Many nonresidential designs will include areas of seating, dining, or sleeping that are treated in the same way they would be in a residence. However in other cases, the place-ment of furniture and fixtures in nonresidential design will be based on some different determinations. In nonresiden-tial design the list of functions will not always relate to a specific person but rather to a generic need or function. For example, in an office with a receptionist, those who enter should have their attention drawn directly to the reception desk. The reception area must then be placed so that it is the first thing seen as a person enters. The designer will not ask the receptionist if center stage position is agreeable because in this situation the function is not related to the personal likes and dislikes of a specific user. Instead, the best ar-rangement for directing the attention of the public to an area where they can be informed and helped will be considered.

Nonresidential Furniture Types

Nonresidential design often includes placement of fixtures that are quite unlike any furniture used in residential de-sign. For example, in health care facilities, such as doctors' offices, clinics, and hospitals, there will be furniture spe-cially designed for examination and other special proce-dures. The design must reflect understanding of each pro-cedure and the relationship between different procedures so that the fixtures and equipment can be placed for effi-ciency and convenience. This kind of specialized need is

Figure 6.41 Box-shaped grouping.
Figure 6.42 Parallel groupings.
Figure 6.43 Solo grouping.

Figure 6.44 Designer duo Anthony Antine and Mark Polo created this inviting solo grouping in the guest room of the Sara Delano Roosevelt House, a designated landmark in New York City, open to the public. The club chair and ottoman can be

pulled close together, as seen here, to create a comfortable chaise lounge or pulled apart for traditional seating for more than one person. Photo courtesy of DuPont "Teflon" soil and stain repellent.

(A)
Figure 6.45

(B)

Figure 6.45 *(A)* An executive office grouping at the Dollar Dry Dock Savings Bank encourages perform- ance of several tasks: interviewing, giving direction, or independent work at the desk; less-formal conversation within the sofa area; and group planning at the conference table. Photo by Norman McGrath © 1986. *(B)* The office of James Mason, Dean of the College of Fine Arts and Communication at Brigham Young University, incorporates a comfort- able L-shaped seating area with a pleasant residential feeling. This kind of grouping is often used in executive offices because it creates a relaxed atmosphere for conversation. Photo by Andy Battenfield and Kelly Haas.

one of the main reasons designers develop and practice in areas of specialty such as health care design, restaurant design, hotel design, and office planning. Such specialization allows a design group to stay current with the latest technology and developments in each area and with the ways to best implement these developments in a design.

Planning Unseen Areas

In many instances nonresidential design will involve the planning of areas the public never sees. Here function may be paramount. For example, a designer who plans a restaurant will create public areas designed to project an image for the restaurant and create a space that is pleasant and appealing to the public. This public area has the strongest influence on the perception of the designer's ability, but the work area not seen by the public is equally important and must be planned with careful attention to function. The designer must study and research the food preparation process so that the equipment and *fixtures* required for food production can be arranged to save space and economize effort. If the work area is poorly arranged, the design cannot be considered successful regardless of the appeal of the public area.

When a designer begins a project that includes unfamiliar functions, it is probably helpful to examine what other designers have done on similar projects. It is also important to probe beneath the surface of a problem to uncover needs that may not have been identified in like projects. Sometimes designs and furniture arrangements that appear well done and aesthetically appealing when we see them in photographs without users are in fact unpleasant and frustrating when put to real use; for example, consider seating arrangements in airports. Most of those arrangements seem to be designed without consideration for the users and appear to be planned for people without long layovers, whose planes are on time, and who travel without hand baggage. In actual practice, seats often end up being used for stacking personal belongings, and when planes are delayed and conditions are crowded, walkways are used as a holding space for luggage and other personal goods. This makes the use of these spaces under such circumstances an unhappy experience. A good design will take every possible eventuality into consideration, and subsequent planning will make that environment as free from frustration as possible. Only careful analysis of function before planning will achieve that goal.

Planning for Systems Furniture

Many businesses and institutions are designed with large open work spaces for many users. To make efficient use of such spaces, designers often specify *systems furniture* (discussed in chapter 7, Furniture Selection). These are prefabricated modules that can be arranged in a number of different ways to create spaces and workstations for an endless number of different needs and functions. Systems furniture provides a great deal of flexibility, but determining space and function needs for each area is an enormous undertaking. This task is made much simpler by the use of computer programs, often provided by the systems furniture manufacturer, for collecting and analyzing data on needs and functions. These programs help generate specifications for the types of modules that best meet the users' needs. The process of laying out the furniture on large-scale projects can also be simplified by the use of *computer-aided design* programs for planning furniture arrangement. Such technology is a boon to the designer, particularly on projects where gathering and controlling vast amounts of information are such superhuman endeavors. Those who represent the manufacturer and sell the systems furniture are also available to help the designer specify the right components and plan their correct arrangement.

Circulation

Many of the basic problems of circulation and traffic control are the same for residential and nonresidential design. Principles or solutions observed in one setting can be applied in the other. For example, like residential design, many nonresidential environments are designed with *open plans* where those coming in enter directly into open areas. Spaces with open plans have a particular need for traffic control. In retail stores and restaurants, furniture and fixtures are often used to define areas for traffic. In restaurants the placement of tables will create aisles for circulation; the patterns can be altered by rearranging the tables. In retail stores, fixtures such as clothing racks or display tables are used to create lanes for traffic. By plotting natural patterns of circulation and then determining where traffic should go, open plan spaces with carefully placed furniture or fixtures can function as well as if they had actual walls or dividers to control traffic.

Barrier-Free Public Spaces

By law, clearances for nonresidential design must include *access* for the physically impaired.[5] Access to all spaces and levels of spaces used by the public must be provided to the *handicapped* by means of specially designed ramps, elevators, or special lifts. Doorways must be a minimum of thirty-two inches wide to allow a wheelchair to enter. A primary path for wheelchair circulation that allows two-way passage should be from fifty-four to sixty inches wide, and a secondary path allowing one-way passage should be from thirty-six to forty-two inches wide. Space required to turn a wheelchair 360 degrees is a circle sixty inches in diameter (a square sixty inches by sixty inches).

Other public spaces have designated requirements of accessibility and clearance. For example, toilet facilities must be provided for wheelchair users. The toilet stall should be sixty inches by sixty inches with a thirty-two-inch door that swings outward, a grab bar, and an elevated toilet. Hand-operated drinking fountains and telephone facilities should be provided with the standard sixty inch by sixty inch turnaround space.

Physically disabled people should be able to enter a dining space without using the kitchen or service areas, and they should be able to choose a variety of dining spaces without being confined to a single area designated for the handicapped. Access aisles should be a minimum of thirty-six inches wide and sixty inch by sixty inch turning spaces should be provided every fifty feet or more. Cafeteria-type food service lines should provide a minimum clearance of forty-two inches between tray slides or counters and control barriers. Vending machine areas should allow standard turning space of sixty inches by sixty inches.

To accommodate the handicapped, dormitories should be planned with a minimum of fifty-two inches between the major fixtures or furniture. A space of thirty-eight inches should be allowed between beds and walls.

Lecture halls, theaters, stadiums, and other public spectator facilities should be designed with easily accessible spaces for wheelchair users. The number of wheelchair spaces required increases according to the capacity of the structure. These spaces should be level and clear of traffic patterns.[6]

In spite of the law, those who are physically challenged still have a very difficult time finding environments that are completely free from frustration. If you study environments through the eyes of such a person, you will find conditions woefully inadequate. Be aware of the problems caused by the lack of complete planning. Wheelchair users may find that even if the toilet stall is large enough for the wheelchair, the grab bars will be missing or the toilet will be too low—at standard height. Parking spots designated for the handicapped may not have side space for a wheelchair to maneuver, or worse yet, the parking stall is often taken by someone without a handicap. Awareness of these needs leads to more sympathetic and complete planning of barrier-free design.

Notes

1. For a complete set of anthropometric data, see Julius Panero's *Anatomy for Interior Designers*. (New York: Whitney Library of Design, 1981).
2. Hall, Edward T. *The Hidden Dimension*. (New York: Anchor, 1969), p. 1.
3. Panero, Julius. *Anatomy for Interior Designers*. (New York: Whitney Library of Design, 1981), p. 19.
4. Hall, Edward T. *The Hidden Dimension*. (New York: Anchor, 1969), p. 172.
5. Public Law 90-480 requires that buildings and facilities be accessible to and usable by the handicapped.
6. For a more complete listing of barrier-free data, see Reznikoff's *Specifications for Commercial Interiors*. (New York: Whitney Library of Design, 1979).

Bibliography

Better Homes and Gardens New Decorating Book. Des Moines: Meredith, 1981.

Curran, June. *Profile Your Life-Style*. Los Altos: Brooks, 1979.

Dreyfuss, Henry. *The Measure of Man: Human Factors in Design*. New York: Whitney Library of Design, 1967.

Faulkner, Sarah. *Planning a Home*. New York: Holt, Rinehart and Winston, 1979.

Gilliatt, Mary. *The Decorating Book*. New York: Pantheon, 1981.

Hall, Edward T. *The Hidden Dimension*. New York: Anchor, 1969.

McCormick, Ernest J. *Human Factors Engineering*. New York: McGraw-Hill, 1970.

Panero, Julius. *Anatomy for Interior Designers*. New York: Whitney Library of Design, 1981.

Panero, Julius, and Martin Zelnik. *Human Dimension and Interior Space*. New York: Whitney Library of Design, 1979.

Reznikoff, S.C. *Specifications for Commercial Interiors*. New York: Whitney Library of Design, 1979.

St. Marie, Satenig S. *Homes Are for People*. New York: Wiley, 1973.

FURNITURE
SELECTION

A nineteenth-century English chair maker's pattern sampler highlights the range of chair backs awaiting the interior designer's selection; beneath it, a slipper chair, all from the collection of Chelsea Custom Corporation of New York. Photo by Ted Spiegel.

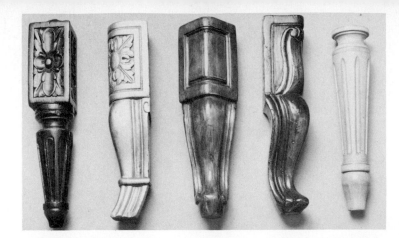

Pages 158 and 159: Knowledge of furniture style allows the interior designer to practice the art of furniture specification. Here, by choosing between Devon Shop's variations of the French Provincial armoire, painted for use in the boudoir or with glass doors for dining room display. This New York custom workshop also offers its professional clientele a wide range of furniture finishes, legs for tables or sofas, and carvings to decorate beds or cabinets. Photos by Ted Spiegel in cooperation with Devon Shops.

Page 160, top right: Noel Jeffrey, a leading New York designer, shows how furniture selection will vary in relation to the client's express taste. In a New York apartment, matching yellow satin damask sofas are complemented by equally formal Louis XVI tables of various shapes and functions. The Neoclassic side chairs upholstered in an appropriately striped fabric echo the vertical lines of the moldings and fireplace-flanking pilasters. In the fireplace, there is a custom-etched glass fire screen with nautical motifs. Photo courtesy of Noel Jeffrey. *Page 160, bottom:* A New York penthouse utilized Art Deco style for its custom-made furniture. Repeated tubular forms in the upholstery pieces give a softly sculptural effect, carefully designed to meet the spatial requirements. Clean, rounded lines in the glossy black dining pieces, edged in brass, add drama and deco sophistication. Relief from the severity of the forms is established with abstract modern art and radiating plant forms. Photo courtesy of Noel Jeffrey. *Page 161:* A more casual life-style is evident in this Brentwood, California, home. A range of seating styles is seen in the sofa with arms, two armless chairs placed together to form a love seat, a large round ottoman, and a chaise lounge, anchored with two heavily scaled tables and balanced with one of clear tubular steel and brass. Note the repeated and harmonious use of circle and rectangles seen in the furniture and accessory shapes and the pleasing distribution of positive to negative space. An East Indian wall hanging establishes a dramatic counterpoint to the chaste, structural furniture. Photo courtesy of Noel Jeffrey.

Page 162, top right: At the Rio Condominium in New York City, interior designer Michael Wiener has created a show, or model, apartment to demonstrate to potential buyers how a small apartment can offer a spacious feeling. The adroit use of a wall mirror and glass block visually expands space. The lack of pattern in the textiles combined with simple, clean, and rounded furniture shapes, such as the open, flowing lines of the dining chairs, allows the eye to travel rhythmically around furnishings rather than to be stopped by decorative motifs. The floor-to-ceiling windows frame the Manhattan skyline, a vital part of the apartment's decor. Photo by Ted Spiegel. *Page 162, bottom:* In the same New York apartment, a wall storage unit cum bedstead makes the most of a narrow bedroom, concealing belongings while offering clean lines, no clutter, and space-expanding, smooth, white surfaces. Photo by Ted Spiegel.

Page 163, top: *Much of the seating provided through an interior designer is made to order. At the New York workshops of Smith and Watson, classic chair designs are faithfully reproduced by master craftsmen. The firm offers more than three hundred antique styles for quality reproduction. Seen here is a set of six paterae-back Neoclassic chairs, behind which are a pair of Regency and a pair of Queen Anne chairs, with a third variation of a Queen Anne partially stained. A gold-leaf American Empire piece sits to the right of a Chinese Chippendale chair and love seat. Photo by Ted Spiegel.* **Page 163, bottom:** *In the frame shop—Sidler Brothers—utilized by Brickel Associates, a Ward Bennett design is reproduced fifteen hundred times for use in a midwestern bank tower. Contract furniture selection can result in significant monetary commitment: Competition for these orders makes furniture selection a difficult task—with cost, comfort, aesthetics, and durability all part of the consideration. Photo by Ted Spiegel.*

Furniture as a Symbol

It is interesting to note how furniture became a symbol of status. During the Medieval era only the most important people had chairs; those of lesser importance used stools. The term cathedral was used to distinguish regular churches from the seat of the bishop. In order to be a cathedral, a church had to contain the bishop's chair, or *cathedra*. Today, when a university wants to establish a faculty position of great status, it will endow a "chair," and when a committee or department is formed, the one most responsible will be called the chair or chairperson, a cultural carryover from the Middle Ages. During the seventeenth century, King Louis XIV of France gave patronage to the manufacture of furniture. His royal support inspired the design and construction of fabulous pieces. Those who were able spent great sums of money to acquire furnishings like the king's because they were beautiful and a source of recognition. Nicolas Fouquet, finance minister to young King Louis XIV, created such a lavish setting at Vaux-le-Vicomte, his château near Paris, that he was sent to prison and his furniture was confiscated by the king. Happily, today such drastic consequences are not associated with the furnishing of an environment, and furniture choices can sensibly be balanced between quality, aesthetics, function, and value. However, even today fine furniture is still a symbol of status or taste.

Determining Quality

In order to make the best possible selection when specifying furniture, it is important to understand relative quality and its relationship to price. Only when the quality of design, materials, and construction are in line with the price can furniture be considered a good value. Consequently, some knowledge of materials and construction is important to making wise selections.

Figure 7.1

Figure 7.1 The baby grand piano is a much-desired status symbol as well as an often used and appreciated furniture selection in both traditional and contemporary homes and nonresidential settings. This rich vignette also features another traditional favorite, used here as a music storage cabinet, the Townsend and Goddard block-front chest from the Late Georgian era. Photo courtesy of the Baldwin Piano and Organ Co.

Figure 7.2

(A)
Figure 7.3

(B)

(C)

Wooden Furniture

Wood is an excellent material for furniture construction and has been utilized by craftsmen for thousands of years because of its inherent qualities. It is a renewable resource that can be regenerated by reforestation, or replacing trees that have been cut down for lumber with seedlings. Wood is strong yet relatively easy to cut, carve, join, finish, and refinish. Wooden pieces are easily cared for, and if well constructed and carefully maintained, they will become better looking with age and may last almost indefinitely. Beautifully finished wood appeals to our senses because of the unity and infinite variety of its grain patterns and the warmth of its colors. Wood was once part of a living organism, and even after the tree has been felled and the wood cured, worked, and finished, wood still has that appealing quality of life.

Hardwood and Softwood

Woods are categorized as hardwood or softwood. *Hardwoods* such as oak, pecan, walnut, birch, maple, cherry, mahogany, and ebony come from broad-leaved deciduous trees that lose their leaves in the winter. These tend to have tighter *grains* than softwoods and consequently are stronger and harder and can be carved and worked in more detail. *Softwoods* such as pine, cedar, cyprus, spruce, fir, and redwood come from conifer or cone-bearing trees. These trees do not drop their needles and grow more rapidly than hardwoods. Softwood has generally been less expensive than hardwood, making it well suited as a building material. Because it is less costly and can easily be worked without expensive, sophisticated machinery, it has been widely used by provincial craftsmen for furniture construction. Softwood has a more open grain than hardwood and in the proper setting adds simple warmth and character to an environment.

Figure 7.2 Wooden case goods bookshelf and reading desk look onto a beautifully executed carved wooden sleigh bed from the French Empire period. Wood furniture, particularly when combined with sensitively selected fabrics, can create an inviting, a secure, and a traditional look much favored by young and old alike. Textiles by and photo courtesy of Schumacher.

Figure 7.3 Furniture that grows with the family, Child Craft offers honey oak Chesapeake II. *(A)* Starting out as a crib, *(B)* it converts to a daybed for a growing boy or girl *(C)* or for a guest room. Photos courtesy of Child Craft.

Other Forms of Wood

Wood in several other forms is also used for construction of furniture.

- *Plywood* is used as a substitute for solid woods and is made by *lamination*—laminating (gluing) thin sheets (*plies*) of wood or other materials, sandwich fashion, in successive layers to make a panel. When each ply is rotated a quarter turn so that the grain of each layer runs perpendicular or at a ninety-degree angle to the layer below it, a material of great strength is created. If the grain of each layer is laminated running the same direction, the plywood can be bent and shaped with heat, pressure, and chemicals to create beautiful furniture designs like Eames' (see Eames' lounge chair).

- *Particleboard,* or chipboard, is made by compressing flakes of wood with resin under heat and pressure to form a solid panel. Particleboard will not warp and can be used as a base for veneers of wood or plastic laminates and can be vinyl wrapped for use in drawers.

- *Hardboard* is also made by compression with heat. Wood fibers are bonded together to make a strong material that is often used for drawer construction, dust panels between drawers, and backing on mirrors and case goods. Hardboard can also be used as paneling in solid colors, with simulated wood grains and textures or drilled with holes for attaching hooks and brackets.

Figure 7.4

Figure 7.4 This very personally styled bedroom in the Sara Delano Roosevelt House in New York City exudes the kind of warmth that comes only with patience and the careful selection of pieces that work well together although they are not a matched set or suite. The Queen Anne highboy on the wall between the windows is colored with an unexpected antique white finish. Case pieces such as this can be used to create secondary focal points that increase the visual interest of a room. Anthony Antine and Mark Polo, interior designers. Photo courtesy of DuPont "Telfon" soil and stain repellent.

Case Goods

Furniture pieces made without upholstery such as desks, dressers, cabinets, and chests are called *case goods* by the furniture industry. Some case goods are made of solid wood, but many pieces are made using other combinations of materials.

- *All-wood construction* means that the visible parts of the piece are made of wood.
- *Combination* indicates that more than one type of wood is used on the exposed parts of the piece.
- *Genuine* denotes the use of veneers of a particular wood over hardwood plywood on all the exposed parts of a piece.

- *Solid* refers to the use of solid pieces of a certain wood in the construction of all the external (visible) parts.
- *Veneer* is a thin slice of beautifully grained wood bonded to plywood or particleboard. Veneers have been used since earliest times to create pieces of great appeal and strength. Because beautiful pieces of wood are used in thin slices, handsome effects with matched grains and inlaid patterns (called *marquetry*) can be achieved with veneers. One frequently used type, burl veneer, comes from the scarlike growths where trees have been diseased or repeatedly pruned. This results in an irregular growth pattern that becomes a beautiful and complex grain in the finished piece of furniture.

Figure 7.5

(A)
Figure 7.6

(B)

Figure 7.5 A modular entertainment system by DAVID L, shown in birch wood. The system features a large TV screen, enclosed speakers, sliding shelves, and bar. "Wood dimensions" can be custom-specified in a variety of wood selections, cabinet configura- tions, and TV-screen size (up to 40 inches). Photo courtesy of DAVID L.
Figure 7.6 *(A)* Walnut burl dramatically sweeps across charcoal cherry wood in the entertainment unit, Witnova 735, in sleek Art Deco style, opening up the world of entertainment inside. *(B)* Sliding doors open for the fully customized storage space within, selected for television and stereo equipment, bar, or computer work space. Photo courtesy of Witnova.

Wood Grains

By using several cutting methods, different grain patterns can be revealed in most woods.

- *Plain slicing* is when the half log (*flitch*) is cut parallel to a line through the center of the log producing a vaulted or cathedral-like grain.

- *Quarter slicing* indicates that the quarter log (also called a flitch) is cut so that the blade meets the grain at right angles to the growth rings, resulting in a generally straight, striped grain.

- *Rotary slicing* shaves a continuous, thin layer of wood from a log mounted to a lathe. It is as if the log were being unwound like a roll of paper. The grain produced by this method is broad, open, and bold.

Joining Methods

A well-made piece of wooden furniture is assembled by fastening pieces of lumber together in junctions or closures called *joints*. There are several ways of joining and reinforcing furniture. The most common of these are corner blocks, double-dowel joints, dovetail joints, miter joints, and mortise and tenon joints:

- *Corner blocks* are triangular pieces of wood that are glued and screwed into place at an angle. These blocks are not considered true joints but rather reinforcements. Corner blocks are used in points requiring extra strength such as points where legs join tabletops, frames for case pieces, or frames for chair and sofa seats.

- *Dowels* are a third piece of wood used to join the other two parts of the frame together. The rounded dowel is glued into holes that have been drilled into the other pieces. The quality of this type of joint relies on the strength of the dowel.

- *Dovetail* joints are used to secure drawer fronts and sides. This joint takes its name from a series of dovetail or fan-shaped notches carved into one piece and projections on the other that are carved to fit the notches.

Figure 7.7

- *Miter* joints are two pieces of wood that meet at a forty-five-degree angle. Mitered corners must be reinforced with screws, dowels, nails, or metal splines in order to be strong and functional.

- *Mortise and tenon* is an ancient method of joinery that imparts great strength. It is formed by two pieces of wood that have been carved to interlock. Into one of the pieces a square hole (mortise) is carved, and the second piece is carved with a projection (tenon) that fits into the hole. Mortise and tenon joints make secure connections for furniture frames.

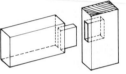

Wood Finishes

Finishes are applied to wood for its protection and to enhance grain characteristics that cannot readily be seen in unfinished pieces. The first step in the finishing process is the preparation of the surface by smoothing and sanding to remove any unevenness and imperfections. The wood may then be filled with a liquid or paste *wood filler* to level the pores inherent in the natural grain. After further sanding, color may be applied to the wood.

Color is generally added in the form of *stains* mixed with water, oils, or other agents; the natural color of the wood grain can be lightened by *bleaching*. Paint can also be used to color a finish. When a paint of darker value is applied over the top of a lighter value and then wiped away leaving highlights and shadows, the finish is called *antique finish*. When no color is added to or extracted from the wood, the finish is referred to as natural. The next step in the finishing process is the application of a transparent film to protect the piece from moisture and stains. One of the oldest finishing films is *shellac*, made by dissolving the waste of

Figure 7.7 Furniture joints are crucial to the construction of chairs like these. Corner blocks will reinforce the legs, whereas dowels and, perhaps, mortise and tenon joints hold arms and backs together. These chairs are part of the Window Chair collection designed by Lee Mindel, manufactured by Luten Clarey Stern, Inc., and is the Seventeenth Annual Product Design Award Winner in the Traditional Adaptation Residential Seating Collection/Group category. While the frame of each chair is identical, the back can be inserted with one of six window designs reminiscent of various architecturally historic periods. Groups of the same style could be used together, or a series of dissimilarly backed chairs could be used together to create a coordinated and highly complementary grouping. Shown here are a window grid design and a quatrefoil tracery design. Photo courtesy of Resources Council, Inc.

(A)

(B)

Figure 7.8

- Drawer interiors should be smooth and free from splinters that might snag clothing.
- Pieces should be checked for quality of joinery and presence of corner blocks.
- Check for *back panels* and *dust panels* between drawers.
- Sanding and finishing of unexposed surfaces can be examined for smoothness.
- *Hardware* can be examined for quality and style.
- The exterior finish can be checked for clarity and possible defects.

the lac bug in denatured alcohol. Shellac produces a beautiful finish that, unfortunately, is not resistant to moisture, alcohol, and heat. A much stronger finish can be obtained with *varnish*. Varnish, a preparation of resinous substances dissolved in oil or alcohol, can be used on almost every surface and is very durable as well as moisture and alcohol resistant. *Polyurethane* is a synthetic resin used to give today's varnish its outstanding properties. *Lacquer* is a resin that has been dissolved in ethyl alcohol. With the addition of pigments to the lacquer, beautiful colored finishes are possible. Interestingly, lacquer is also used as a finish remover. Consequently, a sealer must be applied between stains or other finishes and the lacquer in order to keep the lacquer from softening the previous finish.

Finishes are frequently polished with mild abrasives to soften or refine the finish film. Waxes and oils are used to polish and protect finished wood surfaces; the manufacturer's instructions for specific care of wood should be followed so finishes will not be damaged.

Some furniture is *distressed* to make it appear used and worn like an older piece of furniture or an antique. The surface of the wood is intentionally dented, scratched, and flecked with dark paint as part of the finishing process. As with any phase of the furniture manufacturing process, this can be done very well or in a poor manner. It is the care that is taken at each step together with the quality of the materials used that determines the value of a piece of wooden furniture.

In instances where case goods are being purchased directly from a showroom floor, or even when a selection is being made from a catalog and comparable pieces can be seen in the showroom, simple quality checks can be made.

- Doors and drawers should fit tightly without sticking.
- Drawers should slide easily on *glides* or ball bearings.

Metal Furniture

Like wood, metal is an important material for furniture construction and has been used as such for thousands of years. Metal has great durability and strength and can be worked in many different ways. It can be cast into solid forms, rolled into thin sheets that can be manipulated into an infinite variety of pieces and components, and *extruded* (forced through an opening) into tubes and other shapes that can also be bent and formed into beautiful furniture pieces.

Types of Metal

Though furniture could be made from most metals, only a few are commonly used.

- *Aluminum* is used for some outdoor furniture because it is lightweight and does not rust. It is also used for window frames and can be enameled, left its natural silver color, or anodized a dark bronze color. Aluminum is *anodized* with an electrolytic process, whereby it is subjected to a chemical solution together with an electrical charge.
- *Brass* is a gold-colored metal made from an *alloy* (combination) of zinc and copper. It is used either in solid form or as a plating for furniture and accessories.
- *Chromium*, or chrome, is used as a plating on steel furniture. It is known for its brilliant silver shine. Chromium is also used as a plating on lighting fixtures and plumbing accessories.
- *Iron* is a strong black metal that can easily be wrought (worked) to create indoor and outdoor furniture, railings, grates, grills, and accessories. Iron will rust and must be protected with paint.

Figure 7.8 (A) A Louis XV fauteuil armchair in natural finish, hallmark of French interiors, is here surprisingly upholstered in a bold, contemporary printed fabric. This beloved chair lends itself to nearly any textile from tapestry to plaids to prints to solids. This is, in part, due to its unpretentious nature and classically beautiful curved lines. Photo courtesy of C & A Wall Coverings and Textiles. (B) From Casa Stradivari, an imported hand-painted four-drawer commode in an antique finish of crackled pale cream background with peach and light green stenciled ornamentation with trompe l'oeil (painted to fool the eye) marble top. Photo courtesy of Casa Stradivari.

Figure 7.9

Figure 7.10

- *Steel* is an alloy of iron and carbon. The combination has greater hardness and strength than iron but still can easily be worked. Steel is used extensively for nonresidential furniture and fittings, office systems and furniture, as well as residential pieces. Steel furniture is usually chrome plated or painted.
- *Stainless steel* is an alloy of steel with chromium. The addition of chromium makes the steel rustproof. Stainless steel is used for furniture hardware and trim, as well as for a variety of fittings in nonresidential applications.
- Other metals such as silver, gold, pewter, bronze, copper, tin, and lead are used principally for accessories or for specific functions within the building structure.

Most metals can be finished in several ways. If the unfinished metal is left exposed to the natural elements in an environment, it will tarnish or rust. This quality is sometimes exploited by the designer to create a desired effect. Copper weathers to a beautiful blue-green color and *A 588* steel weathers to a self-protecting coat of rich reddish brown rust. Metals can be polished to a high gloss and maintained with a coat of lacquer or with continued polishing, and if a less-lustrous finish is desired, the metal can be *brushed*. Metal pieces can also be painted or plastic coated in every conceivable color.

The quality of metal pieces will depend on the care and craftsmanship used in their construction. Like a fine automobile, the components of a piece of metal furniture should fit together tightly and the finish should be smooth and free from imperfections. Metal furniture can be found in many ranges of price and quality, and because of its durability and aesthetic flexibility, it can be used in almost every environment.

Other Furniture Materials

Over the years, creative designers have used every material imaginable from animal horns to *papier-mâché* to create furniture. Today a range of natural and synthetic materials other than wood and metal are available to those who design and manufacture furniture. The most common of these are *plastic, wicker, rattan, cane,* and *rush*.

Plastic

Plastic is a type of nonmetallic compound, produced synthetically, that can be molded and hardened for a wide range of design uses. It is a complex product that is in a constant state of development and redevelopment. Consequently, it may be difficult for the interior designer to stay abreast of new technology in this field. Fortunately, of the thousands of plastics that have been created, only a few are used for furniture and interior design. Families of plastics such as *vinyls, acrylics, polyurethanes,* and *melamines* (laminates) are the most common. Each of these families belongs to a larger group of either *thermoplastics* or *thermoset plastics*:

- Thermoplastics change their form by heating and can be damaged by too much heat. Acrylics and vinyls are thermoplastics.
- Thermoset plastics use a combination of compounds that are set by heat and are not easily damaged by it. Melamines are thermoset, and polyurethanes are both thermoset and thermoplastic.

Plastics today can be foamed, molded, *vacuformed*, sprayed, *calendered* (rolled), or blown in just about any weight or consistency, from spongy to rigid, to create a surprising variety of forms. This great flexibility makes plastics an ideal material for creative expression as well as function. Plastics have been maligned because they are often used to imitate natural materials or intricately de-

Figure 7.9 Plexus, a seating system appropriate for indoors or outdoors, can withstand a high-traffic setting. Steel is the primary material because of its superior strength and durability, whereas wood and fiberglass add visual height and softness to the products. Soft forms, nylon powder coating, and contrasting materials and finishes enhance the overall desirability. This Seventeenth Annual Product Design Award Winner in the Indoor/Outdoor Casual Furniture category was designed by Nicola Balderi and manufactured by Landscape Forms, Inc. Photo courtesy of Resources Council, Inc.

Figure 7.10 The Arco chair is a sophisticated combination of sewn and saddle-stitched leather and polished chromed steel, communicating an immediate image of both comfort and style. Although designed for the contract market, the graceful lines and workmanship of this "sculpture for use" would make it appropriate in a residential setting. Designed by Paul Tuttle and manufactured by Arconas Corporation, this chair is the "Roscoe" Winner of the Seventeenth Annual Product Design Award in the Contract Seating Furniture—Individual Product Entry category. Photo courtesy of Resources Council, Inc.

(A)
Figure 7.11

(B)

Figure 7.12

signed details traditionally executed by hand. Yet when plastics are used in the context of their own potential, novel pieces of great aesthetic value are possible.

Because technology changes so rapidly, it is important for the designer to make certain the specifications for a particular plastic are clearly understood before selecting it. Some plastics may be highly flammable, and some may give off poisonous or explosive gases if they burn. Since the designer is often liable for the health and safety of the user, understanding the performance of the material under every condition is most important. Care of plastics should be according to the manufacturer's directions.

Wicker, Rattan, Cane, and Rush

Wicker, rattan, cane, and rush are all natural materials used to make furniture or certain furniture components. These materials tend to be rather informal, although cane is used to make formal pieces as well. Following are some considerations of these materials:

- Wicker is not a specific material but rather the term used to identify any piece that is fashioned from small twigs or flexible strips of wood. Chairs, tables, baskets, or any piece the craftsman might execute from these materials is referred to as wicker.
- Rattan is made from the unbranched stem of a certain Indian palm and is used to manufacture wicker furniture. Rattan poles are flexible, can be bent into beautiful forms, can be stained, lacquered, or painted, and unlike bamboo, which is brittle and hollow, can be nailed or screwed.

- Cane is made from grasses, palm stems, or plants such as rattan or bamboo. Thin strips of these materials are woven to form a mesh that is fitted into the seat or back of chair frames. The mesh allows air to pass through and is strong yet has the ability to give, providing a degree of comfort. Cane has been used throughout history to create beautiful pieces of furniture; today manufacturers continue to use it on pieces of classic design.
- Rush is a type of long grass that is twisted to form a thin cord for weaving provincial chair seats. Rush is a strong and long-lasting material with great appeal and has been used to weave floor mats as well as chair seats. Today, rush is sometimes duplicated with strong paper cords. The paper version is nearly identical to real rush and is particularly well suited to dry climates where rush can dry out and split.

Upholstered Furniture

The quality of fabric-covered furniture is more difficult to assess than case goods because upholstered pieces are "blind" items; you cannot see what is inside. This means that one must rely on written specifications of a particular product as well as the information that a sales representative might furnish about the product. Because quality is important to the durability of a design, we often choose

Figure 7.11 (A) This Quatrefoil table is made of Avonite R, a man-made solid surfacing material. The Quatrefoil, a stylized four-petal floral design, comes from medieval ecclesiastical architecture and is seen here in the pedestal base and tabletop, repeated also in the pickled wood inlays. Custom table sizes, woods, and colors are available. Manufactured for Peter Charles by Plexibility. Photo by Robert Riggs. Photo courtesy of Plexibility. (B) This Sheraton-style console features a two-tone Avonite R serving top commissioned by Antine Associates. The imperceptible seaming and modified ogee edge attest to Plexibility's technical skill and Avonite R's inherent elegance. Photo by David Fishbein. Photo courtesy of Plexibility.
Figure 7.12 A beautifully upholstered chaise lounge chair by Brunschwig and Fils contrasts its elegance with the rustic log walls and twig table and chair. Twig furniture is America's answer to rattan and wicker furniture. Photo courtesy of Brunschwig and Fils.

manufacturers and products with which we are most familiar and whose quality we know and trust. Understanding the construction and composition of fine upholstered goods leads to the selection of pieces of quality and value.

Frames

Frames for upholstered furniture are made from the same materials as case goods: wood, metal, or plastic. Wooden frames are made of hardwood since softwoods generally lack the necessary strength and may split when joined. Wooden frames should be securely joined with double dowels and glue, and the corners should be braced with blocks or metal plates and securely glued and screwed into place.

Springs

Springs are generally of two types:

1. *Coil springs* are attached to a tightly woven webbing of rubber and metal, linen, jute, or synthetic. The webbing is stretched across and attached to the bottom of the frame and serves as the base for the springs, which are then tied together at the top in at least eight places per spring.
2. *Sinuous wire,* or no-sag, *springs* are fashioned from a single wire that is bent in a continuously curved zigzag and attached to the frame. This type of spring is used in chair backs or in upholstered pieces with particularly thin profiles because it requires less vertical space than traditional coil springs.

Cushioning

A layer of burlap protects and supports the padding and keeps it from working into the springs. The *padding* is a soft layer of *batting* made from a fibrous material such as cotton or polyester that covers the springs and frame and is used to give shape and form to the upholstered piece. A *casing* of muslin holds the padding in place and keeps the final cover from abrading the padding.

Some seating pieces are designed with *loose cushions* for reasons of aesthetics and comfort. Such cushions or pillows can be filled with foam-covered springs, down and feathers, foam, polyester fiberfill, or a combination of these materials.

Down is considered luxurious and is distinguished by its rumpled look. Because down and feathers are not resilient, such cushions require frequent plumping. Down cushions are increasingly rare due to cost. The most common cushioning material is *polyurethane foam* with a wrapping of polyester batting. Polyurethane foam comes in a variety of densities and is resilient, nonallergenic, and impervious to moisture. The polyester fiberfill gives added softness and comfort to the cushion and has the quality of resilience missing in down fill. *Reversible cushions* can help extend the life of an upholstered piece because the cushions can be turned. Lower quality furniture typically has solid foam or *laminated* (sandwiched) *foam,* where the thinner outer layers are less dense and resilient than the thicker middle layer, giving some of the feeling of more costly polyester-wrapped foam.

Coverings

Coverings have a major impact on the aesthetic quality of a finished piece of upholstered furniture. Identical pieces covered in dissimilar covers will each have a very different finished appearance. Because the cover is such a visible part of the piece, it will often be a major influence in the selection process.

Covers are available in a wide range of materials and qualities; manufacturers use the cover quality as a means to set prices for upholstered goods. A piece may be covered in material the client has obtained through a designer or elsewhere. These goods are referred to as *C.O.M.* (customer's own material) and are shipped to the manufacturer for upholstery on the selected piece. The manufacturer also maintains a supply of fabrics in several grades of quality that can be specified and ordered from catalogs and sample books supplied by the manufacturer. Each sample is assigned a grade corresponding to its quality; different prices are listed for each grade of material. A piece may be ordered with upholstery in muslin for use with custom-made *slipcovers* that can be changed seasonally or as they wear out.

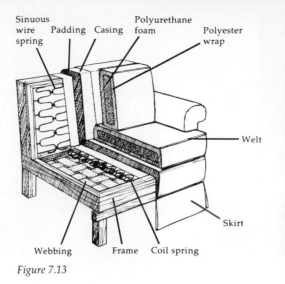

Figure 7.13

Figure 7.14

Figure 7.13 Upholstered piece.
Figure 7.14 Alice, an armless slipper chair from the Jubilee collection of upholstered furniture, designed by Georgina Fairholme for Lee Jofa, features an inviting, deep-cushioned shape with curving, tufted back, neat bolster pillow, deeply fringed skirt, and decorative welting trim. This style is an adaptation from the Victorian era. Each piece in this furniture line has an exceptional range of custom variations. Each may be skirted or plain, shirred or pleated, button or tufted, channeled, fringed, braided, tasseled, or perfectly plain and upholstered in a broad selection of beautiful fabrics. Photo courtesy of Lee Jofa.

The quality of the covering is dependent upon the material and finesse used in tailoring the piece. The materials used for upholstery are discussed in chapter 11, Fabric.

It is often necessary to order goods from catalogs without actually inspecting the pieces; one must rely on manufacturers who have an established reputation for quality and service. However, in some cases where pieces are available in showrooms, quality can be observed firsthand.

- The comfort of the piece can easily be judged by sitting in it.
- Check for careful matching of patterns or *naps* (direction of pile).
- Look for smooth seams and straight *welts* (covered cords) without puckering.
- Verify that cushions fit properly.
- Be aware of loose or hanging threads that might indicate poor craftsmanship.
- On *tufted* pieces, buttons should be tight.
- If a fabric has been quilted, the quilting should be carefully executed.

Figure 7.15

Human Factors

Function

The first consideration in selecting individual pieces of furniture and built-in fittings and fixtures for an environment is the users and the tasks they will perform in the environment.

Each environment has a certain function or group of functions for which it is designed. It is important to be familiar with all of these functions so that furniture and fittings can be designed or selected to enhance the desired function. For example, soft, deep, low-seating pieces for casual television viewing and music listening are very different from the kinds of seating one might choose for work at a sewing machine or computer. Such pieces should provide proper height and back support and should be based on actual human dimensions.

Anthropometrics, Ergonomics, and Biotechnology

Anthropometry is the study of human physical dimensions including height, weight, and volume. *Ergonomics* and *biotechnology* are the study of human relationships to the furniture and products that fill our environments. These terms may seem formidable, but their application to furniture design is simple: The human form, its dimensions, and its need for movement are the bases for functional and comfortable furniture design.

The ideas of comfort and function are often linked to culture. For example, people in parts of Asia and South America learn from childhood to sit on their haunches in

Figure 7.16

squatting fashion. Given the choice of a stool or a grassy spot by the roadside, these people might opt for the grass. Those from other areas of the world could certainly argue the relative comforts of sleeping in hammocks, on a Japanese futon mattress atop tatami mats, or on more conventional mattresses filled with water or coil springs. The ancient Egyptians developed sleeping arrangements with a headrest that today appears anything but comfortable.

Regardless of cultural influences, the best measure of function and comfort is the human form. Ideally furniture and fittings should be scaled to the average human form, but unfortunately, there is no such thing as an average person. Hertzberg, Daniels, and Churchill measured 132 different features of four thousand Air Force flyers and found that there were no men who fell in the average range on ten key measurements.[1] Nonetheless, most design is

Figure 7.15 The upholstery on this chair is an example of tufting.

Figure 7.16 Selecting the right chair for office work is paramount for not only comfort but physical well-being, as well. In the Knoll International showroom at the Interior Design Center, New York, in Long Island City, designers discuss the ergonomic

relationship of human dimensions to furniture forms. Knoll office furniture is displayed on the floor and suspended on the wall track near a shadow illustration of ergonomic forms. Photo by Ted Spiegel.

keyed to an average set of dimensions. These average measurements will not be optimum for everyone but will likely cause less inconvenience than if furniture, fittings, and fixtures were designed for the very short or the very tall. Personal environments can be custom designed to the dimensions of extreme individual sizes, and where possible, this should be an important goal of the design.

With all the research and developments in furniture design, it is interesting to note how little the overall form and dimensions of furniture have changed over the millenia. Today's ergonomic superchairs (see Nonresidential Considerations at the end of this chapter) differ very little in general dimensions from the chairs used in ancient Egypt.

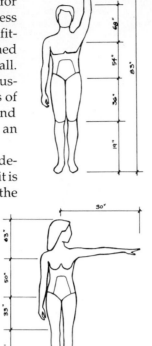

The Classics

Ancient Egypt may seem far removed from today's designs, but cultures of the past and the designs they produced can be a key to understanding the aesthetic appeal of well-designed furniture. As fashions change and styles fall from popularity, certain pieces remain appealing. These pieces that have the power to endure the passage of time are considered *classics*. A knowledge of the classics is a solid foundation for the selection of furniture that will always be pleasing to the senses. Because some furniture manufacturers have taken classic pieces and styles and adapted them poorly, some bad design has resulted. Consequently, some people have an aversion to certain historical styles, yet some furniture makers do build historical pieces of exquisite style and quality. The following list does not include every possible classic design but rather pieces that are frequently seen either as *antiques*, fine quality reproductions, or modern classics in contemporary residential and nonresidential environments.

Pieces from History

The Thebes stool design is based on an Egyptian prototype and was registered with Liberty of London in 1884. This stool was among the first products of Liberty's Furnishings and Decoration Studio, established in 1883 by Leonard F. Wyburd, the designer of the Thebes stool.

Figure 7.17

Figure 7.18

Figure 7.19

(A)
Figure 7.20

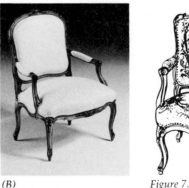

(B)   Figure 7.21

Figure 7.17 Thebes stool.
Figure 7.18 Klismos.
Figure 7.19 Régence fauteuil.
Figure 7.20 (A) French Louis XV side chairs in fine damask are placed around a gaming table in the trophy room of Filoli, a National Trust Property Georgian mansion open to

the public outside San Francisco. Photograph by Peter Vitale. Textiles by and photo courtesy of Brunschwig and Fils. (B) A French Louis XV fauteuil armchair is seen here with classic Rococo lines and hand carving. The curved cabriole legs add grace and charm to this highly favored

occasional chair. Photo courtesy of Casa Stradivari.
Figure 7.21 Louis XV fauteuil.
Figure 7.22 Louis XVI fauteuil.
Figure 7.23 Louis XVI bergère.
Figure 7.24 A French bergère in the Neoclassic Louis XVI style. A loose pillow seat cushion and fine, hand-

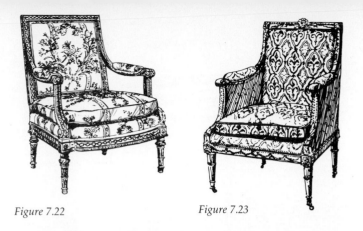

Figure 7.22

Figure 7.23

Figure 7.24

Figure 7.25

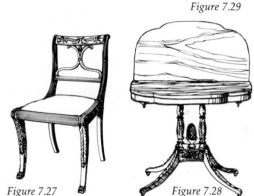

Figure 7.26

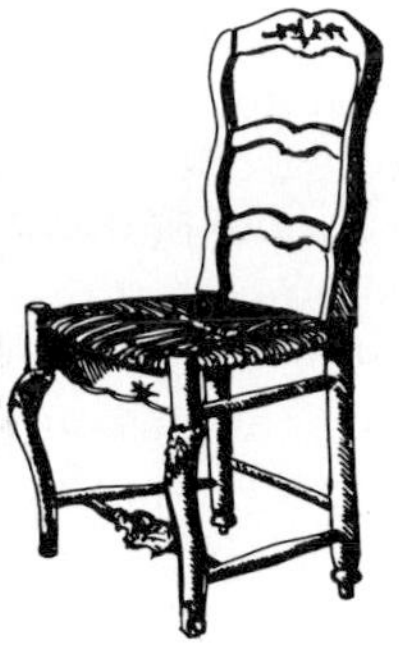

Figure 7.29

Figure 7.27

Figure 7.28

The klismos chair is one of a group of beautiful reproductions of Greek furniture pieces taken from depictions on archaeological artifacts. The pieces, designed by T. H. Robsjohn-Gibbings (1905-1976), are made in Greece by Saridis S. A. and are distributed in America by Gretchen Bellinger, Inc.

The French Règence fauteuil is an open *armchair* from the period of French Règence (1715-1723) between the reigns of Louis XIV and Louis XV. The piece is characterized by the use of cane for the back and seat, *cabriole legs*, and *stretchers* between the legs.

The Louis XV fauteuil is an open armchair from the *Rococo* (1723-1774) or *Louis XV period.* The lines of the chair are curvilinear, it has no stretchers, and it has an upholstered seat and back. The line of the cabriole leg continues without a break into the line of the *apron.*

The Louis XVI fauteuil is an open armchair from the French Neoclassic (1774-1793) or *Louis XVI period.* The piece is characterized by the rectilinear lines of classical design. The chair back is generally either oval or rectangular, and the straight tapered legs have no stretchers.

The French bergère is an upholstered armchair with fully upholstered sides. The fauteuil has an open space between the armrest and the seat, but on the *bergère* that space is filled with cushioning and fabric. Because the bergère was popular during several of the French periods, it is seen in more than one style. The piece pictured (fig. 7.23) is in the Louis XVI style.

The French Empire and English Regency are styles from the beginning of the nineteenth century during the reign of Napoleon in France and George IV in England. Much of the furniture from this period was heavy, based on designs from Rome, yet some of the chairs from the period were amazingly light and delicate, inspired by a new appreciation for the designs of classical Greece, and maintaining much of the delicacy of the previous Louis XVI and Sheraton styles. The Empire and Regency designs made their way to Northern Europe and America where the styles are known respectively as *Biedermeier* and *American Empire* or *Regency.* Duncan Phyfe (1768-1854), a Scottish cabinet-

maker who worked in New York, is famous for his delicate Regency-style furniture. His designs often incorporated the lyre or harp as a prominent motif. Until recently, only the Duncan Phyfe designs from this period had widespread popularity. However, today the heavier *French Empire* and Biedermeier styles are beginning to find wide acceptance as antiques and are being manufactured in larger numbers as reproductions.

The chaise á capucine or fauteuil á la bonne femme is a ladder-back chair with a rush seat from the provinces of France. Provincial designs were influenced by court styles, so the chair may feature straight or curved lines depending on the influence. Most of the fine reproductions feature curved back slats and legs.

carved wood trim in country maple make this chair richly appealing. Fabric cover is a floral glazed chintz. The chair is available in a selection of custom antique finishes and lacquer colors and, of course, any upholstery fabric. Photo courtesy of Casa Stradivari.

Figure 7.25 Empire console table.
Figure 7.26 An English Regency side chair and armchair, based on designs influenced by French Empire and Regency styles. These chairs, japanned black with gold accent trim, combine classic simplicity in outline with elegant decoration of Roman,

Greek, and Egyptian origin. The armchair has a falcon's head detail. This look is favored by designers of traditional and eclectic interiors. During Federal/American Empire years, the foremost designer of this style was Duncan Phyfe. This

adaptation is offered by KPS, Inc. Photo courtesy of KPS, Inc.
Figure 7.27 Duncan Phyfe chair.
Figure 7.28 Duncan Phyfe table.
Figure 7.29 Chaise à capucine (fauteuil á la bonne femme).

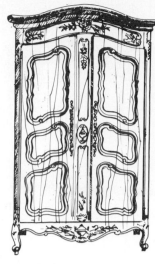

Figure 7.30

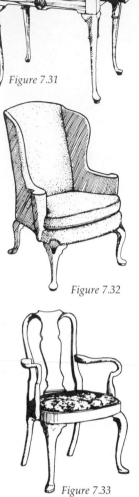

Figure 7.31

Figure 7.32

Figure 7.33

Figure 7.34

The Country French armoire is a large carved wardrobe used for storage. Like the fauteuil á la bonne femme, the design of the *armoire* was influenced by the designs at court and may show asymmetrical elements common to the Rococo style or the rectilinear qualities of Louis XVI designs.

The Queen Anne tea table was a popular piece in eighteenth-century England and America as tea drinking became increasingly fashionable and the serving of tea a highly refined art. The *tea table* is characterized by its cabriole legs with *club feet*. Unlike the French Rococo cabriole leg, the *Queen Anne* cabriole leg does not continue into the line of the apron but rather makes a distinct and abrupt connection with the apron where they meet. Below the apron, the knee of the leg is often carved with a shell or other motif.

The Queen Anne wing chair evolved from a seventeenth-century sleeping chair; the wings provided support for a nodding head. The *wing chair* is upholstered and has typical Queen Anne cabriole legs, some versions with stretchers, others without.

The Queen Anne chairs feature upholstered seats, round shouldered hoop backs with a vase- or fiddle-shaped *splat*, cabriole legs generally without stretchers, and club feet. The *side chair* is armless, and the armchair has open arms in various forms, the most common of which is the gooseneck or shepherd's crook arm with its beautifully shaped curve.

The Queen Anne lowboy and highboy are important case pieces from the eighteenth century. The *lowboy* is a raised chest on cabriole legs, generally with two drawers or a single wide drawer and two smaller square drawers in the curved apron below. The *highboy* is created when a chest of four or five drawers is placed on top of the lowboy. The top of the highboy may be crowned with some type of *pediment*, but most often will be flat with a slight cornice.

Figure 7.35

The Chippendale chairs were designed during the middle part of the eighteenth century by Englishman Thomas Chippendale II (1718-1799). His book of designs, *The Gentleman and Cabinet-Maker's Director*, published in 1754, featured 160 plates with drawings of furniture pieces. Be-

Figure 7.30 Country French armoire.
Figure 7.31 Queen Anne tea table.
Figure 7.32 Queen Anne wing chair.
Figure 7.33 Queen Anne armchair.

Figure 7.34 A lovely recreated Early Georgian interior shows contemporary preference for Queen Anne furniture, such as the armchair in the foreground, the walnut highboy, and the upholstered Queen Anne wing chair. These pieces were developed from museum antiques made by early American craftsmen and reproduced today. Photo courtesy of Hickory/Kaylyn.
Figure 7.35 Queen Anne highboy.

Figure 7.36   Figure 7.37   Figure 7.38

Figure 7.43

Figure 7.39

Figure 7.40

Figure 7.42

Figure 7.41

The Chippendale camel-back sofa is an upholstered piece with a *serpentine*-shaped back that dips and rises from rolled arms to a hump in the center. The sofa has either cabriole legs with claw and ball feet or Marlborough legs with and without stretchers.

cause the designs were published in book form, any skilled craftsman could build or adapt them, and as a result, their popularity soon spread throughout the British Isles and America. Chippendale's drawings showed the influence of French (Louis XV), Chinese, *Gothic*, and Neoclassic designs. The Chippendale chair is characterized by its upholstered seat, cabriole legs with a claw and ball feet, a yoke-shaped back with an ornately carved splat. The backs might be carved in the form of ribbons, in Gothic *tracery*, in Chinese *fretwork*, or into pierced slats forming a ladder-back. The Chippendale cabriole legs joined the apron in the same manner as the Queen Anne cabriole legs. On some pieces a straight square leg known as the *Marlborough leg* was common.

The Chippendale wing chair is similar to the Queen Anne wing chair but generally has either cabriole legs with claw and ball feet or Marlborough legs.

The blockfront is a furniture detail associated with John Goddard (1724-1785) of Newport, Rhode Island. The *blockfront*, which was applied to Chippendale-style case pieces, consists of a front panel divided into three alternating vertical convex and concave sections. The inside section is concave, the two outside sections are convex, and the top of each section is finished with a carved convex or concave shell. The piece pictured in figure 7.43 is a chest.

The Chippendale breakfront is a case piece designed in such a way that the front plane of the piece is broken, i.e., part advancing and part receding. The *breakfront* was commonly built as a *secretary* or a china cupboard and had an enclosed cabinet below and open shelves with glass doors above. The breakfront was also popular in succeeding periods and appears in several styles.

The Chippendale highboy, like the Queen Anne highboy, consists of a low two drawer chest on legs (lowboy) with an additional chest of drawers above. The chest is topped by a scroll pediment with a *finial*. In the eighteenth century, Philadelphia, Pennsylvania, was an important center for furniture manufacture. The Philadelphia highboy, with its magnificent carving, is a particularly beautiful example of the American version of the Chippendale style.

Figure 7.36 Chippendale chair.
Figure 7.37 Chinese Chippendale chair.
Figure 7.38 Chippendale ladder-back chair.

Figure 7.39 Chippendale wing chair with Marlborough legs.
Figure 7.40 Chippendale camel-back sofa.
Figure 7.41 Chippendale breakfront.

Figure 7.42 Chippendale Philadelphia highboy.

Figure 7.43 Block-front chest.

Figure 7.44

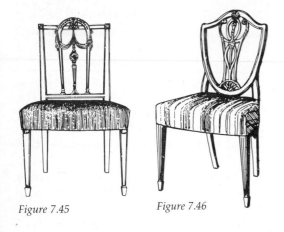

Figure 7.45   Figure 7.46

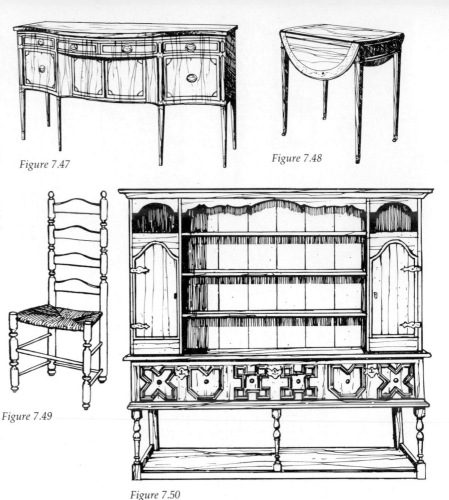

Figure 7.47

Figure 7.48

Figure 7.49

Figure 7.50

The Hepplewhite/Sheraton chairs are typical of the delicate Neoclassic style of the latter part of the eighteenth century. In 1788 George Hepplewhite (d. 1786) produced a book called *The Cabinet-Maker and Upholsterer's Guide*, which contained furniture designs inspired by the work of *Robert Adam* (1728-1792), one of the foremost interior designers and architects of the day. Thomas Sheraton's (1751-1806) *The Cabinet-Maker and Upholsterer's Drawing Book*, published in 1791, was filled with variations of Hepplewhite's designs. Because both men worked in the same style, it is often difficult to distinguish between their designs. The distinctions are usually based on very slight differences in detail such as the direction of the curve on a drawer front or the shape of a chair back. Their chair designs featured straight square or *reeded* round tapered legs without stretchers. The chair with the rectangular back is considered typical of the Sheraton style; and the shield- or heart-shaped back chairs, typical of Hepplewhite designs.

The Hepplewhite/Sheraton sideboard or buffet is a serving piece with drawers, raised on straight tapered legs. If the side drawers are concave, the piece is considered a Hepplewhite *sideboard or buffet;* if they are convex, it is considered a Sheraton sideboard.

The Hepplewhite/Sheraton pembroke table is an *occasional (drop-leaf) table* with drop leaves and a drawer in the apron. The top, when open, is oval in shape, and the legs are straight and tapered, without stretchers.

The American ladder-back chair is an important piece based on an English prototype. It has a frame made of straight members turned in a fashion that resembles a string of sausages (called sausage *turnings*) and joined with stretchers. The *ladder-back chair* would often appear in more humble homes or in the kitchens and servants' quarters of grander homes. Like some other provincial chairs, the ladder-back chair has a seat of woven rush.

The Welsh dresser or *hutch* is a side piece with cupboards and drawers and a set of open shelves above. The *Welsh dresser* is descended from a sixteenth-century French kitchen cupboard and was popular in England in the seventeenth century as well as in Early America.

Figure 7.44 Hepplewhite/Sheraton side chairs with exquisitely hand-carved heart-shaped backs and Neoclassic motifs. Chair cover and wall coverings/textiles are full-bodied adaptations of American Federal-striped fabric designs. Photo courtesy of C & A Wall Coverings.

Figure 7.45 Sheraton chair.
Figure 7.46 Hepplewhite shield-back chair.

Figure 7.47 Hepplewhite sideboard (buffet).
Figure 7.48 Hepplewhite/Sheraton pembroke table.

Figure 7.49 American ladder-back chair with rush seat.
Figure 7.50 Welsh dresser (hutch).

Figure 7.51

Figure 7.53

Figure 7.52

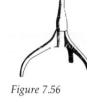

Figure 7.54

The American Windsor chair, as the name implies, is based on an English prototype. The *Windsor chair* is characterized by its saddle-shaped seat, turned legs with stretchers, and spindle back. The early versions were invariably painted. The most common backs are the curved bow or loop back and the comb back. Some later Windsor chairs featured legs turned to resemble bamboo. The English Windsor chair has a pierced splat and may have cabriole legs.

Figure 7.56

Figure 7.55

The Hitchcock chair was designed by *Lambert Hitchcock* (1795-1852), a Connecticut designer. The chair shows the influence of Sheraton and Regency designs and is characterized by its black painted finish, turned legs, rush or cane seat, and gold stenciled fruit and flower decoration.

The Belter chair is typical of the designs of *John Henry Belter* (d. 1865). A New York craftsman, Belter created heavily carved pieces of furniture from laminated rosewood. Both his upholstered and case pieces were curvilinear and showed the influence of French Rococo design. These pieces are a good example of *Victorian* taste for revival styles.

The Shaker chair and rocker are particularly simple in contrast to contemporary Victorian designs. The *Shakers* were a nineteenth-century religious group whose beliefs included the design of furniture free from excessive decoration. The chair has straight legs with straight stretchers and straight uprights with simply formed slats or a woven back. Like the woven backs, the seats are generally webbed with cotton tapes. The uprights and arms might be finished with simple finials, and the top rail was sometimes designed to accommodate a blanket.

The Shaker candlestand is a small *tripod pedestal table* of beautiful proportions and delicate lines. Like other Shaker pieces, it is remarkable because of the purity of its design and its suitablity in contemporary environments.

Figure 7.51 American Windsor chair.
Figure 7.52 Hitchcock chair.

Figure 7.53 Belter chair.
Figure 7.54 Shaker rocker.
Figure 7.55 This stoic scene represents the Shaker style. The ladder-back chair can be hung on the wall pegs when not in use. Utility table and round boxes further

demonstrate simple, classic lines and superb craftsmanship for which the Shakers have been justly famous. Wood window by and photo courtesy of the Anderson Corporation.
Figure 7.56 Shaker candlestand.

Modern Classics

The Vienna café chair, corbu chair, and bentwood rocker are pieces designed by German Michael Thonet (1796-1871) and manufactured in Austria during the last half of the nineteenth century. Thonet invented a bentwood process for bending wood that gives these pieces their beautiful curvilinear design and eliminates the need for complex joinery. Today these chairs are manufactured by Thonet.

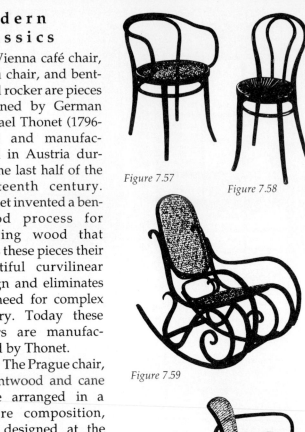

The Prague chair, a bentwood and cane piece arranged in a square composition, was designed at the turn of the century by *Josef Hoffmann* (1870-1956), a member of the *Vienna Secession* and founding member of its offshoot, the *Wiener Werkstäte* (Vienna Workshop).

The Fledermaus chair with its distinctively shaped back and ball *pendants* is Josef Hoffmann's 1905 design. The Fledermaus and Prague chairs are available from Thonet.

The Hill chair is a striking perpendicular piece created in 1903 by *Charles Rennie Mackintosh* (1868-1928) for the Hill House in Glasglow, Scotland. It is constructed of black ebony with a padded seat and is distinguished by a high grid back treatment. The Hill chair, considered an extraordinary design for the period, was particularly influential with the Secessionists in Vienna. The Hill chair is distributed by Atelier International.

The Parsons table was designed by Jean-Michel Frank (d. 1941) of France and *Joseph Platt* of New York in the 1920s. The original design was a low occasional table finished in black or white plastic and was named for the Parsons School of Design in New York. The piece is manufactured today in several different forms by many manufacturers.

Figure 7.57

Figure 7.58

Figure 7.59

Figure 7.60

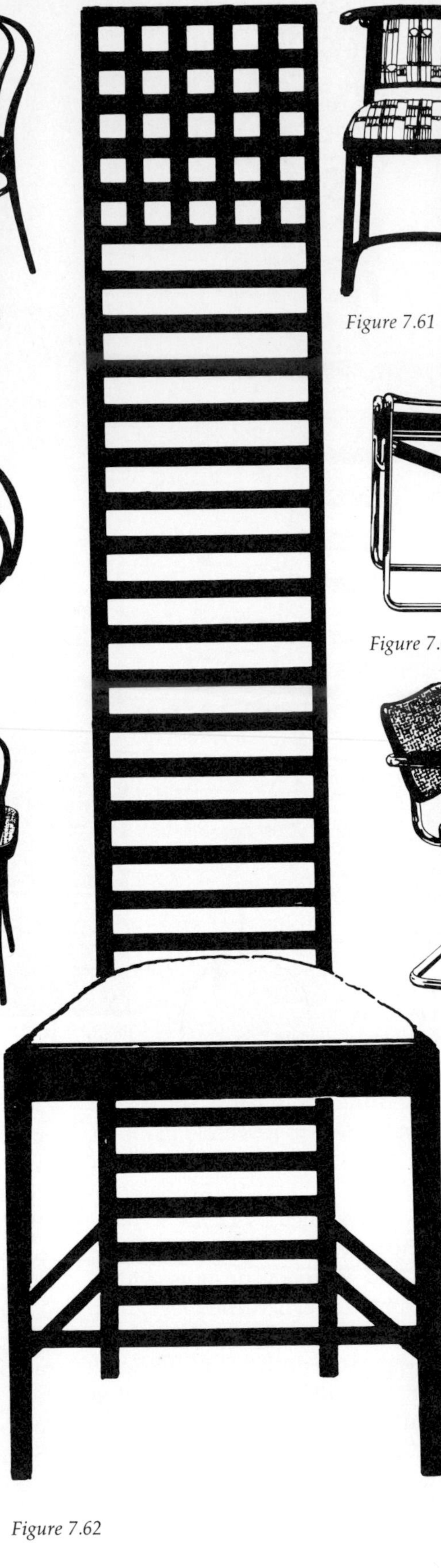

Figure 7.61

Figure 7.62

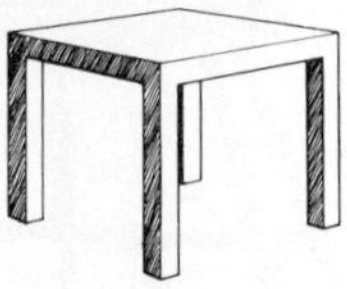

Figure 7.63

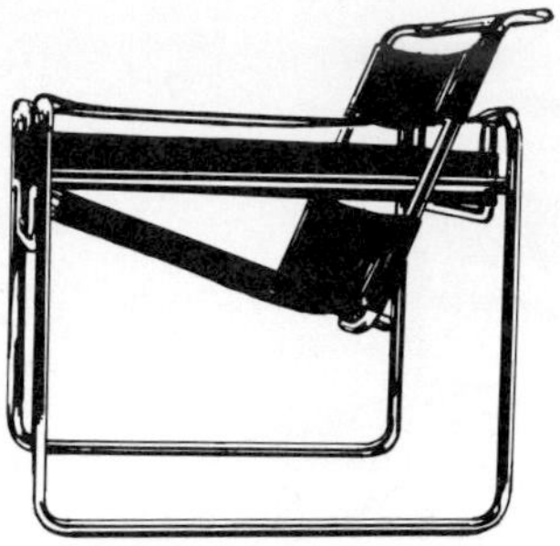

Figure 7.64

Figure 7.65

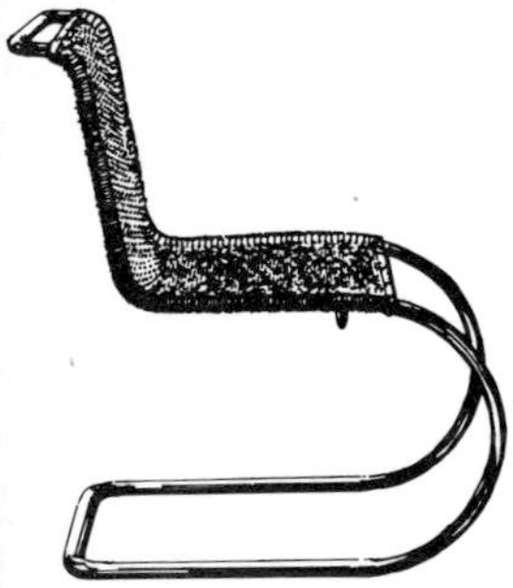

Figure 7.66

Figure 7.57 Corbu chair.	***Figure 7.61*** Fledermaus chair.	***Figure 7.64*** Wassily lounge chair.
Figure 7.58 Vienna café chair.	***Figure 7.62*** Hill chair.	***Figure 7.65*** Cesca chair.
Figure 7.59 Bentwood rocker.	***Figure 7.63*** Parsons table.	***Figure 7.66*** MR chair.
Figure 7.60 Prague chair.		

Figure 7.67

Figure 7.68

Figure 7.69

Figure 7.70

Figure 7.72

Figure 7.71

The Wassily lounge chair (1925), the world's first bent tubular steel chair, was designed by *Marcel Breuer* (1902-1981), one of the foremost designers of the Bauhaus in Germany. The *Bauhaus*, a school of art, architecture, and design, attracted some of the world's finest designers from 1919 to 1933. The chair was named for *Wassily Kandinsky*, an important artist and Bauhaus faculty member. Breuer was one of the first of many designers to take advantage of the possibilities of this versatile combination of materials.

The Cesca chair is another bent tubular steel design by Marcel Breuer. The Cesca chair has a wood-framed seat and back of cane mounted on a cantilevered frame. The *cantilever* design has no back legs and was a remarkable breakthrough made possible by the strength of the metal. Both the Wassily lounge and Cesca chair are manufactured by Knoll International and Thonet.

The MR chair is a tubular steel and wicker or tubular steel and leather piece designed in 1926 by *Ludwig Mies van der Rohe* (1886-1969), the last director of the Bauhaus. The MR chair, like the Cesca chair, is designed on the cantilever principle.

The Barcelona collection was designed by Ludwig Mies van der Rohe for his German pavilion at the Barcelona International Exhibition of 1929. The Barcelona chair and Barcelona stool are constructed on a double X frame of polished stainless steel and are meticulously upholstered in tufted leather. The Barcelona table has an X-shaped frame of polished stainless steel with a glass top.

The Brno chair is Mies van der Rohe's 1930 design for the Tugendhat House in Brno, Czechoslovakia. The cantilevered design has great strength and visual appeal. The Brno chair, the Barcelona collection, and the MR chair are all manufactured by Knoll International, Inc.

The Grand and Petit Confort chairs were designed in 1929 by Swiss-born French designer *Charles-Edouard Jeanneret-Gris* (1887-1965), better known as *Le Corbusier*. The Grand Confort has a basketlike frame of bent tubular steel with a series of leather cushions forming the seating unit. The Petit Confort is the same design in smaller scale.

The Basculant chair was designed by Le Corbusier in 1928. The chair has a frame of tubular steel with seat and back of calf skin and arm straps of leather.

The Pony chaise, designed by Le Corbusier in 1928, is an adjustable chaise lounge with a frame of chromium-plated tubular steel, a base of matte textured steel and pony skin or leather upholstery. These three Le Corbusier designs are manufactured by Atelier International.

Figure 7.67 Barcelona chair.
Figure 7.68 Classic modern furniture is at ease on hard-surface tile and with the clean lines of the walls, cabinetry, and vertical window blinds. The dining table in the center and desk stool at the far left are from the Warren Platner Wire Grouping (Knoll International, Inc.). Bar stools are Magistretti (Atelier International, Inc.) and the Brno chairs were designed by Mies van der Rohe (Knoll International, Inc.). Photo courtesy of Italian Tile.

Figure 7.69 Brno chair.
Figure 7.70 Grand (and petit) Confort.
Figure 7.71 Basculant chair.
Figure 7.72 Pony chaise.

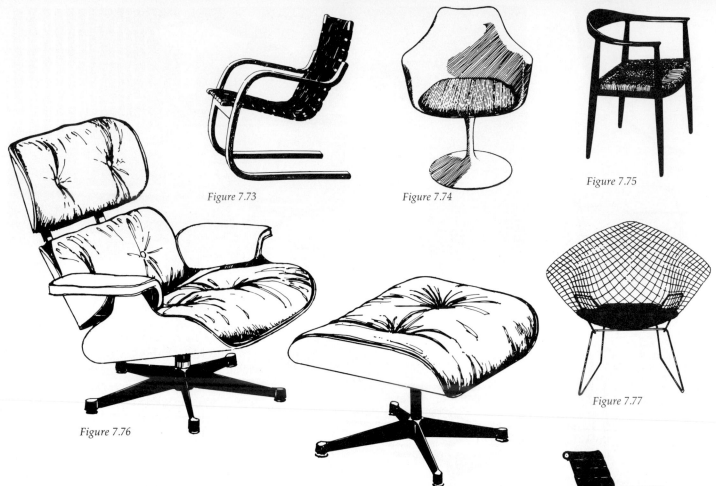

Figure 7.73

Figure 7.74

Figure 7.75

Figure 7.76

Figure 7.77

Figure 7.78

Armchair 406 is a 1935 cantilever design by *Alvar Aalto* (1899-1976) of Finland. The flexible bent laminated plywood frame has a seat and back of woven fabric. Armchair 406 is manufactured by ICF.

The Pedestal group was created by *Eero Saarinen* (1910-1961) in 1956 and was a significant design of a furniture collection without the traditional four legs. The single base of the table and chairs is made of aluminum, and the shell of the seating pieces is made of fiberglass. The tabletop may be marble, glass, wood, or laminate. The Pedestal group is manufactured by Knoll International.

THE chair is a classic Scandinavian design by Denmark's *Hans Wegner* (b. 1914). The 1949 piece is the epitome of fine craftsmanship featuring a beautifully joined wooden frame with a seat of cane or upholstery. THE chair is manufactured by D.S.I.

The Eames lounge chair was designed in 1956 by *Charles* (1907-1978) *and Ray Eames*. The lounge was designed for comfort featuring a chair and *ottoman* with metal bases, bent laminated wood frames, and carefully padded leather upholstery. The lounge was a great success and, like many of the classics, has been widely copied. The original design is manufactured by Herman Miller.

The Bertoia Wire Group by Italian-born *Harry Bertoia* (1915-1978) is a sculptural approach to seating design. The chairs are formed of lattice and are made of a steel rod frame with or without cushions and upholstery. The Bertoia chairs, originally designed in 1956 for Hans and Florence Knoll, are still produced by Knoll International.

The Aluminum Group was also designed by Charles and Ray Eames in 1958. The chairs consist of a cast aluminum star base with horizontally ribbed seat and back of fabric or vinyl attached to a curved aluminum frame. The design offers a great deal of flexibility because the pieces are available in a variety of sizes. Herman Miller is the manufacturer of the aluminum group.

GF 40/4 stacking chair by *David Rowland* was created in 1964 to meet the need for a well-designed nonresidential chair that could be stacked in large numbers. The GF 40/4

Figure 7.73 Armchair 406.
Figure 7.74 Pedestal chair.

Figure 7.75 THE Chair.
Figure 7.76 Eames lounge chair.

Figure 7.77 Bertoia wire group.
Figure 7.78 Aluminum group.

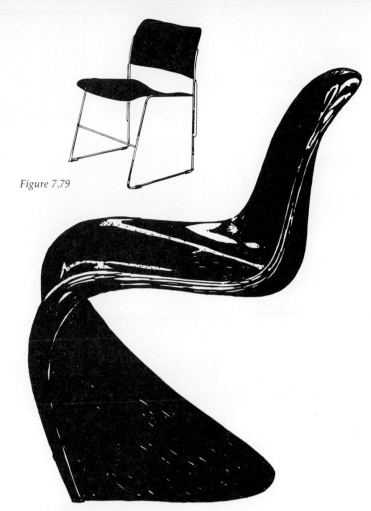

Figure 7.79

Figure 7.80

Figure 7.81

Figure 7.82

Figure 7.83

Figure 7.79 GF 40/4 stacking chair.
Figure 7.80 Panton stacking chair.
Figure 7.81 Soriana chair.
Figure 7.82 Plia chair.
Figure 7.83 Platner wire grouping.

has strong legs made of bent steel rods with a seat and back of thin sheets of rolled steel. The chairs can be loaded in a four-foot stack, forty chairs deep, on a specially designed trolley. The GF 40/4 has been adapted and copied by various companies. The original Rowland design is manufactured by GF Furniture Systems.

The Panton stacking chair is significant because of the way its design takes advantage of the possibilities of plastic. Danish-born Swiss designer *Verner Panton* (b. 1926) designed the chair in 1960 using a single piece of plastic providing great strength and beautifully controlled form. The Panton stacking chair is manufactured by Panton Design.

The Soriana chair is representative of Italian design and was created by *Tobia* (b. 1935) *and Afra* (b. 1937) *Scarpa* in 1970. It is a series of folded and rolled fabric or leather cushions held in place by a metal frame. The Soriana chair is manufactured by Atelier International.

The Plia chair was designed by *Giancarlo Peretti* (b. 1940) of Italy and is a classic folding chair. The piece is characterized by a simple hub containing the entire folding mechanism. The Plia chair is manufactured by Castelli.

The Platner Wire Grouping, designed by *Warren Platner* (b. 1919) in 1967, consists of tables, chairs, and stools modeled from wire rods in a repeating linear design. Some of the pieces may have as many as 1,400 welds. The wire grouping is manufactured by Knoll International.

Nonresidential Considerations

Custom Designs

Nonresidential (and residential) designs often include needs and functions that require specialized fittings and furniture that may not be available from manufacturers. Such pieces can be *custom designed* and built to meet an exact set of specifications. For example, a restaurant design may include a long padded bench (banquette) against a wall, intended for seating with a series of tables. Such pieces must be custom designed and built for a particular set of dimensions because they cannot be ordered from a catalog. Custom designs help establish a distinctive look for an interior because they are one of a kind, created for a unique set of requirements.

Systems Furniture

To meet the challenge of flexibility created by complex and changing needs in offices, laboratories, and production facility designs, product designers have developed *systems furniture,* manufactured in modules that can be assembled and reassembled in different configurations. The spaces created may be open, private, semiprivate, or a combination. The modules might consist of full or partial height

Figure 7.84

Figure 7.84 Herman Miller's Action Office Encore system was introduced in 1986, two decades after the first Action Office system was developed. This grouping clearly demonstrates the flexibility that systems furniture allows. The designers have also planned for personalization of the space with tacking surfaces for pictures and mementos. Photo courtesy of Herman Miller, Inc.

Figure 7.85

Figure 7.86

panels or divider units to which coat racks, filing cabinets, bookcases, storage bins, writing surfaces, chalkboards, computer stations, work surfaces, drawing surfaces, and drawer units can be attached. The systems can also be integrated with freestanding furniture components. These systems contain all the wiring for *task lighting*, ambient lighting, telephones, computer links, electric power, and the systems designed for laboratories even provide flexible plumbing connections.

The wide acceptance of systems furniture is the result of its tremendous flexibility. The inflexibility and permanence of wall construction is eliminated by the use of modular dividers and components that define space in much the same way as conventional constructed walls. These modules also allow users to reclaim unused space or space whose designated function has changed with very little effort or disturbance. Because of their wide use, manufacturers have deemed it worthwhile to invest in the aesthetic design of modular components; the result is exciting lines of systems furniture with great appeal as well as utility.

Ergonomic Superchairs

In today's society many people spend the greater part of their day in work situations where they must be seated. In order to be functional, seating must offer its human users sustained comfort. Because of this need, there has been much research that has led to the design of highly flexible

seating pieces. These self-adjusting chairs are designed to sustain and support the human form and to accommodate the body, which is constantly shifting and changing. These chairs absorb the shock of sitting down and support the body in an upright position until the user decides to lean back. When reclining, the chair shifts to transfer body weight from the buttocks to the back, legs, and thighs. The feet remain on the floor as the user tips back, and the back of the chair flexes to provide constant support for the lumbar area. The result is sustained comfort, reduced physical strain, and less tiring of the lower back. This kind of comfort is a boon to productivity and satisfaction.

Notes

1. McCormick, Ernest J. *Human Factors Engineering.* (New York: McGraw-Hill, 1970), pp. 385-87.

Bibliography

Better Homes and Gardens New Decorating Book. Des Moines: Meredith, 1981.

Boger, Louise Ade. *The Complete Guide to Furniture Styles.* New York: Charles Scribner's Sons, 1969.

Chippendale, Thomas. *The Gentleman and Cabinet-Maker's Director.* New York: Dover Publications, Inc., 1966.

Diffrient, Niels, Alvin R. Tilley, and Joan C. Bardagjy. *Humanscale 1/2/3.* Cambridge: The MIT Press, 1974.

Dreyfuss, Henry. *The Measure of Man: Human Factors in Design.* New York: Whitney Library of Design, 1967.

Fitzgerald, Oscar P. *Three Centuries of American Furniture.* Englewood Cliffs: Prentice-Hall, Inc., 1982.

Figure 7.85 A continuous seating unit forms a waiting space for several users in this reception area. The curved form of the piece helps create a focus by drawing the eye into the framed painting and memorial plaque honoring the person for whom the building is named. Photo by Andy Battenfield and Kelly Haas.

Figure 7.86 The Ergon 2 chair is the second generation of ergonomic seating produced by Herman Miller. It was designed by Bill Stumpf and features smooth edges that support without restricting circulation, a specially curved back that provides support for the lower back, and back and seat that are adjustable to height and tilt tension. Photo courtesy of Herman Miller, Inc.

Gilliatt, Mary. *The Decorating Book.* New York: Pantheon, 1981.

Hepplewhite, George. *The Cabinet-Maker and Upholsterer's Guide.* New York: Dover Publications, Inc., 1969.

The History of Furniture. Anne Charlish, ed. London: Orbis Publishing, 1976.

Lucie-Smith, Edward. *Furniture: A Concise History.* New York: Oxford University Press, 1979.

McCormick, Ernest J. *Human Factors Engineering.* New York: McGraw-Hill, 1970.

Meadmore, Clement. *The Modern Chair.* New York: Van Nostrand Reinhold Company, 1979.

Murphy, Dennis Grant. *The Materials of Interior Design.* Burbank: Stratford House, 1978.

Panero, Julius. *Anatomy for Interior Designers.* New York: Whitney Library of Design, 1962.

Panero, Julius, and Martin Zelnik. *Human Dimension and Interior Space.* New York: Whitney Library of Design, 1981.

Pegler, Martin M. *The Dictionary of Interior Design.* New York: Fairchild Publications, 1983.

Riggs, J. Rosemary. *Materials and Components of Interior Design.* Englewood Cliffs: Prentice-Hall, 1989.

Sheraton, Thomas. *The Cabinet-Maker and Upholsterer's Drawing Book.* New York: Dover Publications, Inc., 1972.

Stimpson, Miriam. *Modern Furniture Classics.* New York: Whitney Library of Design, 1987.

Whiton, Sherrill. *Interior Design and Decoration.* Philadelphia: J.B. Lippincott Company, 1974.

ARCHITECTURAL DETAIL

Architectural detail should be considered as structural sculpture. Drawing upon classic tradition, Boscobel, built by the Dyckman family in the eighteenth century in the Hudson River Valley, is one of America's finest Federal-period museum houses. In the dining room, moldings, carved paterae motifs, and a delicate leaded glass fanlight with repeated elliptic shapes display the superb craftsmanship available in New York during the early days of our Republic. Photo by Ted Spiegel.

Page 188, top: Just as a successfully designed house must have consistency between various elements of its exterior, so should the architectural details of the interior be compatible with its exterior. In the facade of Boscobel, we see many Neoclassic "Adam-inspired" motifs that are repeated with variation within. Photo by Ted Spiegel. **Page 188, bottom:** The architectural detail at Boscobel offers some of the finest work in America. The grand staircase at the core of the house frames a Palladian window arrangement that fills two floors with north light. A wide staircase divides at the landing, its graceful turn lining up precisely with the outer pilaster of the architectural molding. White stringers with stained wooden stair treads compose rhythmic gradation as the eye ascends. The wallpaper is designed to create trompe l'oeil three-dimensional bas-relief blocks. Photo by Ted Spiegel. **Page 189, left:** The consistency between the doorway with its sidelights is an element of both the exterior and the interior (in any home) and should be considered as a portion of the interior's design. Note that raised-panel double doors here are only two feet wide, making it necessary to graciously open both doors to accommodate guests. Four feet is a comfortable width for two people to walk through together. Photo by Ted Spiegel. **Page 189, right:** Details of frieze corner blocks above pilaster columns on four Neoclassic fireplaces from four different rooms display the adaptability of the plaster anaglypta reliefs. Originally carved in wood, these classical Greek and Roman motifs—urns, human figures, paterae and acanthus leaf, and intertwining ellipses—were cast in plaster to be reproduced as needed. Photo by Ted Spiegel.

WEST ELEVATION

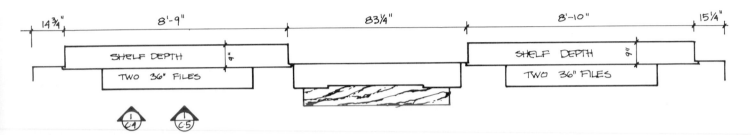

Page 190: *Custom-cut Brazilian mahogany in various shapes formed the raw material of a formal library/ writing room in New York City. Craftsmen from Chelsea Custom Corporation, following the interior design specifications (top) of Nancy Mannucci, ASID, install cove molding atop bookshelves. The bookcase base is mahogany-faced lateral file drawers. Whereas most of the cabinetry is milled at the woodworking shop, the saw in the center of the room (bottom) testifies to the need to cut precisely mitered edges that are skillfully joined on location. Photo by Ted Spiegel.*

Page 191, top: *A closeup of the moldings of the finished library/ writing room, a handsome and rich environment for composing script and text. Cabinetry, a cross between furniture and architecture, is often designed for the interior after the building itself is complete, adding to the visual and monetary value of the interior. Photo by Ted Spiegel.*

Page 191, bottom: *Interiors of contemporary design are often created without "historical" architectural details. The impact of this showroom design for Brickel, an important supplier of nonresidential chairs, lies in the fact that the architectural detail has been kept to a minimum. This simplicity allows the chairs, fabric samples, and leather swatches to be the center of focus. The curve of the arch in the background and its repetition in the radial foreground wall add important visual interest without detracting from the principal intent of the design. Interior design by Edward Schwartz. Photo by Ted Spiegel.*

Walls

In common dwellings from many periods, the wall treatment was generally the same as the building materials. For example, medieval interiors often included a timber framework and stucco infill as a wall treatment. They might also have stone walls left plain, stuccoed with rough plaster, or simply whitewashed. Panels of wood that were joined (fitted together) and carved like furniture were used in the great churches of the Middle Ages. This type of paneling was also used in castles and manor houses as a barrier from the dampness of stone walls and as a form of decoration. This paneling, which usually reached above the level of the doors, was called a *wainscot*. The wood was framed in small vertical panels (approximately one foot by nine inches) that were carved with a motif resembling a stylized piece of folded linen called *linenfold*. Wainscoting in this style was also popular in the medieval-style interiors of the nineteenth and twentieth centuries. These more recent wainscots were frequently finished at the top with an appealing *plate rail* (a narrow shelf used to display plates).

The Renaissance brought with it a return to classicism, and the designs of Rome became the basis for most wall detailing. The Roman temple was built with columns resting on a raised podium. The columns supported a complete *entablature*, including an architrave, frieze, and cornice (see chapter 14, Exterior Style). During the Renaissance the exterior details of the Roman temple were translated into interior wall details, executed in materials such as wood, plaster, and marble. The podium became the *dado* (the lower portion of a wall set apart by moldings or other treatments). The columns were applied decoratively as flat *pilasters* with appropriate bases and capitals (also treated in a flat manner), and the entablature was interpreted as a series of moldings where the wall meets the ceiling. The spaces between the pilasters were filled with molded panels that varied in size and style. During certain periods the pilasters disappeared, leaving just the simple panels. These basic classical details have been reinterpreted many times in every culture touched by the Renaissance.

Certainly, one of the most popular treatments through the years has been panels of wood. However, in more recent years the influence of the International style with its lack of historical ornament and the rising cost of fine historical detailing have made historical paneling less common. In some historically styled homes and in certain nonresidential settings requiring a traditional feeling, paneled walls are still appropriate.

Wood Paneling

The three most common panel types are traditional, board and batten, and tongue and groove (types of wood, finishes, and joints are discussed in chapter 7, Furniture Selection):

- Traditional paneling is made with panels that may be flat, *beveled* (perimeter of panel is cut at an angle to meet the frame), or raised (panel projects beyond the frame). These are framed with *stiles* (vertical part of the frame) and *rails* (horizontal part of the frame). The frames are joined with mortise and tenon or dowel joints (see chapter 7). The frame is grooved where the panel and the frame are joined, and a small space is left to allow for expansion and contraction of the panel.

- Board and batten is paneling made from wide vertical boards. The gap between the boards is covered with a one-inch by two-inch strip of wood called a batten. This type of paneling was used in America during the seventeenth century to cover the fireplace wall, creating what was referred to as the *palisade wall*. Reverse board and batten produces an opposite effect of boards with a wide groove between.

- Tongue-and-groove paneling consists of boards *coped* (cut to fit an adjoining piece) with a projecting tongue on one edge that matches and fits into the recessed groove on the opposite edge. The two edges of the board are generally beveled producing a V-groove where the boards meet. The groove hides any

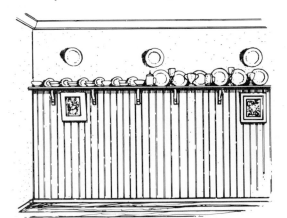

Figure 8.1

Figure 8.2

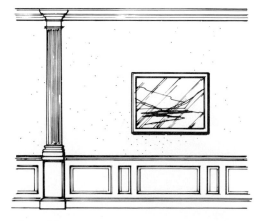

Figure 8.3

Figure 8.1 Wainscot with plate rail.
Figure 8.2 Linenfold panel.
Figure 8.3 Dado and pilaster.

irregularities in the thickness of the boards. Inexpensive plywood paneling sheets are produced to imitate the look of genuine tongue-and-groove paneling.[1]

Moldings

Moldings are trims used to create decorative effects. At the same time, they may cover the unfinished ragged edges of the wall, left in the construction process. Moldings are made of wood that can be worked easily—most often pine and oak. *Mitering* the corners (cutting and fitting together the trim at a forty-five-degree angle) allows for a pleasing fit where pieces are joined. Trims may be stained or painted. When they are painted the same color as the walls, they tend to have less visual importance. When they are painted to contrast with the walls, they become a more dynamic feature of the room. Following is a list of trim types:

- *Base* describes the piece used to finish the corner where the wall meets the floor. Any workable material, including rubber or plastic, could be used to make a base.

- *Baseboard* designates bases of wood. The base hides any slight irregularities in the level of the floor and keeps the wall from being scuffed by vacuums or other equipment. This trim is sometimes called a mopboard because it protects the wall during cleaning.

- *Chair rail* is a molding placed at the usual height of a chair back to protect the wall from damage. If the section below the rail is paneled, dado fashion, the trim is called a *dado cap*. The portion below the rail is alternately called a wainscot, which is not incorrect. However, wainscot is a term better used to describe a door-height section of paneling. The height of the chair rail may vary from approximately thirty to thirty-six inches.

Figure 8.4

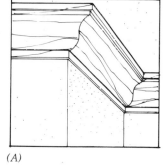

Figure 8.6   Figure 8.7   Figure 8.8

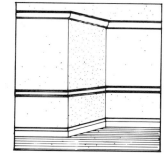

Figure 8.9   (A)

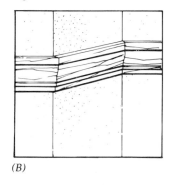

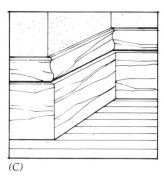

(B)   (C)

Figure 8.5

Figure 8.4 In the sitting room at Filoli, a forty-three room mansion now National Trust Property located outside of San Francisco, rich detail gives resplendence to the Beaux Arts Georgian architecture. Stone bolection molding on the flush-face fireplace is surrounded by rich walnut-colored wood paneling. Photo by Peter Vitale. Upholstered furniture, textiles by and photo courtesy of Brunschwig & Fils.
Figure 8.5 Traditional paneling.

Figure 8.6 Board and batten paneling.
Figure 8.7 Tongue-and-groove paneling.
Figure 8.8 Mitered corner.
Figure 8.9 (A) Crown molding. (B) Chair rail. (C) Base.

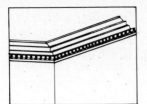
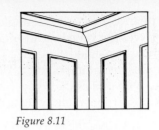

Figure 8.10

Figure 8.11

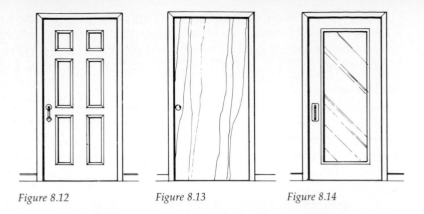

Figure 8.12   *Figure 8.13*   *Figure 8.14*

- *Crown or bed moldings* are placed where the wall meets the ceiling to add a finishing touch to traditionally styled rooms. They are generally simple; the more complex and ornate ceiling molding is called cornice molding.
- *Cornice moldings* often include decorative ornamentation such as the acanthus leaf, egg and dart, modillions, or dentils (see chapter 14, Exterior Style).
- *Cove molding* is rounded and makes a clean smooth transition from the ceiling to the wall. When ceilings are unusually high, a smaller molding can be attached to the wall below the cove. The ceiling, cove, and wall section can then be painted the same color, and the effect of a lowered ceiling is achieved.

A Note of Caution

Moldings are sometimes used to fashion frames on plain walls to give the feeling of traditional panels. This type of treatment requires particular attention to scale in order to prevent the appearance of spindly, tacked-on sticks. If this kind of treatment is done with moldings or combinations of moldings of the proper scale and if the panels are well proportioned, the effect may be fine.[2]

Doors

The selection of the right door is important for practical reasons. Major considerations must be security against breakage and unlawful entry, upkeep with regard to climate and the amount of wear and tear it will receive, and protection against fire burn time. Beyond these crucial safety and maintenance factors come the considerations of initial cost and upkeep cost. Upkeep means determining if the door will need repeated painting or refinishing or whether it will break or shatter, for example. The initial cost should be balanced with the upkeep costs. These considerations should come first, and when they are met, aesthetics will be the determining factor in style selection.

The doorway sets the tone of the building. The scale of a large door can inspire awe and indicate the importance of the structure. The captivating doors of London, painted bright "London bus" red, cornflower blue, butter yellow, shiny black, or Georgian green, trimmed with brass hardware, are a striking counterpoint to the white stucco or somber brick of the town houses. They also provide the touch of individuality that a door demands. The doors on the interior of a house serve more common functions but are no less worthy of attention. Interior doors are framed with moldings to conceal the ragged space between the door frame and the wall. Doors are made of wood and several other *materials* and in several decorative styles. Wooden doors fall into two basic categories: paneled doors and flush doors. Doors are also made of metal, glass, and plastic.

- Traditional *paneled doors* of wood are made in the same manner as traditional wooden wall panels. This type of door consists of wooden stiles and rails that secure the molded panels. This traditional method is rather costly and for a few years was virtually replaced in mass building by flush doors.
- *Flush doors,* as the name indicates, are flat with no raised or sunken panels. They are made of wood using two principal methods. The first utilizes a *solid core* of wood and is also called *lumber core.* In this type of construction, a thin cross banding (veneer with a horizontal grain) is laminated (glued) to a core of wood blocks that has been framed with rails and stiles. The door is finished with a vertical-grained face veneer. The second type is *hollow core,* which is made with a stile and rail frame filled with a lightweight honeycomb of cardboard and covered with as many as three veneers of thin wood. These doors are not as strong as the lumber-core type, but because they are inexpensive, they are widely used in residential and some nonresidential construction.
- Metal doors, once used only for areas with serious security problems, today have become quite acceptable in most settings. They are now made of aluminum and filled with a core of high-density polystyrene or polyurethane plastic foam, which makes them well insulated. Metal doors are less subject than wooden doors to dimension changes resulting from radical temperature shifts. They can be formed in tra-

Figure 8.10 Cornice molding.
Figure 8.11 Cove molding.
Figure 8.12 Paneled door.
Figure 8.13 Flush door.
Figure 8.14 Wood- or metal-framed glass door.

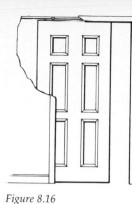

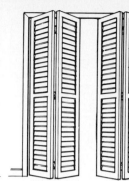

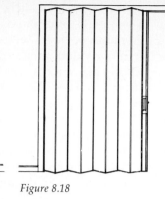

Figure 8.15

Figure 8.16

Figure 8.17

Figure 8.18

ditional paneled styles or fitted with panes of glass, and when painted, they are sometimes indistinguishable from wooden doors.

- High-strength *tempered glass doors* in metal frames, or unframed, are functional because they permit visibility in areas of high traffic and allow passersby to see into areas where products or services are available.

- Glass doors with metal or wooden frames make inviting entrances to patios or balconies or attractive dividers between rooms. When the glass is leaded (smaller pieces held together with lead strips), beveled (edges cut at an angle), or stained (colored leaded glass), it creates beautiful effects with light and can be an important decorative feature of the interior. Sliding glass doors have become less popular because they are heavy and difficult to open and close. They often develop problems with their glides (sliding tracks) and are also difficult to secure.

- Molded plastic doors in many designs, including the traditional paneled type, are available today. They may be embossed with a faint wood grain or perfectly smooth. When they are painted they have the appearance of a wooden door.

There are several styles of doors seen in today's interiors. Among the most important are pocket doors, bifold doors, accordion doors, louvered doors, French doors, Dutch doors, and Shoji screens.

- *Pocket doors* glide on a metal track from which they are suspended. When they are opened, they slide into a recessed pocket in the framing of the wall. They come as a preframed package that is installed during the framing phase of the construction process. They are particularly advantageous in areas where a door that swings open would be in the way.

Figure 8.19

Figure 8.20

- *Bifold* are hinged doors with two sections. One section is anchored on the side, both top and bottom, so that the doors pivot and glide freely. They are kept in place by a small wheel fixed to the top of the unanchored section that guides the door along a metal track fixed to the top frame of the door. They stack against the doorjamb and project slightly into the room when open. They are also used in double configurations with four sections that stack on both sides of wider doors.

- *Accordion doors* are made with narrow panels of wood, metal, or plastic. They fold accordion-style on a track from which they are suspended and stack neatly in a small space. They can be manufactured as tall as sixteen feet and are used to temporarily divide large spaces.

- *Louvered doors* are wooden framed with angled louvers or slats like shutters. Louvered doors allow circulation of air yet still provide visual privacy. They are commonly installed on closets or other spaces where air circulation is advisable. Louvered panels are used on pocket doors, bifold doors, and standard doors.

- *French doors* are double doors that open inward. They are like paneled doors, but the wooden frames are filled with glass rather than wooden panels. One

Figure 8.15 Sliding glass door.
Figure 8.16 Pocket door.
Figure 8.17 Bifold doors.
Figure 8.18 Accordion door.
Figure 8.19 Louvered doors.
Figure 8.20 French doors.

door is often kept latched in place and the other is used for passage. New French-type doors with one permanently stationary door are frequently replacing sliding glass doors. These are called *atrium*, or *patio, doors* and are energy efficient and seal tightly when closed.

- *Dutch doors* break horizontally in two sections so that each can open or shut separately or the two can be latched together into a single door. They may have windows in the top section. Dutch doors were originally designed to admit fresh air through the opening above and to keep out animals by closing below. In nonresidential settings, Dutch doors are used for service areas to keep out un-authorized traffic yet still allow commu-nication or act as a service counter.[3]

- *Shoji screens* are Japanese sliding panels made with wooden frames filled with oriental paper (or frosted glass or Plexi-glas). A grid is placed on one or both sides to divide the screen into panes that resemble traditional windows. The grids can be simple rectangles or quite com-plex and ingenious in their design. They were used like sliding walls as dividers in the traditional Japanese house and are used today in some American interiors for the same purpose or for a purely decorative effect (see also chapter 9, Wall, Window, and Ceiling Treatments).

Windows

Windows are two-way objects. Through them we look out at the world and the world looks in at us. The placement of windows in the wall is not only important to the wall composition of the interior but largely determines the fenestra-tion (architectural arrangement of windows) that is a crucial part of the style and character of the exterior. Some major considerations in the selection and placement of windows should be

- Security. Windows are the easiest point of unlawful entry; the greater the quan-tity and the more accessible and poorly lit the windows on the exterior, the greater that risk.

- Orientation and solar gain. Where solar gain is desirable, windows should be most plentiful on the south of the build-

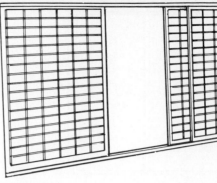

Figure 8.21

Figure 8.22

Figure 8.23

Figure 8.21 Dutch door.
Figure 8.22 Shoji screens.
Figure 8.23 A carved acanthus leaf graces the keystone at the height of this arch flanked by fluted pilasters. French doors and a handsome fanlight window frame a water pond scene from the Tea House at Filoli, a 1919 Georgian-style mansion outside San Francisco. Photo by Peter Vitale. Textiles by and photo courtesy of Brunschwig & Fils.

ing, and the least on the north. Limiting the number, strategically placing them, and protecting against bright sun on the east and the west orientations are imperative. Light is clearest and most steady from the *north*, most warm and constant on the *south*, clearest and brightest on the *east*, and most colored and hottest on the *west*.

- Quantity of light desired. Great quantities of light can be healthful to mind and body, yet when accompanied by heat and glare, light can be emotionally and physically unhealthful. Too much light and heat without window treatment protection can also be damaging to interior furnishings.
- The view. Windows should be planned to frame any pleasant view looking out from the interior. The view can serve to visually expand space and bring the exterior into the interior as an extension of the design.
- Privacy. The location, the height of the wall, and the number of windows can largely determine the amount of privacy afforded the occupant. Windows high in the wall give greater privacy, as do smaller windows.
- Interior window treatments—type and budget. Windows should be covered unless there is no need for privacy, light and glare control, and energy conservation against heat and cold. Large expanses of windows make this consideration a costly one.

There are few architectural details that can compare in elegance to beautifully designed windows. The exquisite Federal-style fanlight with its delicate tracery and the boldly handsome Palladian window are treasured features of many older buildings (see chapter 14, Exterior Style). They represent the finest of architectural historic development. Like doors, windows are trimmed in appropriately styled moldings to complete their finished appearance.

Over centuries of development, glass has been an important part of the evolution of windows from crude openings draped with animal skins to medieval leaded panes to

Figure 8.24

Figure 8.24 Interior designer Ira D. Cohen created a contemporary yet elegant interior for this designer showcase interior in the Guggenheim Mansion, Sands Point, Long Island. The outstanding architectural feature, two rows of traceried windows, clearly dominates, with understated yet rich furnishings. Photo courtesy of the International Linen Promotion Commission.

large Late Renaissance windows to the glass houses of the twentieth century. Setting the glass in place is called *glazing* and can be done with one or more sheets of glass.

- A single layer of glass is called single glazing.
- Double glazing or thermal pane is two sheets of glass sandwiched in a frame to deter heat and/or cold transfer.

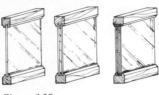

Figure 8.25

- Energy efficiency can be further enhanced with the addition of a third sheet of glass to produce triple glazing. These are often winter storm windows or tinted or summer storm windows that act like sunglasses on the window in hot climates.

Windows that can be opened mechanically or by hand are termed *operable.* The obvious advantage to operable windows is their ability to admit fresh air. Certain types of operable windows also offer the advantage of being easy to clean because both inside and outside glass surfaces can be reached from the inside. Fixed, stationary, or inoperable windows are used where ventilation is unnecessary or undesirable, where the window is out of reach, or where a view is to be framed without being interrupted by a divider bar. Fixed windows are also easier to fabricate and less expensive because they have no moving parts.

Windows are made in a wide range of styles. Each style is appropriate to a historical style or to a functional purpose. Following are common window styles:

- Arched and round windows have been appreciated for centuries. The *Palladian window,* previously mentioned, is an arched window with two lower sidelights framed with classical columns, pilasters, and moldings. The *fanlight* is also an elliptic arch form of the Neoclassic era. Round porthole windows were especially popular during the Victorian era and may be seen in some vintage houses. Hexagonal windows are a six-sided variation of the rounded window. Contemporary architecture utilizes many arched and rounded windows, because we still appreciate their beauty and the relief they give to the straight lines of architecture.
- *Awning windows* are hinged on the top to swing outward at an angle like an awning. They may be

(A)
Figure 8.26

(B)

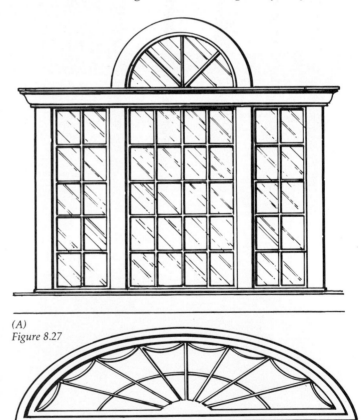

(A)
Figure 8.27

(B)

Figure 8.25 Single, double, and triple glazing.
Figure 8.26 *(A)* (Before) This drafty porch at the rear of a 1930s New Jersey English-style manor house was unused. *(B)* (After) The three open sides of the porch were fitted with glass doors and stationary windows with slender stationary skylights on the southern exposure. The skylights fit between preexisting exposed wood beams, maintaining the style of the house. Photo courtesy of the APC Corporation.

Figure 8.27 *(A)* Palladian window. *(B)* Elliptic fanlight.

stacked or grouped in horizontal bands along a high wall, clerestory fashion for privacy. They may also be used as the bottom component in a sashlike window or other window arrangement. They have the advantage of being able to remain open in a rain storm.

- *Bay and bow windows* are projecting windows. The bay is *canted* (angular) or projects straight out, and the bow is a curved projection. Bay and bow windows are attractive features on a building. They also add extra space to the interior, as well as admit light. They may, however, be costly to drape because they require custom drapery rods.
- *Casement windows* are side-hinged, swinging windows. They are an important historical style popular in many countries. Double, *French casement* windows are generally two panes wide and vary in height. Casement windows are also used as operable

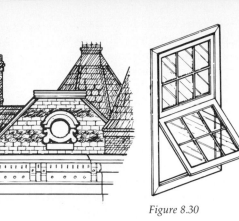

Figure 8.29

Figure 8.30

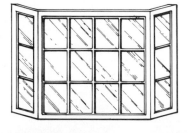

Figure 8.31

Figure 8.32

Figure 8.33

Figure 8.28

(A)
Figure 8.34

(B)

Figure 8.28 This modified Victorian-style Palladian wood-framed window arrangement is in keeping with the raised wood panels and wooden balusters in this nostalgic setting. New insulative windows that replace old ones can still have historic integrity. The U-shaped stair with two turns has a wide landing making stair climbing easier, with a spot to rest and enjoy the view. Photo courtesy of the Anderson Corporation.
Figure 8.29 Round porthole window.
Figure 8.30 Awning window.
Figure 8.31 Bay window.
Figure 8.32 Bow window.

Figure 8.33 French casement window.
Figure 8.34 (A) Exterior and (B) interior of a Colonial-style angled bay window looking out onto Downington, Pennsylvania. The side windows are operable sash windows, and the center of the bay is a stationary, or fixed, window. These window frames are made to look like wood but consist of maintenance-free solid vinyl. Photo courtesy of CertainTeed Corporation.

sections beside large fixed picture windows. They have great appeal because they provide maximum ventilation, and if they swing out, they keep the interior free for draperies or other window treatments. Apart from their functional aspects, casement windows are usually attractive and charming.

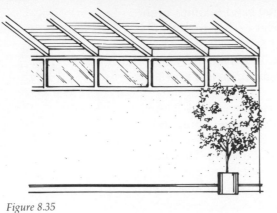

Figure 8.35

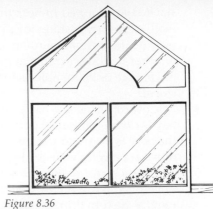

Figure 8.36

- The clerestory was the highest story in the Gothic church, and today, *clerestory windows* are still those that are set high in the wall. These windows may be for light only or for light and ventilation. They may be almost any style window; it is their location at the top of the wall that makes them clerestory. They provide a clear, even light that is pleasant in most interiors.

Figure 8.37

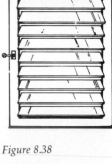

Figure 8.38

- *Cathedral windows* are angled, A-frame windows that follow the pitch of the ceiling. They embody a strong architectural quality that makes them particularly well suited to contemporary interiors. They work best in settings with pleasant views where no window coverings are necessary.

- The *greenhouse window* is a projecting glass box used to catch the sun's rays. Some may be just large enough to fill a kitchen window and others may be room sized. Like botanical greenhouses, they make great places for plants; the room-sized version is a favored spot for dining and relaxing. They can also be designed as sunrooms with hot tubs or spas or comfortable areas for conversation and relaxation.

- The *jalousie window* is made with a set of louvered slats that tilt open and closed. The principal benefit of this window is the ability to provide ventilation while restricting entrance of rain. The name is French for jealousy. A wooden blind, slatted like the jalousie window may have allowed jealous lovers to see without being seen.

- The *sash window* is made with two window panels designed to slide up and down in a vertical channel of the window frame. These may be larger, single sheets of glass or divided into several smaller panes. The smaller paned windows were designated historically by the number of lights (panes) in each panel; for example, twelve over twelve indicates

twelve panes in the top frame and twelve in the bottom, and six over six indicates six above and six below. A *single-hung sash window* has an operable lower window that can be raised and lowered. In the *double-hung sash window*, both sashes are operable, allowing good circulation of air. Cooler air enters through the lower opening, and warm air rises out through the top. The traditional sash window, divided into smaller panes, is

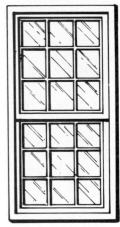

Figure 8.39

a classic. Those that are well proportioned and well built add a clear note of distinction to traditionally styled houses. Because they are so popular, manufacturers have been experimenting with new methods of fabrication. Some have designed wooden grids that fit over a single pane, giving the appearance of individual panes. The grid can easily be removed and then snapped back into the frame, making it easier to wash the windows. Others have placed metal grids between two panes of glass to create the impression of panes. The traditional framing method with individually glazed panes is called a *true divider* system.

Figure 8.35 Clerestory window.
Figure 8.36 Cathedral window.
Figure 8.37 Greenhouse window.
Figure 8.38 Jalousie window.
Figure 8.39 Sash window (nine over nine).

- A *sidelight* is a narrow window next to a door. A pair of sidelights is used to flank a door. A *transom* is a rectilinear window above a door. Arched windows above a door are called fanlights. In older buildings, operable transoms were often used between rooms to improve air circulation.
- *Skylights* are custom-installed or prefabricated units mounted in the roof and ceiling to bring natural light into interiors that have no direct access to windows and would otherwise be dark. The skylight is made of glass, plastic, or Plexiglass.
- *Attic windows* are operable pivoting windows placed in an angled roof in lieu of dormers. They are less expensive than framing a dormer and admit more light. They are being utilized in new construction and remodeling projects where unused attic space is being transformed into living or working space.

Figure 8.40

(A)
Figure 8.44

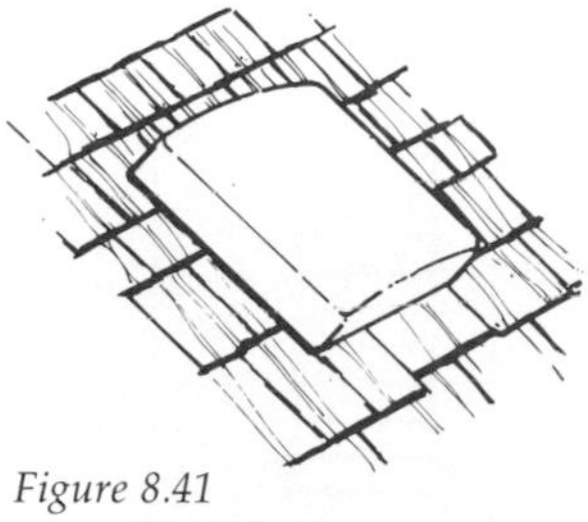

Figure 8.41

Figure 8.42

Figure 8.43

Figure 8.40 Sidelights and transom.
Figure 8.41 Skylight.
Figure 8.42 Attic window.
Figure 8.43 Sliding window.

Sliding windows are technically the same as sash windows. However, the aluminum-framed windows that are used so frequently today are usually referred to as sliding rather than sash. These may slide vertically or horizontally and may also be a single operable panel of a larger window. As well as aluminum, sliding windows may also be framed in wood or vinyl-clad wood.

Stairs

During the Middle Ages, stairs were tucked into tiny turrets (towers) or hidden between walls. In the Renaissance the stairway became more imposing, and by the eighteenth century, it was often a dramatic focal point of the house. These same choices govern the design of stairs today. They may be functional and unobtrusive or a very dramatic part of the design. Stairs often have some romantic memory associations such as sliding down banisters or hiding on stairways decked with pine bows to sneak an early peek on Christmas morning. They may conjure up mental pictures of a grand entry on the night of a first date or of children watching and listening from an upstairs landing as guests arrive for a party. Stairways can be a beautiful and exciting part of an interior. Because the components from which they are assembled may be unfamiliar, they are listed, defined, and illustrated.

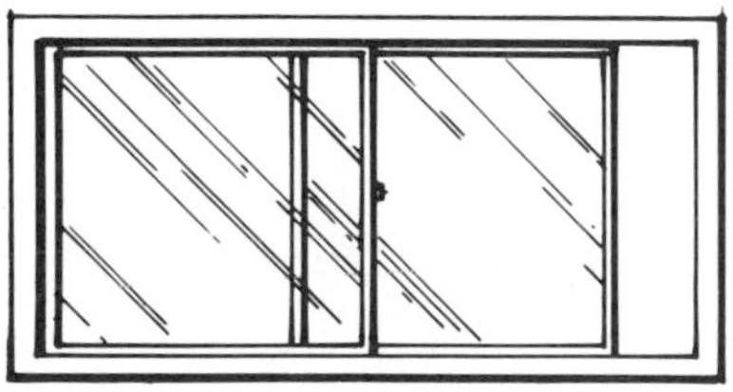

- *Stringers* are the diagonal, notched structural piece that supports and gives form to the stair. On the completed stair,

(B)

Figure 8.44 *(A)* Arches, angles, and deep muted colors combine to make a grand entrance with Neoclassic flavor. The newel posts, reminiscent of Doric columns, head the wide staircase that leads to a mirror on the landing. Durable Italian tiles by Marazzi are used to create a subtle geometric pattern of inset diamonds for the high-traffic area at the base of the steps. Photo courtesy of Italian Tile Center. *(B)* Ideal for application where space is at a premium, this alternating-tread design, fifty-six degree stair is an option to spirals and steep conventional stairs or ladders. Photo courtesy of Lapeyre Stair, Inc.

these structural stringers do not appear because they are usually covered by the treads and risers. On the finished stair, the diagonal molding on the wall next to the steps is also called a stringer.

- Treads are the flat, horizontal pieces where the foot touches when we go up or down a stair.
- Nosing is the rounded edge of the tread. The nosing makes the stair less sharp and dangerous. It also prevents carpet on the stair from wearing against a sharp edge.
- The *riser* is the vertical member between the treads. It is the riser that acts as a toe kick as we ascend the staircase. In certain designs the riser is omitted, creating an *open riser stair.* Some people feel nervous and insecure on open riser stairs because they may not appear solid.
- The *starting step* is the first step of the stair. It is often *bullnosed* (with a rounded curve) on the open end to support a newel post.
- *Landings* are the intermediate platforms on a stair (often where they turn) or the area at the bottom and top of the stair. These are important because they allow the stair to turn and because they make the stair safer. Those who have difficulty climbing stairs are able to rest on the landing. The landing also provides exciting design possibilities. It makes a perfect place for a beautiful window.
- The *handrail* or banister is the piece that follows the pitch of the stair and is held by the hand. *Easements* are the short bends that allow for a change of direction in the handrail. A *volute* is the spiral or scroll end of the handrail that rests on the newel post. Handrails may be the traditional carved type, or they can be formed with metal pipes or tubes or flat pieces of wood or metal or any device that is compatible with the design of the stair.
- The *baluster* is the vertical member that supports the handrail. In traditional stairways the balusters are usually turned wood. However, they could also be bent metal, square wooden pieces, or panels of glass. The balusters, handrail, and newel posts together make a *balustrade,* or railing.
- The *newel post* is a larger baluster that supports or receives the handrail at critcal points of the stair, such as the starting step, the landing, and the top of the stair. The design of the newel post can be elaborate or simple. Victorian newel posts were often massive and highly decorative.
- The *stairwell* is the open space in which the stair is set. Its shape and size will vary with the design of the stair.[4]

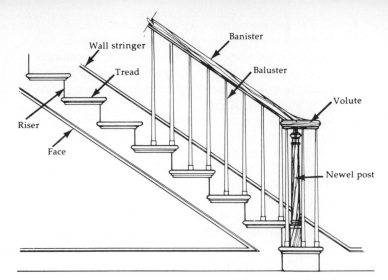

Figure 8.45

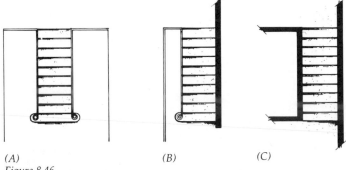

(A)
(B)
(C)
Figure 8.46

Stairs may take several different forms. The most common forms are listed here.

- A stair whose sides are not attached to any wall is termed an *open stair.*
- A *semihoused stair* is connected to the wall on one side and open on the other.
- A stairway with walls on both sides is called a *closed or housed stair.*
- A straight stairway without any turns is said to have a *straight run.*
- A stairway that turns ninety degrees at a landing is a *one-turn stair.*
- A *double-turn stair* makes two ninety degree turns at two separate landings.
- A *U-stair* turns 180 degrees at a single landing.
- A *spiral staircase* twists around a central axis like a corkscrew. This type of stair takes the least amount of space but is often difficult to negotiate and makes moving furniture extremely difficult.
- A *curved stairway* may be open or semihoused and is graceful and dramatic.

Figure 8.45 Stairway components.
Figure 8.46 Stair forms. (*A*) Open stair (no walls). (*B*) Semihoused stair (wall on one side). (*C*) Closed stair (enclosed by walls).

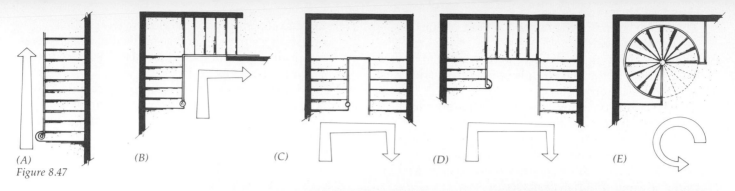

(A)   *(B)*   *(C)*   *(D)*   *(E)*

Figure 8.47

Fireplaces and Chimneypieces

The fireplace is another detail often associated with pleasant memories. The leap and flicker of constantly changing flames and the crackle of the burning wood create a mood of warmth; the memory of a chilly winter evening by a fire with family or friends is pleasant.

For thousands of years, fire was the only source of heat in buildings. During the Middle Ages, when someone discovered that a hole in the wall with a hood could siphon the smoke from a fire, the design significance of the fireplace was instantly elevated. Before that, the fire had been built in a pit in the floor and the smoke escaped through cracks or vents in the roof. The hood provided new possibilities for design. Because it was a source of warmth, the fireplace was the logical focal point in the room, and designers lavished it with attention. Through the years, the basic technology of the fireplace has changed very little. It is the design of the decorative *chimneypiece* that has changed the most. Each new period saw changes in the style of the chimneypiece that gave the fireplace the proper character for its surroundings. The projecting shelf of a chimneypiece is called a *mantel*.

A fire requires fuel, heat, and oxygen. As it burns, the fire consumes oxygen, which creates a draft as more air is drawn in to feed the fire that warms the air. The fireplace works on the principle that warm air rises, drawing the

Figure 8.48

smoke off as it ascends and radiating some heat into the room. The rising air creates a suction that also pulls air from the room. As the intensity of the fire dies, it begins to suck precious warm air from the room. To keep the warm air in the house from escaping, it is necessary to close the front of the fireplace with glass doors or metal doors.

The fireplace is made of several component parts.

- The *hearth* is the noncombustible slab that forms the base for the fire and projects into the room to prevent embers or sparks from charring the floor.

Figure 8.47 Stair forms. *(A)* Straight-run stair. *(B)* One-turn stair (with landing). *(C)* U-stair (with one landing). *(D)* Double-turn stair (with two landings). *(E)* Spiral staircase.

Figure 8.48 This unique fireplace utilizes architectural detail such as dentil trim, quoins, and keystone in the elliptic arch. Trimmed with blue tile, the result is a one-of-a-kind fireplace. Round Georgian arch windows, a narrow Gothic arch, and

a spire on the newel post are eclectic architectural features in this hospice designer showhouse. Carolyn Gutilla/Plaza One, interior design. Fabric and furniture by and photo courtesy of Brunschwig & Fils.

- The *firebox* contains the fire and is built of masonry on top of the hearth.
- The *surround* is the noncombustible piece that frames the opening of the firebox. It is frequently made of tile, marble, or other stone.
- The *flue* is the chimney pipe and is separated from the firebox by a movable *damper* that controls the flow of air and escape of smoke.
- Zero-clearance fireboxes are self-contained units with triple-insulated walls that allow them to be placed in walls without firebrick or masonry.

Fireplaces could be built in any form, imagination and function being the only real restrictions. However, the most common types are flush-face, projecting, hooded, corner, raised, freestanding, and stoves.

- The *breast* (face) of the *flush-face fireplace* is even or flush with the plane of the surrounding wall. Because the flush-face tends to be less decorative, it is well suited to contemporary interiors where it often consists of a surround and a simple molding. Several historically styled fireplaces are also flush faced with or without a mantel shelf.
- The breast of a *projecting fireplace* projects into the room forming a mantel. This type is adaptable to clean contemporary versions as well as more decorative historical types.
- A *hooded fireplace* incorporates a projecting hood that may be formed in nearly any shape from rounded to angled to boxlike. This was the first type of fireplace to be built during the Late Middle Ages and Early Renaissance. These were large-scaled, fanciful designs ornamented with Gothic tracery or classical columns. Smaller, less-ornate versions were also common in provincial houses well after the Renaissance.
- The *corner fireplace* is located in the corner of a room, and may have a hood or may be built like a standard fireplace. Because they cut off the corner of a room, corner fireplaces often have inherent problems of balance and line and may present challenges in furniture placement. Corner fireplaces are a feature of the Southwest adobe houses where they form a pleasing, smooth rounded extension of the walls.[5]
- Many fireplaces are designed with a *raised hearth* in front of the firebox. The raised hearth may be built just in front of the firebox or extend the entire length of the wall. With a raised hearth, the firebox is elevated so it can be seen more easily through the furniture grouping that often surrounds a fireplace. The raised hearth requires less stooping and has the added advantage of making the fireplace easier to fuel and clean. This type of hearth also makes a nice place to sit next to the warmth of the fire.
- A *freestanding fireplace* is a metal unit or other fireplace that is placed in the room away from the wall,

Figure 8.49

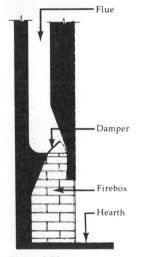

Figure 8.50

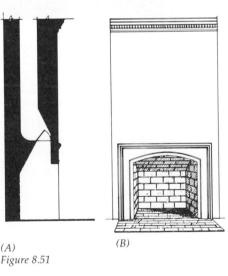

(A)   *(B)*
Figure 8.51

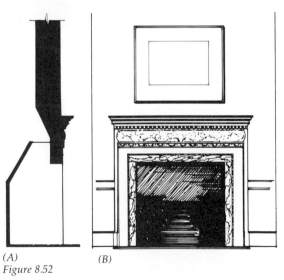

(A)   *(B)*
Figure 8.52

Figure 8.49 A grand old Victorian home with the hallmark rounded arch, inspired by the penchant of Victorians for historical architectural detail. The rounded stone fireplace chimneypiece has carved grapes as decorative motifs, whereas sliding pocket doors display a profusion of etched Neoclassic motifs. Through the doors, a glimpse of Rococo-revival filigree work is seen as a cornice in the adjoining room. Textiles by and photo courtesy of Laura Ashley.

Figure 8.50 Fireplace components showing the hearth, firebox, damper, and flue.
Figure 8.51 Flush-face fireplace. *(A)* Side cutaway section view. *(B)* Front view elevation.

Figure 8.52 Projecting fireplace. *(A)* Side cutaway section view. *(B)* Front view elevation.

Figure 8.53

Figure 8.55

with the flue or chimney pipe exposed. The fireplace unit may be placed on a raised platform or may rest at floor level. The freestanding fireplace is less popular today than stoves that are similar in concept but far more efficient.

- Until the advent of central heating, the pot-bellied stove was a standard fixture in homes, churches, schools, and stores in

(A)   (B)

Figure 8.54

Figure 8.56

every part of the country. Today, in areas with cold winters, *stoves* are being used again in some homes. These are generally freestanding units placed in front of a noncombustible wall with clearance space between the wall and stove. Fireplaces can also be fitted with enclosed stove units called *fireplace inserts* for more efficient use of fuel and little loss of warmed house air. Some stoves and fireplace inserts are designed with forced-air systems that can heat most of a medium-sized house. These draw air from outside; the air is warmed by the stove then forced by a fan into the house, creating positive pressure. When a vent or window at the opposite end of the house is opened slightly, the warm air will be drawn to that part of the house. A fresh air intake pipe to the stove will eliminate drafts caused by combustion in stoves.

Figure 8.57

Figure 8.53 Nelson Ferlita's dining room features a hooded fireplace with stucco walls, floor tile and trim, and furniture echoing the feeling of the early Spanish and French Renaissance. Italian ceramic tile by Omega. Photo courtesy of the Italian Tile Center.

Figure 8.54 Hooded fireplace. (A) Side cutaway section view. (B) Front view elevation.
Figure 8.55 Molded walls with niches and rounded fireplace opening recall the authenticity of the Southwest adobe interiors. Carpet by and photo by Anso V Worry-Free Carpet by Mohawk.

Figure 8.56 Corner fireplace in a Colonial or Territorial Southwest adobe home.
Figure 8.57 Wood stoves are used in place of open fireplaces where clean burning and heating efficiency are desired. This smokeless stove with

maximum efficiency is Intrepid II. Stoves are ideal where space for a full fireplace is limited or where a free-standing fireplace is desired. Photo courtesy of Vermont Castings.

Ceilings

Ceilings are literally the crowning glory of a room. For example, the great hammer-beam ceilings of Early Renaissance England with their Tudor arch-shaped trusses supported on magnificently carved brackets are awe inspiring. And the delicate-patterned plaster ceilings, designed by Robert Adam in eighteenth-century England, are still a beautiful example of the importance a ceiling design can have in a room. Today, we have a vast selection of ceiling materials and types from which to choose. Ceilings may be decorative or structural and may even serve the important function of covering, yet providing access to, mechanical sytems located in the ceiling. Ceilings can provide dramatic changes in plane or space. A low cozy fireplace area can suddenly open to the main body of the room that soars to the rafters. Angled ceilings are interesting because of the variety of line and form they create. Ceilings can be formed in many ways. The materials used to cover ceilings are discussed in chapter 9, Wall, Window, and Ceiling Treatments. The most common types of ceilings are the plain flat, vaulted, domed, coffered, and coved (baffled and suspended ceilings are discussed later under Nonresidential Considerations).

- The simplest type of ceiling is flat plaster or Sheetrock. This plain treatment is ideal when the intent of the design is to emphasize other areas of the room. The flat ceiling may be embellished with textured plaster, raised patterns, moldings, or medallions, which may be painted to harmonize or contrast with the ceiling. These are called *anaglypta*, which is the Greek word for raised ornament. Today, anaglypta patterns are frequently made of hardened plastic foam.

- A *vault* is a ceiling constructed on the principle of an arch. Therefore, a vaulted ceiling may be round (barrel vault) or pointed like the Gothic church ceiling. In today's interiors, the tall, open, cathedral ceiling belongs to this group. Rooms with barrel vaulted ceilings often have rounded ends with half-domed ceilings called *niches*.

- *Cathedral ceilings* are pointed with two slopes. Those with one slope are *shed* ceilings. These can be exciting because of

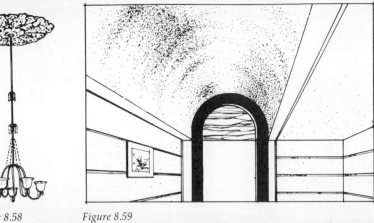

Figure 8.58   Figure 8.59

Figure 8.60

Figure 8.58 Anaglypta, or decorative molded plaster, especially popular during the Victorian Era.
Figure 8.59 Vaulted ceiling.

Figure 8.60 Dramatic slants in the shed ceiling of this contemporary home are accentuated by a skylight that creates sculptural interest and adds height and another light source to the room. APC Long Lites' sleek silhouette allows the interruption in the ceiling to be subtle yet effective. Photo courtesy of APC Corporation.

the way they open up the space. A relatively small room with a high ceiling feels much larger than it actually is. Large spaces such as churches or buildings with tall atriums are awe inspiring.

- *Domes* are bowl-shaped, rounded ceilings. When the dome covers a drum-shaped room, the space is called a *rotunda.* Domes may be quite flat and dish-shaped or deep and high. Because its form is the shape of the heavens, the dome draws the eye upward and

creates a feeling of expanse. In public spaces such as capitol buildings, the dome creates spaces of great dignity and grandeur. In a residence, a shallow recessed dome in an entry or dining room expands the visual space.

- *Beamed ceilings* frankly expose the rafters or trusses as a decorative feature of a room. They can be very simple and rough or richly carved or painted. Beams can impart a provincial or rustic feeling to an environment. The

buildings of the Southwest incorporate large pine beams called vigas (see chapter 14, Exterior Style) as structural support for the smaller crossbeams, called latillas, which form the ceiling. Logs add a rugged feeling to cabins and ski lodges in any geographic setting. Squared, finely finished hardwood beams trimmed with molding are favored in rich traditional interiors such as law offices, libraries, and luxury housing. Since buildings are

Figure 8.61

Figure 8.61 Arched beams and a sculptured chimneypiece look to the Spanish Colonial vigas and molded fireplaces for inspiration. Architectural interest can be clean and

contemporary, as evident in this interior. Vertical louvers by and photo courtesy of Del Mar Window Coverings.

(A)
Figure 8.63

Figure 8.62

generally no longer made of timbers, these will usually be false beams used just for their effect. Metal trusses are left exposed in some of today's designs, because like their wooden counterparts from earlier times, they have interest and strength as design forms.

- Coffers are decorative boxes constructed in the recesses between beams and crossbeams. Some of the most magnificent *coffered ceilings* were built in France during the Renaissance.
- *Coved ceilings* are formed with a curved radius or straight angle where the wall meets the ceiling. This is accomplished by actually structuring the ceiling in that fashion or by the application of cove moldings. The absence of a sharp right angle has a softening effect on the room.

Cabinetwork

Cabinetwork, or *cabinetry*, is finished interior woodwork such as shelves and cabinets. *Finish carpenters* are craftsmen of custom freestanding and built-in units. Cabinetwork is manufactured in two basic ways. Cabinets are mass-produced on an assembly line in standard sizes or crafted to custom specifications in large or small woodworking shops by skilled finish carpenters. These units are brought to the site as components and installed, fitted, and trimmed with molding.

(B)

Figure 8.62 Historical three-dimensional coffered ceiling.

Figure 8.63 (A) Hand craftsmanship is clear to be seen and appreciated in the wood cabinetry in this vintage library. Wood blinds echo the mellow gleam of the cabinetry, and Rococo swirls are repeated in the carpet and frieze above the windows. Window blinds by and photo courtesy of Del Mar Window Coverings. (B) Kitchen cabinetry in this Dallas, Texas, showcase house indicates that today's homeowner can enjoy modern conveniences without sacrificing warmth, tradition, and good looks. Interior design by Gerald Tomlin. "Country Wood" blind by and photo courtesy of Hunter Douglas, Inc.

Figure 8.64

Figure 8.65

Figure 8.66

Mass-produced cabinetwork is installed wherever standard sizes will fit the space and where a tight budget demands economy. Prefabricated units may be purchased at home improvement stores and builder supply houses.

Custom pieces are planned by the designer and executed by the cabinetmaker or finish carpenter; for example, custom cabinetwork is seen in living/dining rooms, kitchens, bathrooms, laundry rooms, and sewing areas of luxury homes. One area of the home where custom cabinetwork is particularly impressive is the home office, study, den, or library. Custom details make these interiors more individual, distinctive, and functional.

Nonresidential Considerations

Many of the details used in residential design are the same as those in nonresidential design. However, the following details are more common to nonresidential design:

- Today, coffered ceilings are formed when concrete is poured over inverted "pans" or forms in such a way that when the concrete has set and the pans have been removed from below, a wafflelike pattern of coffers is produced. This process is called concrete slab construction.
- A *baffled ceiling* is hung with wooden or metal slats or fabric banners. These are installed in parallel or grid patterns that act as a screen for the lighting system and also serve as an acoustic treatment. The fabric banners provide an excellent opportunity to add color and texture. The wooden and metal slats also create patterns that add an interesting quality to the environment.
- *Suspended ceilings* are metal grid systems hung from the superstructure of the building with wires. The *plenum,* or space between the grid and the building structure above, contains ducts for the HVAC (heating, ventilation, and air-conditioning) system, as well as plumbing and electrical systems (see chapter 13, Building Systems). The grids are filled with acoustic panels that can be removed and replaced, allowing easy access to the equipment above the ceiling. Lighting systems, sound systems, sprinkler systems, smoke detectors, and vents for the HVAC system are often integrated with the suspended ceiling.
- Custom cabinetwork is extremely common in nonresidential design. For example, the reception desk in a hotel is not a stock item. It must be designed to fit the physical and aesthetic requirements of the project. The same is true of a nurse's station in a hospital or the cashier/host station in a restaurant. All of these kinds of pieces are custom designed and manufactured.

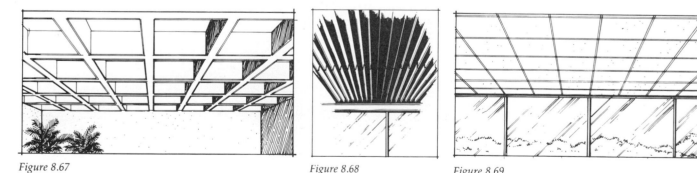

Figure 8.67

Figure 8.68

Figure 8.69

Figure 8.64 This heavily scaled stair forms an important focal point in the very large space of the Utah State capitol building. The marble construction lends visual solidity and durability in an area of relatively high traffic. Photo by John Wang.

Figure 8.65 The beautifully controlled curve of the banister and the stately forms of the newell post and balusters make a striking design feature in this traditionally styled professional building. Photo by Stuart Grigg.

Figure 8.66 The bookcases in the conference room of this law office demonstrate the way in which custom milled cabinetry can be designed and adapted to the specific needs of a user. The beautiful wood tones together with the texture of the books are important aesthetic features of the space. Photo by Stuart Grigg and Jennifer Smith.

Figure 8.67 Contemporary grid pattern in a coffered ceiling.

Figure 8.68 Baffled ceiling.

Figure 8.69 Suspended ceiling.

A Historical Overview

The following chart shows the relationship of interior architectural details to many of the building styles discussed in chapter 14, Exterior Styles. Each style is identified by name, monarch or significant designer, period, building styles where the details might be seen, and the description of the details.

Chart 8.1 Historical Overview

The Tudor Style

Monarch or Significant Designer:
Henry VIII—England
Period: 1500-1558
Related Buildings Styles: Tudor, Beaux Arts, Contemporary Tudor
Description of Details
Floors: Wood plank, parquet wood
Walls: Small wood panels, plain or filled with linenfold carving
Windows: Casement with leaded panes
Doors: Paneled, in the flattened Tudor arch form
Chimneypiece: Flush, Tudor arch-shaped opening
Ceiling: Flat, beamed, or decorative plaster
Stairs: Double turn, wooden, decorative balusters, and newel posts

Tudor

The Rococo Style

Monarch or Significant Designer:
Louis XV—France
Period: 1714-1774
Related Building Styles: Rococo, Beaux Arts, Contemporary French
Description of Details
Floors: Parquet
Walls: Large, rectangular, painted wooden panels, often with carved or painted asymmetrical, curvilinear designs. French paneling is called *boiserie.*
Windows: Long French casement or French doors
Doors: Paneled, double doors
Chimneypiece: Projecting, ornate carved marble, curvilinear opening
Ceiling: Flat, plain, cove molding
Stairs: Stone U-stair, with ornate wrought iron balustrade

Rococo

The French Neoclassical Style

Monarch or Significant Designer:
Louis XVI—France
Period: 1760-1789
Related Building Styles: French Neoclassic, Beaux Arts, Contemporary
Description of Details
Floors: Parquet wood
Walls: Large, rectilinear, painted, wooden panels
Windows: Tall French casement or French windows
Doors: Paneled, double doors
Chimneypiece: Projecting, carved marble, rectilinear with corner-block designs
Ceiling: Flat, plain, with decorative cornice
Stairs: Stone U-stair, with wrought iron balustrade

French Neoclassical

Adam

American English Medieval

The Adam Style

Monarch or Significant Designer:
 Robert Adam—England
Period: 1770-1810
Related Building Styles: English
 Neoclassic, Federal, Beaux Arts,
 Contemporary
Description of Details
Floors: Hardwood
Walls: Plain plaster with panels of
 anaglypta and niches
Windows: Tall sash windows
Doors: Paneled, with classical
 moldings
Chimneypiece: Classical, projecting,
 with columns or pilasters; entabla-
 ture frieze divided into three ap-
 proximately equal panels; center
 panel raised and decoratively
 carved
Ceiling: Vaulted or flat, decorated with
 delicate but profuse anaglypta
 patterns
Stairs: Wooden or stone U-stair, with
 wrought iron balustrade

The American English Medieval Style

Monarch or Significant Designer:
 None; a vernacular development
Period: 1620-1720
Related Building Styles:
 Seventeenth-century English
 Medieval, Cape Cod, and other
 vernacular houses
Description of Details
Floors: Wide wooden plank
Walls: Stucco
Windows: Small casement with leaded
 panes
Doors: Doors made of planks (later
 paneled)
Chimneypiece: Large, open, brick
 fireplace for warmth and cooking;
 large wooden mantel beam; board
 and batten palisade wall

Ceiling: Beamed
Stairs: Simple, modified, wooden
 double-turn, with wooden balustrade

The Early Georgian Style

Monarch or Significant Designer:
 Influence of Christopher Wren
Period: 1699-1750
Related Building Styles: Early Georgian,
 Beaux Arts, Contemporary
Description of Details
Floors: Wooden plank
Walls: Large raised wooden panels,
 unpainted; also, plain plaster with
 chair rail
Windows: Sash
Doors: Paneled
Chimneypiece: Flush, framed with simple,
 projecting *bolection* molding
Ceiling: Flat, plain
Stairs: Wooden U-stair with turned
 balusters

The Late Georgian Style

Monarch or Significant Designer:
 Influence of James Gibbs
Period: 1750-1790
Related Building Styles: Late Georgian,
 Beaux Arts, Contemporary
Description of Details
Floors: Wooden plank
Walls: Large raised wooden panels,
 painted; also, dado with wallpaper
 above
Windows: Sash
Doors: Paneled, moldings with *ears*
 (molding breaks to form squares at
 corners)
Chimneypiece: Flush, with bolection
 molding with ears, and often with
 cornice and frieze; cornice forms
 mantel
Ceiling: Flat, plain or decorated with
 anaglypta
Stairs: Wooden U-turn, turned balusters

Early Georgian

Late Georgian

Continued on next page.

Chart 8.1 *Continued*

The Federal Style

Monarch or Significant Designer:
Thomas Jefferson, Samuel McIntire, Charles Bullfinch
Period: 1790-1830
Related Building Styles: Federal, Beaux Arts, Contemporary
Description of Details
Floors: Wooden plank
Walls: Plain plaster; also dado with wallpaper above
Windows: Sash
Doors: Paneled, with fanlights used as transoms
Chimneypiece: Projecting, classical, in the Adam style, with a raised panel in the center of the frieze
Ceiling: Plain, plaster with cornice molding
Stairs: Various configurations; wooden with turned balusters

Federal

American Empire Style

Monarch or Significant Designer:
Duncan Phyfe
Period: 1820-1860
Related Building Styles: Greek Revival
Description of Details
Floors: Wooden plank
Walls: Plain plaster or chair rail
Windows: Sash or French doors
Doors: Paneled
Chimneypiece: Projecting, classical, black marble
Ceiling: Plain with crown or cornice molding
Stairs: Several configurations; curved was popular; wooden with turned balusters

American Empire

The Victorian Style (Rococo Revival)

Monarch or Significant Designer:
Queen Victoria
Period: 1837-1901
Related Building Styles: Victorian
Description of Details
Floors: Wood plank
Walls: Plain plaster with wallpaper
Windows: Sash
Doors: Paneled; some sliding pocket doors
Chimneypiece: Projecting carved marble, with a roundheaded arched opening
Ceiling: Mass-produced crown moldings, anaglypta patterns, and chandelier medallions of plaster
Stairs: Various configurations, straight run favored; wooden with turned balusters and elaborate newel posts

Rococo Revival

The Country French Style

Monarch or Significant Designer:
None
Period: Seventeenth century–present
Related Building Styles: Provincial French, Contemporary
Description of Details
Floors: Wooden plank, red tile
Walls: Stucco or papered
Windows: French casement
Doors: French doors
Chimneypiece: Simple version of Renaissance hooded fireplace; also, carved natural wood version of Rococo chimneypiece with curved opening
Ceiling: Plain or beamed
Stairs: Various configurations of wooden stairway with plain balusters

The Southwest Adobe Style

Monarch or Significant Designer:
None
Period: Seventeenth century - present
Related Building Styles: Southwest Adobe, Contemporary
Description of Details
Floors: Wood plank or tile
Walls: Stucco
Windows: Casement
Doors: Plank or paneled
Chimneypiece: Irregular, rounded, stuccoed adobe, corner fireplace with a round, arched opening
Ceiling: Vigas and latillas (see chapter 14, Exterior Style)
Stairs: Early versions generally one story; contemporary versions incorporate various configurations and styles

The International Style

Monarch or Significant Designer:
Ludwig Mies van der Rohe, Philip Johnson
Period: 1920 - present
Related Building Styles: International, Contemporary
Description of Details
Floors: Hard, smooth, marble, or tile
Walls: Plain plaster, glass
Windows: Large areas of glass with minimal framing
Doors: Flush
Chimneypiece: Simple rectangular opening with no trim
Ceiling: Plain plaster
Stairs: Open riser, no embellishment

Country French

Southwest Adobe

International Style

Notes

1. Riggs, J. Rosemary. *Materials and Components of Interior Design.* (Reston: Reston, 1989), p. 99.
2. Whiton, Sherrill. *Interior Design and Decoration.* (Philadelphia: Lippincott, 1974), pp. 420–26.
3. Riggs, pp. 142–45.
4. Architectual Woodwork Institute. *Architectural Woodwork Quality Standards, Guide Specifications and Quality Certification Program.* (Arlington: Architectural Woodwork Institute, 1984), p. 77.
5. Riggs, pp. 153, 157.

Bibliography

Architectural Woodwork Quality Standards, Guide Specifications and Quality Certification Program. Alexandria: Architectural Woodwork Institute, 1978.

Friedman, Arnold, John F. Pile, and Forrest Wilson. *Interior Design.* New York: American Elsevier, 1970.

Ramsey, Charles George, and Harold Reeve Sleeper. *Architectural Graphic Standards.* New York: Wiley, 1981.

Reznikoff, S.C. *Interior and Design Graphic Standards.* New York: Whitney Library of Design, 1986.

Riggs, J. Rosemary. *Materials and Components of Interior Design.* Reston: Reston, 1985.

Tate, Allen, and C. Ray Smith. *Interior Design in the 20th Century.* New York: Harper & Row, 1986.

Whiton, Sherrill. *Interior Design and Decoration.* Philadelphia: Lippincott, 1974.

WALL, CEILING, AND WINDOW TREATMENTS

Architectural elements—walls, windows, and ceiling—are often found to be bland and boring until they are treated. Treatments can give zest and beauty to interiors that are not architecturally interesting. In this updated historic bedroom, coordinated fabric and wallpaper are utilized on wall and window, as well as on the bed; the ceiling is treated as a fifth wall with overbed pelmet or valance directly attached. Fabric, wall coverings by and photo courtesy of Schumacher.

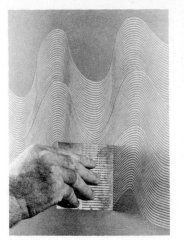

(A)

(B)

(C)

(D)

Page 216, top, left to right:
Painter Curt Hineline of Ridgefield, Connecticut, demonstrates four key techniques of custom painting used to texturize and faux (paint to imitate natural materials) walls, ceiling, and other surfaces. Shown, here are (A) combing, (B) marbling, (C) sponging, and (D) rag rolling. In all of these demonstrations, the application of the second coat to the surface is followed immediately by surface treatment. The metal comb subtracts paint, as does the rolled up newsprint, which gathers paint with a sharp randomness. The sponge leaves a softer pattern as it picks up the wet paint. Faux marbleizing utilized a newsprint-rolled field, or background, for subtraction of paint by an eraser's corner and the addition of white veins by a turkey feather. Photo by Ted Spiegel. Page 216, bottom:
The Pinechas home in Ridgefield, Connecticut shows faux marbling and sponging by master painter Curt Hineline. Photo by Ted Spiegel. Page 217, top: Boscobel Restoration, this lovely Federal-style symmetrical window treatment and valance is seen in the guest bedroom, echoed in the draped canopy of semisheer, fringed fabric.
Page 217, bottom, left to right:
Elsewhere in the home, American Empire treatments are seen in asymmetrical and symmetrical treatments, a style much copied, adapted, and generally revived in recent years. On the ceiling are moldings—the design for many interiors call for specialized artisans to add ceiling detail in this way for interiors inspired by historic styles. In this way, otherwise plain and uninteresting ceilings take on significance and richness. Courtesy of Boscobel Restoration. Photos by Ted Spiegel.

Page 218, top: The Japanese spirit pervades in this Greenwich, Connecticut, home. Shoji screen walls are seen in the background in the traditional and serene horizontal-rectangle arrangement of panes and in the foreground in a complex shoji design—a hand-crafted and expertly joined set of screens. Although shoji screens are considered both doors and window treatments, they can also make handsome wall treatments, overriding the need for any further decoration. The tokonoma (niche) displays simple art selections. Burnt timber ceilings convey the samurai influence on its owner-designer, a prominent financial executive. Here the ceiling treatment becomes not only a great design statement but it is important in the structural support of the building. Photo by Ted Spiegel, courtesy of Paul Kramer Construction. *Page 218, bottom:* Skilled craftsmen restore the beauty of this English Renaissance-style plaster ceiling in a Ridgefield, Connecticut mansion by fashioning replacement sections such as the one at the left. The panels are formed by pouring fiberglass and gypsum into a rubber mold (bottom left) made at the site from existing panels. Courtesy of Curt Hineline. Photo be Ted Spiegel. *Page 219:* An Art Deco masterpiece, the lobby ceiling at the Netherland Plaza in Cincinnati, Ohio, gives travelers a fanciful welcome. Not only is the architectural shape and lofty space impressive but so are the magnificent tooled metal panels that are rich in motifs from the 1930s. Gazelles gracefully leap over the lobby walkway through a "sky" filled with rolling clouds and a compass sunburst complete with greetings in Dutch and French. Photo by Norman McGrath © 1989.

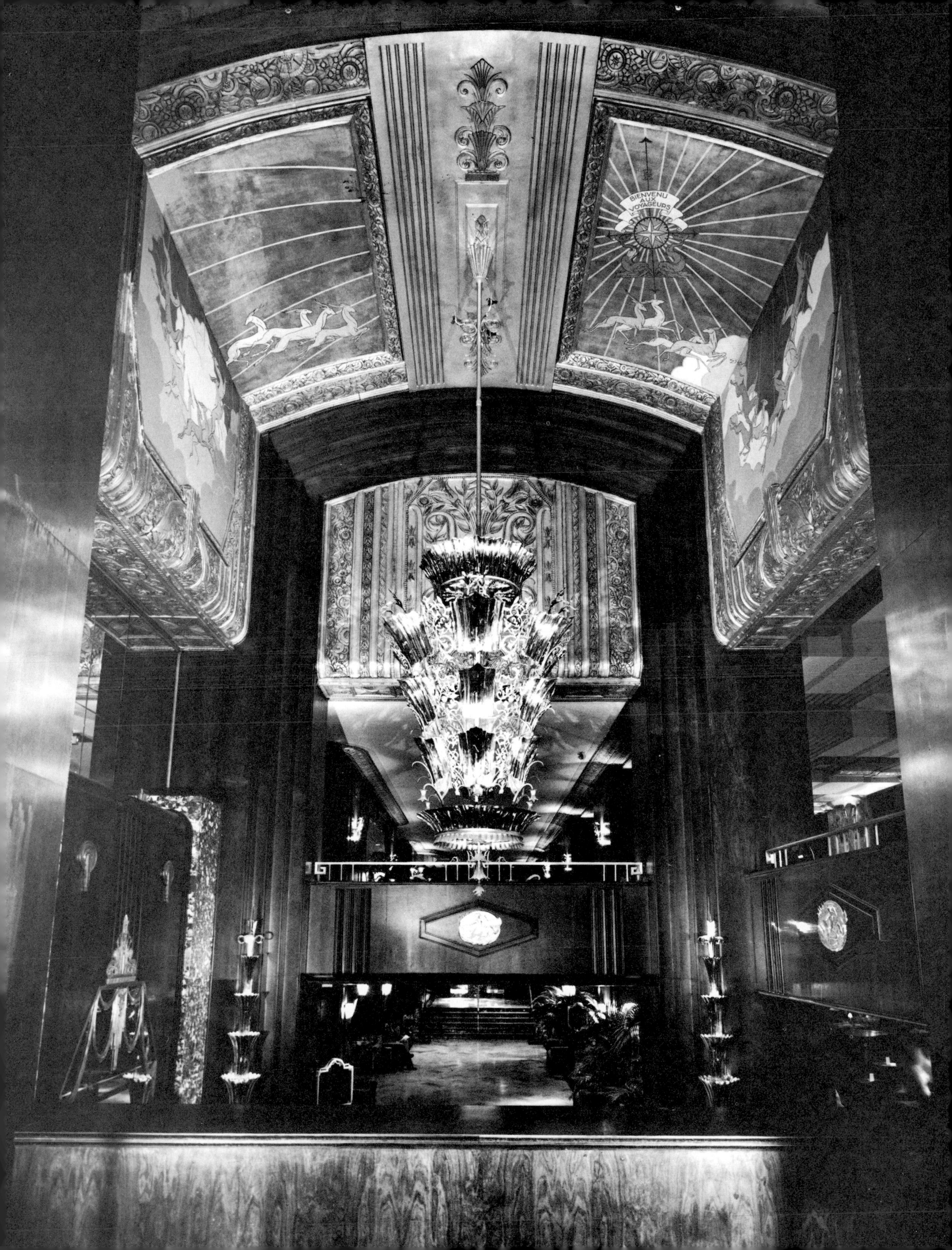
BIENVENU
AUX
VOYAGEURS

Wall and Ceiling Materials

Materials in use today for walls and ceilings come from a variety of sources, both natural and man-made. Although many of the materials used on walls and ceilings are the same as those used on floors, there are many others that are appropriate only for walls and ceilings. Wall and ceiling materials may be hard and rigid, flexible or soft. They may be heavyweight, medium weight, or lightweight. Just about the only restricting factor for materials used on walls is the limitation of the imagination—if it can be thought up, it can be installed. In this chapter, we will examine the materials used for walls, for ceilings, and for window coverings. Chart 9.1 overviews the selection of materials and gives brief guidelines to their selection.

Making the Right Choice

It is evident from charts 9.1 and 9.2 and the information that follows in this chapter that there are many, many selections for wall and ceiling coverings. Making the right choice can be a difficult and sometimes agonizing dilemma. Some of the following guidelines will simplify the choices:

- Generally, hard materials will echo and reflect or amplify more sound; flexible and soft materials will absorb sound.
- Materials that are permanent installations will initially cost more but may be the least costly in the long run because they require no finishes, replacement, or upkeep. These include natural materials such as stone, wood, tile, and brick. The time frame of occupancy must also be a factor in selecting permanent materials. A long occupation can justify the costs, whereas frequent moves will not.
- Interiors need to be flexible for change. Shifts in the life-styles of occupants will benefit from flexible materials that can be replaced, such as paint, wall coverings, or fabric.
- Pattern on the walls will lock in a style or color scheme and can potentially be restrictive if the pattern becomes tiresome and dated before the finances are readily available to change the scheme.
- Upkeep is a major consideration where busy life-styles do not accommodate much time for cleaning or where traffic or age group would tend to soil, mark on, or damage the wall surfaces.
- Authenticity and ambience or style are factors in selecting wall materials. The reproduction of a period room or the general look or feeling or level of formality will largely dictate the actual surface and visual texture as well as the pattern. Sensitivity to the need for unity is paramount in selecting wall materials.
- The size of the space can be a determining factor in wall material selection. Heavy textures, large patterns, and dark or intense colors will close in spaces,

making them appear smaller. Likewise, smooth or subtle textures, small patterns, and light or dull colors will visually expand the space.

- The purpose or function of the interior will determine the durability of wall material choices. Heavily used areas need impervious materials; little-used areas can accommodate more fragile treatments. High levels of humidity or moisture in the air or smoke and fumes or airborne oils or dirt can dictate nonabsorbent materials.

Hard or Rigid Wall Materials

Most materials that are hard or rigid will be permanent installations and, as such, have some common characteristics. They will usually be costly to purchase and to install and will often require little or no upkeep, depending on the finish or character of the surface. Hard or rigid materials can be very beautiful because of their inherent natural texture or pattern, and many have withstood the test of time and are considered classic wall and ceiling treatments. Examples include the rough-hewn beams and rough stucco walls seen in many rustic, provincial, or country settings. Smooth paneling, molding, and smooth or cast plaster have served more formal interiors throughout every period of history. Earthy materials such as stone, wood, and plaster or stucco are always appropriate for rustic informal settings. Metal, smooth stone such as marble or travertine, and glass are choices for interiors where glamour, drama, or sleek sophistication is sought. Chart 9.2 presents details on each type of hard or rigid wall and ceiling materials and includes a description of the material, its applications, the required maintenance, special considerations, and the cost structure.

Chart 9.1 Wall and Ceiling Materials—An Overview:

Materials and Considerations in Their Selection

Brick Heavy, hard, costly material, expensive to install. Lasts indefinitely and is structurally handsome. No upkeep.

Cork Very lightweight, flexible, sound absorbent, costly material but moderate installation. Handsome and subtle appearance. Easy upkeep.

Concrete Heavy, hard building blocks or cast slabs. Can be painted or left natural gray or colored before casting. Cold to the eye and touch. Moderate cost of material; can be costly to install. No upkeep unless painted.

Fabric Flexible, sound absorbent, three-dimensional; can carry out a fabric scheme by coordinating with other furnishing fabrics. Several methods and styles of applications. Can be changed at will. Cost of fabric varies from low to high; installation is moderate. Easy upkeep.

Glass Architectural glass (windows), glass block, stained glass used as transparent or translucent building materials. Can be very structural and moderately to very decorative. Costs vary from moderate to expensive. Upkeep varies according to use and environment. Glass tile requires little upkeep, but cost is high as an imported item. Fiberglass is used in tub surrounds and is costly. Upkeep requires nonabrasive cleaners.

Metal Aluminum, brass, bronze, copper, stainless steel, and tin are costly to purchase and install. Effects are rich whether structural or decorative. Permanent material. Upkeep depends on finishes and location or use. Most require little or no upkeep.

Paint The least expensive of the wall treatments, but it must be applied over a prepared, rigid surface such as Sheetrock or wood. Color range and effects are unlimited, and paint can be reapplied at will. Paint can imitate many materials, such as marble and wood. Professional painting services are costly. Upkeep depends on the use and the environment and the type of paint used.

Plaster Versatile, from very smooth to very rough stucco. Can be casted into decorative anaglypta moldings and ornament to document a particular period. Cost is moderate; upkeep depends on the type of paint or finish the plaster is given.

Stone Fieldstone, flagstone, granite, marble, and travertine are all heavy, costly materials that are also expensive to install. Weight dictates a properly reinforced flooring beneath. Structural or decorative effects, but all with natural beauty and little or no upkeep. Lasts indefinitely.

Cultured stone (imitation onyx and marble) is used for tub and shower surrounds and countertops or cabinet tops.

Lightweight; moderate cost; requires nonabrasive cleansers.

Tile Acoustical ceiling tile absorbs sound. Set into a grid framework, lightweight, decorative or structural, moderate cost, no upkeep—tiles that become stained are replaced.

Ceramic, quarry, Mexican, and mosaic tile installations are heavy and costly in terms of material and labor to install. Permanent material, little or no upkeep. Tile is also popular in bathing or hot tub areas as a countertop or cabinet-top material.

Wallboard Sheetrock, masonite, wood paneling, particleboard—all come in sheet form to cover large areas and are referred to as wallboard or drywall. Sheetrock (*gypsum-*

board) is the most common wall and ceiling material and requires painting or wall coverings. Moderate material and installation cost. Upkeep depends on finish methods and materials.

Wall coverings A variety of paper, vinyl, or cloth products that come in rolls or bolts. Subtle and structural to very decorative patterned effects. Low to moderate cost of goods, moderate installation costs. Upkeep depends on final layer (fabric, paper, vinyl) and placement and use. Generally little or no upkeep.

Wood Planks, paneling, molding—wood is a costly material to purchase but modest installation expense. Wood has lasting beauty. Wood can be stained, sealed, or painted. Little or no upkeep.

Chart 9.2   Rigid Wall and Ceiling Materials

Brick

Description: Clay, shale, and water mixed and shaped into solid or hollow rectangular blocks, then baked or fired to harden. Brick is colored according to the clay used (red is most typical) or the dyes added before firing. Brick used for constructing walls is typically 7 to 8 inches long by 3 to 4 inches wide and 2 to 3 inches thick.
Applications: Interior and exterior walls and fireplace surrounds, vaulted or arched ceilings, residential and nonresidential.
Maintenance: Low upkeep—dust or use a mild soap and water solution. Often no upkeep whatsoever is required.
Special Considerations: Brick should be treated with a sealant such as polyurethane that will prevent the brick from absorbing oil-based spills.
Cost Structure: Moderate to high.

Cork

Description: The outer layer of the oak tree of the birch family that grows in the Mediterranean area. It is light in color, elastic, and very insulative. It is resilient and may be treated with a vinyl coating, making it a more

durable product. It is sound absorbent.
Applications: Residential and nonresidential settings where a quiet, clean surface is required.
Maintenance: Dust or vacuum; little or no upkeep.
Special Considerations: Due to its insulative properties, cork should not be used where solar gain is desired. It will absorb bumps well but can be broken off and is very difficult or impossible to repair.
Cost Structure: Moderate to high.

Concrete Block and Slab

Description: Large porous bricks made of concrete with air pockets that make the material lightweight enough to handle and also make it somewhat fragile during handling. Poured slabs of concrete form walls and can be relatively smooth or very rusticated or brutalistic.
Maintenance: Little or no maintenance. Concrete block surfaces are usually painted, then treated as any porous painted surface. Concrete slabs are almost never painted but are used as a frank and structural building material.
Special Considerations: May be used for an exterior building

Figure 9.1

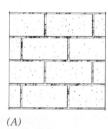

(A)
Figure 9.3

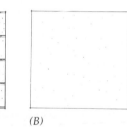

(B)

Figure 9.2

Continued on next page.

Figure 9.1 Brick wall.
Figure 9.2 Marble has for centuries been preferred finish material in large public spaces, such as seen here in the Utah State Capitol building. Columns, walls, and floors are stone, a material that provides a sense of permanence and stability and one that will last

through generations of hard traffic. In the middle background is seen the rotunda, the round floor area with curved walls lined with niches beneath the dome. Photo by John Wang.
Figure 9.3 (A) Concrete block. (B) Concrete slab.

Chart 9.2 *Continued*

material; then it must be sealed against water permeation. Cost is low to moderate, although installation or labor to install is high.

Cost Structure: Low to moderate.

Glass

Architectural Glazing

Description: Transparent or translucent brittle material of molten sand, potash, lime, and perhaps metal oxides for color or for reflecting and screening properties. Flawless glass is made by the float-glass process (extruded and suspended onto a flat liquid); other methods include rolled, calendered, and cast glass, which may be textured, patterned, or colored.

Applications: Window glazing, curtain wall construction (glass walls over a steel skeleton frame), both residential and nonresidential; interior office walls and dividers.

Maintenance: Transparent glass will show the dirt easily and needs occasional maintenance with a glass-cleaning solution. Professional window washers are usually employed for nonresidential installations.

Special Considerations: Glass for angled (skylight, greenhouse) installations must be tempered for strength (known as tempered or safety glass). Low-E (low-emission) glass screens out the harmful ultraviolet rays. Single glazing is one layer of glass; *double or twin glazing* is a window filled with two layers and is more insulative. Triple glazing is the most effective plain glass insulation and is often accomplished with an interior or exterior winter or summer storm window. Architectural glass may also be soundproofed, made into one-way visibility glazing, and coated with metal oxides to reflect excess solar gain (known as tinted and mirrored glass).

Glass Block

Description: Transparent or translucent glass pressed and formed as two halves and fused together. The semihollow blocks offer light diffusion and transmission and good insulation. Designs may be imprinted on one or both sides. Blocks for

Figure 9.4

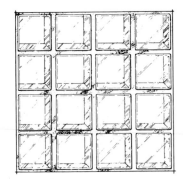

Figure 9.6

Figure 9.5

floor paving are solid glass (not hollow) and are tempered for strength.

Applications: Residential and nonresidential applications where light diffusion is needed with some privacy. Glass blocks are not for use in load-bearing situations. Glass blocks for floor paving give light to basements or lower floor levels and may also be used in ceiling installations with artificial light behind the blocks.

Maintenance: Little upkeep. If the blocks become dirty or greasy, soap and water will clean them. Polishing is not necessary.

Special Considerations: Variations of glass block include a fibrous glass insert that controls glare, brightness, and excessive heat gain. Solid glass blocks are also available for wall installations for greater protection against breakage and forced entry.

Cost Structure: Moderately high.

Fiberglass

Description: Glass fibers spun or pressed into a lightweight, insulative mass; translucent or opaque.

Applications: Wall panels and dividers, bathtub and shower surrounds and units. Fibrous fiberglass "wool" is an insulative material used in wall and ceiling structures. Fiberglass panels are sometimes used for corrugated ceiling panels and patio covers. Both residential and nonresidential applications.

Maintenance: Fiberglass panels and pressed forms are easily scratched and need to be cleaned with a nonabrasive spray or foam cleanser.

Special Considerations: Used where little hard use is anticipated, as it loses its shiny finish with abrasion or hard-water deposits.

Mirror

Description: Flawless float glass backed with a coating of silver or silver alloy. May be bronzed

or grayed, antiqued (smokey) or veined with gold color, or etched with a design.

Applications: Walls, ceilings, residential and nonresidential.

Maintenance: Clean with glass cleaner; polish with soft cloths or paper products.

Special Considerations: Mirrors will visually expand the space and may be set in place as flat, flawless panels or shaped into patterns such as tile. Mirrors may be used on folding screens or sliding closet doors.

Cost Structure: Moderately high.

Plexiglass

Description: Not a glass product but a thermoplastic resin product, which is a trademark of the Plexiglass company. It is formed into transparent, colored or printed sheets that are lightweight and nonbreakable.

Applications: Window glazing where breakage or break-in is a major concern. Examples include institutions such as hospitals

---

Figure 9.4 Architectural glazing.
Figure 9.5 Walls made of glass, supported by a steel skeleton are termed "curtain wall construction," meaning that the vast expanse of

glass may need protection against glare and excessive solar heat gain. Often, however, glass walls are left untreated, and the structural beauty is appreciated whenever possible. This is seen in these doors at the Caroline

Hemenway Harman Continuing Education Building at Brigham Young University. The glass reflects majestic mountains, part of the Wasatch range. Photo by Andrew Battenfield and Kelly Haas.
Figure 9.6 Glass block.

whose patient safety or control is paramount or stores in high-risk areas. Also used in dividers. Ceiling panels of Plexiglass may be printed to simulate real stained glass.

Maintenance: Low maintenance. Use a nonabrasive spray cleaner that will not cause a chemical reaction with the plastic. A mild solution of soap and water is best. Plexiglass scratches easily.

Special Considerations: Cost is generally higher than glass for glazing, but the factors of safety and durability may justify the expense. Gives off toxic fumes in case of fire; large quantities are generally not used because of this and the problem of scratching of the surface.

Cost Structure: Moderately high.

Stained and Art Glass

Description: Transparent or translucent glass that is colored with metal oxides and formed by casting, rolling, or pressing a design (calendering). Art glass may be frosted or etched. The color may be solid throughout the piece or flashed with layers of color. The colored glass, plus clear glass, is cut into shapes and held together with strips of lead caming or copper foil (or one of several other less-common methods) and formed into a design or picture.

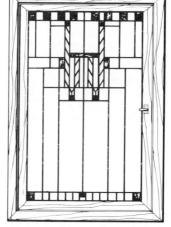
Figure 9.7

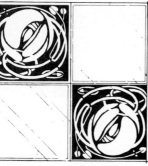
Figure 9.8

Applications: Window primary or secondary glazing; art hung in front of windows or framed and backlighted with artificial lighting or used as door inserts; ceiling panels or skylights. Used in both residential and nonresidential settings.

Maintenance: Low upkeep unless handled frequently or exposed to airborne dirt or storms. Clean as any glass product.

Special Considerations: Priced by the square foot, by the complexity of the design, and by the artisan's reputation. May need protection against breakage.

Cost Structure: Moderately high.

Glass Tile

Description: Solid, tempered, impervious tiles of glass that are colored and glazed; produced in France.

Applications: Walls and countertops, residential and nonresidential installation.

Maintenance: Plain water and sponge; soap and water if surface becomes oily.

Special Considerations: Heavy traffic may abrade and remove the surface glazing.

Cost Structure: Moderately high.

Metal

Aluminum, Brass, Bronze, Copper, Stainless Steel, Tin

Description: Metal is an extremely durable material, which is used in several forms. Sheets of aluminum, brass, bronze, copper, and stainless steel may be cut and fitted in place; strips of metal may be installed on clips. Metal panels are available, solid or perforated. Tin panels, tiles, or squares are again being produced with stamped patterns that document designs from the Victorian era.

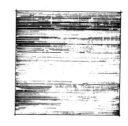
Figure 9.10

Applications: Window primary or secondary glazing; art hung in front of windows or framed and backlighted with artificial lighting or used as door inserts; ceiling panels or skylights. Used in both residential and nonresidential settings.

Applications: Walls, ceilings, and custom installations such as wrapped columns. Used occasionally in custom residences but more often in businesses, banks, hotel lobbies, and other nonresidential installations.

Maintenance: Little upkeep. If surfaces should become spotted from handling, use a metal polish preparation. Painted metals can be washed with soap and water. Follow manufacturer's instructions for cleaning. Most metals are treated to be impervious to oil, dirt, and corrosion.

Special Considerations: Tin panels are often painted. Metals are available in shiny or brushed surfaces. Metal surfaces may be costly background finishes, but they give an exclusive and expensive look. Some metal ceiling systems are designed to be installed over existing ceilings in renovation or remodeling work, making it possible to maintain existing heating and air-conditioning ducts and wiring. Finishes (discussed in chapter 6, Furniture Selection) include anodized satin, polished, and brushed.

Cost Structure: Moderately high to high.

Plaster

Description: A paste mixture of lime, sand, and water that hardens as it dries. May be applied as a finish material to be smooth, textured, or rough. Rough plaster is called *stucco*, and may be a smooth or rough consistency, depending on the fineness of the sand used. Plaster may also be cast into decorative ornaments or cornices, generally called anaglypta or anaglyphs, that can imitate hand-carved wood and be nailed or glued in place and painted or antiqued.

Applications: Walls, exterior and interior, ceilings; anaglypta ornament, moldings. Authentic smooth plaster walls are coated over *lath*, thin strips of wood nailed to the wall studs horizontally about three-eighths inch apart, or plaster can be applied over wire mesh. Today, plaster is more often applied over plasterboard or *Sheetrock* (see Wallboard) made of

Figure 9.9

Continued on next page.

Figure 9.7 Frank Lloyd Wright-inspired modern stained glass.
Figure 9.8 Glass Tile.

Figure 9.9 The ceiling in this modern kitchen is made of an aluminum strip system by Hunter Douglas Company. Plastic laminate and wood cabinetry and walls are contrasted with commercial-strength Italian ceramic tile by Marazzi. Photo courtesy of the Italian Tile Center.

Figure 9.10 Brushed metal wall material.

Chart 9.2 *Continued*

gypsum or concrete block. Plaster is most often used as a finish material. It is applied as a mud to seal the perfatape, which conceals seams in the wallboard, or applied as rough-textured stucco. It is also sprayed on as a texture in various thicknesses and sanded into the desired texture. A light application of blown plaster is usually called orange peel and is common in some residential and nonresidential settings. Plain plaster applications are more common in nonresidential settings. A frothy mixture called blown acoustic plaster is sometimes used on ceilings.

Maintenance: Upkeep of plaster depends on the use or abuse. Plaster can chip, crack, and peel. It scratches and mars easily, and smooth plaster is difficult to touch up with paint. Washability depends on the type of paint used, with oil-based paint being the most durable and scrubbable.

Special Considerations: Today smooth plaster walls applied over Sheetrock are more costly than sprayed or textured walls. New lath-and-plaster walls are nearly nonexistent because of the labor involved.

Cost Structure: Moderate.

Stone

Description: Natural stone includes flagstone, granite, marble, and terrazzo, all described in this chart. In addition, other general types fit the definition of stone.

1. *Ashlar* is stone that is cut into rectangular shapes so that it can be fitted together into a geometric pattern with grout.
2. *Cobblestone* (or river cobbles) are large, rounded, somewhat smooth rocks used to face walls and fireplaces in rustic settings.
3. *Fieldstone* is a rugged type of large rocks that may or may not be rounded and smooth. When laid, fieldstone has a random pattern.
4. *Sandstone* is a soft, reddish stone that is a type of fieldstone and may be cut into ashlar shape.
5. *Rubble* means rough uncut stone or stone that is not uniform.
6. *Artificial stone* is man-made to imitate rubble or ashlar.

Figure 9.11

Figure 9.12

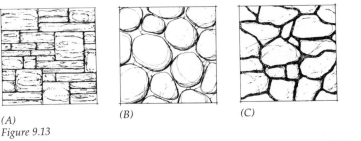

(A)
Figure 9.13

Figure 9.14

Granite

Description: A very hard crystalline rock with small amounts of feldspar, quartz, and other minerals in crystal or grain form. The size of the crystals varies from very fine to fairly coarse.

The colors vary from light to dark values and variations of gray, pink, green, brown, and black and may be combinations such as greenish or pinkish gray. May be dull or highly polished.

Applications: Walls, countertops, fireplace surrounds. Used in both residential and nonresidential settings.

Maintenance: Low upkeep; sweep or vacuum; damp mop if necessary.

Special Considerations: Exact color match will need to be carefully coordinated between the designer and the quarry or supplier.

Cost Structure: Very high.

Marble

Description: A metamorphic limestone, granular or crystalline, white or colored, often with streaks. The hardest and typically the most expensive of the stones. May be cut into thin sheets or slabs. Can be polished to a high sheen. Cold to the touch. Terrazzo is a composite flooring of broken chips of marble set into cement and polished to a sheen. This is a practical use of marble, as up to 50 percent waste occurs from breakage at the quarry.

Applications: Walls, fireplace surrounds, tiles for special or custom installations. Expensive look for both residential and nonresidential installations.

Maintenance: Clean with warm water and infrequently with soap and water.

Special Considerations: The most formal of the stones; rich-looking finish material.

Cost Structure: Very high.

Figure 9.11 Smooth plaster or plasterboard (Sheetrock) walls are painted a clear yellow, setting the tone for this light, refined traditional living room. Wood trim and fireplace mantle and surround are painted clean white. Photo courtesy of the National Paint and Coatings Association, Washington, D.C.

Figure 9.12 Rough stucco plaster is the correct choice for this Southwest interior. The rustic quality of the walls is compatible with Mexican tile floor, vigas and lattias ceiling, and accessories from the great Southwest. Wood window blinds are softened with an asymmetrical sheer swag

slung over projecting vigalike projections. Window blinds by and photo courtesy of Hunter Douglas, Inc.

Figure 9.13 *(A)* Ashlar. *(B)* River cobbles. *(C)* Fieldstone, sandstone, or rubble.

Figure 9.14 Flagstone.

Travertine

Description: A light-colored limestone rock formed near mineral springs. Trapped gas in the stone causes holes and interesting textures that can be filled according to the intended use.

Applications: Walls, fireplace surrounds and hearths, bathrooms. Used frequently in nonresidential settings and as accents and for custom installations in residential interiors.

Maintenance: Wash when necessary with clear lukewarm water. Wash no more often than every six months with soap and water and rinse thoroughly. On vertical surfaces it needs little if any cleaning.

Special Considerations: Travertine is slightly less formal than marble and widely used.

Cost Structure: High.

Tile

Acoustical Tile

Description: Acoustical tiles or panels are made from mineral fiberboard or from fabric or plastic-clad fiber, fiberglass, and even metal.

Applications: Primarily ceilings in both residential and nonresidential settings; occasionally for walls.

Maintenance: Depending on location and human contact, maintenance is usually low. Ceiling installations will not show soil easily, except around air distribution openings. Follow manufacturer's directions for cleaning. Tiles that become stained are often simply replaced.

Special Considerations: Acoustical tiles may not be tiles at all but strips of insulative materials. Square, rectangular, and strip materials are usually mounted on a track or grid system, making them relatively easy to install.

Cost Structure: Moderate.

Ceramic Tile

Description: Fine, white clays formed into tile shape (bisque) and fired at very high temperatures. Ceramic tiles are glazed before the first firing or before a second firing. Glazed finishes vary from shiny and smooth to patterned to rough and matte (dull). Mosaic tiles are very small tiles that were historically used to create permanent patterns and pictures on walls and floors. Today mosaic tile

Continued on next page.

(A)
Figure 9.21

(B)

Figure 9.15

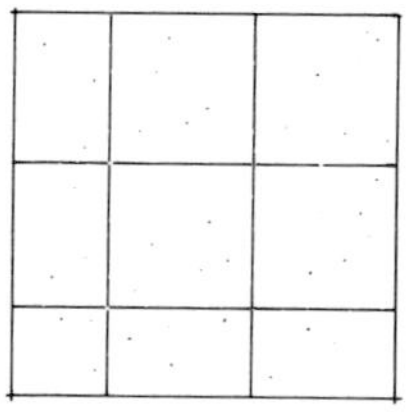

Figure 9.16 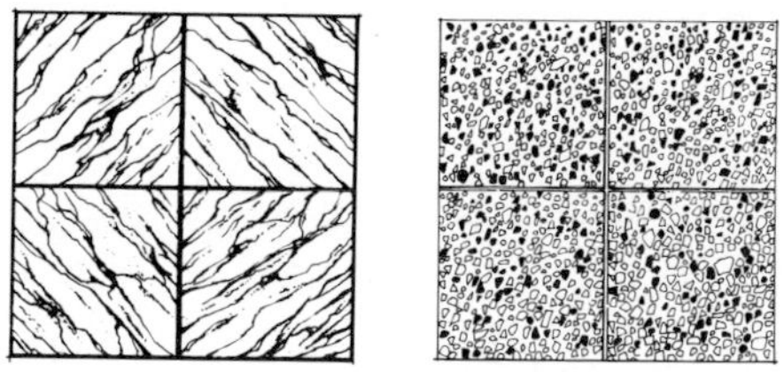   (A) *Figure 9.17*   (B)   Figure 9.18 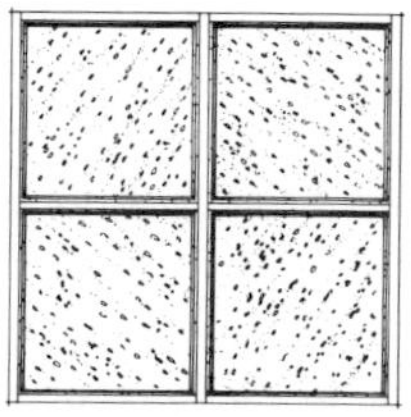   Figure 9.19 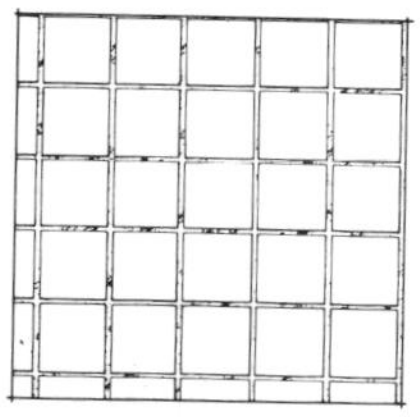   Figure 9.20

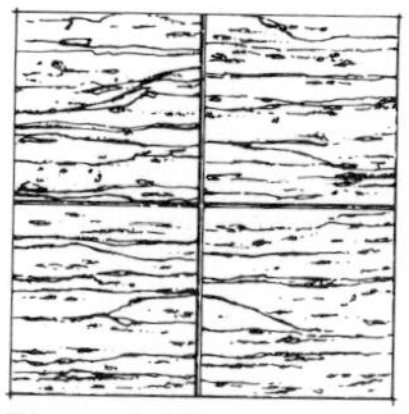

Figure 9.15 Impervious to heat and stains, this countertop and backsplash of granite stone will wear more than a lifetime. Window shades by and photo courtesy of Del Mar Window Coverings.

Figure 9.16 Granite.
Figure 9.17 (A) Marble. (B) Marble terrazzo.
Figure 9.18 Travertine.
Figure 9.19 Acoustical tile.
Figure 9.20 Ceramic tile.

Figure 9.21 (A) Heat-proof and easy-care Italian ceramic tiles in the kitchen make cooking and cleaning a breeze. Decorative border tile adds cheerful pizzazz to this all-white kitchen. (B) Lively new ceramic tiles from Italy show their colors in a variety of hand-painted decorations, ranging from floral or stripes to minipatterns in a wide range of styles. They can be used alone or in combination with solid tiles to create a design, make a decorative panel, or cover an entire wall in bright patterns. Patterned tiles are often preferred for borders and accents. Photos courtesy of the Italian Tile Center.

Chart 9.2 Continued

comes in preset sheets, a face mount or back mount, ready to be set with grout.

Applications: Walls, floors, counters, backsplash areas, ceilings. Ceramic tile is used extensively in nonresidential settings because of its durability. Ceramic tile is often used in bathrooms, kitchens, and solariums or in any room in warm climates.

Maintenance: Low upkeep. Dust or wipe with clear water, vinegar water, or soap and water for heavy dirt. Grout may soil and discolor. Silicone treatments will make grout less susceptible to soil. Newer developments in grout are more resistant to stains.

Special Considerations: Durable surface that maintains good looks indefinitely. Ceramic tile breaks, is cold and very hard (hard on the body for standing for lengths of time), and is slippery when wet (especially smooth surfaces), making it dangerous in bathrooms.

Cost Structure: Low to high—costs vary considerably in ceramic tiles. Imported tiles from France and Italy can be expensive. Labor to install is also high. However, because it is permanent, the life-cycle cost is low.

Quarry Tile

Description: Quarry tile is made of fine clay and graded shale, with color distributed through the body of the tile. Most is a terra-cotta rust/red, the color of the natural clay. It may be glazed but usually is left natural. Typical square or hexagonal shapes are most popular.

Applications: Walls, counters, backsplashes, ceilings, residential and nonresidential applications, similar to ceramic tile.

Maintenance: Same as for ceramic tile.

Special Considerations: Natural terra-cotta color gives quarry tile a timeless appeal.

Cost Structure: Tile cost is low to moderate, although installation is costly.

Mexican Tile

Description: Hand-shaped clay taken from the ground and left to set before firing. These tiles are a cottage industry product

(families working together), reflecting imperfections of hand labor that add to their charm. They are thick and fragile, rustic and handsome. Smaller tiles may be hand painted and glazed.

Applications: Large squares are not often used on walls; smaller, glazed tiles are used for decorative effects on walls, countertops, backsplashes, stair risers, and doorway surround trim.

Maintenance: A porous surface that should be treated with linseed oil or paste wax and buffed. Rewax or re-oil when it shows signs of wear. Glazed tiles clean the same as ceramic or quarry tiles.

Special Considerations: Mexican tile is durable, but if not sealed it is susceptible to oily stains. The softest of all the tiles, it can be chipped or broken more easily than quarry or ceramic tile.

Cost Structure: Tiles are low to moderate cost; installation is costly.

Other Tile Materials

Many materials are available as finish wall and ceiling materials in tile form. Among them are leather, mirror, metal, carpet, glass block, brick, and stone.

Wallboard

Description: A general category of drywall goods including Sheetrock or *gypsum board* (made of crushed and processed gypsum rock). It is available in sheets four feet by eight feet or four feet by twelve feet and is hung with nails or screws to wooden or metal studs. Seams are sealed with perfatape (paper) and covered with plaster mud, smoothed out to be inconspicuous. The wallboard may be left smooth or textured. Smooth wallboard is best for wallpaper installations.

Applications: The most common of the wall finish materials for both residential and nonresidential settings. It is a basic material that may be finished as described or overlayed with wall coverings or fabric.

Maintenance: Upkeep will depend on the texture and finish given the wallboard. Paints vary in their ability to withstand

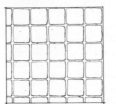
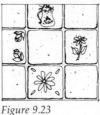
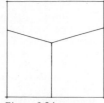

Figure 9.22   *Figure 9.23*   *Figure 9.24*

Figure 9.25

repeated cleanings, as do wall coverings and fabric.

Special Considerations: Economical wall-covering material. It is also fragile. It will dent and scratch and can be punctured with door knobs or other hard objects thrust against it.

Cost Structure: Moderate to high.

Wood
Millwork

Description: Stock and custom-milled wood applied to walls and as cabinetry in the form of flat and raised panels, shelving, and moldings. The wood may be

hardwood or softwood, plywood or solid wood.

Applications: Walls in residential and now, to a substantial extent, in nonresidential work.

Maintenance: Depends on the finish it is given. Oiled or waxed wood may need protection against moisture and will show fingerprints. Millwork is usually sealed with lacquer, acrylic, or urethane, which then is easy to clean with a mild detergent solution.

Special Considerations: Installation is considered to be part of the architectural detail and hence a permanent part of the building that is rarely

Figure 9.22   Quarry tile.
Figure 9.23   Mexican tile.
Figure 9.24   Wallboard—Sheetrock or gypsum board.
Figure 9.25   Knotty pine planks and rustic beams give an earthy quality to this contemporary kitchen. The

ceiling appears lower because of the color and texture of the wood. The brick fireplace wall is harmonious with the natural ceiling. Vertical blinds by and photo courtesy of Hunter Douglas, Inc.

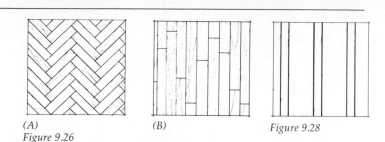

(A)
Figure 9.26

(B)

Figure 9.28

Figure 9.27

Paint

Paint is used as a finish material more often than any other material on walls and ceilings. The reasons are diverse and all valid.

- Paint is an extremely versatile material. It is flexible as a liquid and dries to a hard, protective finish with various textures and types of finish.
- Compared to other materials, such as wall coverings, stone, wood, brick, or tile, paint is an inexpensive wall finish and relatively simple and easy to apply.
- Paint offers infinite color and texture variety and assures protection to the surface.
- Painted smooth or textured walls can reinforce the interior architecture through neutral, noncompetitive colors.
- Paint has contrast and graphic ability; colors and values may contrast and provide excitement or drama. Graphics can be accomplished with careful planning and painting.
- Paint can add richness and subtlety to interiors through low-contrast, deep, or soft colors.
- Paint can accent or draw attention to surfaces and furnishings.
- Dark-colored paint reflects little light, which makes

(A)
Figure 9.29

removed unless remodeling takes place. It gives visual richness to the interior, particularly when stained rather than painted.
Cost Structure: Moderate to high, depending on whether the millwork is paint grade (less costly) or stained wood (high cost).

Wood Paneling

Description: Solid wood paneling comes in four- by eight-foot sheets of hardwoods. More typical, however, is high-quality veneer plywood (sandwiched) with a thin layer of hardwood (veneer) laminated to the surface. Prefinished plywood has a surface of good quality capable of being finished.
Hardboard is made of wood fibers compressed under heat or pressure. These may have a veneer or a photo reproduction of wood applied to the surface and grooved to represent a plank wall material. They may also be formed with a surface texture to imitate carved wood panels. Tongue-and-groove strips (milled to interlock) are

also used for walls as a paneling. Palisade walls are long strips of wood with narrow strips or lath nailed or screwed over the seams.
Applications: Walls and ceilings. The quality of the wood will determine the type of residential or nonresidential application.
Maintenance: This depends on the surface of the product. Paneling may be oiled, waxed, urethaned, or treated with acrylic or other products, or it may have a plastic finish, which varies from a very thin coat to a durable, permanent finish capable of withstanding the wear of any contract installation. Wall-cleaning products are available for wood only or follow the manufacturer's instructions. Durable finishes may be washed with soap and water.
Special Considerations: Wood paneling ranges from a do-it-yourself project look to a very exquisite and costly appearance.
Cost Structure: Moderately low to moderately high. Solid wood will cost the most.

Wood Molding

Description: Narrow strips of hardwood or softwood formed into flat, concave, and convex shapes.
Applications: Baseboard, doorway trim, chair railing, cornice, and dado trim (see chapter 8, Architectural Detail).
Maintenance: Depends on the finish. Should be durable enough to be washable.
Special Considerations: Wood trim molding can create an effect of solid wood walls or ceilings when it is painted to match raised wall panels. It can lend an air of historical significance and richness.[1]
Cost Structure: Moderate to moderately high. Labor to install may be high.

(B)

Figure 9.26 *(A)* Herringbone parquet wall. *(B)* Random plank wood wall material.
Figure 9.27 Millwork wood wall.
Figure 9.28 Palisade wall of board and batten.

Figure 9.29 *(A)* Stenciled roses form an arched frame around this simple turn-of-the-century powder room. Stenciling as a painter's art has once again become a popular and economical alternative to wall-covering borders. Photo courtesy of the National Paint and Coatings Association. *(B)* Artisan Elise Heinline stencils delicate sprays of roses and festooned ribbons in the home of photographic team Ted and Signy Spiegel. Stenciling can give authenticity and one-of-a-kind individuality to an interior. Photo by Signy Spiegel.

the surface seem to advance, and light-colored paints can visually expand spaces. These properties allow the design to visually alter sizes and shapes, perhaps creating architectural interest where none had existed.

- There is a vast number of ways that paint can give character and interest to walls and ceilings. The chromatic and textural variety of paint allow it to evoke other materials—wood, marble or other polished stones, tortoiseshell or fabric, for example. These are discussed under Preparation, Finishes, and Textures.
- *Trompe l'oeil,* painted three-dimensional scenes that trick the eye, adds architectural interest and sometimes humor by painting scenes of architecture, accessories, or even people that are not really there.
- Paint can be the least expensive of the background materials to apply. With the advice of the local paint store experts or painting handbooks, painting can be accomplished by the amateur.
- The services of a professional painter can be a great asset for large, new, or special projects. Skilled professional painters can produce texture and pattern, contrast and camouflage; they can create imitations of nearly any type of material. Professional painting is not inexpensive, although the cost to paint faux (false or imitation) marble, for example, is far less than surfacing with real marble.[2]

Painting Guidelines and Cautions

Because paint has great variety in versatility and ease of application, paint must be used with great discretion. Reckless abandon in painting can only bring about sloppy, haphazard work and probably garish results as well. Careful planning and preparation are imperative to achieve truly beautiful results.

Some guidelines and cautions for using paint include the following:

- Paint is sometimes assumed to have the power to cover and renew surfaces that have blemishes and flaws. This assumption is often met with disappointment if the surface has not first been properly prepared. Old paint that is cracked, bubbled, flaked, or peeling must be removed or sanded. Wallpaper must be removed. Cracks, holes, and damaged areas must be patched and sanded smooth. The surface must be clean and free from dust and sanding particles. A smooth surface will help assure a flawless finish and has a great deal to do with the success of a painted wall or ceiling. Call in experts or consult painting manuals or books for detailed information. Paint stores, interior design bookstores, and home improvement stores will have selections of books on

(A)
Figure 9.30

(B)

Figure 9.30 *(A)* A painted perspective in this intimate reading alcove gives the illusion that the room extends a greater distance. Such painted scenes that fool the eye are termed *trompe l'oeil*. Sara Delano Roosevelt House, New York City. Photo courtesy of DuPont "Teflon" soil and stain repellent. *(B)* Real marble on the floor in contrasting values sets an authentic stage for theatrical trompe l'oeil wall treatments. The giant blocks, reminiscent of the great Egyptian pyramids, are faux or painted as is the scene from antiquity—the columns, landscape, and sky, a realistically surprising vista. Photo by Norman McGrath © 1989.

Figure 9.31

watercolor paints (a less costly way to experiment). Colors achieved can be duplicated by any reputable paint company.

- Consider *glazing* (transparent paints) for unique light-revealing effects or any of the texturizing techniques presented later in this chapter. Experiment with different color combinations; for example, a light color with two or more colors glazed over it.
- In rooms where the painted walls and ceilings (or floors) become important architectural or decorative backgrounds, it is important to not overfurnish the room and thereby destroy the effects of the paint by competing with backgrounds or by changing the apparent proportions of the room. Paint can be not only a background but also an artistic backdrop that may require few furnishings to make it effective.
- Select textures and patterns that are appropriate for the room setting and the surface. Avoid mixing textures; for example, a marbleized wall and tortoiseshell woodwork will likely be overpowering and busy. This is particularly true where various moldings and paneling exist in the room.
- Consider orientation and climate when selecting the hue for painted

this topic. Professional painting contractors may advertise, or you may learn of experts through personal recommendations.

- Before selecting paint colors, textures, or patterns carefully evaluate the room itself. Look at the dimensions, the moldings, the architectural assets and defects. Evaluate the number of windows, the direction they face, and the amount of light pouring in. Remember, there is no such thing as an ugly room; any room can become quite handsome with intelligent planning.
- Select a color scheme by painting a small wall, portions of the wall, or a paper that can be taped to the wall with quarts from the paint store. Small paint chips provided by the paint store will often look different and usually darker when an entire wall is painted that hue. Larger swatches on the wall will allow a judgment of the color during different times of the day and under different types and directions of light. Another good method is to mix poster or

walls. For example, a lively yellow may be warm and comforting in a cool room with a north exposure or in a cooler climate, whereas that same color would visually and psychologically bake the inhabitants of an interior with a broad, southern exposure or in a hot season or climate.

- Evaluate what contrast in the paint will do to the room. High-value contrast (very light hues against very dark hues) will accentuate and draw attention to that contrast. This can be dramatically effective where the contrast is in large planes and busy if the contrast is, say, around every door and window or painted as graphic stripes on the walls. On the other hand, low-value contrast (light values next to medium ones or medium values near dark values) can provide depth and richness but certainly not the clarity of the high-contrast graphic approach. The program and the master design plan should dictate the way that value contrast is handled.[3]

Figure 9.31 High-contrast drama is accomplished through light- and dark-value paint on the ceiling of this traditional living room. The walls are painted a vivid red, with rich colors echoed in the textiles. Photo courtesy of the National Paint and Coatings Association.

- Consider the psychological effect of the color. The way people feel about color is often based on experiences and prejudices of the past, and these feelings are very real. If the user detests green, for example, it would be most unwise to paint the walls any shade of green. The detestation may be deep-rooted. Certainly color preferences and prejudices should be discovered in the design program research. Further, warm colors are desirable for people who tend toward depression or when, for some other reason, the interior calls for lively or warm welcoming colors. Cool colors that calm and provide a restful, restrained environment are selected for personalities or situations where these needs must be fulfilled.

Paint Types

The selections in paint are sometimes confusing to both the designer and the lay person. It is helpful to understand the types and characteristics of each type of paint so that the best paint for the purpose can be selected. It is also wise to describe the project to painting contractors or retail paint store specialists who can recommend a suitable product. (See chart 9.3.)

Preparation, Finishes, and Textures

There are several lusters or finishes in paint. The luster can be selected for a desired result or effect. Chart 9.4 lists the types of finishes available in paint today, as well as their advantages.

Paint-Texturizing Techniques

Visual texturizing can be achieved in many ways; just about any effect the design calls for can be accomplished by a skilled painter. Chart 9.5 lists some of these techniques.[4]

Chart 9.3   Types of Paints

Acrylic paint is a synthetic resin water-based paint. It is odorless, quick-drying, durable, and easy to use. It cleans up with soap and water and is moderately priced.

Alkyds and alkyd enamels are resins, oil modified, that dry faster and harder than oil paints. Alkyd enamels produce a glossy surface. Alkyds are moderately priced, are easy to work with, and have very good coverage and color range. Cleanup is with solvents or paint thinners.

Artists' paint are paints—oil or acrylic—that come in small bottles or tubes and can be thinned with mineral spirits or water, respectively, and used as glazing for transparent color overlay painting techniques.

Enamel paints are oil-based or sometimes water-based paints that usually come in gloss or semigloss (may have flattening agents added for a matte finish). These paints are used most often for their hard, glossy, smooth finish.

Epoxy paints come already mixed or have hardeners mixed in at the site. Epoxies can be used to paint metal and water-holding surfaces such as bathtubs and swimming pools.

Fillers and sealers are used prior to staining or painting. Fillers are putty or stick-putty materials that fill in holes or cracks. Sealers are liquid preparations that make a smoother surface.

Finishes refer to the relative shine (see chart 9.4). Finishes also consist of a separate group of liquid sealants used on cabinetry and furniture, including shellac, lacquer, polyurethanes, and acrylics.

Flame-retardant paints are widely available from nearly every major paint company. These paints retard the spread of flames or the toxic fumes and smoke given off by burning paints. Most specifications for new or remodeled nonresidential buildings will require paints to meet a Class A flame spread, the lowest possible.

Latex paint is the least costly of the paints. Latex paints vary in their quality and durability. They are easy to apply and dry quickly, reducing recoating time. They have an excellent color range and are fairly durable but must be protected from freezing temperatures. They are not as scrubbable as alkyds but do have the ability to breathe, allowing moisture to escape. Cleanup is with soap and water.

Oil-based paints were for several years considered the best paint to buy. They were thought to be the most durable, were the most expensive, had the strongest odor, and took the longest to dry. Cleanup of oil-based paints is with paint thinner or solvent. These paints have largely been replaced with alkyds.

Primers are liquid sealers applied to some surfaces before the paint. It fills in small pores and helps the paint become more durable.

Solvents are liquids that dissolve resins, gums, or oils and are used to thin or clean up oils, alkyds, and oil-based enamels.

Stains are thin liquids that are used to color woods by penetrating the porous surface. Stains come in water base, oil base, varnish, and waxes.

Chart 9.4   Paint Finishes

Flat, or *matte, paints* reflect very little sheen. They are appropriate for walls and ceilings to give a soft, velvetlike texture. Flat paints are the least washable of the lusters. Flat paints are available in enamel, often called *eggshell enamel,* which gives a matte finish and is more washable.

Satin or eggshell paint has a small amount of light-reflecting quality and hides fingerprints better, as well as being more washable.

Semigloss paint is perhaps the most widely used luster in residences. It has some sheen that hides marks and is a more washable paint than flat or satin. It also contrasts nicely with either flat or gloss paints.

High-gloss, or *gloss enamel, paint* is the shiniest of the paint lusters and the most durable and scrubbable. Its reflecting qualities, however, will show every flaw on a surface that has not been properly prepared for painting.

Texturizing paint also comes in various textures. While the majority of the paints used are smooth, there are some thicker paints available that can be applied to give the effect of stucco or of suede. These texturizing paints will absorb more sound as well.

Chart 9.5 Paint-Texturizing Techniques

Smooth textures are achieved by using one of the four most common methods of applying paint—brush, roller, pad, and spraying. These techniques may produce an even surface appropriate in many period settings and modern interiors where woodwork and architectural detail are not important. They also make appropriate backgrounds for the broken and textured paint techniques presented in this chart.

1. *Brush painting* is used for corners and small, hard-to-reach areas and for detail work such as window grids and moldings.
2. *Roller painting* is very useful for large areas such as walls and ceilings. Small rollers are handy for narrow areas. A different sleeve should be used for each color. Rollers do spatter somewhat, and the roller should never be too full of paint.
3. *Pad painting* is useful for smaller areas and will not spatter. Pads cover evenly and are easy to work with.
4. *Spray painting* takes on two forms. *Airless spraying* uses fluid pressure and undiluted paint giving a better coverage and using more paint. *Air compression spray guns* use diluted paint with less-complete coverage. Spraying is common in new buildings, both residential and nonresidential. It is fast and economical. It should be followed with a roller to even out the paint.

• *Antiquing* means to make a surface look old, to soften and blur slightly in imitation of the mellow patina that naturally accompanies the aging process. Techniques frequently used in antiquing include color washing, glazing, spattering, and dragging.
• *Color washing* is a technique of applying a coat of thinned, sometimes translucent paint over a white or colored background. It is versatile and attractive and easy to use, giving effects from rugged texture (over rough walls) to shimmering translucence (over smooth walls).
• *Dragging and combing* are techniques that produce fine lines and may be used in wood

(A)

Figure 9.32

(B)

graining. Dragging or coasting a dry brush over a wet glaze reveals a base color and can imitate fine fabric yarns. Combing uses any hard comblike tool. Dragging and combing can be done in straight lines or in curving lines or fan shapes. Cross-hatching by combing can produce a fabric burlaplike texture; by dragging with a brush, a variety of interesting crosshatch textures are possible.
• *Glazing* is a technique where transparent colors are overlayed in sequence, thereby producing various gradations of color. Artists' paint taken directly from a tube and mixed with water or mineral spirits will maintain the purity of the color while making it transparent.
• *Marbling* is the technique of imitating polished marble stone and can be done by artisans with a high degree of skill and artistic sense where the marbled surface cannot be distinguished from the real stone, or it can simply be a mottled whirling, moving flow painted onto the surface.
• *Outlining* means painting contrasting colors or white values on architectural molding. *Picking out* means highlighting features on molding, such as dentil trim or carved bas-relief.
• *Porphyry* is a granitelike texture achieved by crisscross brushing, then stippling, spattering, and finally *cissing*

(dropping mineral spirits on the splatters to dilute and make shadows of the spatters).
• *Ragging and rag rolling* are the basis for marbling where the wet paint or glaze is partially removed by dabbing with a rag or rolling the paint off with a rolled rag. A variety of textures is possible. It works best with pastel colors.
• *Shading* is the technique of blending color values from light to dark across a wall or ceiling. For example, a light color at the bottom of a wall shading to a darker color of the same hue at the ceiling can make the ceiling visually lower. The lighter values at the top blending to lower values at the bottom of the wall will make the ceiling appear higher. Walls can be darker around the perimeter or vice versa, as can ceilings. Different hues can be shaded together with a prismlike effect, although this takes skill, careful planning, and considerable discrimination.
• *Spattering* is achieved by filling a brush and flipping the paint onto the base color to produce uneven spots or spatters. Lighter or darker colors can be used, with lighter or darker base colors. Spattering can vary from tiny irregular dots to large globs of paint, and the spacing can be very close or sparsely spattered on an open ground.

• *Sponging* (or paint applied with sponges) produces a broken, splotchy effect. Larger sponge pores will produce a more coarse-looking texture and a larger splotch than finer sponges. Sponging can yield rich-looking walls and ceilings, somewhat akin to granite when more than two colors of very carefully coordinated paint or two or more shades of one hue are used. Oil-based paints will look more crisp; latex paint will look softer.
• *Stippling* is similar to sponging but uses a stippling brush to dab on a colored glaze or paint, revealing some of the base color. The result is finer than sponging.
• *Tortoiseshell* is a technique of imposing layers of tinted varnish through dabbing, dragging, and crisscrossing to produce a look of tortoiseshell or the mottled, blended colors of tortoiseshell butterfly wings. Colors typically vary from light golden to auburn to deep chestnut, with some backgrounds seen in dark turquoise. Small areas must be produced because the varnish dries quickly.
• *Wood graining* is done by brushing on a glaze and drawing wood grains and lines with an artist's brush. Techniques vary according to the type of wood being imitated. When well-done, wood graining can be very beautiful.

Figure 9.32 *(A)* Architectural pilasters and moldings painted ebony flank faux-marble (painted imitation) panels with surprising realism. The ceiling is airbrush painted to produce a subtle cloud-and-sky effect and visually ties together the deep violet and blue-on-black values of the marbled insets. *(B)* Marbling is skillfully employed in the corner of this bathroom as faux-marble columns and wall materials. The arched window with a balloon shade provided the inspiration for the keystone arches and perspective marble insets. Photos courtesy of the National Paint and Coatings Association.

Wall Coverings

Wall covering categories include wallpaper, vinyl and textile wall coverings, and fabric. These three types of wall coverings provide tremendous variety in pattern, color, texture, sound absorption, and flexibility. Walls and ceilings benefit from the many wall coverings that add visual and architectural interest. The reasons for utilizing wall coverings include the following:

- Colors, patterns, and textures of wall coverings are unlimited. There are styles and colorways to suit every type of interior design.
- Wall coverings can imitate natural materials such as stone or wood or brick or tile at a fraction of the cost of those materials.
- Costs vary, but they can be modest. Installation can be done professionally or by the lay person.
- Three-dimensional fabric wall coverings absorb sound and give a sense of quiet or peace to the interior.
- Wall coverings can cover badly cracked walls, old paint, and even camouflage architectural flaws or defects.
- Fabric installed on the wall can coordinate with ensemble—fabric used in other areas of the interior. Likewise, many wall covering companies offer companion fabrics to match wallpapers.
- Wall coverings can provide instant decor—they can add charm, beauty, and character to interiors.
- Fabric wall coverings can be installed flat, pleated, shirred, draped, or folded (see chart 9.8), thereby allowing creativity in the way the fabric pattern, color, or texture is utilized.

Figure 9.33

Wall Covering Guidelines and Cautions

Wall coverings are more popular today than at any other time in history. They are so extensively used as instant decorating that there must be some inquiry into the appropriateness of great quantities of wall coverings. In this respect, some guidelines and cautions are listed for careful consideration.

- Select wall coverings that are compatible with the style of furnishings and with the architecture of the building. Formal Baroque or Renaissance designs in a modern building are not only out of character but they may insult the integrity of both the wall covering and the architecture.

Figure 9.33 Four vignettes of wall coverings and appropriately selected accessories from interior designer Mary Gilliatt's Edwardian Garden collection. Contemporary wall coverings are available in an unlimited variety of dots, stripes, plaids, florals, abstracts, and textures. Photo courtesy of Sandpiper Studios.

Chart 9.6 Wall Covering Terms

- *Single rolls* contain thirty-six square feet, or about twenty-eight feet long by twenty-seven inches wide. When calculating wall covering quantity, figure a single roll will cover thirty square feet, which allows for waste. In Europe, there are twenty-eight feet per single roll of wall coverings. Wallpapers are priced as single rolls and may be purchased by the single roll. It is abbreviated S/R.
- *Double roll* is the equivalent of two single rolls rolled into one and usually contains about seventy-two square feet. It saves waste and is therefore more economical. The price of a double roll is the price of two single rolls.
- *Triple roll* equals the footage of three single rolls in one length, about 108 square feet, and is the most economical use of the paper; it is priced as three single rolls. Narrow wall coverings, eighteen to twenty inches wide, are normally packaged in double and triple rolls. Wider wall coverings are also available in double and triple rolls.

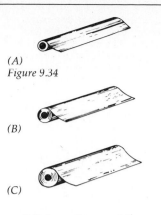

(A)
Figure 9.34

(B)

(C)

- *Bolt* is another word for a roll of wall coverings.
- *Dye lot* is a single run of colors or a single production. The dye lot shades may vary, as may the color of the background paper. If it becomes necessary to reorder, always specify the dye lot number (included on a piece of paper with the roll) or send in a swatch of the paper. It is not always possible to obtain the same dye lot, so it is best to be generous when ordering.
- *Paste* or *adhesive* comes as a dry powder to be mixed as needed at the site, or it may

come as a premixed paste. There are various types of paste, which are manufactured to be compatible with different wall coverings. The type of paste should also be compatible with the type of sizing used.
- *Pattern repeat* comes in two directions. A vertical pattern repeat is the complete motif or pattern (there may be more than one) from the top of one length to the top of the next. A large pattern repeat is more wasteful, as a complete pattern repeat must begin at the top of each length. A horizontal pattern repeat means that the pattern can be matched straight across or drop-matched by lowering the next length of paper.
- *Peelable wall covering* means the top layer of the wallpaper will peel off, leaving a substrate (lining) material that can be papered over again.
- *Prepasted wall covering* means the paper has a dry coating of paste and will only need to be moistened to apply. The back of the paper usually has a sandpaperlike texture.
- *Pretrimmed wall covering* means ready to hang. Hand-

printed wallpapers have a selvage (border) with separate printed information, including blocks of color used in the paper. This must be trimmed off before the paper is hung. Pretrimmed papers have the selvage cut off. *Semitrimmed* has only one side of the selvage trimmed so that the selvage left on is under an overlap or is trimmed off at the site.
- *Scrubbable* denotes a wall covering that can withstand repeated wet cleaning. Most vinyl wall coverings are scrubbable.
- *Sizing* is a thin liquid painted onto the wall surface that reduces the amount of paste absorbed by the wallpaper, gives the surface "tooth" or enough abrasiveness to stick well, and seals the surface so alkali cannot penetrate into the wallpaper. Sizing and adhesive should be selected to be compatible.
- *Strippable* is a term applied to papers that can be stripped off the wall completely without scraping or steaming.
- *Washable* means the paper can be cleaned gently with a little soap and water.

- Choose the pattern carefully and with great discrimination. Consider how long a pattern will stay stylish and aesthetically appealing. There are a great number of bright, loud, or busy patterns offered for sale today. A general rule is that the more dramatic or flamboyant the pattern, the more quickly it will become tiresome.
- Limit the number of patterns in an interior and coordinate them to provide harmony from one area to another. Patterns that differ in style or color will be discordant, and if two or more clashing wall coverings can be viewed from any one vantage point, the effect can be disastrous.
- Obvious patterns on the ceiling can visually lower the ceiling and can be psychologically disturbing.
- Patterns that clash with fabrics in the interior are poor choices. Keep in mind how often the furnishings may be changed or replaced.
- Many textured wall coverings are lovely and sophisticated, and their subtle qualities establish pleasing transitions from room to room or area to area.

However, some textures are cheap imitations such as plastic grass cloth, or are so brightly colored that they cannot be considered good design.
- Installation is a key factor in how nice a wall covering looks. Professional wall covering installers will make a great difference in the effectiveness and beauty over a careless or unskilled do-it-yourself job.

Prepackaged wall coverings have several terms in common that are useful in selecting and ordering wall coverings. These terms, listed in chart 9.6, are helpful in determining the type and quantity of wall coverings.

Types of Wall Coverings

One need only visit a wall covering store to discover the enormous variety of wall coverings available. As the color, pattern, and texture are a matter of careful coordination with other background materials and interior furnishings, the selection can be an almost overwhelming task—so great are the number of choices. Yet the basic types of wall coverings remain relatively constant; the following chart should provide some guidance.

Figure 9.34 *(A)* A single roll of wall covering contains thirty-six square feet and will cover approximately thirty square feet. *(B)* A double roll contains seventy-two square feet. *(C)* A triple roll contains 108 square feet.

Chart 9.7 Types of Wall Coverings

Figure 9.35

(A)
Figure 9.36

(B)

• *Coordinating or companion fabrics* are now available with many wall coverings. This is a convenient, although not inexpensive, way to coordinate fabric installations with wall coverings.

• *Cork wall coverings* use cork, which is a natural resilient material, that can be cut into very thin layers and laminated to a paper backing. It is insulative and left natural, sometimes mounted onto colored papers that may show through holes in the cork. Cork comes in square tiles or bolts of wall coverings.

• *Embossed wall coverings* are those that are calendered to produce a three-dimensional, raised pattern. *Anaglypta wall coverings* are embossed to resemble sculptured plaster, hammered copper, or hand-tooled leather.

• *Fabric or textile wall coverings* are fabrics laminated to a paper backing and sold in rolls or bolts. The most common fabric wall coverings are linen, jute, and wool. These may be woven or simply yarns laid parallel to each other. Linen and wool are quite costly. They do, however, give a rich natural-textured look and are very appropriate for both residential and nonresiden-

tial interiors. Wool is inherently flame resistant, while linen and jute become resistant when paper-backed.

• *Custom paper-backed fabrics* are either custom fabrics or designer fabrics that may be mounted to paper for wall installation.

• *Fabric-backed wall coverings* are used for heavy-face papers or vinyl. The cotton cheesecloth, Osnaburg, or twill fabrics give strength to the installation. Most nonresidential wall coverings and heavy vinyl residential wall coverings are fabric-backed.

• *Flocked wallpapers* use flocking, which is a process of gluing tiny fibers in a pattern to the surface of the paper. It is a decorative effect, in imitation of fine damask and brocatelle.

• *Foam wall coverings* are thin layers of foam laminated with papers. They come in bolts or as squares and are highly noise and temperature insulative.

• *Foil/mylar wall coverings* have a shiny, highly reflective quality. They may be patterned or flocked.

• *Grass cloth* is made of dried grasses that are left natural or dyed a color and woven into a textile with fine cotton threads (a more refined product) or other grasses as the warp (coarser looking). Grass cloth is versatile and fits nicely in both formal and informal interiors. It is costly but has little need of being replaced, as it is a classic. Grass cloth comes in widths up to fifty-four inches.

• *Hand-printed wall coverings* are those that are block printed or silk-screened by hand as a limited edition or for a custom installation. They are usually on heavy paper and may be vinyl coated with a paper backing. They are usually not pretrimmed and sometimes come with coordinating fabrics. Hand prints tend to be more expensive and may be custom designed to coordinate with a textile application.

• *Kraft papers* (paper used for wrapping packages for mailing) are sometimes used as a basis for hand prints. They should be treated to resist oil and grease stains.

• *Leather* is a luxurious and quieting wall covering. Squares or tiles of leather, the tanned

Figure 9.35 This handsome bathroom vignette illustrates richness in wall covering and coordinated fabrics with the formal stripe in the foreground and a rich paisley in the background and as a portiere (doorway curtain). The reflection in the mirror shows a coordinated classic Country French toile pattern. Wall coverings and fabrics created by Richard Felber Designs, Inc. Collection offered by Pelican prints of Design Directions, Inc. Photo by Leslie John Koeser Associates. Photo courtesy of Wallquest, Inc.
Figure 9.36 (A) Linen warp wall covering from the Xcaliber collection is a subtle background suitable for both residential and nonresidential interiors. This woven fabric wall covering is protected with Scotchguard and is paper-backed for ease of application as a wall covering. Photo courtesy of Wallquest, Inc. (B) Subtle, handsome linen wallcovering textiles from the Beaumont II Collection by J. M. Lynn Co., Inc. These linen and linen-blend wall coverings meet class A ratings in the ASTM E84 Flame Spread Tests, making them suitable for both residential and nonresidential settings. Photo courtesy of the International Linen Promotion Commission.

Figure 9.37

hide of cattle and swine, are dyed brown or colors and possibly embossed with patterns. Because leather is very costly, it is often used in small areas or in exclusive settings. The subtle, mellow quality of leather will age gracefully. Tanned leather is one type that may be used on walls; suede, which is leather with a brushed nap, achieved through different finishing processes. Many vinyl wall coverings are produced to imitate leather and suede. There are also fabrics that imitate suede, called suede cloth. Some of these wall coverings and fabrics can give a remarkably authentic leather look.

• *Murals* are printed scenic wallpapers that come in panels. They have traditionally been scenes of romantic or faraway places, sometimes ruins of ancient civilizations.

• *Trompe l'oeil* are papers or wall coverings that are printed into realistic, three-dimensional "trick-the-eye" scenes.

• *Vinyl wall coverings* come in several types, from light to heavy weight. They are *vinyl-protected wall coverings*, a thin layer of vinyl applied over a wallpaper to make it more washable and durable; *vinyl*

Figure 9.38

latex, paper impregnated with vinyl and applied to a fabric or paper backing; *coated fabric*, coated or laminated before the pattern is applied, then the pattern is usually coated with more vinyl. Vinyl wall coverings are the heaviest of the wall coverings, the most scrubbable and strippable, and possibly even reusable. Vinyl wall coverings are more difficult to hang because of their weight. They may imitate wood, leather, tile, marble, or any other natural or man-made hard material.

Figure 9.39

Fabric Wall Coverings

Fabric installed or upholstered onto a wall or ceiling has many advantages. It is the most *flexible wall covering*, as it can be applied flat or gathered (shirred) or pleated or folded. Fabrics can change their character with the different methods of installation. A patterned fabric laid flat looks quite different than one which is shirred, pleated, or folded. Installations can be quite temporary, permanent, or semi-permanent.

Fabrics are highly insulative against both noise and temperature extremes. They offer visual comfort as well as physical softness. Perhaps most important is the ability to use the same material on other installations, such as upholstered furniture, bedspreads, and accessory items.

Fabrics used on the wall may be subject to soiling and may discolor or stain when spot cleaned, making upkeep difficult. Fabrics should not be used in heavy traffic areas where people, particularly children, tend to touch the wall frequently.

Ceiling Treatments

All of the materials discussed thus far in this chapter may be applied to ceilings. However, the most common of the ceiling treatments will be drywall, plaster, glass and other glazing materials, metal, and wall coverings or fabric. Keep in mind that ceilings may need to be visually lowered or heightened and that patterns, dark or bright colors, or texture will lower the height. Smooth surfaces or light, pale, or dull colors will visually raise the height. Horizontal bands or beams will visually lower a ceiling, whereas angled ceilings with beams or bands that carry the eye upward will increase the visual height. Fabric is sometimes upholstered on a ceiling or draped in sunburst or tentlike

Figure 9.37 Historic adaptations in architecture and furnishing materials are brought boldly to the present in front of this hand-printed wall covering and fabric from the Air Brush collection. Photo courtesy of Schumacher.

Figure 9.38 An innovative collection, Malabar and Kebaya, designed by Danny Recoder and produced by China Seas, Inc., is the winner of the Traditional Adaptation Patterns/ Collections/Groups category of the Seventeenth Annual Product Design Award. Both wall covering and fabric possess an abstracted overall design

reminiscent of traditional paisley patterns. All products in the collection are suitable for contract or residential use. Photo courtesy of Resources Council, Inc.
Figure 9.39 Walls are pleated and draped lavishly in this retreat designed with a sumptuous use of

fabric on the chairs and the table skirt. Fabric on walls may be pleated, shirred, or installed flat—each technique producing a different effect. Fabric and furniture by and photo courtesy of Lee Jofa. Photo by Phillip H. Ennis.

Chart 9.8 Methods of Installing Wall Fabric

• *Covered frame method* is a good technique for temporary installations. A lath frame (one inch by two inch wooden strips), is laid on the back of the fabric, then the fabric is pulled tightly over the frame and stapled. The result is a blind wooden frame with top and sides covered with fabric. This can be mounted or hung on protruding nails as panels and may not cover the entire wall. Smaller fabric-framed panels may be accessory items.

• *Direct pasteup* uses fabrics that come prepared for installation as a wall covering with a paper or foam backing, or the installer may apply a spray backing or iron on a stiffening fabric backing. Sometimes the preparation or paste causes the fabric grain to slip, making it difficult to match patterns horizontally. A skilled professional is an asset in direct fabric pasteup. A less-permanent method is to sponge liquid laundry starch onto the wall or dip the fabric in it. The fabric will stick to the wall until it is remoistened and pulled off.

• *Hook-and-loop fasteners* may be used to install fabric where the fabric needs to be taken down frequently for cleaning. The best known brand of hook-and-loop fasteners is Velcro. One-half of the tape, square, or circle fasteners is sewn to the fabric, and the companion part is applied to the wall.

Figure 9.40

• *Lath method* is where wood lath strips are nailed to the wall perimeter, then the fabric is stapled, glued, or fastened with Velcro hook-and-loop tape. This saves the effort of preparing badly damaged walls or stiffening the fabric for direct pasteup.

• *Panel-track method* can use several brands of metal or plastic tracks that are on the market for the professional, usually nonresidential installation of fabric on the wall; these include office systems furniture, a flexible wall where fabrics can be changed when necessary.

• *Stapling* with a staple gun is a fast, easy method of applying fabric to the wall. The staples are usually covered with trim such as welt or gimp or braid or with wood or plastic molding.

• *Strapping tape method* is a very inexpensive and easy method. Simply roll lengths of strapping tape into circles and apply to the wall then press the fabric in place. High humidity or certain paint surfaces may make this method unsatisfactory, however.

• *Upholstered walls* mean that there is a layer of batting applied first to the wall in the form of polyester or cotton batting or foam. The fabric is then stapled over the padding, and a trim is placed on top. This gives extra sound absorption and insulation values.

---

fashion, which not only can absorb sound but can create a cozy atmosphere. Fabric panels or acoustical panels (see chart 9.1) absorb sound and are appropriate in many settings. Textured acoustical plaster also absorbs sound, although it is extremely difficult to paint over—it catches dust and collects soil from ceiling-mounted ducts. Ceilings are frequently given a textured finish before painting to cover blemishes and reduce upkeep. Chapter 8, Architectural Detail, discusses and illustrates different architectural ceilings.

Window Treatments

The window treatment industry has matured significantly in the past decades to include a greater spectrum of choices than at any point in the past and from many competitive manufacturers.

The free-enterprise system has opened doors of opportunity to research, develop, and market new and

Figure 9.41

Figure 9.40 Pavarini-Cole Interiors created an adult environment to absorb extraneous sound. Individually wrapped fabric sections combine to create a textile brick-patterned wall. Sara Delano Roosevelt House, New York. Photo courtesy of DuPont "Teflon" soil and stain repellent.

Figure 9.41 This skylight ceiling, as seen from the mezzanine of the Utah State capitol building, casts full-spectrum, balanced natural light through the voluminous space. Further, because of the lightness, the ceiling appears to be even higher than it actually is. Photo by John Wang.

innovative types of window coverings and to improve the standard treatments that have withstood the test of time. Because of consumer demands for beauty, privacy, energy conservation, comfort, and cost efficiency, today's window treatments have so many options that they would form an enormous section in this book. Consequently, the most significant are discussed here. Interior designers and retailers alike strive to keep abreast of the continuing technical advances in window coverings.

Window treatments are generally divided into two categories—soft and hard. *Soft window treatments* include curtains, draperies, fabric shades, and top treatments; *hard window coverings* include a wide array of art glass, horizontal and vertical slat blinds, screens, shades, and shutters. These treatments are presented in charts 9.9 through 9.15. Making a window treatment selection is often a difficult decision because styles, types, and colors vary so greatly. Recent trends have favored layered treatments, of two or more fabric treatments or of practical and durable hard treatment—a blind, shutter, screen, or shade—layered over with a soft fabric treatment of curtain, drapery, shade, or top treatment. Whether one, two, or more layers at the window, well thought-out considerations will assure a sensible choice.

Window Treatment Considerations

Many factors go into making a wise choice for a window covering. These include *aesthetic coordination, privacy, energy consciousness, light control,* and *operational control.*

Aesthetic Coordination

Aesthetic coordination is the careful selection of window treatments not only to be beautiful but to blend with and support the interior and exterior design and architecture. Where the building is structural and modern, for example, window treatments should

Figure 9.42

likewise be no-nonsense and simple, acting as an appropriate background for the often dramatic, sculptural furnishings of the modern interior. Or where architecture and interior design are historical, a treatment that supports that style or is an adapted, updated traditional treatment will be a good choice. Exterior appearance is a consideration when selecting window coverings. Generally, the more consistent the treatments in each window, the more pleasing the exterior of the building will be. Bright colors at the window can be aesthetically disturbing because they do not harmonize with the exterior. Likewise, treatments that are excessively ruffled in one window and straight and severe in another will not produce a harmonious exterior.

Look carefully at the overall plan for the interior—the colors, textures, and patterns used in the floors,

Figure 9.42 The grand paneling serves as the perfect background for these valance and draw drapery window treatments made from a linen and cotton print called Filoli Tapestry. Inspired by the flowers and fruit trees just outside, this large-scale design has a Jacobean flavor. Fabric is repeated on the Chippendale side chairs. Photographed by Peter Vitale at Filoli, a Georgian-styled mansion outside San Francisco, now a National Trust Property. Filoli is known for its magnificent gardens. Photo courtesy of Brunschwig & Fils.

walls, furniture, and art and accessories. Window treatments should complement these elements, not compete for attention by being too ornate or overbearing. On the other hand, the treatment should not leave the interior unsupported by undertreating the window or leaving it barren. Successful aesthetic coordination requires discrimination and knowledge and much looking and adequate research into appropriateness, style, and authenticity.

Aesthetic coordination also requires sensitivity to good proportion. Window treatments that are top heavy, too wide, overdone or on the other hand, too skimpy can throw off the proportions of the entire room. This is because the window itself is a justly important architectural feature that will inevitably draw attention because of the light and view. If the window treatment is aesthetically disturbing, the interior will seem incomplete and lacking in harmony, no matter how handsome other furnishings are. Further, simple, well-proportioned treatments will have longer aesthetic appeal than treatments that are excessively fussy or fancy. It is well worth the time and effort to assure that the window treatments beautifully support and complement the interior design.

It helps to judge proportion by sketching the window treatment to scale (one-fourth inch equals one foot is a standard scale). Calculate the overall dimensions and judge these in comparison to the size and scale of the room. Look carefully at the pattern and use of trimmings and at the lines and fullness of the treatment itself as it relates to the needs and furnishings of the interior.

Privacy

Perhaps the most important consideration to personal comfort and safety in the selection of window treatments is privacy. Privacy can be achieved by restricting or completely blocking out the view into the interior. Such privacy protects valuable belongings against burglary. If it can be seen, it can be stolen. Privacy also gives a psychological sense of well-being to many people and makes a space more useable after dark.

During the day a sheer, semisheer, or casement fabric curtain, drapery, or shade will provide privacy. A pleated fabric shade, horizontal or vertical blind, partially opened shutter, woven wood, bamboo shade, roller shade, and translucent and pierced or lattice screen—all give good daytime privacy.

At night, any translucent treatment will not give privacy. Treatments that have holes or slats that do not close completely (pleated shades, horizontal blinds, woven woods, shutters) will provide considerable privacy but not 100 percent privacy. Only opaque treatments that can be closed fully will provide complete nighttime privacy. These include opaque draperies and shades, solid vane vertical louvers, lined woven woods, and opaque pleated shades with hidden cords.

Figure 9.43

Figure 9.44

Figure 9.43 A beautiful window treatment graces a beautiful window in this Neoclassic interior furnished with Laura Ashley's Blueberry fabric. The rope and tassel ties are placed high on the shirred curtain, exposing as much window as possible while framing the arch in complementary swags. The arch over the window is an architectural detail that forms a bonnet over the glass. Photo courtesy of Laura Ashley.

Figure 9.44 In this office as well as in the home, a screening fabric filters the light and reduces the glare and ultraviolet rays that damage furnishings. Photo Andy Battenfield and Kelly Haas.

Chart 9.9 Calculating Yardage

Calculating yardage for curtains and draperies includes the following steps:

1. Determine rod width (end of rod to end of rod).
2. Add on for overlaps (for traverse draperies that meet in the center) and returns (around the corner to the wall), if applicable. Twelve inches are standard for a single-hung layer, sixteen inches for a double-hung layer, and four inches for an underlayer.
3. Divide by twenty inches to determine the number of widths or cuts (a typical forty-five to forty-eight inch fabric will pleat or gather down to about twenty inches including side hems).
4. Determine the *finished length* desired, then add for hems, headings, and any ruffles to find the *cut length.* Hems are usually four inches doubled, or eight inches. For pleated headings add eight inches. Ruffled headings will need six to twelve inches added depending on the depth of the ruffle and the width of rod—figure the finished length plus the rod pocket and ruffle plus two inches again for the self-lining and hem, which is turned under.
5. Multiply the cut length by the number of widths or cuts to find the total inches, then divide by thirty-six inches to yield the number of yards. Always round up. For pattern repeats, figure

the number of complete pattern repeats needed for each cut, then multiply that number by the inches in one pattern repeat for the total inches needed per cut. There will be waste in pattern repeat fabrics because the pattern must start at the same point at the top of each cut. Yardage will be an average of 20 percent greater.
6. Costs to sew and install (charged by the width or foot) and for the rods are additional.

To calculate yardage for balloon shades:

1. Determine finished width, then divide by twenty inches for number of cuts or widths.
2. Add six to eight inches for hems and headings, then add twelve inches for the pouf at the bottom.
3. Ruffle yardage is figured in widthwise or lengthwise strips, total inches of ruffle needed will be multiplied by two or three (for desired fullness), and the depth of the ruffle doubled plus one inch for self-lining. These dimensions are calculated or sketched out in scale into the width of the goods either widthwise or lengthwise.
4. Cost to sew is figured per square foot (ruffles are extra, charged per linear foot), and fabrication costs are greater if the shade is operable.

5. Installation board and cost to install are priced per linear foot. Board may be included in cost of shade fabrication.

For Austrian shades:

1. Determine the finished width; divide by twenty inches for number of cuts or widths.
2. Multiply the finished length by three for the cut length.
3. Multiply the number of cuts or widths by the finished length and divide by thirty-six inches for total yardage, rounding up to the next whole yard.
4. Labor for fabrication or sewing is priced per square foot and will usually include installation board. Installation is per linear foot across the top.

To calculate yardage for flat, shaped, and pleated valances:

1. Determine whether the width should run vertically in cuts or horizontally (railroaded) with no seams. Railroaded fabrics may appear a different color than the curtain or shade beneath it because of the way the light hits the weave.
2. Determine the cuts or widths (if selected) as previously determined for curtains, eliminating the overlap but figuring in returns. Multiply the cuts by doubling the finished length for self-lining, plus two to four inches for seams, or multiply by finished length plus two to four inches if lining fabric

is used. Divide by thirty-six inches for yardage, then round up. Order the same quantity of lining fabric if the fabric is not to be self-lined.
3. Railroaded valances and curtains/draperies turn the width to run the lengthwise direction of the goods. Multiply the finished width by two and one-half (or fullness desired) and divide by thirty-six inches for yardage. For valances, figure strips this way—finished length—face only or self-lined measurement divided into the width of the goods.

For swags and cascades:

1. Determine the number of swags or festoons by sketching them in the configuration desired and determining the overlap and width of each swag. Measure for desired depth.
2. A self-lined swag up to twenty inches wide and twelve inches deep will need one to one and a half yards each; a self-lined swag up to forty inches wide and twenty-four inches deep will need three yards each.
3. Cascades and jabots need yardage equal to double their finished length. Costs to sew are determined by the workroom. To sew on ruffles or trimmings will cost extra (trimming yardage is two and a half times the top of the swag); installation is per swag or cascade or per linear foot of installation board.

Energy Consciousness

Energy consciousness is important for two reasons: (1) the cost of heating or cooling a room can be reduced through energy-efficient treatments, and (2) the comfort of the room can be enhanced by controlling excess *heat gain* and *heat loss.*

Heat gain or *solar heat gain* can be a problem not only in hot climates and in the summer but anytime heat from the sun becomes uncomfortable and begins to fade or damage interior furnishings. Heat gain controlling treatments are referred to as shading devices. The ideal shading device is actually on the exterior, preventing the sun from hitting the glass. These devices include sunscreens; awnings; rolling, angled, or movable shutters; deciduous trees; vines; trellises; and projecting architectural elements.

Once the sun hits the glass, temperatures between the window and the interior window treatment can climb to as high as 300 degrees Fahrenheit, not only heating the room but causing damage to the window treatment, too. The

most effective interior shading devices are those that can reflect a high percentage of sunlight back through the glass. Metallized (fabrics and pleated shades) and light-colored treatments (hard and soft) do this best. Room-darkening treatments also effectively control heat and brightness. These include roller shades; woven woods; some shutters; horizontal and vertical blinds; and fabric curtains, draperies, and shades, particularly when lined and interlined.

Heat loss is a problem in moderate to cold climates in the winter. It takes place when heated interior air rises and travels toward the window, coming in contact with cold glass, thereby cooling the heated air, which then drops to the floor and circulates at ankle level, causing us to feel a draft. Preventing the warm air from striking the glass is the best preventative for heat loss. Sealed insulated fabric shades sealed on the sides and at the bottom and insulated shutters are the best treatments. Opaque roller shades and lined, solidly woven woods and heavy lined/interlined draperies that reach to the floor and are securely attached to the walls and have sealed top treatments are also good choices. The heavier and more solid the treatment, the better it insulates. Many treatments on the market claim to be energy efficient in winter, and some are—to a degree. Any treatment is better than a bare window, and some treatments allow light and view while offering a limited amount of heat loss protection. However, the best treatments during the cold winter are heavy and opaque.

Light Control

Control of light is a major consideration in selecting window treatments. Certainly the light-controlling needs must be noted in the research phase of programming in the design process. If the room needs to be completely darkened, for example, then only certain treatments—opaque draperies, perhaps coupled with window shades—will fill that need. Light control also means heat gain control through shading devices. Light is often desirable. The undesirable aspect is not heat gain as much as control of glare (too bright, directional light), which causes irritation and fatigue. Glare control is a relatively simple need to fill, because many treatments will do a fair to an excellent job— draperies, curtains, shades (of light to medium weight), all types of vertical and horizontal blinds, pleated and translucent shades, louvered shutters, screens, bamboo shades, and woven woods are all good choices.

Within an interior, the need for light and glare control may vary according to the *orientation*, or direction the windows face. Whereas north-facing windows may need little light control, the bright east light, constant south light, or hot, piercing west light may require shading devices during particular times of the day when the sunlight comes directly through that window.

Operational Control

The selection of a window treatment should also be based on whether or not it needs to be operable, and this will largely be dictated by the needs previously discussed. Stationary treatments—tieback draperies, ruffled curtains, top treatments, stationary screens—cannot be dropped for privacy nor can they be removed for desirable solar gain or maximum light penetration. Ventilation may be inhibited by a treatment that is difficult to operate or that will not adequately stack out of the window area.

For many treatments on cord- or pulley-operated hardware, motorized units can operate the opening and closing of the treatment. Many situations can benefit from motorized units, from hard-to-reach controls, such as solarium shades, to control by a disabled person to the convenience of automation or remote control. There are mechanisms that can sense by light or temperature change when to close treatments, thus enhancing energy efficiency.

Soft Window Coverings

Fabric is used at the window more frequently than on walls because of the softness it gives to an inherently hard and poorly insulative material. Fabric at the window provides both sound and temperature insulation, visual comfort, and interest through color, texture, and perhaps pattern. In addition, light-filtering fabrics can give daytime privacy (and be layered with opaque fabrics or hard materials for nighttime privacy) and can effectively reduce or eliminate glare, which is harsh directional light. Fabrics can be installed on *traverse rods* to be drawn off the window. Fabrics also can be made into many decorative shapes, giving architectural support, authenticity, or decorative effects. There seems to be no limit to the styles and combinations of fabrics used at the window, making the window perhaps the most creative of the background material installations.

Curtains

Curtains are soft window treatments that make up a group of treatments. Curtains are often shirred, or gathered, onto a rod, making them stationary or hand operable. *Shirred curtains* may be formal or informal. Curtains can also have a variety of headings depending on the use. Chart 9.10 lists the types of curtains.

Draperies

Draperies are pleated fabric panels hung on a rod. Draperies may be opaque or casement (semiopaque) or translucent. There are many types of pleats, the most common being the French or pinch pleat. See chart 9.11.

Fabric Window Shades

Fabric shades are panels of fabric that operate top to bottom. In Great Britain they are called blinds. See chart 9.12.

Top Treatments

Top treatments are used for a number of reasons: to hide rods or pleats, to cover the area from the top of the window to the ceilings, to give a soft and finished look to the room. Top treatments may be shaped according to architectural detailing or inspired by furnishings. Fabric is often an effective medium to unite a room and carry the eye gracefully along the top of the walls. Types of top treatments are discussed in chart 9.13.

Drapery Hardware

Much of the versatility possible in soft window coverings is due to the many kinds of hardware that have been developed during this century. The basic types of hardware are presented in chart 9.14. Many variations of each type are available through interior designers and window treatment specialists.

Chart 9.10   Types of Curtains

• *Cottage curtains* are short lengths, shirred and hung in informal style within or on the window frame. They may be *tiered*, or layered to slightly overlap one another, and may include a ruffled curtain valance and longer side panels under which are café curtains.

• *Café curtains* cover the bottom half of the window and were originally used in French cafés where those seated by the window could enjoy privacy and passersby could look in to see the posted menu. Café curtains may be shirred, pleated, flat, or scalloped panels.

• *Priscilla curtains* are a form of cottage curtains that fill the window with a sheer, semisheer, or muslin fabric. Priscillas have a ruffle sewn on the front leading and bottom edges and on the tiebacks and have a ruffled valance. They meet in the middle or crisscross with one panel in front of the other.

• *Country curtains* are a takeoff of the more traditional Priscilla curtains. These meet at the center and are gathered up to five times the fullness with deep, sometimes layered ruffles. They are often quaint cotton prints in one or more patterns.

• *Sash curtains* are sheer or semisheer fabrics shirred at the top and bottom and installed most often on casement windows and French doors so as to swing with the casing. The curtains may not cover the entire window but leave the top bare, being a form of café curtains.

• *Tab curtains* are flat panels with straps of fabric sewn to the top and looped over dowel rods.

(A)
Figure 9.45

(B)

(C)

(D)

(E)

(F)

(G)

(H)

(I)

Figure 9.45   Curtains. *(A)* Cottage curtains. *(B)* Tiered cottage curtains. *(C)* Café curtains. *(D)* Center-meet Priscilla curtains. *(E)* Crisscross Priscillas. *(F)* Country curtains. *(G)* Sash curtains. *(H)* Tab curtains. *(I)* Bishop's sleeve side panel curtains.

Chart 9.11 Types of Draperies

- *Draw draperies* are installed on a traverse (cord-operated) rod and may be pulled or drawn open and closed.
- *Privacy draperies* are installed under a transparent fabric or separated tiebacks to give nighttime privacy or insulative control.
- *Sheer draperies* include transparent and translucent fabrics, often placed next to the glass and historically called *glass curtains*.
- *Side draperies* are stationary panels hung to the side of sheers or an undertreatment for softness and framing.
- *Tieback draperies* are ideally slender stationary panels that meet in the center on narrow windows or are separated on wider windows. They are tied back with fabric bands (ties) or metal holdbacks.
- *Casement draperies* are draw draperies made of a woven or knit fabric with novelty yarns and a strong textural look. They are popular in nonresidential settings, such as offices, and in casual settings at home. They screen light and cut down on glare but do not provide nighttime privacy.

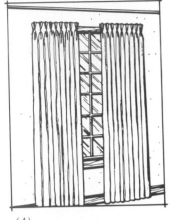

(A)
Figure 9.46

(B)

(C)

(D)

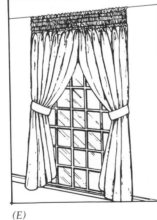

(E)

Figure 9.46 Types of draperies. *(A)* Pinch- or French-pleated draw draperies. *(B)* Pencil-pleated, closed draw draperies. *(C)* Butterfly-pleated tieback draperies. *(D)* Sheer draperies and box-pleated side panels. *(E)* Tieback draperies with smocked heading.

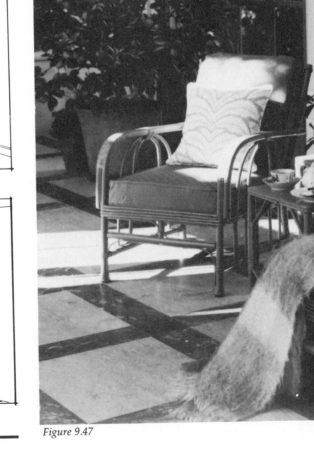

Figure 9.47

Figure 9.47 Balloon shades with an interlocking leaf design adapted from an early American block-printed wallpaper, c. 1800. This sun-filled room with rattan furniture is at Filoli, a Georgian mansion outside San Francisco, now a National Trust Property. Photo courtesy of Brunschwig & Fils.

Chart 9.12 Fabric Window Shades

- *Austrian shade* fabric is sewn into soft horizontal scallops and gathered vertically. Formal theaters often use Austrian shades. In homes and formal offices they are often made of sheer or semisheer fabrics, edged with fringe.
- *Balloon, pouf, or cloud shades* are billowy at the bottom, forming large poufs or balloons. The top may be shirred, flat box pleated, French pleated, etc. They may be tailored or fancy with ruffles and trimmings.
- *Pleated shades* are factory-made products of semisheer polyester fabric, plain or printed, that fold up accordion fashion. They may have a metallized backing for insulation against solar gain and winter heat loss. They may also be opaque.
- *Roman shades* are sewn in horizontal folds that raise and lower accordian style with a draw cord. They may be pleated first to give more fullness to the shade. Roman shades may also be interlined with batting, heavy lining, and moisture-barrier material to make an energy efficient shade.

(A)

Figure 9.48

(B)

(C)

(D)

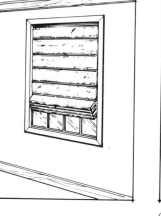

(E)

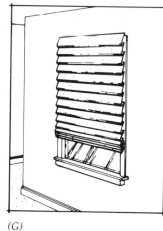

(F)

(G)

Figure 9.48 Window shades. *(A)* Austrian shade. *(B)* Balloon shade. *(C)* Ruffled balloon shade. *(D)* Pleated shade. *(E)* Flat Roman shade. *(F)* Soft-fold Roman shade. *(G)* Pleated Roman shade.

Chart 9.13 Types of Top Treatments

• *Austrian and balloon valances* look like the shades previously described. Balloon or pouf valances are more casual and airy; Austrians are more formal and traditional.

• *Shirred and double-shirred valances* are gathered on the top and on the top and bottom, respectively. Smocked valances are a variation of double shirring and tucks in a diamond-shaped pattern. Top-shirred valances may have shaped or scalloped bottoms.

• *Pleated valances* have several different forms. They may be French or pinch pleats, flat box or inverted box pleats, or

variations such as rounded cartridge pleats, pleat and scallops, pencil pleats, or any number of unconventional pleats.

• *Shaped valances* usually have straight tops and scalloped or shaped bottoms, although the top may also be shaped or curved. The shape might carry out a theme, document a historic period, or be a shape found in a piece of furniture—the back of a chair, for example. Fabric and lining are interlined with a stiffening material to give body to the flat fabric valance.

• *Quilted valances* may or may not be shaped. Often these are

outline quilted, following a printed or woven pattern. The quilting may also be done in an all-over pattern or emphasize a certain motif.

• *Swags and festoons* are individual half-round fabric treatments that can be installed in overlapping arrangements. A festoon usually refers to a single swag. Swags are perhaps the top treatment most often used throughout history. Many widths, depths, and variations are possible.

• *Cascades and jabots* often frame swags and festoons. Some are placed on top, and some underneath. A cascade has a

straight outside edge (at the end of the window) and a zigzag fold next to the swag. A jabot is a pair of cascades sewn together so that both outside edges form the zigzag fold.

• *Cornices* are straight or shaped wooden top treatments. When covered with padding and fabric, they are called *upholstered cornices.* When cornices extend down both sides to the floor or partway, they become lambrequins or cantonnieres and may also be upholstered. These are energy efficient as they keep warm and cool air from exchanging at the window.

(A)
Figure 9.49

(B)

(C)

(D)

(E)

(F)

(G)

(H)

Figure 9.50

Figure 9.49 Types of top treatments. *(A)* Double-shirred valance. *(B)* Shirred valance. *(C)* Austrian valance. *(D)* Balloon valance. *(E)* Flat valance with box-pleated corners. *(F)* Shaped valance or cornice or pelmet. *(G)* Swags and cascades. *(H)* Architectural cornice.

Figure 9.50 The window treatment in this child's room is of two colors of miniblinds, topped with a printed fabric finger swag valance tied at the corner with bows. Coordinating

fabrics give charm and intimacy. Interior designer: Margot Gunther, ASID. Photo courtesy of Hunter Douglas, Inc.

Chart 9.14 Types of Drapery Hardware

- *Conventional traverse rods* are cord-operated rods with carriers to hold the drapery hooks. White is the usual color, and brown is available. Conventional traverse rods come in single-hung (for one pair of draperies), *double-hung* (for two sets of draperies), with a plain curtain rod underneath or a curtain/valance rod on top. They also come in one-way draw for stacking draperies to one side.
- *Curtain rods* come in slender (one-inch) round or oval shape or extra wide (four-inch) sizes. They may be separated or hinged to swing in or out. Some curtain rods are made with spring tension so no brackets are necessary on an inside frame mount. Curtain rods also come in round brass and white finishes with attached finials and may have brass rings to hold drapery hooks or clips to clip onto pleats or panels.
- *Tieback holders* come in decorative rosette patterns and as concealed (clear plastic placed under the drapery) holders.
- *Decorator rods* have special carriers that look like rings but operate as traverse (cord-operated) rods. They come in wood colors, white, antique, brass, chrome, and black finishes.
- *Wood rods* come plain and fluted, natural, white, wood, and black and may be painted any color or covered with fabric or wallpaper. Curtains may be shirred onto wood rods, fabric draped over in loose swag fashion, or the wood ring carriers will hold drapery hooks, which must be hand operated.
- *Bay and bow rods* are available in nearly as many varieties as listed for conventional traverse rods.
- *Special rodding* is available to bend to any shape or angle.
- *Architectural rodding* comes in several varieties, and each company has patented names for their products. Nonresidential or architectural rods have sturdy ball-bearing carriers, and many of the styles are operated with a wand rather than a cord, which eliminates many problems of cord-operated rods in places such as hotels, offices, and institutions. Often nonresidential rods are for flat panels or for draperies with less fullness and simpler pleats. Components can be specified separately for any type of custom installation.
- *Motorized rods* are for hard-to-reach draperies or large installations or simply for the convenience of pushing a button rather than pulling on a cord or drawing a wand. Motorized systems are common in nonresidential settings. They are less common in residences, due to the extra cost and potential maintenance.

Hard Window Treatments

Today we are at an apex of selection in window treatments. We enjoy not only historical hard materials that have endured as classics but we also have new styles and hardware that are continually being improved through keen market competition. Hard materials are generally very durable and require little cleaning. They can be clean and contemporary or very traditional, crossing boundaries in many cases. They are versatile backgrounds and are often simple statements that will coordinate with many styles of furnishings. Some can be inexpensive and offer both privacy and light control. Types of hard window treatments are discussed and illustrated in chart 9.15.

Chart 9.15 Types of Hard Window Treatments

Art glass includes beveled, etched, leaded, and stained glass.

- *Beveled glass* is accomplished in two ways: (1) by authentic grinding and buffing glass held together with lead strips and (2) by molding or pressing. The prismlike effect is beautiful.
- *Etched glass* is done by hand or with an abrasive and is a surface design usually done on plain or frosted glass.
- *Leaded glass* is made of clear glass cut into shapes or designs and held together with lead strips called came or caming.
- *Stained glass* is likewise held together with lead or with copper foil or other materials. Stained glass comes in many colors, types, and thicknesses. The patterns range from very traditional to very contemporary.

Figure 9.51

The charm of stained glass as a hard window treatment lies in the many moods it produces according to the light at different times of day and night.

Blinds are slats of wood or metal.

- The oldest are *venetian blinds,* which are two inch wide metal or wooden horizontal slats, held together with braid. Metal venetian blinds used during the 1940s and the 1950s were synonymous with the clinical office look. They controlled light and glare.
- *Miniblinds* came onto the market during the 1960s and the 1970s and have been widely used since then. They are one inch wide and of thin concave baked-on enamel-coated aluminum. The band

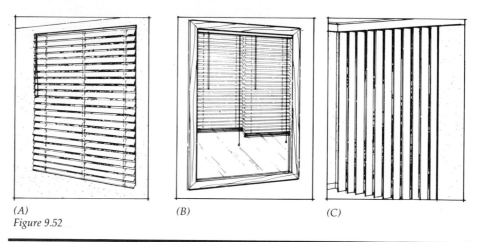

(A)
Figure 9.52   *(B)*   *(C)*

Continued on next page.

Figure 9.51 Stained glass in the Victorian/Art Nouveau style.
Figure 9.52 *(A)* One-inch miniblinds.
(B) One-half-inch micro-miniblinds.
(C) Vertical louvered blinds.

Chart 9.15 *Continued*

cording was replaced with tough nylon cord in matching colors. Colored slats can be arranged in custom sequences. Miniblinds control glare, give privacy, are clean and contemporary, and can be good undertreatments. They stack up to a very small area. Miniblinds are available as stock items in department stores and as custom-made items.

• *Micro-miniblinds* are one-half inch wide slats and provide an even sleeker look than miniblinds, but they are not as strong.

• *Wood blinds* are flat slats of stained or painted wood, one inch wide. They are handsome and can provide the classic look of shutters without the side vertical and horizontal rails and stiles. However, wood blinds are comparatively expensive and take a great deal of stacking room.

• *Vertical louvered blinds* are typically made of three inch wide slats of PVC (polyvinyl chloride), polyester fabric, wood, or various other materials. Vertical louvered blinds are very popular in both residential and nonresidential interiors. They control light and glare, have very low maintenance, can be energy efficient, and are available in a wide range of colors, patterns, and textures. Wallpaper or fabric may be inserted into the grooves.

Screens are sliding or folding panels placed or installed in front of windows.

• *Grid screens* are custom units that resemble vertical or diagonal garden trellises. They protect against glare but offer little privacy unless the slats are double and can slide to cover the open spaces.

• *Pierced screens* such as those from India are freestanding units that make interesting hard treatments.

• *Japanese shoji screens* and their Chinese fretwork counterparts are considered classics, befitting modern and updated traditional as well as oriental interiors. Shojis are symmetrical panes set into a wooden frame and glazed with mulberry or rice paper. They may have hip boards at the bottom (solid wood panels). Shoji screens are translucent and do not provide a

Figure 9.53

Figure 9.54

Figure 9.55

Figure 9.56

view nor do they give 100 percent privacy. They may be freestanding screens but are usually custom made to slide as panels in front of the window or as wall divider units.

Shades are woven or nonwoven materials that roll or fold up and down.

• *Pull shades* are mounted on spring rollers or are operated by a pulley chain. They are made of solid vinyl extruded into sheets from thin translucent to heavy opaque (which are energy conserving). Pull shades can also be made of tinted plastic or reflective mylar to cut down on solar gain. Among the least expensive of the hard window treatments, pull shades make good undertreatments as they roll out of the way and provide privacy when lowered. They may be custom ordered and installed to pull from the bottom up.

• *Bamboo or matchstick shades* are made of split bamboo woven

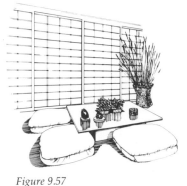

Figure 9.57

Figure 9.53 Sleek lines in the miniblinds provide not only light control and privacy but a clean architectural statement in this handsome eclectic interior. Photo courtesy of Hunter Douglas, Inc.
Figure 9.54 Miniblinds are fitted into windows beneath a large glass arch, giving light control and privacy to

this dining/study area while respecting the architecture above, leaving it untreated. Photo courtesy of Levolor Lorentzen.
Figure 9.55 Shiny aluminum miniblinds installed in an angled window are harmonious with the materials in this international modern setting: the glass coffee table and

mirror, and the classic chaise lounge in chrome and leather by Le Corbusier. Photo courtesy of Levolor Lorentzen.
Figure 9.56 Hard textures in this contemporary room are complemented with the fabric vertical louvered blinds in the window treatment. The architectural lines of

the window frame further add clarity to the interior design. Photo courtesy of the Dixie Verticals division of Hunter Douglas, Inc.
Figure 9.57 Japanese shoji screen.
Figure 9.58 Types of hard window treatment shades. (A) Vinyl pull shade. (B) Pull shade with scalloped hem and separate valance. (C)

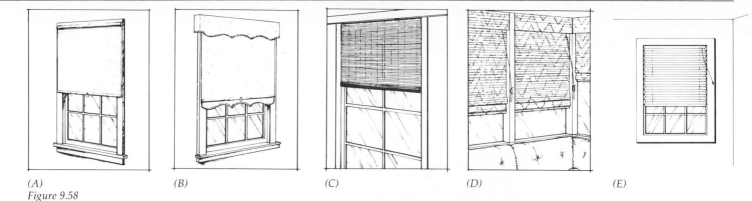

(A)　　　　(B)　　　　(C)　　　　(D)　　　　(E)

Figure 9.58

Figure 9.59

Figure 9.60

(A)　　　　(B)　　　　(C)　　　　(D)

Figure 9.61

together with cotton yarn. They are casual and used for interior as well as exterior shading devices.

• *Woven wood shades* are slats of stained or painted wood woven together with cotton or rayon yarn in stripes, textures, or Jacquard patterns. They are costly, are durable, and can provide privacy and insulative value. They can be ordered as spring-roller shades, as Roman shades, to drop from the top or to be raised from the bottom, and to be used as curtains and draperies (turned sideways).

• *Pleated shades* are made of sheer, transluscent, or opaque polyester fabric heat set into one-inch accordian folds. When metallized on the reverse, they reflect solar heat gain and help to keep winter heat in. They offer the sleek look of miniblinds with the softness of fabric and easy maintenance.

Wood shutters are perhaps the oldest and most classic of the hard window-covering materials. The basic types of shutters are raised panel, slat shutters, movable louvered, nonmovable louvered, and vertical louvered.

• *Raised-panel shutters* have solid panels that are raised in the center. These are formal and may be stained a wood color or painted. A variation of these are solid-panel shutters, both of

Continued on next page.

Bamboo or matchstick shades. (D) Woven wood shades, Roman-shade style. (E) Pleated fabric shade.
Figure 9.59 Interior designer Mikel Wenslow solved the problem of too much sunlight and too little nighttime privacy in this bath by selecting Duette pleated fabric shades with a top-down installation. The shade offers energy efficient qualities and translucence that allows light emission, creating a play of shape and form from the trees outside. Photo by Tom McCavera, courtesy of Hunter Douglas, Inc.
Figure 9.60 These woven wood shades are seen here in a country setting, and fold up from the bottom in Roman shade fashion. A continuous valance conceals the headrail. Woven wood shades are flexible; besides stripes, they come in many woven textures and abstract patterns such as Elizabethean flame-stitch and patterns taken from Southwest Native American motifs. Valances may be scalloped and trimmed, or can be deleted. Photo courtesy of Kirsch Company.
Figure 9.61 Types of window shutters. (A) Formal raised-panel shutters. (B) Raised-panel shutters. (C) One-inch movable louvered shutters. (D) Two- to four-inch plantation shutters.

Chart 9.15 *Continued*

which are used in residential and nonresidential interiors. They may be filled with insulation or solid wood, both of which provide good energy conservation.

• *Slat shutters* are vertical slats of wood nailed together with horizontal top pieces. These are rustic and charming. Usually stained a natural wood color.

• *Movable louvered shutters* are the most popular for interiors. These have a center guide bar that lowers or raises the louvers. Shutters may be stained or painted a color. Movable

louvered shutters are classics. They are available in varying louver widths. One inch is the traditional width, but louvers up to three inches are available. Wide louvers, called *plantation shutters*, were originally used to shade plantation houses during the hot, humid southern summers, permitting ventilation. The louvers may also be placed vertically.

• *Vertical louvered shutters* have blades that run vertically and provide an interesting alternative to the standard horizontal louvers.

Figure 9.62

Figure 9.63

Figure 9.62 Classic elegance of the grand piano is underscored with the bay window of rich brown stained shutters. Shutters control light and view, allowing daylight to enter while protecting the occupants with the degree of desired privacy. Photo courtesy of Pinecrest, Inc.

Figure 9.63 Wide louvered blades classify these as plantation shutters. Seen here in natural light wood color, these shutters have rolling coaster feet attached to the bottom so they can smoothly glide to stack off the sliding glass door. Photo courtesy of Pinecrest, Incorporated.

Nonresidential Considerations

Materials for nonresidential wall, window, and ceiling materials often differ from those used in the home. These differences are threefold. Nonresidential materials generally must be

1. more durable—able to withstand harder abuse from greater traffic in less-controlled situations;
2. less patterned and more textured in appearance— nonresidential materials are comparatively plain compared to the variety of decorative materials used in homes; and
3. flame-retardant, fire resistant, or fireproof and static- and microorganism-resistant in order to meet state and local building codes for public safety.

Durability

Because of the durability requirement, permanent hard materials are often used in nonresidential settings. It is not uncommon to see stone, such as travertine, or tile or brick used not only on the exterior but on the interior of a nonresidential installation. This allows people to touch, bump, soil, or abrade the surface without worry that the surface will be damaged. Wall covering materials are specially made to be durable for nonresidential applications. For example, vinyl and fabric wall coverings can withstand a great deal of physical abuse, and many *nonresidential wall coverings* have been tested and rated so the architect or designer can match up the durability rating to the traffic classification required by code or building specification.

• Class I are wall coverings that are decorative.
• Class II are decorative and serviceable wall coverings. Serviceability includes colorfastness (low) and washability.
• Class III are decorative wall coverings that have good serviceability. Serviceability includes colorfastness (low to moderate), washability, scrubbability, and resistance to abrasion, breaking, crocking, and stains.
• Class IV are wall coverings that are decorative with full serviceability including colorfastness (low to moderate), washability, scrubbability, and resistance to abrasion, breaking, crocking, stains, and tears.
• Class V are medium commercial serviceability wall coverings that include colorfastness (very good), washability, scrubbability, and resistance to abrasion, breaking, crocking, stains, tears, heat aging, cracking, and shrinkage.
• Class VI are full commercial serviceability wall coverings the same as Class V but with greater resistance to tearing.[5]

Nonresidential wall coverings are also typed either

Figure 9.64

Figure 9.64 Textured wall coverings and a baffled grid ceiling create a cozy ambiance and muffle sound in this Holiday Inn at Fort Lee, New Jersey, lounge area. Nonresidential walls and ceilings must meet more stringent needs of durability and noise control than those in the home because of the greater numbers of people in close proximity who are carrying on different tasks or conversations. Here the window treatment limits the amount of light, whereas a well-planned lighting system is encased in the suspended ceiling. Interior design by Christine Battersby. Photo by Norman McGrath © 1986.

Figure 9.65

non-mildew resistant or mildew resistant. They may also need to meet fire code restrictions, which makes the product selection somewhat different than residential wall coverings. The range of selection tends to be more textured and subtle, without the many changing designer patterns found in residential wall coverings.

Nonresidential wall coverings are often fifty-two to fifty-four inches wide and contain thirty square yards, which is more convenient and economical for large installations. However, this much weight is unwieldy and requires expert installation.[6]

Nonresidential Ceiling Treatments

There are many materials and types of treatments used in nonresidential interiors that are worth mentioning. These include acoustical ceilings in tile or larger panel sections, mounted on dropped grid systems. Ceilings are often dropped to accommodate HVAC (heating, ventilation and air-conditioning) systems, lighting systems, communication systems, and fire-extinguishing systems. The ceiling must be selected to allow access to these systems in case of

breakdown of the system or a component. Ceilings may consist largely of indirect lighting; they may contain soffits for lighting or accommodating the previously mentioned systems. The ceiling may be of glass, such as a solarium ceiling, in which case it must be safety glass (see chart 9.2).

Nonresidential Window Treatments

Window treatments for nonresidential interiors must be able to withstand operation from many different people who might not know how to smoothly or carefully operate them. Therefore, mechanisms are usually engineered to be trouble free insofar as possible. Drapery rods without pull cords are often specified. Draperies are often slid open and closed one panel at a time with a wand attached to the leading carrier. This not only prevents breakdowns that would otherwise occur in a cord-and-pulley system but discourages the handling of the fabric to find the cords, which can so easily soil and damage it.

Window treatment materials must be able to cut down glare for office use, a particularly important facet for those working on computer terminals (glare on the screen must be minimized or eliminated). Daytime privacy in

Figure 9.65 Small wooden strips are a good choice to follow the vaulted line of this bank's ceiling. The effect is somewhat like a tambour door, similar to a roll-top desk lid. Sunlight streams through the wall opposite the curved ceiling. Photo by John Wang and Doug McIntosh.

working/nonresidential situations is also of prime importance. Hard window treatments are used frequently for these purposes in nonresidential settings. Of these, the most popular are miniblinds, vertical louvers, roller shades (opaque and film), and pleated shades with metallized backings. Casement draperies—generally an open-constructed cloth—are a standard item in offices and situations where glare control and softness are required.

Window treatments may also be required to provide any or all of the following six energy conservation functions:

1. allow winter solar heat gain
2. allow daylighting all year
3. reflect summer solar heat gain
4. "seal" the window from the room air when mechanical heating and air-conditioning are operating
5. insulate against heat and cold extremes
6. allow for natural ventilation during temperate weather[7]

Nighttime privacy is a need in some installations, and this means a hard treatment that can close fully or a fabric that is lined or opaque or a combination of hard and soft materials, such as a casement fabric over a blind or shade. Printed fabrics are sometimes used in hospitality and medical facilities. Hotels, for example, will often have coordinated or matching draperies and bedspreads; hospitals and clinics may have patterned draperies in patient rooms and sometimes as cubicle curtains. These are finished with soil- and stain-resistant treatments. Patterns are good choices where the fabric will be handled. Patterns will not readily show soil and will hide wear better than plain fabrics, unless, of course, the patterns fade from sunlight, which makes them look worn-out prematurely.

Less Pattern

Most of the materials used in nonresidential installations, however, do not include much pattern. Rather, texture is seen for nearly every surface installation. Hard materials (stone, brick, tile, concrete) often have natural patterns that read as texture and cannot be removed. Where plaster is used, it is often textured, as well. Flexible wall coverings are frequently given textures that imitate natural materials such as grass cloth, leather suede, or stones, such as marble. Fabric wall coverings can be amazingly durable as well as handsome. Natural linen and wool coverings are fine quality examples of beauty combined with durability. Man-made fibers can also make tough, good-looking wall covering fabrics and are often used in wall partitions or dividers in open office planning where they serve to absorb sound. Acoustical ceiling tiles, likewise, have texture and very subtle pattern, as do other ceiling panel materials—metal or fabric, for example. Textures show less soil and wear and will last longer under use and abuse than will plain fabrics.

Whereas patterned fabrics and wall coverings soon become dated and the color schemes last only a few years, textured fabrics do not go out of style as quickly as do patterns. This is important in nonresidential settings where the design scheme may not be changed for many years.

Safety Codes

Safety codes are laws that ensure the safety of the occupants in public spaces. Codes routinely govern fire safety, static resistance, and protection against microorganism and bacteria growth. Of these, fire safety is the most important concern for wall, ceiling, and window materials. The architect or designer must find materials that meet either building codes or written building specifications that require materials to meet minimum public safety standards established by law. These are materials that have been tested and rated for their resistance to fire, static, and microorganisms. Most materials will have been tested in most of these areas, and the information will be written on the samples (part of product specifications) or available from the manufacturer in written form. The documentation of these ratings is of prime importance in designer liability. Fire safety is obviously the most crucial of these standards. The material should also have been tested for smoke density and for the emission of toxic or poisonous gases while burning or smoldering. Flammability terms are presented under Nonresidential Considerations in chapter 11, Fabric.

Notes

1. Riggs, J. Rosemary. *Materials and Components of Interior Design,* 2d ed. (Englewood Cliffs, N.J.: Prentice-Hall, 1989), pp. 5–64, 73–115.
2. Hemming, Charles. *Paint Finishes* (Secaucus, N.J.: Chartwell Books, Inc., 1985), p. 7.
3. Ibid.
4. Ibid., pp. 12, 53–131.
5. Reznikoff, S.C. *Specifications for Commercial Interiors: Professional Liabilities, Regulations, and Performance Criteria* (New York: Whitney Library of Design, 1979).
6. Riggs, J. Rosemary. *Materials and Components of Interior Design,* 2d ed. (Englewood Cliffs, N.J.: Prentice-Hall, 1989), pp. 85–86.
7. Reznikoff, S.C. *Specifications for Commercial Interiors: Professional Liabilities, Regulations, and Performance Criteria* (New York: Whitney Library of Design, 1979), p. 131.

Bibliography

Blandy, Thomas, and Denis Leamoreau. *All Through the House: A Guide to Home Weatherization.* New York: McGraw-Hill, 1980.

Brady, Darlene A., and William Serban. *Stained Glass: A Guide to Information Sources.* Detroit: Gale Research Co., 1980.

Burch, Monte. *Tile, Indoors and Out.* Passaic (NJ): Creative Homeowners Press, a division of Federal Marketing Corporation, 1981.

Conran, Sir Terence. *New House Book: The Complete Guide to Home Design.* New York: Villard Books, 1985.

Fishburn, Angela. *Curtains and Window Treatments.* New York: Van Nostrand Reinhold Co., Inc., 1982.

Hand, Jackson. *Walls, Floors and Ceilings.* New York: Book Division, Times Mirror Magazines, Inc., 1976.

Helsel, Marjorie B. ed. *The Interior Designer's Drapery Sketchfile.* New York: Whitney Library of Design, 1969.

Hemming, Charles. *Paint Finishes*. Secaucus, NJ: Chartwell Books.

Innes, Jocasta. *Paint Magic*. New York: Van Nostrand Reinhold Co., Inc., 1981.

Jackman, Dianne R., and Mary K. Dixon. *The Guide to Textiles for Interior Designers*. Winnipeg: Peguis Publishers, Ltd., 1983.

Judson, Walter W. *Introduction to Stained Glass*. Los Angeles: Nash Publishing, 1972.

Kent, Kathryn. *The Good Housekeeping Complete Guide to Traditional American Decorating*. New York: Heart Books, 1982.

Kicklighter, Clois E. *Modern Masonry*. South Highland (IL): Goodheart-Willow Co., 1977.

Landsmann, Leanne. *Painting and Wallpapering*. New York: Grosset and Dunlap, 1975.

Langdon, William K. *Movable Insulation*. Emmaus, PA: Rodale Press, 1980.

Neal, Mary. *Custom Draperies in Interior Design*. New York: Elsevier Science Publishing Co., 1982.

Nielson, Karla J. *Window Treatments*. New York: Van Nostrand Reinhold Co., Inc., 1990.

Percival, Bob. *The How-to-Do-It Encyclopedia of Painting and Wallcovering*. Blue Ridge Summit (PA): TAB Books, Inc., 1982.

Professional Drapery Institute. *How the Professional Installs Custom Draperies and Window Coverings*. Pittsburgh: Professional Drapery Institute, 1985.

Reznikoff, S.C. *Specifications for Commercial Interiors*. New York: Whitney Library of Design, 1979.

Riggs, J. Rosemary. *Materials and Components of Interior Design*, 2d ed. Englewood Cliffs, N.J.: Prentice-Hall, 1989.

Schuler, Stanley. *The Floor and Ceiling Book*. New York: M. Evans and Co., 1976.

Shurcliff, William A. *Thermal Shutters and Shades*. Andover, MA: Brick House Publishing Co., 1980.

Sowers, Robert. *Stained Glass: An Architectural Art*. New York: Universe Books, 1965.

Time Life Books. *Paint and Wallpaper*. New York: Time Life Books, 1976.

Time Life Books. *Walls and Ceilings*. New York: Time Life Books, 1980.

FLOOR MATERIALS AND COVERINGS

Beautiful flooring and floor coverings appeal to everyone. Fine rugs are prized both within the cultures where they are handmade and in western societies where they are sought for well-designed rooms. Here a little girl is intrigued with an enchanting Portuguese Kilim garden rug in wool from Stark Carpets. The gamut of oriental, folk, European handmade as well as machine-made rugs is vast; there are rugs for every taste, for every style of interior. Photo by Ted Spiegel.

Page 254, top right: Hard surface materials also come to us through much hand-labor, such as marble chiseled from the great quarries of Carrara in Italy. Marble has been esteemed as the most elegant and formal of the nonresilient flooring materials; its natural graining and gentle streaks of color evoke mystique and respect for the thousands of years required to create this and other stone materials. *Page 254, bottom left:* Oriental rugs woven by hand on an upright loom are produced in a vast array of colors and patterns, each one a treasure. Generations of skilled and patient artisans working in both cottage industry and in large manufacturing centers have given us a legacy of fine, intricate design. The pattern of the Russian Azerbijan (north of Iran) rug being woven in the background is taken from the two-dimensional "cartoon" design. Photo by Ted Spiegel. *Page 254, bottom right:* When Mario Buatta, ASID, designed this room, he used Stark Carpet's Trellis Fleur Design from their Boucle Collec-

tion. This carpet is woven on a twelve-foot Wilton loom and comes in a variety of colorways. The lavish use of fabric in this English design-inspired interior is fitting for the broadloom carpet that originated in Wilton, England. Woven patterned wool broadloom carpeting, so often used in the Victorian Era, has once again achieved status in both residential as well as nonresidential interiors. Photo courtesy of Stark Carpet. *Page 255:* This single-needle, hand-tufted rug was custom designed to compliment the oriental flavor of this interior. A rich finishing effect (copied from authentic Chinese rugs) is achieved by "sculpturing"—hand-carving at a beveled angle around the motifs. Designer rugs as well as many oriental rugs today are woven to meet color, design, and size specifications of western designers and suppliers. When the interior designer works with custom carpet companies, virtually any design is possible today, an important tool in bringing together fine interior design. Photo courtesy of Stark Carpet.

Page 256, top: *The most popular hard floors are of wood or tile. Bruce Hardwood Floors offers a broad range of tones and textures in their parquet line. Wood offers warmth and visual comfort, retaining its life-telling grain, a natural pattern that never loses its design appeal or flexibility. Wood floors make ideal backgrounds for any of the types of rugs examined in this chapter, and by itself wood is an ultimate statement of fine design. Photo courtesy of Bruce Hardwood Floors.* Page 256, bottom: *Tile floors are renowned for their easy upkeep and handsome appearance. Tile's ability to withstand heat and water make it ideal for kitchen and bath use. This small sample of Elon, Inc.'s tile is an indication of the broad range of tiling available from a wide spectrum of domestic and overseas suppliers. The kitchen was designed by Gloria Kaplan-Sandercock Associates. Photo courtesy of Elon Tiles.* Page 257, top: *When Spiros Zakas designed this Chicago restaurant, he utilized three types of flooring: vinyl tile, industrial rubber matting, and spattered paint on concrete. These combine to create a lively field for his nostalgic design. Photo courtesy of Zakas-pace.* Page 257, bottom: *In this tie store, Spiros Zakas counterpointed the vividly colorful tie display with a classic black and white marble flooring, thus illustrating that a dramatic flooring is as elegant to an interior as a man's tie can be to his wardrobe. Photo courtesy of Zakaspace.*

"Before the world sees your home, your automobile or your wife's jewelry, it sees your necktie." Montague

Page 258: In Stark Carpet's generously sized warehouse, woven rugs are laid out for inspection and finishing/stabilizing. Rugs come in sizes and varieties that can boggle the mind; here is just a sampling. In the foreground a French Savonnerie design full of majestic Empire swirls and medallions that not just Napoleon but any aristocratic taste might enjoy. Lengthwise next to it is a machine-woven rug imitating a primitive "Ikat" design where warp threads were originally printed or tie-dyed, then slipped into a water-mark design. Other rugs come from collections offered by Stark in broadloom designs. Sizes, border selections, and even colors are custom specified through interior designers. Photo by Ted Spiegel.

Page 259, top left: Texture is often the key element in carpeting and is accomplished with various thicknesses of yarn, height contrast, and finishing techniques such as sculpturing, which is carving the outline to make the design stand out in relief. Whereas most uncomplicated carpets are tufted, patterned carpets are either broadloomed for large quantities (Axminster or Wilton are most common), or tufted by hand for one-of-a-kind designer rugs. This sampling represents the spectrum offered by Stark Carpet. Photo by Ted Spiegel. *Page 259, top right:* In Stark Carpet's showroom, needlepoint rugs display the western European taste that continually enjoys popularity in America. A fine rug will often form the basis for the entire design, where carefully selected furnishing elements compliment and enhance the inherent beauty and quality of these floral carpet works of art. Photo by Ted Spiegel. *Page 259, bottom left:* Flat folk rugs, seen here from the Stark Carpet collection, include Romanian kilims and Indian dhurries. These economical rugs have been prolifically used in contemporary and rustic interior settings because of their refreshing, simple designs often based on stylized floral or abstract folk art patterns. Flat folk rugs are reversible, and since there is no pile, they can safely be folded as well as rolled. Photo by Ted Spiegel. *Page 259, bottom right:* Oriental rugs from Stark Carpet's selection of imported carpets from Iran, Iraq, India, Turkey, China, and other oriental countries. Even a modest-sized rug such as this classic open-field medallion pattern will take months of pain-staking labor to accomplish. Oriental rugs have been treasured possessions in western civilizations since the Middle Ages. Today oriental rugs are a symbol of prestige and discriminating taste and are appropriate selections for traditional, eclectic, or contemporary interiors in both residential and nonresidential design. Photo by Ted Spiegel.

Flooring Requirements and Specifications

When a home or new building is designed, the finish materials specified for floors are often permanent selections. The criteria that determine the choice include:

1. the durability needed and/or maintenance necessary,
2. cost of materials, of installation, and of maintenance in terms of time, effort, and expenses,
3. aesthetic considerations, such as establishing a particular or authentic architectural style,
4. the necessity of acoustic control of noise,
5. applicable insulative and solar absorption or reflection needs, and
6. the fire or building codes that must be met to make the interior safe.

Floor materials are calculated and priced per square foot or per square yard. Hard materials such as stone, wood or wood combined with another material, and some tiles are calculated per square foot and are costly, although they are very durable. Sheet vinyl and carpeting are calculated per square yard and cost less than most hard materials, though they are less durable. To find the square footage, multiply the width (in feet) times the length (in feet) of the room. Divide this figure by nine to find the square yardage (nine square feet in one square yard). Calculating yardage is a bit more complex, however, because roll goods (vinyl and carpet) must be installed all the same way with no quarter turns. Designers and specifiers will plot roll goods to determine exact widths and cuts (vinyl is usually six feet wide; carpet twelve feet wide). Each cut (width) is multiplied by its length, then divided to determine the yardage to be ordered.

Installation costs for stone and tile are high and figured per square foot according to the charges of the installer ($2.00 or more per square foot—pr/sq/ft). Wood installation is also costly and may further need professional finishing (acrylic or polyurethane), also charged by the square foot ($1.00 or more pr/sq/ft), and brick may need a sealant. Carpet costs are figured per square yard and generally include pad or underlay and installation in a tackless strip method or the glue and installation in the direct glue-down method—usually $3.00 and up (carpet underlay and installation are discussed later in this chapter).

Flooring materials are divided into three categories—hard, resilient, and soft. *Nonresilient flooring materials* include brick, concrete, stone, tile, and wood. *Resilient* flooring materials are asphalt tile, cork, fabric, leather, linoleum, rubber, and vinyl. Soft floor coverings include wall-to-wall carpeting and a wide selection of area rugs.

Guidelines for Selecting Hard and Resilient Floor Materials

Hard and resilient floor materials form a substantial basis for the character of an interior. The integrity of flooring is so important that it is impossible to create successful interiors if the flooring is cheap looking, a poor imitation of a natural material, or shoddy design or quality. Whether the flooring is to be any of the hard or resilient materials listed in charts 10.1 and 10.2 or whether it is a rug or carpet (discussed later in this chapter), it will be a wise choice if it is, in itself, beautiful. We should not look at a floor covering only as a background but as a material that will provide years of satisfaction, both in terms of beauty and durability and upkeep or maintenance.

- The first consideration, then, is to determine whether the flooring material is inherently beautiful and has good design merit and integrity. It should be appealing even if there are no furnishings whatsoever in the interior.
- The material should provide a graceful and harmonious background for a variety of furnishing styles over a period of years. This means that neutralized colors, subtle textures, and a lack of definite pattern are usually desirable. The exception here is where the flooring provides drama or focus as a planned part of the interior design.
- Look at the way the material will age and consider how long the flooring will be in place. Hard and resilient flooring is often in place for ten to twenty years, and quality hard materials (stone, brick, tile, and wood) can last for hundreds of years, as seen in many important historic interiors.
- Consider subfloor preparation. If stone or heavy tile or brick is to be used, then the floor must be structurally strong enough to hold it. Thick floor materials will raise the floor level, as well. For thin resilient floors such as vinyl, the subfloors must be smooth and free of irregularities since these flaws will show through the finish flooring.[1]
- Look at the cost of the material in comparison to the number of years the flooring will last. For example, stone, brick, tile, or wood can last indefinitely, whereas vinyl, cork, and leather may have limited life spans. The total cost of the installation divided by the number of years of expected use will yield the predicted cost per year. This may, surprisingly, reveal that the more costly product is actually cheaper in the long run because it will never need replacing.
- Consider using materials that possess real longevity, since these not only look good for many years but they also gleam with patina, a mellowing of the finish as it ages and a quality often present in great interiors that have endured the test of time.

- Consider upkeep. Hard flooring materials generally require little maintenance, whereas some resilient materials may need special upkeep. A wisely selected flooring will be appropriate for the amount of soiling it will receive. Natural materials are particularly good at camouflaging tracked-in soil. Upkeep also entails the relative ease of cleaning. For example, grooves or indentations can trap dirt, which can be quite difficult to remove, requiring more labor and time in maintenance.
- Take into account the ability of the material to withstand traffic. Will the material resist wearing down, and will any finish wear off in areas of heavy traffic?
- A functional consideration is that smooth hard and resilient flooring tends to be slippery when wet unless texture is used to prevent slippage.
- Flooring for the aged and handicapped require special considerations, such as no glare and avoiding three-dimensional patterns or abrupt pattern changes. Flooring for the wheelchair-bound must not impair the chair's smooth operation by being too rugged or by carpeting *pile* being too deep.
- Stone will withstand heavy traffic but may become scuffed or scratched. As it is very hard, it should not be used in areas where long periods of standing will take place or where fragile items may drop and break.

Hard Floor Materials

Hard flooring materials have a common set of advantages.

- Nonresilient materials are noted for their strength and durability.
- They are nonabsorbent and relatively impervious to soiling.
- They are easy to maintain and clean.
- They tend to be "classics," with aesthetic appeal to last indefinitely. This is particularly true of brick, stone, tile, and wood, which may be used as suitable backgrounds for many styles of interior design furnishings.
- Several varieties of these materials are available, giving the designer the flexibility to create interiors that are formal or informal, structural or decorative, textured or patterned.
- In addition, the heavy and substantial nonresilient materials such as brick, tile, stone, or concrete can serve as the structure as well as the finish materials for some floors and walls.

Disadvantages of hard flooring materials include the following:

- Hard materials have a high initial cost. For example, wood is considerably more costly to purchase and install than resilient sheet vinyl. In the long run, however, wood may actually cost less than a type of vinyl that must be replaced every five or ten years. This is referred to as life-cycle costing.
- Special preparation is required to support floors of heavy finish materials, such as brick, tile, stone, and concrete.
- It is possible for nonresilient materials to be damaged or broken by dropping a heavy object on a tile floor or throwing a hard ball through a glass wall, for instance.
- Hard materials tend to be cold to the touch unless heated artificially or by sunshine.
- Since they are nonporous, they reflect sound and even seem to amplify noise. Because of this, hard materials are often used as backgrounds for soft materials such as area rugs.

Following is a chart of the hard flooring materials. Each type includes a description, applications (where used), maintenance guidelines, special considerations when selecting each material, and the cost structure of the flooring material.

Chart 10.1 Hard Floor Materials

Brick

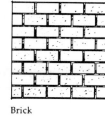

Brick

Concrete

Description: Clay, shale, water mixed and shaped into solid or hollow rectangular blocks, then baked or fired to harden. Brick is colored according to the clay used (red is most typical) or the dyes added before firing. Solid brick used for paving is three-fourths to two inches thick and is referred to as "pavers."

Applications: Interior and exterior floors, patio paving, residential and nonresidential.

Maintenance: Low upkeep: sweep, dust, vacuum, damp mop, or buff.

Special Considerations: Should be treated with a sealant such as polyurethane to prevent the brick from absorbing oil-based spills.

Cost Structure: Moderate to high.

Concrete

Description: Portland cement, sand, gravel, or rock aggregate and water mixed and poured into forms or slabs and possibly texturized. Hardens as it sets. Naturally gray but may be colored.

Applications: Subfloors, floors may be cast or formed into shapes. Nonresidential floors in high-rise office buildings, apartment houses, dormitories, hospitals, and retail buildings.

Concrete may be both the structural element and finish material.

Maintenance: Concrete maintenance depends on how it is finished. Raw concrete will absorb stains and generate dust; painted or sealed concrete will be impervious to stains as long as the paint or finish remains intact. Sweep, damp mop, or hose off where possible.

Continued on next page.

Chart 10.1 *Continued*

Special Considerations:
Concrete is rarely used unfinished as an interior flooring, except in high-tech designs and warehouse situations. It is, however, a low-cost flooring and is frequently used as a subfloor, especially in basements where it is easily covered with another flooring material. It is cold to the touch yet is excellent as a thermal mass and is often used alone or as a subfloor under tile, brick, or stone in solariums. It will crack with temperature and humidity fluctuations, and if joints are scored into the paving (giving the appearance of tile, for example), then cracking will be minimized. Slippery when wet unless surface is given rough finish.
Cost Structure: Low to moderate.

Exposed Aggregate

Description: Also called pebble tile or pebble concrete. Aggregate (smooth rocks or small pebbles) set or rolled into wet concrete. Part of the concrete is hosed off before it dries in order to expose the aggregate. Appearance will depend on the size, shape, and color of the aggregate used.
Applications: Interior and exterior paving or flooring where heavy traffic requires exceptional durability and where the textured look is desired. Residential and nonresidential applications.
Maintenance: When sealed with a polyurethane or other finish, exposed aggregate has very low upkeep. A brush vacuum is the easiest method of sweeping, and damp mopping may be unnecessary as it is impervious to dirt penetration.
Special Considerations: Very hard surface and hard on the body and legs when standing for prolonged periods.
Cost Structure: Moderate to high.

Flagstone

Description: Flagging is a term that describes exterior or interior paving. Types of flagstone include bluestone, quartzite, sandstone, and slate. It is cut rough and left uneven in thickness. Sizes vary from one to four feet square.

Applications: Used for flooring in residential and nonresidential settings. Shape can be regular or irregular and surface will be fairly uniform.
Maintenance: Little upkeep: sweep, vacuum, damp mop if necessary.
Special Considerations: Heavy stone that requires strengthened floor preparation and a deeper area for setting and grout due to variations in the thickness of the stone. Rough texture is safe when wet.
Cost Structure: High.

Stone

Granite

Description: A very hard crystalline rock with small amounts of feldspar, quartz, and other minerals in crystal or grain form. The size of the crystals varies from very fine to fairly coarse. The colors vary from light to dark values and variations of gray, pink, green, brown, and black and may be combinations such as greenish or pinkish gray. May be dull or highly polished.
Applications: Floors; used in high-end residential and nonresidential settings.
Maintenance: Low upkeep: sweep or vacuum, damp mop if necessary.
Special Considerations: Polished surface slippery when wet.
Cost Structure: High.

Marble

Description: A metamorphic limestone, granular or crystalline, white or colored, often with streaks. The hardest and typically the most expensive of the stones. May be cut into thin sheets or slabs. Can be polished to a high sheen. Cold to the touch. *Terrazzo* is a composite flooring of broken chips of marble set into cement and polished to a sheen. May be tiles or poured as a solid floor. This is a practical use of marble, as up to 50 percent waste occurs from breakage at the quarry.
Applications: Floors, fireplace hearths. Exclusive material for high-end residential and nonresidential installations.
Maintenance: Clean with warm water and infrequently with

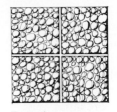

Exposed aggregate

Ashlar

Cobblestone

Sandstone or rubble

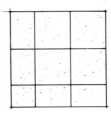

Flagstone

Granite

Figure 10.1

Figure 10.2

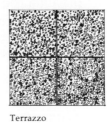

Marble parquet   Terrazzo

Figure 10.1 Nonresilient marble flooring offers reverberating acoustics to this music alcove. Marble requires little or no upkeep and looks classic indefinitely. Vertical louvers by and photo courtesy of DelMar Window Coverings.

Figure 10.2 Travertine is used extensively in this luxury bath, on floors, walls, and tub and vanity areas. This material would be especially desirable where the climate is warm. Note also the oriental rug, a traditional Persian design. Photo courtesy of Kohler Co.

soap and water, taking care to rinse well, as soap residue will render the floor slippery.
Special Considerations: The most formal of the stones, possibly the coldest and the slickest. Rugs set on top of marble floors will need nonskid pads. Rich-looking finish material. The most slippery of the hard flooring materials, particularly when wet.
Cost Structure: Very high.

Figure 10.3

Slate

Description: A metamorphic, finely grained, hard rock that cleaves or splits naturally into layers, making it possible to cut slabs from one-half to one inch thick. The surface may be treated in three ways: fairly rough if a natural cleft or split; be rubbed with sand to achieve an even plane; or honed, which produces a smooth finish and has a patina or mellow glow. Colors vary from grays to greenish or reddish grays to blacks and browns.
Applications: Slate is used as a paving or flooring in both residential and nonresidential settings.
Maintenance: Low upkeep: sweep, vacuum, mild soap and water. Do not wax.
Special Considerations: Slate has been used historically as early as the 1500s in England and France. It is an authentic floor material for rustic settings as well as very contemporary ones.
Cost Structure: Moderate to high.

Travertine

Description: A light-colored limestone rock formed near mineral springs. Trapped gas in the stone causes holes and interesting textures. When used as flooring, the holes are filled with cement or epoxy.
Applications: Floors, stair treads, fireplace hearths. Used frequently in nonresidential settings and as accents and for custom installations in residential interiors.
Maintenance: Vacuum, wash when necessary with clear lukewarm water. Wash no more often than every six months with

soap and water and rinse thoroughly to prevent a slippery surface.
Special Considerations: Travertine used as flooring should have the holes filled in with an epoxy resin filler. This may be opaque, which does not reflect light, or transparent, which takes on the sheen of the polished stone. Travertine is slightly less formal than marble and widely used. As slippery as marble when wet.
Cost Structure: High.

Tile

Ceramic Tile

Description: Fine, white clays formed into tile shape (bisque) and fired at very high temperatures. Ceramic tiles are glazed before the first firing or before a second firing. Glazed finishes vary from shiny and smooth to patterned to rough and matte (dull). *Mosaic tiles* are very small tiles that were historically used to create permanent murals on walls and floors. Today mosaic tile comes in preset sheets, a face mount or back mount, ready to be set with grout.
Applications: Floors; used extensively in nonresidential settings because of its durability. In high-end residences, ceramic tile flooring is often used in bathrooms, in kitchens, as flooring and walls in solariums, or in any room in warm climates.
Maintenance: Low upkeep: sweep, vacuum, damp mop, or soap and water for heavy dirt. Grout may soil and discolor. Silicone treatments will make grout less susceptible to soil.
Special Considerations: Holds up well to heavy traffic, and baked-on (kiln-fired) shiny glazes are permanent. Slippery when wet, particularly in smoothly finished tiles. Textured tile is safer against slippage.
Cost Structure: Low to high—costs vary considerably in ceramic tiles. Imported tiles from France and Italy can be expensive. Labor to install is also high. However, because it is permanent, the life-cycle cost is low.

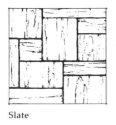

Slate

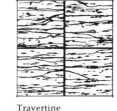

Travertine

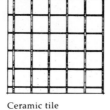

Ceramic tile

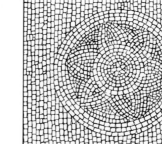

Mosaic tile

Continued on next page.

Figure 10.3 A crisp chrome and black and white kitchen and breakfast nook takes on a bold effect with recessed lighting and Italian ceramic tiles on the floor. The natural glaze of the tiles reflects both natural and artificial light and resists abrasion and greasy food spills. Photo courtesy of the Italian Tile Center, New York.

Chart 10.1 *Continued*

Quarry

Description: Quarry tile is made of fine clay and graded shale, with color distributed through the body of the tile. Most is a terra-cotta rust/red, the color of the natural clay. It may be glazed but usually is left natural. Typical square or hexagonal shapes are most popular.

Applications: Flooring where a less formal, durable flooring is desirable.

Maintenance: Same as for ceramic tile.

Special Considerations: Natural terra-cotta color gives quarry tile a timeless appeal. Smooth surface is slippery when wet.

Cost Structure: Low to moderate (installation is costly).

Mexican Tile

Description: Hand-shaped clay taken from the ground and left to set before firing. These tiles are a cottage industry (families working together) product, which reflects imperfections of hand labor and adds to the charm of these tiles. They are thick and fragile, rustic and handsome. Smaller tiles may be hand painted and glazed.

Applications: Large squares are useful for flooring in both residential and nonresidential settings. Infrequently used on walls. Smaller, glazed tiles are used for decorative effects on walls, countertops, backsplashes, stair risers, and doorway surround trim.

Maintenance: A porous surface that should be treated with linseed oil or paste wax. Sweep, dust mop, wax, and buff. Rewax or reoil when it shows signs of wear.

Special Considerations: Mexican tile is durable, but if unbaked it is susceptible to oily stains. The softest of all the tiles, it can be chipped or broken more easily than quarry or ceramic tile.

Cost Structure: Low to moderate (installation is costly).

Vinyl

Poured Seamless Vinyl

Description: A nonresilient vinyl that comes as a liquid, formed, or poured onto a clean, level surface. The base coat may be vinyl, epoxy, polyester, or urethane, over which vinyl chips are sprinkled or sprayed. The top coat or wear layer is the same material as the base.

Applications: May be used in residential settings but more often used in nonresidential settings such as veterinary offices, where no seams and a surface that can be kept very clean are paramount.

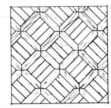

Quarry tile

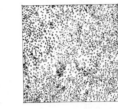

Mexican tile

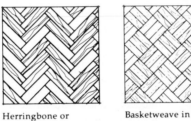

Seamless vinyl floor

Random plank

Herringbone or chevron parquet

Basketweave in diagonal

Basketweave and octagonal parquet

Figure 10.4

Maintenance: Damp mop, may be waxed.

Special Considerations: Surface is nonskid or not slippery. May be coved to form continuous flooring up to baseboard, which eliminates areas where dirt and bacteria can accumulate. Slippery when wet.

Cost Structure: Low to moderate.

Wood

Solid Wood Planks and Parquet

Description: Oak, maple, or teak hardwood strips range from one and one-half to two and one-fourth inches wide and two to seven feet in length. Random plank widths range from three to eight inches, typically installed in three varying sizes. Strips and random plank are tongue and groove to fit snugly together. *Parquet* is the arrangement of strips or squares of wood preset into squares or into shapes such as herringbone (chevron or zigzag) or various geometric patterns. Parquet may also be installed in custom designs at the site.

Applications: Flooring; residential and nonresidential. Solid wood may come prefinished, and some products are available impregnated with stain (color) and acrylic, making an extremely durable surface for nonresidential settings.

Maintenance: Depends on the finish it is given. Oiled or waxed wood will need protection against moisture, require dust mopping frequently, and rewaxing. Soft wax such as paste wax is rarely used; hard (liquid) wax has taken its place. Two finishes used frequently today are polyurethane and acrylic, which are applied after the floor is in place. These require only sweeping, dust mopping, or vacuuming, and damp mopping with a water-vinegar solution. Acrylic-impregnated floors have similar upkeep.

Special Considerations: Wood can be dented and scratched. It is easier on the body for long periods of standing than hard materials; consequently, fragile items dropped on wood are less likely to break. Wood is the warmest of the nonresilient materials, and it is the most versatile in terms of design flexibility. Installation is easy, and the look of wood is classic in both formal and informal settings. Waxed and polished wood is slippery, particularly when wet.

Cost Structure: Moderate to high.

Figure 10.4 In this dramatically designed office/master bedroom suite, Herringbone parquet in Gunstock stain is the flooring selection. The rich effect is further enhanced with the use of the same parquet on the wall by the travertine desk. Wood is a warm and comforting, long lived floor material that has endured and will continue to withstand the test of time, both in terms of wear and fine aesthetics. Photo courtesy of Bruce Hardwood Floors.

Figure 10.5

Resilient Floor Materials

Resilient materials are those with some flexibility or give. These include *asphalt tiles, cork, fabric, leather, rubber,* and most *vinyls.* Like hard materials, resilient flooring materials have common sets of advantages and disadvantages.

The advantages of resilient flooring are:

- Initial cost is generally lower than hard materials.
- Resilient floor materials are warmer to the touch than nonresilient materials.
- They absorb more sound and thereby produce quieter, more comforting interiors.
- They are easier on the body for standing and thereby produce less fatigue.
- Items dropped are less likely to break, and less damage is done to the floor itself because of its ability to give (resilience).
- There is a wider variety of designs or patterns, colors, and even visual textures (particularly in the vinyl flooring types).
- The maintenance is relatively low depending on the finish and the durability of the finish.

Disadvantages of resilient flooring include the following:

- Resilient materials may require more maintenance and cleaning if the surface has no protection or the no-wax treatment of the surface wears off (due to harsh detergents or high traffic). Damp mopping no-wax floors with water and a small amount of

vinegar will clean without removing the shine.

- Resilient floors may be damaged, dented, or torn by dropping sharp objects such as kitchen knives or by dragging furniture or appliances across the surface.
- Resilient flooring is less durable than hard floor materials, making them a costly choice in the long run due to the necessity of replacing the material.
- If poorly installed, seams will open and become worn.

Soft Floor Coverings

Carpeting

Carpet, particularly wall-to-wall installed carpet, has become a standard item in interior design. In fact, *broadloom carpet* (twelve foot wide average) can be used in any and every area; its use is restricted only by the aesthetic and maintenance requirements of the room. Selecting carpeting is often a difficult task; there is a vast selection of carpet companies who produce carpets in many fibers in a seemingly endless array of colors, textures, and prices. Further, the quality of the carpet and how well it will wear are very difficult to determine when examining the store sample. Further, the small size of most carpet samples makes it hard to visualize the effect of an entire area covered in that carpet. The following guidelines can assist in making wise carpeting selections.

- Understand which fibers are used in carpeting (chart 10.3) as well as the advantages and disadvantages of each.
- Be aware of the many carpet constructions and the selection of textures available.
- Look for carpet brands that are well-known, national companies who have a reputation for quality merchandise and who will stand behind their product in case of flaws (holes, streaks, color variations) or problems that develop after the carpet is installed (such as fading, premature crushing, or pile loss).
- It is wise to purchase carpet from local carpet dealers who are known for their business integrity and will provide quality installation and will gladly service your needs if problems in the carpet arise.
- Be aware that poor quality, inexpensive carpets that appear similar to moderately priced carpets may have inferior quality yarns, less latex glue to hold the primary and secondary backing together (see Tufted Carpets), and quality cut in other ways that are not apparent to the eye. Ask sales personnel to recommend carpets that will stand up to the wear, traffic, and number of years of use you will expect of it, and check to see if there is a written guarantee as to the quality and durability.

Figure 10.5 Quarry Lane floor tiles by Armstrong are nine inches by nine inches. Their resemblance to ceramic tile is enhanced by particles of quartz embedded in the no-wax surface.

Vinyl flooring can imitate many materials. Vinyl is easy care and warm underfoot. Photo courtesy of Armstrong World Industries, Inc.

Chart 10.2 Resilient Floor Materials

Asphalt Tiles

Description: A composition with some asphalt content formed into thin sheets and cut into tiles.
Applications: Flooring; existing in older residential and nonresidential installations.
Maintenance: Damp mop, wax.
Special Considerations: Little asphalt tile is on the market. Like linoleum, it has been replaced with vinyl. Asphalt tile is brittle and easily damaged by solvents, mineral oils, or animal fats. Dents easily and is hard and noisy. Slippery when waxed and particularly when wet.
Cost Structure: Low.

Cork

Description: The outer layer of the oak tree of the birch family that grows in the Mediterranean area. It is light in color, elastic, and very insulative. Resilient cork flooring is usually treated with a vinyl coating or impregnation, removing some of its resiliency but making it a more durable product. It is sound absorbent.
Applications: Residential and nonresidential settings where a quiet, surface is required for low or limited traffic.
Maintenance: Vinyl-cork floors may be damp mopped or buffed. They tend to show dust and footprints easily.
Special Considerations: Due to its insulative properties, cork should not be used where solar gain is desired or over floors with radiant heating systems.
Cost Structure: Moderate to high.

Fabric

Description: Fabric may be bonded between heavy layers of PVC (polyvinyl chloride) and installed by the direct glue-down method.
Application: Primarily residential.
Maintenance: Sweep, vacuum, damp mop.
Special Considerations: Fabrics bonded between vinyl will be a custom specification. Installation methods and costs will vary. Fabric may be used as floor cloth rugs.

Cost Structure: Low to high, depending on the cost per yard of the fabric selected.

Leather

Description: Squares or tiles of leather, the tanned hide of cattle and swine. Dyed brown or colors. Embossed with patterns historically. Leather may also be cut into strips and made into shag-type area rugs.
Applications: High-end residential in small, low-traffic areas. Quiet flooring.
Maintenance: Damp mop with very mild detergent; no saddle soap.
Special Considerations: Leather is a very costly installation and generally used only in small areas.
Cost Structure: Very high.

Linoleum

Description: A mixture of ground cork and wood, color pigments, gums, and oxidized linseed oil poured onto a canvas or burlap backing. This smooth and washable flooring was popular for several decades but is no longer on the market. It has been completely replaced by vinyl. The term linoleum is still sometimes used out of habit to describe vinyl products.

Rubber

Description: Tiles made of butadiene styrene rubber and synthetic materials come in two forms: a flat surface with a marbleized pattern and a raised disc or squares—a solid colored three-dimensional surface. The latter was designed to knock dirt off shoes and to provide water drainage off the surface.
Applications: Primarily nonresidential flooring, though the aesthetic appeal of the raised patterns and the durability are making it useful for homes as well.
Maintenance: Sweep or vacuum. May be washed with detergent and water. Rinsed and mopped with a water and 5 percent liquid bleach solution. Buff for shine return. New floors will require more buffing.
Special Considerations: A good selection for entrances because

mud and dirt are knocked off and fall down into the lower area. Very resilient flooring. Good traction, used in areas when wet floors need to be safe floors.
Cost Structure: Moderately high.

Vinyl

Description: Vinyl is a shortened name for polyvinyl chloride, a plastic solution that hardens to a solid film. Many materials may be coated with vinyl, such as cork and fabric. Resilient materials that are primarily vinyl include vinyl composition/asbestos, sheet vinyl, and vinyl tile.

Vinyl Composition

Description: A blended composition of vinyl, resin, plasticizer, and coloring agents formed into sheets under pressure and heat. Sheets or tiles.
Applications: Both residential and nonresidential settings.
Maintenance: Sweep, vacuum, damp mop; detergent. May be waxed.
Special Considerations: Noisy flooring. Resists stains, acids, alkalies, cleaning compounds, and water. Historically, it contained asbestos, which is still in existence in older installations. It has not been considered a health hazard unless the floor is sanded or abraded to set the asbestos fibers loose in the air. Slippery when wet.
Cost Structure: Moderate.

Sheet Vinyl

Description: Sheets of vinyl come in six-, nine-, and twelve-foot widths. There are basically two kinds of sheet vinyl. One is a solid or *inlaid vinyl*, built up with successive layers of vinyl granules that are usually plain or patterned with a suggestion of texture. The other method, called *rotogravure* or *roto*, is a printed pattern, such as a wood or patterned tile. The surface is coated with vinyl or vinyl/urethane (a thinner layer) called the wear layer. Both types of vinyl may or may not have a cushioned backing.

Applications: Flooring, both residential and nonresidential. Nonresidential vinyls are thicker or have a thicker wear layer.
Maintenance: Most sheet vinyl is given a no-wax surface to help maintain a shiny surface. However, heavy traffic or furniture movement and harsh detergents may remove the shine. Damp mopping with a water and vinegar solution will help keep the shine. Vinyl floors may be waxed.
Special Considerations: Thicker wear layers of vinyl and thicker inlaid vinyls (nonresidential) will be the most durable. The excessively patterned and brightly colored vinyls may become visually tiring, although they may show less dirt than the plain and textured vinyls. Patterned vinyls may also be embossed, a process that makes permanent indentations in the surface to accent the pattern. These may catch and hold dirt. May be slippery if not a textured surface.
Cost Structure: Moderate.

Vinyl Tile

Description: Solid vinyl composed of PVC, plasticizers, pigments or coloring agents, mineral fillers, and stabilizers. Solid colors, plus patterns such as marble, travertine, slate, brick, stone. Some vinyl tiles may have a wood veneer sealed between layers.
Applications: Flooring, both residential and nonresidential.
Maintenance: Sweep, vacuum, damp mop (as for sheet vinyl) without detergents, which can dull the floor.
Special Considerations: This composition is also used to form vinyl baseboard or wall base.
Cost Structure: Moderately low.

Vinyl floor

- Quality can be determined to an extent with hand tests. By bending back the face of a tufted carpet, the fabric into which the carpet is tufted (the primary backing) is revealed. This is called making the carpet "grin." If there is a lot of primary backing exposed, then the tufts are not close together and the carpet will be more likely to mat or crush under traffic. When the tufts are close together, the carpet will have more resilience or the ability to bounce back. Also try untwisting the pile to see if it may become fuzzy, pull at the pile to determine if the face will lose a lot of fibers.

Figure 10.6

- If it is possible, secure a sample or scrap of the carpet (or of two or three for comparison), and take it home or to the site where it will be installed. Lay it down to evaluate color during different times of the day and at night with artificial light, and walk on it to determine whether it will show footprints or crush easily. Drop thread or other debris on the surface and evaluate whether it will readily show soil.
- Where carpet will be used in a heavy traffic area, it is wise to select a color that is medium in value (not too light or too dark) and low in intensity (fairly dull). This will hide the inevitable shadows and soiling that accompany foot traffic. Further, patterned carpet will virtually double the life span of a carpet under heavy use because pattern can effectively hide both the soil and the wear.
- Look at the expected life span of the carpet as compared to its aesthetics. A vivid or demanding color may prove tiresome sooner than would a more neutralized carpet. Neutral (browns, grays) or neutralized (dulled) colors generally prove more flexible for redecorating, which typically takes place several times during the life span of a carpet.
- Select a quality padding (carpet underlay; see Installation Methods and Padding at the end of this chapter), and check to see that the padding that is delivered to the site is the very one you selected in the carpet showroom.

- Keep in mind that the quality of installation may determine how the carpet looks, lays, and performs to an extent. Insist on the best, most-skilled carpet installers that can be hired in your vicinity.

Understanding Carpet Fibers

When selecting a carpet, it is wise to have an understanding of the fibers commonly used, their advantanges and disadvantages, the maintenance required, and the cost structure. This information is valuable in choosing carpeting for specific purposes and in helping to realize that no one fiber has all desirable qualities.

The designer and consumer will also discover that there are an increasing number of carpets that are made of blended fibers, such as 65 percent wool and 35 percent acrylic, or a blend of 80 percent nylon and 20 percent wool or polyester. These and other blends are appearing on the market for three reasons:

1. A blend will possess positive qualities of each fiber, to become both pleasing to the touch and possess durability.
2. A more costly fiber can be extended with the combination of lesser expensive fibers.
3. Cross-dying effects can be obtained by coloring the yarn with a single dyestuff, where two different fibers take the dye differently, creating a two-tone effect.

Chart 10.3 contains a list of individual carpet fibers, with a listing of the source, advantages and disadvantages, maintenance requirements, and cost structure. It is very important to realize that there are many quality levels of each of these fibers, both natural wool and synthetic man-mades. Higher quality fibers will make the carpet perform better and last longer and will be reflected in a higher cost per square yard.

Woven Broadloom Carpet

As the name implies, broadloom carpets are wide, six, nine, or the typical twelve or thirteen feet wide and woven or tufted by machine. The first two woven carpets originated in England and are named after the towns where they were first loomed. A *Wilton* carpet is woven on the complex Jacquard loom. It allows complex patterns to be constructed, and its hallmark is that each color in the carpet is carried as

Figure 10.6 A grand feeling infuses this traditional living room furnished with a mix of contemporary fabrics, carpeting, and prize antiques. The lovely Saxony carpet is Anso V Worry-Free Nylon, featuring permanent, built-in resistance to soil, stain, and static. Interior design by Carl Mitchell of Wilds & Mitchell Design, Inc. Photo courtesy of Anso V Worry-Free Carpet by Wunda Weve.

Chart 10.3 Carpet Fibers Comparison

Wool

Source: Wool is the fiber taken from domesticated sheep and varies from very fine to very coarse. Wool also varies in length; the shorter staple lengths are used in lesser quality, and longer staple lengths in higher quality wool carpets. Wool may be dyed any color or left in its natural white, cream, brown, or gray hue, as are berber carpets.

Advantages: Wool has long been used for a standard of comparison as the most durable carpet fiber. Wool is very resilient due to the overlapping scales of the staple (short-length) fiber. This resiliency gives wool its long life and resistance to crushing. Wool takes dyes beautifully and is woven and tufted into carpets of high quality. It is traditionally used in pile for Oriental, folk, and fine designer rugs. Wool can absorb up to 25 percent of its weight without feeling damp.

Disadvantages: Wool carpets must be treated for moth resistance. When wet, wool emits a distinctive animal smell. Some people are allergic to wool. Wool is susceptible to fuzzing (fibers working loose) and pilling (fibers working into small balls or pills). Wool is the most costly of the carpet fibers.

Maintenance: Wool should be vacuumed regularly and spots cleaned up immediately. Wool takes a long time to dry but may be wet cleaned. Professional dry-cleaning methods are recommended. Avoid scrubbing brushes that could untwist or encourage pilling.

Cost Structure: High.

Nylon

Source: A manufactured synthetic based on the raw materials phenol, hydrogen, oxygen, and nitrogen. Nylon is heated into a solution, then extruded into long threads that may be texturized and cut into short fibers or staple to meet requirements of the many textures found in nylon carpet.

Advantages: Nylon is the most widely used carpet fiber on the market today, accounting for over 90 percent of all carpeting sold alone or combined with other fibers. It is a flexible fiber that is used for level-loop carpets as well as cut piles, both tufted and woven, and used often for accent or *scatter rugs.* Nylon is strong and durable, resilient, and abrasion resistant. Nylon possesses good color retention, hides dirt, and has excellent bulk. There is a minimum of fuzzing and pilling; it is nonallergenic and mildew and insect resistant. Nylon has good flame resistance.

Disadvantages: First and second generation (early chemical composition) nylons were prone to static electricity, had a harsh sheen and unpleasant touch, and took colors too vividly. However, in third and fourth generation nylons, all these weaknesses have been overcome. Fifth generation nylons now are guaranteed against stains and soiling. However, there are many qualities of nylon, and some of these problems may still exist.

Maintenance: Nylon cleans exceptionally well. It should be vacuumed regularly and spot cleaned as needed. Steam or wet cleaning is effective if the secondary backing is jute and not kept wet. Accent or scatter rugs may be machine washed and dried.

Cost Structure: Moderate.

Acrylic

Source: Acrylic is a synthetic fiber composed mainly of acrylonitrile, a colorless liquid that is boiled and extruded into long-chain polymers or single threads that can be texturized and cut into staple fibers and spun into a bulky yarn.

Advantages: Acrylic is the fiber that is most similar to wool. It is warm to the touch and looks similar to wool, so it is often combined with wool to lower its cost. It is soft and warm to the touch. Acrylic is often used to imitate wool berber carpet (neutral colored with natural wool color irregularities).

Disadvantages: Acrylic has low resiliency, mats easily, fuzzes and pills, and has a relatively short life span as compared to wool or nylon. The life span is dramatically increased when blended with either of these two fibers. Acrylic is vulnerable to oil-borne stains, which are difficult to remove.

Maintenance: Acrylic responds well to wet cleaning, but care must be taken to avoid brushing and untwisting the fibers, as the fiber will mat down and pill more easily when the fibers have been loosened. Vacuum acrylic regularly and remove spots immediately if possible, as acrylic absorbs oil-borne stains that are difficult to remove once they are set.

Cost Structure: Moderate.

Modacrylic

Source: Modacrylic is a synthetic long-chain polymer primarily of acrylonitrile modified by other polymers; literally a modified acrylic.

Advantages: Modacrylic is inherently flame resistant, making it a good choice to meet code or fire safety. Modacrylic is a soft, bulky fiber, historically manufactured into an imitation fur-type pile, and used as accent or scatter rugs. In broadloom carpeting it is sometimes combined with acrylic to improve flame resistance. Modacrylic dyes well and is insect and mildew resistant and has fair abrasion resistance.

Disadvantages: The softness of modacrylic makes this fiber mat down or crush easily, hence, it is not suitable alone as a broadloom fiber. It also fuzzes and pills (loose fibers working into balls).

Maintenance: Accent rugs— shake or vacuum, machine or hand wash, warm. Machine dry (low setting) or line dry. Rugs of fake fur (imitation floccati rugs) require occasional professional dry cleaning. In broadlooms, modacrylic is as cleanable as the other fibers with which it is blended.

Cost Structure: Moderate.

Olefin/polypropylene

Source: Olefin and polypropylene carpets are made of ethylene or propane gas constituted into a synthetic long-chain polymer. Polypropylenes are modified olefins as propylenes are added and polymerized.

Advantages: Olefin is lightweight, inexpensive, durable, strong. It resists fuzzing, pilling, and abrasion. Used for indoor-outdoor carpeting, nonresidential carpeting and carpet tiles. Also used for artificial turf.

Disadvantages: Olefin has a plastic feel and is not soft to the touch. Must be treated for resistance against sunlight fading and deterioration. Has low-melting point. Lower qualities may crush.

Maintenance: Stain and soil resistant. Vacuum regularly. Cleans well; is unaffected by moisture and most chemicals and acids. Olefin or polypropylene carpets installed outdoors (patios, around swimming pools, around nonresidential settings, and as artificial turf) may be hosed off.

Cost Structure: Low to moderate.

Polyester

Source: Polyester is a synthetic long-chain polymer derived from a reaction between dicarboxylic acid and dihydric alcohol.

Advantages: Polyester takes and holds dyes well; colors are often some of the nicest available in man-made fibers. Next to acrylic, it most closely resembles wool because of its dyeability and softness to the touch. Polyester is mildew and moth resistant, nonallergenic, nonabsorbent. It is a durable fiber that resists fuzzing and pilling. Polyester is soft and cool to the touch, an advantage in warm-weather climates.

Disadvantages: Polyester lacks the resilience and strength of nylon and must, therefore, be heat set to maintain yarn twist. Heat-set polyesters are good selections for most residential areas except heavy traffic lanes. Polyester lacks warmth of wool, nylon, or acrylic.

Cost Structure: Moderate to moderately high, depending on the quality of the fiber.

(A)   (B)

Figure 10.8

Figure 10.7

(C)

a separate weft beneath the face of the design. This means the carpet can be very heavy and substantial. Designs vary from Empire and Victorian large-scale designs to contemporary small-geometric patterns. Wiltons are nearly always of quality wool and are very costly. They are seen most often in exclusive areas of nonresidential interior design.

Axminster carpets are also Jacquard woven but without the extra warps. Only the colors needed are inserted, making complex patterns possible without great expense. Axminster carpets are of wool or nylon and are seen in many kinds of nonresidential settings such as restaurants, theatres, retail businesses, and hotels. Axminster carpets are readily adaptable to custom design, and where they are still cost prohibitive for every area of a installation, carpeting can be printed to imitate the design.

Velvet weave carpets are also woven but without any design. They may be solid or woven of variegated yarn, usually of wool or a wool and nylon blend.

Tufted Broadloom Carpets

Tufted carpets make up the majority of carpets sold in America today. They are constructed on a loom that employs multiple needles threaded with the yarn. The carpet yarn is punched into the primary backing in a zigzag pattern. The zigzag holds the yarn more securely in case of a loose tuft that is pulled. The tufts are held securely with a latex coating (rubber-based glue) that holds on a secondary backing made of woven jute or polypropylene fabric. Jute stretches somewhat but will rot if kept moist. Polypropylene will not be affected by moisture, but has very little flexibility. There are some tufted carpets that have no secondary backing, and custom hand-tufted carpets have a layer of latex (rubber-based glue) to which is affixed a loosely woven scrim textile that adds some stability to the construction. *Rubber-backed tufted carpets* are tufted into a thick rubber-cushioned backing and directly glued to the surface. *Fuse-bonded carpets* (such as artificial turf) are tufted into a heavy layer of latex and are also directly glued down without padding. There are many levels of quality in the construction of tufted carpets.

Other Carpet Constructions

Knitted carpets are constructed of knitted yarns held together with a latex backing. They account for very few carpets on the market.

Needlepunch carpets are masses of fibers rather than yarns that are held together by an interlocking fiber-punching machine. They are inexpensive and durable and come in yardage and square tiles with or without a latex backing. They may be installed over a pad or glued down directly.

A carpet seldom seen is the *flocked carpet*, which is made by electrostatically charging nylon fibers that are blown onto a glue-covered fabric. These carpets have a short-pile velvet texture.

Figure 10.7 Broadloom carpeting in the form of Wilton and Axminster weaves is utilized as "in stock" carpet patterns as well as individually designed carpets for custom installations, such as this one. Here the carpet was loomed of fine wool to document fluttering ribbons and floral garlands, motifs of the Neoclassic/Federal era in America for the front drawing room at Boscobel. Photo courtesy of Boscobel Restoration Incorporated.
Figure 10.8 Results from a wear test in a Hong Kong subway station, where a half-million commuters walked across it. (A) Armstrong's Anything Goes! carpet cleaned beautifully, with excellent tip retention and surface appearance. (B) An ordinary saxony with similar density and thickness, subjected to the same half-million commuters, lost its tuft twist and remained frayed and matted looking even after cleaning. (C) Armstrong's Anything Goes! carpeting is an example of the most-popular residential carpeting, saxony or plush, a cross between a shag and a plush carpet cut pile. Saxony carpets are available in a wide array of colors and yarn thicknesses. Photos courtesy of Armstrong World Industries, Inc.

Carpet Textures

The texture of the carpet refers to the pile surface. This is where most of the variety of a carpet is possible. The yarns may vary in thickness, in pile height, and in level. The following textures are the most common:

- Cut pile surfaces are tufted, then sheared to one short height. The tufting can be dense, or tightly packed, or less dense with fatter yarns. Early cut piles included *plush carpet*, dense and one color. During the 1960s and 1970s, *shag* carpets with very deep pile but generally not densely tufted became popular. Today, high-quality shags are often of wool and are densely tufted. *Saxony*, is a combination of a shag and a plush. The density approaches a plush, while the depth is between a plush and a shag. Very tightly twisted yarns are termed *frieze* cut piles and are sturdy and durable carpets.

- *Sculptured carpets* are made of two levels of cut pile, or of a higher cut pile and a lower level loop. They may also be multihued or of several values, tufted of variegated yarn, or dyed to be colorful and form a busy pattern. Many quality levels of sculptured carpets exist, with the best design and quality found in the carpets that are only slightly variegated in color or value and where the sculpturing is understated, forming strength and resilience to the pile height rather than a dramatic difference in pile height, which can easily mat down.

- *Level loop carpets* are tufted or woven without being sheared into a cut pile. They are sometimes called *wire construction,* or *round wire tufting,* as the yarns are looped over wires for uniformity; the wires are then removed. If the wires are razor sharp, they cut the yarn to form a cut pile when removed. Variations of the level loop include the *random shear,* where some loops are woven slightly higher then sheared off. The surface then somewhat resembles a very dense cut pile, looking more luxurious but with the strength of the loops to prevent crushing. A *level-tip shear* is the same as random shear, where the loops are the same height as the sheared loops. Another loop texture is the *multilevel-loop,* or *sculptured-loop,* or *embossed-loop pile,* where the loops are tufted at two or more levels, producing a pattern.

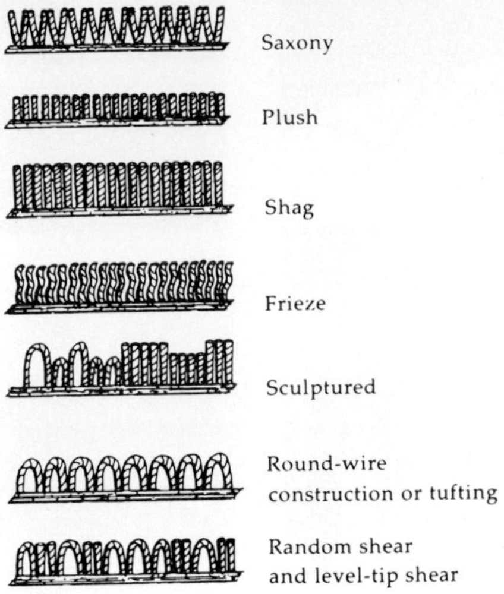

Saxony

Plush

Shag

Frieze

Sculptured

Round-wire construction or tufting

Random shear and level-tip shear

Figure 10.9

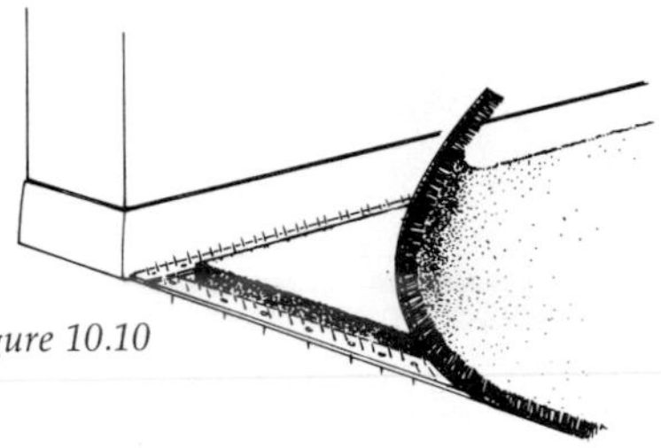

Figure 10.10

Installation Methods and Padding

There are basically two types of installations: direct glue-down and the pad and tackless strip method.

Direct glue-down is possible for any type of carpet; no separate cushion is used. The reasons for direct glue-down include: (1) heavy traffic, where the constant walking could cause the carpet to develop ripples, which are potentially dangerous; (2) carpet installations where no softness is required; and (3) saving the expense of the pad, tackless strip, and labor to install two layers.

Tackless strip is a thin board with tacks embedded so that they protrude at an angle toward the wall. The strip is nailed near the wall, and the pad is stapled, nailed, or glued to the floor just inside this perimeter. The carpet is then laid over the pad and hooked over the tacks with carpet installation equipment that stretches, then pounds the tacks into the carpet.

Padding, or carpet underlay, is available in several types.

- *Sponge rubber pads* combine natural and synthetic rubber and fillers to form a flat or a waffle sponge; suitable for light to medium traffic. With heavy traffic, these pads tend to crush and lose their resiliency.
- *Foam rubber pads* are firmer flat sheets made from natural or synthetic rubbers; suitable for medium traffic.
- *Urethane foam* is made from synthetic polymers and is available in varying sheet thicknesses. It may be formed to be extra dense. Chopped urethane foam may be *bonded,* or *rebonded* (as it is sometimes called), into sheets with additives such as paper, vinyl, fabric-backed foam, or wood chips. This factor makes bonded foam subject to many quality levels. Both urethane foam and rebonded foam are popular choices for padding.
- *Felt padding* was originally of animal hair, though *animal hair felt padding* is now rare; a *combination felt padding* made of some animal hair and some synthetic fibers is more common, and *fiber felt padding* is all synthetic. Felt padding has less resiliency and is an excellent choice for Oriental rugs because too much resiliency can damage the rug's backing.

Figure 10.9 Carpet textures.
Figure 10.10 Tackless strips are nailed next to the wall, then padding or underlay is stapled down (if subfloor is wood), and carpet backing is hooked into angled staples to anchor it securely to the floor.

Carpet Maintenance and Cleaning

The appearance and life span of a carpet often depends on the way it is maintained. Although carpet that receives greater traffic will wear out faster than carpet that receives little use, keeping the carpet clean is a key to good looks and to increasing its life span. Soil allowed to stay on the surface of a carpet is not only unsightly but the longer it is left, the more difficult it is to remove. When dirt, grit, or sand settles to the bottom of the pile, it can abrade the yarns at the base, wearing them off, and eventually destroying the carpet.

In heavy traffic areas such as hallways and rooms that contain traffic lanes, carpeting should be vacuumed every day. Areas of little traffic, such as bedrooms, usually require vacuuming only once a week. A light vacuuming is three times back and forth, and a thorough vacuuming is seven times back and forth. Repetitive vacuuming loosens and pulls the dirt from the base to the surface, then finally sucks it up into the machine.

Spots should be removed as quickly as possible and never allowed to remain on the carpet long enough to become set. Mild detergent and clear water are useful for many stains, and oil- or tar-based stains can be removed with a commercially prepared dry-cleaning solution. Carpet stores will often recommend products or sell kits for cleaning spots.

Carpets should be wet or dry cleaned when they become so soiled that the vacuum or spot-cleaning of the carpet can no longer keep the surface looking good. There are several methods of cleaning carpet.

- Wet cleaning is done in various ways. Steam extraction forces very hot detergent solution into the carpet, then extracts it immediately with a suction or wet vacuum. Wet cleaning can also be done by spraying a dry cleaning chemical solution onto the carpet then mopping the carpet with circular pads. Steam cleaning is safer in that it will not untwist the yarns. However, both methods run the risk of wetting the carpet too much, which can damage a jute primary or secondary backing, and the detergent and chemical solution may attract dirt more quickly. Rinsing the carpet with a mild vinegar and water solution will remove most of the residual detergent.

- Dry cleaning is done by sprinkling the carpet with a powdered or sawdust-like preparation then using a rotating brush machine to work the compound into the carpet. The compound is then extracted with a vacuum. It may run the risk of leaving cleaning compound behind that will attract and hold dirt more quickly after cleaning.

Oriental and Area Rugs

Oriental and area rugs can give character and richness to interiors. Often a fine rug will be the basis for the decorative scheme and will seem to finish the room. The basic categories of area rugs are *Oriental, folk, European handmade, designer, and natural fiber.* All of these may be called *area rugs,* as they generally vary from four by six feet to eighteen by twenty-four feet, defining spaces such as a conversation area or dining area. Within each of these categories are several types of rugs. A basic knowledge of these will lead to a better understanding of their use in interiors.

Oriental Rugs

Oriental rugs are knotted or tied by hand by native craftsmen from Iran, Turkey, Romania, the Caucasus, Afghanistan, Pakistan, India, and China. The finest Oriental rugs originated in what was called Persia at the height of the rug-weaving era, today primarily Iran. An Oriental rug is composed of a cotton warp, pile knots of wool or sometimes silk, and a cotton weft inserted after every two rows of knots. The design and colors are drawn on graph paper and called a cartoon. Patterns are symmetrical, often mirroring the design on all four corners. The finer the warp and knots and the greater the number of knots per square inch, the more intricate the patterns possible (finest rugs have four hundred knots or more per square inch). A fine rug can take months to weave in a rug-weaving center and years if the weaver is working alone (as with a nomadic tribe).

Figure 10.11

Figure 10.11 A symbol of artistry and laborious skill handed down for countless generations, the oriental rug brings prestige and profound elegance wherever it is laid in both residential and nonresidential design. On polished stone flooring surrounded by fine architectural detail, this Persian oriental rug makes a statement of highest culture and impeccable taste. Photo by Norman McGrath © 1989.

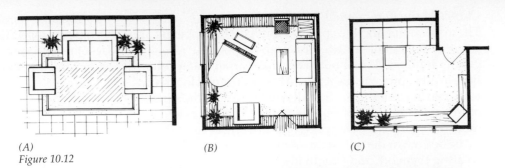

(A)
(B)
(C)

Figure 10.12

Oriental rug weaving has for centuries been recognized as an art and skill of the highest order, which is reflected in prices of the finer rugs. Antique Oriental rugs (older than seventy-five years) are the most costly if they are in good to excellent condition. Semi-antiques are those from twenty-five to seventy-five years, and new rugs are less than twenty-five years old. Oriental rugs will often increase in value over the years despite some wear. This is true even of new rugs if they are authentic and woven in the area where they originate, called the traditional rug-weaving area. Nontraditional rug-weaving areas, such as India, have made traditional designs readily available. These rugs are not as valuable, however. It takes an expert to evaluate and appraise a rug. It is best to shop for an Oriental rug at a reputable dealership that specializes in them.[2]

Oriental rugs are divided into Persian, Caucasian, and Chinese rugs. *Persian rugs* have intricate curving patterns, often floral, and have high knot counts. Persian rugs from Iran are considered the finest rugs, although there is a great variety in quality. Persian rugs are also produced in India and surrounding countries. The best-known types are the Hamadan, Hereke, Herez, Isfahan, Kashan, Kerman (Kirman), Nain, Qum, Sarouk (Saruk), Senneh, Sereband, Shiraz, Shirvan, and Tabriz.

Caucasian or Turkish rugs are generally those from the Caucasus region of the USSR, and Turkish rugs originate in Turkey, though many are produced in Afghanistan, Pakistan, and India. These rugs are generally coarser, of brighter primary colors, and with simpler and geometric designs. Best known are the Afghan, Belouch, Bokhara, Kazak, Kurd, Qashqa'i (Kashkai), Tekke (Tekke Turkoman), and Yomut (Yamout).

Chinese rugs are woven with a deeper pile of coarse wool (fewer knots per square inch). By law, all modern Chinese rugs have the same number of knots per square inch. Designs may be traditional with open background, central medallion and a large-scale border, typically in cream, ming blue, gold, and/or red, or they may copy designs from Persia, France, or they may be contemporary patterns. All these will be sculptured or beveled on both sides of the design, giving a deeper, richer look and emphasizing the design.

Rugs from India have flooded the market in recent years. Since labor costs are low and skills are high, rugs of all types are produced there. By law, all wool is native, and these factors combine to make Indian rugs less valuable as investments. Persian, Turkish or Caucasian, and Chinese rugs are all made in India. Chinese rug depth and sculpturing is applied to French patterns and termed Indo-Aubusson rugs. In addition, flat folk rugs are produced in great quantity in India. Indian rugs are fine selections if investment and resale are not important to the buyer.

Folk Rugs

Folk rugs comprise a very large category of rugs. A loose definition is any rug woven by an ethnic group or reflecting the native heritage of a country. Folk rugs are flat, reversible rugs, generally of wool. These come from India, Romania, Scandinavia, Colonial New England, South America, the southwestern United States, and pile rugs from Africa, South America, Scandinavia, and Spain. The best known of the folk rugs are the following:

The *dhurrie (dhurry, durry)* and *kilim rugs* have been produced for

Complex Persian Oriental rug. Fine rugs have over 400 hand-tied knots per square inch; more knots yield curved lines.

A Persian prayer rug

Figure 10.12 (A) An area rug, defining an area such as for conversation. (B) A room-sized rug, a loose rug large enough to nearly cover the room—within one foot to a few inches from the wall. (C) Wall-to-wall carpeting, installed by direct glue-down or tackless strip and underlay or padding.

Caucasian or Turkish rug

Chinese rug

Romanian kilim

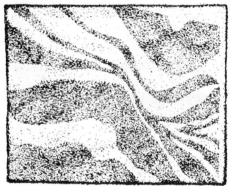

Scandinavian rya rug

Indian dhurrie rug

Navajo rug

Navajo rugs are made in the southwestern United States—Arizona and New Mexico, primarily. These flat tapestry rugs reflect native American tribe (Indian) motifs and colors—geometric, angular simple patterns in gray, cream, white, black, brown, rust, and red. Navajo rugs can be fairly valuable as investments, although they are imitated by Mexican and Japanese craftsmen who produce knockoffs, which are not valuable. The types of Navajo rugs include the Chinle, Crystal, Ganado-Klagetoh (Ganado Red), Shiprock-Lukachukai (Yei and Yeibechi), the Storm Pattern, Teec Nos Pos, Two Gray Hills, and Wide Ruins.[3] Of these, the finest weave and most valuable are the Two Gray Hills rugs.

The *rya and rollikan rugs* are the two best known of the Scandinavian rugs. The rya is a hand-knotted deep pile rug in abstract designs and contemporary colors. The rollikan is a flat tapestry rug that reflects the simplified, modern tastes influenced by the folk arts and flowers of Scandinavia.

centuries in India and Romania, respectively. Indian dhurries were traditionally of cotton, so few authentic antiques exist; Romanian kilims were of wool. In both rugs, folk designs are woven with no pile. They are reversible, and vary from dark and vivid to pale colors. Designs are often geometric but may be based on floral patterns or have only textures and no patterns. Today the designs and colors are largely dictated by European and American tastes, since the Western market has received these rugs so well.

Rag, braided, and hooked rugs are the New England colonists' contribution to folk rugs. These rugs were made of clothing that was no longer usable (rags) and turned into utilitarian floor coverings. Rag rugs are plain weave, flat rugs, originally woven on a floor or hand loom. Braided rugs are made of strips of fabric, braided and sewn into an oval or circle. Both rag and braided rugs are also manufactured by machine today. Hooked rugs are made by inserting strips of fabric into a heavy scrim or burlap backing cloth; they form simple patterns, usually floral.

Moroccan rugs are pile rugs that are geometric and vividly colored. Berber rugs may have natural colors —beiges, browns, and blacks—and perhaps some pattern. Moroccan *Rabat* rugs reflect the oriental designs, much simplified.

Central and South American rugs include those made by native craftsmen of Central and South America. Either flat tapestry or pile rugs, they most often reflect the pre-Columbian influence of native tribes, such as the Inca, Maya, and Aztec, in geometric patterns and bright or neutral colors similar to those used by the Navajo.

European Handmade Rugs
The best known of the European rugs are the French Savonnerie and Aubusson, the Portuguese needlepoint, and the Spanish rugs.

Savonnerie rugs have been produced at the Savonnerie factory in France for over three hundred years. These rugs are a hand-knotted pile, traditionally with deep, rich, vivid colors and large-scale patterns. The Savonnerie rugs produced there today may be of very contemporary patterns as well as the historical French motifs.

Aubusson rugs are named after the factory where they were first produced and today bear the name even though they are no longer produced at

the Aubusson Tapestry Works. These French rugs are flat tapestry weaves, historically of Oriental rug-inspired motifs in faded or muted colors. These rugs were particularly favored during the reign of Louis XVI when light-scaled Neoclassic designs were in vogue. Today Aubusson rugs may have a floral pattern, or they may have very abstract and modern patterns.

Portuguese *needlepoint rugs* are produced in several countries including America. However, the authentic needlepoints originated in Portugal. Although some needlepoints are machine made, authentic needlepoints are still hand-embroidered wool on a heavy scrim. The characteristic round stitches are usually formed into lovely floral patterns.

Spanish rugs are hand- or machine-woven pile rugs called Mantas. They have designs that appear three-dimensional and have subtle shadings, although the colors are bright and vivid.

Designer Rugs
Designer rugs are made to custom specifications by several companies in America. The rugs are most often hand or machine tufted of quality wool onto a canvaslike fabric, then

coated with a latex to hold the stitches in place. There may be a heavy fabric sewn onto the back as a secondary backing. The value of designer rugs lies in the freedom and creativity possible. The rug may be a simplified, enlarged version of a selected textile. It may have large- or small-scale patterns and a variety of pile heights and yarn textures. The size and shape are also totally custom. In nonresidential applications, designer rugs may center around a corporate logo or carry

French Savonnerie rug

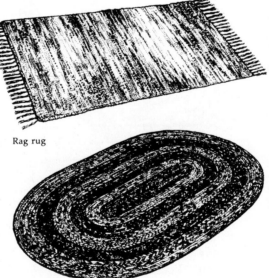

Rag rug

Braided rug

French Aubusson rug

Figure 10.13 Winner of the Traditional Adaptation Rugs category of the Seventeenth Annual Product Design Award, this rug designed by Mark Saley and Teddy Sumner is available through F. Schumacher & Co. The hand-stitched needlepoint employs a Victorian motif of roses in a design suitable for many uses. Made

out a specific theme. Designer rugs can be used as focal points or wall tapestries. They may be pictorial, reflecting regional histories, architecture, geology, or industry. And surprisingly, designer rugs are not as costly as many people think. Manufacturers have professionals who work with the designer toward the exact colors, textures, and designs for these fine rugs.

Natural Fiber Rugs

Natural fiber rugs include *animal skins, berber rugs, cotton rugs, floccati rugs, sisal/maize mats, tatami mats, and wool rugs.*

Animal skins include zebra, black, brown, and polar bear skins, and any other animal skins laid on the floor or hung on the wall. The use of animal skins has been curtailed in recent years due to conservation efforts.

Berber rugs, originally woven by the Berber tribal natives of North Africa, are made of wool that is not dyed but left in its natural color state—cream, brown, and black. The wool hues are mixed to frankly expose the natural flecks of the various colors. Berber rugs come in off-white, various beiges, darker browns, and charcoals. Berbers today are most often machine-tufted broadlooms for nonresi-

Portugese needlepoint rug

Figure 10.13

Figure 10.14

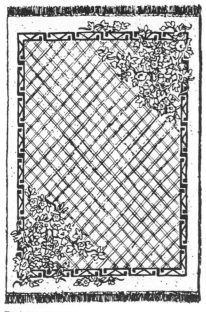

Designer rug

Figure 10.15

of 100 percent wool, the standard size is nine feet by twelve feet, and custom sizes are available. Photo courtesy of Resources Council Inc.
Figure 10.14 Designer rug Sheba from the Saxony Carpet Company's Srinigar collection, a group of twenty 100 percent wool handwoven designs ranging from large and small florals

to intricate geometrics. This design is an allover traditional English floral in lush colors. Designer rugs can be custom designed, colored, and sized. Courtesy of Saxony Carpet Company.
Figure 10.15 Created with the aid of a custom computer-aided design program, each Fire in the Lake rug by Carleton Designs is limited to an

edition of fifteen and available on a custom basis with color and size specified by the client. Colors are hand-mixed from Swiss acid dyes with excellent wash and light fastness, allowing for extensive use of shading known as abrash. Flat,

reversible weave. Winner of the Contemporary Rugs category of the Seventeenth Annual Product Design Award. Design by Carolyn & Vincent Carleton. Photo courtesy of Resources Council Inc.

dential and residential application. A berber area rug may be a portion of a broadloom with bound edges, cut or shaped to cover an area.

Cotton rugs are woven by hand or machine and left neutral or yarn dyed to form simple patterns and textures. Cotton rugs may be machine washable and dryable if they are small rugs, and in larger installations they absorb dirt but clean up nicely.

Floccati, or flokati, rugs originate in Greece. They are tufts of sheared goat's hair woven into a knit or woven fabric. They have a deep, luxurious pile. Floccati rugs are used in both informal and formal settings and have been favored area rugs in contemporary settings for many years. They are available in off-white and brown and are surprisingly inexpensive. They must be professionally drycleaned.

Sisal and maize mats are also available in squares or tiles, so the installations can cover small or large areas. They are not known for their comfort; sisal is particularly prickly to the touch. But these natural fibers form interesting and handsome floor textures.

Tatami mats are traditional floor coverings for Japanese homes and are seen in contemporary Western residences as well. They are woven of dried sea grasses and edged with black fabric and are set together in geometric patterns. The thickness of tatami mats vary from about one to four inches. They offer good insulation as well as a fine appearance.

Natural wool rugs are often woven or tufted into neutral, subtly patterned area rugs. Surface textures vary from cut pile to beveled designs to level-loop construction.

Accent Rugs

Accent rugs form a broad category of rugs that are generally smaller and of man-made fibers, such as nylon, rayon, and polyester. Most are machine washable and dryable and are used in kitchens, in bathrooms, and near entries. They may be tufted into a deep pile. Also included in the accent rug category are *domestic Oriental rugs*, which are machine Oriental rug designs woven of wool or nylon. While domes-

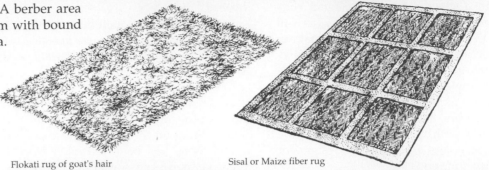

Flokati rug of goat's hair   Sisal or Maize fiber rug

Figure 10.16

tic Orientals are not washable, they are durable and may be comparatively inexpensive. There are many quality levels of domestic Oriental rugs. Small decorative accent rugs are sometimes called art rugs.

Nonresidential Considerations

In addition to the considerations listed in this chapter for selection of residential flooring, nonresidential flooring has further criteria and considerations.

Hard and Resilient Floorings

Hard flooring is frequently specified by interior designers for nonresidential settings. Factors that dictate this decision include the flooring budget and the traffic level or classification. A class *A* or *I* traffic rating indicates extremely

Figure 10.16 Intriguing one-point, vanishing perspective is accentuated with the grid lines of the ceramic tile floor in this New York subway station. Ceramic tile can withstand years of hard nonresidential abuse and still look good. Photo courtesy of Italian Tile Center, New York.

Figure 10.17

advantage in that they are resilient and will not be damaged easily; they are easier on the feet and legs because of this resiliency; and they are quieter than nonresilient flooring.

Rugs and Carpeting

Carpeting selected for nonresidential installations varies somewhat from residential settings where color, price, and durability are the criteria, respectively. Nonresidential carpets must meet some or all of the following requirements:

1. Cost of all nonresidential carpets must meet budget limitations.
2. Construction is an important criterion. In order for a nonresidential carpet to be durable, minimum requirements must be filled for *pile density,* which means the number of *tufts or stitches per square inch,* together with the distance between rows and the pile height. The more dense the tufting or the weave, the stronger the carpet is likely to be. The strength of the *tuft bind,* or how tenciously the face yarn is held onto the primary and secondary backings, is also a construction criterion. A thin layer of latex, for example, may not prevent the yarn from unraveling when pulled.
3. Weight of the face yarn will be one measure of carpet durability. Heavier *face weights* will indicate the amount of yarn used per square measure. *Finished pile weight* includes the backings as well.
4. Abrasion resistance includes the type and quality of fibers, the type, thickness, and twist tightness of the yarn, as well as the density.
5. Resilience means the carpet must have the ability to withstand light, medium, heavy, or extra heavy traffic without undue crushing or matting.
6. Appearance means the carpet will hide and release soil, resist staining and fading, fuzzing and pilling.
7. Maintenance is an important factor. Carpets that show dirt easily or are difficult to clean will have high maintenance, often an excluding factor in specification. The majority of nonresidential carpets are patterned because they show about 50 percent less wear and soiling than an unpatterned carpet.
8. Static resistance is important where delicate machinery such as computer terminals may be affected or where highly flammable materials are present.
9. Flammability resistance forms a stringent requirement in many public buildings. Testing for flammability is often conducted, and ratings are available to the client through the designer.
10. Sanitation is a requirement for carpet cleaning and maintenance in clinical and institutional facilities.[4]

heavy traffic flow. Many residential floorings such as medium-grade vinyl or tufted saxony carpeting would wear out quickly under heavy traffic. Thus, the manufacturers of flooring produce materials that are durable for these situations. These include solid vinyl, rubber, and particularly tile, brick, and stone. Although initially very costly, tile, brick, and stone will outwear any other flooring because they are intended to last indefinitely under even very heavy traffic. Because of their weight, the subfloor must have extra strength and support. Another advantage of hard materials is that they will generally not show dirt or traffic-pattern shadows and will be easy to clean and maintain. Little damage can take place to tile, brick, and stone unless a very hard blow is struck, then the material will need to be replaced. Rubber and solid vinyl have the

Figure 10.17 Patterned carpet in warm, stimulating colors is a key element in the interior design of this hotel lobby. Patterned carpet has a life span double that of a plain carpet; it hides both the soil and the wear. Photo by Andy Battenfield and Kelly Haas.

Notes

1. Riggs, Rosemary. *Materials and Components of Interior Design*, 2d ed. (Englewood Cliffs, N.J.: Prentice-Hall, 1989), pp. 22–23, 28.
2. Jerrehian, Aram K., Jr. *Oriental Rug Primer*. (New York: Facts On File, 1980), pp. 28–77, 116–76.
3. James, H.L. *Posts and Rugs: The Story of Navajo Rugs and Their Homes*. (Globe, AZ: Southwest Parks and Monuments Association, 1976), pp. 36–89.
4. Jackman, Dianne R., and Mary K. Dixon. *The Guide to Textiles for Interior Designers*. (Winnipeg: Peguis Publishers, Ltd., 1983), pp. 148–59.

Bibliography

Arizona Highways Department. Arizona Highways, Vol. L, No. 7. Phoenix: Arizona Highways Department, July, 1974.

Burch, Monte. *Tile, Indoors and Out*. Passaic (NJ): Creative Homeowners Press, a division of Federal Marketing Corporation, 1981.

Eiland, Murray L. *Oriental Rugs: A Comprehensive Guide*. Boston: New York Graphic Society, 1973.

Hand, Jackson. *Walls, Floors and Ceilings*. New York: Book Division, Times Mirror Magazines, Inc., 1976.

Herbert, Janice Summers. *Oriental Rugs: The Illustrated Buyer's Guide*. New York: Macmillan, 1978.

Jacobsen, Charles W. *Checkpoints on How to Buy Oriental Rugs*. Rutland (VT), 1969.

James, H.L. *Posts and Rugs: The Story of Navajo Rugs and Their Homes*. Globe, 1976.

Jerrehian, Aram K., Jr. *Oriental Rug Primer*. New York: Facts On File, 1980.

Kahlenberg, Mary H., and Anthony Berlant. *Navajo Blanket*. New York: Praeger, 1972.

Kicklighter, Clois E. *Modern Masonry*. South Highland (IL): Goodheart-Willow Co., 1977.

Kopp, Joel, and Kate Kopp. *American Hooked and Sewn Rugs*. New York: Dutton, 1975.

Neff, Ivan, and Carol Maggs. *Dictionary of Oriental Rugs*. London: A.D. Donker, 1977.

Petsopoulos, Yanni. *Kilims: Flat-Woven Tapestry Rugs*. New York: Rizzoli, 1977.

Reznikoff, S.C. *Specifications for Commercial Interiors*. New York: Whitney Library of Design, an imprint of Watson-Guptill Publications, 1979.

Riggs, J. Rosemary. *Materials and Components of Interior Design*, 2d ed. Englewood Cliffs, N.J.: Prentice-Hall, 1989.

Salter, Walter L. *Floor and Floor Maintenance*. New York: Halstead Press, 1974.

Schuler, Stanley. *The Floor and Ceiling Book*. New York: M. Evans and Co., 1976.

Schurmann, Ulrich. *Caucasian Rugs*. London: Allen & Unwin, 1964.

Time Life Books. *Paint and Wallpaper*. New York: Time Life Books, 1976.

Time Life Books. *Walls and Ceilings*. New York: Time Life Books, 1980.

FABRIC

There are perhaps more selections of style in fabric than any other component of interior design. A glimpse into the range of fabric colors and textures is seen in this selection from a line offered by F. Schumacher, Inc. Photo by Ted Spiegel.

Page 280, top left: *The design studio at Boris Kroll has been asked to modify a fabric for a contract. Samples to be color coordinated are found in the rug-in-hand's tuft. The three yarn samples at the left are coming out; three yarn samples in the center are to be added in their place. The three at the right will remain constant in the textile. Photo by Ted Spiegel.* **Page 280, top right:** *The "cartoon," or grid-sheet drawing, of the textile on the loom (also in the previous photo) where each square represents a single interlacing of warp with weft. The tufts of yarn that are used in this colorway of the loomed textile lay atop the cartoon. The vertical wires are heddles, which are threaded with individual warp yarns and are raised and lowered in different combinations to alter the interlacing of the weft or filler yarns, thus creating the pattern. Photo by Ted Spiegel.* **Page 280, bottom:** *A fabric designer at Boris Kroll Fabrics examining a Jacquard-woven Renaissance pattern as it is loomed. This damask, which would reveal opposite coloration on the reverse, has colored bands of warp yarns. The traditional pattern emerges through the insertion of filler yarns to create this trial piece. Here the designer is judging how various filler colors work with the warp, and which do not work. This judgment can only be made when it is on the loom, where the designer's pattern is proven, prior to mass production. Photo by Ted Spiegel.* **Page 281:** *Close-up of a Boris Kroll textile as it is being loomed. The warp, or lengthwise yarns, are at the top and are seen threaded through the comblike reed, or beater bar, that tamps down the weft, or filler yarns, as they are woven by the shuttle. The selvage is being trimmed on the side of the fabric. Displayed on the fabric are the colorways, or color combinations, available as stock fabric in this design. Boris Kroll produces fabrics for residential and contract work but focuses on nonresidential textiles. Photo by Ted Spiegel.*

Page 282, top: Interior designer Susan Thorn used harmonious, co-ordinated textiles from Waverly Fabrics to create this intimate, inviting guest room in the Red Lion Inn, a New England country inn. Patterns are based on Colonial motifs and hand-stitched appliqué quilt patterns. Colors are restful and fulfilling. Photo by G. Allsop, courtesy of Home Decorating and Remodeling. Page 282, bottom left: A close-up of one of the pillow ruffles. Photo by Ted Spiegel. Page 282, bottom right: Fabrics used in the guest room. Photo by Ted Spiegel. Page 283, top left: Inger McCabe Eilliot (right) of China Seas is assembling a new fabric collection with her designer Shannon Mulligan. Fabric companies, such as China Seas, offer coordinated florals, abstracts, geometrics, stripes, and solids in compatible textures, designs, and colors. These samples are then produced for use by interior designers in individual small and large swatches and in fabric books. Clients order through interior design firms, who in turn order textiles from the fabric houses, who do not sell directly to the public. Large "memo samples" measuring approximately one yard square may be borrowed by the designer to try out the textile where it will be installed and there it can be judged against the lighting and other materials and furnishings with which it is to be used. Photo by Ted Spiegel. Page 283, top right: Inspiration for new fabrics offered by fabric houses is always a challenge to textile designers. Here we see the evolution of a new textile inspired by this original museum quality hand-printed batik document that is over one hundred years old. Photo by Ted Spiegel. Page 283, second from top right: The artist's rendering with individual repeats for use by the Swiss cotton mill in the conversion process—dyeing and printing the textile as contracted with China Seas for a new fabric. Page 283, third from top right: The artist's rendering of the interior border from which the textile printers or converters will create their grid-sheet cartoons, mix their dyes, and use as a standard with which to match the finished textile. Photos by Ted Spiegel. Page 283, bottom right: The finished line, based on the document batik, emerges as Jardin Exotique, shown here with complimentary samples, and is ready for marketing. Photo by Ted Spiegel.

Page 284, top left: The introduction of new fabric lines takes place at most fabric houses twice each year, in the spring and in the fall. Here the Schumacher Company has utilized professional interior designers to create mock-up rooms, or vignettes, to acquaint the trade (designers) and the public alike with their newest textiles. Promotional materials advertised in design periodicals also keep the designer and interested clients abreast of new textile lines and new style trends by showing their textiles in use. Entire new lines are introduced to the trade and hence to the public about every six months. Previous fabrics that are not selling well are discontinued. The search for new designs is an unending one. Inspiration in this photo is a lighthearted Queen Anne floral. Photo courtesy of Schumacher. Page 284, top right: Elizabethan England inspires a flame-stitch pattern. Photo courtesy of Schumacher. Page 284, bottom left: The Rococo French Era provides a basis for fine design. Photo courtesy of Schumacher. Page 284, bottom right: The Art Deco lines and motifs from Radio City Music Hall in New York City form the basis for classic contemporary design. Photo courtesy of Schumacher.

The Fabric Industry

Fabrics for interior design travel an interesting road from their natural or compounded raw goods state to our homes and the places where we work or visit. The fibers discussed in this chapter are woven, knitted, or extruded into goods that need an average of six finishes to become marketable. During that time, the production has many different levels.

A horizontal operation is production at only one level. The company may only produce *greige* or *gray goods* (raw, woven, untreated fabric), for example, or it may only color or finish the fabric (called conversion). A vertical operation is one that does several steps in the production of textiles, perhaps weaving gray goods, finishing and coloring the fabric, and selling it to regional jobbers who then buy, sample, and distribute fabrics to designers and stores. A conglomerate is a very large corporation that does all or nearly all of the steps from obtaining raw materials to producing fibers and fabrics, coloring and finishing, sampling and marketing.[1]

While some fabrics stay on the market for several years, there is an amazing turnover in current fabrics. Every six months, new fabric lines are introduced to the interior design marketplace (the spring line and the fall line), reflecting current styles, trends, favored fibers, colors, and finishes. Design inspiration is sought the world over for design trends in color, pattern, and texture.

Fabrics obtained from interior designers are purchased through a jobber (who buys "job" or dye-lot yardage) who sells cut orders to the trade. In metropolitan locations, the designer may take a client to an open showroom where samples of the "lines" carried by a fabric company (or fabric house) are displayed. Showrooms that do not allow the client to accompany the designer are termed closed showrooms. These wholesale fabric companies may order fabrics from converters who display their wares at fabric shows such as the New York show, attended by wholesale companies from across America. Some companies will custom design fabrics so that only they will have those fabrics; this is termed exclusive design. Fabrics imported from abroad may also be contracted by a company to carry certain fabrics with exclusive rights. What all this means is a head-spinning array of fabrics, a continually evolving kaleidoscope of goods that are varied enough to meet any need and any situation.

Fabric — The Champion of Versatility

Fabric is indeed three-dimensional and versatile—a malleable element that can be used in more ways than any other material. Fabric softens the straight lines of the interior while complementing and establishing an interesting counterpoint to them. Fabric is used at the window as draperies and curtains, shades, top treatments, and trimmings. On furniture, fabric serves as upholstery, slipcovers, pillows, trimmings and throws (blankets or afghans). In the kitchen and bath, fabric "linens" dry and caress both us and our precious and everyday objects. Fabrics function as floor cloths and wall and ceiling treatments.

Because of its affordability and availability, fabric can be utilized in every room in the house. This is in itself a remarkable achievement of our civilized and modern society, for in past centuries, even nobility did not enjoy the quantity and easy care of luxurious fabrics that we take for granted today. Today we also have the ability to keep our

Figure 11.1

Figure 11.1 Evoking a luxury of the past, today's textiles, such as this bed linen ensemble of 100 percent cotton in Martex's Liberty of London, is easy care and can be affordably mixed and matched in many coordinating designs and solids. Photo courtesy of Cotton Incorporated.

fabrics clean, fresh, and appealing. We know how to extend the life span of fabrics as we respect their limitations and maintain them properly.

We are free to change or rotate our use of fabric—where and how it is used. If we so desire, we can change the interior design by rotating fabrics seasonally or by keeping up with current color and style trends that last only one to three years. We can replace fabrics as they wear out or as our life-styles change or our personality needs evolve.

We can choose durable and timelessly beautiful fabrics for the long "haul" fabrics that produce deep satisfaction; fabrics that will be just as appealing in ten or twenty years as the day we bring them home. In this sense, fabric can be like a trusted old friend— a familiar face each time we walk through the door.

As a versatile medium fabric may be used lavishly or sparingly. However it is to be applied, a valid area of concern is filling out work-order form completely and accurately for correct fabrication and installation. Since fabric and labor are so costly, it is crucial that interior designers be well trained to shoulder the responsibility of overseeing correct specification, fabrication, and installation.

The Human Touch

Fabric, more than any other tactile element in design, has the ability to humanize our interiors. Fabric can establish a feeling of quietude and seclusion as it absorbs the spoken word and the din of machinery and electronic equipment. Fabric can give a sense of personal space, since so often fabric is selected with personal preference as a prime criterion. As we return to fabric surroundings that are appealing and uplifting, fabrics that meet emotional or psychological needs, we are greeted with a sense of cordial hospitality— of welcome home. Seeing a familiar fabric, whether it is a handmade heirloom or a store-bought textile, gives us a sense of belonging, which is, in large measure, why we come home at all. Through the selection of colors, patterns, and textures, we not only can express the uniqueness of individual and collective family personality, but we can visually make statements about our philosophy of life and our interpretation of the beauty it has to offer. As we freely select our fabrics and how we want them used, we manifest to all who live in or visit our homes what values and life-styles we have chosen for ourselves.

In past centuries, smooth, elegant fabrics considered sensually appealing were the exclusive right of the wealthy. As fabrics became more readily available and as man-made fibers imitated fabrics of luxury inexpensively, the wealthy saw, to their dismay, that anyone could achieve a pseudo elegance. Those with money and taste have often turned to a new sensual pleasure of handwoven, unique, one-of-a-kind fabrics, rustic or refined—fabrics that are costly because of the complexity of the construction and finishing

Figure 11.2

Figure 11.3

processes or the relative obscurity of their source. Sometimes these types of textiles are brought back from travels to exotic ports of call or obtained through exclusive interior design firms to establish a look that (they hope) cannot be duplicated. In this way, fabric not only appeals to the senses, it even establishes identity and status.

Figure 11.2 The welcome-home quality of Colonial New England is enhanced with a printed textile that may become as familiar as an old friend. Warm apricot colors and richly colored woods suggest hospitality and stability. Photo courtesy of Laura Ashley.

Figure 11.3 Inviting down comforters and exquisite white bed linens beneath upholstered linen wall fabric, custom dyed in Italy in tender green from Glant Fabrics, provide a soothing bedroom in the home of author Barbara Taylor Bradford. Interior design by Jane Victor. Photo courtesy of International Linen Promotion Commission.

Figure 11.4

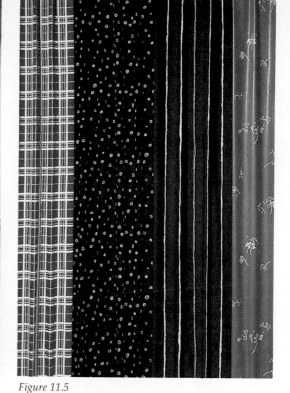

Figure 11.5

Fabric does appeal to the visual, tactile, and emotional senses; it can stimulate or excite, be dramatic or theatrical, even produce a sense of intrigue and fascination. Fabric can enliven and cheer us through light, bright, or pastel colors and patterns; it can draw us to the earth with coarse, ruggedly romantic textures, patterns, and colors; and fabric can lift us above earthly cares with soothing texture, neutralized color, and subtle pattern, thereby helping us cope with today's high-stress life-styles.

Fabric can establish seclusion and privacy. Fabric can shut out the world, lending the wonderful satisfaction of owning and controlling a space. In proxemics, this is known as "territoriality" (see chapter 8). Fabric can satisfy the deep human craving for indulgence in that which gives pleasure—warm, deep, aesthetic pleasure—which is what artistic design is all about.

Fabric Aesthetics

Often a fabric is preferred because of its beauty and emotional appeal, and this is as it should be, providing the fabric is also a durable and an appropriate selection. Three attributes—color, pattern, and texture—form the basis for personal choice. We can judge not only the appropriate use of the fabric through color, pattern, and texture but whether the fabric is in itself good design and whether fabrics brought into combination with other fabrics are tastefully and discriminately used.

Color

Color is the most emotional and personal of fabric's attributes. It is often finding just the right color in a fabric that clinches it as the selection for a particular use. Color preferences are often deep-rooted and should always be respected. Color affects the mental and physiological health and well-being of those who live with it. Certainly persons who suffer from depression—physiological or conditional—should not be forced to live around depressing, serious colors. The emotional effects could be disastrous. Rather, they will need warm and reassuring, lighthearted, or happy colors. On the other hand, a person in a high-stress life-style needs to be soothed and calmed with fabric color, not stimulated or further excited. (Refer also to the psychology of color, discussed in chapter 3.)

For most situations, there are guidelines in selecting color for fabric coordination that will give security to both the professional and the layperson when making fabric color decisions. These guidelines are listed in chart 11.1. Further information is found in chapter 3, Color.

Pattern

Pattern establishes the character and personality of a fabric. Pattern can firmly tie a fabric to a period—Victorian lace or Georgian Renaissance floral sprays or delicate Federal

Figure 11.4 An artistic expression of territoriality, this sumptuous draped bed clearly gives satisfaction of personal space to its owner. Richly colored white-on-deep blue toile provides a dramatic focal point in lush folds of patterned fabric. Interior design by Michael Zabriskie, McMillen, Inc. Textiles, furniture by and photo courtesy of Lee Jofa.

Figure 11.5 Fabric designer Leoda de Mar created extravagant, fresh colors with lighthearted motifs for Thibaut fabrics and wall coverings. Color is an important consideration in fabric selection because color evokes strong emotional response in interiors. Photo courtesy of Du Pont "Teflon" fabric and wall covering soil and stain repellent.

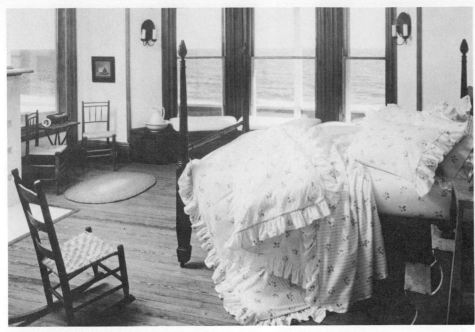

Figure 11.6

Figure 11.7

Chart 11.1 Fabric Color Coordination Guidelines

- Colors are typically either pure and clear or neutralized and dulled. Colors should be used together with other colors from the same families.
- Colors have warm or cool undertones, produced by mixing other colors into the dye. Cool colors can have warm or cool undertones, and warm colors can have warm or cool undertones. In complementary schemes, either the warm or the cool hue should dominate.
- Consider the color of the light and how it will affect the fabric colors. Always try out fabric combinations *in situ* to be certain they will really coordinate under lighting conditions in that room. It may become necessary to change the quality, type, and direction of the light to coordinate and enhance the fabric color scheme.
- Look carefully at the orientation and needs of the room and its inhabitants. Is it a cold, north room that needs cheerful colors, or is it a hot south or west exposure that cries for cooling hues?
- Vary intensity or brightness within the fabric color scheme. If all the fabrics are intense, the scheme may prove unlivable, and if all colors are dull, the scheme may prove uninteresting. The law of chromatic distribution has proven its validity over the centuries of interior design: "The largest areas are most neutralized, and as the area becomes smaller, the intensity or brightness increases proportionately." In other words, large areas are dull and neutralized (light, medium, or dark), and only small areas are really bright. In-between objects are in-between intensities.

Certainly this law can be broken and surprisingly wonderful color schemes can result when the designer is truly skilled and aims for a particular result.
- Be sensitive to value distribution. Light values above, medium around, and dark colors below have consistently proven pleasing. However, some schemes can be very successful as all light (high-key), all medium, or all dark (low-key) values. Some schemes even reverse the standard distribution to light below, dark above. High-value contrast (light next to dark) is stimulating and dramatic; low-value contrast (blended values) is soothing and pleasant.
- Consider what colored fabrics do to each other. Colors should enhance, support, and beautify one another, never compete or cause visual irritation.
- Avoid too many coordinated fabrics with exactly the same dyes in varying colors and patterns. Although these coordinated "designer fabrics" can be lovely, there is also pleasure derived from searching many sources and finding fabrics that do not perfectly match as much as they beautifully blend and complement. This approach takes effort and time but is inevitably worth the hunt.
- Fabric color schemes that are sensitively coordinated will feel natural and interesting, with an almost destinylike rightness. One should sense that these fabrics were somehow meant to be used together. It is, of course, the skill in the coordination that produces this effect.

stripes or broad, bold American Empire stripes. Period styles and their motifs or patterns look good together because they evolved around a cohesive spirit of the times where one social, political, or artistic/architectural thrust was paramount. This spirit or character must remain consistent in order for the patterns to coordinate and look right. Some guidelines for coordinating fabric patterns are included in chart 11.2.

Texture

To the touch and to the eye, fabrics are textural. From smooth and refined (satin, velvet, damask, brocade) to sturdy and coarse (tweed, matelassé, frieze, bouclé), fabric is aesthetically appealing because of textural relief. Relief is the way the surface reads—the peaks and valleys, highlights and shadows. This added third dimension gives depth and interest to fabric and accounts for much of its appeal. Guidelines to careful texture coordination of fabric are suggested in chart 11.3.

Figure 11.6 Selecting textiles takes into account the rightness of the pattern and style for the setting and such things as the direction and quantity of the light. Here, designer Eileen West's 100 percent cotton flannel sheets, Snow Cherries for J. P. Stevens' Utica brand, are at home in an informal Shaker-inspired bedroom with plenty of unobstructed light at the seashore. Photo courtesy of Cotton Incorporated.
Figure 11.7 Vibrant pattern designed by Jay Spectre for Ametex first appeared at the Southern Furniture Market on wicker seating by Century Furniture. The glowing, fresh color and vivid designs suggest both casual and exotic interiors. Photo courtesy of Du Pont "Teflon" fabric and wall covering soil and stain repellent.
Figure 11.8 A living area filled with patterned fabric used as draperies, upholstery, and pillows, this large-scale pattern graciously saturates this elegant interior. Occasional chairs employ small geometric patterns, and a plaid fabric on the round table

Figure 11.8

Chart 11.2 Guidelines to Coordinating Patterned Fabric

- Look to the source of the fabric, its period or inspiration. If it is an adaptation, does it still possess the integrity or spirit of the original period from whence it came? Look at the colors of the patterns as they relate to the source. For example, a delicate Federal or Neoclassic fabric in bright yellow or brilliant orange would be out of character with the pattern itself.
- The pattern itself should be handsome, well proportioned, and livable, whether or not it is authentic.
- When bringing together more than one pattern, vary the scale of the fabrics, for example, a large pattern with a small one.
- Add appropriate support patterns and textures, such as correctly scaled stripes and

geometrics with a floral pattern and, of course, plain textured fabrics.
- Consider the goals of the overall look of the interior. If, for example, the fabrics are to replicate the look of Country England, then several seemingly conflicting patterns of block-printed textiles will work because they are authentic. The seemingly haphazard appearance looks lived in, hence its strong appeal. If the look is American Country, then several small-scale calico-chintz or sateen fabrics will pull off the look well. If a formal look is desired, say, a Georgian or French room, then the patterns should not only support each other but they should support the ambience that is the end goal of the interior.

Figure 11.10

Chart 11.3 Guidelines for Coordinating Fabric Textures

- The character of textures used together must be compatible. For example, leather is not usually compatible with refined damask or brocade but is wonderful with matelassé or tweed. Lace is not in character with dramatic modern textures, but it beautifully complements moiré or velvet.
- Harmony is a key to good texture coordination. There must be a theme or ambience, a period or style, a look that holds together and relates all fabrics in a scheme. However, there must also be variety within unity, which is the accurate description of harmony. For example, in a formal setting there may be a velvet, a damask, a satin, a

sheer, a moiré, and other different textures of the same character. In a Country French provincial setting, we may see a heavy tapestry, a ticking, a toile de Jouy, a tweed, and a woven herringbone or plaid.
- The textures should be appropriate to their intended use. Fabrics as upholstery should feel comfortable. Wall fabrics should coordinate with the level of formality, and all appointments should be selected to be pleasing for their use. Refer to chart 11.6 for a comparison of fabric weights and applications or uses. Also refer to the decorative fabric glossary at the end of the chapter for definitions, weights, constructions, and finishes of fabrics by name.

Period furnishings proved their worth in the coordination of color, pattern, and texture. As we create contemporary fabric schemes, we can continually learn from the rightness of these schemes. Chart 11.4 categorizes major architectural periods and gives an overview of these periods as guidelines for sensitive coordination in adapting these beautiful styles from the past. These are periods that are copied and stylized today.

Figure 11.9

balances the floral print. Furniture and fabrics by and photo courtesy of Brunschwig & Fils.
Figure 11.9 A selection of textured fabrics chosen by interior designer Lynn Wilson for the presidential suite in the Ocala Hilton. Clockwise from the upper left: a gauze casement from

Henry Calvin Fabrics; Japanese Armour (linen-wool) woven pattern from Hinson & Co.; Derby, a diagonal print (linen-cotton), and Balantine, a bold houndstooth plaid, both from Missoni at Coraggio Design. Paper-backed textured woven wall coverings are from OJVM; and the

subtle striped high-sheen Gautier (linen-silk) is from Kirk-Brummel Associates.
Figure 11.10 An original textile wall hanging of subtly shaded cords highlighted with white creates a dramatic focal point in the Sara

Delano Roosevelt House, New York City. The background wall and chaise lounge are upholstered in the same textured fabric. Design by Mayo-Delucci Interiors; photo courtesy of Du Pont "Teflon" soil and stain repellent.

Chart 11.4 Period Fabrics—Color, Pattern, and Textures Overview

The Orient: Japan and China

Colors: Natural, dull, or neutralized punctuated with colors such as peony pink, chrysanthemum gold, jade green, Ming blue, Imperial red, and peacock blue.
Patterns: Japan—the cherry blossom branch, Mt. Fuji, ladies in headdresses and kimonos, Japanese architecture, birds, flowers, clouds, waves. China—complex fretwork; vertical, mystic mountains; bamboo and flora; birds; clouds; waves.
Textures: Smooth silks, brocades, damask, complex woven textiles; wild, nubby silk fabrics—pongee, shiki, shantung.

Italian Renaissance (c. 1450–1650)
Baroque (France: 1632–1750, England: 1650–1714)

Colors: Rich and vibrant reds, blues, golds predominantly.
Patterns: Large-scale florals, the artichoke, the pomegranate, the crown, classical urns.
Textures: Plain and figured velvet, tapestry, silk brocade, and damask.

French Rococo (1730–1760)
Country French (1730–1760)

Colors: In the court, colors were soft and feminine. Turquoise, rose, warm creamy yellow, pale sage green. In the provinces, the colors were deeper and more somber—royal blue, cranberry red, goldenrod yellow, rich avocado green, accents of black. Printed textiles sported light, lively florals.
Patterns: Shells were quite popular, along with ribbons, scrolls, love knots, country folk in country scenes, and Chinese chinoiserie motifs—pagodas, architecture, nature scenes, fretwork, and Chinese people in native dress.
Textures: In the court, fabrics were very refined and smooth. Taffeta, *chiffon*, damask, brocade, velvet, lampas, *batiste*. In the provinces, fabrics included tapestry, printed toile de Jouy, and floral fabrics, sturdy twill ticking, and woven tweeds such as houndstooth and herringbone.

Figure 11.11

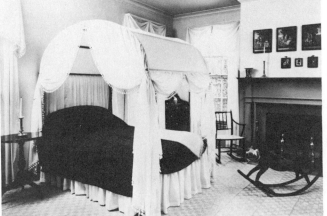

Figure 11.12

Figure 11.13

Figure 11.11 This French Provincial farmhouse has rough-hewn, exposed rafters and stucco set between. The textiles Country French interiors are compatible with rustic elements; printed or tapestry floral or paisley, plaid or stripe, they suggest durability as well as busy yet charming aesthetics combined to create the endearing Country French conviviality that accounts for its continuing popularity. Wall coverings and textiles by and photo courtesy of Raintree Designs, Inc.

Figure 11.12 High contrast is evident in this historic interior with light, tassel-fringed batiste at the window and bed drapery in the Neoclassic manner. Pastel colors and neutrals were commonly used throughout history, much of it from natural dyes. The dark, hand-quilted coverlet would become a treasured heirloom as years passed. Photo courtesy of Boscobel Restoration, Inc.
Figure 11.13 Sunnyside, overlooking the picturesque Hudson River Valley, was the home of literary celebrity Washington Irving. Textiles used at the window echo his eclectic taste.

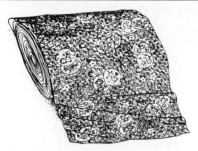

Figure 11.14 Oriental

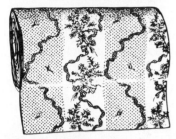

Figure 11.15 French Rococo

Figure 11.16 Country French

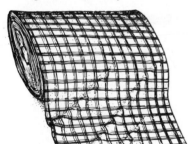

Figure 11.17 Colonial

Figure 11.18 Early Georgian

Early American Colonial (1650-1790)

Colors: Natural colors or neutrals (off-white, brown, gray) and colors that came from natural sources—madder or cranberry red, indigo blue, dull gold from birch leaves or other plants.

Patterns: When they were found, simple stripes and checks, stenciled or embroidered floral or folk patterns.

Textures: Homespun, muslin, flannel, broadcloth, burlap, ticking, hand-spun coarse textures.

American Early Georgian (1700-1750)

Colors: Williamsburg (dull, medium value) blue, green, or rose were predominant, influenced by the Renaissance. The colors at places such as Colonial Williamsburg and Mt. Vernon, Virginia, have undergone recent tests that reveal that these colors may have originally been more vibrant than what we see today.

Patterns: Authentic or adapted Renaissance floral sprays.

Textures: Woven damasks and brocades, velvets, and some plain or satin textures.

English Georgian (1714-1770)

American Late Georgian (1751-1750)

Colors: Baroque and Rococo influence. More vivid colors, red, gold, blue, and turquoise or teal, and rich coral sometimes lightened to soft peach.

Patterns: Renaissance patterns still in use and strong influence of Chinese and Rococo motifs. English garden *block-printed* patterns.

Figure 11.19 Late Georgian

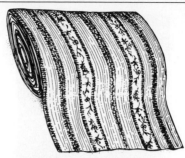

Figure 11.20 French Neoclassic

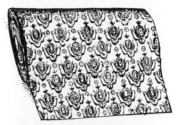

Figure 11.21 English Neoclassic

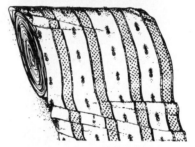

Figure 11.22 American Federal

Figure 11.23 French Empire

Figure 11.24 American Empire

Textures: Smooth silklike textures in damask and brocade, printed *cotton* fabrics from slightly coarse to very refined. Some velvets.

French Neoclassic (1760-1789)

English Neoclassic (1770-1820)

American Federal (1790-1820)

Colors: Pastel, light, creamy dull colors accented with white or a little rich color.

Patterns: Fine stripes, garlands, bows, ribbons, oval shapes, classic Greek and Roman urns and motifs, tiny florals; in America also the pineapple (symbol of hospitality).

Textures: Plain satin, refined damask and brocade, plain and antique taffeta, batiste, moiré, voile, chintz (crisp cotton textures).

French Empire (1789-1820)

American Empire (1820-1860)

Colors: French-inspired color schemes included rich vivid red, gold, deep green, brown, and royal purple. These were also used in America and were sometimes softened to pale mauve, spun honey, dull greens and browns, and dull gray-violet.

Patterns: Plain satin background with isolated small motifs such as the laurel wreath, the star or snowflake, honeybee, or classical urns; also the griffin, festooning, both broad and blended satin stripes.

Textures: Plain satin, antique taffeta and silk textures, various sheer and semisheer fabrics.

English Victorian (1837-1910)

American Victorian (1840-1920)

Colors: Called the mauve decades—many varieties of dull, somber reds. Also deeper values of green, blue, violet, and gold. Backgrounds were often off-white or black.

Continued on next page.

The Hepplewhite/Sheraton settee and side chair are upholstered in a restrained satin stripe from the earlier era, whereas the velvet daybed/chaise in the corner reflects Irving's travels throughout Moorish-influenced Spain. Photo by Ted Spiegel.

Chart 11.4 *Continued*

Patterns: Copied and adapted, stylized and combined from many sources including Gothic, Egyptian, Byzantine, Oriental, Neoclassic, Rococo, Renaissance, with plenty of large- and small-scale floral and lacy patterns.
Textures: Velvets of every description, woven *Jacquard* fabrics from very smooth to very heavy, cotton prints, lace, and heavy trimmings.

Figure 11.25 Victorian

Spanish Colonial/Southwest Indian Influence (1790-present)

Colors: Authentic Spanish colors are either dramatic and bold, red, gold, and black (all used sparingly as accents) or dull, sun-drenched, very livable colors. The dull pastel colors have influenced Western trends of recent years. The influence from Latin America gives accent colors of brilliant blue-green, chartreuse, vivid violet, and sunshine yellow.
Patterns: Geometric patterns, stripes.
Textures: Heavy, coarse matelassé, tweed, homespun textures, leather.

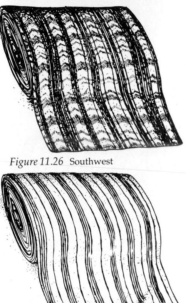

Figure 11.26 Southwest

Modern (1919-present)

Colors: Several color palettes have been evident during the twentieth century. Bright primary colors are one, natural neutrals are another. Dulled, neutralized colors and even psychedelic or vivid chroma colors have all been used, according to decades; now, modern trends are established every one to two years.
Patterns: Where pattern did exist, it has been abstract and stylized, often reflecting modern art and architectural grid systems. Some patterns were adapted from nature forms.

Figure 11 27 Modern

Textures: Texture is the hallmark of modern design. Leather, handwoven textures (authentic or machine produced), nubby semisheer and casement fabrics, geometric three-dimensional woven textures have all been very popular.

Fabric Weight and Application

Fabric may be categorized in two ways: by weight and by specific use or application. Following is a listing of four basic categories of weight and the common uses for fabrics that fall in each category. In the decorative fabrics glossary at the end of the chapter, each fabric is given a weight designation that can be cross-referenced to the information in chart 11.5.

Chart 11.5 Fabric Weight and Applications

Weight	Application and Use
Sheer, thin, very lightweight fabrics	Bed hangings, canopies, bed curtains, window curtains, sheer curtains/draperies, window semisheer casement and contract draperies, soft top treatments, thin table coverings, wall curtains
Lightweight fabrics	Accessory items and trimmings, casements, curtains, draperies, shades, top treatments, kitchen linens, lamp shades, supported bedspreads, table cloths
Medium-weight fabrics	Bedspreads, pillows and accessories, bath linens, slipcovers, supported upholstery, wall and partition upholstery, window treatments—draperies, heavier curtains, shades, stiff top treatments
Heavyweight fabrics	Bedspreads (tapestrylike), floor cloths, wall upholstery, wall hangings and tapestries, upholstery

Figure 11.28

Figure 11.29

Performance and Durability

Other important criteria for selecting residential fabrics include:

- Cost limitations, both initially and for upkeep. Some low-end fabrics as well as some costly fabrics may need more frequent cleaning, thereby costing more than is planned for in maintenance labor and money. Look at the fabric's ability to hide soil and still look great. Check the cleanability of the fabric based on fiber content, construction, and durability of finishes.

- The durability of the fabric. Some fabrics will wear out faster because of the fiber, the yarn, and the construction, necessitating replacement. Some fabrics will only wear out aesthetically, because the colors, patterns, and textures date too quickly or because of functional weaknesses such as *fuzzing* (tiny fibers working to the surface) or *pilling* (fibers working into balls or pills) or problems with fading or *crocking* (color rubbing off) or the lack of serviceability (cleanability).

Figure 11.28 Light- to medium-weight fabrics are ideal for draperies and curtains, bedspreads, tablecloths, pillows, furniture and wall upholstery, and slipcovers. Rose designs in pinks and greens highlight this fabric collection by Cyrus Clark Company. Photo courtesy of Du Pont "Teflon" soil and stain repellent.

Figure 11.29 Deep values and Victorian motifs are recreated in these needlepointlike tapestries by Brunschwig & Fils. Heavyweight fabrics are most often used as upholstery and are also suitable for rugs, wall hangings, and heavy bedspreads.
Figure 11.30 (A) Reconstituted and regenerated cellulosic, rayon and acetate, are man-made fibers that come from cotton linters, wood pulp, and chemicals. (B) Man-made synthetic fibers come from complex chemical formulas based on such ingredients as petroleum, air, coal, and natural gas. A generic name is granted by the Federal Trade Commission when the composition and resulting fiber are significantly different. The most widely used man-made fibers in interior design are rayon, acetate, nylon, acrylic, modacrylic, polyester, and olefin.

Fibers

A knowledge of fibers is essential to both interior designers and consumers. This is because fibers do vary in strength, dimensional stability, and a host of other criteria. When selecting fibers, a close look should be given to the level of expectation for the given installation. No one fiber can do everything and meet every need. For this reason, fibers may be blended, either in the viscose-solution stage (man-made fibers) or the raw-fiber stage (natural fibers), or threads may be spun together to make intimate blends, or two or more fibers can be used in fabrics, one as a base the other(s) as pile or as one direction of yarns (the warp or the weft). The reasons for blending fibers are threefold:

1. to extend a costly fiber with one that is less expensive,
2. to strengthen a weaker fiber with a stronger fiber, and
3. to give different characteristics such as bulk, texture, and different color reactions to one dye.

Fibers are of two general types: natural and man-made. *Natural fibers* come from two sources: cellulose and protein. *Cellulosic fibers* are derived from plants—from the fruit, such as cotton, or from plant leaves, stems, or stalks, called *bast fibers*, such as *linen* (from flax), *jute*, ramie (China grass or linen), sisal, coir (coconut), piña (pineapple), maize (corn), Oriental grasses, and other, less-common fibers.

Protein fibers come from animals (wool of sheep, hair of goats, camels, horse, rabbit, and other animals) and insects (silk from the silkworm caterpillar). *Sericulture* is the tedious process of producing silk under cultivation.

Man-made fiber also consists of two basic categories: *cellulosic* and *noncellulosic or synthetic*. *Rayon* and acetate come from cellulose—cotton linters or wood chips—to which various chemicals are added. Noncellulosic or synthetic fibers—*nylon*,

(A)
Figure 11.30

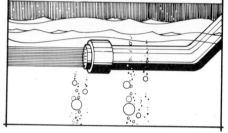
(B)

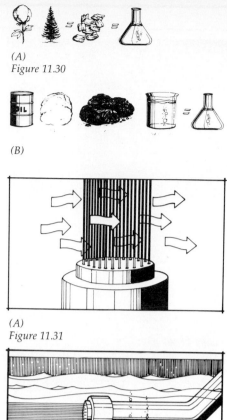
(A)
Figure 11.31

(B)

acrylic, *polyester, saran, olefin, vinyl,* and many others not frequently used in interior design—begin with organic compounds such as petroleum, natural gas, coal, air, and water. Man-made *generic* fibers are produced by hundreds of companies, over four hundred worldwide, who manufacture them for specific end uses. These companies issue trade names or trademarks to identify their fibers.

An independent fiber category is natural/mineral fibers that must be processed in ways similar to man-made fibers. These include asbestos, rubber, and metal.

All man-made fibers are formed in much the same way. The compound is made into liquid or viscose form, then forced through holes in a showerheadlike orifice called a *spin-*

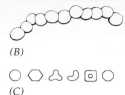
(A)
Figure 11.32

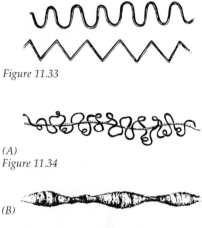
(B)

(C)

Figure 11.33

(A)
Figure 11.34

(B)

(C)

(D)

(E)

(F)

nerette. The size and shape of the openings can build in certain fiber characteristics. Variety in the yarns comes through *texturizing* the *filaments,* through types of yarn formations, and through the tension and direction of the yarn twists. In addition, generic fibers may be combined in the viscose stage, making blended fibers that can be engineered to meet specific needs.

Chart 11.6 lists the source of the major fibers on the market, their natural types or man-made *trademarks,* positive and negative characteristics, uses in residential and nonresidential settings, the care and cleaning of each fiber, its relative cost structure, and its flammability rating.

Figure 11.31 Close-ups of the extrusion process. The viscose solution of man-made fibers is forced through tiny, shaped holes into warm or cool air or into a solution where the syruplike strands solidify into continuous monofilaments, ready for spinning or texturizing.
Figure 11.32 (A) The Man-Made Fibers Industry logo showing polymer chips made from natural and chemical sources, the

spinnerette and monofilaments being extruded and spun into yarn. (B) The composition of a long chain polymer, the enlarged chain of molecules that make up man-made fibers. (C) Some of the shapes possible in extrusion of man-made fibers.
Figure 11.33 Texturizing the yarns if often done by crimping the yarn into curves or zigzags to offer bulk and resilience to the fabric.

Figure 11.34 Some specialty or novelty yarns that give texture to fabrics. (A) The bouclé yarn, a tightly curled yarn wrapped around a core yarn, often held on with a nearly invisible thread. (B) A slub yarn, thick and thin. Hand-spun slubs are uneven; machine-spun slub yarns are predictable. (C) A crepe yarn, so tightly twisted that it turns back on itself, producing a slightly

pebbled surface to the fabric. (D) A thick and thin yarn that has been abraded to imitate chenille. (E) A ratiné yarn that zigzags across a core. Bouclé and ratiné yarns are examples of complex yarns. (F) A true chenille yarn, woven with vertical spaces so that the weft yarns can be brushed and abraded to make a fuzzy yarn.

Chart 11.6 Fiber Comparison Chart

Natural Cellulosic Fibers

Cotton

Sources: Fruit of the cotton plant, a member of the mallow family. Needs extended sunlight and a long growing season.

(A)   (B)
Figure 11.35

Types: Short, long, and extra long, carded, combed, mercerized. Egyptian and Sea Island are the finest cotton fibers.

Positive Characteristics: Versatile, dyes and prints well; good *hand*, dimensionally stable; absorbent fiber.

Negative Characteristics: Wrinkles, fades, shrinks unless mercerized and preshrunk. Mildews if kept moist. Eventually rots from sunlight exposure. Low abrasion resistance.

Residential Uses: Draperies, walls, upholstery and padding, slipcovers, bed and bath linens, trimmings, accessories, rugs.

Nonresidential Uses: With a flame-resistant finish, used for draperies, upholstery, and accessory items.

Care and Cleaning: Washable or dry-cleanable. Washing removes more finishes, dry cleaning recommended. May require ironing. Remove spots with mild detergent.

Cost structure: Depending on grade, varies from low to moderately high.

Flammability: Burns readily; flammable. Must be chemically treated for flame resistance.

Linen

Source: Fibers within the stalks of the flax plant; a bast fiber. Grown well in moist, moderate climates such as Great Britain and the low European countries.

(A)   (B)
Figure 11.37

Types: Two linen (short *staple*), demiline, line linen (long staple). Ramie or China grass cloth is a bast fiber with some similarities to linen.

Positive Characteristics: Crisp, strong fiber. Appealing natural texture in tow linens. Dyes well, maintains good appearance. Absorbent. Line linens are smooth, lustrous. Durable.

Negative Characteristics: Brittle, stiff, inflexible; sun fades; short fibers have low abrasion resistance. Stains are difficult to remove. Permanently creases.

Residential Uses: Upholstery, slipcovers, drapery, semisheer casements, wall coverings, fine table linens (line linen), kitchen linens.

Nonresidential Uses: When treated for flame resistance, wall coverings, casement draperies, upholstery blends.

Care and Cleaning: Dry-clean. Table and kitchen linens may be washed in hot water and machine dried. Ironing is required for table linens.

Cost Structure: Depending on fiber length and finishes, medium to moderately high.

(A)
Figure 11.36

(B)

Flammability: Flammable, burns readily. Must be treated for flame retardance in nonresidential settings. Paper-backed, adhered linen wall coverings are inherently flame resistant, receiving a class *A* rating.

Jute

Sources: Fibers within the stalks of the jute plant; a bast fiber.

Types: Burlap, gunnysack cloth.

Positive Characteristics: Dyes bright colors, inexpensive, strong when dry.

Negative Characteristics: Will rot if kept damp; fades, brittle.

Residential Uses: Crafts, carpet backing, wall covering. Draperies and curtain blends.

Nonresidential Uses: Carpet backing.

Care and Cleaning: Hand wash, dry thoroughly. Dry cleaning recommended.

Cost Structure: Low.

Flammability: Burns readily; flammable.

Natural Protein Fibers

Wool

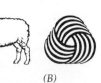

Sources: Wool of sheep; hair of goats and camels.

Types: Virgin— 100 percent new wool;

(A)   (B)
Figure 11.38

worsted—longer staple; woolen—short-, medium-staple fibers. Mohair: Angora goat hair.

Positive Characteristics: Great resiliency, dyes well, durable, flame resistant. Appealing hand. Dimensionally stable. High absorbency.

Negative Characteristics: Some wools are scratchy, and some people are allergic to wool. Susceptible to moths. No resistance to alkalis. Low tensile strength.

Residential Uses: Upholstery, draperies, casements; wall coverings. Broadloom carpets; area, designer, folk, and Oriental rugs, and carpets.

Nonresidential Uses: Upholstery; carpeting and rugs, (designer, folk, Oriental) wall upholstery accessory items, draperies.

Care and Cleaning: Dry-clean or by professional wet method.

Cost Structure: Moderately high to very high.

Flammability: Flame resistant; slow to ignite, self-extinguishes when flame is removed.

Silk

Source: Filament of domesticated or wild silkworm cocoons.

Types: Cultivated, reeled—Bombyx Mori produced by sericulture. Wild (raw)—off-white tussah silk with slubs from A. myllita and A. perny moth species.

(A)
Figure 11.39

(B)

(C)

(D)

(E)

Positive Characteristics: Lustrous, smooth to slubby, dry hand, excellent drapability. Strong when dry. Dimensionally stable. Resists organic acids. Not harmed by wetting.

Negative Characteristics: Subject to sunlight deterioration. Soil, moisture decomposition. Low resistance to alkalis. May be eaten by carpet beetles.

Figure 11.35 *(A)* The cotton plant, a member of the mallow family, needs long growing seasons and plenty of water to produce the cotton boll, or fluffy white fruit. *(B)* The Cotton Council and Cotton Incorporated logo. Cotton is a highly versatile designer fabric.

Figure 11.36 *(A)* Two 100 percent cotton textiles. Chevrons and Chinchester are two

English textiles of understated elegance and quiet sophistication. *(B)* La Vigne, a recalled medieval tapestry, woven in France, is available in 100 percent cotton. Photos courtesy of Kirk-Brummel Associates, Inc.

Figure 11.37 *(A)* The flax plant, grown mainly in the British Isles and lowland European countries, produces linen. *(B)* The logo of the International Linen Promotion Commission. Linen, the oldest of the fibers,

is crisp, absorbent, versatile, and highly regarded by interior designers.

Figure 11.38 *(A)* Wool, the product of domestic sheep, offers exceptional resilience, long wear, and warmth. *(B)* The Wool Mark, the symbol of pure wool textiles.

Figure 11.39 The life cycle of the Bombyx Mori moth. *(A)* The mature adult moth and *(B)* its eggs, carefully screened for disease,

then hatched into larvae and finally *(C)* silkworms (actually caterpillars), which *(D)* spin cocoons. The majority of cocoons in sericulture are subjected to heat to kill the moth before it escapes. *(E)* Some are allowed to escape so that the life cycle may be perpetrated. Silk is lustrous and costly and often called the queen of textiles.

Figure 11.40 *(A)* Two silk textiles from Gretchen Bellinger, Inc.: (top) Coppelia, a

(A)
Figure 11.40

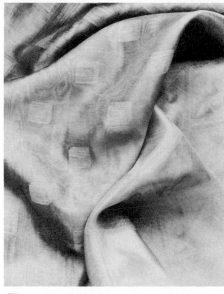

(B)

Figure 11.41

Residential Uses: Draperies (must be lined), trimmings, upholstery, wall hangings and coverings, fine Oriental rugs. Accessories—pillows, scrolls, embroidered art fabric.
Nonresidential Uses: Draperies, fine trimmings, luxury upholstery.
Care and Cleaning: Dry cleaning recommended. Some silks are washable.
Cost Structure: Moderately high to very high.
Flammability: Burns slowly. Self-extinguishes when flame is removed.

Leather

Source: Hides or skins, cattle, swine.
Types: Full, top grain, split leather. Sueded, buffed, embossed, glazed. Analine, pigment dyed.
Positive Characteristics: Extremely durable. Wears well and long. Resists fading, tearing, stretching, cracking.
Negative Characteristics: Quality varies according to hide, tanning, and company branding, marks, holes, tears.
Residential Uses: Upholstery, desk tops, book bindings. Rarely for floor tiles, wall coverings, and area rugs.
Nonresidential Uses: Upholstery, desk tops, book bindings. Executive situations—floor coverings and wall coverings.
Care and Cleaning: Mild soap and water; no saddle soap.
Cost Structure: High.
Flammability: Flame resistant/fire retardant. Emits no toxic fumes.

Man-Made Cellulosic Fiber
Rayon

Source: Regenerated cellulosic from wood chips and cotton linters.
Trade Names: *Avril, Coloray, Colorspun, Enkrome,* Jet-spun, *Zantrel, Bemberg, Rayon, Cordura, XL, Fibro,* Beau-Grip.
Positive Characteristics: Imitates silk in luster, *drapability*. Good solvent, insect resistance.
Negative Characteristics: Low abrasion resistance, susceptible to sun, moisture resistance; will mildew.
Residential Uses: Draperies (should be lined), trim, bedspreads, upholstery, slipcovers, scatter rugs.
Nonresidential Uses: Blends—(some) draperies and upholstery fabrics.
Care and Cleaning: Dry-clean.
Cost Structure: Low to medium.
Flammability: Flammable—ignites readily; melts before burning.

Acetate

Source: Reconstituted cellulosic, wood chips, cotton linters, and acetic acid.
Trade Names: Airloft, *Celanese, Chromespun, Estron,* Acele, *Celaperm, Lanese, Loftura.*
Positive Characteristics: Also a silklike sheen and hand. Stable fiber, low absorbency; good solvent resistance.
Negative Characteristics: Low abrasion resistance; susceptible to sunlight deteriora-

Continued on next page.

Figure 11.42

dupion plain weave custom woven in Italy, and (bottom) Isadora, a pleated silk custom woven in France. Photo courtesy of Gretchen Bellinger, Inc. *(B)* Hologram Square is a sheer composed of two layers of transparent gauze—one an all-silk organza, the other linen and silk, woven as a single cloth. The two layers interact visually to create a motif of squares. When played against the light, these shimmering, almost metallic, surfaces produce a dramatic moiré pattern. Designed by Mark C. Pollack, manufactured by Jack Lenor Larsen, the "Roscoe" Winner of the Seventeenth Annual Product Design Award in the Woven Fabric—Individual Product Entry. Photo courtesy of the Resources Council, Inc.
Figure 11.41 The Belvedere Seating Group, designed by Brian Kane and manufactured by Metropolitan Furniture Corporation, is shown upholstered in leather, with details such as welting and zippered gusset skirts that can be opened or closed. This group is at home in both formal and informal settings. Winner of the Contemporary Residential Seating Collections/Groups in the Seventeenth Annual Product Design Award. Photo courtesy of Resources Council, Inc.

Figure 11.42 Nylon is the fiber of choice in many nonresidential settings, both as carpeting and as upholstery. These nylon velvet sofa and chair coverings look and feel plush and exclusive but will be sturdy and easily maintained through the life of the interior design. Photo by John Wang.

Chart 11.6 *Continued*

tion. Poor resistance to acids. Mildew will discolor. Weakens with age.
Residential Uses: Bedspreads, draperies (should be lined), curtains, fiberfill, mattress ticking, *lining*, slipcovers, upholstery.
Nonresidential Uses: Blends—(some) draperies.
Care and Cleaning: Dry-clean. Some acetates are washable.
Cost Structure: Low to medium.
Flammability: Flammable—ignites readily; melts before burning.

Man-Made Noncellulosic/Synthetics

Nylon

Source: Amide linkages attached to two aramid rings.
Trade Names: Anso, Antron, *Cadon, Caprolan, Cumuloft, Nomex, Perlon, Quiana, Cantrese, Courtaulds, Cordura, Ultron, X-Static, Zefran, Zeflon.*
Positive Characteristics: Strong, stable, durable, resilient, versatile. Sheer to thick. Not affected by water, moisture, insects, microorganisms, aging. Resists alkalis, acids, solvents.
Negative Characteristics: Conducts static electricity; sheen, harsh hand; low sunlight resistance.
Residential Uses: Bedspreads, carpets, curtains, mattress pads, scatter rugs, slipcovers, upholstery, wall coverings.
Nonresidential Uses: Carpets, curtains, upholstery, wall coverings.
Care and Cleaning: Dry-clean or wet-clean.
Cost Structure: Low to medium.
Flammability: Some flame resistant; melts before burning; self-extinguishes when flame is removed.

Acrylic

Source: Over 85 percent acrylonitrile units, synthetic long-chain polymer.
Trade Names: Acrilan, *Bi-Loft, Creslan, Dolan, Dralon, Fina,* Leacril, *Orlon, Zefran.*
Positive Characteristics: Excellent resilience. Soft woollike texture, hand, and appearance; dyes well. Resists alkalis, acids, solvents, mildew, insects, and aging.
Negative Characteristics: Oleophilic—holds oil-borne stains; variable strength and stability; may fuzz and pill.
Residential Uses: Carpets, upholstery blends, curtains, draperies.
Nonresidential Uses: Carpets, wall coverings.
Care and Cleaning: Dry cleaning recommended.
Cost Structure: Low to medium.
Flammability: Flammable, melts, then burns slowly.

Modacrylic

Source: Between 35-85 percent acrylonitrile units, long-chain polymer.
Trade Names: Acrilan, *Dynel, Kanekalon, Elura, Sef, Verel.*
Positive Characteristics: Soft, buoyant, good hand, drapability, texture. Resists water, aging, insects, alkalis, acids.
Negative Characteristics: Restricted application, low abrasion resistance; heat sensitive; moderate strength.
Residential Uses: Casement draperies, fake fur blends, upholstery.
Nonresidential Uses: Casement curtains, draperies, walls.
Care and Cleaning: Dry cleaning recommended.

Cost Structure: Medium.
Flammability: Flame resistant; burns only with flame source; self-extinguishes when flame is removed.

Polyester

Source: Synthetic polymer ester of substituted aromatic carboxylic acid.
Trade Names: Alvin, *Blue C, Caprolan, Dacron, Encron, Fortrel, Hollofil, Kodel, Lanese, Quintess, Shantura, Spectran, Strialine, Tergal, Terylene, Textura, Trevira, Twistloc, Vycron, Zefran.*
Positive Characteristics: Resists sunlight fading and deterioration, mildew, insects, dimensionally stable, good strength. Soft hand, dyes well, resembles wool appearance. Water, heat, aging have no effect.
Negative Characteristics: Susceptible to abrasion, low resilience; oleophilic—holds oil-borne stains; pills.
Residential Applications: Sheer curtains, draperies, wall fabric, upholstery, slipcovers, carpets, awnings, fiberfill battings.
Nonresidential Applications: Curtains and draperies, wall fabric, upholstery.
Care and Cleaning: Wash or dry-clean.
Cost Structure: Low to medium.
Flammability: Flammable; will burn with flame source; self-extinguishes when flame is removed. Easily flame-retardant treated.

Olefin

Source: Long-chain polymer of ethylene, propylene, or other olefin units.
Trade Names: Durel, *Herculon, Marvess, Polybloom, Polypropylene, Vectra,* Patlon, *Fibralon.*
Positive Characteristics: Durable, economical, good resilience. Oily stains easily

---

Chart 11.7 Fabric Maintenance Guidelines

• Vacuum regularly upholstery and window treatments as well as floor textiles. This will prevent soil from becoming embedded into upholstery fabrics and prevent dust from combining with humidity and air impurities to become sticky grime on window coverings.
• Remove spots promptly with a dry-cleaning solution or very mild detergent or a weak water and vinegar solution, depending on the fiber and finish (1 teaspoon detergent per quart lukewarm water). Always blot the excess, lifting it out, rather than rubbing it in.

• Vacuuming and spotting can prevent the necessity of major cleaning. This is desirable for a number of reasons:

1. Repeated cleaning can weaken fibers.
2. Cleaning solutions can remove finishes and fade colors.
3. Repeated cleaning can take body out of fabric, causing it to hang limply or lose shape.
4. The cost of cleaning and time and effort are involved.

• When selecting professional cleaners, inquire as to method, and guarantee and seek personal recommendation for quality work.

Fabric Maintenance

Although chart 11.6 does list care and cleaning of fibers, there are some general guidelines available that make a difference in how long a fabric lasts and how handsome it remains over years of use. These are suggested in chart 11.7. The designer is not liable for the way a fabric is cared for once it is installed, but it is professional courtesy for the designer to recommend safe methods of fabric maintenance.

Fabric Construction

Fibers are made into fabric in a variety of ways; textiles may be woven or *nonwoven*, knitted or *needle constructed*, *layered* or *compounded*, and *extruded*.

Woven fabric, still the way that the majority of fabrics are made, is constructed on looms, which vary from simple hand-operated instruments to sophisticated, computer-controlled elaborate machinery. Weaving is the interlacing

removed with water and detergent. Resists acids, alkalis.
Negative Characteristics: Low melting point, susceptible to sunlight and heat deterioration; oily, rough texture.
Residential Uses: Awnings, carpets—face and backing, upholstery, floor mats.
Nonresidential Uses: Indoor-outdoor carpeting, upholstery, carpet backing, artificial turf.
Care and Cleaning: Dry-clean or wet-clean.
Cost Structure: Low to medium.
Flammability: Flammable; burns slowly. Melts and burns when flame is removed.

Saran

Source: Long-chain polymer vinylidene chloride.
Trade Names: Enjay, Saran.
Positive Characteristics: Resists sun damage. Moderate strength. Dimensionally stable. Not affected by water, aging, insects, microorganisms, acids.
Negative Characteristics: Plasticlike feel, nonabsorbent, heat sensitive. Colors may darken in sunlight.
Residential Uses: In blends for upholstery; webbing, outdoor upholstery, stretch upholstery.
Nonresidential uses: Curtain; some fabric blends.
Care and Cleaning: Wet- or dry-clean.
Cost Structure: Medium to high.
Flammability: Will not burn; fire retardant. Softens and scorches.

Spandex

Source: Segmented polyurethane.
Trade Names: Lycra, Spanzelle, Vyrene, Duraspan, Estane, Fulflex, Glospan, Interspan.
Positive Characteristics: Dyes readily. Exceptional strength and return. Good chemical, sunlight, moisture resistance.
Negative Characteristics: Low strength, but stretch increases tenacity.
Residential Uses: Stretch upholstery.
Nonresidential Uses: Stretch upholstery.
Care and Cleaning: Wash or dry-clean.
Cost Structure: Medium to high.
Flammability: Melts, self-extinguishes.

Vinyon/Vinyl

Source: Vinyl chloride, long-grain polymer.
Trade Names: Naugahyde, Valcren, Vinyon, PVC, Phovyl, Eibranyl, HH, Leayl, Teylron, Thermoyyl, *Cordelan.*
Positive Characteristics: Imitates leather; many colors/textures.
Negative Characteristics: Splits; holes difficult to repair.
Residential Uses: Artificial leather upholstery, wall coverings.
Nonresidential Uses: Artificial leather upholstery, wall coverings.
Care and Cleaning: Mild soap and water solvents for ink removal.
Cost Structure: Low to medium.
Flammability: Melts, self-extinguishes.

Mineral Synthetics

Latex

Source: Rubber.
Trade Name: Latex.
Positive Characteristics: Dimensionally stable.
Negative Characteristics: Not used as a face fabric.
Residential Uses: Coated lining to stabilize fabrics.
Nonresidential Uses: Fabric backing, coating.
Care and Cleaning: Wash or dry-clean.
Cost Structure: Medium.
Flammability: Melts before burning.

Fiberglass

Source: Glass.
Trade Names: Fiberglass, PPG, Beta.
Positive Characteristics: Dimensionally stable. Inherently fireproof. Strong. Resists chemicals, moisture, sunlight.
Negative Characteristics: Low resistance to alkalis. Abrasive touch, poor drapability.
Residential Uses: Insulation, bathtub enclosures.
Nonresidential Uses: Insulation, historically used for draperies.
Care and Cleaning: Wash or dry-clean.
Cost Structure: Medium.
Flammability: Flameproof.

Metallic

Source: Minerals.
Trade Name: Bekinox, Brunsmet, *Lurex, Mylar.*
Positive Characteristics: Adds glitter, shine. Most will not tarnish and are washable.
Negative Characteristics: Limited use.
Residential Uses: Threads in upholstery, drapery, slipcovers, trimmings.
Nonresidential Uses: Threads in upholstery, drapery, slipcovers, trimmings.
Care and Cleaning: Dry-clean, some may be washed. Usually plastic-coated.
Cost Structure: Medium to high.
Flammability: Flameproof.

(A)
Figure 11.43

(B)

Figure 11.43 (A) Linen yarns are wound on bobbins to be used to weave cloth. Yarns for fine or sheer linen fabrics are spun by a wet process, whereas fibers for heavier fabrics and wall coverings are spun dry. *(B)* Automatic looms are guided by people and computers to produce plain or fancy woven cloth, such as dobbies, jacquards, velvets, and herringbones, with great speed and accuracy. Photos courtesy of the International Linen Promotion Commission.

of lengthwise continuous *warp yarns* that are strung on the loom with crosswise *filling* or *weft yarns* to form a fabric. The order of interlacing determines the type of weave. There are five basic types of weaves accomplished on looms. These are *plain, twill, satin, Jacquard,* and *pile.* A fabric may be composed of a single weave, or variations of a single weave, or a *combination* of weaves.

The Plain Weave
The *plain, regular, tabby,* or *taffeta weave* is formed by interlacing yarns one over, one under (1/1) in regular sequence. Variety is introduced through different-sized yarns or by *cramming,* adding extra yarns in one direction, or by altering the weave itself.

Balanced weaves are equal, one over one, two over two (the *basket weave* variation), three over three. *Unbalanced* plain weaves vary the interlacing, such as this sequence 1/3, 2/4, 1/3. The *oxford weave* variation floats two fine warp threads over and under one heavier weft thread.

Another variation is the *leno* or *doup weave* in which the warp threads form an hourglass twist where they interlace the filling threads. The dobby attachment weaves in small geometric one-color figures, and the *lappet* and

(A)
Figure 11.44

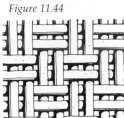

(B)

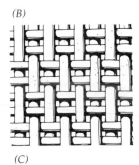

(C)

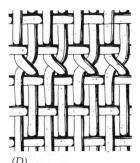

(D)

swivel attachments embroider isolated designs onto plain-weave fabrics. A host of fabrics are plain weaves, including chintz, broadcloth, ninon, batiste, and tweed, for example.

The Twill Weave
The warp-face twill weave is made of an interlacing pattern that floats one warp thread over two or three weft threads, then under one, called a weft tiedown. This order produces a diagonal *wale.* Steep wales are the result of floating over two, low-pitch wales float over three. A horizontal or weft-face twill floats weft threads over warp threads. Warp- and weft-face twills are *balanced twills. Unbalanced twills,* or *novelty twills,* are formed by reversing or altering the order

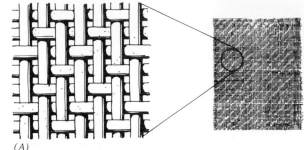

(A)
Figure 11.46

of interlacing, such as the herringbone (a zigzag *chevron* pattern) and the houndstooth (a four-pointed star, or a square with a tooth projecting from each side). Twills can be incorporated into complex Jacquard-woven patterns, as well. Duck and serge, as well as houndstooth and chevron, are twill fabrics.

(B)

Figure 11.45

Figure 11.47

Figure 11.44 The plain weave. *(A)* Warp and weft float over and under two in a balanced, equal weave. Chintz and broadcloth are two of the plain weave fabrics. *(B)* A balanced basket weave, here with two yarns under, two over. *(C)* Oxford weave, often used for printed cloth, floats one heavier warp thread over and under two thinner weft threads. *(D)* The leno or doup weave forms an hour glass twist where warp thread occasionally twist to create pattern and fabric texture, often used for casement fabrics.
Figure 11.45 The balanced plain weave interlaces one warp (lengthwise) yarn with one weft (crosswise) yarn as seen in Edinburgh plaid and Glasgow stripe Missoni fabrics by Coraggio Design. Photo courtesy of the International Linen Promotion Commission.
Figure 11.46 The twill weave. *(A)* A balanced twill, where both warp and weft are interlaced under and over two. Denim is a common example. *(B)* A steep angle is achieved when the warp-face twill floats over two, then ties down under one weft. The diagonal lines that result are called the wale. Calvary twill has a steep, crisp wale.
Figure 11.47 Close examination will reveal this Tartan plaid collection as examples of the twill weave, coordinated with Scotland Plain Weave in the upper corner. Photo courtesy of Brunschwig & Fils.

The Satin Weave

The *satin weave* floats one warp yarn over four or more weft yarns, then is tied down with one thread (4/1, 5/1, 6/1, 7/1, or 8/1). The order of interlacing is staggered so the result is a smooth face with no wales. Many satin-weave fabrics are woven in very fine threads that increase the luster of the cloth. Satin weaves are also used intensively in cotton decorator fabrics. Satin weaves that float weft or filler yarns on the face of the goods are termed *horizontal satins, satinets,* or *sateens.* In addition, satin weaves often form the background for damask and brocade.

The Jacquard Weave

Early in the eighteenth century, a Frenchman named Joseph Marie Jacquard invented a loom attachment that became known as the Jacquard loom. It resembled the early computers in that hole-punched cards were utilized strung in sequence high above the loom. As the wires carried each card into position above the loom, the holes would allow some of the threads to raise and would keep others in position. Thus, large, complex patterns were woven at a fraction of the cost of handwoven fabrics. This loom today takes a very long time to

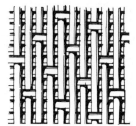

(A)
Figure 11.48

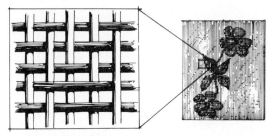

(B)

thread and set up, but once the loom is ready to operate, large runs of fabric can be produced at relatively little expense and time. Jacquard fabrics include matelassé damask, brocade, brocatelle, and figured velvets.

The Pile Weave

The *pile weave* inserts a supplementary warp or weft set of threads into the fabric as it is woven. The extra threads may be looped or cut pile. Examples are velvets, corduroys, and terry cloths.

Figure 11.50

Figure 11.49

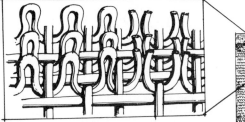

Figure 11.51

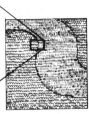

Figure 11.52

Figure 11.48 The satin weave. *(A)* Warp yarns float over a minimum of four yarns to create a smooth surface. Here the sequence is 7/1—over seven, then tie down under one. *(B)* Weft yarns that float over warp yarns make a sateen, satine, or horizontal satin.
Figure 11.49 Satin weave striped fabric sets a sumptuous tone for this selection of

passementerie, or trimmings, that include braid, cord, light and heavy fringes, and tassels. These luxurious examples represent the significance of trimmings in historic and formal textile applications. Photo courtesy of Brunschwig & Fils.
Figure 11.50 The Jacquard weave. A woven-in pattern made possible with the complex Jacquard loom. The loom is slow

and difficult to thread and set up but fast and economical to weave. Jacquards include brocade, damask, and matelassé.
Figure 11.51 The Jacquard loom produces complex woven designs such as this classic paisley pattern. Designs may be large or medium sized and may contain many colors. Although slow to thread, once the

Jacquard loom is set up it can produce thousands of yards of complicated patterns in a short amount of time. Photo courtesy of Brunschwig & Fils.
Figure 11.52 The pile weave showing the supplementary warp or weft yarn with both cut and uncut loops. Terry cloth is an example of an uncut pile, velvet is a cut pile.

Nonwoven Textiles

These are fiber mats or webs or extruded (flowed on, then solidified) textiles used for fabric backings or for upholstery, wall, and carpet padding.

Needle Constructions

An increasing number of fabrics today are needle constructed through the processes of knitting, *tufting*, and interlocking. *Knitted fabrics* comprise the majority in constructions such as single and double knits and rachel or warp knits for casement draperies. Arnache and malimo needle machines use multiple needles to chain stitch or interlock threads onto a cloth as it is formed. Lace is also a needle-constructed fabric.

Layered or Compounded Fabrics

As the name layered implies, this group of fabric constructions takes more than one production step to complete. Examples of *layered or compounded fabrics* include *embroidery: hand*, *crewel*, and *schiffli* (machine embroidery). Appliqué, the layering of additional fabrics by gluing and/or stitching, is also a compound cloth. Tufting is yet another example and is the method by which the vast majority of carpets are constructed today. Tufting punches yarns into a base fabric. In carpet, the tufted yarn is held in place with a layer of latex adhesive, then adhered to a secondary backing of jute or polypropylene. (See chapter 10.) Early American chenille bedspreads are another example of tufted fabrics.

Finishes

Finishing is the process of converting textiles from their raw or gray goods or greige state (dingy grey without pattern, color, or textural interest) into an identifiable fabric for interior design. *Finishes* can be broken into two main categories: *finishing* and *coloring*. Both of these processes take place at a variety of times. For example, the fabric may receive prefinishing steps,

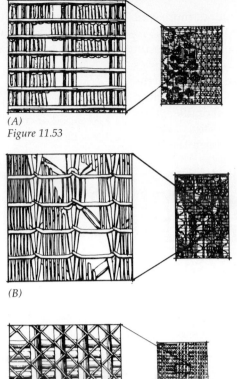

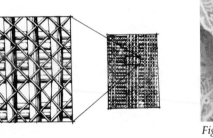

(A)

Figure 11.53

(B)

(C)

then be dyed, and further finished for aesthetics and/or durability. Or, the cloth may be dyed first, then treated with finishes later. Most fabric goes through an average of six different finishing steps or processes before it is ready to market.

Coloring

Coloring of fabric takes place in two general ways: by *dyeing* and by *printing*. There are certain terms that are used that will help us understand the materials and processes used in the coloring of fabric. These are presented in chart 11.8.

Prefinishes

Prefinishes are steps that prepare fabrics for coloring or other finishes. Natural and man-made fibers receive prefinishes in the unconverted or greige (gray goods) state. Prefinishes are listed in chart 11.9.

Figure 11.54

Figure 11.55

Figure 11.53 Needle-constructed fabrics include *(A)* lace construction, *(B)* malimo and arnache, where banks of yarns or nonwoven fibers are knitted in, and *(C)* Rachel knits, where chain stitches hold yarns together.

Figure 11.54 Needle constructions produce many textiles, such as tufted and knitted fabrics. Here the needles have yielded a large floral bouquet and finely detailed borders of this Scottish lace. Lace is particularly delightful to filter sunshine and contribute old-world charm. Photo courtesy of Lee Jofa.

Figure 11.55 Layered or compound textiles are the result of embroidery and appliqué detailing of fine linen napkins often seen in quality restaurants where attention to detail is prized. Photo courtesy of the International Linen Promotion Commission.

Chart 11.8 Fabric Dyeing and Printing

Dye: A water-soluble coloring matter that is mixed with water and chemicals to make a liquid solution or dye bath.

Pigment: A nonsoluble coloring agent that is held onto the surface of fabrics with resin binders. It looks more like paint, and white is typically printed as a pigment.

Stock dyeing: Dyeing natural fibers before they are spun into yarn.

Solution or dope dyeing: Adding *dyestuff* to the man-made fiber solution before extrusion.

Yarn dyeing: Dyeing the yarn by the skein, by the package, on a beam, or through space dyeing (different colors of the skein, package, or beam).

Piece dyeing: Dyeing a full length of woven fabric (45 to 150 yards long). Types of dyeing include beck, jig, padding, pressure jet, union dyeing, and cross dyeing.

Dye lot: When a new dye bath is constituted, several pieces are dyed at once. The new solution may vary slightly from previous batches of the same color, so may not to perfectly *match* other dye lots.

Affinity: The attraction of certain chemical compositions to certain fibers. Chemical affinities must be carefully matched.

Cross dyeing: Two fibers of different affinities dyed in the same bath, accepting the dye in different ways.

Hand printing: Techniques that print fabric through hand-only labor, including batik and tie-dye.

Batik: A hand-printing process where areas of the cloth not to be colored are covered with a specially prepared wax. The waxed cloth is immersed in a dye bath, then the wax is removed. Other layers of wax and differing colors of dye create interesting patterns.

Tie-dye: A hand-resist method of coloring where strings or knots are tied around or in the fabric that is dyed, and abstract patterns emerge.

Block printing: Carved wooden or linoleum blocks are inked, then stamped onto a cloth to create block prints. Large florals in many colors on fine cotton and linen fabrics are classically traditional English patterns, where block printing originated.

Silk-screen printing: A stencil technique using a thin fabric with a film painted or transferred. Ink is squeegeed across, penetrating where the film is absent. A new screen is needed for each color.

Figure 11.56

Flat bed screen printing: A semiautomated silk-screen process where the screens are automatically raised and lowered.

Rotary screen printing: A fully automatic silk-screen process where the screens are wrapped around circular drums that rotate the ink onto fabric that moves along beneath the rotary screens.

Roller printing: A mechanical printing method employing a large engraved metal cylinder, which is continuously inked as fabric moves around it.

Resist or reserve printing: A mechanized process where a pattern is printed with a chemical paste that resists the dye. The background is colored and the design is light and neutralized.

Discharge printing: Removes the dyed color in patterned areas and replaces it with another color.

Heat-transfer printing: Decals are dispersed-transferred from waxed paper to the cloth under heat and pressure.

Air-brush printing: Hand-operated mechanical pressure ink jet guns that spray dye over a stencil.

Etch or burn-out printing: Prints a design with a chemical that dissolves one of the two or more fibers in a fabric to leave some areas more sheer and the nonprinted areas more opaque. Typical is burning out cotton in a cotton-polyester semisheer.

Colorfast: Resistance to fading.

Chart 11.9 Prefinishes

- *Boiling or scouring* removes natural grease, gum pectin, or sizing.
- *Preshrinking* subjects fabrics to very hot water and dry heat to shrink the fabric before finishing.
- *Bleaching* whitens the gray goods or greige materials.
- *Mercerizing* subjects cotton or linen to caustic soda, increasing the fiber's ability to absorb dye, increasing luster, causing yarn to become rounder and more consistent, and making better body.
- *Singeing* burns out vegetable matter or short fibers.
- *Brushing* pulls out unwanted short fibers.
- *Stabilizing and heat setting* sets the weave; in polymer fabrics it sets in creases or pleats by heating the fabric to a high temperature where the fabric begins to melt then cooling it quickly, forcing the fabric to be permanently creased or pleated.
- *Durable finish* is a finish that will withstand repeated cleaning.
- *Nondurable* or *soluble finish* is a finish that will be removed with cleaning and will need to be reapplied.

Chart 11.10 Standard Finishes

- *Antibacterial, antiseptic,* or *bacteriostat finishes* inhibit the growth of mold, mildew, and rot—important in humid climates and where allergies are a factor or where a sterile environment is desirable.
- *Antistatic finishes* reduce static electricity or conduction.
- *Carefree finishes* provide wrinkle-resistance.
- *Flame-retardant finishes* inhibit the fabric's ability to burn and to spread fire (see also Nonresidential Considerations at the end of the chapter).
- *Insulative finishes* are a *foam* coating or layer applied to the back of fabrics to insulate against heat and cold.
- *Mothproofing* guards against destruction by insects.
- *Soil-release finishes* increase a fabric's ability to absorb water and thereby release soil through wet cleaning.
- *Soil-repellent* or *soil-resistant finishes* make soil removal easier.
- *Water-repellent finishes* protect against stain and humidity disintegration.

Figure 11.57

Standard Finishes

Standard finishes are also called *chemical, wet,* or *functional finishes.* Their purpose is to improve the performance of the fabric or its resistance to environmental factors. Standard finishes may be durable or nondurable. Many types are listed in chart 11.10.

Decorative Finishes

Decorative finishes also may be durable or nondurable. These are also termed *mechanical* or *surface treatment finishes* and may determine the decorative identity of the fabric. Decorative finishes include those listed in chart 11.11.

Figure 11.56 Roller and screen printing are the most common printing techniques, producing fabrics such as this Covington Fabrics Corporation Paper Roses collection inspired by eighteenth-century European fabric motifs. Photo courtesy of Du Pont Company.

Chart 11.11 Decorative Fabric Finishes

Figure 11.58

- *Calendering* flattens and shines the fabric through hot, heavy roller pressing.
- *Embossing* calenders with engraved rollers to produce a pressed-in pattern.
- *Moiré* is an embossed watermark pattern.
- *Friction calendering* produces a glazed surface.
- *Ciré calendering* produces a resin-wax gloss finish.
- *French wax calendering* produces a high-gloss ciré.
- *Palmer calendering* adds softness.
- *Schreiner calendering* embosses tiny lines for sheen.
- *Durable press calendering* resin pressing for durability and pattern impressions.
- *Flocking* adheres tiny fibers to the surface in patterns.
- *Napping* brushes up a nap or very short pile.
- *Etch* or *burn-out printing* prints a fabric with acid that burns out one fiber, usually cotton in a blend, to produce a sheer pattern.
- *Brightening finishes* add optical brighteners that reflect light.
- *Softening finishes* are chemical finishes that produce a softer hand or feel.
- *Delustering finishes* use chemicals that diffuse light, making a duller finish.
- *Stiffening finishes* apply starch and resin to add crispness to the surface.
- *Texture finishes* are chemical treatments that pucker or otherwise produce a surface texture.

Nonresidential Considerations

Fabrics installed in nonresidential buildings must meet minimum requirements for durability, colorfastness, and fire safety. These minimum acceptable standards are written as specifications by an architect or interior designer. The interior designer

Figure 11.59

Chart 11.12 Criteria for Written Specifications for Fabric

- *Cost:* Nonresidential installations typically have a strict budget, and all selected fabrics must stay within their allottment.
- *Durability:* The ability of a fabric to exist for a long time without significant deterioration. Durability includes:
  Abrasion resistance—The fabric's ability to withstand friction, rubbing, or grinding.
  Colorfastness—Resistance to both sun fading and fading from cleaning.
  Resistance to crocking—Crocking is the rubbing off of color onto another fabric or onto the skin.
  Strength or *tenacity*—The actual or physical strength of the fiber. The strength of a fabric is based also on the way the yarns are spun and plied, the closeness of the weave, and the thickness of the fabric.
- *Dimensional stability:* The ability of a fabric to maintain its original size and shape dimensions. This includes:
  Resistance to sagging—Elongation (or sagging) may occur in fabrics that absorb moisture (*hydrophilic* fibers) when humidity is high or the fabric is wet-cleaned.
  Resistance to hiking: Hiking up or shrinkage can occur when humidity drops or fabrics dry out. The lack of dimensional stability in hung fabrics through sagging and hiking is called the *yo-yo effect* and the bottom hem becomes quite uneven.
- *Resilience:* The fabric's ability to return to its original shape after stretching or elongation. In upholstered fabrics, dimensional stability also includes resilience, or the ability to bounce back to its original shape. Resilience is the result of two qualities:
  Flexibility—Stretching and rebounding.
  Strength or *tenacity*—A fabric lacking strength, which tears easily, is termed *tender.*
- *Resistance to static electricity:* An important consideration where static

electricity buildup may affect delicate instruments, such as computers, or where they may be a source of fire ignition.

- *Resistance to insects and microorganisms:* Necessary to prevent fabric disintegration and the spread of disease, particularly in hospitals and institutions.
- *Flame resistance:* Fibers in nonresidential settings must meet the rigid fire code.
  Flammable or *inflammable*—Fabrics that catch fire easily or are highly combustible, such as cotton, linen, rayon, and acetate.
  Flame resistant—Natural fibers that do not ignite easily and are slow-burning and will often self-extinguish. These are wool, silk.
  Fire-retardant—Man-made fibers that are flame resistant (not easily combustible, slow burning, may self-extinguish). These are modacrylic, saran, polyvinyl chloride, nomex, and novoloid. Fire-retardant fabrics may be flammable natural fibers (cotton, linen, rayon, and acetate) that have been given chemical finishes to inhibit their flammability. These treatments are termed *flame-retardant finishes.*
  Non-flammable or *flameproof*—Fibers which will melt but will not burn are asbestos, metal, and fiberglass.
- *Flame-retardant finishes:* These are, chemical applications that enhance a fabric's ability to withstand or resist combustion. Most flame retardants provide one of the following degrees of durability:
  Nondurable—A water-soluble compound that is removed with wet cleaning, requiring reapplication.
  Semi-durable—A compound that will resist wet-cleaning but not dry-cleaning solutions.
  Durable—Treatments that will withstand repeated dry cleaning and are permanent, lasting the lifetime of the fabric.[2]

then selects fabrics that meet the specifications or requirements listed in chart 11.12.

Contract Specifications Tests

Although countless tests can be performed on textiles, there are three general types of tests that are routinely performed on both fabrics and carpeting. These tests are for durability, colorfastness, and flammability and are discussed in chart 11.13.

Chart 11.13 Durability, Colorfastness, and Flammability

• Durability is tested in part by abrasion tests that rub the fabric back and forth or in circles. Abrasion tests yield numerical results that are guidelines for upholstery specifications.

• Colorfastness tests are conducted with instruments such as Fadeometers, which measure resistance to sunlight fading by simulating strong exposure from ten to two-hundred hours. Drapery fabric is generally tested for eighty hours. Colorfastness may also be tested by washing and dry cleaning and by subjecting the fabric to a gas fading chamber to test the colorfastness of fabrics that will be exposed to nitrogen oxides in heating or lighting gases.

• Flammability tests measure the rate of ignition of a textile, the rate of flame spread once the source of the fire is removed, how long the fabric continues to burn, whether or not it self-extinguishes, how long it remains in a red-glow state, and the density and toxicity of the fumes. Flammability-tested fabrics that meet stringent test requirements yield ratings useful for selecting textiles for nonresidential situations.[3]

Figure 11.60

Notes

1. Jackman, Dianne R., and Mary K. Dixon. *The Guide to Textiles for Interior Designers.* (Winnipeg, Peguis, 1983), pp. 13-14.
2. Reznikoff, S. C. *Specifications for Commercial Interiors: Professional Liabilities, Regulations, and Performance Criteria.* (New York: Whitney Library of Design, 1979), p. 154.
3. Jackman, Dianne R., and Mary K. Dixon. *The Guide to Textiles for Interior Designers.* (Winnipeg, Peguis, 1983), p. 126.

Decorative Fabrics Glossary

antique satin
A lightweight drapery fabric in a sateen or horizontal satin weave with slubs that imitate spun shantung silk. Most antique satins are one color, though the warp and weft yarns may be dyed different colors to produce iridescence; may also be printed. Suitable for bedspread fabric if quilted.

armure
Medium-weight fabric in one color with small woven repetitive dobby figures. Plain-weave ribbed background cloth.

arnache
Needle-constructed lightweight casement cloth. Weft threads are inserted just ahead of the multiple-needle lockstitch knitting.

batik
A lightweight to medium-weight hand-printed textile. Certain areas are waxed, then the fabric is dyed. For two or more colors, each preceding wax layer is removed, and wax is reapplied in a different pattern. A crinkled pattern is achieved by crumpling the fabric and cracking the wax. Primitive or ethnic batik patterns from Indonesia and Africa are reproduced by mechanical silk screen or roller printing.

batiste
A thin, semisheer curtain/drapery fabric.

bengaline
A medium-weight horizontal or weft-ribbed fabric produced with fine warp and plied or grouped filling yarns. Strong and refined cloth.

bird's-eye
A lightweight to medium-weight fabric with small dobby woven all-over diamond patterns in one color. Originally a toweling/linen fabric, cotton is used most often.

bouclé
Medium-weight to heavyweight knitted or woven cloth. Looped bouclè novelty yarns give a tightly curled, bumpy surface texture to the fabric.

bouclé marquisette
Fine leno-weave sheer marquisette with bouclé weft or filler yarns. Originally glass curtains of nylon; today of polyester and used as lightweight casement fabric.

broadcloth
Lightweight cotton plain taffeta weave with fine horizontal ribs. Yarn twist or tightness is slightly irregular. Also a finely napped twill weave wool in various weights.

brocade
Medium-weight formal Jacquard weave with supplemental warp or weft woven into the fabric to give an embroidered often colorful design. Background weave is often satin. Threads not tied down are carried as "floats" on the back of the fabric. Cut floats make *broche* brocade.

brocatelle
Medium-weight Jacquard fabric with slightly heavier and puffier surface than damask. Fine cloth with two sets of warps and wefts.

buchram, buckram, or crinoline
Lightweight fabric, in width three, four, or five inches, stiffened and used as drapery heading interfacing. Plain weave or non-woven web of cotton, linen, jute, or synthetic fiber.

burlap
Medium-weight jute fabric in plain, loose weave, also called *gunnysack cloth.* Coarse texture, solid colors. Natural and synthetic fibers imitate jute burlap.

burn-out
A method of printing designs into semisheer or lightweight casement cloths. Usually a cotton-polyester base fabric printed with an acid design that eats or dissolves the cotton. Edges around the burn-out area are often printed with pigment ink to seal edges. Also used to produce eyelet holes. Also called *etch-printing.*

calico
Lightweight cotton or cotton/polyester fabric similar to broadcloth. Usually printed in small country-style all-over multicolored floral patterns.

cambric
Semisheer to lightweight plain weave cotton or linen fabric, often printed. May be finished dull and soft or stiff with a sheen. Also called *handkerchief linen.*

canvas
Versatile medium-weight to heavyweight cotton fabric in plain or twill weave. May be dyed any color and has many uses such as upholstery, shades, and awnings.

casement
Lightweight to medium-weight casual drapery fabric. Plain or combination weave or needle-constructed fabric. Interesting texture, color, and pattern through dyed novelty yarns and weave variations. May be semisheer, translucent, or opaque.

chambray
Lightweight cotton or blend fabric in plain, balanced weave. Yarns are slightly slubbed in both directions. Usually white warp and colored weft or filling.

chenille
Medium-weight to heavyweight fabric with chenille yarns that are fuzzy and resemble soft pipe cleaners. Velour textures are common.

chevron
Regular and repeated zigzag pattern, also called *herringbone,* formed by reversing the twill weave. Fabric is of natural and/or synthetic fibers. Medium weight to heavy-weight.

chiffon
Sheer, very lightweight ninon or voile drapery fabric. Also a soft finish given to a fabric, such as *chiffon velvet.*

chintz
Lightweight fine cotton or cotton/polyester plain weave fabric. Solid colors or floral or exotic prints. Most often sized or glazed, hence, *glazed chintz.* It is a multipurpose fabric.

corduroy
Medium-weight to heavyweight pile weave cotton or cotton blend fabric. Lengthwise cords or wales are named according to width:
   pinwale corduroy Narrow wales.
   wide wale corduroy Large wales.

crepe
A fine yarn that is twisted so tightly that it gives a pebbly or crinkled surface in woven fabrics. Crepe may be plain or satin weave and includes the following types:
   canton crepe Heavy fabric with ribs.
   chiffon crepe Soft finish thin crepe
   crepe-de-chine Sheer, very thin, limp crepe.
   crepon crepe Heavy crosswise ribs.
   faille crepe Fine horizontal ribs.
   flat crepe Smooth, fine surface.
   plissé crepe Puckered or crinkled surface.

cretonne
Medium-weight unglazed printed cotton fabric slightly heavier than chintz. Versatile decorative fabric similar to toile.

crewel embroidery
Medium-weight compound fabric. Base cloth is basket weave of cotton, linen, or wool, with hand or machine embroidery of worsted wool. Patterns are meandering vine and floral motifs based on English interpretations of the Eastern Indian tree-of-life motifs.

crinoline
Same as buchram.

damask
Medium-weight Jacquard fabric with reversible pattern, historically a large floral or Renaissance design. Contemporary damasks are medium weight in a variety of designs; multiple-use fabric.

denim
Medium-weight sturdy twill cotton or cotton/polyester cloth. Navy colored denim is *jeans fabric,* cream or white denim is *drill.*

dimity
Thin, very lightweight semisheer fabric in plain weave with a crisp finish. Vertical warp spaced ribs or cords are formed with heavier or piled threads. Checks may also be woven in. One color or contrasting thread may form the ribs, cords, or checks.

dotted swiss
Plain or leno weave *swiss:* sheer curtain fabric, within tiny embroidered or flocked dots or squares in spaced sequence.

double cloth
Same as matelassé.

duck
Durable medium-weight cotton fabric in oxford weave similar to canvas. Different-sized weft threads and the addition of colored stripes may vary the appearance.

embroidery
A thread or set of threads sewn onto a fabric for surface ornamentation. Types include:
   piece work Embroidery done by hand.
   crewel embroidery Tree-of-life motifs originating in India done by hand-guided machine using a looped crewel stitch.
   schiffli embroidery Decorative machine embroidery for mass production.

eyelet
Lightweight cotton, cotton/polyester, or other blend, plain weave fabric with schiffli-embroidered designs and small burn-out or etched dots that are part of the design. The fabric is usually a solid white, cream, or pastel color with matching or accenting embroidery. Also comes in smaller widths, usually five, seven, eleven, and fourteen inches, which are scalloped borders.

faille
A lightweight, finely woven fabric generally of cotton, silk, acetate, or rayon, or blends, with horizontal or weft ribs that are slightly heavier and flatter than taffeta. When these ribs are pressed or calendered in a water-mark design, faille becomes *moiré.*

felt
A nonwoven fabric made of wool and perhaps hair and cotton fibers compressed with moisture, heat, and agitation. Felt comes in many weights, from craft felts to heavy hat and interlining felts.

fisheye
A medium-weight piqué of dobby-weave cloth with an all-over diamond pattern. Larger diamond motifs are called *gooseye.*

flamestitch
A pattern originally from the Early English Renaissance that represents the flames of a fire and is loosely a chevron design.

Flamestitch patterns are multicolored and may be embroidered, woven, or printed on various weight cloths.

flannel
Any fabric that is woven then brushed to achieve a soft nap. Types include:
cotton flannel, flannelette Lightweight, thin fabric used for flannel sheets.
outing flannel Medium weight, suitable for upholstery; pilling may be a problem.
french flannel Fine plain weave flannel.
melton flannel Heavyweight cotton and/or wool dense plain weave. Used for interlining and stiffening as a support fabric.
suede flannel Two-sided nap, trimmed and pressed.

foam back
Loose adjective for a latex or other synthetic coating laminated, flowed, or sprayed onto the back of drapery and upholstery fabrics to increase energy efficiency and/or dimensional stability.

frieze or frisé
Heavyweight, sturdy nylon upholstery fabric with a looped pile. May be a Jacquard weave to achieve a sculptural or ribbed effect.
grospoint Frieze in even or staggered rows with large loops. May also be Jacquard woven.
petit point Very small loops; resembles fine hand needlepoint.

gabardine
Steep-pitched twill fabric woven or natural of synthetic yarns; lightweight to medium weight. Surface has obvious diagonal ribs that are tightly woven of fine, lustrous yarns.

gauze
Very thin, sheer or semisheer, loosely woven fabric used for curtains and draperies.

gimp
Narrow braid trimming in many designs for drapery and upholstery. Also term for metallic cording.

grenadine
Thin, sheer leno weave curtain fabric. May be flocked or swivel lappet embroidered with small dots or designs.

grosgrain
Narrow trimming ribbon or textile with round, even, heavy ribs in the weft or horizontal direction.

herringbone
Originally a medium-weight wool fabric. Pattern is a novelty or complex twill that is a regular zigzag pattern. Named after the spinal structure of the herring fish. May also be woven or printed on lightweight, medium-weight and heavyweight fabrics and in a variety of natural or man-made fibers.

homespun
Coarse, lightweight wool, linen, or cotton fabric from Early American hand spun and handwoven plain weave textiles. Today in nearly any fiber, a textile that imitates this look. May be natural colors with flecks or vegetable matter. May also be simple stripes or checks.

hopsaking
Similar to plain homespun yet less sturdy. Usually woven in a loose, semiopen basket weave and given a soft finish. Lightweight casement fabric.

houndstooth
Medium-weight to heavyweight fabric with woven twill pattern in contrasting color that resembles squares with projecting toothlike corners called four-pointed twill stars. Originally a coarse provincial wool fabric, now in a variety of fibers and may be woven in finer yarns.

interfacing
A lightweight, stiffened woven or nonwoven fabric that is usually placed between a decorative and a lining fabric to give body and firmness. White or solid colors.

interlining
A thick, lofty woven or nonwoven textile of natural or synthetic fibers used to insulate against noise or heat and/or cold. May be a polyester batt or lambs' wool batt, for example.

Jacquard
Any textile woven on the Jacquard loom, which permits large designs to be machine woven (see Weaving). Used for both cloth and carpeting, Jacquard fabrics are brocade, brocatelle, matelassé, lampas, tapestry, and moquette velvet.

jersey
Single vertical knit fabric that includes tricot and some stretch knits. Fabric is usually lightweight, though some upholstery stretch jersey fabrics are medium weight.

khaki
Multipurpose twill or plain weave fabric of a greenish, dusty, earthy beige. Lightweight to medium-weight cotton or blend fibers.

knit
Knit fabrics are produced on multiple needle knitting machines and include:
rachel, raschel knit Warp knit casement fabrics.
single or jersey Lightweight knit with weft ribs used for fabrics such as tricot.
double knit Heavier knit textiles.
stretch knits Elastomeric threads for stretch upholstery.
knit terry cloth Knit toweling.

lace
A lightweight machine or handmade, needle-constructed fabric of natural or synthetic yarns. Open, floral, or geometric patterns sometimes on a net background, lace is typically used for curtains, draperies, and table settings. Geometric lace for contract settings are sometimes termed architectural lace.

lampas
Medium-weight Jacquard fabric with a plain or satin background and figures of contrasting colors in both the warp and weft direction in ribbed, plain, or twill weave.

lappet
Swivel or discontinuous (no floats carried on back) embroidery accomplished with an attachment to the plain or dobby loom.

lawn
Fine, thin fabric that is the base cloth for batiste, organdy, and printed sheer fabrics. Usually cotton, linen, rayon, or blends.

leno
Also called *doup*, a variation of the plain weave where pairs of warp threads are twisted in hourglass fashion as they interlock weft threads to give strength and texture. Used in thin, very lightweight, marquisette sheers as well as lightweight casement fabrics.

lining
A lightweight support fabric in plain or sateen weave in cotton or synthetic fibers or blends that are sewn onto or used as separate backing for the decorative fabrics.

malimo
Casement, contemporary fabric where groups of weft yarns are chain stitched together in clear monofilament thread with multiple needles. Groups of warp threads may also be laid and stitched into the top of the weft groups.

marquisette
A thin, sheer curtain or drapery cloth of natural or synthetic fibers in a leno or doup weave. Slightly heavier than ninon or grenadine.

matelassé
A heavyweight textile in Jacquard weave of two sets of warps and wefts. Background surface appears puffy or cushioned since the sets of threads are woven together only where the pattern is. Also called *double cloth* or *pocket weave*.

moiré
Lightweight to medium-weight faille fabric embossed with a watermark moirè pattern. A versatile fabric.

muslin
Thin cotton cloth of a plain balanced weave similar to lawn, but stiffer. Muslin forms the base for several cotton fabrics. May be natural (bleached or unbleached), dyed, or printed. Also lower thread-count bed sheets.

mylar
Trade name of the DuPont Corporation for a clear or metallized extruded material. Used in flat sheets such as reflective wallpaper backgrounds or cut into ribbons, texturized, and woven to achieve a novelty-textured fabric.

needlepoint
Heavy upholstery-weight textile of tight hand-stitched wool yarn on art canvas net.
petit point Finer needlepoint, very tiny stitches.
grospoint Coarser, larger embroidered stitches.

net
Historically made by hand as a base for lace, now a machine, needle, and open construction, thin textile with a background of square, diamond, hexagonal, or irregularly shaped mesh.

ninon
Very fine sheer drapery and curtain fabric in pair *warp thread plain weave variation.* Usually of polyester in varying widths up to 118 inches seamless. It has excellent drapability, crisp body, and a lustrous appearance. Sometimes called *French voile, triple voile,* or *tergal voile.*

organdy
Plain weave sheer curtain and drapery cloth of natural or synthetic fibers (originally cotton), which is given a stiff, very crisp finish. A semisheer organdy is called *semiorgandy.*

ottoman
Natural or man-made fibers woven medium to heavy in a fabric with broad, round weft threads that produce a horizontal rib. Fine warp threads cover completely the large-, even-, or alternate-sized filling yarns.

oxford cloth
A lightweight cotton or cotton/polyester fabric in an oxford variation of the plain weave: pairs of warp threads are grouped together and carried over and under a heavier filling yarn. Often used as a base cloth for decorative prints and may be woven with slightly heavier yarns to produce a medium-weight fabric. Oxford cloth is traditionally a finely woven shirting cloth.

paisley
A pattern printed onto natural or synthetic, lightweight or medium-weight fabrics. The curved pear, leaf, or water drop shape originated in India but is named for a city in Scotland where woolen paisley shawls have been produced for centuries.

pellon
Stiffening interfacing fabric that is a trademark of the Pellon Corporation.

percale
Lightweight plain weave cotton or cotton/polyester fabric in a fine yarn and high thread count. Finely woven bed sheets are generally percale. Percale is finished to a variety of lusters from soft to stiff, or given a textured plissé finish.

pile fabric
Medium- to heavyweight fabric with an extra set of warp or weft threads that are woven or knitted into the fabric to produce a deep surface texture. Examples include velvets, terry cloths, friezes, and corduroys.

piqué
Lightweight to medium-weight versatile cloth in a plain weave variation, which inserts raised cords, stripes, or geometric patterns. The rib or cord usually runs lengthwise in the face of the goods. Types included:
   birds'-eye Lightweight diaper cloth, small geometric three-dimensional weave.
   goose-eye Larger bird's-eye with diamond-shape pattern in relief, lightweight.
   dimity Thin, semisheer fabric with lengthwise ribs of heavier threads.
   ribcord or pinwale Medium-weight fabric with lengthwise ribs often used for bedspreads and draperies.

   embossed piqué Design pressed or calendered into face of fabric.
   waffle piqué Three-dimensional square patterns.

plaid
Lightweight, medium-weight, or heavy-weight yarn dyed, woven, or printed design consisting of stripes in both warp and weft directions that cross at intervals to form different colors in square or rectangular patterns. Plaids may be plain or twill weave. Variations include:
   tartans Scottish clan plaids.
   plaidback Reversible plaid.

plissé
A sheer, thin, or lightweight fabric given a blistered or puckered surface through chemical treatments.

polished cotton
Lightweight to medium-weight plain or sateen weave cotton fabric with smooth, lustrous yarns. Sateen weave is also called *glosheen. Unglazed chintz* may be classified as polished cotton.

poplin
Lightweight to medium-weight fabric with pronounced horizontal ribs. Weft threads are heavier than warp. Often a base cloth for many decorative print fabrics.

quilted fabric
Any fabric that is lined and usually interlined with a lofty batt, then hand or machine stitched through so that stitches show both front and back. Pinsonic quilting is often used for mass-produced bedspreads, where layers are fused together with ultrasound heat in a predetermined pattern.

rachel, raschel knit
Also called warp-knit casements, a light-weight drapery fabric where knitted warps form the body of the fabric.

rep, repp
A horizontally or vertically ribbed fabric in plain weave with heavier threads in one direction. Durable medium to heavy fabric with many applications. High-quality reps are often of wool.

sailcloth
Same as duck, sometimes heavier.

sateen
A horizontal satin fabric in lightweight to medium-weight. Used for linings and printed decorator fabric in natural or man-made fibers.

satin
A basic type of weave where warp threads float over four to eight weft threads, then are interlaced or tied down with one weft thread. Fine thread yields a smooth, lustrous surface. Lightweight to medium-weight. Types include:
   antique satin Horizontal slubs to imitate silk shantung.
   lining satin Lightweight drapery lining fabric.
   ribbed satin Resembles faille or calendered into satin moiré.

   satin damask Background satin with Jacquard pattern—lighter weight known as ticking satin.
   upholstery satin Heavier weight satins, may be the base cloth for Jacquard weaves.

schiffli
Any fabric with machine-embroidered designs, other than dotted swiss, eyelet, and swivel or lappet embroidery. Threads may be one color or variegated. Embroidered on fabric from very sheer to very heavyweight and in simple to complex patterns.

scrim
Very thin plain weave cloth with loose construction. Types include:
   theater scrim Sheer, curtain-weight, softer, more drapable.
   upholstery scrim Woven or nonwoven web dust cover fabric for the bottom of upholstered pieces.

seersucker
Lightweight to medium-weight cotton or cotton blend plain weave fabric. Crinkled or puckered surface usually in spaced stripes or plaids, permanently woven. Occasionally induced through chemicals that produce more permanent puckers than plissé.

serge
Lightweight to medium-weight fabric in natural or synthetic fibers (originally silk) in durable, crisply finished twill weave.

shade cloth
Plain or plain weave variation, such as canvas, poplin, or oxford. Medium weight to lightweight, it is stiffened to become roller shade fabric. Also called *holland cloth.*

shantung
Originally a spun silk fabric with slubs that formed interesting and exotic textures. Shantung today may be of natural or synthetic fibers. Fabrics that imitate shantung are *antique satin* (sateen weave rayon/acetate) and antique taffeta (plain weave). Shantung is a lightweight fabric.

sheer
A translucent or transparent thin, very lightweight curtain or drapery fabric. Examples include ninon, chiffon, grenadine, marquisette, swiss, and voile.

strié
Also called *jaspé,* meaning shadow stripes, a sateen or satin weave with colored warp threads that produce a finely blended vertical stripe. Lightweight to medium weight, multipurpose fabric in natural or synthetic fibers or blends.

suedecloth
A lightweight to medium-weight synthetic knit or woven textile with brushed nap that imitates genuine suede.

swiss
A very thin, semisheer curtain fabric of plain weave. It is a crisply finished fabric and may be embellished with woven or flocked dots or figures. Originally of cotton, today it is often polyester. Also called *swiss muslin.*

taffeta
A plain, balanced weave in lightweight fabric of natural or man-made fibers. Weft threads are slightly larger, creating a fine horizontal rib. Types include:
  moire taffeta Calendered as moiré—pressed ribs make the classic water mark pattern.
  faille taffeta Heavier ribbed taffeta.
  antique taffeta Horizontal slubs, a reversible fabric.
  paper taffeta Very crisp finish, often woven in plaid patterns.

tapestry
A plain weave technique used to produce heavy, complex, handwoven European pictorial tapestries. These are now most often Jacquard weave fabrics with multiple warps and wefts and are very heavy fabric. Tapestry techniques are also used for handmade flat, reversible folk rugs and further apply to a large category of fabric and nonfabric wall hangings or textiles. Tufted wall hangings may also be referred to as tapestries.

terry
Medium-weight pile weave used for absorbent cotton terry cloth toweling. Loops may be cut for a plush or velour surface texture or left uncut as loops.

ticking
Originally a twill navy blue and cream vertically woven striped fabric used to make ticks (mattress and pillow casings). Today a woven or printed stripe, in one color on cream or white. Multi-use fabric. Mattress ticking may also be a satin damask fabric, called *damask ticking* or *ticking damask.*

toile
A fabric of cotton or linen similar to muslin or percale in plain or sometimes twill weave. It is similar to a heavier unglazed chintz. Toiles are typically roller or screen printed in one color: navy, cranberry, or black on a cream background. Types include:
  toile de Jouy eighteenth- and nineteenth-century rural scenes and people; originating in Jouy, France.
  federal toile American federal buildings and eagles.
  country toile Contemporary provincial floral patterns.

tricot
Nylon jersey knit that has a weft-only stretch. Lightweight, limp fabric.

tufted fabric
A pile fabric that is formed by tufting a yarn into a woven background. Early American tufted bedspreads are one example. Some upholstery fabrics and all tufted carpets utilized this method. The fabric may be tufted with a small hand-held tufting gun or on a large machine that utilizes multiple needles, tufting entire sections in rapid sequence.

tweed
Heavy upholstery-weight textile in plain balanced or variation weave or (originally) twill weave variation. Plain and twill weaves may also be combined. Made first of wool in Scotland, today's tweeds may be of wool, nylon, or a combination of natural and man-made fibers in solid colors, a heathered effect, or plaid.

union cloth
A coarse, medium-weight cloth that is approximately 50 percent cotton, 50 percent linen. Yarns are calendered or flattened somewhat. Union cloth may be dyed one color or printed and often resembles a very coarse chintz. Versatile fabric with many uses.

velour
A heavy pile fabric with a soft, velvetlike texture that includes some velvets and all plush-pile surface cloths, as velour terry.

velvet
Woven pile fabric with a soft yet sturdy face. May be of one or more fibers, including cotton, linen, wool, silk, rayon, acrylic, and nylon. Types include:
  antique velvet Streaks pressed or woven in: slubs on woven back, or slight strié effect.
  brocaded Etch-printed or burn-out pattern, often exposing the woven background.
  chiffon velvet Thick, soft surface finish velvet.
  crushed velvet Varies from light to heavy crushing of pile.
  electrostatic velvet Flocked, rather than woven pile, usually bold color and pattern.
  embossed velvet Bas-relief roller calendering to produce pressed-in pattern.
  moquette velvet Exposed ground with floral historic patterns of cut and uncut looped pile in Jacquard weave.
  panne velvet Pile lays flat, pressed in one direction.
  plush velvet Deeper pile, sometimes crushed.
  upholstery velvet Deep thick pile and sturdy back.
  velveteen Short, cotton-faced pile and back.
  printed velveteen Roller or screen printed, typically in floral or geometric patterns.

vinyl
Extruded polyvinyl chloride (vinyon) synthetic fabric flowed onto a woven, knitted, or nonwoven base cloth. Medium-weight to heavyweight upholstery fabric, which is also called *imitation leather* or *artificial leather.*

voile
Sheer, transparent fabric in plain weave with tightly twisted yarns. Often has a stiff finish. May have novelty effects such as piqué stripes, printed patterns or stripes, or woven with nubby yarns for *novelty voile.*

Bibliography

American Fabrics Encyclopedia of Textiles. Englewood Cliffs, NJ: Prentice-Hall, 1980.

Belgium Linen. New York: The Belgium Linen Association, n.d.

Birren, Faber. *Color for Interiors: Historical and Modern.* New York: Hill and Wang, 1963.

Clouzot, H., and F. Morris. *Painted and Printed Fabrics.* New York: Metropolitan Museum of Art, n.d.

Corbman, Bernard P. *Textiles: Fiber to Fabric.* New York: McGraw Hill, 1983.

Cowan, Mary L., and Martha E. Jungerman. *Introduction to Textiles.* New York: Appleton-Century-Croft Educational Division, 1969.

DuBois, M.J. *Curtains and Draperies: A Survey of the Classic Periods.* New York: Viking Press, 1967.

"Facts About Man-Made Fibers." New York: Celanese Fibers Marketing Co., n.d.

Farnfield, C.A., and P.J. Alvey. *Textile Terms and Definitions.* New York: State Mutual Book and Periodical Service, 1975.

Gakyu, Shobo, ed. *Japanese Interiors.* San Francisco: Japan Publication Trading Center, 1970.

Grosicki, A. *Watson's Textiles Design and Color.* London: Newness-Butterworth's, 1975.

Hall, A.J. *The Standard Handbook of Textiles.* Woburn, MA: Butterworth, 1980.

Hardingham, Martin. *Illustrated Dictionary of Fabrics.* New York: MacMillan, 1978

Hoffman, Emmanuel. *Fairchild's Dictionary of Home Furnishings.* New York: Fairchild Publications, Inc., 1975.

Hollen, Norma, and Jane Saddler. *Textiles.* New York: MacMillan, 1979.

Hussey, Christopher. *English Country Houses: Early Georgian.* (1955); *English Country Houses: Mid-Georgian.* (1956). *English Country House: Late Georgian.* (1958). London: Country Life.

Interplay: The Story of Man-Made Fibers. Washington, DC: Man-Made Fibers Producers Association, 1975.

Jackman, Dianne R., and Mary K. Dixon. *The Guide to Textiles for Interior Designers.* Winnipeg: Peguis Publishers, 1983.

Joseph, Marjory L. *Essentials of Textiles.* New York: Holt Rinehart, and Winston, 1980.

Klapper, Marvin. *Fabric Almanac.* New York: Fairchild Publications, 1971.

Labarthe, J. *Elements of Textiles.* New York: MacMillan, 1975.

Larsen, Jack Lenor, and Jeanne Weeks. *Fabrics for Interiors: A Guide for Architects, Designers, and Consumers.* New York: Van Nostrand Reinhold, 1975.

"Leather, The Revealing Facts." Signal Hill, CA: Lackawana Leather Co., n.d.

Lewis, Ernst. *Encyclopedia of Textiles.* New York: MacMillan, 1953.

Lewis, Ethel. *The Romance of Textiles.* New York: MacMillan, 1953.

Lyle, Dorothy Siegert. *Modern Textiles.* New York: John Wiley, 1983.

Man-made Fibers Fact Book. Washington, DC: Man-Made Fiber Producers Association.

Moller, Sven Erik, et al. *Danish Design*. Copenhagen: Detdanske Selskab, 1974.

Performance of Textiles. New York: John Wiley & Sons, 1977.

Reznikoff, S. C. *Specifications for Commercial Interiors: Professional Liabilities, Regulations, and Performance Criteria*. New York: Whitney Library of Design, 1979.

Textile Fibers and Their Properties. Greensboro, NC: American Association for Textile Technology/Burlington Industries, 1977.

The Story of Cotton. Memphis: The Cotton Council, n.d.

The Story of Wool. New York: The Wool Bureau, n.d.

Tortora, Phyllis G. *Understanding Textiles*. New York: MacMillan, 1982.

Whiton, Sherril. *Interior Design and Decoration*. New York: J.B. Lippincott, 1974.

Wilson, K. A *History of Textiles*. Boulder, CO: Westwiew Press, 1979.

Window Treatments Through the Ages. Sturgis, MI: The Kirsch Company, 1976.

ART AND ACCESSORIES

Art and accessories are not only the finishing touch in interior design; they are often the component that gives personality and individual character to an otherwise plain interior. In the bedroom of photographic team Ted and Signy Spiegel, an antique Aubusson tapestry of Amour, framed in a symbolically endless circle, hangs above decorative bed linens by Laura Ashley. Reflecting the image is an antique mirror with candle sconces and a charming array of personally selected objets d'art. The rhythmic quality of the circular forms is carried around the top of the room with a custom-stenciled festoon border just visible above the tapestry. Interior design and photo by Signy Spiegel.

Page 310, top left: New York interior designer Ruben de Saavedra's eclectic room at the Place des Antiquaries features a pair of Empire obelisks. He feels that the assembling of art and accessories is the "icing on the cake" for the interior designer. Page 310, top right: One of de Saavedra's favorite foraging sites is Objets Plus, a New York Shop which features European and Oriental art and accessories. Page 310, bottom: Another of de Saavedra's favorite sources is at the Place des Antiquaries—The Gallery of A. R. Broomer, Ltd. He is always on the lookout for the right accent, such as an antique Chinese export porcelain. Photo by Ted Spiegel. Page 311, top left: At the annual Manhattan Antiques show, New Jersey based "St. James Place" offers antique American decorative glass as well as cast iron toys. Page 311, top right: At the booth of "Haymarket" from Caliopolis, Michigan, the broad range of decorative arts, folk carving, quilts, Shaker baskets, sinage, all lend themselves to "country" decor. Photos by Ted Spiegel. Page 311, bottom: With the accent on simplicity, Rachel Newman, Editor of Country Living magazine, gracefully blended contemporary with antique art and accessory "finds" in her fanciful examples of majolica ware from around the world seen in the step-back cupboard (left), and the Czech "sgrafitto" collection, mostly of pre-1939 vintage, which reveals Ms. Newman's passion for checks (cupboard at right). Photo by Keith Scott Morton, courtesy of Country Living magazine.

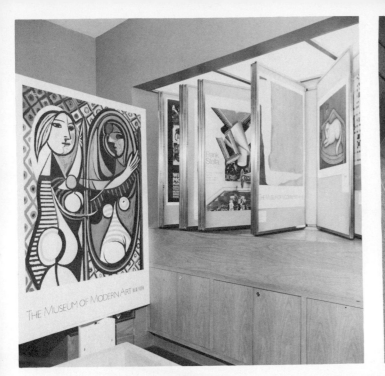

Page 312, top left: *The poster selection at the Museum of Modern Art (MOMA) in New York offers an economical access to famous modern art. Museum shops everywhere sell reproductions of their well-known works, as well as posters that advertise travelling exhibits with the name of the museum, the name of the artist, and the date in graphic lettering. Photo by Ted Spiegel.* *Page 312, top right:* *The Museum of Modern Art's Contemporary Design Collection includes the Tizio lamp, the Bauhaus chess set, the Aalto vase, Russian Suprematist porcelain, and a coffee table designed by Isamo Noguchi, all available in reproduction at reasonable prices. Photo by Ted Spiegel.* *Page 312, bottom:* *The wall-sized abstract painting by Robert Natkin makes an appropiate and fitting backdrop for the original Henry Moore reclining figure sculpture. Together with the custom designed granite and steel table, the simple art and accessory grouping makes a dramatic welcome in the entrance foyer of this New York City apartment. Photo courtesy of Noel Jeffrey, ASID.* *Page 313:* *The offices of Robert K. Lewis, ASID, demonstrate the inspiration of 18th and 19th century art and accessories. Lewis first found in an antique store a Houdon bust of the Marquis de Lafayette, commissioned by a Virginia Governor. Lewis then located the Governor's miniature portrait and placed it on the bust pedestal, which is complemented by the Robert Adam graphic-inspired Neoclassic window treatment. The vase, a Roman treasure, is seen in both print and three-dimensional reproduction. Photo by Ted Spiegel.*

Fine Art

The *fine arts* are concerned with the creation of two- and three-dimensional works of art, designed as expressions of beauty and faith or as a statement of the personal meaning or feeling of the artist. The great *masters* are those throughout the ages who have excelled in the creation of art and whose work has passed the test of time to become what we call classics. Every era has its masters, and these men and women were often aware of each other and the work produced by each artist. This mutual awareness often produced similarities in philosophy, technique, subject matter, or other areas of influence. Art historians have classified the work of the masters into *schools* according to these similarities and influences. Many of the masters were equally comfortable drawing with a pencil, painting with a brush, or working sculpture with their hands. The fine arts include *sculpture, painting, mosaic, drawing,* and *printmaking.*

Figure 12.1

Sculpture

Sculpture is a three-dimensional art form created by carving or assembling stone, working clay, wood, or other materials, or casting or assembling metal. Sculpture may represent the human form, animal forms, or other forms from nature in a realistic, conventionalized, or abstract fashion.

Bas-relief is French for low relief. It is a type of sculpture carved or cast in a flat manner where the design is slightly raised from the background to create a three-dimensional effect. Bas-relief is often seen in friezes (sculptural panels or bands) used on exteriors, in interiors, and even on furniture and small decorative objects.

Painting

Painting is a one-of-a-kind, two-dimensional art form created with colored *pigments* and a number of different *vehicles* (substances that give the paint form and body). The paint can be thinned with different *media* and manipulated by pouring, dripping, or splashing or applied with brushes, sponges, or *palette knives* to many different surfaces such as plaster, wood, canvas and other textiles, paper, glass, or any material or surface capable of holding the paint.

Figure 12.2

- *Oil paint* is colored pigment mixed with linseed oil or varnish and thinned with turpentine. Oil painting is probably the most versatile painting technique because the color can be applied thick or thin and opaque or transparent. Oils tend to be one of the most permanent types of painting, which may account for their popularity with collectors.
- *Watercolor* is colored pigment mixed with *gum arabic* and thinned with water. The pigments are slightly transparent. Because the water used as a medium dries quickly, the artist must work rapidly to complete the painting. The quickness imparts a fresh, underworked quality to the finished piece.

Figure 12.1 The bronze statue "Coppelia" by Charpentier is a fitting accessory for this sophisticated mix of modern and antique furnishings in the high-style living room of author Barbara Taylor Bradford, whose photograph is an important personal accessory atop the antique Irish console table of hand-carved mahogany. Floral arrangements balance the clean lines with light, airy qualities. Photo courtesy of the International Linen Promotion Commission

Figure 12.2 Two-dimensional art hung over the fireplace mantle is at the center of the focal point grouping in this contemporary room. Red walls and lamp bases are echoed in the red flowers at the center of the painting. A gold-accented molded frame suggests richness without becoming overly traditional, thus in harmony with the room's vivid chroma, modern furnishings, and Oriental accessories. Interior design by Rona Levine for the Sara Delano Roosevelt House, New York City. Photo courtesy of DuPont "Teflon" soil and stain repellent.

- *Acrylic* can duplicate the appearance of oils and watercolors. It is made of plastic and can be mixed with several kinds of media or thinned with water. Its appearance can be opaque or transparent. The untrained eye may find it difficult to distinguish acrylics from the older, more traditional oils and watercolors. Many artists enjoy the versatility provided by a single medium capable of so many different effects.
- *Tempera*, one of the oldest painting techniques, is pigment mixed with egg and thinned with water. It is somewhat transparent but more opaque than watercolor. Budding artists at kindergarten easels often use a form of tempera to create their bright, fresh, uninhibited paintings, and tempera poster paints are frequently used to create banners and posters. However, the tempera used by fine artists is much more refined than poster paint. Fine tempera is often called *gouache*.
- *Fresco* is Italian for fresh and is a combination of pigment and limewater applied with brushes to fresh, damp plaster. When it dries, the pigment and plaster become unified. The artist had to work quickly, and plaster was applied only as far as the artist could work before it dried. Frescoes were often used to decorate the ceiling and walls of Renaissance buildings and are a particular glory of that age.

Mosaic

Mosaic is an important medium for creating two-dimensional art made of *tesserae* (small pieces of marble, tile, or colored glass) fitted together to form a pattern. The design is held in place with plaster or cement. The Romans used mosaics to decorate their floors, and artists in the Eastern-Roman Byzantine empire developed the art of mosaics to a high level of perfection. The interiors of Byzantine churches shimmer with scintillating mosaic designs of great beauty.

Drawing

Drawings are also one-of-a-kind, two-dimensional art forms produced with pencil, pen and ink, charcoal, chalk, crayon, or grease pencil on paper or other surfaces. Drawing is considered a fundamental but highly important skill for artists. Drawings are produced as finished works and also as preliminary studies in the development of paintings, sculpture, and other art. The work of the masters often includes a large body of drawings that were used as studies for later work and that stand by themselves as treasured art pieces.

Printmaking

Printmaking is a method of mass-producing two-dimensional fine art. Prints are produced in limited editions by the artist who prepares a screen, plate, block, or stone and then makes a numbered set of prints. The artist signs and numbers the prints that are of acceptable quality. The numbers read as a fraction and indicate how many copies were made and the order in which they were printed. For example, 8/10 would indicate that a particular print was the eighth print out of a total of ten. Generally, the smaller the number of prints produced, the greater the value. Several screens, plates, or blocks representing different parts of the design can be utilized to create multicolored prints. When using more than one run of color, each plate, screen, or block must be carefully registered (aligned) to produce a clear and even print.

- Woodcut or *wood-block print* is made by carving a design into the flat surface of a piece of wood. The background is cut away leaving the pattern standing out in relief. The block is then inked and printed creating a negative or reverse pattern on the paper. A wood engraving is executed in the same way, except that the pattern is carved into the harder end grain of the wood, which usually results in a finer and more precise design.
- Linoleum-block print is made by cutting a pattern into a piece of heavy guage linoleum. The process is similar to the woodcut process except that the design will have less detail in the form because of the softness of the linoleum. Woodcut, wood engraving, and linoleum-block printing are all forms of *relief printing* because the portion of the pattern that receives the ink and does the printing stands out in relief.
- *Engravings* are prints made from a metal plate that has lines hand engraved (scratched) with a tool called a burin. These lines make small impressions or grooves in the plate. The plate is covered with ink and then wiped clean leaving ink only in the grooves. The plate and paper are pressed together so that the ink is transferred from the grooves in a negative impression onto the paper.
- *Etchings* are made by covering a metal plate with an acid-resistant substance such as wax. The artist uses a needle to draw through the wax. The plate is immersed in an acid bath that bites or etches the design into the metal wherever the wax has been scratched away. After the plate is etched and the remaining wax removed, the plate is used to print in the same manner as an engraving. Because wax is less difficult to cut than a metal plate, etching designs tend to be less rigid than engravings. Engravings and etchings are forms of *intaglio* where printing is done from the recesses in a plate.

- *Lithographs* are produced on the principle that water and grease repel each other. The artist creates a design on a limestone block or metal plate with a grease pencil or with a brush and tusche (a waxy liquid). The block or plate is then chemically treated to attract ink to the greasy design and water (which repells the ink) to the untouched portions of the stone or plate. The stone or plate is then charged (wetted) with water and ink and pressed together with the paper to create a negative image.

- *Serigraph or silk screen* is a printmaking process that utilizes a fine screen of silk or man-made fiber and cut stencils to create a positive, direct (not reversed) image. The stencils are applied to the screen and ink is *squeegeed* across the pattern, forcing a thin layer of ink onto the surface being printed through the open areas of fabric where there is no stencil.[1]

- *Rubbings* are not a true form of printmaking, though they are often framed and used in much the same way as prints. Rubbings are made by placing a sheet of paper over a flat metal or stone plaque, such as a grave marker, or an architectural or decorative detail that has a rather flat bas-relief or a raised pattern. The paper is then rubbed with a crayon or chalk to create a direct image of the pattern beneath. The quality of the piece is determined by the care and skill of the person doing the rubbing.

- *Reproductions* are copies of the artist's work and are an important educational tool. Without them, those unable to visit the world's museums would find it difficult to study the history of art. Reproductions often vary in size from the original and may be scaled from postcard size to full poster size or larger. Color quality of reproductions may also vary. For example, colors that were red in the original may appear violet in the reproduction. Once the original piece of art is complete, the quality control of the reproduction is generally out of the artist's hands; the quality of reproductions ranges from excellent to poor. Reproductions of great art are a viable means of bringing quality art into the interior.

- *Graphic art* includes posters designed to publicize athletic contests, concerts, plays, shows of artists' works, and other cultural events. These are often worthy of display on the merits of their fine design and, in time, may become very valuable. Posters are an important resource for those who love art but are unable to afford paintings and other art forms. Unfortunately, there are many poster designs available with no aesthetic value, and it is essential that purchasers be knowledgeable and selective. Maps, botanical drawings, architectural drawings, fashion illustrations, book illustrations, and even some mechanical or architectural drawings may also have value as graphic art.

Obtaining Fine Art

Art can be found at many locations in a vast range of prices. The works of the great masters are generally sold for enormous sums at auction houses like Christie's or Sotheby's in London and New York. Some less well-known but important pieces are sold by art and antique dealers who operate retail shops and galleries. Contemporary artists are usually represented by galleries and dealers who act as agents for the artist. Galleries may specialize in a certain type of art such as historic, oriental, or Western as dictated by the tastes of the local market or by tourism. Art-minded communities and organizations often sponsor art festivals where artists informally display and sell their work. Some businesses and corporations sponsor art shows or display artists' works that may be purchased.

Those who have less to spend for acquiring art pieces should know that art teachers and artists who need to finance travels and studies will often sell their work at relatively reasonable prices. Schools of art may have shows of faculty and student work, much of which is for sale. Because they have not usually established a reputation, students tend to sell their work at lower prices.

Economical graphic art posters can be purchased directly from museum shops or from the sponsoring organizations of the event being publicized in the poster, sometimes even without charge. Old posters, prints, and maps can frequently be found at flea markets or bookshops. When collecting art, one should be prepared to pay fair market prices, though the price is less important than the quality and appeal of a piece.

Print shops specialize in graphic designs from museums, galleries, shows, and other cultural events. In addition, this type of shop will often have fine photography in poster format and reproductions of the masters' works in varying sizes of posters. It is important to be discriminating and choose pieces of fine quality and lasting value, because good design is uplifting and becomes more meaningful with the passage of time.

Obtaining art for our homes is certainly a matter of personal taste, but the more we learn about art, the higher our level of enjoyment and appreciation will be. The design of a home is a reflection of personal style, and the art chosen for such settings should also be a statement of discrimination and taste. Unfortunately, many of us are insecure and underexposed to quality art. Designers or consultants could be used to help us make wise selections, but the most pleasing and personal collections belong to those who put forth the effort to become knowledgeable about art and its history. Not everything that is advertised as original art is worthy of collection. Knowledge, training, and exposure are the only means to ensure wise selection. Following are some important guidelines to help develop the confidence to choose fine-quality art:

- Do not be too intimidated by a blank wall—it may have more appeal than a piece of poor art. Take the time and steps necessary to develop confidence in your ability to choose.
- Those who are seriously interested in collecting art will study its history. This can be done formally or informally with classes or independent study. Study of art history builds a sincere appreciation and understanding of art and those who created it.
- Taking art classes and attempting to actually create works of art add profound depth to our appreciation of quality art and helps build the ability to see.
- Visiting museums of fine art to observe firsthand the works of the great masters and contemporary artists sharpens the ability to discriminate. It provides the kind of exposure that enables us to detect the difference between real art and the poor quality pieces we see advertised on television as "original oil paintings."
- Like anything of real value, it takes time and effort to build an understanding and appreciation of art. It is a lifelong pursuit and an important part of the process of developing the ability to discriminate, discussed in chapter 1, The Process of Design. It is a goal worth the effort because of the lifelong satisfaction that fine art provides.

Preparing Art for Display

When purchasing a piece of art, it may be necessary to select a *frame,* a *mat* board (heavy flat paper frame), or some other means of display that will show the piece to the best advantage and add to its quality and character. Frames are available in unassembled kits or ready-made from art shops, from paint stores, and even by mail. In some places there may be hobby shops or specialty shops where customers can cut mats and make and assemble their own frames. However, with truly fine pieces of art, it may be worthwhile to consult a qualified framer who understands art conser-

vation and can advise on the proper method and materials for displaying and preserving art pieces. Following are some suggestions for framing fine art:

- Generally, oil paintings are framed but left unglazed (not covered with glass). They may be framed with heavy, elaborate, period frames that often include a fabric liner to separate the painting from the frame. Contemporary oils and acrylics may be left unframed, or they may be treated with a simple, minimal frame.
- Watercolors, drawings, photographs, and prints are frequently framed behind glass with simple, narrow frames and a mat that keeps the painting from touching the glass. Clear glass is preferable to *nonglare glass* or *Plexiglass.* Nonglare glass does not allow clear color and line transmission. Plexiglass is subject to scratching and bowing. Posters can be framed like watercolors or prints but can also be mounted behind glass with no frame where the glass and backing are held together with clips. When mounting paintings, prints, graphic designs, or reproductions, it is important not to cut or *crop* the piece to make it fit a frame. Cropping destroys the value of the work.

Figure 12.3

Decorative Art

The *decorative arts* include both utilitarian pieces such as mirrors, tableware, baskets, clocks, screens, lamps, books, tapestries, and rugs as well as nonutilitarian pieces like figurines or statuettes, and objects from nature such as plants and flowers and rocks and shells. *Objets d'art, bibelots, and curios* are French terms used to describe both these utilitarian and nonutilitarian objects of artistic value and beauty. Furniture, also considered a decorative art, is discussed in chapter 7, Furniture Selection.

Not all pieces created as decorative art have strict artistic value. *Kitsch* is a German term that describes bad taste and is applied to pretentious or foolish art and design. In our contemporary world we are inundated by objects of mediocre or poor design. As we develop the ability to

Figure 12.3 Framed memorabilia either side of this faux keg lamp allow nostalgic glimpses into earlier eras. Hand-done needlepoint cushions on the inviting chair and ottoman and a handy supply of favorite books complete this private reading corner. Interior design by Richard Fitzgerald. Fabric and furniture by, and photo courtesy of, Brunschwig and Fils.

discriminate, we can sift out the kitsch from our environment and replace it with that which is fine and uplifting. It is worth the effort to find good design because it enriches and deepens our appreciation for true beauty. Today, art has become a status symbol, and vast sums of money are often spent on questionable design. Both good and bad design can be found at every price level, and many times it costs no more to choose good design.

Mirrors

In the fourteenth century the skilled artisans of Venice discovered that a layer of *quicksilver* sandwiched between a piece of tin and a piece of glass (a process called *silvering*) created a mirror. Today, mirrors add depth, a feeling of spaciousness, and sparkle to interiors, and they can be obtained in many sizes. They can be framed to harmonize with period styles or can be used in sheets large enough to cover entire walls. However, caution should be exercised in using mirrors because some people may find it objectionable to be seated or to have to stand and look at themselves in a mirror for prolonged periods. Large areas of mirror on several different walls may visually duplicate the elements of a design in a manner that creates visual confusion and makes the space seem smaller. Mirror finishes or types include clear glass, smoked glass, *Venetian glass* (veined), *beveled glass*, *leaded glass*, and *etched glass*.

Tableware and Cookware

Tableware is the term that describes plates, cups, drinking vessels, and flatware or eating utensils. Artisans through the ages have lavished their finest creativity and the best developments of technology on the creation of beautiful and useful pieces for the table and kitchen. Materials of all kinds have been used to create tableware and cookware, and today plastics and other innovative space-age products are used alongside more traditional materials such as ceramics, glass, wood, and metal for the design of quality pieces. (These same materials are also used to create a wide variety of functional and decorative objects unrelated to table or kitchen such as small sculpture, planters, containers, bookends, desk sets, dressing or grooming accessories.)

Ceramics

Ceramics are made from clay that has been taken from the earth and molded in its softened form into useful shapes that are then fired or baked at high temperatures in an oven called a *kiln*. The soft clay may be molded by hand, formed in molds, or thrown on a potter's wheel run by motor or foot power. Clay mixed with water to the consistency of thick cream is called slip and is used to fill molds and for other functions in the ceramic process. *Glazes* are thin layers of glass fired onto ceramic pieces to produce a glossy surface and colored effects and to make the pieces nonabsorbent

Figure 12.4

Figure 12.5

and sanitary. Glazes may be dull or shiny or clear or colored and can be used by the ceramist to create decorative effects. Following is a list of ceramic types:

- *Porcelain* is the highest grade ceramic body. It is made of fine, white clay (*kaolin*) and *feldspar* (crystalline materials) and fired at very high temperatures that *vitrify* the clay (change it to a glasslike substance), harden the glaze, and make the ceramic

Figure 12.4 This jewellike mirror is incised with Neoclassic motifs, reflecting not only soft light but finely detailed ornamentation. The toilette table, filled with a romantic array of small accessories and luminaires, was part of a Kips Bay showcase house master suite by interior designer Noel Jeffrey. Photo by Ted Spiegel.

Figure 12.5 Sensitive arrangement of crisp textiles, fine porcelain, luminaires, and fresh flowers breathe spring into this boudoir accessory grouping. Fabrics by and photo courtesy of Laura Ashley.

Figure 12.6

Figure 12.7

breakage resistant. Porcelain is sometimes used in the manufacture of fine dinnerware, vases, figurines, and other decorative objects. Porcelain may be plain or decorated with colored glazes and patterns.

- *China* was the designation given by Europeans to the porcelain imported from the Orient. It contains a large percentage of animal bone ash (hence the term bone china) that produces a hard, translucent porcelain. Today, china and porcelain are generally used as synonymous terms.
- *Stoneware* is a heavy, durable, thick pottery used for less-formal dinnerware, serving and cooking pieces, as well as other art objects. Stoneware finishes may be less formal and show flecks and speckles in the clay or glaze. Stoneware finishes vary from natural browns, grays, and bluish grays to bright, lively colored patterns.
- *Earthenware* is the most coarse and inexpensive of the ceramic bodies. It is derived from red earthen clays and often finished like a common clay flower pot. It is fired at lower temperatures, making it softer and less durable. Earthenware products are sometimes referred to as terra-cotta, an Italian term that literally means cooked earth. It is commonly used for baking and serving pieces and other decorative pieces for the interior and garden.

Glass

Glass (also discussed in chapter 9, Wall, Window, and Ceiling Treatments) is used to fashion decorative objects, dishes, serving pieces, and drinking vessels of all shapes and sizes. The quality and design of glassware ranges from inexpensive molded glass to fine lead crystal.

- Molded or *pressed glass* is a method for mass-producing glass. Molten glass is poured into forms or molds of metal or wood. The mold often leaves a seam where the molds meet. The molding process can be used to form simple and functional glass shapes or to imitate the look of cut glass.
- Cut or *etched glass* is decorated with patterns incised with chemicals or abrasives. The cut patterns are quite clear, and the etched designs have a frosted appearance.
- *Enameled glass* is layered with a porcelainlike finish.
- *Cased glass* is a layer of clear glass encased in a layer of colored glass.
- *Gilded glass* has a layer of silver or gold applied to its surface. Enameled, cased, and gilded glass are often engraved or cut to reveal patterns in the sparkling clear glass layer underneath.
- *Crystal* is a high-grade glass containing lead. Because of law requirements, American lead crystal contains less lead than European lead crystal. Higher lead

Figure 12.6 A small collection of majolica earthenware is appropriately grouped in front of a historic painting atop a traditional, antique chest of drawers. Size, selection, and placement yield pleasing proportions of positive and negative space. Design by Anthony Antine and Mark Polo for the guest room in the Sara Delano Roosevelt House, New York City. Photo courtesy of DuPont "Teflon" soil and stain repellent.

Figure 12.7 Glass stemware and service pieces counterpoint the earthy quality of these stoneware and earthenware serving pieces and this dinnerware. Tulips and apples bring life and appetite-stimulating color. The decorative pendant luminaire provides well-placed lighting and a lighthearted approach, supported by the springlike coordinated printed wall coverings and fabrics. Photo courtesy of C & A Wall Coverings.

content makes the glass softer, allowing the glassmaker to cut more intricate designs. Fine lead crystal sparkles beautifully in the light and rings or sings when tapped lightly with a fingernail. Crystal is used to create art objects, serving pieces, and drinking vessels. Stemware is the name given to formal drinking pieces with a slender pedestal and raised bowl.

(A)

Figure 12.8

(B)

Wood

Wood (also discussed in chapter 7, Furniture Selection), aside from its use in construction and sculpture, was used historically to make crude plates, utensils, and serving pieces. Today it is still used to create beautiful art objects, both carved and plain, as well as serving pieces, handles for metal utensils and cookware, spoons, and other cooking implements.

(C)

(D)

Metals and Alloys

Metals and *alloys* such as aluminum, brass, chrome, iron, steel, and stainless steel (discussed in chapter 7, Furniture Selection), together with gold, silver, pewter, bronze, and copper, are common materials used to fashion art objects, cookware, serving pieces, dinnerware, flatware (silverware), fixtures, and hardware.

- Gold, a bright, deep yellow, is the most precious, costly, and prestigious metal and was used historically to create dishes, flatware, drinking vessels, candle holders, and other objects of art. Because of its great expense, gold is used principally today as a plating for metal pieces or as paper-thin sheets applied to objects in a process known as *gold leaf. Gold electroplate* is a type of flatware created by the electrolytic process of layering pure gold over a silver/nickel alloy (silver plate).

- Silver is a bright, lustrous, gray-white metal used in the manufacture of objects of art and tableware. *Sterling silver* is the finest and most costly, being by law at least 92.5 percent pure silver. Sterling will tarnish and must be polished and protected from the air. It becomes more beautiful with use, developing a soft *patina* of almost invisible scratches. *Sterling II* is flatware that combines silver handles with stainless steel blades, bowls, and tines, costing about half as much as sterling silver. *Silver plate* is

made of a silver/nickel alloy electroplated with pure silver. It is the most affordable type of silverware and is also used as a base for gold electroplate.

- *Stainless steel* is also used to make flatware and serving pieces. Affordable stainless steel flatware and serving pieces are readily available today. These pieces are popular because they do not tarnish or scratch easily, and they are strong, durable, and dishwasher safe. Some designs feature handles of wood or colorful plastic.

- *Pewter* is a soft, dull gray alloy of tin, copper, lead, and *antimony* used to create dishes, drinking vessels, candle holders, and other art objects. Historically pewter was considered poor man's silver. However, this description no longer applies. Though it is less costly than sterling, pewter is not inexpensive. Once considered dangerous because of its lead content, today pewter is often made without lead and is safer and easier to care for. Pewter adds character and warmth to informal, *provincial* (country) settings. Less-expensive imitations of pewter are now being made of cast aluminum.

- *Copper* is a bright, shiny, reddish brown metal used principally for cookware, because of its ability to conduct heat. Some copper pieces are coated with lacquer or other finishes that prevent tarnishing. These finishes must be removed if the piece is to actually be used for cooking or if a tarnished finish is

Figure 12.8 These faucets from Kohler show a few of the ways metals, porcelain, and plastics are used in fixture hardware. (*A*) Alterna Flume spout is engineered to eliminate splashing and reveals water flow that is fascinating to watch. The knob inset can be selected to coordinate with the interior design. (*B*) Taboret offers modern styling with distinctive solid brass construction. Removable color indexing rings indicate temperature—red for hot, blue for cold. (*C*) Acrylic diamond handles with beveled corners offer a prismlike alternative to the bath and powder room Alterna faucet line. (*D*) Contemporary European styling is incorporated into the Epicure kitchen faucet. The dual spray head conveniently pulls out of the spout. Photos courtesy of the Kohler Company.

desired. When copper is allowed to tarnish, it turns reddish brown or a beautiful blue-green. To maintain the original copper color and shine, it must be polished with copper paste and a soft cloth unless it has been treated as mentioned.

- *Bronze* is a deep reddish brown alloy of copper and tin used primarily for sculptural pieces or plaques.
- Iron is cast or wrought (shaped and bent with heat) to make lighting fixtures, candle holders, and other decorative accessories. *Cast iron* is molded in its molten form to create substantial cookware and some art objects. *Wrought iron* pieces and heavy cast pieces such as corn pone or muffin molds, skillets, and Dutch ovens are frequently used as decorative accessories in less-formal, country settings .

Plastics

Plastics (also discussed in chapter 7, Furniture Selection) are used extensively to create informal tableware and other accessories for interiors. Plastic is generally less expensive than the other materials discussed in this chapter and can be used to create designs of great appeal and integrity. For example, some contemporary plastic dishes are bright, colorful, and well designed. Because they are relatively inexpensive, one can indulge in a splash of color without undue concern for the budget. Whereas if selecting fine porcelain, such a colorful investment might be unthinkable.

Plastic is sometimes used in a lighthearted manner to imitate natural materials such as glass or metal. This is particularly true in the manufacture of disposable objects that are not meant to be taken seriously. When plastic is used to imitate natural materials in a serious manner, the design becomes questionable. For example, plastic molded to resemble carved wood or fine cut crystal might only be considered kitsch.

Baskets

Baskets are woven for function, each type or shape reflecting its specific use. Woven by almost every culture in the world, they show a frank use of materials such as wicker and willow; weav-

Figure 12.9

ing can form beautiful patterns. Because of their decorative nature, baskets make excellent additions to informal interiors, particularly when they serve a useful purpose such as a container for plants, bread, fruit, or fragrant *potpourri*. Many baskets are beautiful and well made and can be treated as art objects with no particular purpose other than aesthetics.

Clocks

Today, time pieces such as *hourglasses, sundials*, and antique clocks are collected as objects of art. Looking at fine clocks with intricately designed cases, we appreciate the cabinetmakers and furniture designers whose creative genius made scientific instruments into functional and decorative art. The design of clocks has changed over the years. Today's *high-tech* clocks are often the work of industrial or product designers rather than furniture craftsmen, and these frank, sleek designs may be as beautiful in their own way as the handcrafted pieces of the past. Clocks may be wall mounted, displayed on shelves, mantels, or brackets, or they may be floor clocks. Large-scale floor clocks are often referred to as grandfather clocks, and those of a slightly smaller scale are called grandmother clocks. Clocks are frequently included as a feature in appliances such as radios, microwave ovens, stoves, and VCRs. These often utilize a digital display system that indicates the hour and minutes as digits instead of using the traditional clock face.

Screens

Screens are hinged or sliding panels designed to divide and separate spaces or create areas of privacy. For centuries, the Japanese have used wooden-framed panels glazed with mulberry or rice paper called shoji or fusuma screens. In Western culture, screens have often been used to create dressing spaces. In Near-Eastern cultures screens are used as a "blind" to see out without being seen. In today's interiors, screens are used as dividers, wall art, window treatments, and a background for furniture. Screens can be made of wood with solid panels or *louvers, lattice*, pierced wood, or wrought iron. Screens are also custom-made items that might be up-

Figure 12.9 Antique coromandel screens, in a rich shade of chocolate, with oriental figures and landscapes, divide the living area from the formal dining area. Other important accessories include Staffordshire figures, Bohemian blue glass, Synsley bone china, Christofle silver, Baccarat and Waterford crystal. Artwork beyond the coromandel screens is "Central Park" by Bernard Taurelle. Wall fabric and table linens are Glant fabrics. Photo courtesy of International Linen Promotion Commission.

holstered, covered with mirrors, painted, lacquered, papered, or treated in other interesting ways.

- Antique screens from Europe and America with details appropriate to period styles from those countries and cultures are nice additions to interiors as functional dividers or simply as objects of art.
- *Coromandel* are large Chinese black lacquered folding screens, decorated with low relief, all-over patterns. They were introduced into Europe in the seventeenth century by the East India Company.
- *Byobu* are small-scaled folding Japanese screens. They are decorated with scenes painted on silk or paper and are generally used as wall hangings, on tables, or as freestanding pieces in today's interiors.
- Shoji or fusuma are Japanese screens made of oriental papers mounted onto a wooden frame. The frames are set into tracks or grooves as sliding panels or hinged and freestanding and used as partitions. Shoji are exterior sliding panels or window screens, and fusuma are decorative interior sliding room partitions or doors. Translucent *transoms* set above the screens add light through a grid or intricate design patterns.
- Near Eastern are intricately patterned pierced wooden screens from Islamic cultures. Islamic design was taken to Spain in the eighth century by invading *Moors*. The Near-Eastern influence can also be seen today in the screens of Mexico and other countries with *Hispanic* ties. Today, many pierced wooden screens are made in India and imported to Western countries.

Figure 12.10

Figure 12.11

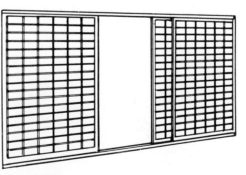

Figure 12.12

Figure 12.13

Figure 12.10 Antique screen with zoological panels.
Figure 12.11 Coromandel screen.
Figure 12.12 Byobu screen.
Figure 12.13 Shoji screen.

Decorative Lighting Fixtures

Lighting fixtures have evolved over the centuries from torches, oil- and gas-burning vessels, and candle holders into the electric fixtures we use today. (Architectural lighting and principles of lighting are discussed in chapter 4, Lighting.) Some of today's most common lighting fixtures are electric versions of historical lighting pieces. It is also common to see decorative objects such as metal *tea caddies* (antique tea containers), *ginger jars*, *cloisonné* (enameled metal) and porcelain vases, as well as figurines and other sculptural pieces made into table lamps. *Luminaire* is the technical term used by lighting designers and engineers to describe table lamps, floor lamps, and ceiling or wall-mounted lighting fixtures such as chandeliers and sconces. This designation is to help distinguish from the current technical usage of the term lamp, which is used to describe what most people still commonly call a light bulb or flourescent tube. Following is a list of the most common luminaires:

- *Table lamps* are designed to sit on the table for general lighting of a space or for reading, writing, and other specific tasks. Traditional designs usually incorporate the use of a shade to diffuse the light.
  - *Floor lamps* serve the same basic purposes as table lamps but are designed to stand on the floor.
  - *Torchére* is a historical term that was used to describe a candle table or candle stand. Today it describes a type of floor lamp that casts its light upward onto the ceiling.
  - *Sconce* is a wall-mounted luminaire of any style that has descended from wall-mounted torches or candle holders.
  - *Chandelier* is a decorative, ceiling-mounted, hanging, or pendant-type luminaire. This type of fixture functions best where ceilings are high enough to accommodate them and where a strong focal point is the intent of the design.

(A)

(B)

(C)

(D)

Figure 12.14

Many antique and contemporary lighting pieces are used simply as objets d'art. Candle holders made of metal, wood, and ceramic and various styles of oil and gas lamps are often collected and displayed because of their aesthetic appeal and not because of a need for light. Candlelight is used to create a special mood, because like firelight, it has a moving and scintillating quality that is not commonly duplicated with electric luminaires. *Neon lamp* designs created for advertising or as pieces of art are sometimes seen in today's interiors. Such pieces are far more important as decorative art than as light.

When selecting luminaires for an interior, it might be useful to consider the following applications of the elements and principles of design:

- The form of the luminaire should be pleasing and the lines should be harmonious with the other elements of the design.
- Proportions should be good, and with traditional luminaires, the proportions of the base and shade should relate well to each other.
- The luminaire should be in scale with the space and with the other furnishings.
- The design should be appropriate to the function of the space.

Books

Books are not only decorative but are also appealing because of their unity

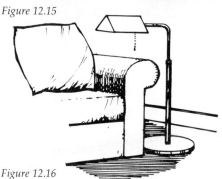
Figure 12.15

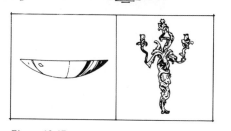
Figure 12.16

Figure 12.17

Figure 12.18

of form and variety of color and texture. They may also lend a certain amount of emotional warmth to a space, because when read, they may be like old friends, associated with all kinds of memories. Second-hand books are sometimes purchased and displayed like stage props. These look attractive in settings such as restaurants and shops where the design is intended to create a homey atmosphere. In a residential setting, books purchased as props will be visually pleasing but may lack the emotional appeal of books that have been read and loved. Books stashed in attics or garages might be an untapped resource that could add a warm touch to interiors.

Books make a suitable background for furniture groupings; they are a welcome addition to almost any interior. They can be carefully interspersed with objets d'art or plants to create pleasing compositions. Interesting books and magazines placed on tables for browsing make stimulating accessories. Entries, living rooms, family rooms, dining rooms, kitchens, bedrooms, even bathrooms are all appropriate locations for books. A library or home office is becoming more practical and fashionable, and a formal dining room used for meals only occasionally might double as a library or study. The table would be useful for reading or writing, and the books would make a pleasant background for occasional dining.

Figure 12.14 Decorative luminaries by Beth Weissman Company represent a few of the wide range available today. (A) Sung Tao, an imported Chinese crackled porcelain jar, is mounted on a carved black ebony base with antique brass accents. (B) Influenced by Art Nouveau, sculpturelike brass tulips float on a disk of acrylic. Crisp angular lines of the shade give a clearly modern feeling to this luminary. (C) The Wyndham, made of gun metal and brass, is an updated version of a chandelier from an eighteenth-century manor house. (D) A traditional antique fruit wood and polished brass floor lamp with an extended arm with a mini-box-pleated shade. The height is 55 1/2 inches. Photos courtesy of Beth Weissman Co., Inc.

Figure 12.15 A contemporary and traditional approach to table lamp design.
Figure 12.16 Floor lamp.
Figure 12.17 Contemporary and traditional sconces.
Figure 12.18 Contemporary and traditional chandeliers.

Textiles

Textiles serve important functional and decorative purposes as accessories. Linen, the name of the natural fiber derived from the flax plant, today is used to describe the fabric products of natural, man-made, or blends of fibers used on the dining table, the bed, and the towel rack. These items are an important part of the appearance of a completed interior and should be chosen in harmony with the other elements of the design. Fine, traditional white linens are still considered classic, but today linens also provide an opportunity to add color and pattern to appropriate settings. Because they are relatively inexpensive, linens tend to reflect constantly changing color and design trends. Textiles are also used in the form of rugs and carpets, *tapestries*, and other types of hangings to add warm finishing touches to interior environments. The following represent some of the uses of textiles as accessories:

Figure 12.19

- Table linens include tablecloths, napkins, place mats, and runners. These are made in every possible shape and of many natural and man-made fibers. The man-made fibers are generally easier to care for, but the natural fibers have a fine look and feel that are difficult to duplicate. A table beautifully set with linens, tableware, and flowers chosen to create a harmonious and stimulating mood can be an important part of the pleasure of a good meal.

- Bed linens are sheets, pillowcases, *pillow shams* (removable, decorative pillow covers), *dust ruffles,* bedspreads, blankets, comforters, quilts, *duvets* (nondecorative comforters) and their covers. These are available in a wide array of colors and styles. Today, bed linens are the domain of the designer and are manufactured in classic whites as well as designs compatible with every type of interior from primitive log cabins to English country houses to postmodern penthouses.

Figure 12.20

- Bath and kitchen linens consist mainly of towels. These are generally made of linen, cotton, or cotton *terry cloth,* all of which are absorbent and easy to launder. Linen (flax) cloths are particularly good for drying glassware, because they are lint free and shine glass nicely.

- Rugs and carpets are discussed with floor coverings in chapter 10, Floor Materials and Coverings. The types of rugs generally considered to be accessories are art rugs, designer rugs, and Oriental rugs, particularly when they are scaled to hang on the wall.

- Tapestries and hangings were used for hundreds of years to provide actual physical warmth to the interior environment. They were used to cover the windows and walls of cold and damp castles; as bed hangings to protect from drafts, to keep in the

Figure 12.19 A romantic place setting for two on a mirror-bright metal table features pure-white Belgian linen traced with Renaissance lace delicate as a butterfly's wings (Sferra) played against the sensuous curves of Cove flatware (Yamazaki). Beauville Peony porcelain dinnerware (Fitz and Floyd) and hand-blown Trellis crystal stemware (Wedgewood) combine elegance in table accessories. Photo courtesy of the International Linen Promotion Commission.
Figure 12.20 Sumptuous bed hangings softly frame luxurious pillows and a collection of oriental containers at the foot of this guest room bed in the Sara Delano Roosevelt House, a designated historical landmark in New York City. Interior design by Anthony Antine and Mark Polo. Photo courtesy of DuPont "Teflon" soil and stain repellent.

warmth, and to provide privacy; and as table covers. Their use today is far more decorative, although they may provide a certain amount of psychological warmth because of their texture, pattern, and color. Traditional tapestry designs from Europe are still being manufactured today, and contemporary artists are creating textile hangings with innovative methods of construction and design.

- *Fabric art* or soft sculpture are handwoven or constructed fabric or textile pieces that hang on the wall. Handmade antique or new coverlets or quilts are also used as wall hangings and table covers.

Objects from Nature

Plants

Caring for green and flowering plants is a satisfying and rewarding pastime. Plants add a quality of life and interest to interiors because they are continually growing and changing and because of their free-flowing and sculptural form. Each type of plant has a distinctive quality of design that makes it better suited to one style of interior than another. For example, the *cactus* has a strong, bristling, hard-edged quality and a dramatic sculptural form making it well suited to clean, structural interiors. The Boston *fern* is soft and feathery—characteristics that make it suitable in both traditional and contemporary environments where it adds textural variety. When selecting plants pay close attention to the shape, texture, and suitability to the area where they are to be placed.

Because plants are living organisms, they require special care. Plants need adequate light, proper temperatures, and careful feeding, watering, and cleaning. These needs vary according to the type of plant. Some are sturdy, whereas others are quite sensitive to environmental changes. In some interiors such as greenhouses and solariums, live plants can or may become the very reason for the room's existence.

Plants look healthy and well formed in floral shops or nurseries because they have been raised in greenhouses under controlled conditions. Yet when they are moved into typically overheated or overcooled or dry human environments, they often become quite sickly. Unhealthy and neglected plants look worse than no plants at all. Living with plants from day to day, it is not uncommon to become unaware of how bad a poorly-cared-for plant might appear.

Those who have the ability to raise and maintain healthy, nice looking plants are said to have a green thumb. Those who do not have green thumbs or whose interior environments are not conducive to healthy plants may need to consider alternatives. One such alternative is the commercial plant service available in many places. These plant services care for greenery on a contract basis and will advise as to the type of plant that does best in a given setting. These firms may even sell or lease the plants and in some cases will offer a warranty for their product and service. Another alternative is to seek professional advice on selection and care so that a plant will thrive in its new environment.

Some plants will survive very well with artificial light, but in dark environments with dramatic lighting like certain restaurants and lounges, artificial plants may be a suitable alternative. Fortunately the quality of artificial plants is improving. Today silk leaves and blooms are combined with actual trunks and plastic stems to create fairly convincing artificial plants, trees, and flowers. The quality of artificial foliage varies a great deal. The better the quality, the more realistic the flora appears. Artificial plants need regular cleaning in order to continue to look their best.

Flowers and Greenery

Figure 12.21

Any time of the year, we can find growing or natural things that can be brought indoors to brighten the environment and lift the spirits. Cut flowers from the garden or florist add color and life to interiors. Arrangements can be very formal and precise, like the Japanese *ikebana* in which flowers are arranged according to strict, ancient rules of placement. Geometric bouquets purchased through florists continue in popularity, but bouquets of spring or summer blooms that appear to have been brought straight in from the garden and loosely arranged in an artistic way are often more pleasing because they have soft flowing lines that imitate the way flowers grow in nature.

Flowers can be used as single blooms or massed in myriads of color and texture combinations, using a wide variety of flowers. But when flowers are not available, or simply as a change of pace, other natural and growing things can be used seasonally to bring life to interiors. For example, wreaths or baskets full of pine boughs and cones can be used all through the winter, not just at Christmas, to add a touch of greenery. In the early fall, branches of bright autumn leaves are cheerful, and in late fall and early winter, bowls, baskets, or sprays of hardy berries like *pyracantha* bring warmth to a cool season. Bowls or baskets full of apples, horse chestnuts, or other late fall delights are attractive and long lasting. Pumpkins, gourds, and winter squash, or piles of lemons, limes, or oranges make fine

Figure 12.21 An informal arrangement of flowers.

winter displays. In the spring, blossoms from fruit trees or pussy willows and corkscrew willows are interesting alternatives to flower arrangements.

In the summer there is a wonderful array of flowers available, but other growing things can be equally exciting. Fresh summer fruits and vegetables in interesting arrangements are beautiful and eventually even edible. Freshly cut herbs from the garden make unusual greenery for flower arrangements and are also very appealing used by themselves in monochromatic arrangements. Dried herbs, grasses, and weeds make long-lived compositions if arranged with restraint and care. Ivy pulled from the garden is also long lasting when placed in water. With so many possibilities, there is no need to despair the lack of a green thumb. Creating arrangements of flowers and other types of plant life is a most rewarding and creative activity.

Selecting the container is a delightful part of the creative process. A beautifully designed vase is a fine way to display flowers, but anything that will hold water is fair game for arrangements. Water-tight containers can often be hidden inside baskets and other porous or leaky objects to make them flower-worthy. Some of the most interesting arrangements may be created in very unusual containers. For example, an old rusty disk from a tiller could hold a fall arrangement, a wicker picnic basket could be filled with summer garden flowers, and a small copper teakettle could complement a sweet country bouquet.

massed together in baskets, glass bowls, or any appropriate container where their beauty can be fully appreciated. Rocks can be displayed in much the same way as shells, massed together or mounted on stands. The beauty of some rocks only becomes evident after cutting and polishing, which often reveals natural designs of amazing beauty.

- Animal skins and hunting trophies may add an exotic or rustic quality to certain interiors. However, some people may object to such things on grounds of sensitivity, concern for conservation, or cruelty to animals. This should be a matter of careful discrimination.

- Fish, like plants, are living organisms and bring a definite quality of life to interior environments. However, like plants, they also require meticulous upkeep in order to be attractive—a dirty aquarium or sick fish are anything but appealing. As with plants, there are also services available in some areas for maintaining aquariums and fish.

Other Accessories

There are a number of other things that appear in our environments that are products of rapidly developing and constantly changing technology. Appliances, computers, video systems, audio systems, and telephones are important

Figure 12.24

Other Natural Objects

Consider this list of other objects from nature that often find their way into interior environments.

- Sea shells and rocks can be displayed as decorative accessories. Large shells can be mounted on specially designed pedestals or displayed on a table or shelf as any other art object. Small shells can be

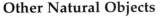

Figure 12.22

Figure 12.23

Figure 12.25

Figure 12.22 Branches with blossoms have interesting forms.

Figure 12.23 Branches of blossoms and a Chinese wardrobe chest create an exotic background for a table of Oriental accessories featuring a cloisonné (brass and porcelain) lamp of fine proportions. The spiraling,

free-form quality of the floral arrangement establishes vertical asymmetrical balance to the visually weighted vessels and containers. Furniture and fabrics by and photo courtesy of Brunschwig and Fils.

Figure 12.24 A bowl of fruit adds life and interest to an interior.
Figure 12.25 An antique washbasin and pitcher make an appealing container for flowers.

elements of a functional interior. These are chosen primarily for their function, although they may be good design as well. They should be considered an important part of the design and be accommodated with sensitivity to their function and aesthetic appeal.

The Use of Accessories
Collections

Many of us enjoy collecting objects, and the collections usually say something about the background, travels, or experiences of the collector. Some collections are worthy of display and help to impart a personal quality · to the environment. These collections might be pieces of fine art, porcelain or other ceramic bodies, antique toys, shells, books, bottles or other glass pieces, stamps, coins, guns

Figure 12.26

and swords, photographs, or any pieces of personal interest. When space in a particular environment is not sufficient to accommodate an entire collection, the finest pieces should be selected for display, grouped, and arranged in harmony with the principles and elements of design.

The Japanese Approach to Displaying Collections

The Japanese are widely esteemed in Western culture for their aesthetic sensitivity. There is much to be learned from the way they collect and display objets d'art in their traditional environments. The traditional Japanese home had a specially designated area called the *tokonoma*, which was a type of shrine for the display of one or two art objects and an arrangement of flowers (ikebana). These displays were changed regularly, and pieces were often chosen to honor a special guest who was seated near the tokonoma. Objects not on display were safely stored for later use. This approach to the display of art objects is characterized by the excitement of bringing out old and treasured pieces that have been packed away for a time and then rediscovered. These possessions become new again and are used with refreshed appreciation.

This clean or minimal philosophy is in harmony with the idea that "less is more"—a concept that has been a hallmark of the modern design movement and is still the favored approach to many designs. Such designs, stripped of all unnecessary embellishment, can be appealing because they create a sense of space and freedom. Neat, well-ordered spaces devoid of mess and clutter can be peaceful and calming as well. Any object placed in this kind of environment is important because it does not compete visually with other elements of the design. Therefore, a carefully selected art piece or accessory can become a focal point in the room.

Figure 12.27

Figure 12.28

Figure 12.26 A collection of plates adds a personal touch to an interior.
Figure 12.27 The less-is-more philosophy in accessorizing is evident in this large-scale modern solo grouping. A single massive plant and pot on a high-tech table, surrounded by a grid pattern in the floor and padded fabric folding screen, is reminiscent of the Japanese tokonoma where only a few, sensitively selected accessories are displayed. Upholstered furniture by and photo courtesy of Brunschwig and Fils.

Figure 12.28 A tokonoma from the traditional Japanese house.

The Victorian Approach to Displaying Collections

During the Victorian era of the nineteenth century, there was a tendency to fill every available inch of space with *nicknacks*. Shelves and tables were crowded with objets d'art. When new pieces were introduced, the others were pushed a little more tightly together to make room for the new piece. Everything was on display.

This approach, not uncommon today, is called organized clutter. Some environments may appear this way due to a lack of organization and planning, a lack of will to part with anything, or a desire to create a feeling of nostalgia. To others, however, each object in the space may have special significance and create a system of emotional support important to their well-being.

Emotionally Supportive Design

Some interiors are appealing because of their clean, streamlined approach to art and accessories, while others are interesting and charming because they are filled with personal treasures. Somewhere between the extremes of Japanese and Victorian philosophies of accessory display lies comfortable and pleasing middle ground that suits the environment and provides the right balance of emotional support for the users.

Art, accessories, and furnishings have the power to provide emotional support because they are often links to esteemed people or events. This is why a piece of furniture or cherished piece of porcelain often serves as a *memento* of a person, time, or place. Those who emigrated from one country to another or who, in years past, moved from civilized surroundings to settle the wilderness, often carried and protected treasured objects from their past into their uncertain futures. To preserve a fragile remembrance from the past and keep it undamaged through the years is a remarkable accomplishment and a source of pride. Today, these same objects are passed from one generation to another with great respect and love.

A photograph, a certificate, and *memorabilia* such as pressed flowers, a tiny christening gown, a watch or medal, and even a map can also preserve a memory and help recall

Figure 12.29

Figure 12.30

an important time in one's life. Objects collected while traveling serve as reminders of exciting places and experiences. Well-designed pieces received as gifts from cherished friends may be decorative and also serve as remembrances of those people.

Drawings and crafts created by children are part of the emotional support system of a family and should be displayed with pride to encourage creativity. Such pieces often have artistic merit, and the child seeing the work on display is encouraged to continue the creative endeavors. These pieces could be matted and displayed in a place of honor or simply taped to the refrigerator door. It is the recognition that counts.

We want to be surrounded by the things we love whether it be in large doses or one object at a time. The clutter approach is not more correct than the minimal philosophy, merely better suited to certain interiors and individual human needs. It is important to determine what kind of a balance is most pleasing to us and appropriate to our interiors so that we can live happily in emotionally supportive interiors.

When planning interiors, we should be careful not to discard well loved pieces simply because we might not be completely confident of the aesthetic quality of the piece. For example, to some, a porcelain figurine might seem to be valueless kitsch. To another it might represent a cherished childhood memory, or it may have belonged to a dear friend or relative. We alone can make those determinations of value, and it is the inclusion of valued art and accessories that makes an environment emotionally supportive as well as a statement of personal experience.

Nonresidential Considerations

Art and accessories in nonresidential interiors create a feeling of finish and add the important element of human interest to spaces that could otherwise be quite impersonal. For this reason, many nonresidential design projects have specific budgets for artwork. The decision on how to spend those budgets usually belongs to the architect or designer,

Figure 12.29 An intimate bedside accessory arrangement of organized clutter displays treasured mementos of times and people now past. Room is left for the teacup and examining stamps while seated nearby or curled up in bed. The Louis XV fauteuil chair is graced with a warm peach-colored reading blanket and lovely vase of peach tulips. Window blind by and photo courtesy of Bali, Carey-McFall Corporation.
Figure 12.30 Organized clutter.

Figure 12.31

Figure 12.32

a committee, or an art consultant. Sadly, sometimes the art budget is extremely limited or consumed by cost overrides in other areas of the design. At the other end of the spectrum are the large corporations who collect art not only for its aesthetic value but for investment as well. Some of these have staff members whose sole responsibility is the acquisition of art and its dispersement to permanent collections throughout the corporation.

Many large nonresidential projects such as offices, hotels, and hospitals benefit from the use of art, though not in permanent collections. These interiors are usually redesigned every few years, and a change in the art is often part of the new design program. Selecting pieces for this kind of design project requires extreme sensitivity, because not only must the art be purchased in large quantities but it must also be chosen for its relationship to the elements of the design, its price, and its aesthetic merit. Success in this kind of art selection is not as common as it should be, but the errors made in these situations can provide one key to understanding how to select quality art.

Figure 12.33

Fine art, regardless of price, cannot be exclusively tied to a decorative scheme by color or some other element—it must have its own aesthetic merit. If a new design program truly demands a change in the art, then the pieces being removed, if they have aesthetic merit, should still be of value in some other setting. If they have no value ten years

Figure 12.31 *Appropriation*, likely to be the buzzword of the 1990s, is the search and procurement of objects from far away places and of unusual historic finds that are blended in often disparate or startling combinations. Here, seemingly unrelated accessories were passionately collected by American pop artist, the late Andy

Warhol, in his New York home. Photo by Norman McGrath, © 1987.
Figure 12.32 Accessories are the key ingredient to the interior design of the Hard Rock Café in Houston, Texas, where fans of Elvis Presley can enjoy memorabilia of the king of rock music. The café is in an old Protestant

church, a setting with fine architectural character. Photo by Norman McGrath, © 1987.
Figure 12.33 Industrial-design educator Doug Stout's office provides the setting for an unusual link with his native Britain and his lifelong fascination with trains. His bookshelf

displays part of his collection of British locomotives and rail cars purchased during visits to England and Scotland. They are not only visually appealing but serve as an important cultural tie with his past. Photo by John Wang and Doug McIntosh.

Art and Accessories   329

Figure 12.34

after their initial installation, then certainly they had no aesthetic merit to begin with. Such pieces of decorator art or motel art will only find their way to incinerators or dusty thrift-store tables. Finding good quality prints, reproductions, or originals at the price points required by large projects may demand some effort. However, the search is worth the impact that good quality art creates in an interior design. When judging a piece of art, it might be wise to ask ourselves, What will be the value of this piece ten years from now? If it can weather the test of time, it will be well chosen. The ability to choose well comes through the process of exposure and training outlined earlier in this chapter.

Some designs such as restaurants and boutiques often require the selection of art and accessories keyed to a theme such as English Tudor or Country French. This kind of project may be like creating a stage setting, and each piece of art and every accessory will be selected because it reinforces the concept for the design. This often requires some research into the history of the decorative arts to ensure that selections are supportive and appropriate to the stated goal or theme.

One of the most crucial aspects of a design is its relationship to the users. Designers may find it discouraging to return to a design for a post-occupancy evaluation and find that things have changed; for example, the pristine reception area has been invaded by the receptionist's personal items, and the secretary's wall is covered with postcards and pictures of the family. It is human nature to surround ourselves with things we love, and design must accommodate that tendency so that the work environment can be pleasant and supportive in every way. If a design is so clean that it forces management to create policies prohibiting personal belongings, then it has failed to meet the emotional needs of its users. It should not be difficult to provide a surface for photographs or cards and a space for personal mementos. Rather than detract, such considerate planning will add vitality to the design.

Notes

1. Knobler, Nathan. *The Visual Dialogue.* (New York: Holt, Rinehart, and Winston, 1971), p. 492.

Bibliography

Allen, Phyllis Sloan, and Miriam Stimpson. *Beginnings of Interior Environment.* New York: Macmillan, 1990.

Better Homes and Gardens. *Better Homes and Gardens New Decorating Book,* Gerald M. Knox, ed. Des Moines: Merideth, 1981.

Gilliatt, Mary. *The Decorating Book.* New York: Pantheon, 1981.

Gombrich, E.H. *The Story of Art.* Oxford: Phaidon, 1979.

Hicks, David. *On Living—with Taste.* London: Frewin, 1968.

Knobler, Nathan. *The Visual Dialogue.* New York: Holt, Rinehart, and Winston, 1971.

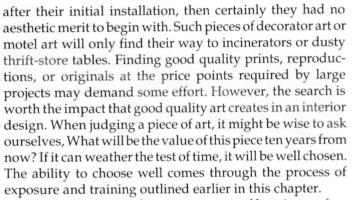

Figure 12.34 The interior of the Salt Lake City International Airport is enriched with large-scale paintings by a Utah artist. The subject for the paintings is the ruggedly beautiful southern Utah landscape, which not only adds the quality of fine art to the interior but also provides a preview of lgeographic sites for arriving passengers. MHT Architects. Photos by Andrew Arnone and Darlene Langford.

THE BUILDING

The building is often as exciting as the interior, especially when we understand and appreciate the systems and architecture that make the structure possible. Architecture exists for the interior, providing the shell for the functions that take place there. The increasingly sophisticated building systems of today make possible higher standards of living, bringing about greater comfort and ease.

Contemporary buildings utilize the most up-to-date building systems. They also often incorporate historic architectural proportions, materials, and details, making it possible for us to enjoy the luxuries and conveniences of the twentieth century along with the timeless architecture of period styles.

In Natchez, Mississippi, where historic homes are lovingly preserved, thousands of people participate in an annual pilgrimage. Stanton Hall, a magnificent antebellum mansion standing amidst rich Southern foliage, reminds us of the romance and culture of a past era. Museum houses around the country and around the wold invite us to relish timeless design.

Whether constructing new or remodeling older buildings, the framework and inner structural systems make possible the shapes, angles, lines, and conveniences of electric, plumbing, and communication systems we often take for granted. Electric wires are threaded through drilled holes in the joists and rafters. Once the finish material, such as Sheetrock or paneling, is in place, it is unlikely that the inner systems can be altered without great expense and labor. The placement of each piece of lumber is here for a reason; all exist to reinforce and make possible the structure, both on the exterior and the interior. Photo by Ted Spiegel.

Figure 13.1

Figure 13.2

Plumbing Systems

Plumbing is a term that indicates pipe installed within a building for carrying a volume of air or water. Plumbing typically means the water intake system, water-conditioning and/or water-heating system (including components of passive or active solar systems discussed later in this chapter), and water disposal systems—drains and sewer lines. Plumbing is carried within the framework or threaded through the masonry block and is termed *rough plumbing*. Copper pipe is generally used for water intake, and cast-iron (more costly but quieter) or plastic (PVC—polyvinyl chloride) pipe for sewer or waste-water disposal pipes. *Finish plumbing* includes hookups to appliances (dishwashers and clothes washers) and installation of *fixtures* (sinks, toilets, urinals). Shower units and bath tubs/whirlpools are installed during the framing before the *Sheetrock* is hung.

Plumbing is also used to facilitate *central vacuum systems* and may also be used for fresh air intake for wood-burning stoves and for furnace (heating) and central air-conditioning (cooling) units.

In nonresidential design, space will usually be allotted for a *plumbing chase* (the thick plumbing wall area) that provides access for maintenance.

Heating, Ventilation, and Air Conditioning

Central heating or *space heating* of the interior is generally handled through a *furnace* and connecting hot water pipes or *ductwork* or *ducts* (run through the walls, floors, and ceiling joists). The furnace heats an element that in turn heats air that passes by it and is blown out, called *forced-air heating*. *Cold air return* vents draw air back to the furnace where it is reheated for recirculation. Warm air typically enters a room at the floor or ceiling level through *registers*. Many types and price ranges of furnaces exist, fueled by electricity, natural gas, coal, or oil. A *high-efficiency furnace* uses less of the resource to heat the interior thereby costing

Figure 13.3

less to run, although these units have a higher initial purchase price. Furnaces may also be fitted with humidifying devices (*humidifiers*) that add moisture to the heated air. (Any method of heating will draw moisture out of the air, which is harmful to health, plants, and furnishings.) *Radiant heat* is produced by using a furnace to heat water in a *boiler*. The hot water passes through pipes to a *radiator* that warms the room. This type of system is not used commonly today, but it may be

Figure 13.1 As winter snows melt, workmen are busy with the remodeling of the exterior. New windows and siding, new paint and trim are part of an extensive face-lift for this grand old home. Beyond the single family residence, older buildings, such as this, are often converted via "adaptive reuse" into professional and

business offices, retail space, and condominiums. The interior designer must understand what exists inside the walls and comprehend the complexity of existing building systems in order to specify removal or remodeling of walls, or updating, moving, or removing existing support systems, such as plumbing and wiring. The finish package, or cabinetry, woodwork,

and metal trim, is also a part of the building's systems. Photo by Ted Spiegel.
Figure 13.2 Solarium spaces are desirable in many homes and buildings and are often built on as a retrofit, if not integrated into the building's blueprints. Here, unusual angles and soaring heights give architectural drama to this solarium living area. Looking through a traditional sash

window, the impression is one of retrofitting a new passive solar space onto an older one. Note the ceramic flooring, important as a thermal mass to slowly collect solar heat, then to slowly release it at night. Photo by Norman McGrath © 1989.
Figure 13.3 A high-efficiency furnace, this one fired by natural gas. Space planning must allow for cool air return for

found in older homes. The furnace is controlled with a *thermostat*, which can be set to maintain a specified temperature. Thermostats for small systems are often programmable to accommodate needs that vary according to the time of day or the use of the building. Large HVAC systems will be monitored and controlled by computer.

Interior furnishings must never obstruct heat registers or cold air returns. Where draperies hang to the floor, clear plastic deflectors can be placed over a vent or register that channel or direct the hot air into the room.

Room or area heating can also be handled through electric or gas-fueled *baseboard units,* by *radiant ceiling panels,* by *radiator units,* by *portable space heaters,* or by *wood-* or *coal-burning stoves* and fireplaces or fireplace inserts. These units also must not be obstructed with furnishings that may combust, or catch on fire. Local building codes will require a *clearance,* or distance (usually about three feet), that restricts placement of combustible materials, including walls and structural components, near the heat source. An exception is for insulated *zero-clearance fireplace units,* which can be placed in combustible walls. (Space and room heating are also discussed under Active and Passive Solar Systems.)

Ventilation and air-conditioning are interrelated terms. *Ventilation* refers to natural breezes or air currents gained by opened windows and doors. The designer must be aware that window treatments and furniture placement should allow for, and not obstruct, desired natural ventilation. Ventilation may sufficiently cool the interior for most of the year, supplemented by air-conditioning only in the hottest seasons. However, hot, arid or humid regions rely heavily on air-conditioning for livable comfort for much of the year.

Air-conditioning can be handled similarly to heating in small-scale settings: by a central system or by cooling one room at a time. A *central air-conditioning system* may be handled through the forced-air furnace unit or by a separate unit located outside or inside the building. In very humid climates, the air-conditioning unit may have a *dehumidifier,* a unit that removes excess humidity (moisture) from the air. In dry climates, an *evaporative cooling system,* or *swamp cooler,* may be less costly to run and may cool more efficiently. The evaporative or swamp cooler works by forcing air through moistened pads or filters and is installed in a wall or window or in the ceiling connected with central ductwork. With this system, windows or doors are kept ajar in the rooms where the cooled air is to be drawn.

The designer should be aware of the heating and cooling system and ductwork in the case of remodeling or structural changes in the interior design. Walls or ceilings that carry ductwork cannot be removed or altered without destroying the heating and air-conditioning. Contractors and HVAC specialists are valuable resources for the designer in this regard and should be consulted before structural changes are made.

Figure 13.5

Figure 13.4

Figure 13.6

recirculation and for exhaust to the exterior of the building. The duct system leads from the furnace to the registers carrying volumes of forced air to living or working areas. Photo by Karla Nielson.
Figure 13.4 Where electric heat is the choice, furnaces may be electric, or heating may take place on a room-by-room basis, such as the baseboard heater in this

bedroom. Providing both privacy and summer shade, the miniblinds at the window do not obstruct the natural wooded landscape. Optix window blinds by and photo courtesy of Nanik.
Figure 13.5 The central air-conditioning unit cools air by refrigerating it. This system can be fitted with dehumidifiers for very humid climates, where evaporative coolers

would be totally ineffective. In dry climates, the cost of operating this system is many times greater than the evaporative cooling system. The central air-conditioning system operates on a sealed-environment principle, making it cleaner and possibly more convenient. Photo by Karla Nielson.
Figure 13.6 The evaporative cooler, used in arid climates, operates on the principle of

forcing air through water-soaked pads, which cools it. Also called a swamp cooler, the unit may be mounted into a wall or window to cool one or more areas, or on the roof, where a duct system carries cool air to registers in each room. To draw the air through the home, a door or window must be slightly ajar. Photo by Karla Nielson.

Other Built-In Systems

Fire Alert Systems

Fire alert systems are single or interconnected networks of *smoke detectors* and heat-sensing devices that alert the occupants of a potential fire hazard. They may emit a shrill whistle or a long or interrupted buzz or beep that will indicate danger.

Security Systems

Security systems guard against unlawful entry. They are sensing devices that take many forms. When activated they may turn on lights, set off alarms, or automatically notify security guards. Security systems can become quite elaborate, even to the point of being connected with the local police dispatcher's unit. Security systems vary dramatically in price and options.

Communication Systems

In the home, the *intercom* system is an effective way of communicating from one area to another without raising the voice. The wiring should be installed when the home is being built, although radiolike units can be purchased and installed at a later date. The intercom can also pipe music to various rooms, and parents can listen to children in other parts of the house with the intercom. Other *communication systems* are discussed under Nonresidential Considerations.

The Smart House System

A new system available in 1990 has been developed by The Smart House Development Venture, Inc., a wholly owned operation of the National Research Center of the National Association of Home Builders (NAHB). This system is one that centrally locates the control of all the systems in a house, based on a closed loop principle for

(A)
Figure 13.7

(B)

(A)
Figure 13.8

(B)

(C)

energy distribution. Small microchips are installed in each appliance and outlet allowing the appliance to identify itself to the system. Gas systems, fire alert systems, security systems, electric appliances, and lighting—all can be controlled from a central location as well as the familiar switch. Monitor screens can be installed in several rooms, and the system can also be controlled via telephone keypad, by a remote controller, by video touch on the screen, and even by voice.

Some benefits of this new system include early fire detection, with screens showing the fire's location, which rooms are occupied, and the safest path of exit. The same information can immediately be relayed to the fire department or emergency monitoring service, and the gas service to the home can be shut off. Doors and windows can be locked and monitored from remote locations. An unauthorized entry can be relayed to the homeowner, the neighbors, or the police. A surveillance camera can also be plugged into any outlet, and the picture appears on a television plugged into any outlet.

The Smart House system calls for a unified cable that performs three functions: (1) power distribution, (2) control or data signal distribution, and (3) audio and video telephone signal distribution. This unified cable would replace the spaghettilike system of wires now being strung throughout the house. The system should simplify gas and electrical system construction because of ease of installation for the builder, fewer subcontractors needed, and less installation time. The result is a home that is safer, offering more convenience and peace of mind to the homeowner. Projected costs vary from $5,000 to $10,000.[1]

Figure 13.7 Overhead systems. *(A)* A residential smoke detector sets off a shrill alarm when smoke fills the air, an important safety feature against fire hazard and smoke inhalation. *(B)* A nonresidential ceiling with HVAC (heating, ventilation, and air-conditioning) in the foreground and in the background, a sprinkler to douse potential fires in this office. Together with lighting, the overhead systems are housed in an acoustic-suspended ceiling. Photos by Karla Nielson.

Figure 13.8 *(A)* The intercom is a means of communication. If the intercom is left on in the home, monitoring of activities, of infants, or of ailing family members can take place. The major advantage of an intercom is to communicate without raising the voice. Intercom systems may contain other features such as a radio and in some models a cassette tape player. *(B)* The intercom wires in the wall surrounded with insulation, ready for installation of the intercom unit. *(C)* The intercom station near the back door. An intercom at the front door would allow monitoring

Passive and Active Solar Systems

Many buildings today incorporate active or passive solar heating. The designer needs to understand the terms and concepts of solar energy so that the interior design may complement and augment, rather than detract from or obstruct, the system. Architectural solar systems require some investment of funds to purchase materials or to create the structure that utilizes the sun's energy for space heating and water heating. The amount spent on the system or on components is compared to the amount it would cost to purchase and run a conventional space- (furnace) or water-heating system. The *payback period* is the number of years required to save enough to pay for the system. If the payback period is less than five to ten years, it is generally considered a good investment (if the occupant will stay in the home or building that long).

Active Solar Systems

An *active solar system* is made of mechanical parts that convert *incident solar radiation* (*insolation*) to thermal energy to warm air space, heat water, and even run air-conditioning units. The system consists of six basic components that may be altered as needed. These components are (1) *collectors* that capture or collect the sun's warmth by means of panels mounted to face the sun at approximately ninety-degree angles. They may be focusing (like a magnifying glass) or nonfocusing (like a greenhouse—heating a material, which in turn heats a gas or liquid medium). This thermal energy is moved by (2) *transport*, usually via a fluid or air, from the collectors. This may require pumps, valves, and pipes for liquid transport or blowers, dampers, and ducts for hot air. The transport component moves the heat to (3) *storage*, a reservoir that stores the thermal energy. It may be simple or complex, made of water, rocks, aluminum oxide, or other materials. The storage ensures warmth at night and on cloudy days when no thermal energy is being collected. (4) *Distribution* carries the heat through pipes and ducts to the space to be heated. It usually requires larger ducts and radiating surfaces than conventional furnace systems. (5) *Auxiliary heating* is usually a central or localized system. Hooked into the solar distribution unit, the furnace is capable of taking over heating needs if the active solar system cannot produce enough heat on successive sunless days. (6) *Control*, perhaps in the form of a thermostat, is an automatic or a manual system to control heat and energy flow.

Active systems can be complex, costly, bulky, and awkward to install. Solar systems may also be subject to breakdown of components, yet they generally provide between 70 to 100 percent of the interior space-heating or water-heating needs. Much research must take place before selecting the exact system best suited for an individual building.

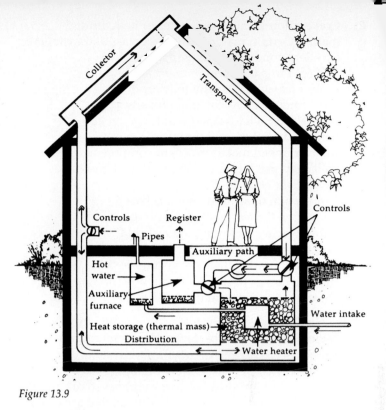

Figure 13.9

Passive Solar Systems

Passive designs share common aspects with active systems. Both collect, store, and distribute thermal solar energy for space heating and water heating. The difference is that passive designs are dependent on natural heat and cold movement. Heat is naturally transferred in three ways:

1. Radiation is the spreading of heat through space, as in the radiating heat from the sun to the earth. Heat from fireplaces and space room heaters where heated elements send forth warmth is radiant heat. The heat waves from the sun, called solar energy or solar gain, are long, strong electromagnetic waves. These waves are strong enough to pass through glass windows, where they refract against floors, walls, ceilings, furnishings, and people. As solar waves bounce off surfaces, some of that energy is absorbed, and what is left becomes shorter, weaker wavelengths that cannot repenetrate the glass windows. Thus, heat is trapped and builds up inside glass-enclosed spaces, a phenomenon known as the *greenhouse effect*.

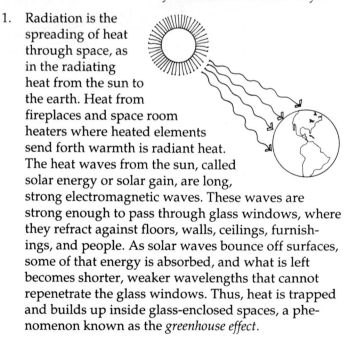

without having to open the door to find out who is there. Intercom systems are often used in city apartment or condominium dwellings that function also as security-entrance systems. Photos by Karla Nielson.

Figure 13.9 Six components of an active solar space- or water-heating system. (1) Collectors capture the sun's warmth through panels. (2) Transport of the heat via a liquid or air. (3) Storage of the thermal energy, which may be simple or complex. (4) Distribution of the energy through ducts and/or pipes. (5) Auxiliary energy such as a furnace to take over heating needs. (6) Mechanical controls to gauge heat and energy flow.

2. Conduction is the transference of heat through matter. Certain materials such as glass and metal are excellent conductors allowing heat and cold to pass through their molecules, which is why they are most often used as cooking utensils. Glass- and metal-framed windows conduct heat and cold into the interior; metal makes excellent components of solar collectors used in active solar systems and in passive water heaters.

3. Convection or air movement is based on *natural thermal flow* (the path of rising warm air moving toward cold and the subsequent falling of cool air). The greenhouse effect warms interior air, making convection work to our advantage through these natural thermal air flows.

When the passive system is augmented by mechanical devices such as pumps, fans or blowers, and ductwork or even connected to an existing furnace system, it becomes a *hybrid solar energy system*. New buildings may integrate passive solar design principles or hybrid systems into the design of the building. Existing buildings that are remodeled, or have additions, to include an active, passive, or hybrid solar system are *retrofitted*. It is important to note that most solar systems are custom designed for the architecture and space; effectiveness will therefore vary.

Direct Gain The simplest form of passive solar heating is *direct solar gain*, which is sunshine coming through south-facing windows. The heat is generally absorbed by a thermal mass (dense material slow to heat and cool) such as floors or walls of concrete, ceramic or quarry tiles over cement or rocks, bricks or stone, or barrels or pools of water or sand. Direct gain may allow too much heat, light, and direct sunshine to enter the interior, causing fading and damage to furnishings, and too much heat loss may take place at night. For this reason, direct gain windows may require light-filtering or shading devices and movable insulation to guard against excessive heat loss.

Indirect and Isolated Gain *Indirect and isolated passive solar gain* means gathering the heat or energy separate from the occupied areas. Listed and illustrated here are some of the most commonly used passive solar systems.

- *Trombe walls* are thermal storage walls named after the French scientist who developed them. A Trombe wall system uses large areas of south-facing glass as collectors. Within a few inches of the glass, a dark-colored masonry of brick, concrete, or stone slowly conducts the collected heat to radiate warmth to the interior at night. The Trombe walls have vents at the top and bottom to utilize a natural convection loop—

Figure 13.10

hot air becomes lighter and rises and vents high in the wall; low vents allow cooler, heavier air to return to the heat trap to be warmed.

- *Thermosiphoning* traps air in spaces in the walls and roof. The air is heated and rises to a point where it can be drawn off with fans through ducts. Fiberglass panels used in the ceilings can also admit translucent light. A thermosiphonic system is less effective than thermal mass Trombe walls but also is less costly.

- *Roof monitors* are window arrangements set high in the wall or ceiling as clerestory windows, skylights, or cupolas (glassed-in extensions, also called sunscoops, in the roof). Monitors admit light, and solar winter heat, and ventilate out summer heat. In the winter the lighter hot air must be circulated to the floor level and the monitors should be protected against heat loss at night.

- *Solar greenhouses* or solariums are the most popular of all indirect passive solar system options, probably because they are the easiest to retrofit and because a greenhouse sun space is a delightful, healthful, and versatile extension of interior space. They are especially popular in restaurants and nonresidential settings, and in homes they can serve as living/dining space, as a hot tub or swimming pool area, or as a gardening greenhouse. A solarium works best with a thermal mass or rock or sand surrounded by rigid insulation. Insulated glass facing within fifteen degrees of due south works best to collect sunshine.

Figure 13.10 A 1950s bungalow with a rabbit warren of small rooms was transformed by interior designers Barbara Ross and Barbara Schwartz of Dexter Design into a bright and easy-to-maintain open space home. The most spectacular change is this greenhouse added on the sunny southern exposure. Originally an enclosed porch with jalousie glass windows, the entire structure was removed. A sound understanding of the old and new building systems was crucial to the designers' successful remodeling, producing this new architectural and interior design. The floor tiles act as a thermal mass and were selected as Perla, twelve-inch-by-twelve-inch ceramic tile by Ceramica Nuova D'Agostino. Photo courtesy of the Italian Tile Center.

Figure 13.11 Types of passive solar heat gain. (A) Direct gain through windows—amplifies the heat that is absorbed by a thermal mass, such as brick, tile, or concrete. (B) The Trombe wall—glass set very near a thermal mass wall with vents to draw off the heated air into the interior and return cool air to the heating space. (C) Thermosiphoning wall and roof—spaces between the outer and inner wall trap heated air that is drawn off via fans and ducts or registers. (D)

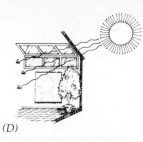

(A)   (B)   (C)   (D)

Figure 13.11

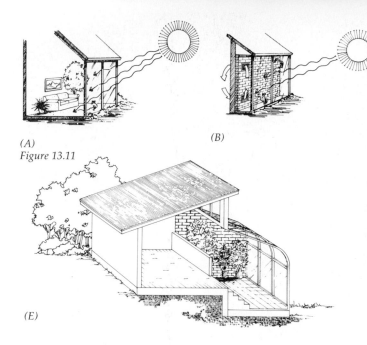

(E)

(A)

Figure 13.12

The thermal mass stores the heat in direct-gain fashion to be released through convection and reradiation in cold weather and at night. The solarium/greenhouse can be designed to close off from the interior at night and during cold, cloudy spells in order to control excessive heat gain and heat loss in the main body of the house or building.

Greenhouses can produce 10 to 50 percent of the heat for the interior, depending on the size and insulation of the building, the climate, the size and orientation of the greenhouse, and factors such as protection from prevailing winds, landscaping, movable insulation, interior air flow (an unobstructed convection loop through the house and back to the greenhouse is essential), and the design and quality of the greenhouse itself. Diagonal glass, used in many greenhouses, is the most difficult to protect against heat loss at night and excessive heat gain in the summer, making it less efficient than vertical glass.

Energy Conservation

The comfort of conventional and solar buildings often depends on the control of excessive heat loss or heat gain to be fully effective. In the winter when the *heat loss* occurs during overcast days and cold nights, the windows or collectors will need either *movable insulation* such as fiberglass insulation panels on the interior or exterior or *insulative window treatments,* such as layered fabric shades, insulating shutters, or lined and interlined draperies.

In the summer, excessive *heat gain* can be a problem and will need control through exterior or interior *shading devices.* Exterior shading devices include awnings, rolling, hinged, or angled shutters, solar screens or sunscreens,

(B)

architectural projections or roof extensions, vine-covered trellises, or deciduous trees. Interior shading window treatments include metallized pleated shades, horizontal and vertical blinds, opaque roller shades, shutters, and soft window treatments (curtains, draperies, shades).

Roof monitors—windows set high in the wall such as clerestory windows that invite sunshine and heat into the interior. (E) A solarium or space-heating greenhouse collects passive solar heat, can provide living space, and may be closed off from the main body of the house during hot or cold spells. This illustration also shows a thermal mass in tile floors over concrete and a brick wall. Adding a solarium on the south side of a building is an excellent way of retrofitting to take advantage of solar energy.

Figure 13.12 In the Sunbelt regions, shading devices are crucial for energy conservation as well as interior comfort. Two window treatments that have proven their success are (A) the pleated fabric shade, metallized on the reverse to reflect heat as well as light, and (B) vertical louvers that can draw open and closed, similar to draperies, or tilt to adjust louvers according to the direction and quantity of light desired. Here, textured strips of fabric are inserted into solid vinyl-grooved vanes, forming an ability to darken the room for heat and light control and complete privacy. Photos courtesy of Del Mar Window Coverings.

Using the earth to insulate is called berming. An earth berm is soil pushed up against the walls, usually on the north side of a building. The berm can be partial, up just a few feet, or it can cover the building up to and even over the roof. The berm may be landscaped, as well, to make it more attractive. Houses submerged into the earth are called earth homes. Some utilize glass on the south for passive solar heating. The constant temperature of the earth maintains even, comfortable temperatures inside the building. However, building construction under the earth can require extra efforts and costs, such as waterproofing against water table seepage and stablization against pressure from the earth.

When air is trapped in or around a home, a natural insulative barrier that conserves energy is formed. This *envelope* concept, originated by architect Lee Porter Butler, has an integral solarium on the building's south side, and vents carry the heated air through channels over the ceiling in the attic, down a double north wall, and through channels under the lower floor. The continuous air convection loop utilizes passive solar gain with or without a thermal mass.

Insulation

Insulation can take several forms. As discussed above, insulation can be movable, as in energy efficient window coverings for the interior or exterior. Insulation also refers to standard materials used in building construction: *rigid panels* or sheets of insulation, *batts* (fluffy fiberglass rolls of insulation), and *blown insulation* (mainly chopped manufactured fiberglass). Strong plastic can aid insulation by forming a *vapor barrier* that will not allow heat or cold to penetrate by convection or air movement.

Window glazing can increase insulative values. Two or even three panes of glass, called *double or triple glazing* will significantly reduce heat loss or heat gain. Triple glazing can be found in the form of storm windows. A tinted "summer storm window" cuts down unwanted solar gain. *Weatherstripping* around doors and windows also helps stop drafts or air infiltration. *Draft dodgers* are any material (heavy rug, fabric tube filled with sand) pushed tightly against a door to prevent cold air infiltration. *Storm doors* and *vestibules* (air lock entries) are other means of keeping out cold air.

Identifying the Professional Roles

Interior design affects not only the finished space but the planning of the space (see chapter 5) and the construction of the walls, units, and systems that are integral to the interior

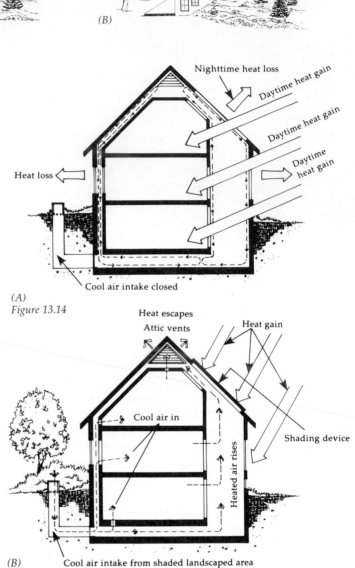

design and architecture. Even if designers do not design the interior structural components, they must be able to communicate with contractors and craftsmen who build, finish, and decorate the space.

When the interior designer does specify a structural change, such as moving a wall, for example, it may be wise to seek the expertise of the architect, general contractor, or structural engineer. By respecting and consulting the professionals in these related fields, the interior design plan can become more feasible and realistic.

Figure 13.13 A house with a bermed north side—earth pushed up against the house and strategically landscaped to buffer against north winds and direct them up over the roof. (A) In the summer, with the sun high overhead, shade is cast on the glass from the foliaged trees and from the wide overhanging eave. (B) On the south, broad windows admit low-angled winter solar gain as filtered through the barren branches of deciduous trees.

Figure 13.14 Envelope system of passive solar design showing (A) the winter heating mode and (B) the summer cooling mode showing air drawn from a cooling tube from the northern, foilage-covered side.

Figure 13.15

All buildings, both residential and nonresidential, must be inspected by a city official, the *building inspector*, who has authority to halt construction if the structure does not meet codes. This is done in order to protect the health and safety of the building's occupants.

The building plans are drafted or executed by a *draftsman* or by the interior designer or an architect, who may draw the plans first in pencil on paper, then in ink on vellum, then reproduced into multiple sets of blueprints. *Drafting* is also done on computers using CAD, or computer-automated design software (see chapter 5, Space Planning).

The working drawings, sometimes called blueprints, are the sets of plans that specify designs, materials, and dimensions to guide each subcontractor or craftsman who works on the home or building. Working drawings include the following:

- Floor plans are drawn to scale (1/4 inch equals one foot or 1/8 inch equals one foot—see chapter 5) and show the layout of the rooms and their relationship to one another. They are used for estimating cost, for scheduling, and actual construction of the building.
- Schedules indicate how various parts of the building are to be finished. Materials and finishes for components such as doors, floors, walls, and ceilings are spelled out in a chart (figure 13.17).
- Site plans show the situation of the building on the land, legal boundaries, slope, key reference points, and possibly information on soils and vegetation. Site plans also indicate details on water, sewer, and electrical system grids (hookups).
- Foundation drawings indicate necessary details on footings, fireplace footings, anchor bolts, breaks in walls, and drains and are used to estimate labor and materials for foundation work.
- Framing plans give projections of the building from the lowest level and up to the roof. It shows sections, key connections, and the layout of the floors and roof, with necessary information on columns, beams, and joists. Details are shown close up or enlarged.
- Cross sections are vertical drawings of a slice through the interior of the building, showing the relationship and scale of the foundation, walls, beams, rooms, stairs, and other architectural elements.
- Exterior elevations are the exterior views of each side of the building (north, south, east, and west, for example) in flat drawings (no perspective) showing the finish building materials, the location and style of doors, windows, architectural detail, roof, chimney, and other details unique to the building.
- Utility plans show a building's mechanical systems: HVAC and plumbing (usually presented separately)

The role of the architect is to interview the clients, work through the programming process (chapter 1) for the building, and design the structure to be functional, structurally sound, strong, stable, and aesthetically pleasing. The interior designer/architect is one who is trained both as an architect and interior designer and who can structurally design or remodel buildings and specify all materials, finishes, and furnishings. The architect may oversee the building and receive a percentage of the total cost of construction as a fee, or the architect may be contracted to design the building and produce the blueprints that are used by a general contractor.

The general contractor is one who may be skilled in many areas of construction and who contracts (hires out) the work to be done in each of the phases of building. The general contractor will work on one of two bases: (1) a turnkey package—the finished building (according to the requirements of the itemized contract) or (2) a cost-plus basis. The turnkey package gives the client the building for a specified amount of money, with the option of adding to the building in the form of extras (items paid for by the client that are not part of the contract). The actual cost of the building may vary from the bid overruns and may be renegotiated at the finish of the building. The general contractor has the option of charging a percentage fee for the building (generally 10%). The cost-plus is billing the client for work done plus a percentage. With this arrangement, it may be harder to predict expenditures, and the client pays whatever the cost of the building when it is completed.

Figure 13.15 Professionals involved in the processes of building systems include the architect as well as the interior designer; both can produce designs and have them blueprinted into plans that are in turn used by the general contractor and subcontractors to execute the jobs. Although some designs today are produced on computer-assisted design hardware and software, the majority are still produced the old-fashioned way—on the drafting board. Photo courtesy of Anderson Windows.

and the electrical and lighting plans. These plans will include layout for other systems such as fire protection, security, and communications (intercom).

- Interior elevations show types of cabinets and millwork (molding, railings) and other special interior features. They are used to obtain bids and construct the items.
- Details are enlargements of construction components where clarification or additional information is needed. This might be a custom window arrangement to be framed.
- Specifications are written documents that describe structural or finish materials or custom work: what is needed, where it is to be located, what quality and craftsmanship level is desired, how it is to be assembled, and any other special considerations needed for correct construction.

- Subcontract is the agreement for specialized work performed by a person or company and specified for a building's construction or finish work. The *subcontractor* will take information from the blueprints, figure out how much labor and materials would be required for the job, and give a bid or solid estimation of the job. The general contractor will usually get three or more bids and select either the lowest bid or the subcontractor with the reputation for the best quality work or select a subcontractor with a reasonable bid and proven quality. The interior design package or parts of it, such as carpeting, window treatments, wall coverings, or furnishings, may also be bid in this manner.

(B)

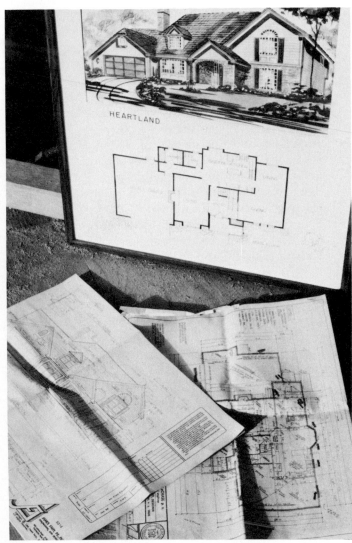

(A)
Figure 13.16

(C)

Figure 13.16 *(A)* The Heartland, a stock plan from Douglas Bennett Associates Architects, was chosen by Brinkerhoff Construction for the Utah Valley Parade of Homes moderate price category. The artist's rendering was displayed at the valley's largest shopping mall to advertise the event. Below the rendering are the sets of blueprints showing the front elevation and, beneath, the main floor plan. *(B)* The finished home, customized and modified to include railing and arched front porch, won top honors as the Best Designed house, inside and out, in its price category. Interior design by Velda Johnson. *(C)* Home shows invariably bring prospective homeowners who want the same home built elsewhere. Here the Heartland is being reproduced in a different locale with modifications, such as utilizing the attic area over the garage as a family room or bedroom. Brick columns will be used in place of the colonial balustrade on the front porch, and the brick and exterior color scheme will vary. Photos by Karla Nielson.

Constructing the Building

When construction begins, the architect or general contractor will set up a method for making everything happen at the right time. A critical path (see figure 13.28) indicates the time frame in consecutive and overlapping order of every step in the building and finishing process. *Scheduling* means setting up and reconfirming dates for the selected subcontractors to arrive on the site and perform their tasks. If one subcontractor fails to meet the deadline for finishing, it could throw the entire schedule out of synchronization. Further, the next subcontractor on the critical path may not be available at a slightly later date because of other job commitments. It is therefore the responsibility of the general contractor, architect, or interior designer to coordinate the schedule by frequently contacting the subcontractors and reconfirming the schedule. This responsibility may affect the work of the interior designer at the finish and/or decoration and furnishing stage. However, the smooth flow of the construction critical path (see figure 13.28) is crucial to the success of the finish critical path, and in many cases, they are not separated. Large interior design firms who specialize in nonresidential work routinely work out complex and extensive critical paths that track the flow of jobs to be performed.

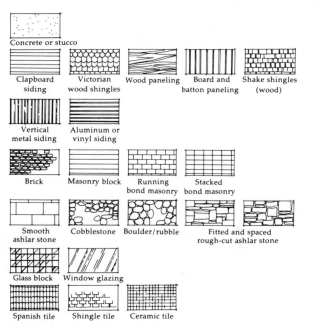

Ⓐ DOOR SCHEDULE

CODE	NO.	W.	HT.	DESCRIPTION		NOTES
A	1	30"	6'-8"		E	W/"E" WINDOW
B	1	30"	6'8	STEEL INSUL.	E	W/ DEAD BOLT
C	1	30"	"	POCKET		
D	2	28"	"	FRENCH	S	W/ GRIDS
E	1	50"	"	"	S	"
F	1	28"	"		S	"
G	2	28"	"	STEEL INSUL.	E	W/ DEAD BLT.
H	3	26"	"		S	
J		26"	"	POCKET		
K		28"	"	"		
L	2	24"	"		P	
M		26"	"	STEEL INSUL.	E	W/CLOSER
N		160"	70"	RUF-TEX GARAGE		
O		24"	6'8"	POCKET	P	
P		40"	"	BI-FOLD	S	
Q	3	24"	"	POCKET	P	
R	3	28"	"		S	
S	1	50"	"	BI-FOLD	S	

Ⓑ WINDOW SCHEDULE

CODE	NO.	W.	HT.	DESCRIPTION	NOTES
A	20	40"		PATIO REPLAC.	NG, NS
B	6	40"		FIXED ALUM.	" "
C	6	40"		ALUM. SLIDER	NG W/SCREEN
D	2	30"		ALUM S.H TRIPLE	W/ GRIDS
E	1	54"		ELLIPTICAL TRANSOM	W/ "A" DOOR
F	2	40"		ALUM. SLIDER	W/ GRID
G	1	40"		" "	NS, NG
H	2	30"	FIXED	PATIO. ALUM FRAME	MULLION
I	1	30"	"	ALUM. SEMI CIRCLE	"
J	1	50"		ALUM. SLIDER.	NS, NG
K	1	30"		ALUM. S.H. INSUL.	W/GRIDS
L	3	30"		" " SH TRIPLE	" "
M	2	60"		PATIO DOOR	NG, NS
N	4	30"		PATIO ALUM FRAME	2/GRIDS 2/WO
O	1	26"		ALUM. S.H.	NG, NS
P	1	30"	FIXED	ALUM. INSUL.	
Q	2	40"		ALUM SLIDER	W/GRIDS
R	1	40"		" "	NG, NS
S	3	2/ 24"		SKYLIGHT DBL.	W/DIFFUSER

(A)

LEGEND:
E - ENTRY LOCKSET W/SER A500
P - PRIVACY " " A300
S - STD. PASSAGE " A100
NS - NO WINDOW SCREENS
NG - NO " GRIDS

Figure 13.17

FINISH SCHEDULE

NO.	ROOM	FLOOR				BASE				WALLS: NORTH				SOUTH				EAST				WEST				CEILING				NOTES:
		WOOD	TILE	VINYL	CARPET	RUBBER	WOOD			SHEETROCK	BRICK	PAPER	WOOD	SHEETROCK	BRICK	PAPER	WOOD	SHEETROCK	BRICK	PAPER	WOOD	SHEETROCK	PAPER	BRICK	WOOD	SHEET ROCK	ACOUSTIC	WOOD	TEXTURED	
101	VESTABULE		•				•			•				•				•				•				•			•	
102	ENTRY				•		•			•						•		•				•				•			•	
103	LIVING RM.				•		•			•				•				•				•				•			•	COVE HOLDINGS
104	DINING RM.				•		•					•				•				•		•				•			•	
105	SITTING				•		•			•				•				•	•			•				•		•	•	CEDAR T&G
106	KITCHEN	•					•			•						•		•				•				•			•	
107	SOLARIUM	•					•			•				•				•				•				•			•	
108	LAUNDRY			•		•				•				•				•				•				•			•	
109	BATH			•		•				•				•				•				•				•			•	
110	LIBRARY				•		•					•				•				•				•		•			•	
111	STAIRWAY				•		•			•				•				•				•				•			•	
112	PANTRY			•		•				•				•				•				•				•			•	
113	GARAGE	CONCRETE																												
20	HALL				•		•			•				•				•				•				•			•	
202	UPPER SITTING	•					•			•				•				•	•			•				•			•	
203	WALK-IN CLO.				•		•			•				•				•				•				•			•	
204	BEDROOM				•		•					•				•				•				•		•			•	
205	BEDROOM				•		•			•				•				•				•				•			•	
206	UPPER SOLAR.									•				•				•				•				•			•	
207	BATH			•		•				•				•				•				•				•			•	
208	MASTER BATH			•		•				•		•		•						•		•				•			•	
209	BALCONEY	•					•			•				•				•				•				•			•	
210	MASTER SIT.				•		•					•				•				•				•		•			•	
211	MASTER BED				•		•			•				•				•				•				•			•	
001	FAMILY			•	•	•	•			•				•				•				•				•			•	
002	STORAGE			•						•																				
003	CEDAR CLO.			•									•				•				•				•					
004	OFF./DEN									•				•																
005	SOLARIUM DN.	•	•				•			•				•				•				•				•		•		EXPOSED
006	BATH			•						•				•				•				•				•				
007	HOBBY RM.				•					•				•				•				•				•				

(B)

Figure 13.18

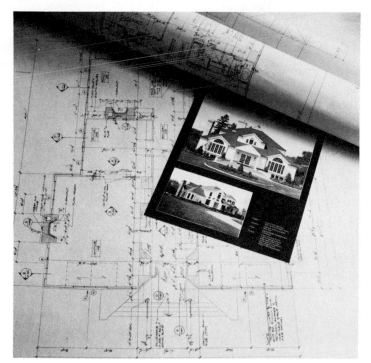

Figure 13.19

Figure 13.17 *(A)* A door and window schedule for a 4,900 square foot home with integral solarium. *(B)* Finish schedule for the same home, indicating materials for floors, walls, ceilings, and baseboards.

Figure 13.18 Representation of finish building materials as indicated on the elevations—part of the blueprint plans.

Figure 13.19 Floor plan specifications for a luxury home in Harrison, New York. Shown here is part of the set of blueprints from which bids are obtained from subcontractors and from which the building is constructed. Many sets of blueprints are made; the general contractor will use one or more, as will the architect who may be involved in the building stage. The owners of the home or building will often keep a set, and various sets will be used by the interior designer, electrician, plumber, framer, sheetrock workman, and so on. Floor plans also include elevations, cabinet details, wiring, plumbing, and cross-sections. Architectural design by Nadler/Philopena, Mt. Kisco, New York. Photo by Ted Spiegel.

The interior designer must understand the aspects of construction in order to communicate with subcontractors, architects, engineers, and other professionals to see a job through to completion. A mutual respect and understanding between designers and these professionals will allow the designer to better communicate structural plans, architectural details, finish materials, and furnishing instructions. It will also allow these aspects to be more successfully completed. The designer has the responsibility to notify the builder of special materials or finishes that could interfere with the critical path. For example, if the designer and client change from carpeting or vinyl to a wood floor, the building must be left empty for work by the floor installers and finishers for a week or longer. This could cause serious problems with the critical path if the designer does not notify the builder in advance of the change in plans. It is the responsibility of the architect or designer and the contractor to see that all aspects of the design are properly and correctly executed.

The jobs performed by subcontractors with whom the designer may communicate on a design job are explained in the following paragraphs. The list is broken into two categories: the structural building components and systems and the interior finish components.

Structural Building Components and Systems

Many kinds of *structural systems* are in use today. A few are quite common, and some are unusual and rarely seen. Building methods vary according to the environment, available materials, and local building code requirements. The designer must become acquainted with regional building methods and variations. The system described here is *wood frame* or *wood truss system construction*, used primarily in homes and smaller nonresidential buildings.

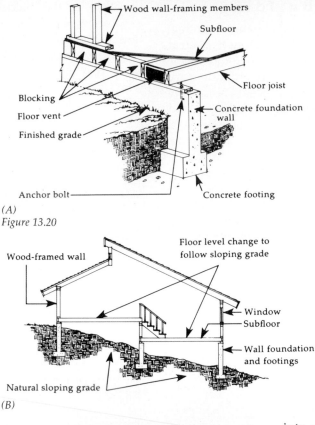

(A)
Figure 13.20

(B)

(C)

The Foundation

After the lot has been surveyed and laid out with chalk lines and the hole for new construction has been excavated, or dug, cement contractors set up wooden and metal frames, pour, and finish foundation footings. Footings are the strips of concrete set into the ground several inches to several feet below the excavated basement or crawl space area. Footings anchor the foundation walls and serve as a base for the weight of the building.

Foundations are the concrete block or poured concrete walls of the basement or sublevel. After the concrete forms are stripped or removed, the walls must cure for a period of time. *Cement* is a dry mixture of lime, silica, alumina, and other minerals used to bring nonadhesive materials together into a strong, cohesive unit. *Concrete* is the building material made by mixing cement and a mineral aggregate with sufficient water to cause the cement to set into a hard mass. Before it sets, concrete is relatively easy to work and may be poured into forms to become a durable material used where strength and stability are requirements and where moisture may permeate interiors (moisture will rot a wooden structure but will not do similar damage to concrete). *Reinforced concrete* has *rebar* (strong, bendable steel bars) or wire mesh set into the wet mixture before it is dried, which gives structural strength and helps prevent cracking. *Flatwork* refers to cement for basement floors, garage floors, driveways, and walkways and may be reinforced and poured over sand, gravel, wire mesh or rebar to minimize shifting and settling that produce cracks.

Another type of foundation frequently used in frame construction is masonry block (concrete block). *Waterproofing* the foundation is done by spraying or rolling a sealant such as a tar mixture and perhaps a sheet of heavy black plastic or tar paper on to the foundation walls before the dirt

---

Figure 13.20 *(A)* A close up, cutaway view of a foundation wall, floor joist system, and subfloor with placement of wood wall-framing members. This illustration shows only a crawl space under the main floor—no basement.

(B) A cross section showing a floor change to accommodate the natural slope of the site grade. Note the depth of the foundation walls. Here the deep footings will give stability to the building. Also, the deeper the frost

line, the deeper the foundation must go into the earth. In northern climates, this justifies digging deep enough to make full basements. *(C)* Framework of the main staircase of the Heartland for its newest homeowner showing stairs four feet

wide, a custom feature suggested by the professionally seasoned builders. The family room is behind the stairs in this view, whereas the stairs are open to a portion of the step-down formal living room. Photo by Karla Nielson.

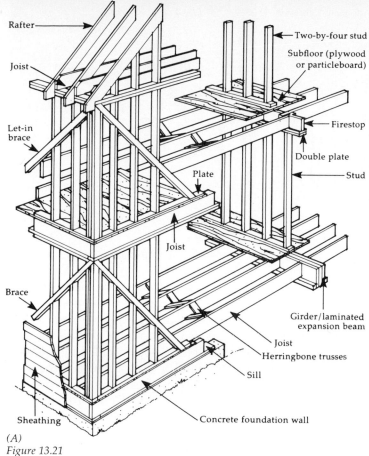

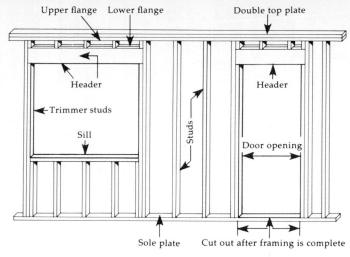

(B)

(A)
Figure 13.21

is backfilled around it. The sealant prevents water seepage into the foundation. The foundation walls may also be insulated with styrofoam board insulation before the back-fill. *Window wells* are corrugated rounded steel or cement units that keep dirt away from a basement window. They may be open at the ground level or can be covered over with ironwork, plastic bubbles, or glass block.

Backfilling and compacting mean that some of the excavated dirt is filled into the area outside the completed footings. Compacting, coupled with wetting the excavated area, hastens the settling process so that the dirt will be prepared for the subgrade or foundation floors.

Plumbing takes place at three stages: (1) before the foundation floor is poured, the underground plumbing brings water and sewer pipe into the sublevel and heating (natural gas lines where applicable); (2) the rough plumbing (both water, including tubs and showers, and systems, such as a central vacuum) is installed and hooked up when the building is framed; and (3) the finish plumbing is the installation of fixtures, such as sinks and toilets.

Framing the next step, is the wood skeleton. This is a crucial step in the construction process, because the wooden frame that is set onto the foundation (called wood frame or truss construction) supports the entire building. In

wood frame construction, *joists* (wood beams) are secured with *trusses* (triangular braces) and form the base for the *subfloors* (plywood or other material) and the walls. Walls are built of two by four studs (eight foot lengths of lumber approximately one and three-fourth by three and three-fourth inches). Load-bearing walls carry the weight of the structure and the roof. The triangular roof truss system is made of rafters and joists and usually are prefabricated to specification and called *roof trusses.* Roof trusses can also be flat.[2]

Once the walls are framed, the interior spaces are firmly established, and although it is possible to move walls after the building is framed, it is costly in terms of time and labor and will likely be viewed as an inconvenience. However, to move walls after the Sheetrock has been hung constitutes major remodeling and is very costly. Framing is finished with the addition of plywood, Celotex, paper-board, styrofoam, or other exterior panel materials. These add stability to the frame, add some insulation, and provide closure.

Interior building systems are now installed, which include the *rough plumbing, rough electrical,* and *rough heating.* Rough plumbing is the installation of pipes that will connect water to the taps and drains from sinks, tubs, showers, and toilets and vents for pressure balance, allowing the pipes to drain. Tubs are set at this time, so Sheetrock can be filled around them. Rough heating includes forced-air ducts (see Heating) and vents run from the clothes dryer hookup. Rough electrical is the wiring from the breaker box to each area of the interior where electricity will be needed for light fixtures, light switches, and electric outlets. Wiring is also installed now for intercoms, telephones, built-in stereo, and media equipment. A master panel is a luxury feature, installed at convenient locations, that can control all electric lights and major appliances.

Figure 13.21 *(A)* An isometric view of a wood-framing system. The floor joists are reinforced with herringbone trusses; upper floors are supported by let-in braces. Subflooring is laid over the floor joist system and is usually plywood or particleboard. Where heavy finish flooring (such as stone, brick, or heavy tile) will be used, the floor system must be engineered and specially prepared to support the strain beyond what the typical load would be on this type of floor. Triangular rafters premade and delivered to the site are called trusses. *(B)* A typical exterior wood-framed wall system showing a window opening and door opening. Building studs are usually sixteen inches apart. For placement of wall-supported design treatments, such as window coverings and art anchored into the walls, it is important to understand what is underneath the finished wall and where the wooden members will fall. Electric boxes for switches and outlets are also anchored into the building studs.

(A)
Figure 13.22
(B)

(A)
Figure 13.23
(B)

Insulation is added at this time, in the form of batts, rigid panels, or blown (loose) insulation. A *superinsulated* structure has a deeper skeleton framework (up to fourteen inches) filled with insulation and layered with a thick *vapor barrier* plastic. Very *tight* superinsulation will require *air-exchange units* to bring necessary fresh air into the interior. Several materials can be used to deaden sound such as *sound board,* which absorbs noise and is used with Sheetrock or plasterboard.

Concurrently with the roughed-in systems windows are set in place and the *exterior veneer* and *finish materials* such as brickwork, siding, and stucco are added. The roof is finished with *tar paper, shingles,* (*shake shingles* are made of wood; *asbestos,* or fireproof, shingles are common) or other roofing materials such as *bartile* or metal shingles or panels.

Exterior finishing includes installing any garage doors, finishing the *soffit* (area under the eaves), the facia (the front of the eaves), *rain gutters* (channel rainfall as it drains off the roof), plastering the foundation, and any exterior painting of trim.

Interior Finish Components

The interior finish materials and components include wall, ceiling, and floor finish materials, woodwork and cabinetry, countertops, optional wall coverings, and optional window coverings. The most common wall and ceiling material is *Sheetrock,* made of pulverized gypsum rock (also called *drywall,* gypsum board, *plasterboard,* or wallboard—see also chapter 9). The Sheetrock is installed by nailing, screwing, or gluing horizontal or vertical panels to the wall studs and ceiling joists. Wallboard panels measure ten by four or eight by four feet and are cut to fit the space. Seams are covered with *perfatape* (three inch wide stiff paper tape), attached and smoothed with plaster called mud. Finishing the walls smooth is more costly than *texturizing* the walls and ceilings: spraying or hand-troweling textures of plaster then lightly sanding the wall or ceiling to a desired smoothness. Light texturizing is called orange peel, and heavy texturizing is sometimes termed brocade texture. Other finish wall materials include wallpaper, ceramic or quarry

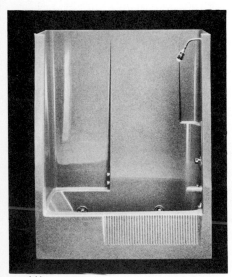

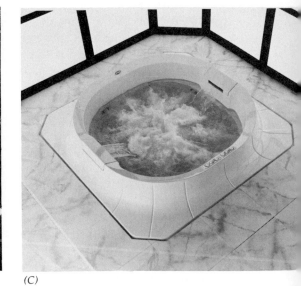

(A)
Figure 13.24
(B)
(C)

Figure 13.22 (A) Within the wood framework of another new home, the duct work for heated and cooled air must be positioned. (B) Plumbing to carry waste water from bathrooms above economically join the plumbing for this powder room in a stacked arrangement. Copper pipes bring hot and cold water to the sink and above to the upper floor. The wiring is also in place for the vanity wall light, which will be installed after the Sheetrock, painting, and any wall coverings are complete. Photos by Karla Nielson.
Figure 13.23 (A) An electrician threads wires through holes he has drilled in the two-inch-by-two-inch building studs. The wires are encased in shock-resistant plastic and rubber outer coatings. The wires will be connected to switches and outlets and for built-in systems such as intercoms, stereo and television systems. (B) A spaghettilike ensemble of wires are being installed to the main breaker box in this new home. Photos by Karla Nielson.
Figure 13.24 (A) Tubs and showers must be installed early as a part of the framing process, then are usually kept covered until the floors are installed and the walls are painted. New products offered include the Barbados bath and shower module in Minralite, featuring a one-piece seamless design, corner ledges, and a fluted front panel. This unit includes a whirlpool and displays Alterna faucets. (B) Inspired by the Oriental tradition of cleansing oneself before entering the bath, this Aventura Shower and Soak™ combines a circular shower adjoining a whirlpool bath in a single unit, allowing users to move freely from one compartment to another without dripping on the floor. The shower utilizes two curved, pivot-style doors and has a slip-resistant finish in the shower receptor and on the steps leading to the shower and the

Figure 13.25

Figure 13.26

tile, wood, stone, cork, and fabric. Other ceiling materials include acoustical tile (suspended ceilings), wood, fabric, and wall coverings (see chapter 9).

The *finish package*—built-in shelves and closet systems, baseboard and door and window trim, and railings—is installed next, then painted along with the walls and ceilings. Doors are removed from the prehung frames, painted or stained separately, then hinged. If wood trim is to be stained, it may be installed after the general painting is done. Any woodwork to be painted is installed at this point. Railings are then installed and finished, cabinets and countertops and any other built-in units (prefinished) are installed, as are *window sills of wood, marble, or tile,* and tub and shower *surrounds* (cultured marble, onyx, or tile). Finish flooring is set in bathrooms/rest rooms and laundry

areas so that the *finish plumbing* (sinks, toilets) can be installed. Finish electric work (lighting fixtures) comes before, after, or concurrently with finish flooring and plumbing. After the finish plumbing and electrical work, any wallpaper is installed, and following that, the carpet or other floors that need some protection, such as wood, is installed, and hardware (door handles and strike plates) is set in place. Appliances are installed, and window treatments may now also be installed. Last is the delivery and arrangement of furniture and accessories.

The Critical Path and the Punch List

The critical path graphically illustrates the overlapping order of everything that must be accomplished in a job. The exact items will vary according to the nature of the job, whether it is new construction or remodeling. The *punch list* is a series of items that must be accomplished as the project progresses. The sample includes spaces for noting the start and finish dates.

Figure 13.28 is a sample construction/finish critical path, and chart 13.1 is a sample punch list. Neither is intended to be exhaustive of details

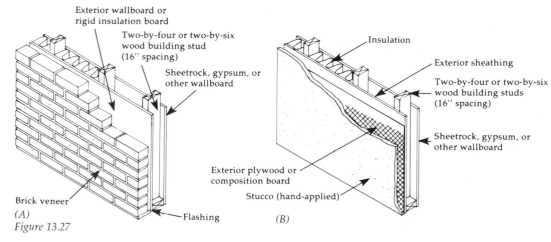

Figure 13.27

(A)

(B)

bath. The five-jet whirlpool features a two-speed pump and individual air and water volume intakes. Photos courtesy of Kohler Co. (C) The Allusian™ whirlpool bath from Jacuzzi Whirlpool Bath is a new design, featuring customized whirlpool hydromassage. It is made of high-gloss acrylic reinforced with fiberglass in a variety of Designer Series colors, with options including a matching skirt for above ground installation and an in-line electric heater for

on-site installation. Photo courtesy of Jacuzzi Whirlpool Bath.
Figure 13.25 Wiring installed in the structural stage of this New York apartment designed by architect Peter Wilson has made possible this media room with custom controls in the wall and projection box. Architectural lighting has been planned in wall fixtures and artistic cold-cathode lighting on the back wall. Photo by Norman McGrath.

Figure 13.26 Taking custom wiring in the structural stage to the ultimate in luxury, this marble bathroom in Oheka Castle, Cold Springs, New York, has a built-in telephone and intercom system. Interior design by Gail and Stephen Huberman. Photo by Norman McGrath, © 1987.
Figure 13.27 Exterior wall construction in a wood-frame system. Two-inch-by-two-inch wood studs spaced sixteen inches apart with insulation shown in the empty space. The

insulation here would be the fluffy batting that comes in rolls the width of the spacing. The space may also be left empty because the exterior sheath is often insulative. Sheetrock or other wallboard is applied to the building studs after the wiring and plumbing systems are installed inside the framing. (A) The exterior brick veneer. (B) The process of applying stucco (exterior plaster) to a mesh attached to the sheathing.

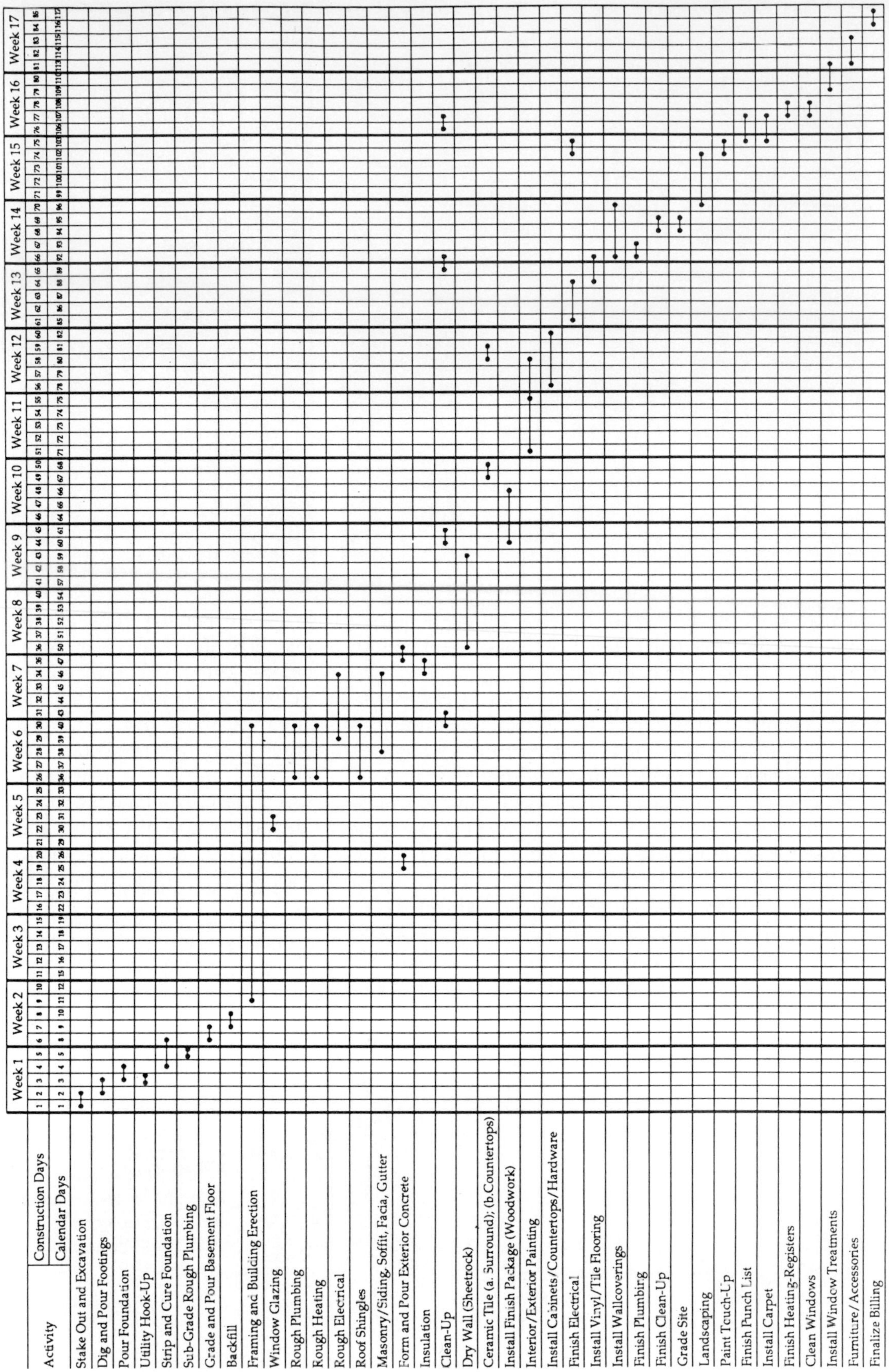

Figure 13.28 A sample critical path for building a three-thousand to five-thousand square foot house. The process is shown to take just over four months and is shown as a single project. There will be variables, depending on the smoothness of the work flow, the weather, and the lack of or existence of problems that may occur. There is also some flexibility as to the order of the items listed in the critical path, although this order has proven its efficiency by professional builders who have supervised the construction of many custom homes.

Chart 13.1 Punch List

	Start Date	Finish Date
Architectural plans	_____	_____
Turn in plans to city	_____	_____
Order temporary power	_____	_____
Lay out lot	_____	_____
Order footing material	_____	_____
Order steel for footing/walls	_____	_____
Dig hole (excavate)	_____	_____
Order concrete for footing	_____	_____
Deliver footing material	_____	_____
Set footing	_____	_____
Call to confirm foundation crew	_____	_____
Pour footing	_____	_____
Strip & stack footing material	_____	_____
Order underground plumbing	_____	_____
Order underground heating hook-up	_____	_____
Caulk footing	_____	_____
Order waterproofing of walls	_____	_____
Call for inspection of walls	_____	_____
Order window wells	_____	_____
Water proofing of foundation	_____	_____
Call for inspection plumb. & heat.	_____	_____
Backfill house & floor	_____	_____
Grading & compaction of floors	_____	_____
Run water and sewer laterals	_____	_____
Order framing material	_____	_____
Pour concrete floor and garage	_____	_____
Deliver framing material	_____	_____
Framing of house	_____	_____
Clean-up after this phase	_____	_____
Confirm windows/doors	_____	_____
Confirm plumbing	_____	_____
Confirm heating	_____	_____
Confirm electrical	_____	_____
Order brick/masonry	_____	_____
Rough heating	_____	_____
Rough electrical	_____	_____
Run dryer/bathroom vents	_____	_____
Install fireplace	_____	_____
Inspection of plumbing, heating, electrical	_____	_____
Clean-up after this phase	_____	_____

	Start Date	Finish Date
Windows set in place/glazed	_____	_____
Bricking/masonry exterior	_____	_____
Order cabinets/built-ins	_____	_____
Order flooring	_____	_____
Ceiling insulation	_____	_____
Order finish package	_____	_____
Hang sheetrock	_____	_____
Clean-up after this phase	_____	_____
Order tub & shower surrounds	_____	_____
Taping & texture walls/ceil.	_____	_____
Confirm painter	_____	_____
Brick interior (fireplaces)	_____	_____
Finish work (wood work)	_____	_____
Clean-up after this phase	_____	_____
Confirm cabinets/counter tops	_____	_____
Interior painting	_____	_____
Confirm tile installer	_____	_____
Confirm flooring installers	_____	_____
Setting of cabinets	_____	_____
Confirm finish plumbing	_____	_____
Confirm heating	_____	_____
Confirm electrical	_____	_____
Setting of counter tops	_____	_____
Setting of marble and tile	_____	_____
Order garage doors	_____	_____
Ceramic tile in entry	_____	_____
Confirm carpet and vinyl	_____	_____
Finish electrical	_____	_____
Set vinyl in bathrooms	_____	_____
Finish plumbing	_____	_____
Finish heating	_____	_____
Install garage doors	_____	_____
Install wall coverings	_____	_____
Finish setting vinyl/carpet	_____	_____
Install hardware	_____	_____
Appliances	_____	_____
Install window treatments	_____	_____
Finish soffit, facia, rain gutters	_____	_____
Clean-up after this phase	_____	_____
Call for final move-in inspection	_____	_____
Set furnishings in place	_____	_____

Note: the Critical Path and Punch List are typically expanded to fit the job requirements. The punch list may consist of several sub-lists, and may include specific items requested by a client as the job progresses.

within the construction/design process although both represent the types of things that are done in new construction, remodeling, and interior design.

This sample critical path (figure 13.28) is a typical time frame for a small home, which can be completed within two months. Larger homes with more features typically take from four to six months or longer to complete. Remodeling projects can take from two weeks to two years, depending on factors such as extent of demolition and reconstruction, funds available, and size of the work force. Small nonresidential buildings will take from three to eight months to build and furnish, and large nonresidential buildings require a time frame of four months to three years.

Not taken into account in this sample critical path is the preliminary design process. Chapter 1, The Design Process, outlines the method involved in gathering data and developing the design before the actual building process begins. This chart also does not include lead time, which is the length of time required to file for and obtain a building permit, time to take the plans to the city and the consequent approval of the structure and its building, time required to survey and establish the relationship of the building to the lot, and time to prepare the property before the excavation begins. Lead time is also required for prequalifying the client for the loan and to begin the loan processing, which can take longer to finalize than it takes to construct and finish the building.

The critical path and punch list are typically expanded to fit the job requirements. The punch list may consist of several sublists and may include specific items requested by a client as the job progresses. A punch list is also used to note unresolved problems observed during inspection tours of a project. These problems must be resolved by the contractor and subcontractors before the project is finished.

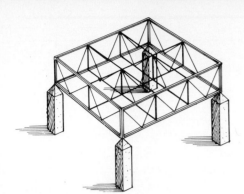

Figure 13.29

Figure 13.30

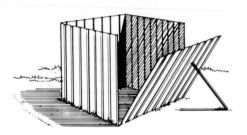

Figure 13.31

Figure 13.32

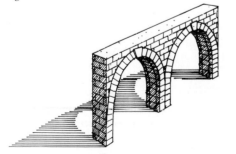

Figure 13.33

Nonresidential Considerations

The Professionals

In nonresidential design work, the architectural team may consist of both architects and interior designers/architects, who follow project development through three stages: 1. establish preliminary client contact, draw up a contract, make a preliminary design, 2. final review, design development, review, costing, final specifications and drawings, review, and 3. construction scheduling, contracting, review, supervision/installation, project completion review. The project may entail a highly complex, computer-produced *critical path*, which outlines every necessary step according to a time frame.

Structural Systems

In large nonresidential buildings and complexes, the systems that are most common are metal or concrete systems.

- The *metal frame* or *space frame* is a three-dimensional truss/beam and column system assembly that creates steel skeleton and is also called *curtain wall construction*. The exterior finish material can be glass or brick veneer or siding, for example.
- Slab system is reinforced concrete ribbed or waffle design that transfers the lateral loads to supporting end beams; slabs can span short distances and are widely used.
- Frame system is made of a rigid steel skeleton sheathed with prefabricated rolled steel or precast concrete.
- *Masonry block construction* consists of walls made of structurally supportive brick, such as concrete block or adobe block.

Some other structural systems include:

- *Arch systems* are stone blocks cut and fitted to form a curved

Figure 13.34

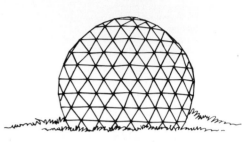

Figure 13.35

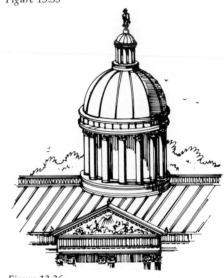

Figure 13.36

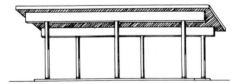

Figure 13.37

Figure 13.29 The metal frame or space frame, also called the steel skeleton, used in high-rise buildings and sometimes referred to as curtain wall construction.
Figure 13.30 The slab system, transporting weight and stress to the exterior support beams.

Figure 13.31 The frame system, showing rolled sheathing anchored onto a frame.
Figure 13.32 Masonry block construction, commonly seen in convenience store/gas station buildings.
Figure 13.33 The arch system, in existence since ancient Romans built viaducts.

Figure 13.34 The vaulted system, used in ecclesiastical and public architecture where lofty spaces are desirable.
Figure 13.35 The geodesic dome, developed in the twentieth century by American architect Buckminster Fuller. Based on the strongest and

most-stable building shape, the triangle, this interlocking system creates lightweight and economical spaces used for a variety of purposes and even for buildings and shelters that need to be transportable.
Figure 13.36 The dome system, most often seen in rotundas of government

shape, anchored firmly in vertical supports and with a *keystone* to stabilize the compression and friction needed to bind the arch together.

- *Vaulted systems* form an elongated arch such as seen in medieval cathedrals.
- *Dome systems,* as seen in rotundas, are an arch rotated about a circular plan, with a compression ring rather than a keystone that stabilizes the dome.
- *Geodesic domes* are constructed of triangular steel skeleton components filled with opaque or transparent materials.
- *Beam systems* are often seen in gas station canopies and are straight, solid structural elements of reinforced concrete, solid or laminated wood, or rolled steel section based on compressive and tensile stress. The load is laterally transmitted along the axis to the vertical support beams.
- *Folded plate systems* are of thin reinforced concrete in a strong, rigid geometric form.
- *Pneumatic systems* are air-inflated or air-supported lightweight, flexible membranes.
- *Tensile systems* are fabric structures stretched over vertical posts or frames like a tent.
- *Cable systems* are based on a vertical column and horizontal slab connected with flexible steel cables.
- *Thin shell membranes* are self-supporting concrete or lightweight foam membranes over a steel reinforcing mesh (like an eggshell) with free-form curvatures.[3]

Heating, Ventilation, and Air Conditioning

HVAC are systems of heating, ventilation, and air-conditioning. In many large nonresidential settings, the windows are fixed or nonoperable, thus

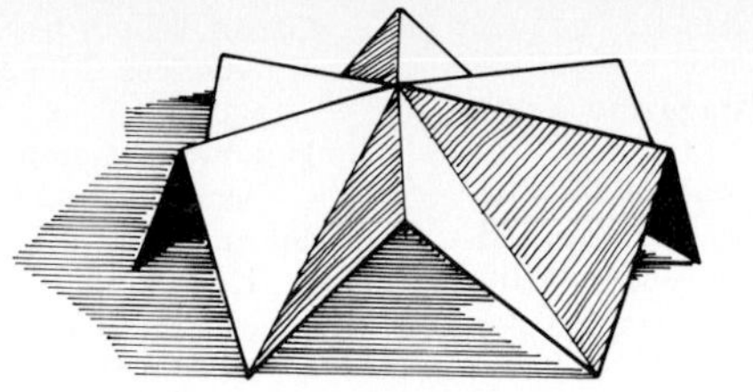

Figure 13.38

Figure 13.39

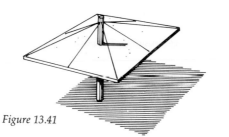

Figure 13.40

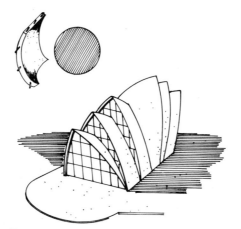

Figure 13.41

Figure 13.42

creating a mechanically *sealed environment* that eliminates natural ventilation. Sealed environments in large buildings and complexes are utilized because they can be efficiently controlled, which is difficult with operable windows. HVAC systems mix warm and cool air to achieve a constant temperature. The rate of air exchange (the infusion of clean, fresh air into an environment, replacing stale air) is sometimes dictated by *code* (see chapter 1).

Communication and Safety Systems

Intercom systems allow occupants to talk through wall-mounted or desk units with persons in other areas of the building. The intercom works much as a walkie-talkie, yet for nonresidential installations, the intercom can become rather sophisticated and complex to include loudspeakers and two-way response without pushing buttons. Telephones also can form intercom systems. The intercom may also carry taped or radio music.

Computer networks link personal computers together or connect *computer terminals,* (a keyboard and monitor, or screen) with a *mainframe computer* (large computer processing unit) and allow workers to call up information and *interface* (compare or put together) information for projects and business dealings. Computer systems that network outside the immediate building are often linked by telephone systems.

Telephone systems connect workstations together, sometimes with a central operator, and allow calls to be transferred, put on hold, computer dialed or placed, and a host of other functions, including computer accessing.

Fire alert systems are mandatory in all nonresidential design. In large complexes, the sensing devices are connected to a central monitor. Additionally, sprinkling systems are required to douse or fight fires.

buildings and in some churches. The dome is a soaring space inside the building and is essentially an arch system rotated around an axis.
Figure 13.37 The beam support system, often seen in canopies of gas stations and a selection of some of the types of steel support beams.

Figure 13.38 The folded plate system made of rigid forms of reinforced concrete.
Figure 13.39 Pneumatic systems are inflated and supported by air.
Figure 13.40 The tensile system is fabric stretched over a frame or support posts, as a tent.

Figure 13.41 The cable system anchors the canopy from its sides and corners to the center shaft with strong metal cables.
Figure 13.42 The thin-shell membrane, based on a spherical form, is lightweight concrete or foam formed over a wire mesh as seen in the cutaway illustration.

Notes

1. *"The Smart House System."* Professional Builder Magazine (December, 1987), pp. 66-82.
2. Feirer, John L., and Gilbert R. Hutchings, *Carpentry and Building Construction.* (Peoria, IL: Chas. A. Bennett Co., Inc., 1976), p. 343.
3. Information Design. *Notes on Architecture.* (Los Altos, CA: William Kaufmann, Inc., 1982), pp. 16-19.

Bibliography

Anderson, Bruce. *Passive Solar Energy.* Andover, MA: Brick House Publishing, 1981.

Anderson, Bruce. *Solar Energy: Fundamentals in Building Design.* Highstown, NJ: McGraw-Hill Book Company, n.d.

Anderson, Bruce, and Michael Riodran. *The Solar House Book.* Harrisville, NH: Cheshire Books, 1979.

Butler, Lee Porter. *Ekoseá Homes: Natural Energy Conserving Design,* 2d ed. San Francisco, CA: Ekoseá Inc., 1980.

Feirer, John L., and Gilbert R. Hutchings. *Carpentry and Building Construction.* Peoria, IL: Charles A. Bennett Co., Inc., 1976.

Friedmann, Arnold, John F. Pile, and Forrest Wilson. *Interior Design: An Introduction to Architectural Interiors.* New York: American Elsevier Publishing Company, 1970.

Garret, Wilbur E. *Energy: Facing up to the Problem, Getting Down to Solutions.* 2d. ed. Washington, DC: National Geographic Society, n.d.

Hawkweed Group. *The Passive Solar House Book.* New York: Rand, McNally, and Company, 1980.

Information Design Inc. *Notes on Architecture.* Los Altos, CA: William Kaufmann, Inc. 1982.

Jones, Robert W., and Robert D. McFarland. *The Sunspace Primer.* New York: Van Nostrand Reinhold Company, n.d.

Passive Solar Design Handbooks. Springfield, VA: United States Department of Energy, 1978.

Pile, John. "The Lighting Direction for Health." *Interiors,* August, 1982, pp. 74-75.

Professional Builder Magazine. December, 1987.

Ramsey, Charles George, and Harold Reeve Sleeper. *Architectural Graphic Standards.* 7th ed. New York: John Wiley and Sons, Inc., 1981.

Strombert, R.P., and S.O. Woodall. *Passive Solar Buildings: A Compilation of Data and Results.* Springfield, VA: National Technical Information Services, 1979.

Whiton, Sherrill. *Elements of Interior Design and Decoration.* New York: J.B. Lippincott Company, 1974.

Wright, David, AIA. *Natural Solar Architecture: The Passive Solar Primer.* 3d ed. New York: Van Nostrand Reinhold Company, 1984.

EXTERIOR STYLE

Montgomery Place, maintained by
Historic Hudson Valley at
Annandale, New York, reflects the
Neoclassic mood of America during
the first fifty years of the Republic.
Though the English interest in
Greece and Rome related to
architectural discoveries, the
American aristocracy saw itself as
continuing the political traditions of
earlier republics. Many of the
exterior architectural themes seen at
this Livingston family mansion are
utilized for interior design. The new
Republic enjoyed these classical
themes as interior as well as exterior
decor. Photo by Ted Spiegel.

Page 354, top: The classic statement of the Classical period of Greece is the Parthenon, a temple dedicated by ancient Athens to its patron Pallas (goddess), Athena. Its Doric columns, friezes, and entablatures have provided endless resource to architects and interior designers alike. Photo by David Beal, Black Star. *Page 354, bottom:* The Parthenon friezes preserved in part in the British Museum as the Elgin Marbles embody the continuing tradition of commissioning art decorate building exteriors and interiors. Many buildings today have a budget for just such artwork. Photo by Ted Spiegel. *Page 355, top left:* In the Roman forum, surviving columns from the time of the Caeser frame a Renaissance church. Photo by Ted Spiegel. *Page 355, top right:* When Palladio built his theater at Vicenza, his permanent set was a Roman city, its details provided by excavations as well as ruins. Banks, theaters, and other public buildings of today draw upon similar themes; even if the details are different, the ordering of elements and perspective is remarkably persistent. Photo by Ted Spiegel. *Page 355, bottom:* Renaissance—rebirth—a period focusing on the arts, saw Florentine palaces built with split personalities. The architectural detail of Rome decorated the stout walls required for defense during an era of turmoil from intracity and intercity feuds. Photo by Ted Spiegel.

Page 356, top left: Philadelphia's Chestnut Street offers a remarkable slice through the development of American urban architecture. This house was built in Colonial times. Photo by Ted Spiegel. Page 356, top right: These twin houses are Federal in style, with narrow sidelights and rounded keystone arches from the Late Georgian era filled with fanlight-shaped glass. Two styles of shutters, raised panel and louvered, flank the three stories of Federal row houses. Photo by Ted Spiegel. Pages 356–357, bottom: These houses reflect the development of the city outside its own traditions to Tudor and Dutch Beaux Arts styles (page 357,

bottom). The semidetached houses reflect the beginning of urban sprawl and were built in the 1920s. All of the housing stock on these pages is now beginning redevelopment as part of urban gentrification (suitable for the gentry). Interior designers find themselves needing to determine the appropriate interior design style for their clients. Photos by Ted Spiegel. Page 357, top: These houses were built right after the Civil War, showing the Victorian influence of Italianate architecture in the arcade on the ground floor and Tuscan Italianate on the upper stories. Photos by Ted Spiegel.

Page 358, top: Lower Manhattan Island presents New York's interior designers with an endless source of contract design work. Materials utilized reflect the architectural taste prevalent during different boom eras in the growth of the financial capital of the world. Photo by Ted Spiegel. Page 358, middle row, left: Glass-walled environments dominate Modernist architecture that drew on the Bauhaus traditions. Page 358, middle row, right: The repeated columns of the Parthenon are emulated in the AT&T office building. Page 358, bottom left: Financial firms find homes in the solidity of steel-ribbed and aluminum-clad towers. Page 358, bottom right: One of the earliest skyscrapers, the Woolworth Building, used ceramic molds to create a ribbed Gothic high-rise complete with stonelike tracery. Photo by Ted Spiegel. Page 359, top left: The Presbyterian Church of Bedford, New York, is a fine example of Carpenter Gothic, a dominant theme of America's Victorian era. Photo by Ted Spiegel. Page 359, top right: The further we go into the future, the more important it is to preserve our past. George Washington's home at Mount Vernon preserves an important part of America's cultural heritage. Photo by Ted Spiegel. Page 359, bottom: The haven known as Olana, belonging to painter Frederick Church, is cherished as a New York state historical site, immortalizing his fascination with the Moorish world. Photo by Ted Spiegel.

Early Influences

The architecture we see today is the result of centuries of influence, development, and change. It is difficult to separate innovations from the factors that shaped them. Even those trends that claim to be free from previous influence have some basis in the experience and technology of preceding generations. And there are innovators who admit freely to the influence of past designs on their work. Some of the most significant designs in terms of their influence were the buildings of classical Greece, the architecture of Imperial Rome, the Gothic buildings of the Middle Ages, and the architectural designs of the Italian Renaissance.

Greece (Fifth Century B.C.)

The Parthenon, considered one of the most beautiful buildings in the world, is the embodiment of classical Greek architecture. This magnificent combination of sculpture and architecture, designed to honor the goddess Athena, rests on an outcropping of rock called the Acropolis in the capital city of Athens. The Parthenon, built during the fifth century B.C., was partially destroyed in 1687 by a bombardment during the Turko-Venetian war. Even in its ruined state, it is an inspiring sight.

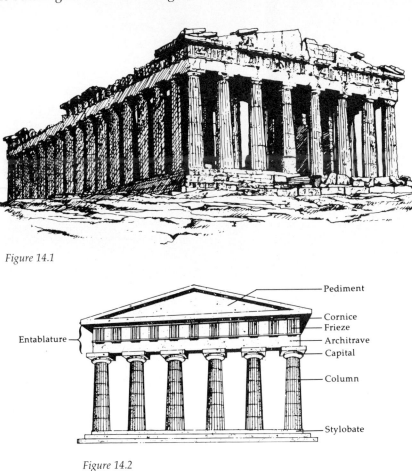

Figure 14.1

Figure 14.2

The construction of the Parthenon is solid marble, generally without mortar. The triangular roof *trusses* were wooden and covered with terra-cotta tiles. The building, designed by Ictinus and Callicrates, is beautifully proportioned. Through minute adjustments to the curvature of the horizontal lines and by manipulation of the shape, placement, and inclination of the columns, optical illusions were created that make the Parthenon appear visually perfect.

One of the Parthenon's finest features was its sculpture, which was executed principally by a sculptor named Phidias. Much of the original sculpture was taken to England during the nineteenth century by British collector Lord Elgin. These extraordinary pieces are now housed as a collection called the *Elgin Marbles* in the British Museum in London.

The Parthenon shows clearly the characteristics of Greek architecture. The entire building rests on a base called the *stylobate*, which can be approached from any angle (the actual entrance was in the rear). The *columns* (supporting posts that carry the weight of the roof) form a *colonnade* (row of columns) around the exterior of the building. A *lintel*, or crosspiece, called the *architrave* rests on the *capitals* at the top of the columns. The capital is a decorative detail that helps distinguish one style or *order* of Greek architecture from another. A second set of beams rests on top of the architrave and runs the length and width of the building. On the exterior, these beams are covered with a decorative panel called the *frieze*. The architrave and frieze form the support for the triangular trusses of the roof. The trusses extend beyond the architrave and frieze and create an overhang called the *cornice*. The architrave, frieze, and cornice together form a combination of the three details known as the *entablature*. The row of roof trusses extends forward and backward to the front and rear of the building. The triangular shape of the roof forms a *pediment* (like a *gable*) at the front and rear. The pediment holds a triangular panel of sculpture called the *pediment frieze.*

The Greek Orders

At some point it was determined that certain types of entablatures were more compatible with other types of columns and capitals, and the idea of distinct styles or orders was born. The three Greek orders are *Doric, Ionic,* and *Corinthian.*

Figure 14.1 The Parthenon of Athens illustrated in its current ruined state. It is considered to be one of the most perfectly proportioned buildings in the world.

Figure 14.2 Classical components as they would appear in a facade copied from the Parthenon.

Figure 14.3   Figure 14.4   Figure 14.5

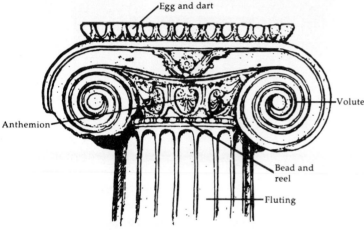

Egg and dart

Volute

Anthemion

Bead and reel

Fluting

Figure 14.6

Figure 14.7

and is fluted with separated semicircular grooves and finished at the bottom with a molded base that rests on the stylobate. The Ionic entablature is narrower than the Doric and features an architrave that rises in three distinct planes. It has an undecorated frieze or one decorated in a continuous band of sculpture and a cornice that projects less than the Doric.

The Corinthian order was not widely used by the Greeks but was adopted by the Romans. The principal difference between the Ionic and Corinthian orders is that the Corinthian capital is shaped like an inverted bell and embellished with two rows of *acanthus leaves*. The bell shape is topped with four small volutes that support each corner of a square abacus. The Corinthian cornice may also be enriched with square *dentil* ornament.

Rome (750 B.C.–A.D. 476)

During the Imperial Age of Rome (beginning in the first century B.C.), Greece was annexed and absorbed into the Roman Empire. At that point, Rome began to take the place of the Greek civilization it had conquered, though the Romans never reached the level of artistic achievement attained by the Greeks. Roman designs were magnificent and showy but never executed with the care and craftsmanship that characterized Greek design. That is probably to be expected because the far-flung Roman Empire had a massive program of building, and such meticulous care would have been impractical. The construction spread to every corner of the Empire from Spain in the West to Asia Minor in the East and from Africa in the South to England and Germany in the North.

The Romans adapted Greek design to suit their needs and added materials and engineering techniques that constitute a unique and important contribution to the history of building. The Romans incorporated the *roundheaded arch* and *barrel vault* and used them along with the post and lintel, often in the same building. The perfection of the arch and vault led to the development of the dome. Bricks and *concrete* made from volcanic ash and lime facilitated rapid and sturdy construction. The brick and concrete were faced with a veneer of marble or plastered with *stucco*.

The simplest and apparently the oldest order is the Doric. The shafts of Doric columns are *fluted* in shallow curved sections and have no base, resting directly on the stylobate. The Doric capital consists of a square *abacus* (plate) at the top and a simple curved *echinus* (dish) below. The Doric entablature has a plain architrave and a frieze divided into *triglyphs* and *metopes*. Triglyphs are blocks divided by vertical channels, and metopes are panels placed between the triglyphs, often decorated with sculpture in low relief.

The Ionic order is a more recent development, though it appears to be related to earlier Egyptian and Near Eastern prototypes. It consists of a capital with two front-facing scroll *volutes*, whose design may have been derived from animal horns or shells. Below is a molding of *egg and dart* with a second lower molding of *bead and reel* or *anthemion* relief designs. The column itself is thinner than the Doric

---

Figure 14.3 Fluted column with classic Greek Doric capital.
Figure 14.4 Greek Ionic capital on a fluted column. The base is added to this column and rests on the stylobate.

Figure 14.5 Greek Corinthian capital—acanthus or Grecian thistle leaves stylized into an ornate work. Fluting and base complete the Corinthian column.
Figure 14.6 Classical motifs and details from the Ionic capital of a Greek ruin.

Figure 14.7 Roman arch, showing angled or splayed stones. The center stone was called the keystone—holding the arch together with pressure from both sides.

The Roman orders include the Doric, Ionic, and Corinthian used by the Greeks as well as two orders developed by the Romans: the *Tuscan* and *Composite*. The Roman Doric order varies most from the Greek original. The Roman version, which incorporates a base on the column, is less massive, and the column is often left unfluted. The Roman Ionic and Corinthian orders are almost identical to the Greek, varying mostly in small details of decoration.

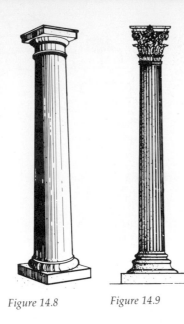

Figure 14.8   Figure 14.9

The Tuscan order is a simplified version of the Roman Doric, without flutes or ornamental moldings. The Composite order, as the name implies, is a combination of the Corinthian and Ionic orders. Large volutes together with a band of egg-and-dart and bead-and-reel moldings are borrowed from the Ionic capital, and two rows of acanthus leaves are taken from the Corinthian order. The resulting design is even more decorative than the Corinthian capital.

The Roman temple was based on the design of Greek temples but differed from them in at least two important ways. First, the Roman temple was built on a raised *podium* instead of a stylobate and was approached only from the front by means of a single set of steps. Second, the interior space (*cella*) was expanded to the edge of the podium and filled the area that would otherwise form a porch at the sides and rear of the building. The exterior walls were lined with half columns that formed a continuous line with the columns of the covered porch or *portico* at the front of the building. The Maison Carrée (c. 16 B.C.), Nimes, France, is an excellent example of a small Roman temple. The Pantheon (A.D. 120) in Rome is an important example of a circular Roman temple. The building, which was dedicated to all the gods and later consecrated as a Christian church, features a large dome (over 142 feet in diameter) that rests on a round drum-shaped cella. The round domed space is called a rotunda. The interior is lighted by an open *oculus* (round opening at the top of the dome), 142 feet above the floor. The exterior incorporates a portico attached to the circular body of the building.

Much of what remains of Roman domestic design is at Pompeii and Herculaneum, cities buried and preserved by the eruption of Mount Vesuvius in A.D. 79. The House of the Vettii, an example of a Pompeian house, opens into an

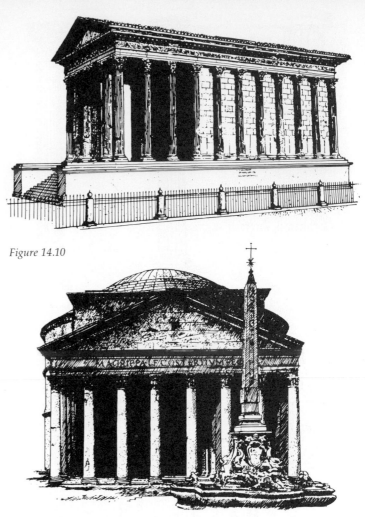

Figure 14.10

Figure 14.11

atrium (a space open to the sky). The atrium contains a pool, which held rainwater collected from the roof. The rear section of the house opened into a colonnaded garden area called the *peristyle*. These houses also typically had libraries, sleeping rooms, kitchens, small rooms for reading and conversation, rooms for sculpture, picture galleries, and dining rooms.

The terms classical and classicism are often mentioned in conjunction with architectural design and detailing. These terms refer to the use or adaptation of Greek and Roman forms, motifs, and proportions in the designs of subsequent periods. The Roman orders and their proportions were documented and preserved in drawings by *Vitruvius*, a first-century Roman architect. Correct classical proportions are often referred to as *Vitruvian proportions.*

The Middle Ages (325–1453)

With official acceptance of Christianity in Rome, the church in Italy began the construction of churches. These were built in a style known as *Early Christian* and were an important influence on the styles that followed. By the year 1000, all of

Figure 14.8 Roman Tuscan column, showing a rimmed capital and simple, rounded base. This column is flat with no fluting.
Figure 14.9 Roman Composite capital and fluted column with exaggerated base.

Figure 14.10 Maison Carrée in Nimes, France (c. 16 B.C.) is a well-preserved example of elaborate Corinthian capitals and detailed frieze in a small Roman temple.

Figure 14.11 The Pantheon in Rome with its Greek temple facade, opens inside to a grand-scale rotunda whose ceiling is the Roman dome. This building strongly influenced Thomas Jefferson in his design for his home, Monticello.

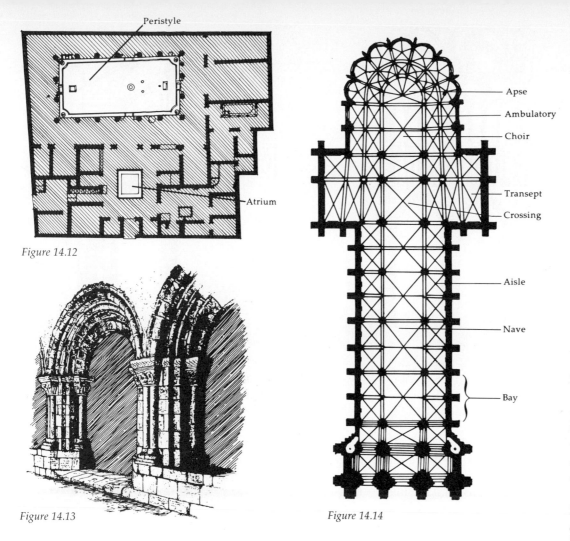

Figure 14.12

Figure 14.13

Figure 14.14

Labels on Figure 14.12: Peristyle, Atrium

Labels on Figure 14.14: Apse, Ambulatory, Choir, Transept, Crossing, Aisle, Nave, Bay

The style that grew out of Romanesque and appeared at the church of Saint-Denis just north of Paris, France, around 1135 is called *Gothic*. The name Gothic, which has become synonymous with design from the Middle Ages, was first applied by Vasari, a post-Renaissance scholar who must have decided that the style was no further advanced than that of the barbaric Goths in the sixth century. He and his contemporaries probably felt that the designers of the Renaissance had corrected the architectural drift away from the classicism of Greece and Rome. The centuries since Vasari have put the Gothic style in perspective, and today, Gothic design and architecture are considered one of the finest achievements of all time.

Gothic architecture incorporates the *Gothic arch* (pointed arch), which led to the development of a very complex and ingenious system of vaulting and allowed the buildings to be built to great heights. These tall spaces draw the eye upward and inspire a feeling of reverence and awe. The churches, often built over the *crypt* (basement) of earlier Romanesque churches, were laid out in the shape of a *Latin cross* or *cruciform*. The main body of the church, where worshipers stand or sit, is called the *nave*. The nave is broken by the *transepts*, which extend outward on both sides from the *crossing* (the area where the nave and transepts cross). Beyond the crossing, the main body of the church is called the *choir* (or *quire*) because the choir stalls and organ were often located there. The rounded end of the main body that frequently houses the altar is called the *apse*. The nave is divided on each side from the *aisles* by an *arcade* (row of arches). The aisles run along the side of the nave and continue behind the choir and apse. The aisles are not as tall as the nave and extend only as high as the aisle arcade. Some churches have windows that open from the aisles to the exterior of the building, while others have small chapels

Europe was Christian. The barbarians who repeatedly streamed out of the North to sack Rome and the rest of southern Europe had intermarried, converted to Christianity, and had in fact become Europeans. The lives of these people were inextricably tied to the church in a manner that is difficult for us to comprehend today. The church took care of every need, whether spiritual, physical, or intellectual, and in return everyone was expected to contribute money and labor to the building of churches.

Many of the Early Christian buildings had been destroyed by fire, and in the eleventh century, a new style of church with a fireproof stone ceiling spread through Europe. These buildings used the roundheaded Roman arch and vault as forms for windows, doors, and ceilings. The French term *Romanesque*, meaning Romanlike, is the designation given to the architecture of this period. In England the same style is generally called Norman after William I (the Conquerer) of Normandy, who conquered England in 1066.

Figure 14.12 Pompeiian house plan, showing no exterior windows. Interior light came from the atrium, a space open to the sky, and the peristyle, an open, colonnaded garden walled in at the rear of the house.

Figure 14.13 Romanesque arch, as seen in European Christian churches. The style was called Norman in England. Note the disproportionately large arches compared to the relatively small heavy-capitaled columns.

Figure 14.14 Plan of a Gothic cathedral, in the shape of the Christian cross.

that are entered from the aisles and run parallel to the nave and choir and radiate off of the apse aisle or *ambulatory*.

The area between each opposing set of aisle arches is called a *bay*. Each bay is divided by tall *piers* (columns) that carry the weight of the ceiling, the trusses, and the roof. The *ribs* that form the framework of the ceiling spring from *brackets* carved as part of the pier and reach across the ceiling to the opposite side creating *vaults*.

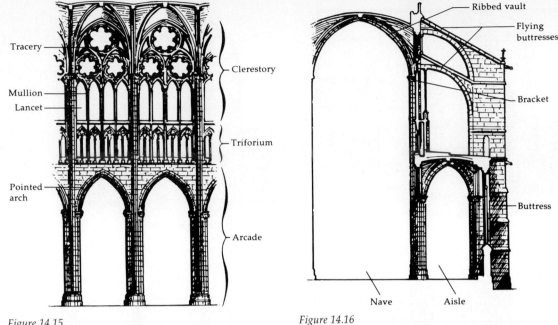

Figure 14.15

Figure 14.16

As the style developed, the vaulting became increasingly more complex and ornate. In some churches, large, decorative, carved medallions, called *bosses*, are attached to the ceiling where the ribs cross.

The wall between each of the piers is pierced at the floor level with the arches of the aisle arcade. Above the arcade is another set of openings called the *triforium*. In some cases the triforium serves as a gallery for looking into the nave and choir. In other churches the triforium is shallow and has no room for passage. The large openings above the triforium are the *clerestory windows*. These windows, as well as the windows on the aisle, are divided into smaller sections by vertical stone dividers called *mullions*. The lower part of the windows are divided into smaller pointed windows called *lancets*. The lacelike pattern of stone above the lancets is called *tracery*. The windows are often filled with *stained glass*. Stained glass is pieces of plain, colored, and painted glass, fitted together with lead strips called *came* to make patterned panels of glass that are fixed to the metal framework between the mullions of the window. Light entering the windows and filling the building was symbolic of the presence of God. The quality of colored light added even further to the feeling of mysticism in the church.

The relatively slender piers support the tremendous weight of the roof and stone ceiling and have a tendency to bow outward unless they are braced. Consequently, the weight of the roof of the nave is carried outward from the wall, above the roof of the aisles, by curved horizontal braces called *flying buttresses*. These connect with tall vertical structures, called *buttresses*, built on the exterior walls of

the aisle. These grow increasingly thick in steps as they reach toward the ground and carry the weight from the flying buttresses.

Each country developed characteristics that distinguished the church designs of that area. For example, elegant flying buttresses were a striking feature of many French Gothic churches. English churches often had two sets of transepts, wide fronts, and tall towers over the crossing. Italian Gothic churches were covered with elaborate patterns in contrasting colors of marble. Every area of Europe produced beautiful Gothic churches, and when one stops to consider the sacrifice, hardship, devotion, and ingenuity required to build them, they become monuments to an age of faith. These beautiful buildings have been preserved, and we can enjoy them and learn about them today.[1]

Late English Medieval domestic design continued well beyond the end of the Gothic Era into the seventeenth century, particularly in the homes of the common people. The common houses from the end of the Middle Ages were constructed of stone, brick, or timber. These houses had steeply pitched roofs, small *casement windows* (that swing in or out) made with *leaded panes* (small panes of glass held together with lead strips, like stained glass). The *timber-framed houses* utilized two types of *infill* to form the walls between the timbers. Panels of woven sticks called *wattle* were fixed, like *lath* (groundwork for plastering), to the timber frame then covered with coarse plaster known as *daub*. The second type of infill was brickwork called *nogging*. The houses often featured an overhang at each story. These may have provided additional space in cramped city settings, but their use in less-crowded areas suggests that

Figure 14.15 Gothic elevation. Note the strong vertical lines, row-upon-row, pointing heavenward. Since domestic living conditions for the masses were very poor, strong church influence directed attention to the cathedrals and church buildings and their religious significance.

Figure 14.16 Gothic cross section. The buttresses and flying buttresses gave stability to the multistoried nave, preventing the collapse of its walls.

Figure 14.17

Figure 14.19

Figure 14.18

The Renaissance (1420–1650)

The *Renaissance* began in Florence, Italy, in the fourteenth century and marked the rebirth of classical influences in architecture, art, and many other areas of human endeavor. The architectural Renaissance moved through Europe by means of *pattern books* containing drawings and descriptions published by leading architects and designers from Italy, France, and Holland. These books along with the writings of Vitruvius, discovered in 1414, had an impact on architecture that continued until the nineteenth century.

The Renaissance palace was a boxlike city fortress with massive gates opening onto an open courtyard or atrium around which the house was built. The exterior of the palace was divided into three distinct stories by means of different textured stone, ranging from *rusticated* on the ground level to smooth on the third story, or by means of protruding rows (*courses*) of stone carved to form entablatures. The entablatures were visually supported by flat, false columns called *pilasters*, which progressed from the Doric order on the ground level to Ionic and Corinthian on the second and third levels. The top of the palace was finished with a very large overhanging cornice. The win-

overhangs were mostly a detail of style. Roofs were frequently *thatched* with bundles of reeds attached to the roof timbers and shaved or cut into smooth rounded curves. *Slate roofs* were made of thin, flat pieces of stone fashioned into shingles. Wooden shingles were also used in some areas. These Late English Medieval common houses were the prototype for the seventeenth-century American houses.[2]

dows on the ground level were small and covered with iron bars. The second floor or *piano nobile* (the noble level) and third floor had larger well-proportioned windows. The *facade* (front face) of the building was arranged in a symmetrical fashion.

The Renaissance architect whose work had the greatest impact on English and, subsequently, American architecture was a sixteenth-century stonecutter turned architect named Andrea Palladio. Palladio's work, centered at Vicenza near Venice, included some public buildings but was focused mainly on the design of villas for wealthy farmers. The most famous of these is the Villa Rotonda (1567). This house sits at the crest of a hill with a fine view in every direction. The basic form of the building is a plain box on a raised Roman podium. A portion of the podium extends outward on all four sides to create staircases. The four sets of steps lead up to four Roman Ionic porticoes. The house has a narrow attic story topped with a *hipped roof* of *terra-cotta* tiles that rises gently to support a low *drum* and shallow dome. The windows of the main floor are topped with triangular pediments supported by curved brackets called *modillions*. The Renaissance architect did not always try to duplicate the designs of Greece and Rome but adapted their proportions, forms, motifs, and orders to create a new and important style.[3]

The English Influence in America

The Seventeenth-Century English Medieval Style (1608–1695)

Settlers arriving in America from England in the early part of the seventeenth century quickly built crude, temporary shelters. However, as soon as conditions permitted, they began to construct permanent buildings of the style they had left in England. Because these settlers were generally not from the wealthy class, they probably had little acquaintance with the Renaissance style. The *Medieval* style persisted in England even after the introduction of some Ren-

Figure 14.17 Hall's Croft, c. 1607, Stratford-upon-Avon, England, is an example of late English medieval domestic design. Note the overhang or jetty, many steep gables and columned chimneys, small window panes, and timber framing with daub and wattle infill.

Figure 14.18 Palazzo Rucellai (1446–1451) in Florence, Italy, is a good example of Renaissance design. The false columns, or pilasters, are placed beneath the entablature. Repeated Roman arches provide rhythm and relief from severe lines and building materials.

Figure 14.19 Palladio's Villa Rotonda. Each of the flat sides incorporates a portico, or covered porch, with classical component facade. This building strongly influenced American Federal and Greek Revival architecture.

aissance motifs and details in the sixteenth century. During the first quarter of the seventeenth century, as America was being settled, English architect Inigo Jones (1573-1653) designed the first truly classical building in Britain, based on the designs of Andrea Palladio. Before the introduction of Inigo Jones' pure Italian style, English designers had superficially applied Renaissance architectural motifs and details borrowed from Dutch pattern books in the design of their buildings. Until Jones traveled to Italy, English architects and builders had never actually seen classical buildings. Consequently, early English Renaissance buildings were still medieval in nature and merely decorated with Renaissance details and motifs. The American settlers were not familiar with Jones' novel style and, instead, were accustomed to medieval construction methods and style.

A few of the American houses showed faint traces of Renaissance design in the form of projecting doorway entries and chimneys shaped like columns. The early Renaissance houses of England were built with *columned chimneys* and ornate entries that often broke forward from the body of the house. The American versions of these details were less elaborate than the English prototypes. Bacon's Castle in Surrey County, Virginia, though essentially medieval, was remarkable for the extent of its Renaissance design. It not only had columned chimneys and a projecting doorway but it also featured *Flemish gables* and a triangular pediment above the doorway. Dutch-inspired Flemish gables, designed with a series of steps and curves, were incorporated on some late sixteenth- and early seventeenth-century English buildings.

Seventeenth-century American houses featured varied use of materials and distinctive characterisitics in each area of the country. Brick was prevalent in the South where lime to make mortar was readily available. In New England, timber

Figure 14.20

Figure 14.21

Figure 14.22

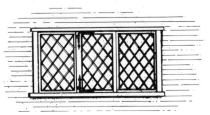

Figure 14.23

houses were often covered with *clapboard*, a sheathing of hand-split oak. Siding houses with clapboard was also common in East Anglia, the English region that had been home to many of the early American settlers. In Rhode Island several houses were built with stone chimneys that covered the end of the building. These houses are called *stone-enders*.

The medieval characteristics of the seventeenth-century American houses were the use of stone, brick, and timber construction, daub and wattle, nogging, overhangs with decorative *pendants*, small casement windows with leaded panes, chimneys built in the shape of Gothic buttresses (*buttressed chimneys*), and steeply pitched gabled roofs. *Saltbox* roofs, though not necessarily medieval, were English. The saltbox slopes to the rear from the ridge of the roof to a level below the line of the front eaves. The saltbox roof covers a lean-to addition at the back of the house. These additions were probably made in response to the need for more space. The saltbox was generally an addition made to an existing house, but by the beginning of the eighteenth century, some houses were built with saltbox roofs. The *gambrel roof,* with two different pitches on each side was also used somewhat during the seventeenth century, but was more popular on the vernacular houses of the eighteenth century. This type of roof, which was English, was practical because it allowed more space in the *garret* (attic).

Characteristics:
- English Medieval construction—brick, stone, timber with daub and wattle or nogging, and clapboard siding
- Steeply pitched gabled roof
- Small casement windows with leaded panes
- Overhang with pendants (optional)
- Buttressed chimneys (optional)

Figure 14.20 The Adam Thoroughgood House, 1640, features brick construction, buttressed end chimneys, diamond panes in the small casement windows, and steep gables. The simple boxlike construction is a departure from the rambling medieval English home, its direct ancestor.

Figure 14.21 The Corwin House, c. 1675, is a half-timber framed home covered with clapboard. The projecting doorway is suggestive of larger English Renaissance homes, and a saltbox roof at the rear tops a practical New England addition. Other medieval characteristics include the jetty, tri-sectioned window, steep gables, and columned chimney. Corner pendants and centralized chimney are American innovations.

Figure 14.22 The Eleazer Arnold House, c. 1687, in Lincoln, Rhode Island, is a good example of a medieval-style stone-ender house.

Figure 14.23 Typical medieval window detail from the seventeenth-century house—three main sections of diamond panes held together with lead came. Only the center section, a casement style, opens. L brackets show Colonial iron craftsmanship.

- Columned chimneys (optional)
- Stone-ender chimneys (optional)
- Projecting entry (optional)
- Saltbox (optional)
- Gambrel roof (optional)

Influences:
- Late English Medieval domestic architecture
- Early English Renaissance architecture

Examples:
- Adam Thoroughgood House (1640), Princess Anne County, Virginia
- Corwin House (c.1675), Salem, Massachusetts
- Eleazer Arnold House (before 1676), Johnston, Rhode Island
- Henry Whitfield House (1639), Guilford, Connecticut
- Whipple House (1638), Ipswich, Massachusetts
- Bacon's Castle (c. 1665), Surrey County, Virginia
- Thomas Clemence House (1680), Johnston, Rhode Island
- Parson Capen House (1683), Topsfield, Massachusetts

Nonresidential:
- St. Luke's Church (1632), Isle of Wight County, Virginia

The Early Georgian Style (1695-1750)

The classical style introduced into England by Inigo Jones began to be widely accepted primarily due to the work of Sir Christopher Wren. Wren was Surveyor of the King's Works (royal architect) in 1666 when the *City of London* was destroyed by fire. Wren was commissioned to rebuild St. Paul's Cathedral as well as fifty-two of the other smaller

Figure 14.24

Figure 14.25

Figure 14.26

City churches. His designs for churches and royal buildings were classical with some of the rich ornamentation that makes them Baroque. The influence of Jones and Wren extended to the building of houses as well. These medium-sized, Wren-Baroque-style houses were the prototype for American houses during the first half of the eighteenth century. Compared to the seventeenth-century medieval houses, the early American Georgian houses seemed splendid. They were, however, versions of middle-class English residences. The very large homes and palaces of the English aristocracy and royalty were not considered as models for homes in the colonies.

At the beginning of the eighteenth century, the American Colonies were prospering, and certain segments of society were ready for more elaborate houses. The new Wren-Baroque style of architecture was introduced in Williamsburg, Virginia, at the end of the seventeenth century. The Wren Building (1695) at William and Mary College in Williamsburg, though much less elaborate than his English designs, is attributed to Sir Christopher Wren and is very much like his Chelsea Royal Hospital (1682) in London.

Residences in the new style began to appear in America after the beginning of the eighteenth century. The first few years of the 1700s saw the death of Queen Anne and the accession to the British throne of George I. He was succeeded by George II, George III, and George IV who gave their name to the *Georgian Era*. The new architectural style popularized by Wren in England a quarter of a century earlier is called Early Georgian in America.

The basic form of the Early Georgian house was a rectangular two-story box, broken by five symmetrically placed bays (sections of wall that include window and door openings). Brick was the preferred building material in the South,

Figure 14.24 The Whitfield House, 1639, shows a buttressed chimney and stone construction. Note the small windows in the two stories and half-story dormers (windows in the attic). Rustic lintels support weight of the stone above the doors and windows on the main floor.

Figure 14.25 St. Luke's Church (1632) is an example of nonresidential English medieval architecture in Virginia. Note the buttresses between the side Gothic-arched windows.

Figure 14.26 This is Westover, c. 1730, before wings were added. This Wren-Barogue style was built for America's upper class, although it was modeled after homes of the

English middle class. Note symmetrical facade with ornate doorway, hipped roof, split-end chimneys, dentil trim, and stringcourse.

painted clapboard or brick were used in New England, and stone was common in the mid-Atlantic colonies. Where brick or stone were used, the first and second stories were frequently divided by a *stringcourse* or *beltcourse*. One or two Early Georgian-style houses built after 1750 include the use of *quoins* (decorative corner block details), which were more common in the Late Georgian style. Because these houses were larger, they required more than one chimney, and the chimneys were frequently placed at opposite ends of the house. Like the English prototypes, the houses had hipped roofs, which slope from the ridge in all four directions to the eaves. The roof was often broken by *dormer windows* that projected to provide light for the attic story. Some builders of independent spirit ignored the English prototype and incorporated gambrel or gabled roofs into their designs. Such variations give these houses a distinctly American feeling.

Medieval details from the seventeenth century such as casement windows with leaded panes were replaced by *sash windows*, and a door flanked with pilasters and crowned with a classical pediment took the place of the simple medieval doorway. The pediments were the simple *triangular* type or rounded *segmental pediments* (the arch is a segment of a circle) or the more ornate, Baroque-style *scroll pediments*. On some of these buildings, pediments were also used above the windows. The rafters were extended far enough to create an overhang that was treated like a classical cornice, often with modillions or dentil trim. A few of these houses had railings or *balustrades* around the ridge of the roof and a windowed tower called a *cupola*. Kitchens, servants' quarters, dairies, and other types of service areas were frequently located in *outbuildings* away from the main body of the house. Some of these outbuildings were attached to the houses during the twentieth century, altering their original appearance.

Characteristics:
- Two-story rectangular block
- Built of brick, clapboard, or stone
- Symmetrical facade with five or more bays
- Hipped roof, often with dormer windows
- Tall end chimneys

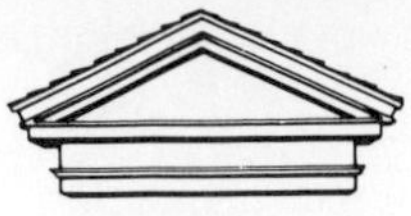

Figure 14.27

Figure 14.28

Figure 14.29

- Sash windows
- Cornice with dentils or modillions
- Stringcourse (optional)
- Pediment and pilasters at doorway or windows (optional)
- Balustrade (optional)
- Cupola (optional)
- Gabled or gambrel roof (optional)
- Quoins (optional)

Influences:
- Inigo Jones and Christopher Wren
- English-Baroque middle-class houses (late seventeenth century)

Examples:
- Westover (c.1730), Charles City County, Virginia
- Governor's Palace (1706–1720), Williamsburg, Virginia
- MacPhaedris-Warner House (1718–1723), Portsmouth, New Hampshire
- Brafferton Indian School (1723), Williamsburg, Virginia
- The President's House (1723), Williamsburg, Virginia
  - Hunter House (1746), Newport, Rhode Island
  - Carter's Grove (1750), James City County, Virginia
  - Wentworth-Gardner House (1760), Portsmouth, New Hampshire

Nonresidential:
- Christ Church—"Old North" (1723), Boston, Massachusetts
- Trinity Church (1725–1726), Newport, Rhode Island
- Independence Hall (1731), Philadelphia, Pennsylvania

The Late Georgian Style (1750–1790)

The style called Late Georgian came to America in English pattern books. These contained drawings of houses, floor plans, and details that could be built by men with little or no architectural training. One of the most significant of these books was James Gibbs' *A Book of Architecture* (1728), which had reached America by 1751 at the latest. His

Figure 14.30

Figure 14.27 Triangular pediment.
Figure 14.28 Segmental pediment.
Figure 14.29 Scroll pediment.

Figure 14.30 Balustrade and cupola. In the maritime Colonies, these sometimes served as protection for the captain who surveyed his ships in the river or harbor. Thus, the balustrade has also been called the captain's walk.

designs had great appeal for Americans because they were conservative in scale and within their means. Also, unlike his contemporaries, Gibbs showed a strong tendency to maintain much of the richness of the Wren-Baroque design. Gibbs' book contained illustrations of homes designed with a central house or block, connected to symmetrical dependencies (outbuildings) by straight or curved passages or wings. Such dependencies created a forecourt in the Palladian manner. Gibbs also designed houses in the Wren-Baroque style— as simple self-contained rectangular houses without wings or dependencies. His designs include the use of rusticated stone, balustrades, quoins, and pilasters, details too ornate for use by other Palladian architects of his time. Gibbs often designed houses with a two-story projecting pavilion or *breakfront*.

Figure 14.31

The breakfront topped with a triangular pediment above the roofline is the most distinctive feature of the Late Georgian-style house. In most other respects, it is similar to the Early Georgian style—a rectangular box with five or more bays, hipped roof, and tall end chimneys. The hipped roof is often lower pitched than the Early

Figure 14.32

Georgian roof and may, in rare cases, feature a balustrade at the eaves that hides the roof. The Late Georgian house may have a portico or a bracketed cornice, as well as pilasters and pediments at the doorway. The door may be crowned with a roundheaded *fanlight* (a rounded, over-the-door window), and the windows in the dormers may also be roundheaded. These houses may also feature a roundheaded arched window with lower rectangular windows on each side called a *Palladian window*. They bear that name because they resemble an architectural detail used by Palladio on several of his designs. When they are

placed above a front door or at the end of an important room, they create an impressive focal point. The standard windows on the Late Georgian house are frequently capped with *crown* or *jack arch lintels*, which are trapezoid-shaped stone pieces with a wedge-shaped *keystone*. Corner trim is plain or quoined or sometimes features two-story pilasters.

Characteristics:

- Same basic form as the Early Georgian house
- Two-story projecting pavilion or breakfront with pediment
- Small portico over doorway (optional)
- Two-story double portico (optional)
- Building massed into symmetrical blocks and connections (optional)
- Palladian windows (optional)
- Doorways with roundheaded fanlights or bracketed cornices or pilasters and pediments (optional)
- Corners untrimmed or trimmed with quoins or pilasters (optional)
- Crown lintels (optional)

Influences:

- James Gibbs and other English Palladian architects
- English pattern books

Examples:

- Tyron Palace (1770), New Bern, North Carolina
- Mount Pleasant (1761), Philadelphia, Pennsylvania
- Longfellow House (1750), Cambridge, Massachusetts
- Mount Airy (1758-1762), Richmond County, Virginia
- Lady Pepperell House (1760), Kittery Point, Maine
- Miles-Brewton House (1765-1769), Charleston, South Carolina
- Brandon (1765-1770), Prince George County, Virginia
- Hammond-Harwood House (1773-1774), Annapolis, Maryland

Figure 14.31 Tyron Palace (1770), New Bern, North Carolina, has a projecting breakfront typical of Late Georgian design. Note extensive dentil trim and bas-relief in the pediment.

Figure 14.32 Mount Pleasant, 1761, has a Palladian window on the second story above the door. It also features quoins on the corner and crown lintels above the windows. The breakfront displays elaborate detail and ornamentation originally inspired by classical Greece and Rome.

- St. Michael's Church (1752-1761), Charleston, South Carolina
- First Baptist Meetinghouse (1774-1775), Providence, Rhode Island
- Redwood Library (1758-1750), Newport, Rhode Island
- Brick Market (1761-1762), Newport, Rhode Island

The Federal Style (1790-1830)

British architect Robert Adam visited the Italian excavation sites at Pompeii and Herculaneum. He returned to England with drawings of ancient Roman and Renaissance design forms that he used to create a Neoclassic style. *Federal* -style houses generally are beautiful adaptations of the Adam style from Georgian England. The typical Federal house has a symmetrical facade of five bays and, like the English prototype, usually has three stories. A few Federal houses have longer second-story windows that extend to the floor. These second-story rooms were the public spaces of the house and were given more importance with the larger windows—a concept related to the Renaissance idea of the piano nobile. The windows on the third level were usually smaller than the other two, a characteristic also typical of the English prototype. The Federal doorway was sometimes covered with a small portico similar to those designed for English *terrace houses* (row houses). The door itself was commonly topped with a roundheaded or delicate elliptical fanlight and flanked with a narrow set of windows called *sidelights*. The elliptical fan shape, discovered on the walls of Herculaneum, was possibly the most versatile and significant motif of the period. It was doubled to form ellipses known as *paterae.* These were used in every possible decorative fashion from furniture hardware to inlaid wood patterns on furniture to plaster patterns for ceilings to elliptical room plans. The roof on the Federal house was low pitched and hipped and often featured a balustrade at the eaves.

The Federal period includes the work of Boston architect Charles Bullfinch, Samuel McIntire of Salem, and English transplant Benjamin Latrobe. Bullfinch's work was widely copied in the pattern books of the day and was likely the basis for much late eighteenth-century, early nineteenth-century architecture in New England. McIntire was a skilled carver as well as an architect, and his interiors and exteriors reflect the master's touch.

Characteristics:
- Five-bay, three- or four-story, box-shaped facade of brick, stucco, or clapboard
- Smaller windows on upper story
- Second-story windows to floor (optional)
- Doorway with fanlights and sidelights
- Flattened hipped roof with optional balustrade at eaves

Figure 14.33

- Classical detail from earlier periods such as the *jack-arch lintel,* portico, Palladian window, stringcourse, and quoins (optional)

Influences:
- Robert Adam
- English Georgian design   Figure 14.34

Examples:
- Pingree House (1804), Salem, Massachusetts; Samuel McIntire, architect
- Pierce-Nichols House (1782), Salem, Massachusetts; Samuel McIntire, arhitect
- Harrison Gray Otis House (1796), Boston, Massachusetts; Charles Bullfinch, architect
- Nathaniel Russell House (before 1809), Charleston, South Carolina
- Amory Ticknor House (1804), Boston, Massachusetts

Nonresidential:
- State House (1795-1798), Boston, Massachusetts; Charles Bullfinch, architect
- Baltimore Cathedral (1804-1818), Baltimore, Maryland; Benjamin Latrobe, architect
- Lancaster Meeting House (1816-1817), Lancaster, Massachusetts; Charles Bullfinch, architect
- United States Custom House (1819), Salem, Massachusetts

Jeffersonian Federal

Thomas Jefferson was not only an important statesman but also a fine amateur architect, and his designs represent an important divergent style during the Federal period. Unlike the mainstream of Federal design, which was based on English prototypes, Jefferson based his work on the designs

Figure 14.33 The Pingree House, 1804, is an excellent example of the Federal-style house. It has a small portico over the front door and a stringcourse between each floor. The elliptical fanlight and sidelights are adaptations of Robert Adam's Neoclassic designs.

Figure 14.34 Fanlight and sidelight detail typical of the Federal style. The ellipse or oval is the motif, called a paterae. Here it is seen cut in half. This fanlight style is sometimes called the spiderweb design.

Figure 14.35

Figure 14.36

Figure 14.37

tury Parisian hôtels (town houses). The work of Thomas Jefferson constitutes a significant and influential departure from the typical Federal style.[4]

The Vernacular Tradition (Seventeenth Century–Present)

In spite of over a century of exposure to classical influences, grass-roots American architecture held tenaciously to the English medieval tradition. Generally it was only the wealthy upper class who built the classically inspired houses discussed thus far. The vast majority of people living in America built adaptations of the new styles using the sturdy medieval house form with its gabled roof, and others remodeled existing seventeenth-century houses, adding new details to make the medieval house more stylish and up-to-date. For example, during the Early Georgian period symmetrically placed sash windows and pilastered and pedimented doorways gave the gabled house a feeling of the new style.

During the Federal period, the addition of fanlights and sidelights at the doorway imparted a sense of belonging to the era. These hybrid houses are referred to as *vernacular*, which literally means common, and implies the houses were adapted by local builders and developed regional characteristics. It also implies a naive, unschooled approach to design quite different from that which attempted to copy faithfully the fine English houses. Vernacular design may be the result of a lack of exposure, or a lack of resources, or it may represent a strong-willed independence or personal preference. Vernacular is not a negative term; most vernacular houses are charming and, in fact, are the most enduring type of house in America. The majority of colonial-style homes built today are vernacular versions of the Georgian- or Federal-style houses. Though vernacular is generally not a style, but rather a quality, some vernacular houses are so distinctive and well known that they have become styles.

The Cape Cod Cottage (Seventeenth-Twentieth Centuries)

The dwellings built in rural Cape Cod, Massachusetts, have become the typical American small house. The Cape Cod cottage is a one-story gabled house usually finished in shingle siding that was allowed to weather to a soft gray in the salty coastal air. In the eighteenth century, the steep medieval roof was lowered and sash windows and classical doorway details were added to make the houses more in step with the times. A few houses had slighty bowed roofs, called *rainbow roofs*, attributed to shipbuilders. (This type of house with a gambrel roof is called a Cape Ann house.) The eaves of the houses are very shallow, which gives them a

of Rome. His architecture is more directly related to original classical types. In his role as statesman, Jefferson traveled to Europe where he saw remnants of Roman culture. He considered the ancient style appropriate for the new American republic and patterned his most famous nonresidential buildings after two well-known Roman temples. The University of Virginia (1822-1826) at Charlottesville is the American incarnation of the Pantheon in Rome, and the State House (1785-1792) at Richmond, Virginia, is a larger version of the Maison Carrée in Nimes, France. His home, Monticello (1768-1782), at Charlottesville, Virginia, features a prominent templelike portico that foreshadowed the ensuing Greek Revival style. The time Jefferson spent in France had a strong effect on the layout of Monticello as well as its dome—both were inspired by eighteenth-cen-

Figure 14.35 Jefferson's Monticello, showing originality with influence stemming from Greek and Roman architecture. The long window, balustrade, and portico direct its classification to American Federal.

Figure 14.36 A vernacular Georgian house, this one of clapboard siding rather than brick, gable roof, modest split chimneys, simple framed windows, yet an elaborate double door with pilasters and scroll pediment.

Figure 14.37 Kendrick House, c. 1790, Orleans, Massachusetts, is a Cape Cod-style house, showing a one-and-one-half story wooden-framed house with shake shingles,

central door, and symmetrical placement of sash windows. The large chimney is centrally placed in the straight, gable roof.

crisp, boxy character. The size of the houses varied from a one-room half house of three bays to the four-bay three-quarter house with one large and one small room to the full-sized five-bay double house containing two full-sized rooms with the doorway in the center. The Cape Cod house is almost as popular today as it was through the seventeenth, eighteenth, nineteenth, and early twentieth centuries.

Characteristics:
- Small half house, three-quarter house, or full-sized house
- One story (some two-story versions built in Nantucket, Massachusetts)
- Gabled roof, less steeply pitched than the medieval houses (some bowed rainbow roofs; gambrel roofs make a Cape Ann house.)
- Sash windows directly under the eaves
- Shallow eaves
- Doorway with simplified pilasters and entablature
- Shingle siding (some clapboard)

Influences:
- Seventeenth-century medieval houses
- Early-Georgian houses
- New England ship carpenters

Examples:
- Kendrick House (c.1790), Orleans, Massachusetts
- Shadrach Standish House (1730), Halifax, Massachusetts
- Hezekia Swain-Maria Mitchell House (1790), Nantucket, Massachusetts

The Greek Revival Style (1820–1845)

The Greek Revival grew out of the spirit of the times and was a natural expression of the growing independence of American culture. Greek mythology, culture, and often even the classical Greek language were part of the educational training during the early nineteenth century. Literature and art were full of allusions to the ancient Greeks, and the Greek war of independence from Turkey had focused the attention of the world on modern Greece. The Greek style was not tied directly to English influences. In fact, the Greek Revival was the first style that was truly harmonious with the American vernacular taste for the gabled house. The gabled end of the house, when turned toward the street, became a Greek temple facade. It was adaptable enough to make it suitable for fine city dwellings as well as regional vernacular houses.

The style found acceptance everywhere in the country that was rapidly expanding toward the west, but it varied so much in its interpretation that it is difficult to identify a single set of characteristics. The one characteristic that seems to be universal is the use of all or part of the Greek

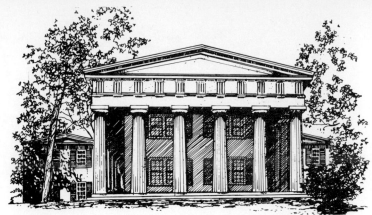

Figure 14.38

temple form on a one- or two-story dwelling. The most extravagant examples feature a full Doric or Ionic colonnade (Corinthian was less common) with a complete entablature, and the most unassuming interpretations are those where the gabled end forms an extremely simple pedimented facade that is turned toward the street. The Greek Revival door

Figure 14.39

opening was generally flanked by sidelights and headed by an oblong *transom* (over-the-door window). The doorway might be framed by a full portico or simply trimmed with pilasters and an entablature; pilasters were sometimes used to give definition to the facade. The basic two-story temple form might be given additional space with one-story flanking wings.

Characteristics:
- Bold forms with an emphasis on strength rather than delicacy
- Greek temple form with pediment (gabled end) oriented toward the front
- Porticoes and colonnades with two-story Greek columns
- Exterior finish of stone, brick, wooden siding, or stucco
- Sash windows
- Door openings flanked with sidelights and headed with oblong transoms or flanked with pilasters and crowned with an entablature

Influences:
- Previous classical styles
- The architecture of classical Greece
- Some French influence

Examples:
- Andalusia (1836), Bucks County, Pennsylvania
- Joseph Bowers House (1825), Northampton, Massachusetts

Figure 14.38 Andalusia was built with a Greek temple facade.

Figure 14.39 Doorway with sidelights and transom typical of the Greek Revival style.

Figure 14.40

- Russell House (1828-30), Middletown, Connecticut (now Honors College, Wesleyan University)
- Shadows-on-the-Teche (1830), New Iberia, Louisiana (see French Influence)
- James Lanier House (1844), Madison, Indiana
- Dunlieth (1847), Natchez, Mississippi (see French Influence)
- Alonzo Olds House (1848), Rushton, Michigan

Nonresidential:
- Philadelphia Water Works (1819), Philadelphia, Pennsylvania
- Girard College (1833), Philadelphia, Pennsylvania
- Second Bank of the United States (1924), Philadelphia, Pennsylvania
- Quincy Market (1825), Boston, Massachusetts
- Hibernian Hall (1835), Charleston, South Carolina
- Congregational Church (1838), Madison, Connecticut

The Victorian Age in America (1837–1901)

The Victorian age in America corresponds to the reign of Queen Victoria of England from 1837 to 1901, though the architectural styles known by her name extended beyond the turn of the century and existed side by side with the radical new architectural developments of the Modern Era. This coexistence was less than peaceful and may account for the scorn that, until recently, was heaped upon Victorian design. Victorian architecture is not a single style but a succession and *eclectic* mixing of styles. Some of the styles have their roots in the philosophies of the nineteenth century. For example, the Gothic Revival was fired by the notion that pagan buildings (Greek and Roman) were not fit for Christian living—the only true and suitable style for Christians was the Gothic. However, those who adopted the styles were likely less concerned with philosophy than with aesthetics.

The nineteenth century saw the full bloom of the Industrial Revolution and a rapid succession of advancements that radically changed the way people lived. The fireplace and stove were replaced by central heating. Gas lighting and, eventually, electric lighting took the place of oil lamps and candles. Indoor plumbing made the outhouse and hand water pump things of the past. The modern lifestyle with its many conveniences, often taken for granted today, was developed by the Victorians.

The advancement of technology also paved the way for migration from the farm to the city where industry was creating a growing middle class and a new wealthy class. This rapid change in society seemed to trigger a proliferation of decorative styles and treatments that have become the hallmark of Victorian design. As each new Victorian style developed, elements of former styles were retained and adapted to create an eclectic design patchwork that signaled the end of classical dominance. Each new variation in style was historical in nature but lacked the authenticity of the original styles upon which they were based. They were re-creations of a distant and romantic past by craftsmen in possession of the new technology of the Industrial Revolution. The most important of these styles were the Gothic Revival, Italianate, Egyptian, Oriental, Mansard, Stick, Eastlake, Queen Anne, Romanesque Revival, and Shingle styles.

General Victorian Characteristics:
- Lively, irregular silhouettes
- *Verandahs* (expansive covered porches)
- Towers
- Large windows made possible by improved glass-making technology
- Frequent use of sash windows often without divisions into smaller panes
- Extensive use of decorative ornamentation
- Eclectic mixing of detail from previous styles

The Gothic Revival Style
Characteristics:
- Steeply pitched gables (sometimes combined with low hipped roof)
- *Crenellated parapets* or *battlements* (notched low walls on the roof)
- Towers, spires, and finials on the roof
- Stone construction (finer houses only)
- Vertical wooden siding of *board and batten* (these wooden houses are called *Carpenter's Gothic*)
- Lacy wooden version of Gothic tracery called *gingerbread* used to decorate eaves and porches
- Pointed Gothic and flattened Tudor arches used for window, door, and verandah framing
- Leaded pane windows

Figure 14.40 The Gothic Revival incorporated narrow pointed arches, sharp gables, and tracery. This example is Carpenter's Gothic, named for the scroll-saw gingerbread trim and vertical wood siding.

Examples:
- Lyndhurst (1838), Tarrytown, New York; Alexander Jackson Davis, architect
- Greystone (c. 1859), Pevely, Missouri
- Town Office Building (1847), Cazenovia, New York; Andrew Jackson Downing, architect

Nonresidential:
- St. Patrick's Cathedral (1858-79), New York, New York; James Renwick, architect
- Brooklyn Bridge (1869-83), New York, New York
- Baptist Church (1878), North Salem, New York
- Calvary Presbyterian Church (1883), Portland Oregon

The Italianate Style
Characteristics:
- Also called Italian and Tuscan, inspired by Italian country houses and Prince Albert's design of Osborn House in England
- Low-pitched hipped or gabled roof
- Wide overhanging cornices with heavy brackets
- Square tower with a low pitched roof (optional)
- *Belvedere* (square tower or cupola)
- Roundheaded windows (optional)
- Ornate versions of classical details such as modillions and pediments
- Often used for New York brownstone and other city row houses

Examples:
- David Mayer Farmhouse (1867), Lancaster, Pennsylvania
- Edward King House (1845), Newport, Rhode Island
- Mills-Stebbins House (1849-1851), Springfield, Massachusetts
- Morse-Libby House (1859), Portland, Maine

Nonresidential:
- Haughwout Building (1857), New York, New York—cast-iron facade
- Sanger-Peper Building (1874), St. Louis, Missouri—cast-iron facade

The Egyptian Style
The Egyptian style was generally not philosophically suited for residential design but was considered appropriate for cemetery gates, tombs, and mausoleums. This was, perhaps, be-

cause of the Egyptian preoccupation with the afterlife and preparation for death. The style, which featured sloping walls with wide cornices, was also used for prisons and churches.

Examples:
- Whaler's Church (1844), Sag Harbor, New York
- Gates, Grove St. Cemetery (1848), New Haven, Connecticut

The Oriental Style
Characteristics:
- Also called Moorish or Persian, inspired by Islamic design
- Pointed and horseshoe Moorish arches used for doorways, windows, and porches
- Bulbous *onion domes* used to crown towers or belvederes

Figure 14.42

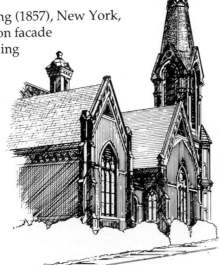

Figure 14.41

Figure 14.43

Figure 14.41 Calvary Presbyterian Church in Oregon is a good example of the Carpenter's Gothic style, with vertical wood siding and much wooden detail around steep gables and Gothic arches. (See also page 374.)

Figure 14.42 The Mayer house, an example of Italianate style, features a heavy-bracketed cornice, cornices over the windows, and a cupola or belvedere.

Figure 14.43 The Whaler's Church (1844) at Sag Harbour, New York, is typical of the Egyptian style, with sloping walls. Wide cornices added importance and decoration to the simple styling.

- Longwood (1860), Natchez, Mississippi
- Olana (1870-72), near Hudson, New York (see page 359)

Nonresidential:
- Wise Temple (1866), Cincinnati, Ohio

The Mansard Style
Characteristics:
- Also called Second Empire and influenced by nineteenth-century French design, or also called General Grant Style because it was popular during the presidency of Ulysses S. Grant
- *Mansard roof* crested with a low wrought iron railing
- Dormer windows that rest on or break through the line of the eaves
- Quoins (optional)

Figure 14.44

Figure 14.45

Figure 14.44 Longwood (1860), in Natchez, Mississippi, reveals romantic details of the Oriental Victorian house—Moorish arches and onion dome belvederes. This octagonal house also incorporates Roman arches and wide, bracketed cornice eaves.

Figure 14.45 The Mansard House was built in the French taste. The gallerie at the edge of the roof was frequently ironwork cresting. Long, simplified French windows are heavily framed in Roman or Greek Revival arches.

Examples:
- Governor's Mansion (1871), Jefferson City, Missouri
- John DeKoven House (1874), Chicago, Illinois
- Governor's Mansion (1878), Sacramento, California
- Iolani Palace (1882), Honolulu, Hawaii

Nonresidential:
- City Hall (1872-1901), Philadelphia, Pennsylvania
- Grand Union Hotel (1872), Saratoga Springs, New York
- McKinley High School (1872), Lincoln, Nebraska
- Hill County Courthouse (1890), Hillsboro, Texas

The Stick Style
Characteristics:
- Victorian version of Late English Medieval house
- Steep gables
- *Stickwork* patterning applied to represent vertical, diagonal, and horizontal timber construction
- Jetties or overhangs

Examples:
- Griswold House (1862-63), Newport, Rhode Island
- Emlen Physick House (1879), Cape May, New Jersey

The Eastlake Style
Characteristics:
- Named for Charles Eastlake, English architect and philosopher of the English *Arts and Crafts Movement*
- Another version of Late English Medieval design
- Decorative effects achieved with different colors of brick or contrasting light stone (*ribbonwork*)
- Flattened Mansard roofs on the porch
- Features projecting bays

Examples:
- Governor's Mansion (1883-89), Raleigh, North Carolina
- Mark Twain House (1874), Hartford, Connecticut

Nonresidential:
- Hart Block (1884), Louisville, Kentucky

Figure 14.46

Figure 14.46 The Griswold House, 1863, features stickwork and Tudor framing. Woodwork is exposed in this adaptation of Late English medieval architecture. Sharp gables and jetties, or overhangs, give charm to this Victorian style.

Figure 14.47

Figure 14.48

The Queen Anne Style

Characteristics:

- Features a variety of decoration and surface embellishments such as stone, rounded *fish-scale shingles*, clapboard, stickwork, *lathwork*, turned *balusters*, and *fretwork*
- Strong horizontal lines or bands
- Combination of gabled and steep hipped rooflines
- Turret (towers) often rounded with round pointed roofs
- Rounded *gazebos*—part of the verandah
- Some use of stained glass

Examples:

- Miss Parks House (1876), Cape May, New Jersey
- Glenmont (1880), West Orange, New Jersey
- Haas-Lilienthal House (1886), San Francisco, California

Nonresidential:

- Hotel del Coronado (1888), Coronado, California

The Romanesque Revival

Characteristics:

- Introduced by architect Henry Hobson Richardson
- Inspired by medieval Romanesque designs
- Heavy stone foundations
- Generally rounded contours
- Use of heavy rusticated stone construction
- Use of stocky Romanesque pillars and heavy, round-headed Romanesque arches

Examples:

- Franklin McVeagh House (1885-1887), Chicago, Illinois; Henry Hobson Richardson, architect
- Hull-Wiehe House (c. 1890), Fort Wayne, Indiana

Nonresidential:

- Crane Memorial Library (1883), Quincy Massachusetts; Henry Hobson Richardson, architect
- Marshall Field Warehouse (1885-1887), Chicago, Illinois; Henry Hobson Richardson, architect

Figure 14.47 Plans for Queen Anne-style houses like this were often found in pattern books. Many materials are held together visually with strong horizontal lines or bands.

- Trinity Church (1887), Boston, Massachusetts; Henry Hobson Richardson, architect

Shingle Style

Characteristics:

- Inspired by colonial seaside dwellings like the Cape Cod, Cape Ann, and Nantucket houses and appearing first as resort houses on the Eastern seaboard
- Covered with shingles
- Small paned windows

Examples:

- Kragsyde (1884), Manchester-by-the Sea, Massachusetts
- Dr. John Bryant House (1880), Cohasset, Massachusetts; Henry Hobson Richardson, architect
- William Low House (1887), Bristol, Rhode Island; McKim, Mead, and White, architects
- Frank Lloyd Wright House (1889), Oak Park, Illinois; Frank Lloyd Wright, architect

Other Influences in America

The Swedish Influence

Scandinavian settlers in the seventeenth-century introduced the house type for which America is most famous—the log cabin. The log house was a typical Scandinavian rural architectural form adapted by eighteenth- and nineteenth-century settlers of many origins. As the American frontier moved toward the Pacific, the log cabin made a strong and quick shelter for those who pushed the borders westward.

Closer to our own time, the simple dwelling has been adapted for the construction of rustic cabins and resort hotels, such as Old Faithful Inn (1904) at Yellowstone National Park.

Figure 14.49

Figure 14.48 Kragsyde, 1884, Manchester-by-the-Sea, Massachusetts, is an atypically large yet characteristic example of the Shingle style.

Figure 14.49 The log cabin is a Swedish contribution to American culture.

Figure 14.50

Figure 14.51

Figure 14.52.

- Washington's Headquarters (1758), Valley Forge State Park, Pennsylvania
- Trout Hall (1770), Allentown, Pennsylvania

The German Influence

The German settlers in Pennsylvania used the plentiful local gray and brown fieldstone to build houses that varied only slightly from the mainstream of American English architecture. The Germans or Deutsch are mistakenly called Pennsylvania Dutch, a designation that has endured.

Characteristics:
- Large, simple, rectangular construction
- Built of roughly finished fieldstone or brick.
- Transoms over front door
- Sash windows
- Gabled or gambrel roof
- A narrow, overhanging rooflike projection between the first and second stories, called a *pent roof* (optional)
- *Cantilevered* (unsupported) triangular portico (optional)

Examples:
- Troxell-Steckel House (1756), Egypt, Pennsylvania
- Thompson-Neely House (1710), Washington Crossing Pennsylvania
- Georg Mueller House (1752), Milbach, Pennsylvania

The Dutch Influence

Nothing remains of the seventeenth-century Dutch buildings in New York City (originally New Amsterdam), and of all the Dutch houses in America, the most distinctive type may not even be Dutch. Historians differ as to whether the so-called Dutch house with the bell-shaped gambrel roof and flaring eaves was an American or Flemish development. Regardless of its origins, the house type has come to be known as Dutch Colonial. Unlike the Dutch who were merchants, the Flemish settlers were generally farmers and built fine farmhouses.

Characteristics:
- Houses of stone, brick, or clapboard
- Gambrel roof with a line that breaks near the ridge
- Flaring eaves that give the roof a bell shape
- Sash windows and doors typical of mainstream English/American design

Examples:
- Dyckman House (1783), New York, New York
- Zabriskie-Von Steuben House (1752), Hackensack, New Jersey
- Richard Vreeland House (1786), Leonia, New Jersey
- Jacobus Demarest House (1719), Bergen County, New Jersey

The French Influence

The funnel-shaped territory that stretches from New Orleans and the Mississippi delta, north to the Canadian border, originally a French possession, was purchased by the United States in 1803. The architectural characterstics of the houses of French settlers in that area were distinctive but not all were strongly tied to the architecture of France. Instead they represented an adaptability to the warm and wet climate and water-logged terrain of that region.

Figure 14.50 The Troxell-Steckel House (1756) has a pent roof and two-story rectangular stone construction, typical of the Pennsylvania Dutch houses.
Figure 14.51 The Dutch houses featured bell-shaped eaves, with the bend high, near the ridge line. End chimneys and a symmetrical facade are similar to the Georgian characteristics. The overhang, or the flaring eave porch, gave protection to building materials. The house was often constructed without a covered porch.

Figure 14.52 Madame John's Legacy had galleries to protect from rain and to shade the house from the sun. This raised basement is indicative of New Orleans French style due to the high water table.

The stucco-covered houses with steeply pitched hipped roofs built by Norman French settlers were soon fitted with an encircling porch called a *galerie*. The roof was extended at a lower pitch to cover the galerie forming a *bonnet roof* ideally suited to the rain and heat. *French doors and windows* opened onto the galerie and allowed the air to move freely through the house. The galerie with French windows and doors was also an important feature that persisted in the design of Greek Revival and Victorian houses of the area. These French details imparted a quality of elegance that is still associated with southern culture. Low piers raised some French houses above the dampness. Some houses were built above a raised basement, used as a service area that also offered protection from flooding or dampness in areas with high water tables.

The French town houses of New Orleans were built around galeried garden courtyards. During the Victorian era of the nineteenth century, with the advent of cast iron, galeries were also added to the front of the houses. These galeries of lacelike cast iron, though found elsewhere, are a symbol of New Orleans and add a touch of character that makes that city particularly charming.

Characteristics:
* Galerie
* French doors
* French windows
* Bonnet roof sometimes with dormer windows
* Frequently built over a raised basement

Examples:
* Madame John's Legacy (c. 1727), New Orleans, Louisiana
* Dunlieth, Shadows-on-the-Teche (see Greek Revival)
* La Veuve-Dodier House (1766), St. Louis, Missouri

* The Fortier-Keller House (1801), St. Charles Parish, Louisiana
* Le Pretre Mansion (1836), New Orleans, Louisiana

The Spanish Influence

The earliest Spanish settlement in America was at St. Augustine, Florida, predating English settlement in Virginia by nearly fifty years. However, due to lack of colonization, frequent destruction and rebuilding, and repeated English inhabitation, nothing of significant original Spanish influence remains.

California Missions

The Spanish also controlled the area along the southwestern border of the United States, from present-day Texas to California. Traces of Spanish influence can be seen throughout that region particularly in the design of missions and churches. These were vernacular designs incorporating Spanish detailing contributed by the missionary-priests and local materials and construction methods employed by the Indian builders.

Examples:
* San José y San Miguel de Aguayo (1768-78), San Antonio, Texas
* San Xavier del Bac (1783-97), near Tucson, Arizona
* San Carlos de Borromeo (1797), Carmel, California

Southwestern Style

In New Mexico, the Southwest Adobe style is more enduring and abundant than in the other areas. Colonists of European extraction arrived in New Mexico early in the seventeenth century and began building houses using the same methods employed by the local Pueblo Indians. The Indian dwellings or *pueblos* were communal structures of *adobe* (clay bricks) several stories high. The Indians reached the upper stories by means of ladders. The thick adobe

Figure 14.53

Figure 14.53 Shadows-on-the-Teche is a Greek Revival-style house that also shows French influence in its galerie.

Figure 14.54

Figure 14.54 San Carlos de Borromeo in Carmel, California, is considered one of the jewels of the California Spanish missions.

bricks are natural insulators in a climate that is hot in the summer and cold in the winter. Adobes are made by forming clay, bonded with straw in wooden frames about one and one-half feet long, and drying the bricks in the sun. Adobe "melts" in the rain and is stuccoed with clay and straw to retard deterioration. The mud imparts a grayish-brown to pink color that varies according to the clay used.

The irregular walls support the large log roof beams known as *vigas*, which are not cut to size but protrude through the walls. These make a convenient place to dry chilies and hang other objects. The beams are covered with thin sticks called *latillas* that are laid across the vigas in parallel fashion or herringbone patterns and form the ceiling of the structure as well as the base for the roofing material. Originally the roof was made of sod or packed earth and required constant repairs (today they are made of more permanent materials). The early pueblos had no windows, but during the eighteenth century, the settlers began to incorporate paned windows deeply set into the thick adobe walls.

The first settlers' houses were built, Spanish style, around an open courtyard. The house served as a fortress, opened to the interior with no exterior windows, and was entered through a sturdy wooden gate. As the threat of attack lessened with the years, the house took on a friendlier aspect, opening to the front, which often includes a covered porch or *portal*. The porch is supported by sturdy posts capped with a carved double *corbel* or bracket called a *zapata*, and topped with lintels. When brick became available, it was used to form a row of trim along the top of the adobe walls. The trim, called *pretil*, is a protection for the weaker adobe and is characteristic of the *Territorial style* frequently seen in Santa Fe. It is a vernacular version of classical design and may feature dentil trim, simple pediments above the windows, and square painted columns in imitation of the Greek Revival.

Special ordinances in Santa Fe and Taos, New Mexico, permit building only in the Adoble (or Territorial) style, giving both those cities a unique architectural continuity found in few other places.

Characeristics:
- Thick, irregular, adobe walls with rounded corners
- Mud-colored stucco finish on exterior walls

- Deep-set windows and doors
- Vigas (log beams) protrude through the walls
- Flat roofs
- Portal (porch) with wooden post and lintels decorated with carved corbels called zapatas

Examples:
- Palace of the Governors (c.1610—restored to its nineteenth-century appearance), Santa Fe, New Mexico
- Casa San Ysidro (eighteenth century), Corrales, New Mexico
- Filipe Delgado House (c. 1872), Santa Fe, New Mexico

Nonresidential:
- San Francisco de Asis (c. 1772), Rancho de Taos, New Mexico
- Mission Church (c. 1710), Santa Ana Pueblo, New Mexico

The California Ranch House

The early California ranch houses (c.1820), like the Southwest houses of New Mexico, were flat-roofed structures built of adobe. However, the flat roof soon gave way to the low-pitched, gabled, red tile roof, which was more practical in a rainier climate. Because there was less need for protection, the house was generally not enclosed with a walled

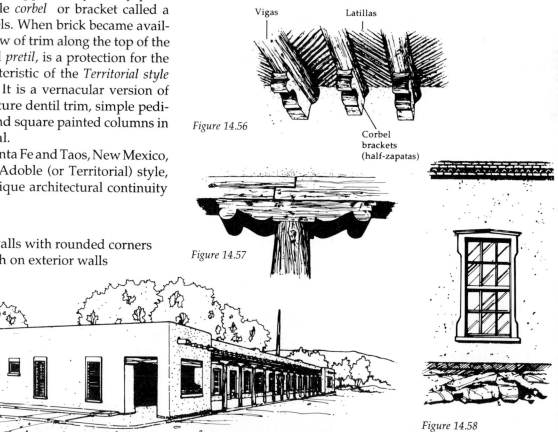

Figure 14.56

Figure 14.57

Figure 14.55

Figure 14.58

Figure 14.55 The Palace of the Governors is a combination of influences. Flat roofs, adobe brick overlaid with stucco are Indian techniques; wood trim and large windows, soft sculpturing are Spanish-American.

Figure 14.56 The interior ceiling of a Southwest adobe home. The vigas often protrude through the walls to the exterior, and the latillas are often laid parallel to each other and are perpendicular (at right angles) to the vigas. The corbel brackets, or half-zapatas, support the vigas.

Figure 14.57 The zapata, the double corbel bracket installed in the Southwest adobe and territorial homes between the post and lintel. It is the Southwestern counterpart of the classic Greek capital.

Figure 14.58 The Territorial variation of the Southwest adobe style features a brick entablature (pretil) and classical or Greek Revival wood trim.

court but open and rambling with a covered porch running the length of the house. The original houses do not exist in numbers sufficient to warrant listing their characteristics. Their significance lies in the fact that they are thought to be the precursor of the twentieth-century rambler or ranch-style house found in many parts of the country. These builder/developer houses, so well suited to the informal California life-style, soon found acceptance in other parts of the country. Many of the newer versions have been adapted to the point where any similarity to the originals is purely coincidental. They may, however, trace their genealogy back to the early California settlements.

Figure 14.59

The Monterey Style

The Monterey house is a California vernacular style with characteristics representative of the mainstream American English influence, local influence, and the ingenuity of the first builder. Thomas Larkin, a merchant from Boston, was the United States Consul to California when Monterey was the colonial capital. The two-story house he built in Monterey was made of local adobe but built with a Georgian central hall floor plan, paned windows, and a low, hipped, shingled roof. Larkin designed the roof to cover a second-story balcony and a porch that surrounded the house like the French galerie (Larkin likely arrived at the design independent of French influence). The Larkin house was the prototype for several other houses and nonresidential buildings in the vicinity, and today the style, built throughout California and the West, is called Monterey.[5]

Characteristics:
- Two stories
- Hipped or gabled roof of tile or shingles
- Second-story balcony, cantilevered or supported with posts
- Generally stucco covered

Examples:
- Thomas Larkin House (1835-1837), Monterey, California
- Los Ceritos Ranch House (1884), Long Beach, California

Nonresidential:
- Thomas Larkin House (1835-1837), Monterey, California (also used as a store)
- Old Customs House (1827), Monterey, California

The Beaux Arts Influence (1881-1945)

Beaux Arts is not a style. Rather, it is the influence on the training of an architect, either direct or indirect, of *L'Ecole des Beaux Arts* in Paris, France. At the beginning of the 1880s, in the midst of Victorian eclecticism and informality, Richard Morris Hunt, the first American architect trained at L' Ecole des Beaux Arts, designed a home for the Vanderbilt family in New York that was elegant, refined, and historically correct. Thus, America was launched on a new sea of historical influence in architecture. The training at L'Ecole des Beaux Arts focused on historical design in its most minute details. This type of training, which became the standard for American architectural schools, produced designers who were capable of creating the magnificent palaces and châteaux demanded by the new rich, as well as accurately styled smaller homes for those of less means.

By the early years of the 1900s, most American architects were being trained in the historical Beaux Arts tradition, and its influence was felt in most areas of the country. Much of the traditional, historical architecture of the Tudor, French, Dutch, Georgian, Federal, Greek Revival, Spanish, and Colonial style houses that dot the pre-World War II neighborhoods of the country, show the Beaux Arts influence. Row houses or town houses also came from the drawing boards of Beaux Arts architects. Without understanding this significant influence, it is difficult to account for much of the period-style architecture that surrounds us.

Characteristics:
- Vary according to the intended style of the building

Examples:
- Biltmore (1890-95), Ashville, North Carolina; Richard Morris Hunt, architect—French Renaissance
- The Breakers (1892-95), Newport, Rhode Island; Richard Morris Hunt, architect—Italian Renaissance
- Marble House (1892), Newport, Rhode Island; Richard Morris Hunt, architect—French Neoclassic
- Hearst Castle (1919-1947), San Simeon, California; Julia Morgan, architect—Spanish Renaissance
- Benjamin Winchell House (1922), Fieldston, New York; Dwight James Baum, architect—Dutch Colonial
- Conkey House (1934), Santa Fe, New Mexico— Southwest Adobe

Figure 14.59 The Larkin House marked the beginning of the Monterey-style house in California. This home is L-shaped, is stucco covered, and features a second-story balcony.

Figure 14.60

The Modern Styles (1885-Present)

It was the Victorians and their technological developments that laid the groundwork for modern architecture. Use of reinforced concrete, structural steel, plate glass, plumbing, and central heating were nineteenth-century developments. The Victorians had also experimented with novel floor plans, as well as new types of architectural massing. We often tend to think of the changes that gave birth to modern architecture as radical. In reality, it is sometimes difficult to know exactly where modern architecture begins. The technology for change was in place. All that was necessary to produce a new style was a break from the cyclical pattern of repeating historical styles. That break is usually attributed to Chicago architects Louis Sullivan and his protégé Frank Lloyd Wright.

Both of these men were familiar with historical architectural types, and the break with that familiarity did not happen all at once. The new modern style grew almost imperceptibly out of experimentation with historical designs. Once the full potential of the new technology was clear, there was no stopping the rapid development of new architectural forms.

The Skyscraper (1857-Present)

The skyscraper is a Chicago phenomenon. It was there that the metal skeleton, which is the basis for skyscrapers, was developed. The installation of the first practical passenger elevator in the New York Victorian cast-iron Haughwout Building in 1857 paved the way for the tall buildings that steel had made possible. The Brooklyn Bridge (1883) had shown that steel could carry far heavier loads than iron. In that same year, William Le Baron Jenney planned the eleven-story Home Insurance Building, using a skeleton framework of steel. This building demonstrated that skyscrapers could reach incredible heights without the support of walls. The walls were for enclosure and could be as thin as glass; the weight of the building was carried on the steel skeleton, and the elevator made the height practical.

The master of the skyscraper was Boston-born Louis Sullivan. To Sullivan is attributed the famous philosophy that "form follows function." He designed a string of im-

Figure 14.61

Nonresidential:

- Boston Public Library (1895), Boston, Massachusetts; McKim, Mead, & White, architects—Italian Renaissance
- Union Station (1907), Washington, D.C.; Daniel H. Burnham, architect—Classical
- County Courthouse (1920), Santa Barbara, California; William Mooser, architect—Spanish
- Woolworth Building (1913), New York, New York; Cass Gilbert, architect—Gothic Skyscraper
- Palace of Fine Arts (1915), San Francisco, California; Bernard Maybeck, architect—Classical
- Grauman's Chinese Theatre (1927), Los Angeles, California; Meyer & Holler, architects—Chinese
- Savoy Plaza Hotel (1928), New York, New York; McKim, Mead, & White, architects—Classical French Château Skyscraper

Figure 14.60 Biltmore, a revival of a French Renaissance château, is an example of the magnificent palaces built in one of the many styles by Beaux Arts designers.

Figure 14.61 The Beaux Arts influence found its way into middle-class homes as well as the palaces of the wealthy. This rambling structure is a picturesque English Tudor, copied from the Late Medieval era. The partial hipped roof is called a jerkinhead roof.

portant skyscrapers (some with partner Dankmar Adler) and started a building trend that has never ceased and has left its mark on almost every corner of the globe.[6]

Examples:
- The Auditorium Building (1889), Chicago, Illinois; Adler and Sullivan, architects
- The Wainwright Building (1891), St. Louis, Missouri; Louis Sullivan, architect
- Monadnock Building (1892), Chicago, Illinois; Burnham & Root, architects
- Reliance Building (1895), Chicago, Illinois; Daniel H. Burnham, architect
- The Guaranty Building (1895), Buffalo, New York; Adler & Sullivan, architects
- Carson Pirie Scott & Co. (1904), Chicago, Illinois; Louis Sullivan, architect

Organic Architecture (1908-Present)

In 1908 with the design of the Robie House in Chicago, Illinois, Wright was able to create a building devoid of historical precedent. The house was low and spread outward from the central chimney, creating a profile that was in harmony with the prairies of the great Midwest. Wright called it organic because it seemed to grow out of its surroundings.

In Pasadena, California, also in 1908, architect brothers Greene and Greene designed a house with far-reaching implications. The Gamble House, with its shingle exterior, low roof, wide overhang, and long low profile, is a Western variation on the organic theme. Bernard Maybeck, a northern California architect, was well schooled in the Beaux Arts tradition but was also disposed to experimentation with new forms. His wooden designs in the San Francisco Bay area are also significant examples of the organic architectural trend. These California architects spawned a new house type that became popular across the entire country. Adaptations of the California bungalow with its low roof and wide front verandah are classics of low-cost housing.

Many contemporary houses share the philosophical legacy of modern organic architecture. Though they may differ from the early modern houses in line and form, designs that make frank use of natural materials such as wood and stone and appear to have grown from their setting are in the spirit of Wright's organic architecture. Houses with soaring veritical shed roofs may seem distant cousins to the very horizontal Robie House. However, in the context of mountains, woods, or even coastal dunes the designs are organic.

Characteristics:
- Materials that harmonize with nature
- Architectural forms in harmony with the setting
- Well-established relationship from the inside of the house to the outdoors
- Flexible floor plan

Examples:
- Robie House (1908), Chicago, Illinois; Frank Lloyd Wright, architect

Figure 14.62

Figure 14.63

Figure 14.62 In the Oak Park suburb of Chicago, Frank Lloyd Wright's Robie House echos the lines of the midwestern prarie. The cantilevers projecting beyond the body of the house reinforce the horizontality of the design.

Figure 14.63 The Greene brothers used natural materials and Japanese design and craftsmanship to create the Gamble House.

- David B. Gamble House (1908), Pasadena, California; Greene and Greene, architects
- Taliesein West (1938), Paradise Valley, Arizona; Frank Lloyd Wright, architect

Nonresidential:
- Church of Christ Science (1912), Berkley, California; Bernard Maybeck, architect

The International Style (1932-Present)

The International style, as the name implies, crossed international borders and drew inspiration from several European schools of thought. From the thinking of the *De Stijl* movement in Holland, the *Bauhaus* in Germany, and *Le Corbusier* in France came the principles that dominated and gave form to the International style.

Though isolated examples existed before, the new style was introduced into the mainstream of American design in 1932 by Philip Johnson and Henry-Russell Hitchcock when they organized the first exhibit of modern architecture at the Museum of Modern Art in New York City and published a book called *The International Style*. The definition of the new style advanced by these men rapidly gained acceptance and established a formula or framework in which less-imaginative architects could design. The style gained further momentum when many leaders of the Inter-national Movement immigrated to America during World War II. Walter Gropius, Ludwig Mies van der Rohe, and Marcel Breuer, all associated at one time with the Bauhaus, became teachers of the new style in the United States.

In some ways, the International style is the antithesis of Wright's organic style. The organic style harmonizes with its setting, while the International style stands out in clear contrast. The materials of the International style are bold and hard edged: concrete, structural steel, glass, and stark white stucco. The architectural approach is minimalist, not adding any unnecessary embellishment, and the plan is open and unencumbered. This architecture is not as "forgiving" as the organic or historical designs. There is little place for the wear and tear of human use and the gentle softening that comes with time. In order to appear pleasing, these clean pure designs must be impeccably maintained. Because of its stark cleanliness, the style has not lent itself to the charming vernacular versions of previous styles.

After the years of historical eclecticism, the International Movement was like a breath of fresh air. There is a purity and cool elegance to this approach that is beautiful and refreshing, but as with all styles, trends never continue unaltered. It is noteworthy that one of the International style's first American proponents, architect Philip Johnson, moved away from strict adherence to its principles to embrace allusions to classical pediments and Gothic spires.[7]

Characteristics:
- Open plan
- Simple, logical, rectilinear structural forms
- Generally flat roofed
- Asymmetrical
- Large areas of glass (often arranged horizontally)
- Use of concrete, stucco, and metal
- Long, uninterrupted white wall planes
- Contrasts with setting

Examples:
- Walter Gropius House (1937), Lincoln, Massachusetts; Walter Gropius and Marcel Breuer, architects
- Glass House (1949), New Caanan, Connecticut; Philip Johnson, architect
- Edgar J. Kaufmann House, Fallingwater (1936), Bear Run, Pennsylvania; Frank Lloyd Wright, architect
- Lovell Beach House (1926), Newport Beach, California; Rudolph Schindler, architect
- Lovell-Health House (1927), Los Angeles, California; Richard Neutra, architect
- Farnsworth House (designed 1946, built 1950), Plano, Illinois; Ludwig Mies van der Rohe, architect

Nonresidential:
- 860-80 Lake Shore Drive (1952), Chicago, Illinois; Ludwig Mies van der Rohe, architect

Figure 14.64

Figure 14.65

Figure 14.64 Walter Gropius' Lincoln, Massachusetts, residence (1939) is a good example of the clean lines and flat planes of the International style.

Figure 14.65 Philip Johnson's own residence (1948) in New Canaan, Connecticut, is a glass house in the International tradition.

- Lever House (1952), New York, New York; Skidmore, Owings, and Merrill, architects
- Crown Hall (1956), I. I. T., Chicago, Illinois; Ludwig Mies van der Rohe, architect
- General Motors Technical Center (1956), Warren, Michigan; Eero Saarinen & Associates, architects
- Seagram Building (1958), New York, New York; Ludwig Mies van der Rohe and Philip Johnson, architects

Art Deco (1925-1940)

Art Deco was a compromise between the fascination with ornamentation of the Beaux Arts tradition and the stark cleanliness of the International style. Art Deco was "slick" modern but at the same time highly ornate and decorative. It was possible for the Art Deco designer to have the best of both worlds. The style represents an extraordinarily rich development in decorative motifs inspired by nature, history, and the machine.

The Art Deco style is characterized by rigid geometric forms, zigzags, chevron patterns, stepped pyramid forms, stylized billows of clouds, stylized human and animal forms. Preferred materials were shiny metals, smoothly cut stone or marble, and etched mirrors and glass.

As an architectural style it was used for the design of skyscrapers, movie palaces, and even some post offices and other government buildings. The style has hundreds of vernacular applications in every corner of the country, and its influence can even be seen in unlikely places such as churches, service stations, and grocery stores.[8]

Its residential application was principally as an interior style and was simply called modern.

Examples:
- Richfield Oil Building (1929), Los Angeles, California
- Chrysler Building (1930), New York, New York
- Empire State Building (1931), New York, New York
- Rockefeller Center (1931-1940), New York, New York

The styles and influences listed in this chapter are only a part of the story. There is no style to end all styles. The development of architecture is an ongoing process, as one style influences another and further variations are born. New technology prompts

Figure 14.66

changes in design, and frequently, some influence of either traditional or modern design reappears. It takes time to determine the value of a design and to put it into the context of a style. In the past, the classification of styles was done in retrospect by historians with a clear overview. The architectural family tree has grown very bushy since the beginning of the twentieth century. We live in an information age filled with self-awareness and are often conscious of every new ism that appears on the scene. For the amateur, this can be confusing and discouraging. It may be comforting to realize that many of the developments in architecture, which have mushroomed along with technology, are still being sifted and judged by time.

A knowlege of the basic styles and influences listed here is a key to understanding the myriad modes that have grown out of the Modern Movement and the thousands of vernacular adaptations of each modern and traditional style. Understanding leads to appreciation and enrichment. We are richer because of our architectural heritage and should cherish it and preserve it for future generations to enjoy.

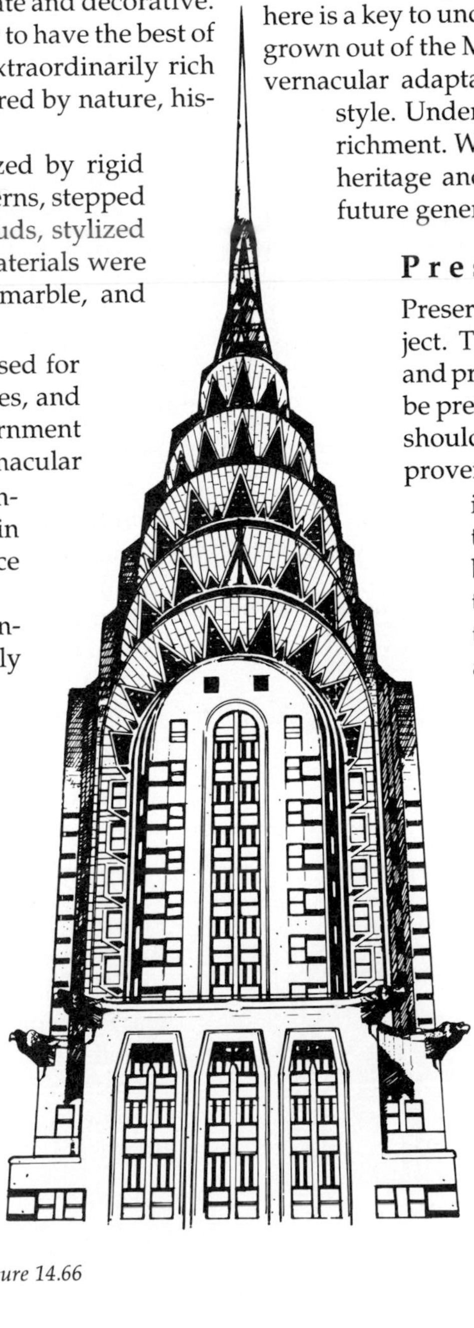

Preservation

Preservation is often an emotion-charged subject. The question arises between developers and preservationists whether a building should be preserved just because it is old or whether it should be removed to make way for new improvements. The delicate issue of time enters into the problem. It often takes time to determine the historic or aesthetic value of a building. At the point where sufficient time has passed to make that determination, the buildings may already have disappeared. To address this problem, preservation societies have been established on both local and national levels. The National Trust for Historic Preservation is the largest of such organizations. This Trust was established in 1949 and today helps determine which buildings, neighborhoods, and historic areas should be preserved. From its headquarters in Washington. D.C., the National Trust maintains museums, assists with restoration and preservation projects, and dispenses information to any who need assistance.

Restoration is a research, demolition, and reconstruction process that returns a building to its original state or to some specific state during its history. *Pres-*

ervation is taking whatever steps are necessary to maintain a building in its present state or the state to which it has been restored. *Adaptive restoration* is where buildings of aesthetic or historic worth are given new life by remodeling and restoring them for new uses. One of the earliest adaptive restorations was at Ghirardelli Square in San Francisco. The old and unused Ghirardelli Chocolate factory (1915) was turned into a pleasant multilevel shopping center with restaurants and landscaped pedestrian areas. Adaptive reuse has spread across the country giving new life to many old spaces that no longer serve the purpose for which they were originally designed. This same concept has been used to turn old buildings into housing, office complexes, theaters, museums, oceanariums, and many other uses.

Notes

1. Yarwood, Doreen. *The Architecture of Europe.* (London: Batsford, 1974), pp. 215-27.
2. Pierson, William H. *American Buildings and Their Architects.* (Garden City: Doubleday, 1970), pp. 14-21.
3. Yarwood, Doreen. *The Architecture of Europe.* (London: Batsford, 1974), pp. 308-21.
4. Pierson, William H., Jr. *American Buildings and Their Architects.* (Garden City: Doubleday, 1970), pp. 240-85.
5. Foley, Mary Mix. *The American House.* (New York: Harper Colophon, 1980), pp. 93-95.
6. Andrews, Wayne. *Architecture Ambition and Americans.* (London: Collier-Macmillan, 1974), pp. 213-20.
7. Foley, Mary Mix. *The American House.* (New York: Harper Colophon, 1980), pp. 241-60.
8. Rifkind, Carole. *A Field Guide to American Architecture.* (New York: Plume, 1980), pp. 217-41.

Bibliography

Andrews, Wayne. *Architecture, Ambition and Americans.* London: Collier Macmillan, 1974.

Cook, Olive. *The English Country House.* London: Thames and Hudson, 1974.

Foley, Mary Mix. *The American House.* New York: Harper Colophon, 1980.

Kidder-Smith, G. E. *A Pictorial History of Architecture in America.* New York: American Heritage, 1976.

Maass, John. *The Gingerbread Age.* New York: Bramhall House, 1957.

Norwich, John Julius, ed. *Great Architecture of the World.* New York: Bonanza Books, 1982.

Pierson, William H., Jr. *American Buildings and Their Architects.* Garden City: Doubleday, 1970.

Rifkind, Carole. *A Field Guide to American Architecture.* New York: Plume, 1980.

Whiffen, Marcus, and Frederick Koeper. *American Architecture 1606-1976.* Cambridge: M.I.T. Press, 1981.

Whiton, Sherrill. *Interior Design and Decoration.* Philadelphia: J. B. Lippincott, 1974.

Yarwood, Doreen. *The Architecture of Europe.* London: Batsford, 1974.

Yarwood, Doreen. *The Architecture of Britain.* London: Batsford, 1976.

In the Dallas, Texas, World Trade Center, a wholesale showroom complex, a breathtaking view from upper levels reveals an impressive space as well as a glimpse into the vast design resources available today.

The interior design profession exists not only to create aesthetic interiors but to protect our health and welfare. Research and soundly conceived design solutions are the requisite responsibility of the profession. Apart from the traditional divisions—residential and nonresidential interior design—the career options in related design professions are rapidly expanding.

As high technology sweeps us into the future, new and innovative design will emerge from the computer as well as the drafting board. However, the role of the designer will remain firmly rooted in meeting human needs for the necessities, comforts, and beauties of life. Photo by David Taylor.

"The professional interior designer is a person, qualified by education, experience and recognized skills, who

• identifies, researches and creatively solves problems pertaining to the function and quality of the interior environment;

• performs services relative to interior spaces including programming, design analysis, space planning, aesthetics and inspection of work on site, using specialized knowledge of interior construction, building systems and components, building regulations, equipment, material and furnishings; and

• prepares drawings and documents relative to the design of interior spaces;

in order to enhance the quality of life and protect the health, safety and welfare of the public."[1]

This definition of an interior designer is endorsed by professional organizations such as ASID, IBD, IDC, IDEC, and NCIDQ. These organizations are listed and defined later in this chapter, and their addresses are found in the Appendix.

Professional interior designers combined efforts to bring this miniature house to reality as a part of the Kips Bay Designer Show House, 1988. Photo by Ted Spiegel.

Page 390, top left: *Kips Bay, a boys' club, annually sponsors the charitable Kips Bay Designer Show House, inviting talented interior designers to furnish one or more rooms. The house (a different mansion every year) is open to the public for two weeks, after which the furnishings are removed. The exposure given to people seeking professional services helps them decide which interior-design firm best suits their tastes and expectations. This venerable Federal-style home selected for 1988 occupies one hundred feet along Park Avenue in New York City. Photo by Ted Spiegel.* **Pages 390–91:** *Three rooms displayed in the Kips Bay Show Houses over a period from 1981-1988 show the evolution and versatility of a particular designer.* **Page 390, top:** *For the 1981 Kips Bay, Noel Jeffrey produced a stunning white-on-white interior, the neutral scheme blending his modern-formed upholstery pieces with rich classic architectural elements. Photo courtesy of Noel Jeffrey, Inc.* **Page 390, bottom:** *This beautifully designed interior by Noel Jeffrey, Inc., New York, was featured in 1985. The prominent curved staircase is as dramatic as the windows. Eclectic furnishings balance the skyward architecture. Photo courtesy of Noel Jeffrey, Inc.* **Page 391:** *In 1988, a master bedroom in neutral colors and increasingly rich furnishings was designed and furnished by Noel Jeffrey. Lavish use of fabric plays a key role in accentuating the elegant poster bed—the prominent feature of the room. Photo by Ted Spiegel.*

Page 392, top left: Fine tufted leather invites the gentleman to his sitting room designed by Mary Meehan Interiors. The Empire-inspired Victorian window treatment and the glass- and bas-relief-tapped wood cabinets suggest a return to and yearning for richness by contemporary homeowners. Photo by Ted Spiegel. *Page 392, top right:* Mary Meehan Interiors was allotted two small 1988 Kips Bay bedrooms, a hallway, and a large bath, which were magically transformed into turn-of-the century lady's and gentleman's sitting rooms. Here the large floral wall covering and Victorian furnishings suggest a genteel retreat of a refinement-seeking era. Photo by Ted Spiegel. *Page 392, bottom left:* Another corner of Mary Meehan's lady's sitting room reveals not only lovely wood furnishings but the lavishness that only fabric can afford in this asymmetrical Empire striped and fringed window treatment—the finishing touch of visual luxury in the suite. Photo by Ted Spiegel. *Page 392, bottom right:* The gentleman's sitting room adjacent to the lady's sitting room sports an antique hutch amply filled with historic porcelain and glassware. The busy wall patterns provide a type of visual companionship to the occupant. Photo by Ted Spiegel. *Page 393, top:* Traditional wood paneling forms a stately background for handsome eclectic furnishings by John Saladino, Inc. The painted wooden floor and dazzling lamé wall hanging, respectively, provide quietude and pizzazz to this second-floor 1988 Kips Bay drawing room. Photo by Ted Spiegel. *Page 393, bottom:* The J. P. Molyneux Studio Ltd., New York, provided Chinese-style furnishing for the 1988 Kips Bay second floor dining room. The design theme was based on the chinoiserie murals installed in the house sixty years ago. The antique storage cabinet is inlaid—a very valuable Chinese piece; Ming-colored porcelain figures parade ceremoniously across the mantle. Chair backs are styled into ornate Gothic-revival arches. Half the chairs were original to the house; the others were matched by Molyneux's shopping expertise. Photo by Ted Spiegel.

Page 394, top: This Napoleonic Empire bedroom was designed for the 1988 Kips Bay by Robert Metzger Interiors, Inc., New York. Bold gold satin, lined with ticking, canopies ceremoniously over the handsome sleigh bed. Behind the bed an excellent secretary/cabinet/writing desk stands in front of a luxurious fabric-draped wall, fashionable during the French Empire as well as now. Photo by Ted Spiegel. *Page 394, bottom:* A surprising high-style blend of antique pieces and modern furnishings creates a study/retreat in a bedroom of the 1988 Kips Bay home. Interior by Paul Siskin of Siskin-Valls, Inc., New York. Photo by Ted Spiegel.

The Evolution of the Design Profession

In past centuries, interiors were often executed by craftsmen who were skilled in many aspects of design. An example is *Robert Adam* (1728-1792), an eighteenth-century English designer of exteriors, interiors, and furniture. His influence was felt as far away as America. *Samuel McIntire* (1757-1811) was an American architect and designer who created exteriors, interiors, furnishings, and details in the Neoclassic Adam style. During the nineteenth century, *William Morris* (1834-1896) produced and designed wallpaper, furniture, tapestries, carpets, stained glass windows, and accessories in the Arts and Crafts style. Most designers of past centuries, however, were specialists, such as artists, cabinetmakers, and craftsmen, who consulted with the client on only those aspects of the design that were produced in his studio or workshop.

By the beginning of the twentieth century, many Americans had attained considerable wealth and status. Consequently, their wants and needs often extended beyond what the architect or specialized craftsman was able to provide for the interior design of homes and businesses. Thus, early in this century, people began turning to knowledgeable and charismatic men and women who acted as specifiers, coordinators, and overseers of the plans, construction, and installation of their interior furnishings. Perhaps the greatest of these society interior designers was Elsie de Wolfe (1870-1950), whose success and credibility also helped pave the way for today's interior design profession.

Beginning with the 1950s, interior design services became affordable to, and demanded by, the general public. This was largely due to the new level of affluence and commercial development and the building and population boom of post-World War II America. Technology developed for war efforts was turned toward the domestic scene, producing a broad spectrum of affordable furnishings and man-made materials. The machine was viewed as a friend to interior design, unlike the attitude of rejection of machine-made products by proponents of the *Arts and Crafts Movement*. The *Bauhaus* (1919-1939), a school of architecture and design in Germany between the world wars, trained designers to produce excellent design incorporating machine-age materials. Bauhaus products included the classic modern tubular steel chairs. When the school was closed, many of these talented architects, artists, and designers came to America, exerting a strong influence on design from the 1950s through today. These designers (discussed in the earlier chapters of this book) included Mies van der Rohe, Marcel Breuer, Walter Gropius, and Wassily Kandinsky.

Designers from Scandinavia (c. 1920-today) also influenced our thinking, combining machine-age materials and techniques with the timeless quality of natural materials and superb quality handcrafting in furniture, textiles, and accessories. American designers, likewise, began to design modern furnishings, based on the simple lines of the International or Bauhaus style and the Scandinavian influence. New trends in design are continually added to the spectrum of contemporary design. Postmodern designers have taken traditional elements, shapes, moldings, and architectural detail and have combined them in new, innovative, and nontraditional ways. Thus, a wealth of not only historical but also innovative new products and materials are now available for interior design.

The Design Profession Today

The interior design profession has matured significantly from the early days of society designers. Today it is a complex and specialized discipline. The interior designer has not only skills and abilities that entail the technical and artistic training discussed in this book but he or she also has resources and considerable knowledge of materials, furnishings, and their application. Further, the designer, in many cases, acts as director or project manager—hiring and becoming responsible for the goods and services and sometimes even the structure and systems that go into a building. Because of this, there are many professionals today who feel that the person who claims the title of interior designer should have earned that right through tests and licensing. At this writing, there are several states that do require licensing; others seem likely to follow. This, in itself, is a step toward greater respect and professionalism, which the field of interior design has earned.

Figure 15.1

Figure 15.1 At the IDCNY—the Interior Design Center, New York—in Long Island City, designers come alone or bring clientele to select furnishings that are sold only to the trade—the interior designer or architect. Here, nonresidential furnishings are the specialty. Design centers are important buildings where the manufacturers display and take orders for their products in showrooms staffed by showroom sales reps. Design centers are located in every major metropolitan city in the United States and require proof that the person entering is indeed a bona fide interior designer. Membership in a professional organization such as ASID or IBD is preferred. Photo by Ted Spiegel.

Today's interior designer not only designs creative and individual interiors but he or she also acts as a specifier, an organizer, and a *buyer* who is knowledgeable about a great number of diverse products, designs, and materials. Although the product of today's designer is the completed or finished interior, the profession has matured far beyond the era of artisans or society designers. The designer today does much more than coordinate background materials and furnishings. Today's designer must be able to perform a variety of professional tasks requiring extensive skill and training. Therefore, the attributes and skills of today's designer are broad and diverse.

Attributes and Skills of Contemporary Designers

Successful interior designers usually have attributes such as insight into personalities and problems, enthusiasm, creativity and flexibility, keen perception, efficiency and organization, attention to detail, and a drive for continual development of creative, intellectual, and professional growth.

Skills required of the designer include business and social skills, artistic and visual communication skills, technical drawing and drafting skills, space-planning skills, research and analytical skills, and technical knowledge skills.

Tasks Required of the Skilled Designer

The interior designer today must have skills, education, training, and experience to perform a variety of tasks, which include the following:

- Preparing documents and letters of agreement pertaining to all contractual aspects of the interior and handling financial and business matters concerned with the design execution.
- Programming, the process and methods used to systematically research and define problems. *Programming* consists of three phases:

  1. Research—examining all the factors such as human factors, behaviors, needs assessments, circulation or traffic patterns, working and living relationships, and social and psychological preferences and considerations. Research also entails architectural evaluations that will meet the needs of the occupants—functions, spacial relationships and requirements, budget, mechanical systems, codes and restrictions, time frames.
  2. Analysis—the process of analyzing, categorizing, assessing information, and establishing priorities.
  3. Synthesis—or the written program. The program may also be referred to as the design analysis.

- Design development or generating and refining the design ideas leading to a design concept.
- Space planning to organize or reorganize residential and/or nonresidential spaces.
- Working with or specifying *building systems*, such as heating, plumbing, and air-conditioning, and all aspects of lighting. The residential designer often works with specialists in these areas.
- Specifying furnishings and materials that fulfill human needs and meet performance criteria such as durability, cleanability, and strength as well as function and aesthetics. This requires a thorough knowledge of all types of floor, ceiling, and wall-covering materials and textile applications and a knowledge of period and contemporary architecture and furnishings.
- Preparing necessary working drawings for cabinetry or interior details that can be executed by a craftsman or subcontractor. Accurate drawings are paramount in assuring that the interiors are correctly constructed.
- Maintaining a good business relationship with many wholesale and craftsman sources and contracts in behalf of the client with those who provide goods and services. The designer is generally considered liable or responsible for these goods and services.
- Oversee the installation and satisfactory completion of all contracted areas of the design project.

(A)   *(B)*   *(C)*

Figure 15.2

Figure 15.2 Professional development and continuing education are musts for designers who participate in a world of progress and continual refinement of new ideas, new products, new technology, and even new directions of design philosophy and aesthetics. At one New York Designer's Saturday, at the D & D Building coordinated by Pauline Delli-Carpini, designers can evaluate new products and learn insights from specialists and other successful professionals.*(A)* Designers take notes in a seminar entitled "Getting Published—A Professional Imperative," where instruction is being given on ways to publish interior design work in design periodicals and other media. *(B)* In this seminar, students and professionals learn specifics of textile design and production from seasoned China Seas president, Inger McCabe Elliot. *(C)* Later they examine firsthand China Seas textiles adapted for contemporary interiors from antique batik fabrics. Photos by Ted Spiegel.

- Post-occupancy evaluation is the thorough evaluation of the success of the design after it is complete. The basis for evaluation is the list of requirements in the program, discussed in chapter one. POE is a required task primarily in nonresidential design, but it is useful in residential design, as well.

The designer may also have the responsibility to educate the client in matters of function, space planning, aesthetics, color, materials, and design.

Professional Development and Continuing Education

Whereas some attributes and talents come naturally to those who become interior designers, there are many personal qualities and abilities that need to be developed or enhanced after a student completes a formal interior design education.

(A)
Figure 15.3

(B)

Figure 15.3 *(A)* and *(B)* Sketching and rendering, skills required of professional interior designers, are means of visually communicating design concepts, materials, and products—their arrangement and potential success. Here, furniture designer Aaron Donner envisions his collection called Delphi for Hickory/Kaylyn—Neoclassic in origin, contemporary in feeling, reflecting the past yet clearly proclaiming the present. Photo courtesy of Hickory/Kaylyn.

Through professional development, designers can keep abreast with new knowledge and technology and increase business and communication skills. *Continuing education* courses are provided by schools, institutions, industry, professional organizations and through on-the-job training. Another means of professional development is through post-occupancy evaluation, POE—evaluating how effectively the design works after a period of occupancy by the users. Professional development and continuing education help designers in the following areas:

- Technical skills and knowledge—Designers are trained to prepare material boards, drafting or technical detailed drawings. Computer skills as well are becoming increasingly important for both design and business management. Interior designers continually increase their working knowledge of construction methods, building systems, codes, architectural specifications, and safety requirements. Designers must stay abreast of innovations in materials, designs, and furnishings.
- Business—Designers develop skills in employee management and relations, *cost analysis* and calculations, *budgeting*, billing and collection matters, purchasing and *lines of credit*, marketing, sales, and public relations.
- Verbal and visual communication—Designers maintain continual collaborative relationships with clients, suppliers, and other professionals. They can improve productivity and increase professionalism by improving their abilities to present ideas, concepts, and contracts in written, verbal, and visual (sketches, *renderings*, and *technical drawings*) form.

Figure 15.4

Figure 15.4 A professional library is essential to the designer, and intriguing to the lay person as well, for few professions reach so deeply into our lives and life-styles as does interior design. At the Interior Design Bookshop at 979 Lexington Avenue (the D & D building) in New York City, information seekers peruse interior design publications, hoping to keep abreast of the history, scope, fashion trends, and technical advances of this complex and ever-changing field. Photo by Ted Spiegel.

Formal Design Education

It is a wise choice to pursue a formal education at an institution that offers an accredited and fully developed interior design program. The time spent in school gleaning from the experience of qualified teachers and learning the skills and knowledge necessary in the profession is well worth the effort.

Some who are currently practicing interior design have entered the field without formal interior design education and have spent many years apprenticing and learning the profession by working on the job. This is a slow and difficult process. Those with good design education backgrounds seem to have little difficulty finding work in design firms, corporations, industry, or any position where interior designers are needed.

Design education is a boon in the working world. Experienced professionals in related fields can sense immediately when one who claims to be a designer knows little about the design process. A competent designer who can demonstrate depth of knowledge will command the respect of architects, contractors, suppliers, craftsmen, and clients.[2]

Educational Programs

Educational programs generally vary from two to six years of study. Additional time is needed to obtain a graduate degree. Curricula at institutions offering a certificate, diploma, or *baccalaureate degree* generally provide students with opportunities to develop their awareness, understanding, and competency in areas such as those listed in Chart 15.1.

Interior design programs are found in schools of architecture and in fine arts or home economics departments of universities and colleges and in design schools. Most schools will have an emphasis or specialty beyond minimum standards. For example, a program may special-

---

Chart 15.1 Topics of Study in Interior Design Education Programs

- Basic and creative arts such as two- and three-dimensional design, fine and applied arts.
- Design theory, human factors and spacial composition.
- Residential and nonresidential design.
- Design for special populations (handicapped, elderly, etc.), special problems (environmental, etc.), and special purposes (historic preservation, adaptive reuse).
- Design materials (materials, textiles, lighting, furniture, color).
- Technical knowledge such as structure and construction, building systems, energy conservation, detailing, materials, laws, building codes, and ordinances.
- Communication skills, such as verbal, written and visual presentation, drafting, and computer systems.
- Professional practice and organization and specification skills.
- History of art, architecture, interiors, furnishings, and materials.
- Research methodologies, survey, literature search, and observation.

---

ize in presentation skills, prearchitecture, historic study and preservation, or business practices. The student should, therefore, look carefully at both curriculum and faculty to determine if the school best meets his or her needs and interests for design education. Many schools also offer apprenticeship or internship options or requirements that allow students to receive academic credit for training received in professional interior design studios and offices.

It is important to realize that design schools do not have the resources to fully prepare a student for every situation encountered by professionals. Every design project will have new circumstances, concepts, and problems to solve. From design education, one should expect to receive a fundamental working knowledge of, or expertise in, most or all of the areas previously listed. Further, a person should expect to learn principles, processes, and creative approaches to problem solving. A person who has been trained to think and adapt will be able to handle new problems and design challenges as they arise.

Interior design programs that meet required standards are accredited by the Foundation of Interior Design Education and Research (FIDER). Although many programs are not yet accredited, a listing of schools with programs accredited by FIDER is available from FIDER. The National Association of Schools of Art and Design (NASAD) also is an accrediting body that evaluates art and design schools and those departments within colleges and universities.

NCIDQ Examination

The National Council of Interior Design Qualification (NCIDQ) exam is administered periodically at many locations around the country. It is now a requirement for full acceptance into several of the professional organizations listed in the following paragraphs. The two-day exam covers the candidate's knowledge of interior design and poses a creative problem that the candidate must solve. A designer who has successfully completed a baccalaureate degree and worked for the minimum two years in the field should be qualified to pass the exam. The *NCIDQ exam* sets a standard of excellence and competence so that professional interior designers may better serve the public. In the future the NCIDQ exam may form a basis for licensing. A strong national effort to encourage states to license interior designers or at least to establish title acts is currently afoot. This promises to protect the public against those who are not qualified to practice interior design.

Professional Organizations

Design organizations exist to research and make available to its members through continuing education new and improved design methods, information, sources, and materials that serve to enhance their design skills and capabilities. These organizations also lobby for licensing and title registration. Each organization has its own standards of excellence, various levels of association, and entrance requirements. A list follows of the organizations to which interior designers or design educators may belong. For further information, refer to the Appendix (at the end of this chapter) for addresses for these organizations.

The American Association of Housing Educators coordinates efforts and shares information with college teachers, government employees, and executives in the residential building industry. It serves to develop a better understanding of the role of housing for the well-being of the public, to increase effectiveness of housing education at all levels, to optimize quality of housing environments, to coordinate efforts among housing authorities. It awards scholarships for its student members and those seeking postgraduate education.

The American Society of Interior Designers (ASID) is the oldest and best known of the design organizations. Its forerunner *AID*, the American Institute of Interior Designers, was founded in 1931 and merged with NSID, the National Society of Interior Designers, in 1975. ASID offers a network of educational seminars, national conventions, extensive design sources, newsletters, and educational materials. ASID sponsors student chapters and activities, which range from design tours to community involvement projects. Information about the profession is frequently available from ASID upon written request.

The Foundation for Interior Design Education and Research (FIDER) is the body that exists to accredit postsecondary interior design schools in the United States and Canada. The agency is recognized by the United States Office of Education in Washington, DC. Its members are frequently members of other organizations, and accrediting teams are drawn from both educational and active professional careers. A list of accredited schools is available on request from FIDER.

The Institute of Business Designers (IBD) is the best-known organization for nonresidential designers. In order to belong to this organization, nearly all design work must fall into the nonresidential category (see Careers in Interior Design). IBD sponsors student and professional competitions, and IBD provides membership for students at a reduced fee, which allows students to participate in IBD professional meetings and activities. Research in new design directions and education is made available to members of IBD.

The Interior Designers of Canada (IDC) is a body of professional designers who are members of various provincial associations. The purposes of IDC are to encourage excellence of interior design in the public interest in Canada, to assist educational institutions in the development of future designers, to encourage continuing education for practicing designers, to assist the provincial associations with research and common organizational information, and to uphold in practice a code of ethics and professional practice.

The Interior Design Educators Council (IDEC) is an affiliate of *The International Federation of Interior Architects/ Designers (IFI)*. IDEC was organized in 1967 with the goal of improving the quality of interior design teaching and education and, thus, raising the quality and level of professional interior design work. IDEC has a network of newsletters, various committees, and a professional journal, *The Journal of Interior Design Education and Research (JIDER)*, which publishes findings of design research conducted by educators and professions. IDEC members join efforts to bring about positive change and improvement in design education.

The International Federation of Interior Architects/ Interior Designers (IFI) is an international, professional body made up of institutions active in interior architecture and interior design. Headquarters are in Amsterdam, the Netherlands.

The National Association of Schools of Art and Design (NASAD) is an accrediting body for schools of art and design that also assists schools to meet standards of excellence in the education and training of artists and designers. NASAD also forms a network whereby professionals and professors can share information, keeping schools abreast of new developments and technologies in the field of art and design.

The National Council for Interior Design Qualification (NCIDQ) serves to identify to the public those interior designers who have met the minimum standards for professional practice by passing the NCIDQ examination (discussed earlier in this chapter). The organization endeavors to maintain the most advanced procedures for examination and continually reviews the examination to include expanding techniques in design development and professional knowledge. A study guide to prepare a candidate for the exam is available on request from NCIDQ (see the Appendix).

The International Furnishings and Design Association (IFDA) (formerly The National Home Furnishing League NHFL) sponsors *The Interior Design Society (IDS)*. IFDA is primarily aimed for retail affiliates and interior design executives who also deal with interior furnishings. IDS, organized in 1973, sponsors educational programs, seminars, and sales supports. These organizations honor and recognize outstanding work and achievement by retail and custom interior design professionals.

Interior Design Resources

An immense number of *trade sources* exist to serve the interior design industry today. Trade sources are companies or vendors that sell to the trade (designers, architects, and specifiers) those goods and services that they purchase in behalf of retail clients. These goods include every element of furnishings needed in an interior. The goods and

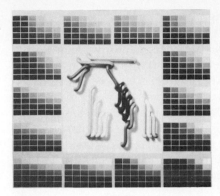

(A)

(B)

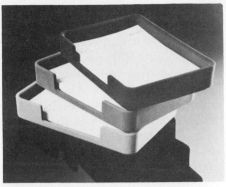

(C)

Figure 15.5

(D)

services are ordered through wholesale catalogs or through manufacturing and product representatives, or reps, or through regional *showrooms*, which may be *closed* (allowing designers only to enter and purchase) or *open* (allowing retail clients to accompany the designer). Craftsmen usually function independently of showrooms and sales representatives; quality craftsmen generally are in demand and have no need to market their services. Most major cities now have design *marketing centers*, or *markets*, which are convenient clusters of trade source showrooms that serve the designer. Many craftsmen are also located near markets.[3]

Interior Design Tools

Interior designers make use of a variety of tools, such as drafting instruments, presentation materials, filing systems, and a seemingly endless collection of furnishings catalogs and fabric/carpet samples, which usually demand semiannual price and/or sample updates. In addition, interior designers benefit by keeping current with new technological advancements that enhance their productivity and design capabilities.

Computers in the Design Profession

Perhaps the most innovative tool available to interior designers today is the computer. The computer has had as much impact in the design profession as in any other field. Not only can client records and billings be kept and easily accessed, and printed out on the computer, but drafting and design, computation of yardage, business and employee management and records, and correspondence also are managed by the computer. Through the computer with special hookups (thermafax, fiber optics networking or telephone systems), items can be ordered from wholesalers and confirmed in seconds. Wholesale companies will soon make catalogs available on software disks, helping to eliminate complete library rooms full of awkward books and saving the designer valuable time with index commands that search and find design items that meet the necessary specifications. The more a designer can incorporate a computer into the practice, the easier his or her job will be.

There are essentially four divisions of computers that interior designers use: the *portable computer*, the *personal computer*, the *mainframe computer*, and the *mini-mainframe computer*.

The portable computer is similar to the size of a briefcase and consists of a keyboard and small monitor and a battery-operated computer drive unit that works off floppy disks where information can be stored and retrieved. These are valuable for travel or on-site computing, but they do not have built-in printing capacities.

A personal computer (PC) consists of the *computer hardware*—a keyboard, a power drive computer unit, a *monitor* or screen (available in black and white or color), a printer, and perhaps a plotter.

A mainframe computer is much larger than a personal computer and up to one thousand times more costly. Mainframe computers are utilized by very large architectural and design firms for large projects and problems. A mainframe has far greater speed and memory and is able to process data that a PC, or personal computer, could not because of limitations in size capabilities. However, several personal computers can be linked to a mainframe, allowing an entire office staff access to the larger, more complex machine. Thus, large and complicated design jobs can be coordinated and synthesized through the mainframe computer.

On the horizon is yet a new generation of computers called mini-mainframes that have more power, more disk space, and greater function capacity than a PC, yet are

Figure 15.5 Winners in the Seventeenth Annual Product "Roscoe" Awards for outstanding creative achievement and for significant contribution to the interior design industry show the latitude of design opportunities for professional designers. Photos courtesy of Resources Council, Inc. (A) The Spectra Color System designed by Alan Tye makes it possible to specify one of over 350 colors for application to any piece of hardware by Modric, Inc. Interior designers use a kit of fourteen color cards with precise colors, computer stored and accurately duplicated and made of heat-cured, modified polyester powder coating. (B) The Minos Series designed by Tom Robbins for Kallista, Inc., is a versatile bath fixture system designed to accommodate a variety of configurations with interchangeable decorative sleeves and with various surface accents, including custom colors, gold or nickel plating, and lapidary or ceramic applications. The lever and base can also adapt to complement numerous spout designs. (C) This desk accessory collection features a soft suedelike textured surface with abrasion-resistant characteristics, resulting from a paint

smaller than a mainframe, comparable in size to the personal computer. Mini-mainframes can work independently or in tandem with other terminals.

Information can also be relayed from *computer terminal* to computer terminal (similar to PCs) via a *computer network* system. Information can be sent to computers in other cities across the country or around the world with amazing speed via satellite or fiber optics or telephone cables.

The *software* consists of *computer programs* available on disks that operate the *hardware*. Software programs are written to accomplish specific tasks, applicable for not only interior design and architecture but for nearly every profession. The types of software programs that have application in interior design include graphics and computer-aided design, word processing, business accounting, desk managing, data bases, and organizational tools. And, as mentioned previously, catalogs will be incorporated as software as the technology progresses and matures.

Figure 15.6

Graphics and Computer-Aided Design

Graphics packages or programs allow the designer to create logos and other graphic designs. Some programs allow word processing and graphics to design flyers, letterheads, or complex billing sheets, for example. Perhaps the most dramatic and high-profile computer application in interior design is the innovation of software programs such as *Computer-Aided Design (CAD)* and *Computer-Aided Design and Drafting (CADD)*. These programs produce technical drawings, drafting, and projections of proposed space. Furniture template components (two-dimensional furniture shapes) can be called up from the *data-base catalog* onto the screen to find the most suitable arrangements. Space planning can be accomplished, then interfaced with high-speed and high-resolution *plotters* (automatic drawing machines) to produce quality plans in a fraction of the time needed for mechanical drawing. CAD software enables designers to plan and experiment in full color and with a variety of textures and patterns. CAD programs vary in scope, abilities, and complexities. CAD programs that oper-

ate on mainframe computers can produce computer-simulated renderings (artists' conception of proposed space in perspective) and can even move the viewer through linear-illustrated movies of a proposed building. Personal computers also can utilize programs with similar but limited capabilities. These programs are continually being refined and further developed.

- *Word-processing* programs are designed for writing. These allow great latitude in composing, rearranging text, working in columns as well as text, and they have the advantage of memory storage, recall, and application of documents to different clients or needs. Uses for interior design include writing programs, *letters of agreement*, client contracts, correspondence, *specifications*, purchase orders, and billing.

- *Business-accounting* packages differ in what may be accomplished for office use. Some options include a general ledger, journals for keeping track of accounts receivable and payable, receipts, sales, purchases, and detailed records. Data or journal entries may automatically post to individual accounts. Accounting programs may produce customized or summarized reports, profit analysis, and billing.

- *Desk manager* programs or packages offer options such as keeping track of personnel schedules, activities, and payments. It may offer a day, week, or monthly calendar, a phone dialer and logger, a financial and/or statistical calculator, an editor, a note and card filer, and various graphic symbols. These can help the designer become more organized and use his or her time more efficiently.

- *Data-base programs* manage, organize, and retrieve files. Files consist of information needed for working on documents, graphics, and CAD. Data bases produce managerial spread sheets, trace inventories, and calculate interior components, such as textile yardage or office planning systems. A data base may be able to sort, summarize, and generate reports, as well as set up and produce forms.

process called Nextel. The accessories combine high-tech aesthetics with function and durability of high-impact plastic. Called Sof-Stone and designed by Tom Janicz, it is part of the Knoll International Smokador collection. *(D)* Aurora Pleated Shades designed by Janet Birch for Graber

Industries introduces a new construction of 100 percent woven metallized polyester, heat set to provide pleat retention. New technology has eliminated metallic bleed-through, making it possible to offer whites, tinted whites, and pastel colors in heat-reflecting metallized fabrics.

Figure 15.6 Utilizing a software program design by Steelcase, a designer is able to produce working drawings on a pen plotter directly from his CAD screen. The photo at

the bottom left shows the actual furniture being utilized by the designer on the computer. Photo by Ted Spiegel, courtesy of Steelcase.

- *Organizational tool* programs offer a variety of options, such as charts, math and graphics capabilities, and data analysis. Organizers may help establish priorities, evaluate ideas, synthesize information, and facilitate decision making. They may produce project management documents, which outline a critical path. They also report on resource interdependencies and generate all needed printed reports. An organizational program may be a tool for writing specifications, as a cross between a word- and an outline-processing program.[4]

State of the Art

The previous list of computer programs is only a portion of the programs available today. Specific programs developed and marketed by independent companies will vary in scope, abilities, complexity, and cost. The *state of the art* continually changes, and competition makes research and marketing software programs profitable. Retail merchants and computer specialists are knowledgeable and have sources of information on current software programs.

Computer Purchase and Training   The purchase of a computer system requires a sizable investment. The actual cost depends on the complexity and capacity of the units and how many software programs are purchased. Personal computer hardware usually constitutes about half of the total cost, since software programs, printers, and plotters will require an equal investment. However, computer systems are a competitive commodity, and they tend to become more affordable with time.

Training in terms of time and personnel pay is also costly. However, given the man-hours saved once training on the computer is complete, the computers will most likely be cost efficient in the long run in both hours saved and quality and quantity of services rendered. Other advantages of the computer are the smooth and efficient filing of information with near-instant file and information retrieval, the central location of information, and the reduction of human error and oversight.

Many design schools incorporate computer-aided design training into their programs. Some have also required or recommended basic courses in word processing, business applications, and other programs such as those previously mentioned. Programs may *interface* (use similar commands), so that a comprehensive knowledge of everything the computer can do is not necessary in order to operate a variety of programs. This makes the computer much less intimidating and makes self-training possible.

User-friendly hardware and software are relatively simple for the users to understand, making specialized training less necessary. Computer applications for design firms may be expanded as needs and skills increase, beginning with simple programs for one or two areas of application and extending to more programs or more complexity as design work expands.

Careers in Interior Design

Interior design is a field of broad latitude in career options. Professional opportunities exist in *interior architecture* and design, in retailing, and in design-related fields.

Interior Design

Interior design involves all the steps of analysis, planning, and execution of services listed at the beginning of this chapter. An interior design firm may function alone or be part of an architectural team, working in tandem on common projects or working independently within the framework of the business.

Because there is more interior design work available than architectural commissions of new buildings, many architectural firms have taken advantage of this economic opportunity by incorporating interior design departments in their firms. In some cases a design unit within the firm may win a bid to do the interior of a building that is being designed by another architectural firm. These interior design departments may even function independently of their architect counterparts within the corporation or architect's firm.

Most interior design firms function independently of architects. Many successful firms began as a single interior designer functioning as a *sole proprietor* whose skills and expertise paved the way for more and more contracts. Hence, many such firms eventually expand into corporations where interior designers, assistant designers, draftsmen, renderers, secretaries, accountants, and resource/studio help are employed.[5]

There are two main divisions of interior design: residential design and *nonresidential design*. Residential design is discussed here; nonresidential design follows at the end of the chapter under Nonresidential Considerations.

Residential Interior Design

Residential firms design interiors for homes, condominiums, mobile homes, vacation houses, apartments, or any residence for the individuals or families who live there. Residential firms may handle dozens of interiors or only four or five larger commissions each year. The firm may deal only with entire interiors, or it may be willing to undertake only certain rooms or portions of an interior.

Retailing

Retailing is an aspect of interior design that also indicates a specialty. Designers who work in the sale of goods and services to the public may specialize in window coverings, wall coverings, or hard or soft floor coverings. Interior design services are often incorporated into quality department stores, and interior designers may be a key to the success of furniture stores where a full range of interior design goods and services may be available.

Interior Design Education

Teaching careers in colleges, design schools, and universities are open to those with proper credentials. Full-time, *tenure-track positions* offer rank advancement from instructor to assistant professor to associate professor to full professor. Advancement is based on teaching effectiveness, creative work and research, degree held, and service to the institution and the community.[6]

Requirements for full-time tenure-track positions usually include professional experience plus a terminal degree—*master of arts* (M.A.), *master of science* (M.S.), *master of fine arts* (M.F.A.), *doctor of philosophy* (Ph.D.). Since only a few institutions offer advanced degrees in interior design, candidates might consider related fields in which to seek terminal degrees. Possibilities might include a selection of architecture, art history, business management, computer-aided design, education, historic preservation, humanities, psychology, or housing.

Teaching design at the high school level or community college level is also an interior design career option. High schools generally offer courses in interior design as a part of their home economics programs. Community colleges frequently offer interior design courses, and some will offer vocational training or associate degrees that may emphasize design. A baccalaureate (bachelor's) degree would be the minimum requirement to teach in either of these situations, and high schools usually require a teaching certificate in addition.

Teaching part-time is also a viable career option. Designers who are active in the profession or in a related field can add immeasurably to the strength of a design program by teaching skills and experiences gleaned from real-life situations. Few design programs exist that do not heavily rely on practicing professionals, which include interior designers, architects, *graphic artists,* rendering artists, draftsmen, lighting specialists, specialists in materials and textiles, color, computer-aided design, and other specialists that fill the needs of each program's emphasis.

Specialized Design

Interior designers with education and work experience often become proficient and skilled in an area of specialty. A design specialist can do work that general interior designers may not be equipped to handle. In the recent past, the design field has witnessed the emergence of lighting specialists, of computer-aided design and drafting specialists, and of specialists in dozens of other areas.

The tendency to specialize is natural as people follow their interests and desires, but the overall picture suggests deeper reasons for specialized design. The world today has become so complex and technical that it is difficult for the interior designer to have a commanding knowledge of, and expertise in, all areas of design. Certainly it is professional wisdom to call in a specialist or consultant when some aspect of a project goes beyond the designer's knowledge or experience. Specializing allows the designer to do the in-depth research to become knowledgeable about the technical aspects of one area. This knowledge coupled with extensive experience in one area is required for a designer to become a specialist.

Yet another justification for design specialization is the ever-increasing risk of litigation through designer liability. Designers are becoming more responsible for the interiors they create, for the safety and well-being of the people who inhabit or visit those interiors. If the designer, through lack of knowledge or experience, makes mistakes or is not thorough in some aspect, the client may readily bring a lawsuit that can be disastrous to the designer's career. Specialization allows the designer to work only in areas where his or her knowledge and experience can help prevent mistakes and consequent litigation.

Careers in Related Fields

In addition to specialization, there are many related design career options open to those with schooling and/or training in design. Some may not require any prerequisite formal education, although a considerable amount of time and effort will be necessary to succeed in a related field.

Many specialties and career options related to design are listed in Chart 15.2. This list is by no means exclusive; ten years ago some of these options were unheard of, but today, they are indispensable. This trend will surely continue, as designers with education, training, and the spirit of entrepreneurship continually open up new careers and specialties that will be important to interior design in the future.

Chart 15.2 Design Specialties and Related Fields

- Acoustic design—planning the sound reflecting and absorbing qualities of an interior through the shape of the space and through specified finishes and materials. Theater design will incorporate acoustics.
- Adaptive reuse—the remodeling of old or historic structures to fit a purpose different from the original. A wharf warehouse, for example, could become a shopping plaza or mall; an old home could become a law, real estate, or insurance office; inner-city buildings could become luxury condominiums or co-ops. Rehabilitation or rehab is bringing any older building up to current standards where it can be inhabited.
- Amusement park design—carrying themes into every item of the park from signs to trash cans and drinking fountains. It also deals with safety, traffic patterns, and efficiency.
- Aquarium design—for homes, offices, and aquatic parks and museums. This specialty could also include maintenance.
- Architectural space planning or floor plan design—drafting by hand or CADD (computer-assisted drafting and design).
- Art and accessory dealerships—selling fine art and/or unique accessories retail to the public or wholesale to interior designers.
- Color consultation—for marketing firms, industry, architectural or interiors design firms, business corporations, government.
- Buying—for large department and furniture stores. *Buyers* select stock or floor merchandise or lines (merchandise offered by particular companies) carried by the company.
- Cabinet, closet, and storage design—custom design to suit individual needs or dealerships in retail modular storage furniture.
- Communication design—working with specialized needs in offices for computer terminal stations, telecommunication conference rooms, and other areas.
- Construction/project management—overseeing the construction and acting as liaison between client and contractor. This may include hiring the architect, engineers, subcontractors, craftsmen, and consultants.
- Drafting and/or computer-aided (or computer-assisted) design.
- Design for corporate parties, charity balls, design shows, or other large gatherings where there must be organization and orchestration of many details within a given length of time.
- Design for the handicapped, aged, or infirm—possibly including design for medical facilities, rest homes, hospices, residences, or product design.
- Energy conservation—an energy specialist acting as consultant to architectural firms or clients increasing energy efficiency (see also solar design).
- Entertainment center design—designing not only the storage units for television, videocassette recorders, stereo equipment, and computers, but media-center rooms, as well.
- Environmental safety—research into materials that will not burn or do not threaten the safety of the users of the environment and consultation to manufacturers and architects.
- Facility management—a fast-growing field where corporations utilize a manager to plan and purchase furnishings and to coordinate and be responsible for all building repairs and maintenance. The facility may be one building or dozens of buildings in dozens of locations; the manager oversees other employees in the facilities department.
- Furniture design—the design of new and innovative furnishing items such as case goods, upholstered furniture, and accessories. Furniture retail sales or rental business—residential and/or nonresidential.
- Forensic consultation—studying a product's construction and appropriate use for manufacturing, for application, or as testimony in litigation proceedings.
- Graphic design and illustration, and signage graphics—such as creating a corporate image.
- Greenhouse and solarium design—designing spaces for healthy plants (including temperature and humidity control); also designing sun spaces for people for dining, socializing, or relaxing in the heated whirlpool.
- Hard-surface floor covering design—including both the actual design of the tiles or vinyl or specializing in the use and application of ceramic tiles, wood, brick, and stone on floors, walls, and ceilings, including mosaic and mural work.
- Hardware design—designing doorknobs, handles, and hinges.
- Health club/recreational facility design—buildings that house swimming pools, indoor ball courts, gyms for workout and aerobics. Safety as well as good design is a criterion.
- Historic preservation and restoration of authentic interiors maintained as museums and restoring fine old buildings to their original state or an adaptation of it. Historic preservation is a growing concern in both residential and nonresidential interior design and requires thorough knowledge of specialized goods and services.

(A)
Figure 15.7

(B)

(A)
Figure 15.8

(B)

Figure 15.7 In the nonresidential categories, two winners of the Seventeenth Annual Product Design Awards, these two pieces by different designers and manufacturers have similar clean styles that are somehow reminiscent of the Chinese Chippendale Late Georgian furniture pieces. *(A)* The uniqueness of the Zipp Conference Table, designed by Rodney Kinsman and manufactured by Davis Furniture Industries, is the tongue-and-groove device that allows easy removal of the tabletop. The base can then be folded for moving or storing, making the table well suited for locations where a permanent conference table would be impractical. Its strong designs make it appealing for office settings as well. The base is powder-coated finished steel, the top is glass or oak-edged plastic laminate. *(B)* Angled into a lounge position for seating comfort, the wafer slim seat and back cushions of the Span sofa, designed by Burkhard Bogtherr and manufactured by Brayton International collections. Photos courtesy of Resources Council, Inc.

Figure 15.8 In the residential categories, two winners in the Seventeenth Annual Product Design "Roscoe" Awards for outstanding achievement and significant contribution to the interior design industry. *(A)* The Pinwheel designed

- Hospitality design—interior design for hotels, convention centers, resorts, restaurants. A large and important area in non-residential design.
- Industrial facilities—manufacturing plants and accompanying offices and support areas.
- In-house corporate design—design, consult with experts, and coordinate components to keep the corporate image prestigious.
- Journalism—magazine, newspaper articles on design.
- Kitchen design—planning the latest in cooking equipment and efficient food preparation and serving areas, plus accommodating a social environment. A Certified Kitchen Designer uses CKD after his or her name.
- Landscaping—design firms specializing in interior landscaping select, sell, rent, and maintain real and artificial plants.
- Law—handling litigation concerning disputes over interior design projects or working toward legislation or serving as advisors concerning design laws, public safety, historic preservation, or a host of other design-related areas.

- Law office design—incorporating specialized needs, equipment, and personnel with an image.
- Library design—meeting needs of different kinds and locations of libraries and all the inherent equipment and space planning.
- Lighting design—a twofold career option: designing lighting plans and specialty lighting needs for interiors and designing the lighting fixtures or luminaires.
- Management—in design firms, in industry, or in design-related business, or as facilities managers.
- Marketing—consultants to wholesale and retail firms and to exporters/importers of design goods.
- Medical facilities—interior design for hospitals, clinics, and other medical care facilities.
- Model home design—renting or selling furnishings to model homes. Similar to residential design but without having to deal with a user who will live there. Luxury models for condominiums, flats, or co-ops incorporate expensive and luxurious design.

- Museum design—planning spaces, meeting specialized needs for display design, background materials, specialized lighting and humidity control as well as traffic flow. Curatorship—directors of museums or archives are yet another career option.
- Office design—a specialty in nonresidential design ranging from small offices to high-rise buildings. Professional offices, such as those for doctors and dentists, are another office specialty.
- Plumbing fixture design—designing sinks, lavatories, bath tubs and saunas, toilets and bidets, and faucets.
- *Product design*—new and innovative furnishing items such as furniture and accessories.
- Product evaluation—consulting with and recommending marketing strategies to companies who are introducing new designs and products.
- Publicity and public relations (PR)—establishing an image or marketing an image for corporations, company products, or other designers.

- Purchasing agent—an interior designer can act as purchaser for large companies, negotiating and overseeing correct ordering of furnishings.
- Real estate developer—interior designers often buy real estate, improve or remodel the building, and sell it at a profit. Building new nonresidential buildings and leasing them is another aspect. Interior designer turned developer can arrange financing and sell homes or nonresidential buildings as well.
- Rendering—artists' conceptions of interior or exterior design.
- Restaurant design—a specialty in the interior design of restaurants, cafeterias, bars, and fast-food services.
- Retail design—from individual boutiques to large department stores and from single shops to entire shopping malls, creative designers are becoming in demand.
- Retail selling—many interior designers own, manage, or work in retail stores whose gross profit of stock merchandise may exceed custom interior design that may also be offered there. Specialty shops might include accessories, selected new or antique furniture, textiles, or fine art. Interior designers themselves are often expert sales personnel.
- Salon design—design of beauty and barber shops, tanning facilities, nail sculpturing, and other beauty services.
- Set design—set design is needed for television, theater, movies, and photographs for furniture companies.
- Showroom designer—the interior design and space planning of permanent and seasonal showrooms of furniture, fabric, carpet, accessories, on a free-lance basis or as a permanent employee of a manufacturing firm.
- Solar design—requiring knowledge of energy efficiency, sun control, and sunlight-resistant materials. Specialists in solar interior design are needed in both residential and nonresidential design.

Continued on next page.

Figure 15.9

by Smith-Chororos for Les Prismatiques is a beautifully crafted coffee table veneered in fiddleback ash. Each of four identical quadrants flows into a curving and tapered leg whose shape echoes the traditional cabriole leg. Hand-painted beading details the edges and accents the fluid lines. It is also available in custom woods and finishes, veneers, and solids. (B) The

Petal chaise, designed by Hector S. Topacio and Ched Bereguer-Topacio for Luten Clarey Stern, Inc. The juxtaposition of iron and rattan creates a look merging the primitive and the contemporary, exemplifying how rudimentary methods and materials can be used to create a chaise that is elegantly modern. Photos courtesy of Resources Council.

Figure 15.9 Thomas Lamb designed this Management Plus Series, winner of the Seventeenth Annual Product Design "Roscoe" Awards contract furniture case goods collection category. This all-wood collection of executive case goods features desks, credenzas, overhead storage units, bookcases, and lateral files in rift-cut

mahogany with solid mahogany moldings. The hallmark of these office components is the new Granite ® (TM) finish on the cases and drawer fronts, which gives a depth to the surfaces and accentuates the mahogany tops and drawer pulls. Photo courtesy of Resources Council, Inc.

Chart 15.2   *Continued*

Figure 15.10

Figure 15.11

(A)
Figure 15.12

(B)

• Textile design for fabrics, wallpaper, or carpeting—working in-house for large conversion companies or free-lancing and selling designs or being paid royalties for textile design. Custom design occasionally calls for one-of-a-kind textiles.

• Training specialists—in areas such as computers, retail sales and marketing, lighting, nonresidential specifications, or other design services.

• Transportation design—including specialties in aircraft interiors (passenger jets to corporate jets), marine design (interiors of luxury liners to private yachts), bus and train interior design, and even automobile design.

• Turnkey design—the designer sells the project and assumes complete responsibility to hire all consultants and subcontractors and finish the project with very little input from the client, who only needs to turn the key and walk in to a completed interior. Vacation homes are one application of this specialty.

• Window treatment design—today so many style and mechanical options exist in window treatments that it takes expertise

to know which treatments to specify. Fabric coordination with overall design and furnishings is also necessary.

• Wholesale representatives, or reps, call on design firms within a designated territory to whom they provide or sell product samples or catalogs. They order stock merchandise and provide

the link between the manufacturer and retailer or designer in obtaining goods and services, providing swifter service, and troubleshooting. Reps also assist the designer in preparing specifications, selecting merchandise, preparing bids, and writing purchase orders.[7]

Figure 15.13

Figure 15.10 Textile design is one career avenue for trained and talented designers. In the Schumacher Textile Studio, two designers are hard at work on the two-dimensional part of the textile design process—pattern and coloration—while large books document current and past textile successes. Since major textile

companies offer entire new lines every spring and fall, the textile designer is always seeking fresh design inspiration and translating these finds to printed and woven fabrics. A line will often consist of several interrelated or coordinated patterns, each in up to five colorways. Photo by Ted Spiegel.

Figure 15.11 Winner of the contemporary wall covering category of the Seventeenth Annual Product Design "Roscoe" Awards, this Semiprecious Metals collection by Steve Jensen and Fred Stahl and offered by SJW Designs was designed to create textured surfaces that add a

feeling of warmth and depth to walls. The textured metallic finish also provides an energetic surface that changes character with changes in light. It is made of enamels, sand, powder pigments, and latex on kraft paper ground and is available in thirty-two colors plus custom, and in

Working with a Professional Designer

People turn to interior designers for a variety of reasons. The most important of these is the designer's knowledge of sources. An interior designer has canvassed the market and is aware of the best sources for the given circumstances, and obtains specialty goods and services in behalf of the client. Most wholesale sources will sell only through a retailer or designer; the designer who can order the items needed for a specific job is an important resource for the client. Closed showrooms will not allow retail customers to enter their premises, but clients may go into open showrooms when accompanied by their interior designer.

A designer can produce materials and finishes presentation boards and sketches or colored renderings of the proposed finished space. These enable the client to visualize the interior and approve in advance the purchases and color schemes. Working with a designer from the outset of planning new construction can help assure better interior spacial arrangements. The designer can supervise remodeling and reconstruction of interior spaces and can custom design special items such as built-in cabinetry, wall paneling, and fireplaces. The designer has a knowledge of quality and value and can control each. He or she will know which craftspeople do the best work and will act as liaison between the worker and the client. Thus the client is spared the frustration of dealing with many workmen and subcontractors.

A designer also will be able to control a set budget and assure that services and goods stay within the limits of the budget while completing the interior.

Perhaps the most important way a designer can help is to draw upon his or her experiences with the application of the elements and principles of design. Since furnishing an interior can be a costly expenditure, a designer can see to it that aesthetic mistakes are not made and that the end product is not only beautifully pleasing but fully supportive of the user's needs.

Designer fees vary according to the circumstance and practice of the firm. Residential interior design is usually based on retail sales or retail less a percentage. This may be combined with a design fee based on the time spent drafting, rendering, shopping, and supervising construction or installation. A designer may charge a flat consultation fee only or base design service charges on an hourly fee, freeing the clients to shop on their own and purchase from whatever source they will.

Design fees may be based on the type and extent of services completed by the designer. These services may include the following:

- Consultation with clients.
- Preparation of analysis or surveys.
- Preliminary budget and cost estimates of required furniture, furnishings, and equipment. Preparation of renderings, color and material boards, floor wall, ceiling, and window treatment drawings. Plans for cabinetry, closets, and other built-ins.
- Plans for lighting.
- Preparation of maintenance manuals.
- Specification services.
- Supervisory services.
- Consultation with third parties such as architects, engineers and general contractors. Suggestions for graphics, uniforms, logos. Fees may be based on the phases of the job, with a flat fee determined for each service mentioned.

Compensation is generally secured in phases, at the completion of certain services, or billed monthly.

Letters of agreement are contracts drawn up by the design firm and signed by the client that become legal documents. A *letter of agreement* will vary somewhat between residential and nonresidential projects, but both will contain the same general information. The letter will specify who the work is for, the location of the work involved, and which specific areas are to be involved. It will outline the services to be rendered by the designer, whether purchasing is to be done by the designer in the client's behalf, and which arrangement (retail, retail less a percentage, or wholesale plus a percentage) is agreed upon. The letter will outline specific phases of the design job, the client's responsibility to third-party contractors and services, compensation arrangements, and collateral matters. Disclaimers (items and services for which the designer is not responsible) will limit the designer's liability and clarify the relationship between the designer and the client. A *retainer fee*, applicable to the design fees or the goods to be purchased, is customarily required to initiate work by the design firm.

Choosing a designer or design firm for residential work may be based on personal reference or upon the quality and appeal of the finished interiors executed by the designer or the firm. The client should always interview the designer to form a judgment of the potential for a good working relationship based on professionalism and rapport. The designer will become thoroughly acquainted with the preferences, needs, and wants of each user and often becomes a personal friend because of the necessity of knowing the life-style and preferences so thoroughly.

panels thirty-six inches wide by nine feet long. Photo courtesy of Resources Council, Inc.
Figure 15.12 Here are two winners of categories in the Seventeenth Annual Product Design Awards. *(A)* The Terri Roese III collection designed by Terri Roese contains floral, abstracted geometric, and small-scaled designs, making it ideal for mixing and matching. Available in Teflon-finished 100 percent cotton in seven styles of various colorways. *(B)* The Caravans collection designed and manufactured by Lee Jofa translates antique documentary designs from museum archives into a group of individual fabrics with a contemporary look, drawn mostly from Middle Eastern sources. Three styles in 100 percent cotton, one style in 100 percent silk in various colorways. Photos courtesy of Resources Council, Inc.
Figure 15.13 The basic vocabulary of the machine aesthetics developed at the Bauhaus is expressed through this 100 percent wool complex Jacquard Wilton weave carpet. Designed by Mark C. Pollack and manufactured by Jack Lenor Larsen, this is the winner of the Seventeenth Annual Product Design residential carpeting category. Photo courtesy of Resources Council, Inc.

The Future of Interior Design

It is clear that the future of interior design will entail greater demand for designers to be knowledgeable concerning the complex and technical aspects of interior design. Increased litigation or lawsuits involving design projects is evidence of the rising liability and accountability of interior designers for the environments they create. Because of this, designers in the future will specialize further to possess a more thorough expertise in one area of design.

As more states pass title registration acts and require licensing, interior designers who are qualified will enjoy increased legal recognition. This trend should further protect the public against those who are not qualified to practice interior design.

Finally, the computer promises to play a commanding role in the future of interior design, being used for coordination of research and documentation, analysis, organization, computer-aided design, and processing of all the documents and paperwork handled by the interior designer.

Figure 15.14

Nonresidential Considerations

Nonresidential work is far less personal than residential work, and the image projected by the designer usually must be creative, yet conservative, and businesslike. The representative of the design firm must present soundly conceived design solutions, often to a board of directors, and indicate that the firm's business practices are likewise sound. The client may visit the design firm to evaluate the level of professionalism. The design firm may also be selected by winning a competitive bid.

Nonresidential interior design firms may do a variety of interiors, but most specialize. The areas of specialty include:

- Commercial office planning and design—incorporating space planning and office systems furnishings.
- Health care and clinic facilities—hospitals, same-day surgery centers, women's care centers, medical and dental offices, geriatric centers, rest homes, and hospices.
- Hospitality—hotels, resorts, and restaurants.
- Model interiors—model homes and condominiums and offices.
- Retail design—everything from shops and department stores to entire retail complexes.
- *Tenant improvement* of offices, or facility planning—the developer sets a budget, and designers work with tenants to select and specify materials and furnish-

ings. The developer pays the cost, with the tenant paying for any desired upgrade in materials over the budget allowance.
- Adaptive reuse of old or historic buildings—giving a building new life as retail spaces, office spaces, or residences.
- *Transportation design*—airlines, buses, trains, and/or cars.
- Industrial design—such as manufacturing facilities.

Certain organizations such as business corporations, retail stores and chains, schools and institutions, government agencies, hotel chains, airlines, and energy companies employ *in-house* (staff) *designers* who are responsible for new and on-going design projects. These organizations benefit from an in-house professional who not only has aesthetic and technical skills but who also understands the procedures and policies of the corporation itself.[8]

Responsibilities of the Nonresidential Designer

In nonresidential design, many of the tasks required of the skilled designer overlap those of the residential designer, although the way they are handled or the specific requirements will vary.

The documents and letters of agreement are standard forms that are legally binding and involve all aspects of the project. Often the financial arrangement will be a cost plus a percentage for very large installations. The designer may contract only to research and design the interior, or the

Figure 15.14 Showrooms at the Interior Design Center, New York (IDCNY) in Long Island City give professionals and their accompanied clients the opportunity to shop for the latest products and designs, place orders, and come away with product literature and samples. Photo by Ted Spiegel.

Figure 15.15

designer may take the project as far as the specification of furnishings, without the responsibility of ordering goods or overseeing their installation. These varying situations are made clear in the contracts.

The programming phase in nonresidential design is conducted in much the same way as in residential design: (1) research, (2) analysis, and (3) implementation. However, the categories of research will differ. The research will focus on working situations and ease of functional interrelationships, public traffic, and specialized needs for the project.

The development of the design and the space planning often take place on a larger scale for nonresidential design, and a single design concept may be adapted for several different areas within the interior, from reception area to working area or to hotel rooms or to hospital rooms and then onto specialized areas (to board rooms or to conference rooms or ballrooms or to examination rooms, for example).

Nonresidential designers coordinate work with specialists who plan and install heating, ventilation, and air-conditioning systems (HVAC). They work with lighting and structural engineers and other specialists; the amount of design in these specialized areas depends on the skills and time abilities of the design firm. Whereas in some cases the designer will design the reflected ceiling plan, in other instances that part will be awarded via contract to a specialized lighting firm.

Materials and furnishings must be specified to meet not only performance criteria and user needs but also state and local codes for safety against fire, bacterial growth, and static electricity.

The nonresidential designer spends a good deal of time preparing working drawings for interior architectural detail such as moldings, cabinetry, freestanding units, columns, and any needed furnishing items necessary for the interior design.

Nonresidential design entails purchasing furnishing items or specifying items for the client's purchasing department to order. The nonresidential designer may oversee the installation and be responsible for subcontractors who install, or it may not be a part of the contract.

In nonresidential design, it is entirely possible for the designer to function as the project manager, where all personnel needed to build or remodel are coordinated and hired under his or her direction, from the architect and engineers to the carpet and wall covering installers and electricians and plumbers.

Nonresidential Design Fees

Nonresidential interior design fees are often based on a flat fee, computing in advance the projected time necessary to complete the design. The flat fee may also be based on a square foot method. When fees are based on time, the salary of each person (principal, project manager, senior, junior designers, draftsmen, secretaries) who will be involved in a

Figure 15.15 A wall of small textile swatches by Schumacher awaits the discrimination of the designer. In addition to small free swatches, large "memo" samples can be checked out for a few days for evaluation of the fabrics under the light of the proposed installation. Shopping the design centers found in most major metropolitan cities can save the designer, whose professional practice is nearby, the expense and space needed to purchase and store countless books of textiles and furnishings. Where the design practice is not convenient to a design center, such a library must be maintained and is serviced by a traveling sales representative (rep) who supplies samples and helps to process orders and take care of special design specification needs. Photo by Ted Spiegel.

project is computed or projected, and the monthly salary of each person is multiplied by three and then by the number of months spent in each phase of the design job (programming, designing, construction, installation supervision). That amount will be multiplied by three to cover wages, overhead, profit, and anticipated overtime spent on the job. Square foot method is used less often but is applicable for large spaces.

Purchasing arrangements for nonresidential furnishings are typically billed at wholesale plus a percentage of 10 percent, 15 percent, or 20 percent. The designer may not purchase for nonresidential jobs but may specify furnishings that are ordered by the purchasing department of the client's firm. Likewise, nonresidential clients are generally responsible to pay for third-party services such as architects, engineers, and general contractors. Billings for design goods and services are billed monthly or in prearranged installments that parallel each phase of the project.[9]

Notes

1. "NCIDQ: National Council for Interior Design Qualifications Examination Study Guide." (New York: National Council for Interior Design Qualification, 1983), p. Introduction.
2. Friedman, Arnold. "Interior Design Education: A Hot Topic in 1986." (Ames, Iowa: *Journal of Interior Design Education and Research*, Vol. 12, No. 2, Fall 1986), p. 7.
3. Siegel, Harry, and Alan M. Siegel. *A Guide to Business Principles and Practices for Interior Designers*. (New York: Whitney Library of Design, 1982), pp. 133-34.
4. "MacUser: The MacIntosh Resource." (South Norwalk, CT: MacUser Publications. February 1987), pp. 142-66.
5. Siegel, Harry, and Alan M. Siegel. *A Guide to Business Principles and Practices for Interior Designers*. (New York: Whitney Library of Design, 1982), pp. 19-25.
6. IDEC: The Interior Design Educators Council. "Appointment, Tenure and Promotion: A Position Paper on Criteria for Evaluation of Interior Design Faculty in Post-Secondary Institutions." (Richmond, VA: IDEC, January 1985).
7. Knackstedt, Mary V. *Profitable Career Options for Designers*. (New York: Kobro Publications, 1985), pp. 24-46.
8. Siegel, Harry, and Alan M. Siegel. *A Guide to Business Principles and Practices for Interior Designers*. (New York: Whitney Library of Design, 1982), pp. 39-43, 50-65, 107-115.
9. Ibid., pp. 32-35, 98-106.

Bibliography

"Appointment, Tenure and Promotion: A Position Paper on Criteria for Evaluation of Interior Design Faculty in Post-Secondary Institutions." IDEC: The Interior Design Educators Council. January, 1985.

Boll, Carl R. *Executive Jobs Unlimited*. New York: Macmillan Publishing Company, Inc., 1979.

Broom, H.N., and Justin G. Longenecker. *Small Business Management*. Cincinnati: South-Western Publishing Co., 1979.

Burnstein, David, and Frank Stasiowski. *Project Management for the Design Professional: A Handbook for Architects, Engineers and Interior Designers*. New York: Whitney Library of Design, 1982.

Dalton, Gene W., and Paul H. Thompson. *Novations: Strategies for Career Management*. Glenview, IL: Scott, Foresman and Company, 1986.

Getz, Lowell, and Frank Stasiowski. *Financial Management for the Design Professional: A Handbook for Architects, Engineers, and Interior Designers*. New York: Whitney Library of Design, 1984.

"Interior Design as a Profession." Richmond, VA: Interior Design Educators Council, 1982.

Knackstedt, Mary V. *Profitable Career Options for Designers*. New York: Kobro Publications, 1985.

Loebelson, Andrew. *How To Profit in Contract Design*. New York: Interior Design Books, 1983.

Morgan, Jim. *Marketing for the Small Design Firm*. New York: Whitney Library of Design, 1984.

"NCIDQ: National Council for Interior Design Qualifications Examination Study Guide." New York: National Council for Interior Design Qualification, 1983.

Siegel, Harry, and Alan M. Siegel. *A Guide to Business Principles and Practices for Interior Designers*. New York: Whitney Library of Design, 1982.

Stasiowski, Frank. *Negotiating Higher Design Fees*. New York: Whitney Library of Design, 1985.

Addresses for Design Associations

American Association of Housing Educators (AAHE)
c/o Jo Ann Emmel
Box 3AE, New Mexico State University, Las Cruces, New Mexico 88003

American Home Lighting Institute (AHLI)
435 North Michigan Avenue, Chicago, Illinois 60611

American Institute of Architects (AIA)
1735 New York Avenue, Washington, D.C. 20006

The American Society of Interior Designers (ASID)
1430 Broadway, New York, New York 10018

Color Association of the United States
24 East 48th Street, New York, New York 10016

Color Marketing Group
1134 Fifteenth Street, NW, Washington, D.C. 20005

Designers' Lighting Forum (DLF)
(Contact Illumineering Engineering Society of North America for
information on local chapters.)
IESNA, 345 East 47th Street, New York, New York 10017

Environmental Design Research Association (EDRA)
L'Enfant Plaza Station, P.O. Box 23129, Washington, D.C. 20024

Foundation for Interior Design Education Research (FIDER)
322 Eighth Avenue, New York, New York 10001

Illumineering Engineering Society of North America (IESNA)
345 East 47th Street, New York, New York 10017

The Interior Designers of Canada (IDC)
168 Bedford Road, Toronto, Canada M5R 2K9.
U.S. address: (A member organization for the National Council for
Interior Design Qualifications—NCIDQ)
118 East 25th Street, New York, New York 10010

Interior Design Educators Council (IDEC)
14252 Culver Drive, Suite A-311, Irvine, California 92714

Interior Design Society (IDS)
220 Gerry Lane, Wood Dale, Illinois 60191

International Association of Lighting Designers (IALD)
c/o Wheel Gersztof Associates
30 West 22nd Street, New York, New York 10010

International Colour Authority
c/o Benjamin Dent & Company,
33 Bedford Place, London WC1B 5JX, England

The Institute of Business Designers (IBD)
1155 Merchandise Mart, Chicago, Illinois 60654

The International Federation of Interior Architects/Designers (IFI)
Waterlooplein 219, Postbus 19126, NL-1000 GC, Amsterdam,
Netherlands

International Furnishings and Design Association (IFDA)
(formerly the National Home Fashions League) 107 World Trade
Center,
P.O. Box 58045, Dallas, Texas 75258

National Association of Home Builders (NAHB)
15th and M Street, NW, Washington, DC 20005-2892

National Association of Schools of Art and Design (NASAD)
11250 Roger Bacon Drive #21, Reston, Virginia 22090

National Council for Interior Design Qualification (NCIDQ)
118 East 25th Street, New York, New York 10010

National Lighting Bureau (NLB)
2101 L Street NW, Washington, DC 20037 CIDQ)
118 East 25th Street, New York, New York 10010

GLOSSARY

A lamp
Designation for an arbitrary-shaped, standard light globe or lamp bulb.

A 588
The designation given to steel that rusts only to a certain point and in doing so creates its own rustproof finish.

AAHE
The American Association of Housing Educators.

Aalto, Alvar (1899–1976)
Important Finnish designer of several modern classic furniture pieces.

abacus
The slab or pillow above the capital at the top of a column.

abrasion resistance
The ability of a fabric to resist wear from friction, rubbing, or other abrasive action.

abstract design
A type of decorative design that may be based on natural or even geometric design, stylized to the point that the source is not recognizable, and the design is therefore open to interpretation.

acanthus leaves
A representation of the lobed leaves of the acanthus plant used as a decorative motif.

accent lighting
Focusing or highlighting; sometimes called artistic lighting.

accent rugs
Small rugs, often called scatter or throw rugs, used for art accents or in areas where water may spill onto the floor, such as kitchens and bathrooms, or to catch dirt where traffic enters the interior.

access
The approach or means of entering an environment or grouping of furniture.

accessible
Capable of entering or exiting a building or an area without obstruction.

accessories
The items in an interior used to give a quality of finish or completion such as paintings, sculpture, books, lamps, vases, flowers, plants.

accordion door
Folding door with small vertical panels that stacks against itself.

acetate
A man-made fiber of reconstituted cellulose and acetic acid.

achromatic
Colors without hue, namely black, white, and gray.

acoustical tile/plaster
Wall and ceiling tiles and plaster that help control noise.

acrylic
A synthetic, man-made fiber of over 85 percent acrylonitrile units; used for the manufacture of textiles and furniture.

acrylic light pipe
See light pipe.

acrylic paint
A synthetic resin, water-based paint.

acrylic sheet
A flat plate or sheet of acrylic (a hard plastic) that can be etched to allow special effects. The most common is the Exit sign.

active balance
Another term for asymmetrical balance where objects that are not alike balance each other, or like objects are placed at unequal distances from a central point. It is termed active because it requires some effort or activity of the eye to analyze or discern the balance.

active solar system
A mechanical system of solar heat collection for space and water heating.

actual density
The three-dimensional, literal mass or density of a piece of furniture.

Adam, Robert (1728–1792)
The most influential of four Scottish architect/designer brothers. His English Neoclassic work was influenced by the uncovering of Pompeii and Herculaneum near Naples, Italy.

adaptive restoration
Restoring older buildings for other than the original purpose for which they were constructed.

adhesive wall covering
Paste or powder to be mixed into paste for hanging wall coverings.

adobe
Large building brick made of clay, baked in the sun.

aesthetics
The philosophy of art and beauty. The part of art and design that is beautiful and appealing to the senses.

affinity
The chemical compatibility of fibers to dyestuffs.

afterimages
When the human eye focuses on a strong color for several seconds or minutes, then focuses on a neutral area, the complement of that color will appear in shadow form.

AID
The American Institute of Interior Designers combined in 1975 with NSID to form ASID, the American Society of Interior Designers.

air-brush printing
Dye sprayed through stencils by pressure ink jet guns.

air compression painting
Spray painting powered by an air compression machine that allows paint to be diluted for application.

air-conditioning
Cool air piped into an interior through an air-conditioning unit or through a furnace unit.

air-exchange unit
Draws fresh outside air into buildings and expels stale, used air. Necessary in a superinsulated and tight structure with few or no windows.

airless paint spraying
Mechanical spraying of nondiluted paint.

aisle
A passageway separated by an arcade, running parallel to the nave of a church.

Albers, Josef (1888–1976)
Color expert in simultaneous and successive contrast. Albers taught at the Bauhaus in Germany and at Yale University.

alkyds, alkyd enamel
Oil-modified resin paints. Alkyd enamels produce glossy surfaces.

all-wood
Wooden furniture construction where all visible parts are made of wood.

allocate space
To assign space; to determine the location and layout of rooms or areas.

alloy
A substance formed by fusing one or more metals or a metal and nonmetal.

alternate complement
A four-color scheme of a triad with the direct complement of one of the hues.

alternation
A type of rhythm where two shapes alternate—one, then the other. A classic example is the egg-and-dart molding seen in chapter 14.

aluminum
A lightweight silvery metal.

ambient lighting
Another term for general lighting.

ambulatory
A place for walking; the aisle in a cathedral.

amenities
Facilities shared by condominium owners or available to renters in luxury apartments. These include swimming pools, tennis courts, entertainment or athletic facilities.

American Empire (1820–1860)
The interior design title of the period concurrent with the antebellum Greek Revival homes. Colors influenced by Napoleonic choices of bold, deep hues.

ampere or amp
The measurement of electrical current in a circuit.

anaglypta
Embossed wall or ceiling coverings that resemble plaster, hammered copper, or hand-tooled leather.

analogous
Colors that are next to each other on the standard color wheel or as they occur in a rainbow or prism. An analogous color scheme usually contains three to six adjacent colors.

analysis
A part of programming where information is assessed and priorities established.

Ancient Greece, the Golden Age (fifth century B.C.)
Era of the Parthenon and height of philosophical development and architectural excellence.

Ancient Egypt (4500–663 B.C.)
Great dynasties whose design still has repeated impact today.

angular lines
Any straight line used in interior design that is neither horizontal nor vertical. Angular lines may be diagonal lines in one direction or even or uneven zigzag lines. Angular lines suggest movement and action.

animal hair felt pad
Moderately resilient carpet underlay of 100 percent animal hair felted into padding.

animal skin rugs
Rugs of zebra, bear, sheep, and other animal skins.

anodize
To put a protective oxide film on metal through an electrolytic process with chemicals and an electric charge.

anthemion
A symmetrical stylized Greek flower motif that radiates from a central point at the bottom of the flower.

anthropometrics
The study and comparison of human body measurements, i.e., anthropometry.

antibacterial finishes
Inhibit the growth of mold, mildew, and rot.

antimony
A silver-white, crystalline, metallic element used in alloys.

antique finish
A finish made to appear older by the application of a darker color over the top of a lighter finish.

antiques
Furniture made before 1840 (U.S. Customs definition).

antiquing
Making a painted surface look old with a mellow patina by color washing, glazing, spattering, and dragging techniques.

antiseptic finishes
See antibacterial finishes.

antistatic finishes
Reduce conduction or static electricity.

apartment
A home or unit housed with other units that are rented for living spaces.

apron
The face or front piece of a table just below the top, the face of a chair just below the seat, the face of a chest just below the drawers, and the front piece below the window sill.

apse
A semicircular or polygonal projection of a church.

arcade
A row of arches and supporting columns.

arch system construction
A building type in existence since antiquity; the arch is held together with a splayed keystone under compression.

architectural elements
The walls, floors, ceilings, windows, doors, fireplaces, cabinetry, and other fixtures or details that are the built-in part of the interior.

architectural glazing
See glass.

architectural lighting
Fixtures or luminaires permanently installed. The wiring must be in place in advance.

architectural rods
Nonresidential drapery and curtain rods that are usually drawn with wands or batons rather than a traverse cord and pulley.

architrave
The lintel or crosspiece in a classical entablature.

area rugs
Define a specific area, such as a conversation area.

armchair
A chair with armrests as distinguished from a side chair without arms.

armoire
The French term for a wardrobe or large movable closet.

Art Deco (1909–1939)
A brief period of design between World Wars I and II that has been repeatedly revived in interior design style and color.

art glass
A general term for stained, beveled, leaded, and etched glass used as primary glazing or as hard window treatments.

Art lighting, or light as art
A term for luminaires or fixtures that are in themselves works of art where light is the medium of artistic expression.

Art Nouveau (1890–1910)
A style of design based on natural floral motifs and colors.

art rug
A rug with a decorative texture or pattern of such interest and quality that it can be considered a piece of art.

artificial light
Man-made light, usually divided into two categories: incandescent and fluorescent. Amount and direction of artificial lighting affect color hue, value, and intensity.

artificial stone
A man-made product that imitates natural stone and is generally used for wall facing.

artistic lighting
Another term for accent lighting.

artist's paint
Oil or acrylic paint in small bottles or tubes.

Arts and Crafts Movement
A school of thought at the close of the Victorian Era that espoused a return to handmade, quality furnishings rather than machine-made items.

asbestos shingles
A fireproof roofing material in several color choices laid in overlapping manner and nailed tight.

ashlar stone
Stone cut into rectangular shapes fitted together with grout.

ASID
The American Society of Interior Designers.

asphalt tile
Hard, nonresilient, durable floor tiles with some asphalt content.

asymmetrical balance
The placement of different objects on either side of a center point where they balance each other. Asymmetry requires a discerning eye and sensitivity to achieve the balance.

atrium
The open entry hall of a Roman house.

atrium door
A French-door pair with one fixed side.

attic window
Pivoting window installed in the pitched roof of an attic.

Aubusson rugs
Flat tapestry French rugs woven in both historic and contemporary colors and patterns.

Austrian shades
Scalloped and gathered shades that fold up. They are full and formal looking.

automatic sensor dimmer
A device that automatically turns on and controls the level of artificial light to supplement natural light in order to keep the light at an even level of brightness.

auxiliary heating
A backup heating method needed for solar energy systems when the sun cannot supply all the heating needs of the interior.

Avril
A registered trademark of FMC Corporation for viscose rayon.

awning window
A top-hinged window that swings out.

Axminster carpet
A Jacquard-woven carpet where colored yarns are inserted as needed. Used extensively in nonresidential carpeting.

B lamp
A designation for a candelabra lamp or bulb that is a smooth, torpedo-shaped oval.

baccalaureate degree
The degree granted by colleges and universities and some design schools following four to five years of general education and specific topic study.

back panel
A panel used to cover the back of a case piece; often made of hardboard.

bacteriostat finishes
See antibacterial finishes.

baffle
A device such as a board or grid that deflects light, either to direct it or to prevent glare.

baffled ceiling
Ceiling hung with panels of wood, metal, or fabric that serve as a screen.

balance
The placement of objects, such as furniture or art, or architectural detail, such as windows or columns, so that they create visual equilibrium.

balanced basket weave
See basket weave.

balanced light
Light from more than one direction so that glare and high contrast of light and dark or unflattering or fatiguing shadows are eliminated.

balanced twill
See twill.

ballast
The connecting mechanism within a fluorescent lamp.

balloon, pouf, or cloud shades
Loosely gathered, full, soft, and billowy shades that pull up from the bottom.

baluster
The member that supports the handrail on a stair.

balustrade
The railing formed by the newel post, balusters, and handrail.

bamboo shades
Also called matchstick shades, woven of split bamboo and a cotton warp.

bank of light
A large, well-lit area of light.

barrel vault
An arched roof with a roundheaded arch shape.

barrier-free design
Design for the handicapped that presents no physical obstacles or barriers to access and free movement in the environment.

bartile
Quarry or clay tile (gray or red) roofing material. It is costly but never needs replacing.

bas-relief (low relief)
The type of sculpture where the figures protrude only slightly from the background.

base
Finish trim used to cover the joint where the wall meets the floor.

base lighting
A light placed next to the floor behind a deflector board that directs light upward.

baseboard
Base trim made of wood.

baseboard units
Plugged-in or prewired units near the floor for room or area heating.

basket weave
A variation of the plain weave where groups of warp and weft threads are carried as one. A *balanced* weave carries the same number in each direction—two over and under two; 3/3; 4/4. An *unbalanced* basketweave carries uneven groups of threads over and under such as 2/3 or 3/4.

bast fibers
Natural cellulosic fibers obtained from the stems and leaves of plants. The best known are linen and jute.

batik
A hand process of resist dyeing. A pattern is drawn with wax onto a cloth, then the cloth is dyed. The wax-covered portion will not be colored. The wax is removed and new wax applied to allow other areas of the pattern to be colored.

batting
Polyester, cotton, wool, or other suitable fibers formed into sheets for upholstery padding.

battlement
A parapet indented or crenellated along the upper line of a building.

Bauhaus
A German school of art, design, and architecture that functioned from 1919–1933 and taught the integration of art and technology for the creation of good design. The Bauhaus attracted many important artists and designers and had a significant influence on the development of modern design.

bay
The section between columns, piers, or buttresses.

bay or bow rods
Traverse or curtain rods that are prebent to a bay or bow window shape.

bay window
Projecting window in a square or canted configuration.

bead and reel
A molding of alternating round bead shapes and oval or disk shapes.

beam system construction
Solid beams of steel, wood, or concrete supported with a series of posts.

beamed ceiling
A ceiling with exposed beams or trusses.

beau-grip
A registered trademark of Beaunit for viscose rayon.

bed molding
Same as crown molding.

beltcourse
A projecting row of bricks or stone on the facade that separates one story from another; also called stringcourse.

Belter, John Henry (d. 1865)
A New York furniture craftsman best known for his Rococo Revival pieces of carved laminated rosewood.

belvedere
A cupola or lantern. The small square towers that rise from the roof of the Italianate buildings of the nineteenth century.

Bemberg
A registered trademark of Beaunit for cuprammonium rayon.

bentwood
A method of softening wood with steam and then bending it into curved forms.

berber rugs
Woven or tufted wool rugs left in their natural color state—white, beige, brown, charcoal, with flecks of light or dark neutrals.

bergère
French term for an upholstered armchair with upholstered side panels between the armrest and seat.

berm
A pile of earth used to create a visual or physical diversion or to add variety to a landscape.

Bertoia, Harry (1915–1978)
A modern Italian furniture designer.

Beta
A registered trademark of Owens-Corning for glass fiber or fiberglass.

beveled glass
Thick, decorative glass with a finished edge that is mitered or beveled at less than ninety degrees.

Bi-loft
A registered trademark of Monsanto for acrylic.

bibelot
French term for a small decorative and often rare object.

Biedermeier
The term used to describe the Empire style as interpreted and built by the craftsmen of northern Europe.

bifold door
A door with vertical double panels that folds back against itself; frequently used for closet doors.

biotechnology
The aspect of technology concerned with the application of biological and engineering data to man-made products and environments.

bisymmetrical balance
Also called formal or passive balance, the arrangement of like parts or objects in mirror image on each side of a central point.

bleaching
A prefinishing process for natural fibers that whitens gray goods. Also chemically lightening the natural color of the wood fiber as part of the wood finishing process.

blinds
Slats or louvers held together with cords or on a pulley system. Blinds may be horizontal or vertical. Sometimes pull of pouf shades are referred to as blinds.

block print
A two-dimensional art form printed from a flat wooden or linoleum block on which the background has been carved away, leaving a raised design pattern.

block printing
A hand-printing technique where blocks (usually wood) are carved then inked with fabric dye that is then pressed onto the fabric.

blockfront
A furniture detail used on the front section of case pieces. The blockfront consists of a series of three panels—the two outside panels come forward and the center panel is recessed.

Blue C
A registered trademark of Monsanto for polyester.

blueprints
Floor plans printed in blue ink and used for construction plans.

board and batten
Vertical wooden siding made of parallel boards with narrow strips of wood (battens) to cover the cracks.

boiling or scouring
A prefinish that removes the natural grease, gum, pectin, or applied sizing from a fabric.

boiserie
French term for wood paneling.

bolection
A rounded projecting molding.

bolt
Another word for a roll containing wall covering and textile yardage.

bonded (rebonded) foam
Carpet underlay (padding) of chopped foam and filler materials bonded together by heat, pressure, and some adhesives.

bonnet roof
A hipped roof with two pitches. The top is steeply pitched and the bottom, which covers a porch, is low pitched; used on houses of French influence.

boss
A projecting ornament at the intersection of ribs in the medieval church.

bow window
A curved projecting window (in the shape of a bow).

bracket
An angle-shaped support.

bracket lighting
A light placed on the wall behind a bracket board that directs light upward and downward.

braided rugs
Strips of fabric braided, then sewn together in ovals or circles. Originated in Colonial New England.

brainstorming
Generation of ideas without imposing judgment as to the quality of the ideas.

brass
A yellowish alloy of copper and zinc.

breakfront
A case piece whose front plane is broken with receding or advancing sections. The projecting section of the facade on Late Georgian houses that is topped with a pediment.

breast
The front of the fireplace and chimneypiece.

Breuer, Marcel (1902–1981)
Important designer/architect associated with the Bauhaus and known for the design of several classic chairs.

brick
Clay and other additives formed into rectangles and dried in the sun or fired in a kiln oven; used for walls and floors.

brightening finish
Applied to enhance color vividness in a fabric.

brilliants
Several pinpoints of light that produce a glitter effect.

broadloom carpet
Woven or tufted carpet typically twelve feet wide.

bronze
A deeply colored, reddish-brown alloy of copper and tin used to make sculptural pieces.

brush painting
Application of paint with a hand-held brush. Ideal for small areas and detail work.

brushed finish
A lustrous, but not shiny, finish achieved by brushing a series of uniform scratches into metal.

brushing
A prefinish process that pulls out unwanted short staple fibers from a fabric.

bubble planning
The first step of diagramming where bubbles represent zones and are placed in proximity relationships.

budgeting
The facet of a design project that dictates the amount of money to be spent on various aspects of the job.

buffet
See sideboard.

buffet-style dining
Where guests serve themselves a meal from a table or sideboard (balancing the plate on the lap to eat may be implied).

building inspector
An official whose job it is to inspect new or remodeling construction for structural soundness and safety features.

building systems
Components of a building that are permanent. These include heating, ventilation, air-conditioning (HVAC), electrical and lighting systems, and plumbing.

built-in lighting
Another term for architectural lighting that is prewired and relatively permanent.

bulb
More accurately the lamp bulb or lamp, it is the glass container that houses the filament of incandescent lighting and in fluorescent lighting contains phosphorus and gas.

bullnose
A 180-degree rounded wooden edge on the starting step (also on a table or cabinet top).

burl veneer
Made from scar-like wood growth or from root wood that imparts a complex, swirling grain pattern to the veneer.

burn-out or etch printing
A pattern printed with acid to remove one fiber, usually cotton in a cotton/polyester blend to leave areas of semisheer design.

business accounting software
Enables computers to keep accounting records.

buttress
A structure built against a wall to strengthen it.

buttressed chimney
In medieval construction, a stepped chimney built in the shape of two buttresses placed back-to-back.

buyer
A person who selects lines or companies whose furnishings are sold in furniture and department stores.

byobu
Small-scaled decorative folding Japanese screens.

byzantine
The style associated with the Byzantine Empire, which flourished from A.D. 394–1453.

Byzantium (A.D. 330–1453)
The eastern capital of the classical Roman Empire known for its colorful tile mosaics.

C lamp
A cone-shaped lamp or light bulb.

C.O.M.
Customer's own material—purchased by the customer from someone other than the furniture manufacturer for upholstery on a selected piece.

cabinetry
Fine finish woodwork, as opposed to rough carpentry.

cable system construction
A method of nonresidential building where a canopy is held in place with steel cables hung from a central column.

cabriole leg
An S-curve leg typical of the Régence and Louis XV periods in France and the Queen Anne and Chippendale eras in England and America.

cactus
Green, fleshy, leafless, spiny desert plant that produces showy flowers.

CAD (CADD)
Computer-aided design (and drafting) software.

Cadon
A registered trademark of Monsanto for nylon.

café curtains
Curtains that cover the bottom half of a window.

calendering
A finishing process of ironing under heat with a large cylinder roller. The roller may have raised patterns to imprint designs, and the fabric may also be glazed with a resin, then calendered to produce a high sheen, or other special finishes.

came
The lead strips used to secure the pieces of glass in leaded or stained glass windows.

camel-back sofa
A sofa with a serpentine back that rises to a hump in the center.

candelabra
A luminaire or light fixture that imitates a large, branched candlestick.

cane
Thin strips of rattan or bamboo used to weave mesh for chair seats, chair backs.

canister
A luminaire shaped like a can that contains a lamp at the top or the bottom.

canted
Beveled or tilted at an angle.

cantilever
A projecting or overhanging structure anchored at one end so that no outside support is required.

Cantrese
A registered trademark of DuPont for nylon.

capital
The decorative head of a column or pillar.

Caprolan
A registered trademark of Allied Chemical for nylon and polyester.

carefree finish
A functional, chemical, or standard finish that provides wrinkle resistance in the fabric.

carpenter
One who builds and repairs items of wood.

carpenter's gothic
The wooden, board and batten version of the Gothic Revival style.

cascades
Zigzag shaped panels of fabric that usually frame swags or festoons.

case goods
Furniture without upholstery such as desks, chests, and dressers.

cased glass
Clear glass encased in a layer of colored glass.

casement draperies
A strongly textural-looking fabric in a woven or knitted construction. Screens light, cuts down on glare, and provides daytime privacy.

casement window
A side-hinged window that swings in or out.

casing
A layer of fabric between the padding and the actual cover in upholstery.

cast iron
Iron cast in a mold.

cathedra
The bishop's chair from which the term cathedral is derived.

cathedral ceiling
A high, open, gabled ceiling.

cathedral window
A pointed window set in the gable of a room with an open ceiling.

Caucasian or Turkish rugs
Oriental rugs of a coarser weave than Persians, in geometric patterns and often vivid colors.

Celanese
A registered trademark of Celanese for acetate.

Celaperm
A registered trademark of Celanese for acetate.

cella
Literally a cell. The interior space of a Roman temple.

cellulosic fibers
A classification of natural fibers that come from plants and are made up of cellulose: cotton and linen being the most commonly used. The two man-made fibers that begin with cellulose are rayon and acetate.

cement
A powder of silica, alumina, lime, and other materials. Mixed with water and aggregate, cement becomes concrete.

central air-conditioning
Cool or temperate air controlled from a central unit and distributed through ducts and vents.

central vacuum system
A vacuum located in one unit with plumbed pipe and outlets where the hose is attached. The wall plate covering the outlet activates the system when it is lifted.

ceramic tile
White clays fired to a point of vitrification. Many sizes, shapes, colors, and patterns; a strong, hard material for walls, floors, and ceilings.

ceramics
The art of modeling and baking in clay.

chair rail
A molding placed on the wall at chair-back height.

chaise longue
A French term that literally means long chair. It has an elongated seat designed for reclining.

chandelier
A decorative, ceiling-mounted, or pendant-type luminaire consisting of several branches for candles or electric lamps.

chemical finishes
See standard finishes.

Chevruel, M.E. (1786–1889)
French chemist who was head of dyestuffs at Gobelin Tapestry Works near Paris. Chevruel researched and published theories that were forerunners to the Standard Color Wheel theory.

chimneypiece
The decorative detail that covers the firebox and flue.

china
Designation given by Europeans to porcelain from the Orient.

Chinese rugs
Oriental rugs woven in Chinese traditional or contemporary patterns in a deep, sculptured pattern.

chipboard
See particleboard.

Chippendale, Thomas II (1718–1799)
An important English cabinetmaker known for the designs published in his book, *The Gentleman and Cabinet-Maker's Director.*

choir
The section of the church where the choir sings; the chancel.

chroma
The relative brightness or intensity of a particular hue or color. Low chroma is dull; high chroma is bright. Chroma is a designation of the Munsell color system.

chromium
A shiny silver metal resistant to rust.

Chromspun
A registered trademark of Eastman Kodak for acetate.

ciré
A calendering finish that produces a high sheen on the fabric surface.

circuit
A wiring hookup that forms a path through which electrical current may flow.

circulation
Movement from place to place within an environment.

cissing
Dropping mineral spirits onto wet spattered paint to make shadows of the spatters.

City of London
The one square mile area that encompasses what was once Roman and medieval London.

clapboard
Thin, horizontal, overlapping, exterior wooden siding.

classic
A work of the highest excellence able to stand the test of time.

Classical Rome (200 B.C.—A.D. 100)
The Roman era of political conquest and architectural achievement. Roman design was discovered by the Western world when the excavation of Pompeii began in 1754.

clearance
Space required by code or law around a combustible or heating unit (stove, fireplace, or furnace) so that nearby materials will not ignite. Also, the clear space between users and the objects they are passing.

clerestory window
Window placed at the top of the wall or in the highest story of the nave or choir of a church.

cloisonné
Decorative objects made by soldering metal strips into a pattern on a metal piece and filling the space between the strips with enamel.

closed floor plans
Floor plans with many rooms that are totally private from other rooms with solid walls and accessed only through a door that may also close.

closed showrooms
A design-oriented store for placing orders of merchandise. They deal only with professional interior designers, and clients are not allowed to enter.

closed stair
A stairway with walls on both sides.

club foot
A round, pad-shaped foot on a cabriole leg.

coated fabric wall coverings
Fabric layered with vinyl to become wall coverings.

cobblestone
Large rounded stones such as river cobbles set into concrete and used mainly as nonresilient hard wall materials.

code
A Federal, state, or local ruling, law, or regulation that stipulates building safety and health requirements. Examples include non-flammable materials or fire-stops.

coffered ceiling
A ceiling formed with recessed boxes or coffers.

coil spring
A cylindrically shaped spring used for upholstery cushioning.

cold air returns
Ducts used in forced-air heating systems to return cooled air to the heat source for warming.

cold cathode lighting
The term for all colors of neon lighting.

collectors
Units to capture the sun's energy or heat for active and passive solar heating.

Colonial America (1640–1770)
The period prior to the revolutionary war that included medieval and Early and Late Georgian interiors.

colonnade
A row of columns, often forming a corridor.

color
An element of design, color is pigment in paint or part of the visible spectrum light that enables us to see hues. It incorporates the study of hue, value, and intensity as well as color schemes, color application, and color psychology.

color harmony
The selection and arrangement of colors to be pleasing to the eye and to the senses.

color group moods
Groups of color that produce emotional response, such as light and bright colors producing feelings of spontaneity and happiness.

color washing
Applying a coat of thinned, sometimes translucent, paint over a white or colored ground.

Coloray
A registered trademark of Courtaulds for viscose rayon.

colored incandescent lighting
Accomplished with colored glass lamps or by colored screens or filters placed over a white light.

colorfast
The ability of a dyed or printed fabric to resist color loss from cleaning, light fading, or atmospheric impurities that could cause color change.

coloring
A general term for the dyeing and printing of textiles.

Colorspun
A registered trademark of American Viscose for viscose rayon.

column
A tall upright supporting shaft.

columned chimney
A chimney formed in the shape of one or more columns.

combination
Wooden furniture construction with more than one type of wood in the exposed parts of the piece.

combination felt padding
Carpet underlay felt pad of some animal hair and some synthetic fiber.

combination floor plans
A floor plan with areas that are open and other rooms that are closed.

combination weave
A fabric employing more than one type of weave; for example, plain and twill weaves seen side by side in a fabric.

combustion lighting
Candlelight and firelight.

communication systems
Intercom, computer network, and telephone systems that connect people within the building or beyond the building.

compartmental bathroom
A bathroom where the separate functions are housed in small rooms that open to each other.

complementary colors
Colors that are in opposite position on the color wheel. Complementary colors have the greatest contrast of all the color combinations, each making the other more vivid. Types of complementary combinations include direct, split, triadic, double, alternate, and tetrad complements.

composite
A Roman architectural capital style composed of volutes from the Ionic order and acanthus leaves from the Corinthian order.

compounded fabrics
See layered fabrics.

computer hardware
The components that make up a computer system: the keyboard, monitor, computer power drive, printer, and plotter. It also includes larger mainframe computers when such a system is incorporated.

computer interface
Where two or more computer terminals can access the same information through a central mainframe computer or a networking system.

computer network
Connective cables that allow computer terminals within an office or design firm to access the same information.

computer programs
The software, or disks, that operate the computer hardware. Programs are instructions, information, and data bases that allow the machine to operate specific functions. These include graphics and CAD, word processing, and so on.

computer terminal
A keyboard and monitor that are connected to a mainframe. Also, a personal computer that can be connected to other computer terminals via a computer network system.

computer-aided design (and drafting) CAD (CADD)
Computer software that enables the designer to draw, draft, arrange furnishing components, and compose simulated perspectives of a proposed interior space.

concept
An idea for the solution to a problem.

conceptual drawings
Drawings that show the concept or idea for a design.

concrete
A mixture of sand, water, and portland cement that dries to a hard material; used for floors and walls, footings, foundations, and exterior flatwork.

concrete block
Large building bricks of concrete.

condominium
A home that is individually owned. The owner pays a monthly or yearly charge to maintain common landscaping and recreation and/or fitness facilities.

continuing education
Skills, training, and knowledge gleaned by the professional interior designer through seminars and networks sponsored by professional organizations, institutions, and corporations.

contrast
The difference that exists between two colors, values, or shapes. A large difference is sometimes sharp contrast or high contrast or vivid contrast; small differences are termed low contrast. Contrast makes individual objects more meaningful.

control
The monitoring unit or thermostat needed for a furnace or an active solar heating system.

conventional design
A type of decorative design taken from nature and adapted, stylized, or conventionalized. The pattern is still recognizable as the nature object (flowers, for example) but is not reproduced in its naturalistic state.

conventional traverse rods
Drapery rods with a cord-and-pulley system for operating pleated draperies.

conversation pit
Seating areas designed and built in as an integral part of the environment. The name pit implies a sunken area, but this type of seating could be designed on a platform or on floor level.

cool colors
Colors found next to each other on the color wheel; they include green, blue-green, blue, blue-violet, and violet.

cool white deluxe fluorescent lamps
A quality, balanced spectrum lamp whose light does not appear cold and unflattering.

coordinating or companion fabric
Decorative fabric printed in the same or a coordinating pattern as a wallpaper.

cope
To cut a section of paneling to fit an adjoining piece.

copper
A bright, shiny, reddish-brown metal used for cookware, tableware, decorative objects, and building components.

corbel
Same as bracket.

Cordelan
A registered trademark of the Japan company for a vinyl/vinyon fiber.

Cordura
A registered trademark of DuPont for rayon and nylon.

corinthian
A Greek and Roman architectural style that features a capital decorated with acanthus leaves.

cork, cork wall coverings
Lightweight, resilient bark of an oak tree belonging to the birch family that grows in the Mediterranean area. Coated with vinyl for floors, used in sheets or tiles or laminated to paper for wall coverings.

coromandel
Large Chinese black lacquered folding screens.

corner blocks
Triangular blocks of wood attached at an angle across the corner of a joint for added strength.

corner fireplace
A corner fireplace situated in the corner of a room.

cornice
A wooden top treatment for draperies, frequently shaped on the bottom. Also, the projecting top section of a classical entablature. Found on the exterior under the eaves and on the ceiling where it meets the wall on the interior.

cornice lighting
A lamp or line of light placed next to the ceiling with a board in front to direct the light downward.

cornice molding
A more ornate form of crown molding.

corridor
A passageway or hallway, usually indicating a nonresidential application.

cost analysis
The proposed budget including the design fee for a project or the economic feasibility of the design work. The result of programming research.

cost per square foot
The total cost of the home or building or the total cost of building one floor divided by the number of square feet.

cottage curtains
Curtains often used in tiers or layers with ruffles around the edges.

cotton
A natural cellulosic fiber obtained from the hairs of the boll (fruit of the cotton plant). Cotton comes in short, medium, and long staple fibers and is an absorbent, soft, comfortable fiber. It dyes easily and is used in many printed decorative fabrics and in toweling.

cotton rugs
Accent, scatter, or area rugs woven of cotton. Many are handwoven from India.

country curtains
Ruffled tieback curtains with extra fullness, up to 500 percent (or five times) fullness, usually in a quaint cotton print.

course
A horizontal row of brick or masonry.

Courtaulds
A registered trademark of Courtaulds for nylon.

cove lighting
A light placed next to the ceiling with a deflector board that directs light up onto the ceiling.

cove molding
A concave, rounded molding placed where wall and ceiling meet.

coved ceiling
A ceiling with a concave rounded radius where the ceiling meets the wall.

covered frame wall fabric method
Fabric wrapped and stapled around a lath frame, then hung or affixed to a wall.

cramming
A ribbed surface texture produced by inserting more threads in one direction.

credenza
See sideboard.

crenellation
The notches or indentations in a parapet.

Creslan
A registered trademark of American Cynamide for acrylic.

critical path
The time frame and overlapping order of every step in the building and finishing process.

crocking
The rubbing off of excess dyestuffs onto another fabric or onto the skin.

crop
To trim or cut an art piece to fit a frame.

cross dyeing
Two fibers of different affinities dyed in the same bath; the colors will be accepted differently.

crossing
The area of a cross-shaped church where the nave and transept cross.

crowding
Where people are grouped together in tightly restricted areas.

crown lintel
See jack arch lintel.

crown molding
Trim placed where the wall and ceiling meet.

cruciform
Floor plan in the form or shape of a cross.

crypt
An underground vault, especially in a church, often used for burial.

crystal
A high grade of glass containing lead.

cubic feet or footage
The width multiplied by the length of a room and then by its height. The volume of space we walk through. Rooms with very high ceilings have greater cubic footage than those with lower ceilings.

Cumuloft
A registered trademark of Monsanto for nylon.

cupola
A small-domed structure rising above a roof.

curio
A rare or curious art object—a curiosity.

curtain rods
Plain or nontraverse rods of metal or wood.

curtain wall construction
See metal frame or space frame system.

curtains
A general term for fabric window treatments that are shirred or sometimes pleated but usually stationary or hand operated.

curved lines
Flowing lines, part of the elements of design. Large curves are smooth and gracious; small curves can give a feeling of activity in the interior.

curved staircase
A staircase with a curved radius.

custom design
Any design that is planned and executed according to individual specifications—not mass-produced.

custom paper-backed fabrics
Paper applied to custom fabric for installing as wall covering.

custom floor plan
One that is executed by an architect or designer to meet the needs of the space—custom tailored to the design program.

cut glass
Glass incised with an abrasive to create decorative patterns.

cut length
The length of unhemmed fabric window treatments.

Dacron
A registered trademark of DuPont for polyester.

dado
A section of paneling that extends from the floor only as high as the chair rail.

dado cap
A molding used to finish the top of a dado.

damper
The movable piece in a fireplace that controls the airflow and escape of smoke.

data-base catalog
Information and graphic symbols programmed into a data-base software program. Useful in computer-aided design and in business applications.

data-base programs
Software programs that manage, organize, and retrieve files used for working on documents, graphics, CAD.

daub
A coarse plaster used as infill wall finish in medieval timber-framed buildings.

David Brewster Color theory
Another designation for the Standard Color Wheel theory.

De Stijl
An early twentieth-century Dutch aesthetic philosophical movement best represented by the work of painter Piet Mondrian.

decorative arts
Arts such as ceramics, metal work, textiles, and furniture that are suitable as decoration.

decorative design
A classification of man-made design where the building, furniture piece, or object is decorated with ornamentation. Decorative design is broken into four categories: naturalistic, conventional, abstract, and geometric.

decorative finishes
A term for a group of finishes that add decorative appeal to fabrics. Examples of mechanical decorative finishes include various calendering, flocking, and napping finishes. Chemical decorative finishes include etch or burn-out printing and finishes that add brightness, softness, texture, stiffening, and delustering.

decorative luminaire
Another term for portable luminaire, consisting of plug-in, movable luminaires such as table and floor lamps. Also refers to an architectural or built-in luminaire that is decorative.

decorator rods
Metal drapery rods that are decorative with traverse cord-and-pulley workings.

dehumidifier
A unit connected to an air-conditioning unit that draws off excess humidity as a part of the cooling system.

delustering finish
A special finish to remove the high sheen from textiles.

demographics
The statistical data of a particular population.

dentil
A decorative trim of projecting rectangular blocks.

design
A term that describes a process of designing a building, furnishings, or composite interiors. Design also refers to the plan or scheme that made the end product possible in its executed form, material(s), and size.

design process
The sequence of steps in creating and executing a design project.

design statement
A short declaration that identifies a design project according to purpose, location, and those for whom the design is being created.

designer rugs
Custom-designed tufted or woven area rugs.

desk manager software
Programs with specific options for managing a business.

detached dwelling
A single home on a lot of its own.

deWolfe, Elsie (1879-1950)
The greatest and best known of the society interior designers who paved the way for the modern interior design profession.

dhurrie rugs
Originally cotton, now wool flat tapestry weave reversible rugs. Most are imported from India to meet Western demands.

diagonal lines
Angular lines that may go one (or more) directions in an interior. Diagonal lines suggest movement and action.

diagramming
The graphic process of planning space on paper.

diffusers
The glass or plastic cover over a luminaire that serves to soften the light and spread it evenly over the area.

dimensional stability
The ability of a fabric to maintain or return to its original shape.

dimmer switch
A mechanism that controls the variable brightness of a lamp. May be manual or automated.

direct complement
Two colors that are directly across from each other on the color wheel.

direct glare
Glare from an insufficiently shielded light source directly into the line of vision.

direct glue down
A method of laying carpeting where a layer of adhesive is applied to the floor, then the carpet is laid directly on top of it, with no pad.

direct lighting
Lighting that shines directly on the area or task being lit.

direct pasteup
Gluing fabric or wall coverings up with paste or adhesive.

direct solar gain
Heating an area through direct exposure of sunshine to the occupied space.

discharge printing
A process that removes the dyed color in patterned areas and replaces it with another color.

distressed
A finish made to appear old or antique by the intentional addition of dents, scratches, and flecks of paint during the finishing process.

distribution
Carrying air heated by active or passive solar systems to the various areas or rooms within a building.

doctor of philosophy
Ph.D., or doctorate degree; a possible requirement for full-time, tenure-track teaching positions in colleges and universities.

Dolan
A registered trademark of Hoechst for acrylic.

dome
An inverted round dish or cup-shaped ceiling.

dome system construction
An arch rotated in a circle to become a dome.

domestic Oriental rugs
Jacquard machine-woven rugs in Oriental rug designs.

dope dyeing
See solution dyeing.

Doric
Greek and Roman architectural style with fluted columns and plain capital.

dormer window
A window that projects from the attic.

double complement
Two sets of direct complementary colors next to each other on the color wheel.

double glazing
Filling a window opening with two layers of glass that provide insulation and increase energy efficiency at the window.

double roll
A roll of wall covering with approximately seventy-two square feet, or double the area of a single roll.

double-hung
Two layers of draperies, an overdrapery and an underlayer. Also, two sets of shutters, one installed directly above the other.

double-hung sash
Sash window where both sections are operable.

double-turn stair
A stair that makes two ninety-degree turns on two separate landings.

double-wide trailer
A mobile home that is fabricated into sections the size of a single-wide trailer, then fitted together to become twenty-four to thirty feet wide and twenty to forty feet long.

doup weave
See leno weave.

dovetail
A series of fan-shaped joints used to connect drawer fronts and sides.

dowel
A type of joint in which a third piece (the dowel) is glued into holes drilled in the two pieces being joined.

down
Soft, fine feathers used as filling in some upholstered cushions.

draft dodgers
A sand-filled tube of fabric or a heavy rug placed against a door to prevent cold air infiltration.

drafting
The drawing by hand, machine, or computer of floor plans.

draftsman
A person who drafts, draws, or produces floor plans and blueprints.

dragging and combing
Produce fine paint lines with a dry brush over a wet glaze or combing with any hard comblike tool.

Dralon
A registered trademark of Bayer for acrylic.

drapability
The characteristic of a fabric to fall nicely into folds as in a draped fabric.

draperies
Pleated fabric hung with hooks on a traverse rod. Also refers to stationary side panels, tied-back fabric, and occasionally shirred panels.

draw draperies
Operable panels hung on a cord or wand-operated traverse rod.

drawings
One-of-a-kind, two-dimensional art forms produced with pencil, pen and ink, charcoal, chalk, crayon, or grease pencil on paper or other surfaces.

drop-leaf
A table with a fixed center section and side flaps that can be lowered or raised and held up with various types of supports.

dropped-pendant lighting
Simple, suspended luminaires or lighting fixtures dropped from the ceiling with a cord or chain.

drum
A cylindrical portion of a building used as the base for a dome.

drywall
Another term for Sheetrock or plasterboard; wall material made of pulverized gypsum rock.

ductwork or ducts
Metal or plastic pipes that funnel heated or air-conditioned air throughout an interior.

duplex
An dwelling that is similar to a twin home—two units sharing one roof and foundation.

durable or permanent finishes
Chemical or decorative finishes that remain on the fabric through repeated cleaning.

durable press calendering
A decorative mechanical finish that resin presses for durability and pattern impressions.

Durel
A registered trademark of Celanese for olefin.

durry rugs
See dhurrie rugs.

dust panel
A panel, usually of hardboard, placed between drawers to keep dust and other objects from passing between levels.

dust ruffle
A gathered, pleated, or tailored fabric covering that extends from the mattress of a bed to the floor.

dutch door
A double door, split in half, with independent top and bottom sections.

duvet
A nondecorative comforter that is covered with a removable cover.

dye lot
A single run of color printing of wallpaper or fabric, using a particular batch of dye. Background and decorative design colors may vary with each new dye lot.

dyeing
The process of coloring done in one of several stages: in the viscose solution (man-made fibers) or stock in fibers (natural fibers), in the yarn state or in the fabric piece goods state.

dyestuff
A water-soluble coloring matter used to make a dye bath solution.

Dynel
A registered trademark of Union Carbide for modacrylic.

Eames, Charles (1907–1978) and Ray
An important husband-wife design team responsible for several modern classic furniture pieces.

Early American (1650–1750)
A general term for American Provincial or country New England interiors.

Early Christian
The architectural period following the official recognition of the Christian church by the Roman government from A.D. 330–800.

Early Georgian (1700–1750)
Architectural period that first brought the design and elegance of the English Renaissance to America.

ears
Moldings on panels, door frames, or chimneypiecs that break to form small molded squares or ears at the corners.

earthenware
Coarse and inexpensive ceramic body used for dinnerware and accessory pieces.

easements
Short bends in the handrail that allow it to change direction.

echinus
An oval-shaped molding between the shaft and the abacus on a column.

eclectic
A mixture of stylistic influences or a mixture of styles.

economy
The relative cost of items as it relates to an allotted budget.

effects of crowding
The effects of crowding are inordinate exposure to sounds, smells, and touch.

efficacy
Lumens per watt is a measure of the efficacy or efficiency of the light source.

egg and dart
A molding of alternating egg shapes and dart or arrowhead shapes.

eggshell enamel
A hard finish semigloss paint.

egress
The way out; the exit.

eight plex
An apartment building containing eight units.

elements of design
The tactile portion of interiors that can be manipulated by the designer. These are space, shape or form, mass, line, texture, pattern, light, and color.

elevation
A flat, two-dimensional drawing of a straight-on (orthographic) view of an object, an exterior facade, or an interior wall.

Elura
A registered trademark of Monsanto for modacrylic.

embellishment
Decoration or ornamentation added to an object or an interior.

embossed wall coverings
Wallpapers with an imprinted, three-dimensional design.

embossing
A decorative calendering finish where a three-dimensional pattern is imprinted into the fabric. The finish is usually nondurable.

embroidery
The hand or machine stitching of threads or yarns to create a pattern on the surface of an otherwise completed fabric.

emphasis
A principle of design that indicates attention is given to a certain area within an interior. Emphasis is also called focal point.

Empire (1804–1820)
The period in France associated with Napoleon. Known as American Empire in the United States (1820–1860).

enamel paints
Oil-based or sometimes water-based paints that are hard and glossy.

enameled glass
Glass that has been encased with an opaque vitreous layer.

Encron
A registered trademark of American Enka for polyester.

energy consciousness
A term often associated with window treatments—covering windows to keep in winter heat and exclude summer solar gain or heat.

engravings
Prints made from a hand-engraved metal plate.

Enjay
A registered trademark of Eastman Kodak for saran.

Enkrome
A registered trademark of American Enka for viscose rayon.

entablature
A decorative architectural section made up of a cornice, frieze, and architrave.

envelope construction
A passive solar building system where air circulates in a double-wall construction around the house including a south-facing solarium.

epoxy paint
Used to paint over metal or water. Contains hardeners.

equilibrium
A state of physical or visual balance or equality.

ergonomics
See biotechnology.

Estron
A registered trademark of Eastman Kodak for acetate.

etch or burn-out printing
A decorative chemical finish printed with acid to burn out one fiber, usually cotton in a cotton/polyester blend, to leave a sheer pattern.

etched glass
Glass that has been engraved with a pattern by hand or by use of an abrasive cutting tool, a corrosive substance, or sandblasting.

etchings
Prints made from metal plates that have patterns and designs chemically etched into their surface.

European handmade rugs
French Savonnerie and Aubusson, Portuguese needlepoint, and Spanish rugs.

evaporative cooling system
Also called *swamp cooling*, the system is based on air flowing through a wet pad. Useful and economical in arid climates.

execution
The final phase of the design process where the design plans are implemented.

exposed aggregate
Pebbles set into and protruding above a concrete base. Hard flooring and wall material.

exterior veneer
The finish building material on the exterior, such as masonry (brick, stone) or siding (metal, wood, stucco).

extrude/extrusion
To force out through a small opening; a method used to form tubular steel. Also, manmade fibers formed by forcing a viscose solution through a spinnerette.

eyeball spotlight
A recessed spotlight that shines at an angle on a wall or object.

F lamp
A flame-shaped, often fluted lamp for decorative fixtures such as a candelabra.

fabric art
Handwoven or constructed fabric or textile pieces that hang on the wall.

fabric shades
Vertically or horizontally operated shades of fabric, including roller, Roman, balloon, Austrian shades.

fabric-backed wall coverings
Heavy wall coverings made sturdy and substantial with a fabric, rather than paper, backing. Used for vinyl and nonresidential wall coverings.

facade
The front or principal face of a building.

face weight
Yarn weight of carpeting per square measure. Heavier weights indicate more face or pile yarn, or greater density.

fanlight
A half-circle or half-elipse shaped window placed above a door or in a pediment.

fauteuil
French term for an open armchair.

federal
The post-revolutionary American period from 1790-1830.

feldspar
Crystalline materials mixed with kaolin to make porcelain.

felt padding
Animal and/or synthetic fibers compressed and needlepunched; used for carpet underlay to protect carpet without great resilience.

fern
A plant with large feathery fronds but no seeds or flowers.

festoon
Another term for swag, a half circle of fabric pleated or folded on the ends.

fiber felt padding
See felt padding.

Fiberglass or glass fiber
A synthetic mineral fiber made of spun glass used for insulation, tub enclosures, and contract draperies in past years. A registered trademark of Owens-Corning for glass fiber or fiberglass.

Fibralon
A registered trademark of Fibron for olefin.

Fibro
A registered trademark of Courtaulds for rayon.

FIDER
The Foundation for Interior Design Education and Research, which establishes standards for design education. Also a design school accrediting body.

fieldstone
Any type of large rugged rocks used for flooring or walls.

filament
The continuous man-made fiber strand extruded through the spinnerette. Filaments are combined and spun into threads or yarns. Natural filaments are silk and horsehair.

fillers
Preparatory materials for surfaces to be painted. Used to fill in nail holes, cracks, or other imperfections.

filling yarns or weft
The set of yarns woven crosswise into the set of long warp yarns that are threaded onto a loom.

Fina
A registered trademark of Monsanto for acrylic.

fine arts
The arts of architecture, painting, drawing, sculpture, and printmaking, as well as music, literature, drama, and dance.

finial
A finishing ornament for a pediment, a post, or spire.

finish carpenter
A craftsman who creates custom woodwork and cabinetry.

finish package
The woodwork in an interior, including items such as built-in shelving, cabinets, case piece units, baseboard/door/window trim, and railings.

finish plumbing
The installation of sinks and toilets and faucet hardware.

finished length
The length of a finished, hemmed fabric window treatment.

finished pile weight
Weight in ounces per square measure of finished carpeting.

finishes
These are a group of finishes that render a fabric more resistant to bacteria, static, wrinkling, flammability, insects, soil, humidity damage and increase insulative qualities. A general term for processes that do one of the following: prepare a fabric for coloring, give functional protection, dye or print a fabric, or add aesthetic or decorative effects to a fabric. Clear liquids used to seal and finish stained or painted surfaces.

fire alert system
A network or single unit that senses heat or smoke then alerts the occupants through a shrill noise that danger is eminent.

fire retardant
Certain man-made fibers such as modacrylic, saran, and PVC which resist burning but are not flame-proof.

firebox
The part of the fireplace that contains the fire.

fireplace insert
An enclosed stove unit that can be placed in an existing fireplace to make it more efficient.

fish-scale shingles
Small shingles with round or pointed sawtooth ends used to create decorative surface effects on the nineteenth-century Queen Anne-style houses.

fixed window
A window that cannot be opened.

fixture, or luminaire
The structural or decorative unit that holds the lamp or bulb and the electric connectors. In fluorescent and HID lighting, it also contains the ballast.

fixture
Something that is fixed in place or an element or feature of a setting. Pieces other than typical furniture that are placed in the environment by the designer, such as pieces of specialized equipment, custom-designed work spaces, or counters. Plumbing fixtures are the sinks, toilets, and various bathtubs and hot tubs. Lighting fixtures are also called *luminaires*.

flagstone
Hard, nonresilient stone that splits into sheets, used for paving and flooring.

flame resistant
A term referring to fabrics such as wool, silk, nylon, olefin, and polyester that do not ignite easily, are slow-burning, and will often self-extinguish.

flame-retardant finishes
Chemical finishes that make a fabric that is constructed of a flammable fiber become resistant to fire ignition and spread. Chemical applications that render a fabric less flammable.

flame-retardant paints
Paints with additives that inhibit combustibility.

flammability resistance
Ability of background textiles to resist catching on fire and/or sustaining a flame. Nonresidential code requirement.

flammability tests
Tests that measure the rate of ignition, the rate of flame spread when the source of the fire is removed, how long the fabric continues to burn, how long it remains in a red-glow state, and the density and toxicity of the fumes. These tests are conducted to meet stringent nonresidential state and local fire codes.

flammable or inflammable
A term that refers to fabrics, such as cellulosic cotton, linen, rayon, and acetate, that easily catch on fire or are highly combustible.

flat
An English term for a rented or owned apartment.

flat paint
Any type of paint that dries to a matte or nonshiny finish.

flatbed screen printing
The traditional method of stencil silk-screen printing where screens are manually or mechanically moved and paint squeegeed across by hand.

flatwork
Concrete laid flat for foundation and garage floors, sidewalks, and driveways.

Flemish gable
A gable incorporating steps, curves, or a combination of steps and curves.

flexibility
The ability of a fabric to stretch and rebound to its original shape; a necessary characteristic in upholstery fabrics.

flexible wall coverings
A general term for wall coverings that may be bent or manipulated to fit a shape or surface.

flickering light
An uneven source of light such as candlelight, firelight, or electric lamps that imitate this effect.

flitch
The half or quarter log that is cut to make lumber for furniture construction.

floccati rugs
Area rugs woven or knitted with tufts of sheared goat's hair left in its natural cream or brown color.

flocked carpet
A method of producing a carpet pile similar to velvet. Fibers are electrostatically charged, then embedded in a glue-coated fabric backing.

flocked wallpapers
Wallpapers with chopped fibers affixed to the surface in a decorative pattern.

flocking
A decorative process of adhering patterns of tiny fibers to the surface of a fabric; often seen in sheers and flocked dotted swiss fabrics.

floodlight
A reflective lamp spotlight with a wide-beam spread.

floor lamp
Luminaires designed to sit on the floor for task or general lighting.

floor plans
The two-dimensional layout of rooms. Part of the working drawings and blueprints used to construct a space.

flowing lines
These are a type of curved lines that suggest graceful continuous or growing movement.

flue
The chimney pipe above the firebox in a fireplace.

fluoresce
To glow or become fluorescent.

fluorescent light
Produced by an arc, or discharge, between two electrodes inside a glass tube filled with very low-pressure mercury vapor that produces ultraviolet (invisible) radiation in wavelengths. These activate the white phosphorus lining of the lamp, causing it to glow and converting the ultraviolet energy into visible light.

fluorescent lighting
Artificial or man-made lighting produced by charging mercury argon gas. Light is clear and relatively shadowless. Cool fluorescent lighting may give colors a bluish cast.

flush door
Flat doors with no raised or sunken panels.

flush-face fireplace
A fireplace whose planes are flush with the wall in which it is built.

flute
A groove in the shaft of a column.

flying buttress
A horizontal brace that spans from the wall to a supporting abutment and receives the outward thrust of the wall.

foam rubber pads
Carpet underlay of foam rubber.

foam wall coverings
Lightweight, insulative wall coverings of foam, often with a printed or embossed pattern, in rolls or squares.

focal point
Also known as emphasis or center of interest, a focal point draws the eye to an area or object and holds the interest of the viewer. Architectural focal points include picture windows and fireplaces.

foil/mylar wall coverings
A mirrorlike shiny or reflective background.

folded plate system construction
A building system of thin reinforced concrete in a folded, zigzag roof pattern.

folk rugs
Flat tapestry rugs handmade by an ethnic group in native design and color.

footcandles
A measurement of the amount of direct light hitting a surface.

footlamberts
A measurement of the amount of light reflected off a surface.

forced-air heating system
A conventional furnace-powered heating system where the hot air is blown through ducts and enters rooms through registers.

form
The three-dimensional shape of an object.

formal areas
The spaces in residential design where structured visiting, dining, and entertaining take place away from kitchen and other work spaces.

formal balance
Another term for symmetrical or bisymmetrical balance.

Fortrel
A registered trademark of Celanese for polyester.

foundation
The cement footings and basement walls that support the building.

four plex
A four-unit apartment building.

frame
A case or border made to enclose a picture.

framing or framework
The wooden or metal skeleton structure used for the majority of buildings today.

Frank, Jean-Michel (d. 1941)
French designer of the Parsons table.

freestanding fireplace
A self-contained fireplace unit that is away from the wall.

French door
Double casement-type door that opens in or out.

French Empire
The period c. 1804–1820 during the time of Napoleon in France.

French Régence
The period from 1715–1723 between the reigns of Louis XIV and Louis XV in France.

French wax calendering
A high-gloss ciré, a resin-wax pressed into the surface of a fabric with a heavy iron roller.

French window
Double casement windows that swing in or out from the center.

fresco
A painting made on fresh wet plaster with pigment and lime water.

fretwork
Patterns of flat interlocking bands or trelliswork.

friction calendering
A nonresin finish that produces a moderately glazed surface.

frieze
A tightly twisted saxony cut pile carpet. Also, the section of the entablature above the architrave and below the cornice. Also, a horizontal band of sculpture or painting.

full spectrum lighting
Light that contains all color wavelengths.

function
A normal or characteristic action or some duty required in work. Used here to refer to anything that takes place within a given environment.

functional finishes
See chemical finishes.

fuzzing
The working loose of fibers to the surface of the textile.

furnace
The mechanism that heats air or water by electricity, natural gas, coal, or oil and blows

the heated air through ducts or pumps hot water to the registers of occupied spaces.

fuse-bonded carpet
Carpet yarns directly tufted into a liquid rubber or latex backing that solidifies to hold in the tufts.

G lamp
A spherical or globe-shaped bulb.

gable
The triangular end of a house formed by the pitched roof.

galerie
A covered porch on the houses of French influence.

gambrel roof
A roof line with a double pitch, flatter at the top, and steeper at the bottom like a red barn.

garret
Same as attic.

gazebo
A small, open garden house.

general lighting
Overall lighting that covers a large area, often in the form of overhead luminaires.

generic
A general type of man-made fiber that is significantly different from other man-made fibers and thereby has been granted a name, such as nylon, by the Federal Trade Commission. Within each generic group are up to dozens of trademarks or trade names produced by various chemical companies.

genuine
Wooden furniture construction with veneers of a particular wood over hardwood plywood on all the exposed parts of a piece.

geodesic dome system construction
A building system enclosing spaces with curved, triangular steel truss work. The interior structure must be independent of the dome.

geometric design
A classification of decorative design based on geometric shapes: circles, squares, rectangles, and triangles.

Georgian
A term used to describe design during the period while Georges I–IV were on the throne of England.

gilded glass
Glass that has been encased in a layer of gold.

ginger jar
A bulbous oriental ceramic pot and lid, designed to hold ginger.

gingerbread
The decorative trim used on Victorian buildings.

glare
Strong, steady, daylight or artificial light that can cause irritation, fatigue, and heat buildup.

glare-free
Lamps that have silvered lining.

glass
A hard, brittle material of molten silica sand and soda or potash, lime, and possibly metal oxides. Clear, transparent, or colored; used for window glazing, mirrors, walls.

glass, architectural glazing
Glass used to fill window openings; term usually refers to nonresidential installations.

glass block
Semihollow blocks of translucent glass primarily for non-load-bearing walls.

glass curtains
A historic term for sheers shirred onto a curtain rod and placed next to the glass.

glass tile
Vitrified tiles of dense glass composition. Imported from France.

glaze
A colored or transparent liquid applied to clay objects that hardens and becomes glasslike when baked at high temperatures.

glazing
The process of filling an opening with glass. Also, transparent paint colors overlayed in sequence, producing various gradations of color in a painting.

glide
The mechanism on the bottom or sides of a drawer upon which it slides.

gloss enamel
Hard, oil-based paint that dries to a shine or gloss.

gold electroplate
A process for creating gold-plated silverware.

gold leaf
Extremely thin sheets of gold used in gilding.

golden mean
A pleasing line of division that is placed between one-half and one-third of the height or length of an object, such as tie-back draperies or a chair rail.

golden section
A theory of pleasing proportions based on the sequence 2:3:5:8:13:21, ad inf., where a portion or section of a line relates best to its neighbors in measurements of these or equivalent increments.

Gothic
A period and style from A.D. 1150–1550 in western Europe, characterized by pointed arches and steep roofs.

Gothic arch
A pointed arch that is the principal form in Gothic architecture.

gouache
Any water soluble, opaque watercolor. Often used as a synonym for tempera.

gradation
A type of rhythm where sizes of shapes gradate from large to small or small to large. Also seen in varying color values from dark to light or from light to dark.

grain
The markings and textures in a piece of wood created by the arrangement of the fibers.

granite
A very hard crystalline rock used for floors and walls.

graphic art
Artwork such as posters, fashion illustrations, and book illustrations created primarily for commercial purposes that have aesthetic merit.

graphic artist
A designer who specializes in two-dimensional sinage, graphics, type, and design motifs or logos.

graphics
The visual signs in a retail space that direct customers to departments or to certain goods. Also, the term used for putting on paper the stages of space planning from bubble diagrams to the finished floor plans.

grass cloth
Woven grasses laminated to a paper backing and used as wall covering.

gray goods or greige
Woven fabrics in their natural fiber state before bleaching and prefinishes. Pieces of bolt length may not be gray but a dingy off-white.

grazing or graze
Light shining at a very steep angle that emphasizes the texture of the surface.

great hall
The large, multipurpose area in the English Medieval house.

great room
An open area in contemporary homes that combines the living room, family room, dining, and perhaps the kitchen, office, and/or library.

Greek Revival (1820–1860)
Architectural style that contained American Empire interiors.

greenhouse effect
The captured solar heat from long sun rays penetrating through glass and bouncing off materials and furnishings, becoming shorter, weaker, and unable to repenetrate the glass.

greenhouse window
Projecting glass box for growing plants.

grid screens
Hard window treatment of slats of wood arranged in a grid and used to filter or diffuse light.

grounding receiver
The third hole in an electric outlet required for fixtures and appliances that consume a lot of power to be connected into the circuit and to prevent electric shock.

gum arabic
A sticky substance from gum trees that is soluble in water and hardens when exposed to air, used as a vehicle for watercolor.

gypsum board
See wallboard.

hand
The relative softness or coarseness of a fabric; the way it feels to the touch.

hand printing
Processes such as batik, tie-dye, block printing, and hand silk-screen and stencil printing.

hand-printed wall coverings
Paper or vinyl-coated wall coverings that are hand silk-screen printed in custom or limited designer patterns.

handicapped
Those who are physically disabled or mentally retarded.

handrail
The rail for grasping while ascending a stair.

hard window coverings
Art glass, blinds, screens, shades, and shutters.

hardboard
Compressed wood fibers formed into panels with embossed designs or a wood/plastic laminated surface.

hardware
The metal fittings on furniture such as drawer pulls and keyhole covers. Also, the machine components that make up a computer: the keyboard, the computer power drive unit, the monitor or screen, the printer, and the plotter.

hardwood
Tough, heavy timber of compact texture taken from trees with broad, flat leaves such as oak and walnut.

harmony
A congruous combination of parts into a pleasing whole; the result of unity and variety balanced together in an orderly, agreeable arrangement.

hearth
The slab that forms the base of a fireplace and extends into the room.

heat gain
Solar heat that penetrates the interior through glass; desirable in winter and undesirable in summer.

heat loss
The interior heat lost in winter back through glass to the outside. To prevent heat loss, movable insulation or insulative window treatments are employed.

heat setting
The setting in of permanent creases or folds in polymer fabrics by heating the fold to the point of polymer flow (beginning to melt), then rapidly cooling the fabric.

heat-transfer printing
Decals that are dispersed-transferred from waxed paper to a cloth under heat and pressure.

Hepplewhite, George (d. 1786)
An important English furniture designer who produced a series of drawings published as *The Cabinet-Maker and Upholsterer's Guide.*

Herculon
Hercules' registered trademark for olefin.

HID (high-intensity discharge) lighting
HID lamps establish an arc between two very close electrodes set in opposite ends of small, sealed, translucent or transparent glass tubes. The electric arc generates heat and pressure high enough to vaporize the atoms of various metallic elements inside the lamp, causing the atoms to emit large amounts of visible-range electromagnetic energy.

high contrast
The difference between small areas of light and the dark area surrounding it.

high key
All colors in an interior that are light or high in value.

high rise
A building containing several levels or floors of apartments, condominiums, or offices.

high tech
A product of high technology.

high values
Light variations of a hue; a hue with various amounts of white added.

highboy
A tall four or five drawer chest mounted on a dressing table (lowboy). Also known as a tallboy.

high-contrast values
A wide division of color value in an interior—very light colors contrasted with very dark colors.

high-efficiency furnace
A furnace that uses less energy and delivers a higher output. The unit costs more initially.

high-gloss paint
Any paint that dries to a very shiny finish.

high-hatter
Luminaire recessed very deep in the ceiling with the lamp high inside the fixture.

hiking up
The shrinking of a fabric that has absorbed moisture then dried.

hipped roof
A roof without a gabled end that slopes in four directions.

Hispanic
Having to do with Spain or Portugal.

Hitchcock chair
See Hitchcock, Lambert.

Hitchcock, Lambert (1795–1852)
An American furniture designer known best for his Hitchcock chair with its black painted finish, stenciling, rush or cane seat, and delicate lines.

Hoffmann, Josef (1870–1956)
Member of the Vienna Secession and founding member of the Wiener Werkstette. He is best known for his design of the Prague chair and Fledermaus chair.

Hollofil
A registered trademark of DuPont for polyester.

hollow core door
A veneered door with a hollow core filled with cardboard honeycomb.

hologram
A three-dimensional image projected by splitting a laser beam.

hooded fireplace
A fireplace with a projecting hood to catch the smoke.

hook-and-loop fasteners
A two-part fastening system of nylon loops on one tape and a fuzzy nylon surface on another that stick together and can be pulled apart. The best-known brand is Velcro.

hooked rugs
A traditional method of making decorative rugs of strips of fabric, punched through a jutelike backing with a special hook.

horizontal lines
Line is an element of design. Horizontal lines serve to visually widen or lengthen an interior and, when dominant, produce feelings of relaxation and repose.

horizontal satin
See sateen.

hourglass
An old piece for telling time with two globes of glass connected by a narrow neck that allows a quantity of sand to pass during a specified time.

housed stair
A stair attached to walls on both sides.

hue
Another word for color, as the hue red. An important designation in the Munsell color notation system.

humidifier
An attachment to a furnace that adds moisture or humidity to the air. Heating interior air strips it of moisture.

hutch
See Welsh dresser.

HVAC
Heating, ventilation, and air-conditioning. In nonresidential architecture, it is the system that maintains an even temperature (around 72 degrees Fahrenheit) and circulates fresh air through the interior.

hybrid solar energy system
A passive solar system augmented with fans, ducts, blowers, or other mechanical devices.

hydrophilic
A fiber that readily absorbs moisture, such as natural and man-made cellulosics and natural protein fibers.

hydrophobic
A fiber that does not absorb moisture. Examples include polyester, olefin, and polyvinyl chloride (PVC).

IBD
The Institute of Business Designers.

IDC
The Interior Designers of Canada.

IDEC
The Interior Design Educators Council.

IDS
The Interior Design Society.

IFDA
The International Furnishings and Design Association (formerly the National Home Fashions League).

IFI
The International Federation of Interior Architects/Designers.

ikebana
Traditional Japanese method of arranging flowers according to strict rules of placement.

illusion lighting
The artistic science of creating illusion, or something that is not real, through specialty lighting.

incandescent lighting
Light produced by heating fine metal filament until it glows. Warm incandescent lighting produces a yellowish cast to colors.

independent living
Elderly or handicapped persons who are able to live at home and care for themselves because the space is planned to accommodate their needs.

indirect and isolated passive solar gain
Solar gain from a source other than the occupied space. Examples include greenhouses or solariums that can be closed off from the living or nonresidential space.

indirect lighting
Produced by throwing light against a wall, floor, or ceiling to light a general area.

infill
Materials used to fill the space between the timber frame of a building.

informal areas
Areas for relaxed, spontaneous living and entertaining.

informal balance
Also known as asymmetrical, optical, or occult balance, it is the state of equilibrium reached through the arrangement of unlike objects or parts on each side of a central point.

ingress
The entrance to a building.

in-house designer
An interior designer who is a salaried staff member of a large organization who is responsible for the interior design or facilities management of new and existing buildings owned by that organization.

insolation
Incident solar radiation, or the energy collected from the sun to power active solar panels/systems.

insulation
A material such as fiberglass that prevents heat transfer. Commonly used in batts (fiber blanket rolls), rigid panels, styrofoam beads, or other materials.

insulative finishes
A light to heavy coating that renders a fabric resistant to heat-cold air transfer.

insulative window treatments
Any window covering that deters heat loss and solar gain.

intaglio
Printing from plates where the design is recessed below the surface of the plate. Those recesses hold the printing ink.

intensity
The relative pureness or brightness of a color, as opposed to the dullness or neutralization of that hue.

intercom
An electrical system that allows people to communicate within a building; also carries taped or radio music heard through speakers.

interface
Interdependency of design phases that must be accomplished simultaneously or consecutively. Also, a computer term where different programs use similar commands. *See* computer interface.

interior architecture
The nonresidential aspect of interior design that may entail remodeling and work with building systems.

interior building systems
The systems that are a part of the interior: plumbing, HVAC, electrical.

intermediate, or tertiary, hues
Six hues on the standard color wheel that are produced by mixing a primary and a secondary color. They are yellow-orange, red-orange, red-violet, blue-violet, blue-green, and yellow-green.

interrelationship of functions
The way areas work together or depend on each other to function effectively.

inventories
Lists of possessions and items that must be accommodated in a design.

Ionic
Greek and Roman architectural style with scroll-shaped capital.

iron
A heavy black metal.

Itten, Johannes (1888–1967)
A colorist who taught at the Bauhaus in Germany and at Yale University. He authored several books, including *The Art of Color* and *The Elements of Color.*

jabot
A fabric top treatment that is essentially two cascades side by side, and usually placed between two swags.

jack-arch lintel
A trapezoidal lintel with a wedge-shaped keystone used as decoration above windows.

Jacquard
A loom attachment named after its French inventor that allows complex patterns to be woven in rapid succession. Jacquard fabrics include brocade and brocatelle, damask, lampas, matelassé, and patterned velvets.

jalousie window
A louvered glass window.

Jeanneret-Gris, Charles-Edouard (1887–1965)
Important architect/designer better known as Le Corbusier. Designer of several modern classic furniture pieces.

JIDER
The Journal of the Interior Design Educators Council.

joint
A closure such as the mortise and tenon where two pieces of wood are fastened together in furniture construction.

joists
The heavy supports that support the floor and rafters.

jute
A cellulosic bast fiber obtained from the inner stalks of the jute plant and grown in India. Its main interior use is as carpet backing.

juxtaposition
Colors that are next to each other or are closely related on the color wheel.

Kandinsky, Wassily (1886–1944)
A Russian artist associated with the Bauhaus.

Kanekalon
A registered trademark of Kanekafuchi for modacrylic.

kaolin
A claylike substance used in making porcelain. The name comes from *Kao-ling,* a mountain in China where kaolin was first mined.

keystone
The stone at the top of an arch that is angled on the sides, stabilizing compression and friction.

kilim rugs
Flat tapestry folk rugs that originated in Romania.

kiln
An oven capable of controlled high temperatures used for baking clay objects.

kitsch
A German term that describes bad taste and is applied to pretentious art.

knitted carpet
A sturdy pile carpet that is constructed by knitting with multiple needles.

knitted fabrics
Needle-constructed interlocking fabrics such as single and double knits, laces, rachel warp knits, arnache and malimo fabrics. Knitted fabrics offer speed of construction, variety in patterns, and lacy effects, and either stretch or dimensional stability characteristics.

Kodel
A registered trademark of Eastman Kodak for polyester.

kraft paper
A heavy plain paper used for wrapping or for craft projects that is sometimes used as a base for hand-printed wallpapers.

L'Ecole des Beaux Arts
A school of art, design, and architecture in Paris, France, noted for its emphasis on historical studies.

lacquer
A type of varnish made from shellac or gum resins dissolved in ethyl alcohol or other quick-drying solvents.

ladder-back
A chair back with a number of horizontal slats like a ladder.

laminated foam
One or more densities of polyurethane foam laminated together to form a single pad.

lamination
The process of building up in layers or attaching a single ply as with plywood, foam, or plastic laminates.

lamp
The technical term for light bulb.

lancet
A narrow, pointed arch window.

landings
The platforms of a stair where it begins, ends, or turns.

Lanese
A registered trademark of Celanese for acetate and polyester.

laser
A device containing a crystal, gas, or other suitable substance in which atoms, when stimulated by focused light waves, amplify and concentrate these waves, then emit them in a very intense, narrow beam.

Late Georgian (1750–1790)
The American period that utilized English Georgian design and Chippendale furniture.

latex
A rubber-based synthetic polymer extruded or sprayed on as a coating or backing to hold woven fabrics or tufted carpets stable.

latex paint
A water-based paint that is easy to apply and cleans up with soap and water when still wet.

lath
Thin strips of wood laid parallel and nailed onto building studs. Historic method of plastering walls is to apply it over lath.

lathwork
Grids or panels made with strips of lath, used as screens, trellises, or decorative trim on verandas.

latillas
Sticks laid across the vigas to form the ceiling of the Southwest adobe houses.

Latin cross
The Western Christian cross with a tail longer than the top and arms.

lattice
A panel consisting of metal or wooden strips, interlaced or crossed to form a grid with regular spaces.

law of chromatic distribution
A rule governing the distribution of color intensity or brightness. The most neutralized colors are used in the largest areas, and the smaller the size or area, the brighter or more intense the chroma proportionately becomes.

layered or compounded fabrics
A group of fabric constructions that require more than one step to complete. Examples include embroidery, appliqué, and tufting.

Le Corbusier
See Jeanneret-Gris, Charles-Edouard.

leaded glass
Glass windows made of small pieces held together with lead caming to form a pattern.

leather
The tanned hide of cattle or swine. Largely used for upholstery. Leather is strong, is comfortable, and has a long life span.

leather tiles
Actual pieces of leather cut into shapes and applied as wall or floor tiles. Resilient semi-permanent material.

leno or doup weave
A variation of the plain weave that has warp thread hourglass twists where the weft or filling threads are woven in.

letter of agreement
The legal contractual arrangement between the design firm and the client that spells out responsibilities and services of both parties.

level loop carpet
Woven or tufted carpet with an uncut pile of even loops. Both residential and nonresidential.

level-tip shear carpet
Woven or tufted carpet with some loops higher than others that are sheared or cut to the level of the lower loops. Surface has a smooth, velvetlike texture.

life-style
The whole way an individual or group lives.

light
An element of design that is broken into two types: natural (sunlight) and artificial.

light pipe
An acrylic pipe that conducts light along its corridor. The light source can be sunlight or artificial light.

light-as-art
A term that employs light as a medium to create artistic effects.

lighted-toe mold
Lighting under the toe-kick area of stairs or cabinets.

lighting plan
The portion of the working drawings or blueprints that show where the lights, switches, and outlets are to be placed in a building and how they are connected to each other and to the circuit-breaker box.

line
The deliberate connection of two points as seen in planes and outlines of shapes. An element of design.

line of credit
The total cost of merchandise that may be purchased by a designer on credit in behalf of the designer's clients.

line or outline lighting
Lighting the perimeter of an object to give emphasis or even lighting.

linen
The best known of the cellulosic bast fibers, obtained from the inner stalks of the flax plant. Linen is strong and absorbent and varies from a coarse jutelike texture to fine table damask linen textures.

linenfold
A medieval panel motif resembling folded linen.

linoleum
A soft resilient flooring of ground wood and cork, gum, color pigments, and oxidized linseed oil. No longer produced.

lintel
A horizontal crosspiece over a door or a window or between two columns.

lithographs
Prints made from a stone or metal plate to which the pattern or design has been applied with a special grease pencil or wax.

Loftura
A registered trademark of Eastman Kodak for acetate.

long-life bulb
An incandescent bulb that lasts from 2,500 to 3,500 hours.

loose cushions
Pillows that are part of an upholstered piece but left unattached in the upholstery process.

Louis XV period
The years between 1723–1774 during the reign of King Louis XV of France. Also known as the Rococo period and characterized by ornate, curvilinear, asymmetrical design.

Louis XVI period
The years between 1774–1793 during the reign of King Louis XVI of France. Also known as the French Neoclassic period and characterized by rectilinear, classically inspired design.

louvered door
Door with louvered panels.

louvers
Horizontal slats in a shutter, screen, or window, sloped downward (or movable) to control light and air passage.

low key
A color scheme in a variety of dark values.

low value
Hues that have been darkened.

lowboy
A low chest of drawers raised on legs, used as a dressing or serving table. With the addition of a tall chest, it becomes a highboy.

low-contrast values
Values near each other, such as dark and medium values or medium and light values or a range of middle values, for example.

low-voltage lamps
Bulbs that consume little energy.

lumber-core door
Same as solid-core door.

lumens
A measurement of the amount of light flow.

luminaire
The technical term for a lighting fixture.

luminous ceiling
Incandescent or fluorescent lights around which a box is framed and finished, with the cover over the lights made of translucent glass or plastic.

luminous panels
Fluorescent or incandescent lights set into a wall or floor and covered with translucent glass or plastic.

Lurex
A registered trademark of Dow Badische for metallic fiber.

luxury condominiums
Very expensive condominiums with many luxury items, details, and amenities.

luxury homes
Spacious or luxurious homes with high quality detail, cabinet work, furnishings.

Mackintosh, Charles Rennie (1868–1928)
Scottish designer/architect, influential with the Vienna Secessionists and designer of the Hill chair.

mainframe computer
A large computer into which smaller computer terminals or PCs can be accessed. Mainframes can handle complex data, problems, and computer-aided design with speed and accuracy.

maintenance
The labor required to maintain a material—tasks such as sweeping, vacuuming, dusting, mopping, scrubbing, waxing.

man-made cellulosics
Rayon and acetate, which begin as cellulosic wood chips or cotton linter, pulverized and blended with chemicals, then cooked into a viscose solution and extruded into a filament form.

man-made fibers
Chemically derived and extruded from a viscose solution.

man-made lighting
Artificial lighting—incandescent or fluorescent.

Mansard roof
A hipped roof with two pitches. The bottom pitch is very steep and the top pitch flatter, so it is usually not seen from the ground.

mantle
The projecting shelf of a chimney piece.

marble
A very hard stone cut into slabs and polished for floor and wall materials. Smooth and formal, white or colored with streaks of color.

marbling
Imitating polished marble stone with paint.

market, marketing centers
Convenient clusters of trade sources that market goods and services wholesale to interior designers.

Marlborough leg
A straight, square leg with a square foot.

marquetry
Patterns created by laminating contrasting pieces of thin wood (and other materials) into a veneered surface.

Marvess
A registered trademark of Phillips for olefin.

masonry block construction
Walls or foundations of cinder block or concrete block without any wooden framework.

mass
An element of design that denotes density or visual weight within an object. Heavier mass or density will often make an object appear larger than one that has little mass or empty space within its shape.

massing
Gathering or forming into a mass. The pulling of objects into a group so that together they have more visual weight or importance than they do separately.

master of arts degree
A degree that may be considered a terminal degree in interior design education.

master of fine arts degree
A degree that may be considered a terminal degree in interior design education. M.F.A. degrees require a fine arts skill and showing of work. It is considered the design education equivalent of a doctor of philosophy (Ph.D.) degree.

master of science degree
A degree that may be considered a terminal degree in interior design education.

masters
Those whose art has passed the test of time to become classic.

mat
A border of mat board or other material, used as a frame or part of the frame of a picture.

match
The same color from one dye lot to another.

materials and finishes board
Boards used to show pieces of the materials and finishes that have been selected for a design.

matte paint
Any paint that dries to a flat, nonshiny finish.

McIntire, Samuel (1757–1811)
An eighteenth-century architect and designer who produced exteriors, interiors, and furnishings in the Federal or Adam style.

mechanical printing
A general term for all color printing processes that utilize automation.

mechanical or surface treatment finishes
A classification of decorative finishes that include calendering, napping, and flocking.

media
The substances used to dilute paint, i.e., water for watercolor and turpentine for oil paint. Also the means or methods an artist uses to produce a work.

medieval
Characteristic of the Middle Ages from A.D. 800-1500.

Medieval Era (A.D. 800–1500)
The Middle Ages or Medieval Era in Europe was a time of poverty for the masses and the period of great cathedral building and colorful stained glass windows.

melamine
A synthetic compound used to make plastic laminates.

mementos
Remembrances or souvenirs of a person, a place, or an event.

memorabilia
Things and events worthy of remembrance.

mercerization
A process of treating natural cellulosic fibers, cotton and linen, with caustic soda to enlarge and make the fibers more uniform, increase the luster, and better accept and hold dyes.

metal
Aluminum, tin, brass, stainless steel, and other chemical compounds that are formed into strips, tiles, or sheets for use as wall and ceiling materials.

metal frame or space frame system
Strong, lightweight steel skeleton framework based on the forms of geometry.

metallic yarns
Historically, threads spun of silver and gold. Today metallic threads are of plastic-based or plastic-encased substances that will not tarnish and contribute glitter and shine to certain fabrics.

metameric shift
Colors appearing different under different lighting due to the spectral energy distribution in the materials.

metamerism
The effect of light on color that causes a color to appear different colors in different types of light.

metope
The space between the triglyphs on the frieze of the Doric entablature.

Mexican tile
Clay tile fired at low temperatures. Natural terra cotta color or hand-painted in bright colors, glazed and unfired.

micro-miniblinds
One-half inch wide concave metal slats held together with nylon cord.

Middle Ages
See Medieval Era.

Mies van der Rohe, Ludwig (1886–1969)
An important architect/designer associated with the Bauhaus. Designer of several modern classic furniture pieces.

millwork
Stock- and custom-milled woodwork in the form of cabinetry, shelving, panels, and molding.

miniblinds
One-inch wide, concave metal slats held together with nylon cord. Slat or louvers are adjustable and are excellent for light and glare control.

mini-mainframe computer
A computer about the size of a personal computer but with greater capacity and power somewhat similar to a mainframe computer.

mirror
Glass with the back coated with silver or a silver amalgam (compound) to give the surface a reflecting quality; used on walls, ceilings.

miter
To cut at a forty-five-degree angle. A joint where two diagonally cut pieces meet at right angles and are nailed or screwed together.

mobile home
A house trailer for temporary or permanent housing.

modacrylic
A synthetic long-chain polymer fiber consisting of 35 to 85 percent acrylonitrile units. It is a soft, buoyant fabric that is inherently flame resistant and used extensively for nonresidential draperies where fire codes must be met.

Modern Era (c.1919–present)
A general term for architecture and interiors of the twentieth century.

Modern International style
Simple, structural architecture and furnishings that began with the Bauhaus in Germany (1919) and spread throughout Europe and America.

modillion
A projecting decorated bracket; also called a console.

monitor
The computer hardware screen component.

monochromatic
A color scheme using one color in any of its varieties, plus some white and black.

Monvelle
A registered trademark of Monsanto for a nylon/spandex fiber.

mood lighting
Low-level lighting that creates an ambience or mood that is cozy or inviting.

Moor
A Moslem of mixed Berber (North-African) and Arab ancestry.

Moroccan rugs
Handmade pile rugs from North Africa. Geometric patterns, coarsely woven.

Morris, William (1834–1896)
A designer of the Arts and Crafts Movement who produced wallpaper, furniture, tapestries, carpets, stained glass windows, and accessories.

mortise and tenon
A joint that utilizes a square hole carved in one of the pieces being joined and a projection that fits the hole in the other.

mosaic
Small pieces of glass or stone fitted together and held in place with cement to create a pattern or design. Often used for floor, ceiling, or wall decorations.

mosaic tile
Small tiles fitted together with grout to form a pattern in floors, walls, and countertops.

mothproofing
A finish that renders a fabric, especially wool, unpalatable to moths and other destructive insects.

motivational lighting
A lighting specialty that utilizes brightness, dullness, and darkness to motivate people to behave in a predicted manner. It utilizes principles of psychology, as well.

motorized rods
Drapery rods that are electronically operable. Used for large or hard-to-reach installations.

movable insulation
Interior or exterior insulation that protects against excessive heat loss or solar gain.

movable louvered shutters
Wooden shutters with slats or blades that can be adjusted.

mullion
A vertical dividing piece in an opening, especially a window.

multilevel living
Housing that contains one or more changes of planes in addition to the main floor: an upstairs, downstairs, or step-down or step-up areas.

multilevel-loop pile carpet
A looped pile carpet with various levels woven or tufted to create texture or a pattern.

multiuse areas
Rooms or areas with more than one purpose or function.

Munsell theory
Based on three attributes—hue, value, and chroma—where exact color matching is possible through a notation system.

Munsell, A.H. (1858–1918)
American colorist whose system, based on hue, value, and chroma notation, is widely used in design.

murals
Wallpapers hung in sequence to depict a scene. Also, a large-scale wall painting.

nap
The fuzzy surface of a fabric formed by short hairs or fibers.

napping
A decorative finish that brushes up short fibers to form a pile on the surface of the fabric.

NASAD
The National Association of Schools of Art and Design.

natural
A wood finish without any added color or stain.

natural fiber rugs
Animal skins, berber rugs, cotton rugs, floccati rugs, sisal/maize mats, and wool rugs.

natural fibers
Come from either cellulosic sources (cotton, linen, jute), or protein fibers (silk, wool, leather) which are derived from natural sources.

natural light
Sunlight.

natural saturation point
The amount of naturally occurring white or black value in a pure hue according to the Munsell system for color notation.

natural thermal flow
The movement of heated air up and/or toward cold air and the consequent dropping of cool air.

natural traffic pattern
The pattern of movement users will follow in an environment if their circulation is not hampered or obstructed.

naturalistic design
A classification of decorative design that is a copy or representation of something in nature. It is realistic decoration or ornamentation.

Navajo rugs
Handwoven flat tapestry rugs in earth-tone neutral colors and geometric patterns. Woven in the southwestern United States by members of the Navajo tribe.

nave
The main section of the church where the worshipers stand or sit.

NCIDQ examination
A two-day, two-part examination administered to interior designers after a minimum of two years of professional work experience. Must be passed for full acceptance into several of the professional design organizations.

NCIDQ
The National Council for Interior Design Qualification.

needle constructions
Fabrics made or decorated with automated sets of needles, including knits, laces, some casements, and schiffli embroidery.

needlepoint rugs
Hand or machine rugs most often from Portugal with small stitches of wool yarn on an art canvas background.

needlepunched carpet
Carpeting constructed of fibers held together by needlepunching or interlocking the fibers by meshing together with barbed needles. Indoor-outdoor and nonresidential applications.

negative space
The area between the forms in a two- or three-dimensional design. Empty or void space not filled in with furnishings, accessories, or mass.

Neoclassic or Classic Revival (1760–1820)
The period in America influenced by the excavations of Pompeii and resultant Neoclassic French and English periods.

neon lamp
A thin glass tube containing a gaseous element (neon) that glows when charged with electricity. The tubes can be bent into any shape for artistic or advertising purposes.

neon lighting
The red spectrum of cold cathode lighting formed with neon gas.

network of lighting
Interconnected wiring of lights indicated on the lighting or wiring plan in nonresidential buildings.

neutralized colors
Any hue that is dulled or grayed or lessened in brightness or intensity.

neutrals
Black, white, and gray. Brown is a hue, derived from orange, but is often referred to as a neutral, as are beige, tan, and the colored spectrum of off-whites.

newel post
An upright that receives and supports the handrail at critical points on a stair.

niche
The rounded half-domed end of a room or a similar recess in a wall.

nicknack
A small ornamental article.

nogging
Brickwork used as infill between timber framing.

Nomex
A registered trademark of DuPont for nylon.

nonarchitectural lighting
Portable luminaires.

noncellulosic fibers
The range of synthetically composed man-made fibers that begin as chemicals and organic substances other than cellulose.

nondurable or soluble finishes
These are fabric finishes that are removed with repeated washing or dry cleaning.

nonglare glass
Clear glass with a faintly textured surface that does not reflect light.

nonresidential design
Interior design work where the client is not a residential occupant.

nonresidential wall coverings
Wall coverings that meet standards or codes for durability, fire safety, and low maintenance. Wider and in longer rolls than residential wall coverings.

nonresilient flooring materials
A category of materials that are hard and have no give or resilience.

nonwoven textiles
Comprise a group of fabrics such as felt, webbing, and films, that are processed into fabrics without going through the yarn stage.

Norman
The name given to the Romanesque architectural style in England.

nosing
The rounded edge of a tread.

novelty twill
A twill weave that chances direction to create a pattern such as herringbone. Also called *unbalanced twill*.

nylon
A long-chain synthetic polymer fiber that consists of amides linked to aramide ring molecules. Nylon is a versatile, durable fiber used extensively for carpeting and upholstery.

objets d'art
French term for any object of artistic worth.

occasional chair
A chair kept away from the main seating area that can be pulled up and used occasionally, as needed.

occasional table
A small table that can be moved and used for any purpose as needed.

occult balance
Another word for asymmetrical, informal, active, or optical balance. The balance is not the same on each side but is achieved through arranging until the composition "feels right" and is therefore somewhat mysterious.

oculus
Literally an eye. The opening in the dome of the Pantheon.

oil paint
Colored pigment mixed with linseed oil or varnish and thinned with turpentine.

oil-based paints
Paints that must be thinned and cleaned up with solvents or paint thinners. Durable, scrubbable finish. Requires a long drying time and has a strong, unpleasant odor.

olefin
A synthetic long-chain polymer fiber consisting largely of ethylene or proplylene. Olefin is durable and economical. Used for carpet face and backing and for upholstery.

one-turn stair
A stair that turns ninety-degrees at a landing.

onion dome
A bulb or onion-shaped dome of Near-Eastern origin.

open floor plans
The use of few or no walls in many areas of a floor plan.

open office planning
A large office space that is divided only by furnishing or module components to form the workstations.

open plan
A concept in interior and architectural planning where areas are left open, without wall divisions. The open areas can be used in a flexible manner to accommodate varying functions.

open riser stair
A stairway that is open because it has no risers.

open showroom
A wholesale trade source that allows clients to accompany the designer into the show-room.

open stair
A stair not attached to the wall.

operable window
Window that can be opened.

opposition
A form of rhythm (a principle of design) where right angles meet.

optical balance
Also known as asymmetrical, informal, active, or occult balance. The balance is judged by the eye, or the optical senses.

optical density
The appearance of a pattern or item as heavy or dense or filled in and therefore judged as heavy mass.

orders
The styles of Greek and Roman architecture.

ordinary bulbs
Incandescent lamps that last from 750 to 2,500 hours.

organizational tool software
Analyze, organize, synthesize information. Used for writing specifications, critical paths, and word processing.

Oriental rugs
Hand-knotted (handwoven) pile rugs from the Near and the Far East woven in complex floral or geometric patterns. Used for area, art, and accent rugs and wall hangings. May be very valuable.

orientation
The direction (N, S, E, W) windows face in a room. The natural daylighting of the different orientations each has a unique effect on colors.

Orlon
A registered trademark of DuPont for acrylic.

Ostwald theory
A system for analyzing color based on the color and the amount of white and black added to the hue.

Ostwald, Wilhelm (1853–1932)
A physicist who won the 1909 Nobel Prize for chemistry and who turned his research to color, producing the well-known book *The Color Primer.*

ottoman
Today, an oversized upholstered footstool. Sometimes called a hassock.

outbuildings
Buildings situated away from a house used historically for kitchens, dairies, carriages, or servants' quarters.

outlet
The electric device where a plug is hooked into the wall.

outlet strips
Prewired or plugged-in casings that contain several outlets in a row.

outlining
Painting contrasting colors or white values on architectural molding.

overcrowding
An excessive number of people working or living within a given space.

overlay
A sheet of velum or tracing paper placed over a rough design to improve and refine it.

pad painting
The application of paint with a flat fibrous pad.

padding
A general term for carpet underlay or the cushioning layer covering the springs in upholstery.

paint
A liquid oil, water, resin, alkyd, acrylic, or epoxy-based material that is applied by spraying, brushing, rolling, or pad painting. Dries to a flat, semigloss, gloss, or high-gloss finish.

painting
A one-of-a-kind, two-dimensional art form created with color pigments and a number of different substances (vehicles) that give the paint form and body.

palette knife
A small, usually flexible knife used to mix paint on the artist's paint tray (palette) or to apply paint to the surface being painted.

Palette theory
Another name for the Standard Color Wheel theory.

palisade wall
A paneled fireplace wall formed of boards and battens.

Palladian window
An arched window flanked on each side by lower sidelights.

palmer calendering
A process of fabric pressing (roller heat and pressure) which adds softness to the fabric hand.

paneled door
A traditional door formed with stiles, rails, and panels.

Panel-track wall fabric installation
Metal tracks available for installing fabric on the wall. Used most often in nonresidential settings.

paneling
Sheets of wood used for wall and ceiling finish materials. May be solid wood, or veneered (sandwiched).

Panton, Verner (b. 1926)
Designer of an important molded plastic stacking chair.

papier-mâché
A material used for the construction of furniture and accessories made from paper pulp and glue. During the nineteenth century these pieces were often painted black and inlaid with mother-of-pearl.

PAR lamp
Reflective parabolic aluminized reflector lamp with heavy, protective glass and a focused beam. Silvering is used to establish the beam spread and the reflective quality.

parapet
A low wall on the edge of a roof, bridge, or terrace.

parquet
The decorative, geometric arrangement of short lengths of wood plank for floors and sometimes walls.

Parsons table
A simple clean-lined occasional table with straight legs that continue at right angles into the line of the apron.

particleboard
A solid panel formed by compressing flakes of wood with resin under heat and pressure.

passive balance
Another term for symmetrical or formal balance where items are identical on each side of a central point, and therefore no judgment of the composition is needed—a passive type of balance.

paste
Thick glue or adhesive used to install wall coverings.

paterae
Oval (or round) shapes used as ornament, often decorated with rosettes.

patina
A finish that comes with time.

patio door
Same as an atrium door.

Patlon
A registered trademark of Amaco for olefin.

pattern
An element of design; the arrangement of shapes and perhaps value (light and dark contrast) or relief (high and low areas) brought together to make a random or predictable design.

pattern book
Books of patterns for houses, furniture, and architectural detail published for general use.

pattern repeat
Wall covering or fabric pattern measurement from the top of one pattern to the top of the next or matching the pattern horizontally.

payback period
The number of years that a solar energy system takes to pay for itself.

pedestal table
A table supported by a single member or pedestal. In order to be functional, the pedestal must flair at the bottom into legs or a wide platform to provide stability. In the eighteenth century, tilt-top pedestal tables were common in England and America.

pediment
A decorative design detail that originated with the triangular section of the Greek trussed roof. The pediment was adapted from a triangle into a rounded segmental pediment, a broken pediment, which is open at the top, and an ornate scroll pediment. Pediments are used for furniture and architectural embellishment.

pediment frieze
The sculptural design within the pediment.

peelable wall covering
Wall covering that can be peeled away from a substrate (backing or lining), which is suitable to be repapered.

pembroke table
An occasional table with drop leaves and a drawer in the apron.

pendant lights
Simple, suspended hanging lights.

pendants
Decorative downward projections used to embellish architectural and furniture designs.

pent roof
A narrow overhanging rooflike structure above the first story on Pennsylvania German houses.

Peretti, Giancarlo (b. 1940)
Italian designer of the Plia chair.

perfatape
A wide paper tape that is applied to Sheetrock seams with plasterboard compound or mud.

perimeter lighting
Lighting around the outside of a room or an area. Perimeter lighting visually expands space.

peristyle
A continuous row of columns around a building. Also used to designate the colonnaded garden area at the rear of the Roman house.

Perlon
A registered trademark of Bayer for nylon.

permanent background materials
Structural or finish materials that are not likely to be replaced due to their cost or difficulty to install or remove.

Persian rugs
The finest of the Oriental rugs, traditionally from Persia, today Iran. High knot count, complex, usually floral patterns.

personal computer
A small computer for home or small-business use.

personal space
The invisible "bubble" of space that surrounds us that we consider to be our own.

perspective sketch
A three-dimensional sketch or rendering of an interior space drawn in perspective with vanishing points.

pewter
A soft, dull-gray alloy of tin, copper, lead, and antimony used to make tableware.

phase
The steps of the design process that include programming, designing, construction, installation, and evaluation.

Phyfe, Duncan (1768–1854)
A New York furniture builder, originally from Scotland, known for his Regency-style pieces.

physics of light
A complex scientific study that includes, among other things, the concept that sunlight is made of a full spectrum of colors that range from red to orange, then yellow, green, blue, and violet. These colors are the portion of the electromagnetic spectrum called the visual spectrum that allows us to see objects and their colors.

piano nobile
The principal floor of a building; usually a raised first floor.

picking out
Highlighting features on molding, such as dentil trim or carved bas-relief, with paint.

piece
One bolt of fabric that varies from 45 to 150 yards.

piece dyeing
Coloring a length of fabric after it is woven into cloth.

pier
Same as a column but without its details and proportions.

pierced screens
Freestanding screens of complex design from India.

pigment
A nonsoluble coloring matter that is held onto the surface of the fabric with a resin binder. A dry powder that is the coloring agent for paint, ink, crayons, and chalk.

pilaster
A flat, false, decorative column.

pile
The surface of a carpeting that has depth. Rounded loops are called uncut pile, while cut loops are called cut pile.

pile density
Closeness of stitches (woven) or tufts of a carpet. Greater or tighter density yields a more durable product.

pile weave
A weave that utilizes a third set of threads that form a depth or a pile in the surface. Types of pile weave include velvet, terry cloth, and corduroy.

pillow sham
A removable decorative pillowcase.

PL lamp
Compact twin fluorescent bulb.

plain, regular, tabby, or taffeta weave
The interlacing of threads or yarns in a one-over, one-under sequence.

plain slicing
A method used to cut a log parallel to a line through its center that produces a vaulted or cathedral-like grain.

plan drawing
A flat, two-dimensional, scaled drawing of an environment as seen from above.

plane of light
A bank of light; a well-lit area.

planned development
A tract of land that is developed into housing of a specific style, size, price range, and type of housing (attached dwellings, single detached dwellings, luxury dwellings).

plantation shutters
Louvered shutters with wide blades. Used in the South during Colonial days as screens to encourage ventilation during the hot months.

plaster
A thick, pasty mixture of sand, water, and lime used for smooth and rough wall and ceiling textures.

plasterboard
Another name for drywall, Sheetrock, or gypsum board, plasterboard is a wall material made of pulverized gypsum rock and commonly used as a wall finish material.

plastics
Synthetically produced, nonmetallic compounds that can be molded, hardened, and used for manufacture of various products.

plate rail
A narrow shelf for displaying plates.

Platner, Warren (b. 1919)
Designer of the wire grouping furniture collection.

Platt, Joseph
Codesigner of the Parsons table. *See also* Frank, Jean-Michel.

pleated shades
Factory-manufactured polyester fabric shades permanently heat set into one-inch pleats. May be metallized on the reverse for energy efficiency.

pleated valances
A fabric top treatment that is given fullness through pleating.

plenum
The space between the suspended ceiling grid and the ceiling. This space often contains mechanical systems.

Plexiglass
A highly transparent, lightweight, thermoplastic acrylic resin made into sheets like glass. Unlike glass, it is not easily broken.

plies
Thin layers of wood laminated together to make plywood.

plotter
A computer mechanical drawing printer that can produce drafting, two- and three-dimensional illustrations, and perspectives.

plumbing
The systems that carry water, sewage, or central vacuums.

plumbing chase
A thick wall containing plumbing.

plush carpet
A tufted carpet with a dense, short, even pile in solid colors. Originally intended to imitate the pile of an Oriental rug.

plywood
A product made of thin sheets of wood glued together in layers.

pneumatic system construction
Air-inflated or air-supported structures.

pocket door
A door that slides into a pocket recessed in the wall.

podium
The base on which Roman buildings are built.

point or pinpoint
Spotlights a tiny area for emphasis or a glitter effect.

Polybloom
A registered trademark of Chevron for olefin.

polyester
A synthetic long-chain polymer fiber of polymer ester. A durable, dimensionally stable fiber that is highly versatile. Most sheer and semisheer fabrics are of polyester. Used for residential carpeting and scatter rugs and for wall covering fabrics that are often used in nonresidential interiors.

Polyproplylene
A modified olefin fiber used for artificial turf, tufted indoor-outdoor carpeting, and nonwoven (needlepunched) carpets and tiles. Also used for a primary and secondary backing for some carpeting. A registered trademark of Thiokol for olefin.

polyurethane
A synthetic resin used to make foam for cushions and as a base for varnish.

Pompeii and Herculaneum (destroyed A.D. 79, excavation began 1754)
Sister cities on the Bay of Naples (Southern Italy) that contained prosperous Classic Roman architecture, preserved by the ashes and lava mud flow of Mount Vesuvius. Archaeological excavations resulted in the introduction of the Neoclassic or Classic Revival style in Europe and America.

pool of light
A circle of light thrown by a downlighter or spotlight.

porcelain
The highest grade of ceramic. Made of fine white clay.

porphyry
A granitelike texture achieved by crisscross brushing, then stippling, spattering, and finally cissing paint.

portable computer
A keyboard, monitor and drive unit that folds into the size of a briefcase.

portable luminaires
Nonarchitectural lighting such as table and floor lamps or plug-in wall lights.

portable space heaters
Small units that produce heat for a small area or a room. Types include electric and propane heaters; they vary in their size, output, electricity consumption, and safety.

portal
The porch on a Southwest Spanish house.

portico
A porch formed by a roof with supporting columns.

Portuguese needlepoint rugs
See needlepoint rugs.

positive space
Space filled in with a two- or three-dimensional form or shape.

post-occupancy evaluation (POE)
The formal process of looking at a design once it is in use to see how well it is functioning.

potpourri
French term for the mixture of dried flower petals used to perfume a room.

poured seamless vinyl
A nonresilient hard flooring that is formed or poured on the site. A smooth, seamless floor that can be kept sanitary.

PPG
A registered trademark of Pittsburg Plate Glass for glass fiber or fiberglass.

Prang theory
Another name for the Standard Color Wheel theory.

prefinishes
Processes that prepare a fabric for coloring, decorative, or functional finishes. Prefinishes include scouring, preshrinking, bleaching, mercerizing, sizing.

prepasted wall coverings
Wall coverings with a dry paste or adhesive preapplied to the back which is moistened then pasted to the wall or ceiling.

preservation
Maintaining a building in its present state or the state to which it has been restored.

preshrinking
A prefinish process of subjecting a cloth to wet or dry heat to cause it to shrink and stabilize before further finishing or coloring.

pressed glass
Decorative glass formed in molds.

pretil
A row of brick trim used to cap the adobe walls of the Territorial-style southwest adobe houses.

pretrimmed wall coverings
Wall coverings with selvages trimmed off at the factory.

primary focal point
The main point of emphasis in an environment. The object, area, or grouping that first catches the eye.

primary hues
Red, yellow, and blue, as based on the Standard Color Wheel theory.

primers
Liquid preparations that seal the surface and prepare it for paint application.

principles of design
Scale, proportion, balance, rhythm, emphasis, and harmony (unity and variety).

printing
Applying color to a finished cloth by hand (batik, tie-dye, stencil) or mechanical processes (automated silk screen, roller, transfer).

printmaking
A method of mass-producing two-dimensional art pieces by various means. *See also* woodcuts, block prints, engravings, etchings, lithographs, and serigraphs.

priscilla curtains
Sheer, semisheer, or muslin curtains with ruffles on all edges, on the ties, and as a valance; they meet at the center or crisscross; a colonial style.

privacy draperies
A white, an off-white, or perhaps a colored fabric installed on a traverse rod next to the window to be drawn closed at night for privacy.

private zones
Areas within a home that dictate privacy: the bedroom and the bathroom, for example.

product design
The design of furniture, accessories, or other components that are marketed in the design field.

profile
An outline of characteristics, habits, background, and design preferences that helps determine the direction a design should take.

program
Everything that happens or must be accomplished in an interior. It also is the written document that describes what does or will take place in an interior.

programming
The research phase of the design.

programs, software
The disks that are programmed to operate the hardware or computer machinery to perform specific tasks.

progression
A type of rhythm (a principle of design) where shapes repeat in diminishing or escalating sizes or where colors gradate from light to dark. Also called rhythm by gradation.

projecting fireplace
A fireplace that projects beyond the wall plane to which it is mounted.

proportion
The relationship of parts to a whole in terms of size, detail, or ornamentation. Good proportion is pleasing and functional.

protein fibers
Natural fibers or fabrics whose source is animal based: wool, silk, leather.

provincial
Rustic; local; from the provinces or countryside; not from the city.

proxemics
The way human beings use space and the way that use is related to culture.

PS lamp
A pear-shaped incandescent lamp, often with a long neck.

pueblo
Communal dwellings of the Pueblo Indians.

pull shades
Flat fabric or plastic material on a roller rod, which is operated with a spring or pulley mechanism.

punch list
A check list of items to be completed before final building inspection and occupation.

pyracantha
A flowering bush that produces clusters of red-orange berries in the fall.

Qiana
A registered trademark of DuPont for nylon.

quarry tile
Rust-colored tiles that are fired at lower temperatures than ceramic tiles and valued for their natural terra-cotta coloration. Typically square or hexagonal shapes.

quarter slicing
A method used to cut logs where the blade meets the grain at right angles to the growth rings, resulting in a straight, striped grain.

Queen Anne Period
The period between 1702–1714 during the reign of Queen Anne of England.

quicksilver
An alloy of mercury and tin used for mirror backing.

quilted valance
Flat top treatment often with a shaped lower edge with an quilted pattern or an outline design.

Quintess
A registered trademark of Phillips for polyester.

quire
Alternate spelling for choir. *See* choir.

quoin
Projecting or contrasting brick or stone laid at the corner angle of a building.

R, ER lamps
Lamps with a built-in, reflective surface.

R-20, R-30, R-40
Indicate the degree of beam spread in reflector lamps.

Rabat rugs
Moroccan rugs in a deep, hand-knotted pile with simplified Oriental designs.

radial balance
A type of balance that is seen in the same way as radiation.

radiant ceiling panels
Electrical conduit or water (steam) heat plumbing in ceilings (or walls) that radiates heat.

radiation
A type of rhythm (a principle of design) illustrated by elements radiating out in nearly every direction from a central point, such as spokes of a wheel or concentric circles.

radiator units
Wall or baseboard units that contain steam heat or another heated fluid medium, permanent or portable.

rag rug
A plain weave rug woven with strips of fabric, historically rags or recycled clothing.

ragging and rag-rolling
Wet paint or glaze is partially removed by dabbing with a rag or rolling the paint off with a rolled rag.

rail
The horizontal section of a frame for a panel or door frame.

rain gutter
The metal gutter and downspouts that channel rain and snow runoff from the eaves down the side of the building to the ground.

rainbow roof
A curved, gabled roof attributed to ship's carpenters, used on some Cape Cod houses.

raised hearth
A hearth built on a platform or cantilevered in front of a raised fireplace.

raised-panel shutters
Solid wood shutters with routed recessed areas framing a raised panel or panels.

rambler
A one-story detached home with or without a basement. The social, work, and private zones are located on the main floor.

random-shear carpet texture
See level-tip shear.

rapid-start fluorescent lamps
Eliminate flickering as the gases quickly activate the phosphorus in the light. May also be controlled with a dimmer switch.

rattan
A climbing palm with slender, tough stems used to make wicker.

rayon
A regenerated cellulosic man-made fiber that imitates the luster of silk at a lower cost. Primarily used for drapery and upholstery.

rebar
Bendable steel bars set into concrete for reinforcement and to deter cracking.

rebonded foam padding
Chopped foam and filler bonded under heat and pressure; a widely used carpet underlay padding.

recessed adjustable lighting
Architectural luminaires that are fixed into the ceiling. The lamps can be adjusted to the desired angle.

recessed downlight
A canister that fits into the ceiling and casts pools of light downward.

recessed luminaires
A general term for luminaires that fit into the ceilings where the light is noticeable but the fixture is not.

reeding
Rows of parallel convex beads or moldings used to embellish a column or leg. If the piece is grooved with concave moldings, it is fluted.

refinement or refining
The process of placing overlays of tracing paper to improve a space plan design.

reflectance
The amount of light that bounces off, or reflects off, surfaces. Light or shiny surfaces are highly reflective.

reflecting glare
A shiny object causing a distraction in a task area.

refraction
The bending of a ray of heat, light, or sound.

Regency
The period or style of English architecture that paralleled American Greek Revival.

Regency (English)
The period between 1811–1820 while George IV was regent.

registers (heat registers)
The metal grill that covers the duct opening of the HVAC system.

regular weave
Another term for a balanced plain weave.

reinforced concrete
Concrete set with rebar or metal mesh to deter cracking and to give strength.

relationship of function
The working association of more than one function, such as the proximity of the food preparation area to the dining area.

relief printing
Printing from a pattern that stands out in relief, as is done with a block print.

Renaissance
The great rebirth of classical art and learning during the fourteenth, fifteenth, and sixteenth centuries.

rendering
An artist's conception or perspective of a finished building exterior or interior, usually done in full color.

repetition
A type of rhythm (a principle of design) where shapes, forms, lines, or colors are repeated in a congruous manner.

reproductions
Printed copies of an artist's work.

research
Examining all factors that influence a design.

resilience
The ability of a fabric or flooring to return to its original shape.

resilient
A material with some give or ability to bounce back.

resist or reserve printing
The fabric with a chemical paste that resists the dye, then dyeing the fabric. The area not printed receives the color.

restoration
A research, demolition, and reconstruction process to bring a building back to a specific state of its history.

retainer fee
A deposit given to the designer upon the client's signature on the letter of agreement that retains or hires the services of the designer.

retrofitting
Adding on active or solar systems to an existing building.

reverberation
Echoing of sound waves.

reversible cushions
Loose cushions that can be turned to avoid excessive soiling and wear.

rhythm
A principle of design seen in an interior as a visual flowing pattern or regular recurrence. Types of rhythm include repetition, alternation, progression or gradation, transition, opposition or contrast, and radiation.

rib
A projecting band on a ceiling or vault.

ribbonwork
Contrasting bands of brick and stone used for decoration on the nineteenth-century Eastlake-style houses.

riser
The vertical member of a stair between the treads.

Robsjohn-Gibbings, T.H. (1905–1976)
Designer of a group of Greek furniture reproductions including the klismos chair.

Rococo
See Louis XV.

roller painting
Paint application with a roller—a sleeve of soft fibrous pile fabric that can hold and release the paint evenly. Faster than brush painting. It tends to spatter but is very useful for large areas such as walls and ceilings.

rollikan
A flat tapestry folk rug from Scandinavia that often incorporates simplified floral patterns and stripes.

Roman shade
A fabric shade that folds up from the bottom accordion style. May be interlined for energy efficiency.

Romanesque
The medieval architectural period from A.D. 800-1150 based on Roman design.

roof monitors
Clerestory windows, skylights, and cupola windows that catch heat from the sun and allow ventilation for excess summer heat.

roof trusses
A joist and rafter system that forms the triangular construction of a roof.

rotary screen printing
A mechanized silk-screen process where the screens are wrapped around a circular drum that rotates the ink onto the fabric moving along beneath the rotary screens. It is a fast and efficient process.

rotary slicing
A method of shaving a continuous layer of wood from a log that has been mounted on a lathe, producing a broad, open grain.

rotogravure or roto
A printed pattern overlaid with layers of vinyl for sheet flooring.

rotunda
A round, domed room.

rough electrical
The wiring installed when the building is framed.

rough heating
The installation of furnace and duct or ductwork system when the building is framed.

rough plumbing
The installation of pipes to carry water and sewage and central vacuum.

round wire tufting/weaving
Carpet construction technique that yields even, round loops.

roundheaded arch
An arch formed in a perfect half circle, not flattened. A Roman or keystone arch.

row house
Another term for town house.

Rowland, David
Designer of the GF 40/4 stacking chair.

rubber
A natural or synthetic composition that yields a resilient, solid or marble-patterned flooring.

rubber-backed tufted carpet
Carpeting tufted into a foam rubber backing that serves as a pad or underlay. Direct glue-down installation.

rubbings
Designs made by placing a sheet of paper over any object with a flat, raised pattern and rubbing it with a special crayon.

rubble
Stone or rocks set or installed to produce an uneven, random surface.

rush
A grasslike marsh plant used to weave chair seats and floor mats.

rusticated
Rough-surfaced masonry or stone.

rya rugs
Deep pile shaglike rugs handknotted with abstract, contemporary patterns from Scandinavia.

Saarinen, Eero (1910–1961)
Architect/designer, creator of the pedestal furniture group.

safety lighting
Lighting required by code or building ordinance to protect the health and safety of the public. Examples include Exit signs, egress and aisle lighting, and lighting for stairs and landings.

sagging
Irregular elongation or stretching of a drapery fabric due to increased humidity or moisture in the air.

saltbox roof
A gabled roof with one slope that is longer and lower than the other.

sandstone
A granular stone that may be used as floor or wall materials, laid at random or in a rectangular, ashlar pattern.

sanitation
The elimination of dirt and infectious disease agents. A requirement for medical and food-preparation facilities.

saran
A synthetic long-chain polymer of vinylidene chloride. Saran is fire retardant and used alone or in fabric blends.

sash curtains
Sheer or semisheer fabric shirred (gathered) onto a rod at the top and bottom of the window frame.

sash window
A double window (one panel above, one below), that is opened by raising or lowering one of the panels that slides up and down in its frame.

sateen, satinet, or horizontal satin
A satin weave where the weft or filler threads float over five to eight warp threads, then are tied down under one in an irregular manner that produces a smooth surface.

satin or eggshell paint
A paint that dries to a finish slightly less shiny than semigloss but more lustrous than flat.

satin weave
A smooth, often lustrous fabric weave where warp threads float over five to eight weft or filling threads, then are tied down under one. There are no ridges or wales.

Savonnerie
A hand-knotted pile rug from France, originally woven at the Savonnerie Tapestry Works and patronized by King Louis XIV. Historic and contemporary patterns.

saxony
A carpet with a dense pile about one inch deep.

scale
A principle of design that evaluates the relative size and visual weight of objects. Classifications of scale include small or light, medium, large or heavy, and grand (extra large).

Scarpa, Tobia (b. 1935) and Afra (b. 1937)
Italian designers of the Soriana chair.

scatter rugs
Small rugs, sometimes called throw or area rugs, often a tufted cut pile used in residential areas where water is likely to spill or where dirt is tracked in. Usually of polyester or nylon.

schedule
The chart that indicates the finish material used on floors, walls, and ceiling and lists types of doors and windows.

scheduling
Arranging for subcontractors and craftsmen who build or finish portions of a building and its interior to complete their work within a time frame.

schematic diagram
The graphic evolution of space from the bubble diagram to the point of producing a finished floor plan.

schematics
Quick drawings used to generate or show ideas.

schools
Groups of artists with like philosophies whose work has similar characteristics.

Schreiner calendering
A heavy roller embosses tiny lines into the surface of certain fabrics to give a sheen or lustrous finish.

sconce
A wall-mounted luminaire.

screen printing
Another term for silk-screen printing.

screens
A general term for a sliding or freestanding frame filled with wood, paper, fabric, or other materials, which may be placed in front of a window or used as a divider.

scroll pediment
A pediment with a flat bottom and two curved volutes at the top, often with a finial between the volutes.

scrubbable
Wall coverings that can be repeatedly washed with detergent solutions.

sculpture
The art of fashioning figures and forms of wood, clay, plastics, metal, or stone.

sculptured carpet
A carpet with more than one height to the pile, which gives a pattern to the whole.

sculptured-loop
A multilevel-loop carpet, the same as embossed-loop carpet.

sealed environment
A building with nonoperable or fixed windows where HVAC provides warm, cool, and clean air.

sealers
A liquid used to prepare a surface for painting.

secondary focal point
The point (or points) of emphasis in an environment that is (are) subordinate to the primary focal point because of size, location, color, or other design factors.

secondary hues
Green, orange, and violet, as based on the Standard Color Wheel theory.

secretary
A desk with drawers below and a bookcase above.

security system
A wiring system that detects unlawful entry.

Sef
A registered trademark of Monsanto for modacrylic.

segmental pediment
A pediment with a flat bottom and a curved radius at the top.

semi-detached units
A term for housing that means portions of walls and roofs are common to two or more units.

semi-durable
A fabric finish that will withstand wet, but not dry cleaning.

semigloss paint
A paint that dries to a luster between flat and shiny; it contrasts nicely with both and hides fingerprints.

semi-trimmed wall covering
Wall coverings with only one selvage trimmed off. The selvage edge is overlapped with the next strip or trimmed off at the site.

semihoused stair
A stair attached to the wall on one side.

sericulture
Cultivated silk production.

serigraph
An art print made by passing ink through a fine screen that has been covered with a cut stencil to form the pattern. Also called silk screen.

serpentine
Literally, like a snake; a line that curves in and out as on a chest front or camel-back sofa.

shades
See pull shade.

shading
Blending painted color values from light to dark across a wall or ceiling.

shading devices
Interior or exterior window coverings that deter solar gain from penetrating the interior.

shag
A very deep pile carpet texture; generally not a dense construction.

shake shingles
Wooden roof shingles, somewhat irregular in width, that weather to a gray color.

Shakers
A late eighteenth-century, early nineteenth-century religious sect whose beliefs included the design of furnishings devoid of excessive decoration.

Shantura
A registered trademark of Rohm and Haas for polyester.

shape
An element of design that is the contour or outline of an external surface of a form.

shaped valance
A flat fabric top treatment with a shaped or curved bottom hem. Interlined with stiffening fabric and/or batting and sometimes quilted.

shed ceiling
A ceiling with a single slope.

sheer draperies and curtains
Transparent or translucent fabric hung next to the glass. Called draperies if pleated and hung on a traverse rod, curtains if shirred or gathered onto a curtain rod.

sheet vinyl
Rolls of vinyl in widths up to twelve feet, glued down directly to a prepared surface. May have a cushioned backing, and the thickness of the vinyl surface may vary with the quality.

Sheetrock
Also known as drywall, gypsum board, or plasterboard; a rigid wall material made of pulverized gypsum rock. See wallboard.

shellac
A finish film for wood made by dissolving the waste of the lac bug in denatured alcohol.

Sheraton, Thomas (1751–1806)
An important English furniture craftsman best known for the designs published in his book *The Cabinet-Maker and Upholsterer's Drawing Book.*

shingles
Wood, asbestos, or tile components commonly used as a finish material on angled (gable or hipped) roofs.

shirred curtains
Fabric gathered onto a rod with or without a ruffle at the top.

shirred valance
A fabric top treatment gathered onto a curtain rod.

shoji screens
Wooden frames and divider grids filled with translucent white mulberry or rice paper. Used in traditional Japanese homes and contemporary Western residential and nonresidential interiors as well.

showrooms
Wholesale businesses usually located in marketing centers where the designer may see lines of merchandise and place orders or buy furnishings.

shutters
Wooden planks, panels, or framed louvers used as hard window coverings. Available in a wide variety of colors, styles, and louver widths.

side chair
An armless chair without full upholstery.

side draperies
Stationary panels hung on each side of a window.

sideboard
A dining room serving piece with space for storing tableware. The French term *buffet* and the Italian terms *credenza* or *credence* are also used to describe this type of piece.

sidelights
A vertical, narrow row of windows used on each side of a door.

silk
A natural protein fiber obtained from the filament of the silk moth cocoon. Silk is lustrous, is smooth to slubby, and has a dry hand. It has long been woven into fabrics of luxury and prestige.

silk screen
See serigraph

silk-screen printing
A traditional method of stencil printing, done by squeegeeing ink through stencils on sheer silk stretched on wooden screens. Originally a totally hand technique, *flatbed printing* automates the moving of fabric under the screens and the raising and lowering of the screens, and *rotary screen printing* further speeds the process by rotating the pattern onto the fabric with no hand labor. Silk screening accounts for a large portion of printed designs today.

silver plate
Flatware made from an alloy of silver and nickel, electroplated with pure silver.

silvering
The process of coating with silver or silverlike substances.

singeing
A prefinishing process of passing the fabric over a gas flame to burn out unwanted vegetable matter or short fibers.

single glazing
Filling a window opening with one layer of glass.

single roll
One bolt of wall covering containing approximately thirty-six square feet.

single-hung sash
Sash windows where only the bottom section is operable.

single-wide trailer
A mobile home that is approximately twelve to fifteen feet wide and twenty to forty feet long.

sinuous wire spring
An essentially flat spring bent in a zigzag fashion used in upholstered furniture.

Sir Isaac Newton (1642–1727)
An English mathematician and philosopher who formulated laws of gravity, motion, and physics.

sisal and maize mats
Natural cellulosic fiber mats that are coarse and rough to the touch.

sizing
A thin liquid painted on a surface before hanging wall coverings. It seals against alkali, lessens the paste quantity needed, and provides some grip for the wallpaper.

sketches
A rough, quick illustration of a proposed space or a detail of the space.

skylight
An opening for light set into the roof and ceiling.

slat shutters
A rustic style of shutters made of vertical planks, slats, or strips of wood held together with two or more horizontal slats.

slate
A finely-grained metamorphic rock used for flooring. Colors vary from grays to greenish or reddish grays to browns and blacks.

slate roof
A roof covered with thin sheets of stone, used like shingles.

sliding windows
Windows that slide horizontally.

slipcovers
Fitted covers that can be placed over the original upholstery and secured with snaps or other fasteners.

smocked curtains
A type of gathered curtain heading.

smoke detector
A fire-alarm device that sounds when triggered by excessive smoke in the air.

social zones
Areas for formal or informal social interaction.

soffit
The trim applied to the eave, or the boxed projection above cabinets or over a sink.

soffit lighting
Architectural lighting built into a soffit.

soft window treatments
Fabric treatments: curtains, draperies, shades, and top treatments.

softening finish
A decorative finish that chemically or mechanically softens the hand or surface texture of a fabric.

software
Computer programs that accomplish specific tasks.

softwood
Light, easily cut wood taken from trees with cones such as pine and redwood.

soil-release finish
Allows a fabric to more readily absorb water and free up soil to be lifted out with mild detergent.

soil-repellent or soil-resistant finishes
These are sprayed onto the surface of a fabric, forming a temporary barrier that prevents soil from penetrating the fabric. If the soil or stain is not removed quickly, it can be forced into the fabric through tiny cracks in the finish as it is walked or sat upon. The soil may then be locked under the finish, making it very difficult to remove.

solar energy
The energy from the sun, called insolation, that heats space and water.

solar greenhouses
A greenhouse living space that is also a passive solar collector; a solarium.

solar heat gain
Heat from sunshine collected through glass walls or windows. May be absorbed, stored, and released through many of the hard background materials such as stone, tile, brick, and concrete.

sole proprietorship
An interior design business that is owned by one person.

solid
Wooden furniture construction with solid pieces of wood in all the external or visible parts of the piece.

solid-core door
A veneered door with a core of solid wood pieces.

solution dyeing
The addition of dyes or coloring matter to the viscose solution in man-made fibers before they are extruded. The dyes then become colorfast and will not fade. The process is more costly than other methods of dyeing and must be done well in advance of the finished product, making solution-dyed color somewhat risky in today's market of rapidly changing color trends.

solvent
A liquid for thinning and cleaning up oil-based paints.

sound board
An insulative material in rigid form that prevents audible sounds from being heard; usually used beneath drywall.

Source
A registered trademark of Allied Chemical for a nylon/polyester fiber.

South American rugs
Folk rugs from natives of countries such as Peru, Bolivia, and other South American countries.

space
An element of design consisting of a continuous expanse of distance without forms, which is divided with walls, partitions, and furnishings. Filled space is termed positive space and empty space is called negative space.

space heating
Heating the area or space where people live and work by passive or active solar means or by mechanical devices such as furnaces or space heaters.

space planning
The allotment of spaces to create a workable floor plan. The organization and division of spaces into rooms or areas to meet specific needs.

space-saving device
Any means of maximizing the existing space thereby making a space seem larger.

spandex
A synthetic fiber composed of segmented polyurethane, which has exceptional stretch, strength, and return. Used in stretch upholstery textiles.

Spanish rugs
Hand-knotted pile rugs with a coarse, sparse weave. Classified with folk rugs.

spattering
A method of adding texture to painted surfaces by flipping extra paint onto a surface with a filled brush.

special rodding
Drapery rods that can be bent and suited to custom or special installations.

specifications
The written list of materials and furnishings, itemized according to company, stock number, color, and other pertinent ordering information, and the location where the goods will be installed. Also, in nonresidential architecture, the criteria of minimum durability, cost, and safety requirements of finish materials.

spectral energy distribution
The inherent color characteristics of an object or material due to the type and amount of dyes or pigments. This can cause the object or material to appear as different colors under different kinds of light; also describes the color of the light source.

Spectran
A registered trademark of Monsanto for polyester.

spinnerette
The showerheadlike device through which man-made fiber viscose solutions are forced to create monofilament. The size and shape of the holes in the spinnerette can be changed to give various characteristics to the fibers.

spiral staircase
A corkscrew-shaped staircase.

splat
The vertical wood panel in the center of a chair back.

split complement
Consists of a hue and the two colors on each side of its direct complement.

split-entry home
A two-level home where the entry is located in the center, and the person entering walks upstairs to the kitchen/living/dining areas and the bedroom/bath areas, and downstairs to the family room, extra bedrooms, and storage areas.

split-level home
A three- or four-level home with half flights leading from one area to the next.

sponge rubber pad
Carpet underlay. The most common example of sponge rubber is waffle padding.

sponge texture painting
Applying paint with sponges for texture and color overlay.

sponging
Applying paint with sponges for texture and color overlay.

spotlight
A luminaire that directs light in one direction, casting a pool of light.

spray painting
Paint application through a spray nozzle. Fast and economical for large applications. Should be followed with a roller to smooth out the paint.

square feet or footage
The width multiplied by the length of a room or building. The two-dimensional floor space.

squeegee
An implement with a strong straight crosspiece edged with rubber, for spreading a thin layer of ink across and through a silk screen.

stabilizing
A prefinishing process that sets in the weave through heat treatments to the fabric.

stain
Color mixed with water, oils, or other agents applied to wood as part of the finishing process.

stained glass
Colored and clear glass set into patterns and hung in front of windows or used as the window glazing itself.

stainless steel
An alloy of steel and chromium.

stains
Liquids that penetrate wood with color.

stairwell
The open space filled by a stair.

Standard Color Wheel theory
Based on three primary colors—red, yellow, and blue—and the variations derived by mixing these plus black and white. Colors are arranged in a circle, with secondary and tertiary or intermediate colors placed between the primary colors.

standard finishes
Applied to fabrics to enhance durability. Also known as wet, chemical, or functional finishes.

staple
Short fibers that vary from approximately one-half to two inches. Staple yarns offer greater bulk, insulation, and area coverage.

stapled wall fabric
Fabric attached to a wall by staples.

starting step
The first step of the stair.

state of the art
The current or latest technology; the newest developments.

static resistance
The ability of a carpet to avoid conducting static electricity.

steel
A hard alloy of iron and carbon.

stemware
Designation given to fine drinking glass with raised bowls, stems, and bases.

sterling II
Flatware with sterling silver handles and stainless steel blades, tines, and bowls.

sterling silver
Finest type of silverware; 92.5 percent pure.

stickwork
Flat battens used on Victorian buildings to create patterns in imitation of medieval timber framing.

stiffening finish
The application of starches or resins, that may optionally be calendered or pressed in, to add crispness or stiffness to a fabric.

stile
The upright section of a frame for a panel or door frame.

stippling
Similar to sponging but uses a stippling brush to dab on a colored glaze or paint, revealing some of the base color.

stock dyeing
The coloring of natural fibers (particularly wool) in their most raw-goods state (stock) before they are spun into yarns.

stock plans
Floor plans from floor plan magazines that are mass-produced and purchased, usually by mail order, by anyone wishing to build that home.

stone
Any hard rock used for flooring or wall materials.

stone-enders
Seventeenth-century houses with stone-covered chimney ends, common to Rhode Island.

stoneware
A heavy, durable, thick pottery used for less-formal dinnerware.

storage
Space planned for keeping foodstuffs, linens, tools, clothing, and other items owned by people. It also refers to needs of a nonresidential interior to keep extra stock merchandise, office supplies, or other goods.

storm windows
Glass or plastic removable windows that add insulation. Summer storm windows are tinted as a shading device.

stove
A freestanding wood or coal burning heating unit.

straight lines
Lines that directly connect two points; horizontal and vertical lines.

straight run
A stair that makes no turns.

strapping tape method
A temporary method of attaching fabric to a wall. Rolls or circles of strapping tape are affixed to the wall and to the fabric.

strength or tenacity
The inherent ability of a material to withstand stress without breaking.

stretchers
Crosspieces used to brace and strengthen table and chair legs.

stringcourse
See beltcourse.

stringer
The supporting member in a staircase.

strip wood flooring
Hardwood tongue and groove strips one and one-half to two and one-fourth inches wide and two to seven feet in length.

strippable
A wall covering that can be stripped or completely removed from a wall. Applies to most vinyl wall coverings.

structural design
A basic or general category of design wherein the design is intrinsic to the structure—one cannot be separated without destroying the other.

structural systems
The components of new or remodeling construction that make up the structure: footings and foundation, the framework (or other systems) that support the building and to which the finish materials are applied.

stucco
Rough textured plaster or cement for covering walls.

stylobate
The base upon which the Greek temple rests.

subcontractor
A person who performs a single task in construction such as foundation work, framing, electrical, plumbing, HVAC, finish (millwork or woodwork), or tile or floor laying.

subfloors
The material (usually wood) nailed to the framework on which the finish floor materials are laid.

sundial
A timepiece that shows the time by a shadow cast by a pointer.

superinsulation
Extra heavy insulation of walls, foundations, ceiling, and attic areas to conserve energy; requires thicker than conventional walls.

surface-mounted fixture
A structural or decorative luminaire that is mounted onto the ceiling.

surface treatment finishes
See decorative finishes.

surround
The noncombustible material that separates the opening of a fireplace from the wall or mantel.

surrounds (tub or shower)
The tile, marble, or imitative plastic finish material used to protect the wall against water in showers and bathtub areas.

suspended ceilings
Ceilings formed of metal grids and acoustic panels, hung from the superstructure of a building.

suspended fixtures
Structural (pendant) or decorative (chandelier) luminaires hung on a cord or chain from the ceiling.

swags
Also called festoons. Semicircles of fabric folded at the corners to form a soft or precise curved fabric top treatment. Often finished with a cascade on each side of the swag or arrangement of swags.

swamp cooler
See evaporative cooling system.

swinging door (one way)
The typical side-hinged door.

symbolism
The use of historic color where each color held significance or symbolized a value.

symmetrical balance
Also called bisymmetrical, formal, or passive balance, it is mirror-image arrangement of parts or elements.

synthesis
Bringing together the research data in the programming process.

synthetic or noncellulosic man-made fibers
The group of fibers that do not begin as cellulose but as chemicals or other natural elements chemically altered or composed into a viscose solution and extruded through a spinnerette. This group includes nylon, acrylic, modacrylic, polyester, olefin, saran, spandex, vinyon, latex, fiberglass, and metallic fibers.

systems furniture
Component pieces that can be chosen and assembled to create work spaces according to the needs of the user. As needs change, new components can be added and unneeded elements can be eliminated.

T lamp
Tubular shaped lamp or bulb.

tab curtains
Flat panel curtains with tabs or strips sewn into loops at the top, then threaded over a dowel rod.

tabby weave
Another term for plain weave.

table lamp
Luminaires designed to sit on a table for task or general lighting.

tackless strip
The thin board with recessed-head tacks or staples protruding toward the wall. The strip is nailed down and carpet attached over the top to hold it in place for wall-to-wall installations over padding.

taffeta weave
Another name for plain weave.

tapestry
A plain or Jacquard weave of heavy decorative textiles.

tar paper
A heavy, black, waterproof paper applied to the roof before the shingles and sometimes on the outside of foundation walls.

task lighting
Bright, concentrated light for accomplishing specific tasks.

tatami mats
Woven sea grass mats in various thicknesses. A traditional Japanese floor material. Will not hold up to heavy traffic.

tea caddy
Metal container used to import tea during the eighteenth century, often decorated with oriental motifs and designs.

tea table
A small table, tall enough to accommodate serving tea from a seated position.

technical drawings
Floor plans, elevations, and detailed drawings of architectural detail, cabinetry, storage, and built-in units.

telephone system
A network of connected telephones within a building or office.

tempera
Paint made with pigment mixed with egg and thinned with water.

tempered glass
Glass toughened by heating and rapid cooling.

tenant improvement (T. I.)
The designer works with the client who will occupy a nonresidential space. The design work within an established budget is paid for by the developer.

tender
A state of weakness in a fabric wherein it easily can tear.

tensile system construction
A tentlike building system.

tenure-track position
A full-time college or university appointment that offers tenure, or the status of holding one's position on a permanent basis.

Tergal
A registered trademark of Rhodiaceta for polyester.

terra-cotta
An Italian term for cooked earth used to describe hard, durable reddish brown clay products, such as that used to make roof tiles.

terrace houses
Matching row houses that became popular in England during the eighteenth century.

terrazzo
Chips of marble set into concrete and polished. A hard nonresilient flooring for residential and nonresidential interiors.

Territorial style
The later, more classical version of the Southwest Adobe-style houses of New Mexico.

territoriality
Personal attachment to a certain territory.

terry cloth
A pile fabric with uncut loops, used for towels.

tertiary hues
See intermediate hues.

Terylene
A registered trademark of ICI for polyester.

tesserae
Pieces of colored glass and stone used to make mosaics.

tetrad complement
A variation of a direct complementary scheme consisting of four colors equidistant, or equally spaced, on the color wheel.

Textura
A registered trademark of Hoeschst for polyester.

texture
The relative smoothness or roughness of a surface read by the eye (visual texture) or with the hand (tactile texture). Texture is produced in several ways: by material, color, line, relief, and finish.

texture finishes
A decorative finish that mechanically alters the texture in the fabric surface, making it more smooth, rough, or puckered.

texturizing
Adding crimp, kink, or waviness to a man-made monofilament thread or yarn to increase bulk and loftiness and to add textural interest. An uneven surface applied to drywall or Sheetrock by blowing on a thin plaster mixture then sanding it semismooth.

texturizing paint
Thick paint that can be applied to imitate stucco.

thatched roof
A roof covered with reeds or straw so as to shed water.

thermal pane
A type of double glazing in which two layers of glass are produced with a pocket of air for insulation.

thermoplastics
Plastics that change their form by heating.

thermoset plastics
Plastic compounds that are hardened by heat.

thermosiphoning
A passive solar system of collecting heat through spaces in the walls or roof, then drawing the heat into ducts and forcing it into the interior through fans and registers.

thermostat
A device that controls the furnace or air-conditioning by maintaining a preset temperature.

thin shell membrane construction
A self-supporting membrane of reinforced (mesh) concrete or sprayed foam.

Thonet, Michael (1796–1971)
A German craftsman best known for his bentwood furniture designs.

tieback draperies
Panels of pleated or shirred fabric tied back at a soft curve and held with ties (strips of fabric), or cords, or metal holdbacks.

tieback holders
Concealed hardware to hold the ties or decorative metal rosettes that hold the draperies in the tieback position.

tie-dye
A hand process for coloring fabric where a fabric is folded into various shapes, then tied in spots with string and immersed in a dye bath. Where the folds and tied portions are thick, the dye will not penetrate, creating interesting abstract patterns.

tiered curtains
Short curtains layered to overlap vertically.

tight
An interior that is sealed or that has few or no windows for natural ventilation; requires HVAC system or air-exchange units for fresh air.

tile
A flat, geometrically shaped wall and floor finish material of kiln-baked clay.

timber frame
A frame of heavy timbers used as the structural support system for a building.

tokonoma
A small alcove with a low, raised platform reserved for display of aesthetic and sacred objects in the traditional Japanese home.

tone
A general term for a neutralized, grayed, or toned-down hue.

tongue and groove
Strips of wood milled to fit together and interlock.

top treatments
Any fabric used as a short covering at the top or above a window or window treatment.

torchére
In history a tall candlestand. Today a floor lamp that casts light upward onto the ceiling.

tortoise shell
Imposing layers of tinted varnish through dabbing, dragging, and crisscrossing to produce a look of tortoise shell.

town house
Another term for a dwelling that is narrow, one or two room(s) wide, and two or three stories high. It shares walls with one or two similar town houses, and one roof spans all the units.

tracery
A term used to describe the lacelike orna-mentation in stone or woodwork of Gothic design, often seen in windows.

track lighting
A track that holds and connects several adjustable spotlights.

trade sources
Wholesale companies who market goods and services to the trade or the interior design profession.

trademarks or trade names
Names given by chemical companies to a generic fiber that identify it as their product. Trademarks are registered with the Federal Trade Commission and may be accompanied by a small TM following the name.

traffic
Movement of users through an area or along a route.

traffic pattern
The pattern created by tracing the movement of a user through an area or along a route.

trailer park
A development where many mobile homes are located and perhaps permanently situated.

transepts
The part of a cross-shaped church that extends at right angles to the nave.

transition
A type of rhythm that leads the eye without interruption from one point or area to another.

transom
A window over a door or the upper section of a window.

transport
Moving the sun's heat through a liquid medium to the storage area in an active solar system unit.

transportation design
A facet of nonresidential design: airlines, buses, trains, and automobiles.

traverse rods
Rods equipped with cords and pulleys to draw draperies opened and closed.

travertine
A light-colored limestone used for nonresil-ient floors and hard wall materials.

tread
The portion of the stair that is stepped on.

triadic, or triad, complement
Three colors equidistant, or equally spaced, on the color wheel such as red, yellow, and blue.

triangular pediment
A pediment in the shape of a triangle.

triforium
A gallery above the arches of the arcade in the nave of a church.

triglyphs
The three decorative vertical grooves on the frieze of the Doric entablature.

triple glazing
Three layers of window glass for insulation.

triple roll
A roll or bolt of wall covering containing approximately 108 square feet, or three times the area of a single roll.

tripod table
A three-legged table. The three legs may converge to form a single pedestal.

Trombe walls
A passive solar system of glass (collect and amplify heat) placed in front of a dark masonry wall (absorbs and slowly releases the heat into the interior).

trompe l'oeil
"Trick the eye." Painted surfaces or wall covering in realistic three-dimensional scenes.

trophies
Mounted fish, animals, animal heads, and skins.

true divider
Windows glazed with individual panes, rather than snap-in grids.

truss
A framework for supporting a roof.

trusses or truss construction
Triangular reinforcing in wood or metal that distributes the load effectively.

Tudor arch
A flattened Gothic arch.

tuft bind
A measurement indicating the strength of the latex layer that holds tufts of carpet yarns in place.

tufted carpets
The method by which most carpeting is produced for both residential and nonresidential interiors. Multiple needles threaded with yarn are simultaneously punched into a loosely woven primary backing. The tufts are held in place with a layer of latex, then adhered to a secondary backing of jute or polypropylene.

tufting
A needle construction technique of inserting yarns into a woven or knitted fabric to create a pile. Examples include many cut pile carpets and traditional patterned chenille bedspreads. Tying back fabric and padding in such a way as to create a patterned, pillowed surface in upholstery (also a type of carpet construction).

tufts or stitches per square inch
A measurement indicating the density of the tufts or woven stitches in carpeting.

tungsten filament
Another name for incandescent lighting.

tungsten halogen lamp
The lamp filament is surrounded with halogen gas that reacts with the tungsten, causing a very bright light.

turnings
Decorative spindles formed by turning a piece of wood on a lathe and cutting designs into the wood with a sharp knife as the piece spins.

Tuscan
A simplified version of the Roman Doric style without fluting on the column.

twill weave
The interlacing of yarns in a sequence such as three over, one under, which creates a distinct diagonal rib or wale. A *regular or balanced twill* will not break the diagonal line, while a *novelty or unbalanced twill* may reverse, creating fabrics such as herringbone or houndstooth.

twin home
A dwelling that may adjoin only one other dwelling. A semi-detached house.

Twistloc
A registered trademark of Monsanto for polyester.

U-stair
A stair that makes a 180-degree turn at a single landing.

UBC
The Uniform Building Code.

Ultron
A registered trademark of Monsanto for nylon.

unbalanced basket weave
A variation of a plain basket weave where groups of threads are interlaced as one in unequal portions, such as three threads over four threads, or any variation from two to five threads or yarns carried as one.

unbalanced twill
See twill weave or novelty twill.

undertones
The addition of a small amount of one hue to another, rendering the latter slightly warm or cool.

unity
A component of harmony (an element of design) that provides a change or relief from sameness in an interior through differences in the design and furnishing elements.

upholstered cornice
A wooden top treatment that is padded then covered with a decorative top treatment.

upholstered walls
Padded, then fabric-covered walls.

uplighters or uplighting
Canisters, spotlights, or floodlights that cast light upward to the wall or ceiling.

urethane foam
Synthetic foam carpet padding.

user
Anyone who will use a completed design.

user friendly
Computer hardware and software that are relatively uncomplicated and easy to operate.

vacuforming
A process of forming plastic in a mold in which all the air is drawn out to form a vacuum that forces the plastic around the mold.

valance lighting
A light over the top of a window placed behind a board that directs light both upward and downward.

value
The relative lightness or darkness of a hue according to the amount of white or black inherent in or added to the hue.

value contrast
Hues or neutrals that differ in value. High-value contrast is seen when light and dark values are used together; low-value contrast places together similar hue or neutral values.

value distribution
The placement of differing values in an interior to create a balanced and pleasing effect.

vapor barrier
A heavy-gauge plastic applied to walls or insulative window treatments to prevent moisture and air penetration.

variety
A subelement of harmony made possible through repetition or similarity of objects or elements in an interior.

varnish
A finish film for wood made by dissolving resinous substances in oil or alcohol.

vault
A ceiling constructed on the principle of an arch. An arched roof.

vaulted system construction
A tunnellike arch system of building.

Vectra
A registered trademark of Vectra for olefin.

vehicle
In painting, the binding agent that holds the particles of pigment together and creates the film that adheres to the surface being painted.

veiling glare
The reflectance of a light source from a shiny surface into the line of vision.

velvet weave carpet
A woven carpet with no design. Colors are solid or utilize variegated yarns.

veneer
A thin ply of beautifully grained wood laminated to plywood or solid woods.

venetian blinds
Metal blinds two inches wide, held together with thin cord or wide braid. May be tilted or lifted up and down with a cord. Wide surfaces tend to catch dust. These have largely been replaced by miniblinds.

Venetian glass
Delicate and fine glassware made at or near Venice, Italy. A term used to describe glass mirrors with an antique or veined appearance.

ventilation
Natural fresh air through windows or through a central HVAC unit that circulates clean air through a building.

verandah
A long covered porch along the front and/or side of a building.

Verel
A registered trademark of Eastman Kodak for modacrylic.

vernacular
Design executed by localized craftsmen, with a regional, naive, or unschooled quality.

vertical lines
Up-and-down lines that lift the eye, and give dignity and formality to interiors.

vertical louvered blinds
Typically three or four inch wide slats or louvers attached to a headrail that allows tilt and open-close draw as a traverse mechanism.

vertical louvered shutters
Movable louvered shutters with vertical rather than horizontal louvers.

vestibule
An air-lock entry consisting of two doors and a compartment-like room that prevents excessive heat or cold from entering the building.

Victorian Era (1837–1901)
The English and American era that coincided with the reign of Queen Victoria. It paralleled the Industrial Revolution, during which time many styles were seen. Victorian design is characterized by revivals of nearly every previous historical style together with rapid technological development.

Vienna Secession
A group of young Viennese artists and craftsmen including Otto Wagner, Josef Hoffmann, and Joseph Maria Olbrich who broke away from the mainstream of traditional art and design c. 1897. The group eventually evolved into a more formal workshop—the Wiener Werksette headed by Josef Hoffmann.

viga
A large pole beam used to support the roof of Southwest adobe houses.

vinyl
Polymerized vinyl (ethylene), essentially a plastic compound, extruded into sheets for floors and as a wall covering, and a coating for wall coverings and fabrics.

vinyl composition/asbestos
A resilient hard flooring of vinyl, some asbestos, and other compounds.

vinyl latex wall coverings
Wall coverings that are vinyl through to the backing, which is usually a fabric. They are usually very durable, heavy, and scrubbable.

vinyl protected wall coverings
Wall coverings, usually paper, with a coating of vinyl, which makes the covering washable.

vinyl tile
Extruded vinyl sheets cut into square tiles.

vinyl wall coverings
Any wall covering with a vinyl surface, including vinyl-protected, vinyl latex, and coated fabric wall coverings.

vinyon
A synthetic vinyl chloride long-chain polymer generally extruded in sheet form, and often imitating leather, suede, or nearly any surface texture. Often called vinyl or PVC: polyvinyl chloride.

visual density
See optical density.

visual proportion
The way a proportion might appear regardless of actual dimensions or proportions.

visual spectrum
Colors within the electromagnetic spectrum that can be seen with the eye.

visual weight
The weight or scale an object appears to have regardless of actual weight.

vitrify
To change into a glasslike ceramic by high heat.

Vitruvian proportions
Correct classical proportions as recorded by Vitruvius.

Vitruvius
A first-century Roman architect and writer responsible for standardizing classical architectural forms.

volts or voltage
The measurement of power that comes through the power line.

volute
A spiral or scroll.

Vycron
A registered trademark of Beaunit for polyester.

wainscot
Medieval wooden paneling that may or may not reach to the ceiling.

wale
A pronounced rib or raised cord that may run vertically with the warp, horizontally with the filling threads or weft, diagonally as in a twill weave.

wall composition
The arrangement of furniture, architectural openings, and accessories against a wall.

wall coverings
Paper, fabric, or vinyl rolls or bolts prepared for gluing onto the wall.

wall washer
A general term for a series of lights that wash a wall. These may be recessed adjustable lights or eyeball spotlights, for example.

wallboard
A term for rigid wall materials installed in sheets or boards: Sheetrock (gypsum board), masonite, paneling. Also called drywall.

warm colors
The hues on the color wheel generally considered to produce feelings of warmth. They are red-violet, red, red-orange, orange, yellow-orange, yellow, and yellow-green.

warm deluxe fluorescent lamp
Contains a warm light spectrum similar to incandescent lighting.

warp threads or yarns
The lengthwise or vertical fabric yarns that are threaded onto the loom and form the basis for woven cloth.

wash
A soft plane of light from spotlights or track lighting.

washable
A wallpaper term meaning that the paper can be gently cleaned with a little soap and water.

water closet
A toilet.

watercolor
Paint made with gum arabic and thinned with water. Also a painting created with this type of paint.

waterproofing
Coating the building's foundation with a tar mixture or with tar paper.

water-repellent finish
A functional, wet, or standard finish that allows the fabric to shed or repel moisture and stain due to condensation or excessive humidity.

watt or wattage
A unit of electric power equal to the power of one ampere (amp) as compared to one volt.

wattle
A panel of woven sticks used as infill for timber framing or as fencing material.

weatherstripping
Thin strips of insulation, usually with a sticky side, that insulate around windows and doors to prevent cold air infiltration.

weft threads or yarns
Also called *filling yarns or woof*, these are inserted into the opened shed of warp threads to create a woven fabric.

Wegner, Hans (b. 1914)
Important Danish furniture craftsman, designer of several modern classic pieces.

Welsh dresser
A side piece with cupboards and drawers and a set of open shelves above; also called a hutch.

welt
A fabric-covered piping cord sewn between two pieces of the covering in upholstery.

wet finishes
See standard finishes.

wicker
Furniture, baskets, or other objects woven from twigs.

Wiener Werkstette
See Vienna Secession.

Wilton
Broadloom carpeting woven on a Jacquard loom. All colors used in the carpeting are carried beneath the carpet face, making a thick heavy carpet.

windbreak
Trees, hedges, or fences that provide protection from wind.

window sill
The horizontal ridge or shelf beneath the glass, usually within the frame.

window wells
The corrugated metal or concrete form that keeps dirt away form basement windows.

Windsor chair
Originally an English chair with cabriole legs and a shaped splat. The Windsor chair became common during the eighteenth century in America and featured a carved seat, spindle back, and turned legs.

wing chair
An upholstered easy chair with a high back and wings on each side for resting the head.

wiring plan or electric plan or lighting plan
The portion of the blue prints or working drawings that indicate placement of all electric wiring, fixtures, switched outlets, and connections.

wood blinds
Thin flat slats of wood made into miniblinds. They take more stacking space and are more costly than metal miniblinds.

wood filler
A paste or liquid used in the wood-finishing process to fill the natural pores of the wood and create a smooth surface.

wood frame or wood truss system
The conventional system of framing a building with wood studs, joists, rafters, and beams, reinforced with the herringbone (zigzag) truss system between joists.

wood graining
Brushing on a glaze and drawing wood grains and lines with an artist's brush.

wood molding
Narrow strips of concave and/or convex wood molding. May also be plastic.

wood plank
Flooring of strips of wood. Planks may be even and laid in strips or random plank, three different widths.

wood rods
Curtain and drapery rods of solid wood, often fluted.

wood shutters
Hinged hard window treatments used most often as movable louvered shutters. Other types include solid- and raised-panel wood, slat or plank, and vertical louvered shutters.

wood- or coal-burning stove
A self-contained stove, usually of cast-iron that burns wood or coal for space heating.

wool
Natural protein staple fibers taken from the fleece of sheep and the hairs of goats. Wool is absorbent, resilient and flame resistant, woven and knitted into high-quality textiles for both residential and nonresidential use. Used for carpeting, Oriental and folk rugs, wall coverings, and some window covering fabrics.

wool rugs
A term for natural fiber rugs or carpeting left in its undyed state. The most common is the berber rug.

word-processing programs
Software programs that offer options in text writing.

work zones
Areas for tasks such as food preparation, office work.

working drawings
The final mechanical drawings that are used to obtain bids and construct a design.

woven wood shades
Thin slats of wood woven into a fabric with vertical warp yarns of rayon or cotton. Used most often as a Roman shade or as accordion fold-up window coverings.

wrought iron
Iron, welded and forged into different shapes.

Wyburd, Leonard F.
English designer of the Thebes stool.

yarn dyeing
Coloring yarn before it is woven or knitted into a fabric.

yo-yo effect
Uneven high and low areas along the bottom hemline of a draped fabric due to alternating humidity absorption and drying out of the fabric.

Zantrel
A registered trademark of American Enka for high wet modulus rayon.

zapata
Carved decorative corbel on the porch of the Southwest adobe house.

Zeflon
A registered trademark of Dow Badische for nylon.

Zefran
A registered trademark of Dow Badische for nylon, acrylic, and polyester.

zero-clearance firebox
Triple-insulated, self-contained firebox unit that can be used without firebrick or masonry.

zero-clearance fireplace unit
A fireplace unit that can be set into combustible walls with no clearance.

zigzag lines
Lines that reverse upon themselves in a regular order, such as a herringbone pattern, or in an irregular order, such as a flame pattern.

zones
Areas that have similar functions or purposes, including work zones, social zones, private zones, and storage zones.

Aalto, Alvar, 182
Abacus, 361
Acanthus leaves, 361
Accent lighting, 92
Accent rugs, 276
Access, 155–56
Accessories, 149
    and art, 309–30
    and nonresidential design,
        328–30
    use of, 327–28
Accordion doors, 195
Acetate, 295–96
Achromatic, 70
Acoustical tile, 225
Acropolis, 360
Acrylic, 170, 296, 315
    and carpet fibers, 268
    paint, 230
    sheets, 92
Action, and line, 42
Active balance. See
        Asymmetrical balance
Active solar system, 337
Activity, playful, 43
Actual density, 40
Adam, Robert, 61, 178, 189, 206,
        211, 312, 370, 395
Adam style, 211
Adam Thoroughgood House,
        366, 367
Adaptive restoration, 385
Adhesive, and wall
        covering, 233
Adirondack Mountain resort, 5
Adjustable fixtures, 96, 98
Adler, Dankmar, 382
Adobe, 378, 379
    style, 212, 213
Aesthetic coordination, and
        windows, 237–38
Aesthetics, and fabric, 287–92
Afterimages, 74
Aggregate, exposed, 262
Agreement, letters of, 23,
        401, 407
AHLI. See American Home
        Lighting Institute (AHLI)
Aisles, 363
A lamp, 89
Albers, Josef, 67, 68
Alice chair, 172
Alkyd, 230
    enamels, 230
Alloys, 169
    and tableware and cookware,
        320–21
All-wood construction, 167
Alonzo Olds House, 373
Alternate complements, 65, 66
Alternation, and repetition, 35
Aluminum, 169, 182, 223
Ambient lighting, 91, 93

Ambulatory, 364
America, and color, 61–62
American Association of
        Housing Educators, 399
American Early Georgian,
        period fabric, 291
American Empire, 175, 216
    period fabric, 291
American Empire style, 61, 62,
        163, 212
American English Medieval
        style, 211
American Federal, period
        fabric, 291
American Home Lighting
        Institute (AHLI), 102
American influence, 18
American Late Georgian, period
        fabric, 291
American Society of Interior
        Designers (ASID), 5, 36,
        115, 191, 208, 244, 254,
        312, 395, 399
Ametex, 288
Amory Ticknor Hose, 370
Ampere (amp), 91
Anaglypta, 206
Analogous harmony, 65
Analysis, cost, 397
Anchoring, 140, 142
Andalusia, 372, 373
Angular line, 41, 42
Angular stability, and line, 42
Animal skins, 275
Annual Product Design Awards.
        See Product Design
        Awards
Anodized aluminum, 169
Anthemion, 361
Anthropometrics, 141, 173
Anthropometry, 141, 173
Antimony, 320
Antine, Anthony, 153, 166,
        319, 324
Antiques
    finish, 168
    and furniture selection, 174
    satin, defined, 303
Antiquing, 231
Apartments, high-rise, 124, 125
APC Corporation, 206
Appliances, planning considera-
        tions, 121
Appropriateness, 49
Appropriation, 54, 329
Apse, 363
A. R. Broomer, Ltd., 310
Arc, and lighting, 99
Arcade, 363
Arches, 35, 39, 361, 363
    beams, 207
    systems, 350–51

Architecture
    detail, 187, 209, 210–13
    elements, 184
    glazing, 222–23
    lighting. See Lighting
    organic, 382–83
    rodding, 245
Architrave, 360
Arco chair, 170
Arconas Corporation, 170
Arco Oil Tower, 26
Area rugs, 271
Armoire, 176
Armstrong, 265, 269
Armure, defined, 303
Arnache, defined, 303
Arrangement, furniture. See
        Furniture arrangement
Art
    and accessories, 309–30
    decorative. See Decorative
        art
    fine. See Fine art
    lighting as, 92
    and nonresidential design,
        328–30
Art Center (Pasadena), 55
Art Deco, 40, 49, 62, 99, 160, 167,
        218, 284, 303, 384
Art glass, 223, 245
Artificial lighting, 70, 88–91
Artificial stone, 224
Artistic lighting, 92
Art Nouveau style, 62, 245, 323
Art of Color, The, 68
Arts and Crafts movement,
        375, 395
Ashlar, 224, 262
ASID. See American Society of
        Interior Designers (ASID)
Asphalt tiles, 265, 266
Associations
    color, 73, 74
    lighting, 102
    See also Organizations
Asymmetrical balance, 32, 34
Atelier International, 180,
        181, 183
Athena, 354
Athens, 354
Atrium, 362
Atrium doors, 196
Attached dwellings, 124
AT&T Building, 25
Attic, 366, 368
    windows, 201
Aubusson, rugs and tapestry,
        274, 309
Auditorium Building, 382
Austrian shades, 243
    calculating yardage, 239
Austrian valances, 244
Automatic sensor dimmers, 95

Avonite R, 171
Awning windows, 198–99
Axminster loom, 258, 269
Azerbijan rug, 254
Baccalaureate degrees, 398, 403
Back panels, 169
Bacon's Castle, 366, 367
Baffled ceilings, 209
Baffles, and glare, 95
Baker Furniture, 26
Balance, 30, 32–35
    asymmetrical, 32, 34
    and furniture arrangement,
        144–46
    radial, 32, 34–35
    symmetrical, 32–33
Balance light, 93
Balderi, Nicola, 170
Ballast, and lighting, 99
Balloon shades, 242, 243
    calculating yardage, 239
Balloon valances, 244
Baltimore Cathedral, 370
Baluster, 202
Balustrade, 202, 368
Bamboo shades, 246–47
Banister, 202, 203
Bank of light, 93
Baptist Church, 374
Barcelona chair, 181
Baroque, period fabric, 290
Barrel vault, 361
Barrier-free planning, 141,
        155–56
Base, and moldings, 193
Baseboard, 193
Base lighting, 97
Basic groupings, and furniture
        arrangement, 150–53
Baskets, 321
Bath, space, 109, 116, 120–21
Batik, defined, 303
Batiste, defined, 303
Batten, 192, 193
Battersby, Christine, 249
Batting, 172
Batts, 340
Bauhaus, 28, 62, 181, 359, 383,
        395, 407
Baum, Dwight James, 380
Bay, 364
Bay rods, 245
Bay windows, 199
Bead-and-reel, 361
Beamed ceilings, 207
Beam systems, 351
Beaux Arts influence, 39, 193,
        357, 380–81, 382, 384
Bed molding, 194
Bedroom, 13
Beltcourse, 368
Belter, John Henry, 179
Belvedere, 374

Bengaline, defined, 304
Benjamin Winchell House, 380
Bennett, Ward, 163
Berber rugs, 275
Bereguer-Topacio, Ched, 405
Berms, 16
Bertoia, Harry, 182
Bertoia Wire Group, 182
Bescherer, Jane, 58
Beth Weissman Company, 323
Beveled glass, 245
Bevelling, 192
Bibelots, 317
Bibliographies, 23, 56, 76–77,
     102, 132, 156, 185–86, 213,
     251–52, 278, 307–8, 330,
     352, 385, 410
Bids, 21
Biedermeier, 175
Bifold doors, 195
Biltmore, 380, 381
Biotechnology, 173
Birch, Janet, 401
Bird's-eye, defined, 304
Bishop's sleeve side panel
     curtains, 241
Bisymmetrical balance. See
     Symmetrical balance
B lamp, 89
Bleaching, 168
Blinds, 208, 245–46
Blockfront, 177
Block print, 315
Blue, and common color
     associations, 74
Blueprints, 110
Board, finishes. See Finishes
Board and batten, 192, 193
Bogtherr, Burkhard, 403
Bolts, of wall coverings, 233
Bombyx Mori moth, 294
Book of Architecture, A, 368
Books, 323
     pattern, 365
Boris Kroll Fabrics, 280
Boscobel Restoration, 30, 35, 144,
     187, 189, 216, 269
Boston Public Library, 381
Boucle, defined, 304
Boucle marquisette, defined, 304
Bow rods, 245
Bow windows, 199
Boyd Lighting, 83
Bracket lighting, 97
Brackets, 364
Bradford, Barbara Taylor,
     286, 314
Bradford, Robert, 12–13
Brafferton Indian School, 368
Braided rugs, 274
Brainstorming, 20
Brandon, 369
Brass, 169, 223
Brayton International, 403
Breakers, The, 380
Breakfront, 177, 369
Breast, of fireplace, 204
Breuer, Marcel, 181, 383, 395
Brick, 261, 361
     and wall and ceiling
          materials, 220, 221
Brickel Associates, 163, 191
Brick Market, 370
Brigham Young University, 28,
     154, 222
Brilliants, 92
Brinkerhoff Construction, 342
British Museum, 354, 360
Brno chair, 181
Broadcloth, defined, 304
Broadloom carpet, 265, 267–69

Brocade, defined, 304
Brocatelle, defined, 304
Bronze, 170, 223, 321
Brooklyn Bridge, 374, 381
Bruce Hardwood Floors, 254
Brunschwig & Fils, 41, 58, 171
Buatta, Mario, 254
Bubble, of space, 142
Bubble planning, 110
Buchram (buckram),
     defined, 304
Budgeting, 397
Buffet, 178
Buffet-style dining, 140
Building, 331–85
     constructing, 343–49
     See also Building systems and
          Exterior style
Building inspector, 341
Building systems, 333–52, 396
     interior, 345
     and nonresidential design,
          350–51
     See also Systems
Built-in indirect lighting, 96
Bulbs. See Lamps
Bullfinch, Charles, 370
Bullnose, 202
Burl, 167
Burlap, defined, 304
Burnham, Daniel H., 381, 382
Burnham & Root, 382
Burn-out, defined, 304
Business-accounting
     packages, 401
Busy line. See Tightly curved
     line
Buttressed chimneys, 366
Buttresses, 364
Buyer, 396
Buy once and buy good
     quality, 20
Byers, John, 60
Byobu, 322
Byzantium, 61
Cabinet-Maker and Upholsterer's
     Drawing Book, The, 178
Cabinet-Maker and Upholsterer's
     Guide, The, 178
Cabinetry, 191, 208–9
     and kitchen zones, 119–20
     and standard sizes of
          fixtures, 122
Cabinetwork, 208–9
Cable systems, 351
Cabriole legs, 175, 176
CAD. See Computer-aided
     design (CAD)
CADD. See Computer-aided
     design and drafting
     (CADD)
Cafe curtains, 241
Calendered plastics, 170
Calico, defined, 304
California missions, 378
California Ranch House, 379–80
Callicrates, 360
Calvary Presbyterian
     Church, 374
Cambric, defined, 304
Came, 364
C & A Wall Coverings, 319
Cane, and furniture, 170, 171
Canes. See Handicapped
Cantilever design, 181
Canvas, defined, 304
Cape Ann house, 371
Cape Cod Cottage, 371–72
Capitals, 360
Careers, in design profession,
     402–6

Carleton Designs, 275
Caroline Hemenway Harmon
     Continuing Education
     Building, 222
Carpenter Gothic, 359
Carpets, 265–71
     installation methods and
          padding, 270
     maintenance and
          cleaning, 271
     and nonresidential
          design, 277
     textures, 270
Carson Pirie Scott & Co., 382
Carter's Grove, 368
Cartoon, and grid-sheet
     drawing, 280
Cartoon design rug, 254
Casa San Ysidro, 379
Casa Stradivari, 169
Cascades, 244
     calculating yardage, 239
Case goods, 167
Casement
     defined, 304
     draperies, 242
     windows, 199–200, 364
Casing, 172
Castelli, 183
Cast iron, 321
Castles on the Sound, 37
Cathedra, 164
Cathedral, 363
     ceilings, 206
     windows, 200
Caucasian rugs, 272
C.A.U.S. See Color Association
     of the United States
     (C.A.U.S.) Ceilings, 206–8
     luminous, 92
     materials, 220
     and nonresidential design,
          248–51
     treatments, 215, 235–36
Cella, 362
Centerbrook, 43, 111
Central American rugs, 274
Century Furniture, 288
Cenzo Custom Design, 97
Ceramica Nuova
     D'Agostino, 338
Ceramics, 318–21
     tile, 225–26, 263
Ceremonial shrine (niche). See
     Tokonoma
Certain wall construction, 222
Certificate, 398
Certified kitchen designer
     (CKD), 110
     CKD Excellence in Kitchen
          Design Competition, 110
Cesca chair, 181
Chairs, 163, 176–83, 185, 393
     occasional, 147
     rail, 193
Chaise lounge, 181
Chambray, defined, 304
Chandeliers, 98
Chapman & Biber, 34
Character, homes of, 11
Charpentier, 314
Chelsea Custom Corporation,
     157, 191
Chemical finish, and fabrics, 301
Chenille, defined, 304
Chestnut Street
     (Philadelphia), 357
Chevreul, Michel-Eugene, 64,
     65, 66
Chevron, 294
     defined, 304

Chiffon, defined, 304
Child Craft, 165
Chimneypieces, and fireplaces,
     203–5
Chimneys, 366
China, ceramic, 319
China Seas, Inc., 235, 283, 396
Chinchester, 294
Chinese style, 393
     Chippendale, 163
     rugs, 254, 272
     See also Japanese style and
          Oriental style
Chintz, defined, 304
Chippendale, Thomas, 176
"Chippendale" building, 25
Chippendale furniture, 25, 48,
     52, 163, 176, 177, 237, 254,
     272, 393
Choir, 363
Christ Church, 368
Christian style, 362
Christie's, 316
Christmas wiring, 95
Chroma, and Munsell theory,
     66, 67
Chromatic distribution,
     law of, 69
Chrome, 169
Chromium, 169
Chrysler Building, 384
Church, Frederick, 359
Churchill, 173
Church of Christ Science, 383
Circular line, 41, 42
Circulation, and furniture
     arrangement, 140–41, 155
City Hall, 375
Civil War, 62, 357
CKD. See Certified kitchen
     designer (CKD)
C lamp, 89
Clapboard, 366
Clarence House, 26
Classical Rome, and color, 61
Classic Revival period, 61
Classics
     and furniture selection,
          174–79
     modern, 180–83
Clearances, standard, 141–42
Clerestory windows, 200, 364
Climate
     site, and orientation, 109, 112
     and weather, 15–16
Clocks, 321
Close, Carolyn, 39
Closed floor plans, 124
Closed showroom, 400
Closed stairs, 202, 203
Cloud shades, 243
Clutter, organized, 328
CMG. See Color Marketing
     Group (CMG)
Coated fabric, 234
Cobblestone, 224, 262
Codes, 19, 22, 23, 351
Coffered ceilings, 208, 209
Coffers, 208, 209
Cohen, Ira D., 197
Cold air returns, 140
Cold cathode lighting, 88, 99
Collections, and accessories,
     327–28
Colonial, 207
Colonial Williamsburg, 33
Colonnade, 360
Color, 30, 37, 45, 46–47, 57–77
     in America, 61–62
     in ancient world, 61
     associations, 73, 74

blindness, 87
complementary, 65, 66
cool, 65
and fabric, 287, 288,
  290–92, 300
-fastness, 303
group moods, 73, 74
harmony, 68
in history, 61–63
influencing factors, 70–72
-ing, 300, 301
monochromatic, 65
neutralized, 69
and nonresidential design,
  75–76
organizations, 77
psychology, 72–74
in residential interiors, 75
and spectra, 87
symbolisms, 73, 74
theory, 64–68
trend market, 63–64
warm, 65
washing, 231
Color Association of the United
  States (C.A.U.S.), 63, 77
Color blindness, 87
Colored incandescent
  lighting, 89
Colorfastness, 303
Coloring, 300, 301
Color Marketing Group (CMG),
  63, 77
Color Primer, The, 68
Columned chimneys, 366
Columns, 360
C.O.M. See Customer's own
  material (C.O.M.)
Combination floor plans, 124
Combing, 231
Combining
  lines, 44
  patterns, 45–46
Combustion lighting, 70, 87–88
Communication
  systems, 336, 351
  verbal and visual, 397
Companion fabrics, 234–35
Compartmental bathroom, 121
Complementary colors, 65, 66
Composite order, 362
Composition, wall, 149
Compounded textiles, 296, 300
Computer
  and design profession,
    400–401
  networks, 351
  purchase and training, 402
Computer-aided design (CAD),
  155, 341, 401
Computer-aided design and
  drafting (CADD), 401
Concept, initial, 20, 23
Conceptual drawings, 20
Concrete, 261–62, 344, 361
  and wall and ceiling
    materials, 220, 221–22
Condominium, 124, 126–27
Congregational Church, 373
Conkey House, 380
Conservation, energy, 339–40
Consolidated Edison, 83
Construction
  all-wood, 167
  certain wall, 222
  See Building systems and
    Exterior style and
    Systems
Context, cultural, 48–49
Continuing education. See
  Design profession

Contract, 23
Contrast, 229
  high and low, 47
  or opposition, 35–36
  value, 72
Contrasting harmony, 65
Conventional design, 51
Conversation distance, 143
Conversation pits, 151
Cookware, 318–21
Cool colors, 65
Cool white deluxe lamps, 90
Coordinating fabrics, 234–35
Coordination, aesthetic. See
  Aesthetic coordination
Copper, 170, 223, 320
Coraggio Design, 289, 298
Corbel, 379
Corduroy, defined, 304
Corinthian orders, 360–61
Cork
  and floors, 265, 266
  and wall and ceiling
    materials and coverings,
    220, 221, 234–35
Corner blocks, 168
Corner fireplace, 204, 205
Cornice, 244, 360
  lighting, 96
  moldings, 194
Coromandel, 322
Corridors, 130
Corwin House, 366, 367
Cost analysis, 397
Cost per square foot, 111
Cottage curtains, 241
Cotton, 294
  defined, 306
  rugs, 275, 276
Cotton Council, 294
Cotton Incorporated, 294
Country curtains, 241
Country French style, 212, 213,
  234, 290
  interiors, 169
  period fabric, 290
Country Living, 310
County Courthouse, 381
Courses, 365
Courthouse, 35
Coved ceilings, 208
Cove lighting, 97
Cove molding, 194
Covered frame method, 236
Coverings, and furniture, 172–73
Covington Fabrics
  Corporation, 301
Crane Memorial Library, 376
Credit, lines of, 397
Crepe, defined, 304
Cretonne, defined, 304
Crewel embroidery, defined, 304
Crinoline, defined, 304
Critical path, 7, 347–49
Cross, 363
Crossing, 363
Crowding, 111, 143
Crown Hall, 384
Crown lintels, 369
Crown molding, 194
Cruciform, 363
Crutches. See Handicapped
Crypt, 363
Cubic footage, 109, 110–11,
  112, 130
Cultural context, 48–49
Cultural relationships, 18
Cumming, Armstrong, 32
Cupola, 368
Curios, 317
Curtain rods, 245

Curtains, 240
  calculating yardage, 239
  types of, 241
Curtain wall construction, 350
Curved line, 41, 42
Curved stairway, 202
Cushioning, and furniture,
  172–73
Cushions, 172
Custom designs, 183
Customer's own material
  (C.O.M.), 172
Custom floor plans, 124
Dado, 192
  cap, 193
Damask, 280
  defined, 304
Damper, 204
D & D Building, 6, 83, 396, 397
Daniels, 173
Daroff Design, Inc., 3, 5
Data-base catalog, 401
Data-base programs, 401
Daub, 364
David B. Gamble House,
  382, 383
David Brewster Color theory, 64
Davis, Alexander Jackson, 374
Davis Furniture Industries, 403
Daylighting, 99
Decorative art, 317–25
Decorative design, 49–51
Decorative fabrics, glossary,
  303–7
Decorative finishes, and fabrics,
  301, 302
Decorative lighting fixtures,
  322–23
Decorative luminaire lamps, 92
Decorative luminaires, 96
Degrees, 398, 403
de Lauwe, Paul Chombart, 143
Delli-Carpini, Pauline, 396
de Mar, Leoda, 287
Demographics, 13
Denim, defined, 304
Density, actual and visual, 40
Dentil ornament, 361
de Saavedra, Ruben, 310
Design
  barrier-free, 141, 155–56
  computer-aided, 155
  conventional, 51
  custom, 183
  decorative, 49, 51
  development, 20–21, 23
  discernment, 52–54
  elements. See Design
    elements
  evaluation, 47–55
  excellence, 52–54
  execution, 21, 23
  foundation, 1–77
  interior. See Interior design
  Naturalistic, 51
  nonresidential. See Nonresi-
    dential design
  principles. See Design
    principles
  process. See Design process
    and Design profession
  Pueblo Indian, 18
  statement, 12, 23
  structural, 49–50
  textile, 406
  theory, 30
  See also associated Design
    entries
Design Directions, Inc., 234
Design elements, 37–47
  chart, 30

and furniture arrangement,
  144–50
and principles, 25–56
and space planning, 109,
  123–24
See also Design and Design
  profession
Designer rugs, 274–75
Designers Lighting Forum
  (DLF), 99, 102
Design principles, 30–36
  chart, 30
  and elements, 25–56
  and furniture arrangement,
    144–50
  and space planning, 109,
    123–24
  See also Design and Design
    profession
Design process, 3–23
  chart, 23
  and space planning, 109
  See also Design and Design
    profession
Design profession, 389–410
  careers in, 402–6
  and computers, 400–401
  development and continuing
    education, 397–99, 403
  evolution of, 395
  future of, 408
  and in-house designers, 408
  library of, 397
  NCIDQ examination, 398
  and nonresidential design,
    408–10
  professional organizations,
    398–99
  resources, 399–400
  skills required, 396–97
  today, 395–402
  tools, 400–402
  See also Design and Nonresi-
    dential design
Desk manager, 401
De Stijl, 383
Detached dwellings, 124–25
Detail, architectural. See
  Architecture
Development
  design, 20–21, 23
  linear, 42
  planned, 124–25
  See also Design and Design
    profession
Devon Shop, 158
de Wolfe, Elsie, 395
Dexter Design, 338
Dhurrie rugs, 258, 272
Diagonal line, 41, 42
Diagramming, and floor plans,
  109, 110–12
Diffusers, 98
Dimensional stability, 302
Dimity, defined, 304
Dimmer switch, 95
Dining, 140
Diplomas, 398, 403
Direct complement, 65, 66
Direct general lighting, 91
Direct glare, 95
Direction, of light, 70
Direct lighting, 91
Direct pasteup, 236
Direct solar gain, 338
Discernment, and design
  excellence, 52–54
Discrimination, 11–12
Display, art, 317
Distance
  conversational, public, and
    social, 143

intimate and personal, 142
Distress furniture, 169
Distribution
    chromatic, 69
    spectral energy, 88
    value, 72
DLF. *See* Designers Lighting
    Forum (DLF)
Doctor of philosophy (Ph.D), 403
Dollar Dry Dock Savings
    Bank, 154
Domes, 207, 374
    systems, 351
Donghia, 58
Donner, Aaron, 397
Doors, 194–96, 378
    swinging, 115
Doric orders, 354, 360–61
Dormer windows, 368
Dotted swiss, defined, 304
Double complements, 65, 66
Double-hung sash window, 200
Double-shirred valances, 244
Double-turn stair, 202, 203
Douglas Bennett Associates
    Architects, 342
Doup, defined, 305
Dovetail, 168
Dowels, 168
Downing, Andrew Jackson, 374
Downlights, 98
Drafting, 341
Draftsman, 341
Dragging, 231
Drapery, 237, 240
    calculating yardage, 239
    hardware, 240, 245
    types of, 242
Draw draperies, 242
Drawers, 169
Drawings, 314, 315
    conceptual, 20
    floor plans, 109, 110–12,
      124, 131
    grid-sheet, 280
    plan, 148, 149
    technical, 397
    working, 21, 23, 110
Dr. John Bryant House, 376
Drop-leaf table, 178
Dropped-pendant luminaires, 98
Drum, 365
Duck, defined, 304
Duncan Phyfe. *See* Phyfe,
    Duncan
Dunlieth, 373, 378
Duplex, 125
Durability, 302, 303
    and fabric, 292
Durability requirements, and
    wall coverings, 248–50
Dust panels, 169
Dutch doors, 195, 196
Dutch influence, 357, 377
Dwellings. *See* Housing
Dyckman family, 187
Dyckman House, 377
Dyeing, 300, 301
Dye lot, 233
Eames, Charles, 182
Eames, Ray, 182
Early American Colonial, period
    fabric, 291
Early Christian style, 362
Early Georgian style, 61, 211,
    367–68
    period fabric, 291
Early Modern era, 62
Earthenware, 319
Easements, 202
Eastlake, Charles Locke, 375
Eastlake style, 375

Economic factors. *See* Economy
Economy, 19–20, 23
    and lighting, 92–93, 100–101
    and space planning, 109,
      112–13
Edgar J. Kaufmann House,
    382, 383
Education. *See* Design
    profession
Edward King House, 374
Eero Saarinen & Associates, 384
Egg-and-dart, 361
Eggshell paints, 230
Egypt, 228, 374
    and color, 61
    and furniture, 174
Eight plex, 125, 860–80
Lake Shore Drive, 383
Elderly, and space planning. *See*
    Handicapped
Eleazer Arnold House, 366, 367
Elements. *See* Architecture *and*
    Design elements
Elements of Color, The, 68
Elevation, and furniture
    arrangement, 146
Elgin Marbles, 354, 360
Elizabethan flamestitch, 247
Elizabethan style, 284
Elliot, McCabe, 283, 396
Elon, Inc., 256
Embossed wall coverings,
    234–35
Embroidery, defined, 304
Emotion, 109
    and space, 123, 131
Emphasis, 30, 36, 45
    and furniture
      arrangement, 146
Empire style, 35, 61, 212, 258, 393
    period fabric, 291
Empire State Building, 384
Empty-nesters, 127
Enamel paints, 230
Energy
    conservation, 339–40
    and windows, 237, 239–40
English Georgian, period
    fabric, 291
English influence, in America,
    365–76
English Medieval style, 211
Engravings, 315
Entablature, 192, 354, 360
Environmenal factors, 15–17, 23
Epaphroditus Champion
    House, 26
Epoxy paints, 230
Equilibrium, 32
Equitable Building, 75
Ergofit, 50
Ergonomics, 50, 173, 185
ER lamp, 89
Etched glass, 245
Etchings, 315
Evaluation
    of design, 47–55
    POE. *See* Post-occupancy
      evaluation (POE)
Evolution, of design
    profession, 395
Examination, NCIDQ, 398
Exciting, and line, 42
Execution, of design, 21, 23
Exposed aggregate, 262
Exterior style, 353–85
    early influences, 360–65
    nonresidential design
      examples, 367, 368, 370,
      373, 374, 375, 376, 379,
      380, 381, 383, 384

Extruded textiles, 296
Extrusion, 169
Eyelet, defined, 304
Fabric, 279–308
    aesthetics, 287–92
    and color, 287, 288,
      290–92, 300
    construction, 296–300
    criteria for written specifica-
      tions, 302
    and fibers, 293
    and finishes, 300–301
    and floors, 265, 266
    glossary, 303–7
    and human touch, 286–87
    industry, 285
    installation methods, 236
    maintenance, 296
    nonresidential design, 302–3
    and pattern, 287–88, 289,
      290–92
    performance and
      durability, 292
    period, 290–92
    and prefinishes, 300, 301
    shades, 240
    and texture, 288, 289, 290–92
    and versatility, 285–95
    and wall and ceiling
      materials and coverings,
      220, 233–36
    weight and application,
      292–96
Facade, 365
Face, of fireplace, 204
Faille, defined, 304
Fairholme, Georgina, 172
Familiarity, and stability, 19
Fanlight, 198, 369
Farbenfibel, Die, 68
Farmhouse in Provence, A, 151
Farnsworth House, 383
Fauteuil armchair, 50
Faux, 216, 228, 231
Federal style, 62, 175, 212, 269,
    357, 370, 390
    Jeffersonian, 370–71
    period fabric, 291
Fees
    and nonresidential design,
      409–10
    retainer, 407
Felt, defined, 304
Ferlita, Nelson, 205
Festoons, 244
Fiberglass, 222, 297
Fibers, and fabric, 293, 294–97
FIDER. *See* Foundation of
    Interior Design Education
    and Research (FIDER)
Fieldstone, 224
Filipe Delgado House, 379
Filler, wood, 168, 230
Filoli, 193, 196, 237, 242
Fine art, display and obtaining,
    314–17
Finial, 177
Finishes
    boards, and materials, 20
    and fabric, 300–301
    paint, 230–31
    wood, 168–69
Finish package, 347
Fire alert systems, 336, 351
Firebox, 204
Fireplaces, and chimneypieces,
    203–5
    inserts, 205
First Baptist Meetinghouse, 370
Fisheye, defined, 304
Fitz and Floyd, 324

Fitzgerald, Richard, 317
Fixtures
    decorative lighting, 322–23
    and furniture
      arrangement, 155
    kitchen and bath, 109, 116–22
    lighting, 88, 96–98
    standard sizes of, 122
fl. *See* Foot lambert (fl), 91
Flagstone, 262
Flame resistant, 302
Flame retardant, 302
Flame-retardant paints, 230
Flamestitch, defined, 304–5
Flammability, 251, 303
F lamp, 89
Flannel, defined, 305
Flat paints, 230
Flats, 125
Flatwork, 344
Fledermaus chair, 180
Flemish gables, 366
Flickering light, 94
Flitch, 168
Floating furniture
    arrangement, 140
Floccati rugs, 275, 276
Flocked carpets, 269
Flocked wallpapers, 234–35
Flooring. *See* Floors
Floor plans, 109, 110–12, 124, 131
    See also Drawings
Floors, 345
    materials and coverings,
      253–78
    and nonresidential design,
      276–77
    requirements and specifica-
      tions, 260
Florence, 354
Flou-Flou sofa, 40
Flowers, 325–26
Flowing line, 41, 42
Flue, 204
Fluorescent lighting, 70, 88,
    89–90
Flush doors, 194
Flush-face fireplace, 204
Fluting, 361
Flying buttresses, 364
Foam, polyurethane, 172
Foam back, defined, 305
Foam wall coverings, 234–35
Focal points, primary and
    secondary, 36, 146, 147
Foil/mylar wall coverings,
    234–35
Folded plate systems, 351
Folk rugs, 258, 272–74
Footage, cubic and square, 109,
    110–11, 130
Footcandle, 91
Foot lambert (fl), 91
Form
    and furniture arrangement,
      148–50
    or shape, 30, 37, 39–40
Formal, and line, 42
Formal balance. *See* Symmetri-
    cal balance
Form follows function, 49, 381
Fortier-Keller House, 378
Forum, 354
Foundation, 344–46
    design. *See* Design
Foundation of Interior Design
    Education and Research
    (FIDER), 398, 399
Fouquet, Nicolas, 164
Four plex, 125

Frames, 350
and furniture, 172
Framing, 345
Frank, Jean-Michel, 180
Franklin McVeagh House, 376
Frank Lloyd Wright House, 376
Freestanding fireplace, 204–5
French casement windows, 199
French doors, 195, 196, 378
French Empire style, 165
period fabric, 291
French influence, 377–78
French Neo-Classical style, 210
French Provincial, 290
armoire, 158
French Revolution, 61, 62
French style, 212, 213, 234
Fresco, 315
Fretwork, 177, 246
Frieze, 354, 360
defined, 305
Frieze carpet, 270
Frise, defined, 305
F. Schumacher & Co., 274,
279, 284
Full spectrum, 87
Function, 13–14, 23, 48
and form, 49, 381
and furniture arrangement,
139–41, 153
and furniture selection, 173
and zones, 109, 129
Functional finish, and
fabrics, 301
Furniture
massing, 146
metal, 169–70
nonresidential types, 153–55
and quality, 164
as symbol, 164
systems, 155, 183–85
upholstered, 171–73
wooden, 165–69
See also Furniture arrangement and Furniture
selection
Furniture arrangement, 133–56
and basic groupings, 150–53
and circulation, 140–41, 155
floating, 140
and function, 139–41
and human factors, 141–44
and nonresidential design,
153–56
and principles and elements
of design, 144–50
See also Furniture and
Furniture selection
Furniture selection, 157–86
and the classics, 174–79
and human factors, 173–74
and nonresidential design,
183–85
See also Furniture and
Furniture arrangement
Fuse-bonded carpets, 269
Future, and lighting, 98–99,
101–2
Fuzzing, 292
Gabardine, defined, 305
Gables, 360, 366
Gain, solar, 196–97, 239
Galerie, 378
Gambrel roof, 366
Garret, 366
Gates, Grove St. Cemetery, 374
Gautier, 289
Gauze, defined, 305
General lighting, 91
General Motors (GM)
Building, 25

Technical Center, 384
Gentleman and Cabinet-Maker's
Director, The, 176
Gentle movement, and line, 42
Genuine, 167
Geodesic domes, 351
Georgian style, 61, 164, 211, 357,
367–70
early and late, 61, 164, 357,
368–70
period fabric, 291
Georg Mueller House, 377
German influence, 377
"Getting Published—A
Professional Imperative,"
396
Ghirardelli Chocolate
factory, 385
Ghirardelli Square, 385
Gibbs, James, 368, 369
Gilbert, Cass, 359, 381
Gilliatt, Mary. See Mary Gilliatt
Gimp, defined, 305
Girard College, 373
G lamp, 89
Glant Fabrics, 286, 321
Glare, 87, 94–95
Glass, 364
art, 245
block, 222
doors, 195
stained and art, 223
and tableware and cookware,
319–20
tile, 223
and wall and ceiling
materials, 220, 222–23
Glass House, 383
Glazing, 198
architectural, 222–23
and paints, 229, 231
Glenmont, 376
Glides, 169
Gloria Kaplan-Sandercock
Associates, 256
Glossary, of decorative fabrics,
303–7
Gloss enamels, 230
GM. See General Motors (GM)
Gobelin Tapestry Works, 64
Goddard, John, 177
Gold, 170, 320
Gold electroplate, 320
Golden age, 61
Golden mean, 32
Golden rectangles, 32
Golden section, 32
Goldfinger, Djerba, 134
Goldfinger, June, 133, 136, 139
Goldfinger, Myron, 133, 136, 139
Goldfinger, Thira, 134
Gonnet, Yves, 26
Good taste, and style, 53–54
Gothic arch, 363
Gothic Revival style, 373–74
Gothic style, 177, 200, 359, 363,
364, 393
Gouache, 315
Governor's Mansion, 375
Governor's Palace, 368
Gracefulness, and line, 42
Gradation, or progression, 35
Grader Industries, 401
Grains, wood, 165, 168, 231
Grand Union Hotel, 375
Granite, 224, 225, 262
Graphic art, 316
Graphics
and computers, 401–2
and floor plan, 109, 110–12
Grass cloth, 234–35

Grauman's Chinese Theatre, 381
Gray goods, 285
Great hall, 113, 114
Great room, 18, 113, 114, 118, 124
Greece, 354
and color, 61
fifth century B.C., 360–61
Greek orders, 360–61
Greek Revival style, 62, 372–73
Green, and common color
associations, 74
Greene and Greene, 382, 383
Greenery, 325–26
Greenhouse, 48, 338–39
windows, 200
Greenhouse effect, 337
Greige, 285
Grenadine, defined, 305
Gretchen Bellinger, Inc., 175
Greystone, 374
Grid screens, 246
Grid-sheet drawing, 280
Griswold House, 375
Gropius, Walter, 383, 395
Grosgrain, defined, 305
Grounding receiver, 96
Groupings, basic. See Basic
groupings
Group mass, 40, 41
Group moods, color, 73, 74
Growth, and line, 42
Guaranty Building, 382
Guggenheim Mansion, 197
Guggenheim Museum, 17
Gunther, Margot, 244
Gutters, 346
Gypsum board. See Sheetrock
Haas-Lilienthal House, 376
Hall, Edward T., 142, 143
Hall's Croft, 365
Hammond-Harwood House, 369
Handicapped, and space
planning, 109, 131, 141,
155–56
Handkerchief linen, defined, 304
Hand-painted wall coverings,
234–35
Handrail, 202, 203
Hardboard, 166
Hard flooring materials, 260–64,
276–77
Hard Rock Cafe, 329
Hardware
computer, 400
drapery, 240, 245
and furniture, 169
Hard window coverings, 237,
245–48
Hardwood
floors, 254
and softwood, 165
Harmony, 30, 36–37
analogous and
contrasting, 65
color, 68
and furniture
arrangement, 148
Harrison Gray Otis House, 370
Hart Block, 375
Haughwout Building, 374, 381
Haworth, Inc., 184
Haymarket, 310
Hazardous conditions, 17
Hearst Castle, 380
Hearth, 203, 204
Heat, loss and gain, 239
Heating, ventilation, air-
conditioning (HVAC), 17,
140, 209, 250, 334–35, 341,
351, 409
Heinline, Elise, 227

Henry Calvin Fabrics, 289
Henry Whitfield House, 367
Hepplewhite, George, 178
Hepplewhite/Sheraton, 178, 290
Herculaneum, 61, 362, 370
Herman Miller, 182
Herringbone, defined, 304, 305
Hertzberg, 173
Hezekia Swain-Maria Mitchell
House, 372
Hibernian Hall, 373
Hickory/Kaylyn, 397
HID. See High-intensity
discharge (HID) lighting
Highboy, 176
High contrast, 47, 229
lighting, 92
values, 72, 73
High-gloss paints, 230
High-hatters, 98
High-intensity discharge (HID)
lighting, 88, 89, 91, 99
High key, 72, 73
High-rise apartments, 124, 125
High value, 72, 73
contrast, 47, 229
lighting, 92
Hill chair, 180
Hill County Courthouse, 375
Hilton, 289
Hineline, Curt, 216
Hinson & Co., 289
Hipped roof, 365
Historical overview, of architec-
tural detail, 210–13
Hitchcock, Henry-Russell, 383
Hitchcock, Lambert, 179
Hitchcock chair, 179
Hoffmann, Josef, 180
Holders, 245
Holiday Inn, 249
Hollow core doors, 194
Holograms, 92
Home, of character, 11
Home Insurance Building, 381
Home Magazine, 110
Homespun, defined, 305
Honors College, 373
Hooded fireplace, 204, 205
Hook-and-loop fasteners, 236
Hooked rugs, 274
Hopsaking, defined, 305
Horizontal line, 41, 42
Hotel del Coronado, 376
Houndstooth, defined, 305
Housed stairs, 202, 203
House of the Vettii, 362
Housing, types of, 124–25
Huberman, Gail, 59
Huberman, Stephen, 59
Hues, 64
and Munsell theory, 66
Hughes, Nina, 36
Hull-Wiehe House, 376
Humanizing, and line, 42
Hunt, Richard Morris, 380
Hunter Douglas Company, 223
Hunter House, 368
Hutch, 178
HVAC. See Heating, ventilation,
air-conditioning (HVAC)
IBD. See Institute of Business
Designers (IBD)
IBM. See International Business
Machines (IBM)
ICA. See International Colour
Authority (ICA)
IDC. See Interior Designers of
Canada (IDC)
IDCNY. See Interior Design
Center, New York

(IDCNY)
IDEC. *See* Interior Design Educators Council (IDEC)
IDS. *See* Interior Design Society (IDS)
IESNA. *See* Illuminating Engineering Society of North America (IESNA)
IFDA. *See* International Furnishings and Design Association (IFDA)
IFI. *See* International Federation of Interior Architects/ Interior Designers (IFI)
Ikat design, 258
Illuminating Engineering Society of North America (IESNA), 99, 102
Illusion lighting, 99
Imposing, and line, 42
Incandescent lighting, 70, 88, 89
Inc. Magazine, 19
Independence Hall, 368
Independent living, planning for, 123
Indian dhurrie rugs, 258, 272
Indirect general lighting, 91
Indirect lighting, 96–97
Indirect solar gain, 338–39
Infill, 364
Informal balance. *See* Asymmetrical balance
In-house designers, 408
Initial concept, development, 20, 23
Insects, 302
Inserts, fireplace, 205
In situ, 68
Institute of Business Designers (IBD), 395, 399
Insulation, 340, 346
Intaglio, 315
Intensity, and Munsell theory, 66, 67
Interaction, and privacy, 18
Interaction of Color, 68
Interest, and line, 42
Interface, 402
Interfacing, defined, 305
Interior, 79–330
    lighting effects, 93–94
Interior building systems, 345
    See also Building
Interior design
    study of, 10
    and well-being, 10
Interior Design Bookshop, 397
Interior Design Center, New York (IDCNY), 100, 173, 395, 408
Interior Design Educators Council (IDEC), 399
Interior Designers of Canada (IDC), 399
Interior design profession. *See* Design profession
Interior Design Society (IDS), 399
Interior finish components, 346–47
Interlining, defined, 305
Intermediate hues, 64
International Association of Lighting Designers, 99
International Business Machines (IBM), 25, 26, 100
International Colour Authority (ICA), 63, 77
International Conference of Building Officials, 22

International Federation of Interior Architects/ Interior Designers (IFI), 399
International Furnishings and Design Association (IFDA), 28, 399
International Linen Promotion Commission, 294
International style, 212, 213, 383–84, 395
Interrelationship of functions, 109
Intimate distance, 142
Inventories, 15
Iolani Palace, 375
Ionic orders, 360–61
Iron, 169, 321
Irving, Washington, 290
Isolated solar gain, 338–39
Italianate style, 357, 374
Italian Furniture Showcase, 100
Itten, Johannes, 67, 68
Jabots, 244
Jack arch lintels, 369, 370
Jacobus Demarest House, 377
Jacomini, Beverly, 26
Jacquard, defined, 305
Jacquard weave, 299
Jacquard Wilton, 407
Jalousie windows, 200
James Lanier House, 373
Janicz, Tom, 401
Japanese style, 42, 218, 246
    and accessories, 327
    See also Chinese style *and* Oriental style *and* Tokonoma
Jaspe, defined, 306
Jeanneret-Gris, Charles-Edouard, 181
Jefferson, Thomas, 370–71
Jeffersonian Federal, 370–71
Jeffrey, Noel, 115, 152, 160
Jenney, William Le Baron, 381
Jensen, Steve, 406
Jersey, defined, 305
Jetties, 375
JIDER. *See* Journal of Interior Design Education and Research (JIDER) J. M. Lynn Co., Inc., 234
John DeKoven House, 375
John Saladino, Inc., 393
Johnson, Philip, 25, 28, 383, 384
Joining methods, 168
Joints, 168
Joists, 345
Jones, Inigo, 366, 368
Jones, Jane, 184
oseph Bowers House, 372
Journal of Interior Design Education and Research (JIDER), 399
J. P. Molyneux Studio, Ltd., 393
J. P. Stevens, 288
Just Lights, 81
Jute, 294
Juxtaposition, 72
Kahn, Adolph, 59
Kallista, Inc., 400
Kandinsky, Wassily, 181, 395
Kane, Brian, 295
Kendrick House, 371, 372
Kershaw, 90
Key, high and low, 72, 73
Keystone, 351, 369
Khaki, defined, 305
Kilim rugs, 253, 258, 272
Kinsman, Rodney, 403

Kips Bay Decorator Show House, 389, 390, 393, 394
Kirk-Brummel Associates, 289
Kitchen, 13
    space, 109, 116–20
Kitsch, 317
Klismos, 174
Knit, defined, 305
Knitted carpets, 269
Knitted textiles, 296
Knoll, Florence, 182
Knoll, Hans, 182
Knoll International, Inc., 173, 181, 183, 401
Knowles, Edward, 38, 44
Kohler, 262, 320
Kraft papers, 234–35
Kragsyde, 376
Lace, 300
    defined, 305
Lacquer, 169
Ladder-back chair, 178
Lady Pepperell House, 369
Lafayette, Marquis de, 312
Laido, Michael B., 110
Laido Designs, 110
Lamb, Thomas, 405
Laminated foam, 172
Lamination, 166
Lampas, defined, 305
Lamps, 88, 89, 90, 322–23
Lancaster Meeting House, 370
Lancets, 364
Landings, 202, 203
Landscape Forms, Inc., 170
Lappet, defined, 305
Larkin, Thomas, 380
Larsen, Jack Lenor, 26, 295, 407
Laser lights, 92
Late Georgian style, 61, 164, 357, 368–70
Latex, 297
Latex paints, 230
Lath, 364
Lath method, 236
Latillas, 379
Latin cross, 363
Latrobe, Benjamin, 370
Lattuca, Vince, 97
Laundry rooms, 121–22
Laura Ashley Company, 17, 37, 41, 110, 238, 309
Lauwe, Paul Chombart de. *See* de Lauwe, Paul Chombart
La Veuve-Dodier House, 378
La Vigne, 294
Lawn, defined, 305
Law of chromatic distribution, 69
Layered textiles, 296, 300
Lead, 170
Leaded glass, 245
Leaded panes, 364
Leather, 295
    and floors, 265, 266
    wall coverings, 234–35
Le Corbusier, 181, 246, 383
LED. *See* Light-emitting diode (LED)
Lee Jofa, 172, 235, 407
Leno, defined, 305
Lenox Hill Hospital, 22
Le Pretre Mansion, 378
Les Prismatiques, 405
Letters of agreement, 23, 401, 407
Level loop carpets, 270
Lever House, 384
Levine, Rona, 314
Levitas House, 32
Lewis, Robert K., 26, 312
Liberty of London, 174

Library, for designer, 397
Life-style, 12
    and function, 139
Light, 30, 37, 46
    combustion, 70, 87–88
    control, 91
    natural, 87–88
    physics of, 87
    pipes, 92
    and psychology, 94–95
    values, 72
    and windows, 197, 237, 240
    See also Lighting
Light bulbs. *See* Lamps
Lighted toe mold, 97
Light-emitting diode (LED), 101
Lighting, 17, 70, 81–102
    accent and mood, 92
    ambient and general, 91
    as art, 92
    artificial, 70, 88–91
    associations, 102
    categories of effects, 91–92
    economy, 92–93, 100–101
    fixtures, 88, 96–98, 322–23
    future, 98–99, 101–2
    indirect, 96–97
    interior effects, 93–94
    motivational, 99–100
    natural, 99
    network of, 100
    and nonresidential design, 99–102
    pipes, 92
    safety, 100
    task, 91–92, 185
    track, 92, 98
    See also Light
Lighting associations, 102
Lightolier Lighting Laboratory, 60, 84
Line, 30, 37, 41–44
    combining, 44
    and furniture arrangement, 148
    lighting, 93
    and linear development, 42
    and *See* Linear Moon
    psychological effects, 42–43
Linear development, and line, 42
Linear Moon, and line, 42
Line lighting, 93
Linen, 285, 294
    handerchief, 304
Linenfold, 192
Lines of credit, 397
Lining, defined, 305
Linoleum, 266
Lintels, 369, 370
Lithographs, 316
Lively, and line, 42
Lively visual stimulation, and line, 43
Living areas, 13
Livingston family, 353
Location, physical. *See* Physical location
Lofty, and line, 42
Log cabin, 376
Longfellow House, 369
Long-life bulbs, 90
Longwood, 375
Loom, 254, 258
Loose cushions, 172
Los Ceritos Ranch House, 380
Louis XIV, King, 11, 164
Louis XV, King, 174, 175, 177, 328
Louis XVI, King, 174
Lounges, 181

Louvers, 207
  blinds, 246
  doors, 195
  shutters, 248
Lovell Beach House, 383
Lovell-Health House, 383
Lowboy, 176, 177
Low contrast, 47
  values, 72, 73
Low key, 72, 73
Low values, 72
Low-voltage
  incandescent lamps, 90
  lighting, 89
Lumber core doors, 194
Lumen, 91
Luminaires, 88, 96–98
  decorative, 96
  portable, 92, 96
Luminous ceiling, 92
Luminous panels, 96
Luten Clarey Stern, Inc., 168, 405
Luxury homes, 125
Lyndhurst, 374
MA. See Master of arts (MA)
Maat, Douglas, 184
MacAulay, Angus, 19
McIntire, Samuel, 370, 395
McKim, Mead, and White,
  376, 381
McKinley High School, 375
Mackintosh, Charles Rennie, 180
McMillen, Inc., 287
MacPhaedris-Warner House, 368
Madame John's Legacy, 378
Maintenance, 20
Maison Carre, 362
Maize mats, 275, 276
Malimo, defined, 305
Manager, desk, 401
Manhattan Antique Show, 310
Manhattan Island, 359
Man-made cellulosic fiber,
  295–96
Man-made lighting. See
  Artificial lighting
Man-made noncellulosic/
  synthetics, 296
Mannucci, Nancy, 191
Mansard roof, 375
Mansard style, 375
Mantel, 203
Mar, Leoda de. See de Mar,
  Leoda
Marazzi, 223
Marble, 224, 225, 228, 262–63
  flooring, 254
  parquet, 262
Marble House, 380
Marbling, 231
Marimekko, 59
Marketing centers, 400
Markets, 400
Mark Hampton, Inc., 57
Mark Twain House, 375
Marlborough leg, 177
Marquetry, 167
Marquisette, defined, 304, 305
Marshall Field Warehouse, 376
Martex, 285
Mary Gilliatt, 45, 232
Mary Meehan Interiors, 393
Mason, James, 154
Masonry block construction, 350
Mass, 30, 37, 40–41
  group, 40, 41
Massing, 40, 41
  furniture, 146
Master of arts (MA), 403
Master of fine arts (MFA), 403
Master of science (MS), 403

Matchstick shades, 246–47
Matelassé, defined, 305
Materials
  and finishes boards, 20
  wall, 220–27
Mats, 275, 276
Matte paints, 230
Maybeck, Bernard, 381, 382, 383
Mayo-Delucci Interiors, 289
Maytag, 110
Mean, golden. See Golden mean
Measurement, units of, 90–91
Mechanical considerations,
  17, 23
Mechanical finish, and
  fabrics, 301
Medieval era, and color, 61
Medieval style, 365–67
Melamines, 170
Memento, 328
Memo samples, 6, 283, 409
Menslow, Mikel, 247
Metal
  doors, 194–95
  frame, 350
  furniture, 169–70
  and tableware and cookware,
    320–21
  types of, 169–70
  and wall and ceiling
    materials, 221, 223
Metallic fabric, 297
Metameric shift, 88
Metamerism, 70
Metopes, 361
Metropolitan Furniture
  Corporation, 295
Mexican tile, 264
Meyer & Holler, 381
Mezzanine, 236
MFA. See Master of fine arts
  (MFA)
MHT Architects, 330
Micro-miniblinds, 246
Microorganisms, 302
Middle Ages, 362–65
  and color, 61
Miles-Brewton House, 369
Military collection, 19
Mills-Stebbins House, 374
Millwork, 226–27
Mindel, Lee, 168
Mineral synthetics, 297
Ming porcelain, 393
Miniblinds, 245–46
Minimalism, 63
Mirrors, 222, 318
Mission Church, 379
Missions, California, 378
Missoni fabrics, 289, 298
Miss Parks House, 376
Mitchell, Carl, 267
Mitering, 193
Miter joints, 168
Mobile homes, 124, 125
Modacrylic, and carpet fibers,
  268, 296
Modern International style, 62
Modernist architecture, 359
Modern styles, 62–63, 381–84
  classics, 180–83
  period fabric, 292
Modillions, 365
Modric, Inc., 400
Moire, defined, 305
Molding, 193–94, 227, 361
MOMA. See Museum of
  Modern Art (MOMA)
Monadnock Building, 382
Monitor, 400
  roof, 338, 339

Monochromatic color
  schemes, 65
Monterey style, 380
Montgomery Place, 353
Monticello, 371
Moods, color group, 73, 74
Moore, Henry, 312
Moorish style, 359
Mooser, William, 381
Moot lighting, 92
Morgan, Julia, 380
Morland, Victoria, 151
Moroccan rugs, 274
Morris, William, 395
Morse-Libby House, 374
Mortgage payments,
  comparison of, 113
Mortise and tenon, 168
Mosaic, 61, 314, 315
Moths, 294
Motif Designs
Motivational lighting, 99–100
Motorized rods, 245
Mount Airy, 369
Mount Pleasant, 369
Mount Vernon, 359
Mount Vesuvius, 362
Movable louvered shutters, 248
Movement, gentle, line, and
  rhythmic, 42
MS. See Master of science (MS)
Muffson, Cindy, 43
Mulligan, Sharon, 283
Multi-level living, 128
Multiplex dwellings, 125
Multiuse area, 113
Munsell, Albert Henry, 66
Munsell Color, 66, 77
Munsell packets, 66
Munsell theory, 66–67
Murals, 234
Museum of Modern Art
  (MOMA), 312, 383
Muslin, defined, 305
Mylar
  defined, 305
  wall coverings, 234–35
Nadler/Philopena, 343
NAHB. See National Association
  of Home Builders
  (NAHB)
Napoleon Bonaparte, 61, 62
Napoleonic Empire, 394
Napple, Richard, 72
Naps, 173
NASAD. See National Associa-
  tion of Schools of Art and
  Design (NASAD)
Nathaniel Russell House, 370
National Association of Home
  Builders (NAHB), 336
National Association of Schools
  of Art and Design
  (NASAD), 398, 399
National Council of Interior
  Design Qualification
  (NCIDQ), 398, 399
National Design Fellowship
  Competition, 28
National Home Furnishing
  League (NHFL), 399
National Lighting Bureau (NLB),
  99, 102
National Trust for Historic
  Preservation, 384
Native American motifs, 247
Natkin, Robert, 312
Natural cellulosic fibers, 294
Natural daylighting, 99
Natural fiber rugs, 275–76
Naturalistic design, 51

Natural light, 87–88
Natural protein fibers, 294–95
Natural traffic pattern, 140
Nature, objects from, 325–26
Navajo rugs, 48, 273
Nave, 363
NCIDQ. See National Council of
  Interior Design Qualifica-
  tion (NCIDQ)
Needle constructed textiles,
  296, 300
Needlepoint
  defined, 305
  rugs, 274
Needlepunch carpets, 269
Negative space, 39, 148, 149
Neoclassic style, 35, 61, 163, 174,
  175, 177, 189, 198, 201,
  204, 210, 269, 290, 312,
  353, 397
  period fabric, 291
Neon. See Cold cathode lighting
Net, defined, 305
Netherland Plaza, 218, 303
Network
  computer, 401
  of lighting, 100
Neutra, Richard, 383
Neutralized colors, 69
Neutrals, 69–70
Newel post, 202
Newman, Rachel, 310
New Mexico style, 16, 18
Newton, Isaac, 87
New York, 359
New York Designer's
  Saturday, 396
New York Subway Station, 276
Nextel, 401
NHFL. See National Home
  Furnishing League
  (NHFL)
Ninon, defined, 306
NLB. See National Lighting
  Bureau (NLB)
Noel Jeffrey, Inc., 390
Nogging, 364
Noise, 16–17
Non-architectural lighting, 96
Nonresidential design
  and architectural detail, 209
  and art and accessories,
    328–30
  and building systems, 350–51
  and color, 75–76
  and design principles and
    elements, 54–55
  and design process, 22–23
  and design profession,
    408–10
  and exterior style examples,
    367, 368, 370, 373, 374,
    375, 376, 379, 380, 381,
    383, 384
  and fabric, 302–3
  and floor materials and
    coverings, 276–77
  and furniture arrangement,
    153–56
  and furniture selection,
    183–85
  and lighting, 99–102
  and space planning, 129–32
  and wall, ceiling, and
    window treatments,
    248–51
  See also Design and Design
    profession
Nonresilient flooring materials,
  260–64, 276–77
Nonwoven textiles, 296, 300

Norman, 363
Nosing, 202
Notes, 23, 55, 76, 102, 132, 156, 185, 213, 251, 277–78, 303, 330, 352, 385, 410
Nylon, 295, 296
    and carpet fibers, 268
Objects from nature, 325–26
Objets d'art, 317
Objets Plus, 310
Occasional chair, 147
Occasional table, 178
Occult balance. See Asymmetrical balance
Oculus, 362
Office planning, 131
O'Hare Airport, 86
Oheka Castle, 15, 59
Oil-based paints, 230
Oil paint, 314
OJVM, 289
Olana, 359, 375
Old Customs House, 380
Olefin, 296–97
    polypropylene, and carpet fibers, 268
Omega, 205
One-turn stair, 202, 203
Onion domes, 374
On memo, 6, 283, 409
Open floor plans, 124
Open office planning, 131
Open plans, 155
Open riser stair, 202
Open showroom, 400
Open stairs, 202, 203
Operable windows, 198
Operational control, and windows, 237, 240
Opposition, or contrast, 35–36
Optical balance. See Asymmetrical balance
Orange, and common color associations, 74
Order, 360
Ordinary incandescent lamps, 90
Organdy, defined, 306
Organic architecture, 382–83
Organizational tool programs, 402
Organizations
    color, 77
    professional, 398–99
    See also Associations
Oriental style, 374–75
    period fabric, 290
    rugs, 254, 258, 271–72
    See also Chinese style and Japanese style
Orientation
    of light, 70, 240
    site, and climate, 109, 112
    and windows, 196–97
Ostwald, Wilhelm, 67, 68
Ostwald theory, 67–68
Ottoman, 41
    defined, 306
Outbuildings, 368
Outlets, and switches, 95
Outlet strips, 96, 100
Outline lighting, 93
Outlining, 231
Overcrowding, 111
Ownership, types of, 126–28
Oxford cloth, defined, 306
Packets. See Munsell packets
Padding, 172
    and carpets, 270
Paint, 227–31
    finishes and textures, 230–31

guidelines and cautions, 228–30
techniques, 230–31
types of, 230
and wall and ceiling materials, 221
Paintings, 314–15
Paisley, defined, 306
Palace of Fine Arts, 381
Palace of the Governors, 379
Palace of Versailles, 11
Palatte theory, 64
Palazzo Rucellai, 365
Palio Restaurant, 75
Palisade wall, 192
Palladian window, 189, 197, 198, 199, 369
Palladio, Andrea, 354, 365, 366
Pallas Athena, 354
Paneled doors, 194
Paneling, wood, 192–93, 227
Panel-track method, 236
Pantheon, 362
Panton, Verner, 183
Panton Design, 183
Papier-mâche, and furniture, 170
Park Avenue, New York, 390
PAR lamp, 89
Parquet, 262, 264
Parson Capen House, 367
Parsons School of Design, 180
Parthenon, 354, 359, 360
Particleboard, 166
Passive balance. See Symmetrical balance
Passive solar system, 337–39
Paste, 233
Pasteup, direct, 236
Paterae, 370
Patio doors, 196
Pattern, 30, 37, 45–46
    character of, 45
    combining, 45–46
    and fabric, 287–88, 289, 290–92
    and nonresidential design, 251
    repeat, 233
    and scale, 46
Pattern books, 365
Patterns, traffic, 109, 115, 130–31, 140
Paul Segal & Associates, 55
Pavarini-Cole Interiors, 236
Pavilion, 369
Payments, mortgage. See Mortgage payments
PC. See Computers
Pedestal table, 179
Pediment, 176, 360, 368
Pediment frieze, 360
Peelable wall covering, 233
Pei, I. M., 26, 103, 104
Pelican Prints, 234
Pellon, defined, 306
Pendants, 366
Percale, defined, 306
Peretti, Giancarlo, 183
Performance, and fabric, 292
Perimeter lighting, 93
Period fabrics, 290–92
Peristyle, 362
Perlini, Paula, 57
Permanent fixtures, kitchen and bath, 109, 116–22
Persian rugs, 272
Personal distance, 142
Personal space, 142
Peter Charles, 171
Pewter, 170, 320

Ph.D. See Doctor of philosophy (Ph.D)
Phidias, 360
Philadelphia, 357
Philadelphia Water Works, 373
Phyfe, Duncan, 175
Physical location, 16–17
Physics, of light, 87
Piano, and symbols, 164
Piano nobile, 35, 365
Piccolo chair, 40
Picking out, 231
Piece work, defined, 304
Pierced screens, 246
Pierce-Nichols House, 370
Piers, 364
Pilasters, 192, 365
Pile carpets, 270
Pile fabric, defined, 306
Pile weave, 299
Pilling, 292
Pinechas home, 216
Pingree House, 370
Pinpoint lighting, 93
Pique, defined, 306
Pit, conversation, 151
Pitney-Bowes, 21, 103, 104, 106
Place des Antiquaries, 310
Plaid, defined, 306
Plain slicing, 168
Plain weave, 298
Plan drawing, 148, 149
Plane of light, 93
Planned development, 124–25
Planning
    appliances, 121
    barrier-free, 141, 155–56
    bubble, 110
    and independent living, 123
    open office, 131
    space, 103–32
    and systems furniture, 155, 183–85
Plans
    floor, 109, 110–12, 124, 131
    open, 155
    wiring, 95–96, 100
Plantation shutters, 248
Plants, 325
Plaster, and wall and ceiling materials, 221, 223–4
Plaster ceilings, 206
Plastic, 321
    and furniture, 170–71
    doors, 195
Plate rail, 192
Platner, Warren, 183
Platner Wire Grouping, 183
Plato, 54
Platt, Joseph, 180
Playful activity, and line, 43
Pleated shades, 243, 247
Pleated valances, 244
Plexibility, 171
Plexiglass, 222–23
Plexus, 170
Plia chair, 183
Plies, 166
Plisse, defined, 306
PL lamp, 89
Plotters, 401
Plumbing, 17, 345, 346
    systems, 334
Plush carpet, 270
Plywood, 166
Pneumatic systems, 351
Pocket doors, 195
Podium, 362
POE. See Post-occupancy evaluation (POE)
Pogo's Disco, 86

Pointed arch, 363
Point lighting, 93
Polished cotton, defined, 306
Pollack, Mark C., 295, 407
Polo, Mark, 153, 166, 319, 324
Polyester, 296
    and carpet fibers, 268
Polypropylene, 296–97
    and carpet fibers, 268
Polyurethane, 169, 170, 172
Pompeii, 61, 362, 363, 370
Pony chaise, 181
Pool of light, 93
Poplin, defined, 306
Porcelain, 51, 318–19, 393
Porphyry, 231
Portable luminaires, 92, 96
Portico, 362
Portuguese kilim garden rug, 253
Positive space, 39
Post-Modernist design, 25
Post-occupancy evaluation (POE), 23, 48, 397
Post-War Modernism, 25
Pouf shades, 243
Power
    and discernment, 52–53
    terminology, 90–91
Prang theory, 64
Prefinishes, and fabric, 300, 301
Prepasted wall covering, 233
Presbyterian Church of Bedford, New York, 359
Presentation, 20
Preservation, 384–85
President's House, 368
Presley, Elvis, 329
Pretil, 379
Pretrimmed wall covering, 233
Price, Carole H., 10
Primary focal point, 146, 147
Primary hues, 64
Primers, 230
Princeton University, 83
Principles of Harmony and Contrast of Colors, The, 64
Principles. See Design principles
Printing, 300, 301
Printmaking, 314, 315
Priscilla curtains, 241
Privacy
    draperies, 242
    and interaction, 18
    and windows, 197, 237, 238
Private ownership, 126
Private zones, 109
Problem, solving, 20–21
Process, design. See Design process
Product Design Awards, 168, 170, 184, 235, 274, 275, 295, 400, 404, 405, 406, 407
    Roscoe Awards, 170, 184, 295, 400, 403, 404, 405, 406
Profession, design. See Design profession
Professional roles, 340–42
    nonresidential design, 350
Profile, 12
Programming, 396
    and research, 12–20, 23
Programs, 12
    computer, 401
    data-base, 401
    organizational tool, 402
    writing, 20, 23
Progression, or gradation, 35
Projecting fireplace, 204

Proportion
  and furniture
    arrangement, 150
  and scale, 30, 31–32
  and space planning, 123–24
Proprietor, sole, 402
Proxemics, 55, 142–43
PS lamp, 89
Psychological considerations,
    17–19, 23
Psychological effects, of line,
    42–43
Psychology, 109
  color, 72–74
  - and light, 94–95
  and space, 123, 131
Public distance, 143
Pueblo Indians, 18, 378
Pueblos, 378
Pull shades, 246
Punch list, 347–49
Purple, and common color
    associations, 74
Pyramids, 228
Quality
  determining, 164
  and windows, 197
Quarry tile, 226, 264
Quarter slicing, 168
Quatrefoil, 171
Queen Anne style, 176, 177,
    284, 376
  furniture, 163, 166
Queen Mary textiles, 110
Quilted fabric, defined, 306
Quilted valances, 244
Quincy Market, 373
Quire, 363
Quoins, 368
Rachel, defined, 306
Rachel knits, 300
Radial balance, 32, 34–35, 36
Radiation, 35, 36, 337
Radio City Music Hall, 284
Ragging, 231
Rag rolling, 231
Rag rugs, 274
Rails, 192
Rainbow roofs, 371
Raised hearth, 204
Raised-panel shutters, 247–48
Rambler, 128
Random shear carpets, 270
Rapid-start fluorescent lamps, 90
Raschel knit, defined, 306
Rasmussen, Antonio, 330
Rattan, and furniture, 170, 171
Rayon, 295
RDI, 400
Rebar, 344
Recessed adjustable accent
    lighting, 98
Recessed downlights, 98
Recessed fixtures, 96, 98
Recoder, Danny, 235
Rectangles, golden. See Golden
    rectangles
Red, and common color
    associations, 74
Red Lion Inn, 283
Redwood Library, 370
Reeded legs, 178
Reflecting glare, 95
Reflective lamps, 89
Refraction, 17
Regency period, 30, 61, 163,
    175, 179
Regular weave, 298
Reinforced concrete, 344
Relationships, 14, 23

Reliance Building, 382
Relief painting, 315
Renaissance, 204, 205, 206, 218,
    258, 280, 324, 354, 363, 365
  and color, 61
  period fabric, 290
Renderings, 20, 397
Rental, 127–28
Renwick, James, 374
Rep, defined, 306
Repetition, and alternation, 35
Repetitive tempo, and line, 42
Repose, and line, 42
Reproductions, 316
Republic style, 353
Research, and programming,
    12–20, 23
Residential interiors, and
    color, 75
Residential space planning. See
    Space planning
Resilience, 302
Resilient flooring materials,
    260–61, 265, 266, 276–77
Resources, design profession,
    399–400
Restful, and line, 42
Restoration, 384
Restrained, and line, 42
Restrictions, 19, 22, 23
Retailing, careers in, 403
Retainer fee, 407
Reverberation, 17
Reversible cushions, 172
Rhythm, 30, 35–36
  and furniture
    arrangement, 146
Rhythmic movement,
    and line, 42
Ribs, 364
Richard Felber Designs, Inc., 234
Richardson, Henry Hobson, 376
Richard Vreeland House, 377
Richfield Oil Building, 384
Rightness, sense of. See Sense of
    rightness
Riley, Jeff, 43, 111
Rio Condominium, 162
Riser, 202
R lamp, 89
Robbins, Tom, 400
Robert house, 44
Robert Metzger Interiors,
    Inc., 394
Robie House, 382
Robsjohn-Gibbings, T. H., 175
Rockefeller Center, 384
Rocker, 49
Rocker switch, 95
Rococo Revival style, 212
Rococo style, 51, 147, 174, 175,
    179, 204, 208, 209, 210,
    284, 290
  period fabric, 290
Rods, 240, 245
Roese, Terri, 407
Rollikan rugs, 273
Rolls, of wall coverings, 233
Romanesque style, 204, 357, 363
Romanesque Victorian
    influence, 35
Roman forum, 354
Roman shades, 243
Rome, 361–62
  and color, 61
Roofs, 365, 366, 371, 375
  monitors, 338, 339
  trusses, 345
Roosevelt, Franklin Delano,
    10, 11

Roosevelt, Sara Delano, 10
  See also Sara Delano
    Roosevelt House
Roscoe Awards. See Product
    Design Awards
Ross, Barbara, 338
Rotary slicing, 168
Rotunda, 207
Roumanian kilims, 258
Roundheaded arch, 35, 361
Round wire carpets, 270
Row houses, 125, 370
Rowland, David, 182
Rubber, and floors, 265, 266
Rubber-backed tufted
    carpets, 269
Rubbings, 316
Rubble, 224, 262
Rugs, 48, 52, 253, 254, 258
  and nonresidential
    design, 277
  Oriental and area, 271–76
Rush, and furniture, 170, 171
Russell House, 373
Russian Azerbijan rug, 254
Rusticated, 365
Rya rugs, 273
Saarinen, Eero, 182
Saavedra, Ruben de. See de
    Saavedra, Ruben
Safety
  codes, and nonresidential
    design, 251
  lighting, 100
  and security, 19
Sagamore Hotel, 5
Sailcloth, defined, 306
Saint-Denis, 363
St. Luke's Church, 367
St. Michael's Church, 370
St. Patrick's Cathedral, 374
Saladino, John, 14, 26
Saley, Mark, 274
Saltbox roofs, 366
Salt Lake City International
    Airport, 88, 330
Samples, 6, 283, 409
San Carlos de Borromeo, 378
Sandstone, 224, 262
San Francisco de Asis, 379
Sanger-Peper Building, 374
San Jose y San Miguel de
    Aguayo, 378
Sante Fe style, 18, 379
San Xavier del Bac, 378
Sara Delano Roosevelt House,
    10–11, 97, 153, 166, 228,
    236, 289, 314, 319, 324
Saran, 297
Saridis, S. A., 175
Sartogo, Piero, 128
Sash curtains, 241
Sash windows, 200, 368
Satin
  defined, 303, 306
  paints, 230
  weave, 299
Sausage turnings, 178
Savonnerie design, 258, 274
Savoy Plaza Hotel, 381
Saxony carpet, 270
Saxony Carpet Company,
    275
Scale
  and furniture arrangement,
    144–46
  and pattern, 46
  and proportion, 30–31
  and space planning, 123–24
Scandanavian style, 395
Scarpa, Afra, 183

Scarpa, Tobia, 183
Scheduling, 343
Schematics, 20
  and floor plan, 109, 110–12
Schiffli embroidery, defined,
    304, 306
Schindler, Rudolph, 383
Schumacher, 409
Schwartz, Barbara, 338
Scottish lace, 300
Screens, 246, 321–22
  Shoji, 195, 196, 218, 246, 322
Scrim, defined, 306
Scroll volutes, 361
Scrubbable wall covering, 233
Sculpture, 314
Sculptured carpet, 270
Sculpturing, 254
Seagram Building, 384
Sealers, and fillers, 230
Secessionists, 180
Secondary focal point, 146, 147
Secondary hues, 64
Second Bank of the United
    States, 373
Secretary, 177
Section, golden. See Golden
    section
Secure, and line, 42
Security
  and safety, 19
  systems, 336
  and windows, 196
Seersucker, defined, 306
Selection, furniture. See
    Furniture selection
Semidetached houses, 125
Semigloss paints, 230
Semihoused stair, 202, 203
Semitrimmed wall covering, 233
Sense of rightness, 32
Sensitivity, 11–12
Serge, defined, 306
Serigraphs, 316
Serpentine shapes, 177
Set, theatrical or stage, 55
Seventeenth-century English
    Medieval style, 365–67
Shade cloth, defined, 306
Shades, 240, 242, 246–47
  calculating yardage, 239
Shading, 231
Shadows-on-the-Teche, 373, 378
Shadrach Standish House, 372
Shag carpet, 270
Shakers, 179, 288, 310
Shantung, defined, 306
Shape, or form, 30, 37, 39–40
  of space, 109, 111–12
  of lamps, 89, 90
Shaped valances, 244
Shaping. See Shape
Shed ceilings, 206
Sheer
  defined, 306
  draperies, 242
Sheetrock, 206, 226
Shellac, 168, 169
Sheraton, 179
Sheraton/Hepplewhite
    sideboards, 30, 52
Shingles, 346
Shirred valances, 244
Shoji screens, 195, 196, 218,
    246, 322
Showrooms, 400
Shutters, 247–48
Sideboard, 30, 178
Side draperies, 242
Sidelight, 201, 370
Sidler Brothers, 163

Sign of the Dove, 83
Silk, 294–95
Silk screen, 316
Silver, 170, 320
Silver plate, 320
Simplicity, 50, 54
Single-hung sash window, 200
Sisal mats, 275, 276
Siskin, Paul, 394
Siskin-Valls, Inc., 394
Site, orientation, and climate, 109, 112
Sizes
    of space, 109, 110–11
    standard, 122
Sizing, and wall covering, 233
SJW Designs, 406
Sketches, 397
Skidmore, Owings, and Merrill, 384
Skylight, 201, 206
Skyscrapers, 381–82
Slate, 263
Slat shutters, 248
Slicing, 168
Sliding windows, 201
Smart house systems, 336
Smith and Watson, 163
Smith-Chororos, 405
Social distance, 143
Social zones, 109
Sociological considerations, 17–19, 23
Soffit, 346
    lighting, 97
Sof-Stone, 401
Soft, and line, 42
Soft floor coverings, 265–76
Software, computer, 401
Soft window coverings, 237, 240–44
Softwood, and hardwood, 165
Solar gain, and windows, 196–97, 239
Solarium, 334
Solarium greenhouse, 48
Solar systems, passive and active, 337–40
Sole proprietor, 402
Solid, 167
    and line, 42
Solid core doors, 194
Solvents, 230
Soriana chair, 183
Sotheby's, 316
Sound board, 346
Sources, trade, 399
South American rugs, 274
Southern Furniture Market, 288
Southwest Adobe style, 212, 213
Southwestern style, 378–79
Southwest Indian, period fabric, 292
Space, 30, 37, 38–39
    allocation, 109
    bubble of, 142
    frame, 350
    and furniture arrangement, 148–50, 155–56
    negative, 148, 149
    personal, 142
    positive and negative, 39
    requirements, 14–15, 23
    -saving devices, 114
    stretching, 109, 114–15
    See also Space planning
Space planning, 103–32
    and design process, 109
    and economy, 109, 112–13
    and elderly and handi-capped, 109

and emotion and psychology, 109
    and nonresidential design, 129–32
    and permanent fixtures, 109, 116–22
    residential, 124
    and storage, 109, 115–16
    and traffic patterns, 109–15, 130–31
    See also Space
Spandex, 297
Spanish Colonial influence, 18, 207, 378–80
    period fabric, 292
    rugs, 274
Spattering, 231
Specifications, 401
    and working drawings, 21, 23
Spectra Color System, 400
Spectral energy distribution, 88
Spectre, Jay, 288
Spectrum, full and visual, 87
Spiegel, Signey, 39, 227, 309
Spiegel, Ted, 227, 309
Spiral staircase, 202, 203
Splat, 176
Split complements, 65, 66
Split-entry home, 128
Split-level home, 128
Sponging, 231
Spotlights, 92
Springs, and furniture, 172
Square footage, 109, 110–11, 112, 130
Stability
    angular, 42
    dimensional, 302
    and familiarity, 19
Stage set, 55
Stahl, Fred, 406
Stained glass, 223, 245, 364
Stainless steel, 170, 223, 320
Stains, 230
Stairs, 201–3
Stairwell, 202, 203
Standard clearances, 141–42
Standard Color Wheel theory, 64
Standard finishes, and fabrics, 301
Standard sizes, of fixtures and cabinetry, 122
Standart, Clinton, 57
Standart, Joe, 57
Stapling, 236
Stark Carpets, 253, 258
Starting step, 202
State House, 370, 371
Statement, design. See Design statement
Static electricity, 302
Steel, 170, 223, 320
Steelcase, 401
Stenciling, 227
Stephens, Katherine, 11
Stick style, 375
Stickwork, 375
Stiles, 192
Stimulation, lively visual, 43
Stippling, 231
Stock plans, 124
Stone, 228, 262–63
    and wall and ceiling materials, 221, 225–26
Stone-enders, 366
Stoneware, 319
Storage
    and space planning, 109, 115–16
    zones, 109
Stout, Doug, 329

Stoves, 205
Straight line, 41, 42
Straight run stair, 202, 203
Strapping tape method, 236
Stretchers, 175
Stretching space, 109, 114–15
Strie, defined, 306
Stringcourse, 368
Stringers, 201–2
Strippable wall covering, 233
Structural building components, 344–47
Structural design, 49–51
Structural lighting, 96
    and nonresidential design, 350–51
Stucco, 361
Style
    exterior. See Exterior style
    good, 53–54
    See also particular individual styles
Stylobate, 360
Subcontractor, 342
Subfloors, 345
Suckle, Abby, 103, 104
Suedecloth, defined, 306
Sullivan, Louis, 381, 382
Sumner, Teddy, 274
Sung Tao, 323
Sunnyside, 290
Superchairs, 185
Surface-mounted fixtures, 96, 98
Surface treatment finish, and fabrics, 301
Surround, 204
Suspended ceilings, 209
Suspended fixtures, 96
Swags, 244
    calculating yardage, 239
Swedish influence, 376
Swinging doors, 115
Swiss, defined, 304, 306
Switches, and outlets, 95
Symbolisms, color, 73, 74
Symbols
    floor plan, 131
    furniture as, 164
Symmetrical balance, 32–33
Synergy, 83
Synsley bone china, 321
Synthetics, 296, 297
Systems
    arch, 350–51
    beam, 351
    built-in, 336–40
    cable, 351
    communication, 336, 351
    dome, 351
    fire alert, 336, 351
    folded plate, 351
    furniture, 155, 183–85
    interior building, 345
    plumbing, 334
    pneumatic, 351
    security, 351
    smart house, 336
    solar, 337–40
    structural, 344–47
    telephone, 351
    tensile, 351
    true divider, 200
    vaulted, 351
    See also Building systems
Tabby weave, 298
Tab curtains, 241
Tables, 178
Tableware, 318
Taffeta
    defined, 307
    weave, 298

Taliesein West, 383
Taos, 379
Tapestry, 237, 309, 324
    defined, 307
Task lighting, 91–92, 185
Taste, good, 53–54
Tatami mats, 275, 276
Taurelle, Bernard, 321
Tea table, 176
Technical drawings, 397
Telephone, 17
    systems, 351
Tempera, 315
Tempered glass doors
Tempo, repetitive, 42
Tenants, 408
Tensile systems, 351
Tenure-track positions, 403
Terminals, 401
Terminology
    of decorative fabrics, 303–7
    of power, 90–91
    of wall covering, 233
Terrace houses, 370
Terra-cotta, 365
Terrazzo, 262
Terri Roese III collection, 407
Territoriality, 143–44
Territorial style, 379
Terry, defined, 307
Tertiary hues, 64
Tesserae, 315
Tetrad complements, 65, 66
Textile, 110, 324–25
    construction, 296–300
    design, 406
    wall coverings, 234–35
Texture, 30, 37, 44–46
    carpet, 270
    and fabric, 288, 289, 290–92
    paint, 230–31
Texturizing paints, 230–31
Theatrical set, 55
Thebes stool, 174
THE chair, 182
Theory, color. See Color
Theory of design. See Design
Thermoplastics, 170
Thermoset plastics, 170
Thermosiphoning, 338
Thibaut fabrics, 287
Thiel, Philip, 73
Thin shell membranes, 351
Thomas Clemence House, 367
Thomas Larkin House, 380
Thompson-Neely House, 377
Thonet, Michael, 180, 181
Thonet bentwood rocker, 49
Thorn, Susan, 5, 6, 7, 8, 9, 283
Ticking, defined, 307
Tieback draperies, 242
Tieback holders, 245
Tiered curtains, 241
Tightly curved line, 41, 43
Tile, 263–64, 265, 266
    floors, 256
    glass, 223
    and wall and ceiling materials, 221, 225–26
Timber-framed houses, 364
Tin, 170
T lamp, 89
Toe mold, 97
Toile, defined, 307
Toilet, 121, 130
Tokonoma, 42, 218, 327
    See also Japanese style
Tomlin, Gerald, 208
Tones, 69
Tongue-and-groove paneling, 192, 193

Tools, interior design, 400
Topacio, Hector S., 405
Top treatments, 240
  types of, 244
Tortoiseshell, 231
Toscana Ristorante, 128
Town houses, 124, 125
Town Office Building, 374
Townsend and Goddard, 164
Tracery, 364
Track lighting, 92, 98
Trade sources, 399
Traffic patterns, 109, 115,
  130–31, 140
Transepts, 363
Transition, 35
Transom, 201, 322, 372
Traverse rods, 240, 245
Travertine, 225, 262, 263
Treads, 202
Tree. See Munsell theory
"Tree-of-life" crewel design, 31
Triadic complements, 65, 66
Tricot, defined, 307
Tric-Trac table lamp, 40
Triforium, 364
Triglyphs, 361
Trinity Church, 368, 376
Tripod pedestal table, 179
Trombe walls, 338
Trompe l'oeil, 228, 234
Trout Hall, 377
Troxell-Steckel House, 377
True divider system, 200
Trump Parc Apartments, 152
Trusses, 345, 360, 364
Tudor style, 209, 210, 357
Tufted fabric, defined, 307
Tufts, 173
Tugendhat House, 181
Tungsten filament, 89
Tungsten halogen lamp, 89
Turkish rugs, 272
Turnings, 178
Tuscan arch, 35
Tuscan Italianate, 357
Tuscan order, 362
Tuttle, Paul, 170
Tweed, defined, 307
Twig furniture, 171
Twill weave, 298
Twin houses, 124, 125
Tye, Alan, 400
Tyron Palace, 369
UBC. See Uniform Building
  Code (UBC)
Undertones, 68
Uniform Building Code
  (UBC), 22
Union cloth, defined, 307
Union Station, 381
United States Custom
  House, 370
Units of measurement, 90–91
Unity, and variety, 30, 36–37
University of Virginia, 371
Upholstery
  furniture, 171–73
  walls, 236

Uplighter, 91
User-friendly, 402
Users, 12–13, 23
U-stair, 202, 203
Utah State Capitol Building, 209,
  221, 236
Vacuformed plastics, 170
Valances, 237, 244
  calculating yardage, 239
  lighting, 96
Values
  contrast, 72
  distribution, 72
  high and low, 72
  and Munsell theory, 66, 67
van der Rohe, Ludwig Mies, 28,
  181, 383, 384, 395
Vapor barrier, 340
Variety, and unity, 30, 36–37
Varnish, 169
Vasari, 363
Vault ceilings, 206
Vaulted systems, 351
Vaults, 361, 364
Vaux-le-Vicomte, 164
Veiling glare, 95
Velour, defined, 307
Velvet, defined, 307
Velvet weave carpets, 269
Veneer, 167
Venetian blinds, 245
Verandahs, 373
Verbal communication, 397
Vernacular tradition, 371
Versailles, Palace of. See Palace
  of Versailles
Vertical line, 41, 42
Vertical louvered blinds, 246
Vertical louvered shutters, 248
Vicenza, 354, 365
Victor, Jane, 286
Victorian Age, in America,
  373–76
Victorian style, 35, 41, 51, 62,
  179, 198, 204, 212, 245,
  254, 328, 357, 359, 393
  period fabric, 291–92
Vienna Sucession, 180
Vigas, 379
Villa Rotonda, 365
Vinyls, 170, 297
  defined, 307
  floors, 265, 266
  tile, 264
  wall coverings, 234
Vinyon, 297
Violet, and common color
  associations, 74
Visual Awareness and Design, 73
Visual communication, 397
Visual density, 40
Visual spectrum, 87
Visual stimulation, lively, 43
Visual weight, 144, 145
Vitruvian proportions, 362
Vitruvius, 362, 365
Voile, defined, 307
Voltage, 91
Volts, 91

Volute, 202, 361
Wainscot, 192
Wainwright Building, 382
Walkers, 141, 155–56
Wall, 192–94
  composition, 149
  materials, 220–27
  and nonresidential design,
    248–51
  treatments, 215
  upholstered, 236
Wallboard, 226
Wall coverings, 232–35
  guidelines and cautions,
    232–33
  terminology, 233
  types of, 233–35
  and wall and ceiling
    materials, 221
Wallpapers, 234–35
Walter Gropius House, 383
Warhol, Andy, 47, 48, 329
Warm colors, 65
Warm white deluxe lamps, 90
Wash, and light, 91, 93
Washable wall covering, 233
Washing, color, 231
Washington, George, 359
Washington's Headquarters, 377
Wassily lounge, 181
Water closet, 121, 130
Watercolor, 314–15
Waterproofing, 344
Wattage, 91
  of lamps, 90
Waverly Fabrics, 283
Weather, and climate, 15–16
Weaves, 296–300
Wedgewood, 324
Wegne, Hans, 182
Weight
  fabric, 292–96
  visual, 144, 145
Weighty, and line, 42
Welsh dresser, 178
Welts, 173
Wentworth-Gardner House, 368
Wesleyan University, 373
West, Eileen, 288
Westover, 368
Wet finish, and fabrics, 301
Whaler's Church, 374
What. See Design statement
Wheelchairs. See Handicapped
Where. See Design statement
Whipple House, 367
Who. See Design statement
Wicker, and furniture, 170, 171
Wiener, Michael, 162
Wiener Werkstette, 180
Wilds & Mitchell Design,
  Inc., 267
William Low House, 376
Williamsburg, 33
Wilson, Lynn, 289
Wilson, Peter, 36, 38
Wilsonart, 110
Wilton carpet, 267

Wilton loom, 254, 258, 269
Windbreak, 16
Windedale Historical Center, 26
Window, 189, 196–201, 364,
  368, 369
  and nonresidential design,
    248–51
  treatments, 215, 236–48
  wells, 345
Window Chair collection, 168
Windsor chair, 179
Wing chair, 176
Wire construction carpets, 270
Wiring plans, 95–96, 100
Wise Temple, 375
Wolfe, Elsie de. See de Wolfe,
  Elsie
Wood
  blinds, 208, 246
  filler, 168
  finishes, 168–69
  floors, 264
  forms of, 165–69
  graining, and paint, 231
  grains, 165, 168
  molding. See Molding
  paneling, 192–93, 227
  rods, 245
  shutters, 247–48
  stoves, 205
  and tableware and
    cookware, 320
  and wall and ceiling
    materials, 221, 226–27
Woodcut, 315
Wooden furniture, 165–69
Wool, 294
  and carpet fibers, 268
  rugs, 275, 276
Wooley, Kevin, 28
Wool Mark, 294
Woolworth Building, 359, 381
Word-processing, 401
Working drawings, 110
  and specifications, 21, 23
Work zones, 109
Woven textiles, 296–99
Woven wood shades, 247
Wren, Christopher, 367, 368
Wren-Baroque style, 367
Wright, Frank Lloyd, 17, 223,
  376, 381, 382
Wrought iron, 169, 321
Wyburd, Leonard F., 174
Yamazaki, 324
Yardage, calculating, 239
Yellow, and common color
  associations, 74
Zabriskie, Michael, 287
Zabriskie-von Steuben
  House, 377
Zakas, Spiros, 99, 256
Zapata, 379
Zest, and line, 43
Zigzag line, 41, 42
Zones
  and function, 109, 129
  and kitchens, 117–18,
    119–20, 129